Brush

Diesel

&

Electric Locomotives

1940 - 2008

Foreword

Brush realised the importance of the diesel engine for use in rail traction many years ago, and combining it with Brush electrical equipment set out to enter the activity of constructiong diesel electric locomotives during the early 1940s. With World War 2 in progress matters were delayed until peacetime came. From these beginnings Brush became a household name within the railway world, not only for supplying locomotives but associated equipment also. It was achieved over some years, but Brush adapted frequently to changing market patterns and demands and retained its important place within the industry.

George Toms worked at Brush in Loughborough for over 48 years and in his latest book he chronicles, in great detail and with first hand knowledge, the Works' output of diesel electric and electric locomotives. This book, the first of two volumes, is intended to be the definitive history of one part of the history of Brush. His book has been written to portray the historical side of Brush locomotives produced from 1940 and tells the story of what Brush did, and what happened to the locomotives in general terms after delivery.

The Brush register of locomotives is followed in approximate chronological order where possible and in doing so, Brush-built locomotives, some locomotives for which Brush supplied equipment, sub-contracted examples and joint Brush-Bagnall efforts are included. More recent years cover repair and re-engineering of Brush locomotives.

From the 1950s through to the first years of the 21st Century Brush has supplied many items of equipment to British Rail and its successors, other home railways and overseas railways, in addition to building complete locomotives.

Encompassing small shunting locomotives right through to the main line Type 2s and Type 4s, not forgetting Falcon and Kestrel, export contracts for Ceylon, Cuba, Nigeria, Rhodesia (Zimbabwe), Tanzania and Yugoslavia, the book will have wide appeal. Fully illustrated and including numerous tables of data for the various types built, the work is further enhanced by the inclusion of general arrangement drawings, publicity material and items such as works plates.

Volume 1 takes the story to the British Rail Class 56 locomotives, finishing the build histories to the early 1980s and covering the service history of each type thereafter. A second volume will continue the build histories and bring the story up to date.

These two books will form the definitive record of this well-known and respected locomotive builder.

Contents

Foreword	5
Introduction & Acknowledgments	9
1 – Early Days	12
2 – The Diesel Era Begins	14
3 – The Brush Bagnall Era	26
4 – The Brush Traction Era of the Type 2s	49
5 – Falcon	98
6 – The Type 4 Era	109
7 – The Hawk Project	198
8 – Kestrel	207
9 – Industrial and Overseas Locomotives of the 1960s	222
10 – Renaissance Under Brush Electrical Machines Ltd 1973	248
11 – Class 56	259
12 – Overseas Miscelleny	288
Index	300

BRUSH

4000 hp diesel-electric locomotive
KESTREL

Introduction & Acknowledgments

This book has been written to portray the historical side of Brush locomotives produced from 1940. It is not the intention to include an exact service history detail of all Brush locomotives, not that all such detail is known to the author, because the availability of such material varies enormously from almost nothing to a host of information that would warrant several books devoted to individual locomotive types.

It leans towards the story of what Brush did and what happened to the locomotives in general terms after delivery, where possible. It is assumed that readers will vary in their chosen aspect of interest; some people are railway enthusiasts (and among them we have a wide spectrum of specific interests), some people are employees or former employees of the various Brush companies and others are interested in the local history aspect of one of their industrial concerns. For some, the technical side of locomotives is of prime interest and for others the sheer nostalgia of recalling what may be familiar. Whatever the interest, it is hoped that there is something to interest most readers. The Brush register of locomotives is followed in approximate chronological order where possible and, in doing so, Brush-built locomotives, some locomotives which Brush supplied equipment for, sub-contracted examples and joint Brush-Bagnall efforts are included. Of course some recapitulation and backtracking is necessary due to the concurrent and overlapping nature of different aspects and events.

From the 1950s through to the 1990s Brush has supplied many items of electrical equipment to British Rail, other home railways and overseas railways to such an extent as to be beyond the scope of this book. Brush Traction in all its guises did not just build locomotives, it was (and still is in a different way) part of a larger concern producing a wide range of electrical products. Perhaps, due to many changes, records have been very short-lived in many instances and have been disposed of from time to time. Six years is the time allowed within Brush before information is disposed of, unless there is good reason to do otherwise. This trend was of help to work in progress, but not to the historian, and outside sources have been most helpful over the years. Perhaps in a purely railway establishment this situation might not have occurred, as the railway tradition of retaining historical records is very strong, though not immune to disposal. It is to the credit of individuals at the Falcon Works that there is a better awareness today of saving historical material for posterity.

It may occur to the reader that relatively few personal names occur within these pages. Unlike railway workshops, other engineering concerns tend not to label products with the name of the chief engineer. Design teams collectively produce their work, which is in turn approved when the required form has been achieved. This happens in most firms, but it is common in industry to only pin the label of the firm on the product, hence the Brush Type 2 and the Brush Type 4 nomenclature. Sometimes events developed and opportunities were seized upon and often there was no 'grand plan', despite railway enthusiast opinions to the contrary, the conception and birth of the Brush Type 4 being one case in particular. Indeed, it is hoped that some of the cherished and sometimes mistaken notions of some railway enthusiasts may be corrected. To Brush it was not important what the works number of a Brush Type 4 was, as long as the locomotive was delivered in sound condition. Conversely, the diligent and observant railway enthusiasts who recorded actual works numbers have made research of the lists in the appendices that much easier than it would have been. Your author has been gently 'accused' of spotting on many occasions, but because the recording numbers and events was a means to an end, fanaticism never entered into matters. When the situation was properly explained, people were most helpful. Restricted areas and their contents were respected at the Falcon Works.

One of the aims of the book is to record the events without too much lapse of time, unlike the case of the earlier steam locomotive history of the Falcon Works. It has also become impossible over the years to justify concentrating solely upon the Brush-built examples of certain Brush locomotive types because of the complete integration of their histories with those built elsewhere. In particular Classes 47 and 56 emphasise this point repeatedly. Both were Brush designs and Brush-equipped, so are worthy of inclusion. Furthermore, Brush employees were aware that Crewe and Doncaster Works built examples under licence as it were, but they may not be aware of the details. I hope that the story will be enhanced with their inclusion.

It may appear to some readers that the problems encountered in service perhaps indicated locomotive

Facing Page: The striking cover of the sales brochure produced for the 4,000hp Kestrel locomotive, the most powerful the Company had produced to that time or since.

G TOMS COLLECTION

design failures, but this is not necessarily so. The Class 47 in particular has had its problems and it is a credit to the original Brush design that many of these were overcome. The choice of engine was not that of Brush, but mainly BR, although it must be remembered that at the time of introduction it was the only engine suitably uprated, so the choice was an obvious one if BR wanted its standard Type 4. That the Brush Type 4 design could allow adaptation for all the myriad of modifications requested or required is truly remarkable. When one compares Brush locomotives operating on BR with some of other manufacturers one fact is prominent – that not one design was a failure sufficient to cause an early demise of a class. Examples are still in active service, some over and many approaching thirty years of age.

Class 56 has always been controversial, but again it is a good design by the standards of the time when it was designed. It was also required in service by BR as quickly as possible. Events overtook it while it was in production, an extended production period at that. It was regarded by BR as an interim design. By the late 1980s technology had advanced greatly and outstripped not only Class 56, but also Class 58, the definitive design of BR.

The 1980s witnessed many changes in motive power and Brush rose to the challenge on more than one occasion. Class 89, for example, showed what the Company could achieve. Despite there being no repeat orders for the design, it must be stressed that eventually the work done was acknowledged in time by the placing of orders for the Euroshuttle and Class 92 locomotives.

During this period I had better access to official Brush material, and the help of many individuals has proved invaluable in many ways. Personal observations have proved invaluable also – they were noted diligently at the time and such taking of notes was the result of lessons learned the hard way in trying to establish what happened many years after the events had occurred.

Recent history produces its own difficulties. Much cannot be revealed for contractual reasons which exist between customer and supplier and more than once I have been informed of what occurred then been told, "but of course you cannot print that!". The course of history behind the scenes is not always clearly cut and often relies upon personal contact and knowledge combined with sheer good or bad luck.

In compiling tables of numbers and dates, there have been many times when I have known published data to be in error, sometimes by many months. These have been corrected where known. A typical example was the report of a locomotive entering the Falcon Works three days before I saw its actual arrival – a case of entering the intended move into the TOPS computer system ahead of time. Clerical convenience has always been with us.

It is hoped that errors remain few. Much effort has gone into eliminating them, and I am always reminded that libraries have two basic classifications, fiction and non-fiction, the latter perhaps a reflection that perfection is rarely achieved. Converting the manuscript from one produced on a word processor to one suitable for use on a personal computer brought more than one headache. Any mistakes that have survived are my responsibility alone.

During the course of researching and writing this part of Brush history the help of many people is acknowledged. The help has varied considerably and in some cases reaches back fifteen years, from the hopeful comment of "I have found this. Is it of use to you?" (when it was a priceless gem) to the hard slog of Peter Barnes who keenly went through the main text, vetting it all in the pursuit of better English and technical accuracy. Peter Evison gradually realised that he had been snared into cross-checking the values of numerous machines ratings and technical descriptions of locomotives. Then there was the search for drawings and technical data, which realised some conflicting evidence and further searching. The long-suffering Neville Mays, now retired from Brush Traction, had to put up with my periodic requests for photographs, and did so willingly. Furthermore, after his retirement he read through the manuscript on behalf of Brush Traction, such was his long association with and knowledge of Brush Traction activities. John Stretton provided several hundred photographs when I took up his kind offer of a couple of years standing. His willingness was most welcome.

During the early days of writing this book I had the quiet encouragement of Bob Dilley, who patiently undertook reading the first drafts as they became available. This brought the history to the time when the first twenty Type 2s were being delivered, then sadly, Bob died. His comments were based on a lifetime of being in the private railway industry and also being a railway enthusiast. He could see both sides of the coin and his contribution was invaluable and this book is a worthy tribute to his memory.

I tried the patience and excellent photographic skills of Nigel Bampton, who spent more hours than he would care to admit, producing some works of art from dubious-looking prints and ancient negatives.

Terry Johnston dug out more than a few items from the archives – the place where old, but un-catalogued material had come to rest, more than once!.

Phil Norris also dug out vital works plate and works number information which had lain buried in filing systems referenced by long numbers!

During one hot summer Mike Hunt of Plymouth pitted his wits against my lists of volts and amps as well as long, long lists of Class 47s, 56s and 60s.

Long ago, a flourishing correspondence with Brian Webb ceased abruptly when he died at a very early age. His opinions were always worth attention.

The various railway societies have contributed enormously, either directly or indirectly through their journals and publications. Among them are the Continental Railway Society, the Railway Correspondence & Travel Society, the Industrial Railway Society, The Stephenson Locomotive Society and Brush Transport Enthusiasts Club.

I eventually tracked down Derek Cook, formerly Chief Mechanical Engineer of Rhodesia Railways, to within a couple of miles from my home! His views, firmly expressed, were also invaluable.

Harold Wood, who came from WG Bagnall 'temporarily', became a leading figure not only at Brush but also Hawker Siddeley. His description of how Brush won the Type 4 contest was an illuminating example of how events unfurled and how Brush was still regarded as a young newcomer to the diesel locomotive scene by some people within BR.

The list of people who have contributed follows in alphabetical order:

M Ap-Thomas; Richard Awde; Nigel Bampton; Peter Barnes; J Batwell; Adrian Booth; T Bralesford; John Buckland; Keith Buckle; Don Chapman; R Chatsworthy; Allan Civil; Derek Cook (RR cme retired); Bob Darvill (IRS); Bob Dilley; Jonathan J Dring (HKMTR); Peter Evison; D Frost; S Holland; Mike Hunt; Terry Johnston; Mike Kennard; John Lewis (RCTS); Neville Mays; David Moore; Peter Needham; Phil Norris; G T Perrins; Mike Riley; Neil Simkins; J Sloane; John Stretton; Mervyn Swetman; Bill Tassell; D M Thorogood; John Tidmarsh; Steve Thompson; J F Williams; F H Wood.

In addition, Bill Petrie, Product Group Chief Executive of the Electric Power Group of BTR and former Managing Director of Brush Electrical Machines Ltd, kindly vetted some of the later chapters, notably that of Class 60. His encouragement was most welcome.

Thanks are extended to Mr David Wells, past Managing Director of Brush Electrical Machines Ltd, Alun Williams, Director and former General Manager of Brush Traction Ltd, and his successor Mr John Bidewell, for clearing the manuscript for publication.

Finally I extend my thanks to my Publishers and record my appreciation of the hard work put into the project by John and Mark Senior, Scott Hellewell and Bob Rowe, and their proof readers David and Mary Shaw.

I hope that I have not inadvertently omitted anyone . To all who have helped in any way go my most sincere thanks.

George Toms
Loughborough

October 2008

On the occasion of his retirement in September 2008, after 48 years with the Company, the Author was both surprised and honoured to be made aware of a new recruit to the ranks of named Brush locomotives.

G TOMS COLLECTION

1 – Early Days

The variety of products that have emerged from the Falcon Works since 1853 is quite remarkable. It ranges from horse-drawn omnibuses, transformers and electrical switchgear, agricultural implements, fuses, steam locomotives, tramcars, trolleybuses, carts, aircraft, motors, generators, steam engines and turbines, diesel engines and domestic heaters to railway locomotives and motor cars. The list is seemingly endless.

The business was founded in 1853 as the Falcon Engine Works on the Derby Road in Loughborough. The work was varied and included a timber business, but it was very much a local business in its operation. Henry Hughes, a young London-born engineer came to Loughborough about 1855 and worked on the Derby Road site. He married a local girl, Emma Heafford, and lived in nearby Regent Street. In 1859 he took over the business; indeed he may well have been groomed for this event by his aunt. By 1861 he had gained a partner, one William March, albeit for the shortest of periods and was advertising railway plant. It is from this period that the first evidence of locomotive building emerges, one being sent to the Cape of Good Hope and of 7ft 0ins track gauge! This must have represented considerable progress for what was a very small concern with premises squeezed between the Derby Road and the Loughborough Navigation. After the exit of William March, Hughes appears to have continued alone, but did rely on the capable foreman at the works, Huram Coltman.

The lack of space for the expanding business led to Hughes seeking new premises. Towards the end of 1863 he secured seven acres of land opposite the rear of Loughborough Midland station and transferred the business gradually to this site. The timber side of the business was first to be moved and as new buildings were built the engineering side moved also. By 1867 the works was deemed complete, at least for the level of business then in hand. A rail link was provided and there was much space for further expansion should this be necessary. Also by this time Hughes had taken Coltman into partnership with the former holding two-thirds financial interest and the latter one-third. Various titles for the business headed various advertisements, but 'Henry Hughes and Company, Engineers' was perhaps the most durable.

Four-coupled saddle tank locomotives were the common output from the two-bay locomotive erecting shop situated at the part of the works that fronted with the railway. Within a short space of time six-coupled saddle tank locomotives were being produced. During the early 1870s variations of the two types appeared according to the needs of customers.

In 1875 Hughes built a steam tramway engine to the order and design of John Downes. In 1876 he produced his own design, the first example of which went on trial in Leicester and elsewhere. Partly to be better placed for entry into the potentially lucrative steam tramway market and partly because his partner wished to relinquish his stake in the business to pursue his own business for the ultimate benefit of his sons, Hughes was obliged to sell the business in 1877.

The new business traded as Hughes' Locomotive & Tramway Engine Works Ltd and was associated with tramway promoters and syndicates, including a tramways operating company. Hughes continued at the Falcon Works as Managing Director, and by now had a residence in Leicester.

For a while business prospered, but because of the many legal restrictions imposed on steam tramway operations a good many of the steam tramway engines were not sold, but rather operated under special contracts. A new line of business, that of building tramcars, was commenced. This was to have long term effects upon the course of events at the Falcon Works. There were several demonstration engines that saw service on trial, not only in Britain but on the continent also. One engine in particular was on exhibition in Paris in 1878, going on trial there the following year. This resulted in at least twelve engines entering service there soon afterwards and suffering some serious problems in the process. Further ill-fated engines went to Lille and many of the Paris engines returned home for repair and further service elsewhere.

In 1880 the business was in financial trouble and so was Hughes. By mid-1881 he was no longer involved with the business and was trying to make his own way as an engineer again, based in Leicester, but living in various locations.

In 1883 he emigrated to New Zealand and was followed by most of his family the following year. They initially suffered appalling hardships, but within a few years regained a comfortable life. Hughes himself died there in 1896. Loughborough unknowingly owes him much credit for a considerable portion of its prosperity over the years.

The company in Loughborough was offered for sale by auction in 1881, but there was no taker, so the following year it was reformed with many of the creditors taking shares in the new company. It was entitled 'The Falcon Engine & Car Works Ltd.'. With a new sense of direction, a new tramway engine design by Norman Scott Russell and relaxed laws that allowed conditions conducive to selling engines rather than hiring, events turned for the better. The tramcar side of the business prospered, indeed it had been a good move to enter this sphere several years before. There was considerable locomotive work gained through agents and Spain became a popular area to supply. It does appear that tender locomotives were produced for the first time under Falcon, quite why such an appearance was left so late is not clear. Certainly, the locomotive erecting shop was extended before the 1870s were out, though not greatly.

The advent of the electric tramcar in the USA drew attention in this country in the 1880s and by 1889 was a practical proposition. Falcon sought ways of entering this new market by contacting electrical concerns to fill in for its lack of electrical knowledge. The Anglo American Brush Electric Light Corporation, which had been established in London in

1879/80, was also wishful to enter the electric tramcar market, but lacked both tramcar-building knowledge and facilities. By the considerable efforts of Emile Garcke of the latter firm negotiations took place whereby the operations of the two businesses were to be united and based at the Falcon Works where there was almost unlimited room for expansion. Thus Brush Electrical Engineering Ltd was born in 1889, combining some very diverse operations indeed and gradually tailoring the works to a more varied range of products.

On the transport side the Rolling Stock Department continued to produce railway coaches, wagons, tramcars, steam tramway engines, locomotives and horse buses. Parallel to this was the range of electrical products for industry and domestic markets, ranging from electric lamps to alternators.

As intended there was a merging of interests in the shape of the electric tramcar, but not quite as originally envisaged. It had been hoped to marry the products of the constituent firms, but experimental fitting of Brush motors adapted for traction use to tramcars showed the motors to be inferior to American products. In the event electrical equipment from the USA was fitted to Brush tramcars during the 1890s and later there were attempts made to improve this equipment and fit it as Brush designs.

There were limited extensions to tramway work in the form of small battery electric locomotives and some electric locomotives. These mainly appeared around the 1905 period, the most notable being the two Bo-Bo electric locomotives built for the North Eastern Railway. One of this pair is preserved in the National Railway Museum at York.

During the 1890s steam locomotive production increased, went into decline, and after the turn of the century declined further, became intermittent and ceased altogether in 1912. It must be pointed out that the Falcon Works was never a locomotive builder on the scale of the North British Locomotive Company or Beyer, Peacock & Co and over a period of fifty years probably never built more than 750 steam locomotives. Brush also built a few non-steam locomotives, including possibly twenty or so battery electric locomotives for the Ministry of Munitions in 1917.

From about 1920 there was a decline in the production of rail vehicles of all types. No railway coaches were being built by the end of the 1920s, wagon production had ceased during the Great War as had any locomotive production. By 1938 even tramcar production had ceased. These sorts of products were replaced by other products, often non-transport items.

There was one slender thread which linked the old era with the new in the form of the resident works shunting locomotive, an inside cylinder 0-4-0 saddle tank built by Brush in 1899 and bearing the name SPRITE and the works number 283. This locomotive later became the first Brush diesel and is described in the next chapter.

SPRITE, the Falcon Works steam shunting locomotive, Brush 283 of 1899. The locomotive was photographed in January 1939. In reality it was an amalgam of parts of various steam tramway engines dating from circa 1880 and a steam locomotive boiler. It was unusual for a Brush locomotive to have inside cylinders.

BRUSH 8706, G TOMS COLLECTION

2 – The Diesel Era Begins

During the 1930s the trials with diesel shunting locomotives on the London Midland & Scottish Railway had not gone unnoticed by Brush. These trials had been protracted and had resulted in demonstrating advantages of diesel traction over steam traction for shunting locomotives. The trials also showed that diesel shunting locomotives fell into two groups; up to approximately 300bhp where the best transmission was by mechanical or hydraulic means and above 300bhp where the ideal transmission was electric. The LMS decided not to immediately pursue the first alternative, but to concentrate on the electric transmission with the higher-powered shunting locomotives. In collaboration with the English Electric Company a standard 350bhp design was finally evolved during World War 2 for LMS use. The subsequent history of this design was its proliferation on railways at home and abroad.

Prior to the collaboration with the LMS, English Electric had produced its own prototype which had undergone trial service on the LMS, indeed that railway eventually bought it and had ten similar machines built by Hawthorn-Leslie on behalf of English Electric. Several similar locomotives were supplied to the GWR and Southern Railway. The mid and late 1930s, therefore, were something of a trial period for this mode of traction and, as related above these events did not go unnoticed at the Falcon Works during the late 1930s. Already there was some interest in oil engines (a description that Brush preferred) for other purposes than traction and further happenings at Brush steered this interest into rail traction.

Severe trading losses had been incurred by Brush during the early and mid-1930s and as a result the company was completely reorganised and refinanced in 1938. Among the new Board of Directors were two particularly influential persons. Sir Ronald Matthews became Chairman and Alan P Good became Deputy Chairman. The former was already a director of the London & North Eastern Railway Company and within months of his Brush appointment became Chairman of that railway. His influences were useful, as indeed was the obvious link that resulted. The latter, at the time was aged only 32 and already a dynamic force in British industry. They entered a business that had commenced the manufacture of oil engines in 1933, low speed engines of 300rpm with horizontally opposed cylinders designed by Mr Herbert V Senior who had joined Brush to take charge of the newly established Engine Department. The engines were intended for prime mover work on generating sets and a business was gradually built up despite the industrial depression of the times.

A P Good, in particular, was very much involved in bringing together various interests and combining resources to produce what was required, by association, purchase or whatever was mutually convenient. Diesel, or oil engines, were his chosen forte. In 1937 he obtained control of Petter Ltd., of Yeovil by the purchase of shares and was appointed Chairman of the Board. He also had a close relationship with Mirrlees, Bickerton & Day, also oil engine manufacturers, and was a director of that company. The following year Brush acquired the assets and goodwill of the Petter business and after Christmas 1938 a start was made in transferring operations to the Falcon Works. The transfer of personnel, equipment and plant was virtually complete by the end of March 1939. One item of equipment, of particular interest here, was a diminutive Fowler 0-4-0 diesel mechanical shunting locomotive named ACE.

ACE had a bigger impact upon events than credited previously. She had been built by John Fowler & Co. of Leeds in November 1931, works No. 19425, and had been fitted with a 35bhp Petter engine. The locomotive was for use as the works shunting locomotive at the Yeovil factory in Somerset, and derived its name from the engine fitted. The 'Ace' engine was a three-cylinder, high speed type capable of speeds up to 1,600rpm, fitted experimentally to ascertain whether or not it was suitable for railway use. Trial running in 1931 and early 1932 showed that this was a successful application. Petter already had a steam locomotive dating from 1866 which was then put on standby for three or four years after the arrival of ACE. The newcomer had a short stay at Yeovil.

The arrival of ACE at the Falcon Works was fortunate. Before the end of 1938, the veteran works steam shunting locomotive broke down within a few days of her equally veteran driver, Mr Yates, falling ill. This locomotive, named SPRITE, was an old Brush 0-4-0 saddle tank with inside cylinders, works No. 283 of 1899. Even when SPRITE was built she was not completely new. Her frames and wheels are said to have been those of an old steam tramway engine, fitted out with a conventional locomotive boiler and a saddle tank. Certainly there had been some old tramway engines lying around the works in the early 1880s and SPRITE was built from some parts readily available on the works and not required for anything in particular. The cause of the breakdown appeared to be a hole in the firebox that had developed as a result of gradual wasting. Repairs would be extensive, but as she had recently received some new boiler tubes, further repairs were considered worthwhile.

The success of ACE at Yeovil was repeated in Loughborough, where the advantages of diesel traction were not lost on those people concerned with the operation and upkeep of the works locomotive. As a result, the suggestion was put forward that SPRITE should be not repaired but rebuilt as a diesel electric instead.

Mr Senior set two students and some apprentices from the Engine Division to work on dismantling SPRITE in preparation. The initial work took place in an old wooden shed or shop end, but prior to this at least two photographs were taken of her as a steam locomotive on 19th January 1939. One was with her driver, one without. By 1st February 1939 she was down to her bare essentials, wheels, frames, running board and cab floor. Three surviving photographs taken on the latter day show her in this condition with a wooden board bearing the chalked legend 'STRIP TEASE'. Obviously her youthful team was not without humour. In the background lay her discarded saddle tank and partly corroded cab; in the foreground, one lately removed spring.

Thus the seemingly long-established Brush habit of manufacturing equipment for use in the works from whatever may be to hand was again invoked.

Two old tramcar traction motors were located near the boiler house, where they had lain for several years, thought to be worth only their copper content as scrap. These, therefore, were brought onto the scene, together with an old direct current generator. There was no doubt that the transmission was to be electric; Brush was an electrical firm, the materials were handy and there was a precedent on the main line railways, particularly the LMS which had converted an old steam locomotive to diesel some years previously. A 50bhp diesel engine was allocated to SPRITE from stock. It is believed that this engine was a Brush prototype example, rated at 80 to 120bhp at 375 to 500rpm, and having two horizontally opposed cylinders. It had been designed several years earlier and a larger version with four cylinders had been fitted into several Dundee Harbour Trust ferryboats. Simple control gear was specially made. Conversion took some considerable time. It was the war that hurried events along due to the need for additional haulage power to deal with the increased traffic within the Falcon Works.

The engine was an unwieldy item to place in position. Various equipment layouts were tried, but only one was feasible, and that was less than ideal. The engine and generator had to be directly coupled and the shafts in line with the locomotive frames, which meant that the wide engine was mounted in such a manner as to cause the rocker boxes to overhang the running boards. It was a compromise situation and it resulted in two peculiar bulges (one each side) in the bonnet, just forward of the cab. This was acceptable since clearances within the Falcon Works were generous. Forward of the engine was the main generator, and forward of this was the auxiliary equipment and fuel tanks. A peculiarly shaped chimney hid from view part of the exhaust silencing equipment and produced one of the most unusually-styled diesel locomotive exhausts seen in this country.

The rebuilt SPRITE is believed to have been rated at about 80bhp, the limiting factor being the electrical output. SPRITE was repainted in an attractive green livery, lined in yellow with indented corners, and edged in black. On the left hand side, partly visible ahead of the engine casing bulge was a compressor. This supplied compressed air to a cylinder for

SPRITE after rebuilding into one of the most unusual, but attractive, diesel electric locomotives in Britain. Photograph taken outside the Turbine Shop, behind Loughborough Midland Station, in 1940.

BRUSH 9667, G TOMS COLLECTION

Above: **SPRITE** was demonstrated to Brush directors around the back of the works, soon after returning to work. The location is believed to be near the tramcar traverser.

BRUSH, G TOMS COLLECTION

Probably grossly overloaded and not moving one inch **SPRITE** appears to negotiate the defile between the Main Offices and the Turbine Shop in November 1940.

BRUSH, G TOMS COLLECTION

engine starting purposes. The engine could also be started electrically. A Klaxon horn was fitted in place of the original steam whistle. The original running board was lower than normal for a standard gauge shunting locomotive, and the wheels were also smaller than usual. This is not surprising because both betray steam tramway engine practice, indeed the wheels were an almost identical pattern to those fitted to the Hughes engine supplied to the Wantage Tramway in 1877. As a consequence of the low running board the high-mounted buffer beams were braced at the rear and the original dumb buffers and lower centre coupler were all retained. Behind the front buffer beam the running boards were encased and the old SPRITE cast brass plates positioned on the casings. Two doleful-looking grille apertures, serving as air inlets, were set into the bonnet front. The original cab was retained, complete with open rear, and instead of the circular spectacle plates on the front there appeared two four-sided windows. New works plates were affixed to the cabsides, recording that she had been a steam engine and had been converted to diesel traction.

Below footplate level each side, there was a metal protective skirt which reached down to just above the wheel centre line. This was picked out in white paint around the edges as a wartime blackout precautionary measure. The coupling rods were not refitted, so SPRITE may be described as 0-2-2-0 under the Whyte notation or Bo under the parlance of the diesel age.

It has been suggested that another locomotive of Yorkshire Engine Co. manufacture substituted for SPRITE during her period out of service, but no verification of this has emerged. ACE certainly did and she did it well. It was the war that hurried events along with the conversion. In September 1940 a steel casting defect in a gearwheel held up matters, but she was completed by the end of October and photographed in the yard between the Turbine Shop and the LMS main lines. Those involved with the conversion held a special dinner at a local hotel to celebrate the successful outcome. This was the 'Brush Sprite' dinner, held at the Bull's Head Hotel, Shelthorpe, on Friday 15th November 1940. A special 'War Sprite' specification was produced depicting old and new with four humorous clauses and a 'test report'. Participants in the conversion were listed with much humour.

On 27th November 1940 she was photographed again, supposedly hauling a rake of wagons and vans alongside the Turbine Shop. She was reputed to be a reliable performer around the Falcon Works, being able to pull away smoothly with twelve loaded wagons. Another source suggested that only four wagons was the maximum load and that her speed was never much more than a walking pace. On 30th November she was photographed at the rear of the works, with a foggy Loughborough Meadow as a backdrop, for several dignitaries. Sir Ronald Matthews was one of these persons and apparently he showed a keen interest in SPRITE. The war upset many plans of many people and one such plan was that Brush should enter into the diesel electric locomotive market.

In the meantime SPRITE and ACE saw much hard work during the war and served the Falcon Works well, but being an amalgam of second hand parts the former was finally laid to rest in 1946, being sold as scrap to Johnsons, a local scrap dealer. Fortunately, someone had the foresight to remove and keep the nameplates for further use, but what a wonderful preservation project she would have made had thought been given to such things in those days. In the event the nameplates were transferred to another diesel shunting locomotive that was to arrive from Mirrlees, a Ruston & Hornsby four-wheeled example built in 1943.

On 19th February 1941, at an Emergency Board meeting of the London & North Eastern Railway authorised the construction of four 350bhp diesel electric shunting locomotives at the company's Doncaster Works. The equipment was to be supplied by English Electric and the design was almost identical to that being drawn up in conjunction with the LMSR. In other words it was to the latest and most refined state of the art. The four locomotives (numbered by the LNER 8000 to 8003 and later BR Nos 15000 to 15003) were completed in 1944/5, the last in March 1945.

Because of wartime conditions Brush progress with regard to entering the diesel locomotive market was slow. In 1941 A P Good, still Deputy Chairman of Brush, and very much involved with other companies, endeavoured to keep the idea alive. His prompting within Heenan & Froude Ltd, of Worcester, saw Mr W M Ratcliffe of that company respond by inviting Mr Marten of Caprotti Valve Gear Ltd, of Worcester Engineering Works, to become involved in an advisory capacity. By October 1941 A P Good was pressing to see Mr Marten personally for discussions. The meeting took place the following month. Mr Marten undertook to prepare a report for Brush on diesel traction with a view to aiding Brush to formulate its future policy.

During February 1942 Good also met Mr H Sammons of Armstrong Whitworth Securities Ltd, presumably gaining further ideas of Armstrong Whitworth's pre-war involvement with the LMS diesel shunting locomotives and certainly discussing the position with regard to types of engine for railcar work. During this period contact with the LNER at Doncaster occurred, no doubt gauging progress on the shunting locomotives. Relevant patent filing in Great Britain was also investigated.

Mr Marten's 'Diesel Traction Report', dated April 1942, was received in Loughborough by 3rd May and then given limited circulation internally and its contents digested thoroughly. The report accurately summed up British involvement to date with diesel rail traction generally, with particular emphasis on shunting locomotives, railcars and to a degree, main line locomotives.

Some comparison with the Brush-favoured Petter SS6 type engine was afforded. American and German practice was included. Brush Director Mr D B Hoseason pencilled in a comment to the effect that Brush should build a 350bhp locomotive for its own use.

Brush consideration during the latter part of 1942 was given to possible Government regulation of post-war exports and gradually some idea of what might be done by the Company emerged. It was outline at best, as the war was far from won at this stage. Certainly the idea of producing shunting locomotives was to be pursued and that of main line locomotives if possible.

In 1943 a Traction Department was set up as part of the Electrical Division of Brush Electrical Engineering Co. Ltd.. It was not solely concerned with rail traction, indeed some of its earliest work was concerned with manufacturing 'Joy' shuttle cars for mining purposes. Another reason for its conception was to provide a further outlet for oil engines manufactured within the sphere of Brush control.

To build a prototype diesel electric shunting locomotive to a specification approved by the main line railway companies in Britain was the next step to take, but this was hampered by wartime controls and restrictions. Negotiations with the LNER resulted in an agreement for a Brush-built locomotive to be accepted for trial in the shunting yards of the Railway and paid for only if extensive operation on regular duties proved it to entirely satisfactory.

By November 1944 the Board of Trade had approved the development of such a prototype under the national scheme for commencing post-war development and it enabled Brush to complete drawings and other work at a much faster rate than previously. By this time also the various details in connection with the electrical equipment had been satisfactorily agreed with the Chief Electrical Engineer's Department of the LNER, but various drawings still remained unfinished. These concerned the Brush equipment regarding its disposition so as to fit in with the design of the mechanical parts already completed for the four locomotives under construction at Doncaster Works. Of course, some modification would be required to allow the fitting of Brush equipment.

In January 1945 Mr H W H Richards, Chief Electrical Engineer of the LNER, suggested that the best procedure would be for Brush to purchase an additional complete set of mechanical parts from the Railway upon which the Company could fit its equipment at Loughborough. If testing of the resultant locomotive proved successful, then the Railway would have the option of purchasing it at an agreed price.

Early in 1945 dreams of what locomotives the post-war era might bring were committed to paper.

BRUSH 00442

The price of the proposed set of mechanical parts was estimated to be £3,200, on the assumption that Brush would supply and erect the diesel engine and generator unit together with all starting and control equipment and supply the traction motors with all gearing, which was to be forwarded to Doncaster Works for pressing onto the axles. Brush was also required to supply and erect the radiator, complete with its equipment, all conduit and cable work.

The Brush Board of Directors had already approved certain LNER proposals and then approved these latest, the confirmation of which was conveyed to the LNER at the end of February 1945.

The influence of Sir Ronald Matthews, with his Chairmanship of the LNER and of Brush, again came to bear when an Emergency Board Meeting of the former company authorised the construction of an additional locomotive utilising Brush and Brush-associated equipment instead of English Electric equipment. Rather than have Doncaster Works build the complete locomotive, the arrangement was confirmed that the mechanical parts of the main structure should be completed there for the installation of equipment to take place at Loughborough. Doncaster Engine Order No. 384 covered construction of the underframe, wheels, superstructure and some mechanical parts. The order was placed on Doncaster Works in February 1946. Meanwhile, Brush commenced work on producing motors, generator, diesel engine and associated control gear and parts. The locomotive shell was noted standing in Doncaster Works yard on 13th December 1946, awaiting despatch to the Falcon Works. It was towed to Loughborough and Brush set to work equipping it out with electrical fittings and the power unit. By some logic the locomotive had been allocated the LNER number 8004, following on from the previous LNER locomotives. It may well be that although a Brush prototype, the intention to sell it to that railway if successful made it worthy of an allocated number in advance. Certainly, a direct comparison in service was desirable and of course an identity for clerical and accounting reasons logical.

The prototype was completed in November 1947 and duly photographed by Brush in a grey livery, but with no markings. The livery was decided in a most informal manner, Bob Dilley, then an apprentice, related how: "We went to the paint store and asked what stock paints they had. As the bulk of the work at that time was for the Admiralty the best stock was 'light battleship grey', so Alf Willerton and I decided to use that, picked out in black."

The outward general appearance made the locomotive similar to the LMS twin motor design, then in production, but followed the LNER examples more closely. Because it was air-started there were no large battery boxes mounted on the running board, although the generator had a starting field, and an empty conduit spanned the engine room, under the sump. These provisions were made so that a starter battery could be fitted, but in fact one never was.

It was fitted with a Petter SS4 360bhp two-stroke oil engine, and Brush 190kW generator with continuous rating at 600rpm. Two traction motors were fitted, each one driving an outer axle through double reduction gearing. The four-cylinder, two-stroke engine was a novel departure from the usual six-cylinder, four-stroke engine usually supplied to such locomotives by English Electric; it was the tentative answer from the Brush engine association and hopes were pinned on this prototype being a contender for orders from railways.

More details are listed below:

Traction motors (2)	Brush, each 135hp at one hour rating and 115hp at continuous rating
Tractive effort, starting	32,000lb
Wheels (6)	4ft 0ins diameter
Length over buffers	29ft 1ins
Wheelbase	5ft 9ins + 6ft 0ins = 11ft 9ins
Weight in full working order	51 tons 8cwt
Fuel capacity	800 gallons
Brakes	Westinghouse direct acting
Maximum speed	20mph

The new locomotive undertook some shunting work in the Falcon Works yards and soon left for LNER territory. November 5th 1947 was the day the prototype left, as part of a freight train. The late Bob Dilley recalled the events:

"At about 10.00 am a Toton - Peterborough freight train made a special stop and we were coupled next to behind the engine (a Fowler Class 4F if I remember correctly). Talk about innocents abroad! There we sat, a machines designer on one seat and a student apprentice on the other, confidently looking forward to a pleasant day's jog through the countryside with only one worry, whether we would get to London in time to catch the 6.30 or 7.10 pm from St Pancras back home.

We got to Syston and made the inevitable stop on the North Curve, so while the engine took water, we dutifully got down on the ground for a walk round and came back to reality with a solid thump! The right hand middle axle box was hot! We 'experts' consulted the driver and decided to try the traditional remedy, plenty of oil and push on steadily in the hope that it would settle down, but the fates were not feeling kind to us. When we stopped at Brooksby to have a look, we could nearly boil our tea on it, so there was nothing for it but to put off into the goods yard to cool off. At least this meant we had our lunch in reasonable quietness. Unfortunately, the rural peace did not last long; the station master objected strongly to

Accompanied by an LMS shunter, the prototype Brush 0-6-0 diesel electric shunting locomotive is seen on the southern exchange sidings at the Falcon Works in November 1947. During 1949 it was taken into British Railways (Eastern Region) stock, and numbered 15004.

BRUSH A613

our presence as he claimed that the local goods was due shortly and would not be able to shunt the yard with us in the way, so as the box had cooled by now, a Coalville-Peterborough goods was stopped, and after a stand up fight (verbal) between the station master and a very reluctant driver, with Control acting as referee and us as spectators, we were coupled on and set off again. With the help of a lengthy traffic stop in the loop at Melton we staggered on to Oakham. By then the box was again too hot to carry on and our driver did not even bother to hide his delight at getting rid of us. He was afraid he would not get through in time to get back to Coalville the same night. As it was by now five o'clock, there was nothing for it but to stop the night and see what the next morning would bring. So, instead of reaching London in the first day we had covered the glorious distance of 25 miles. My partner set off home with his tail between his legs and I found lodgings locally.

Next morning I was joined by a new partner (Fred Williams) who knew a bit more about the mechanical side of diesel electric locomotives, having been in the business practically since diesel electric locomotives were first made. So, with fingers firmly crossed and plenty of oil in what we hoped were the right places, we set off

again, this time managing to reach Stamford, where we spent a couple of hours scouring the town for a spanner large enough to fit the spring hanger nuts. All we found was a giant Stillson Wrench. With the aid of this and the skin off most of our knuckles we managed to take some of the load off the middle axle and then had another try to get to London.

We arrived at Peterborough and were sent straight into the LMS locomotive shed for examination. As we were heading for the LNER the shed staff, after a thorough examination, managed to persuade themselves (and us) that we were fit enough to carry on, so we were sent on the front of the next trip to the East Yard, where the LNER took over. A short debate now took place on precedence; a load of cattle was booked on the next train out as well as us and, according to the rule book, both of us had to be coupled next to the train engine! The cattle wagon looked to be much-travelled and we did not fancy being downwind of it all the way across the fens, so we argued hotly and eventually had our way and travelled next to the engine. The hot box decided to behave itself and we arrived in due course at March, where we spent the night.

Next morning, we had the pleasure of a steam engine all to ourselves, so, by taking the journey in easy stages, we eventually arrived at Stratford locomotive shed, a mere matter of 48 hours late, and were taken straight to the 'Ark', a rather primitive erection of shear legs and a couple of sheets of corrugated iron which was all the facility there was for removing axles."

The facilities at Stratford, primitive though they were, must have been sufficient for the repairs because the locomotive soon started working trials at the Temple Mills Yard there, and later in Whitemoor Yard, March. These trials extended into 1948. During this period the locomotive was borrowed by Brush and brought back briefly to Loughborough to demonstrate shunting in the former LMS goods yard for the benefit of some Siamese visitors. This occurred early in 1949.

After successful BR trials the locomotive was bought by the Railway in April 1949, but by this time the LNER had ceased to exist and British Railways was it successor. An interesting BR minute of 21st April 1949 records the authorisation to purchase the locomotive at an estimated cost of £21,400, "the locomotive having been on trial since 11/47". The Eastern Region of BR inherited the locomotive and it was given the number 15004, following on from the LNER quartet in the BR locomotive list for diesels. Plain BR black livery replaced the 'Bob Dilley grey', with the running number appearing on the side access doors of the bonnet and the new lion and wheel emblem on the cabsides, the reverse of common practice. It was classified DES2, being reclassified DEJ2 in 1954. No works number of either Doncaster Works of Brush was ever allocated to No. 15004, presumably because the LNER regarded it as a Brush locomotive and Brush presumably never considered the matter.

In the same month that it was taken into BR stock 15004 was officially allocated to March, where it had already spent the greater part of its trials, and joined the LNER quartet on similar duties in the Whitemoor yard operating on shunting wagons over the hump. On 9th December 1951 it was transferred to Hornsey, where it commenced trials against former LNER Class J50 steam locomotive No. 68949 for a fortnight on a regular South London goods transfer trip to Herne Hill via the Widened Lines. On 24th December it arrived at Cricklewood for similar trials which began three days later and lasted until 11th January 1952, with 15004 travelling between Brent and Hither Green on a regular basis. Loads were between twenty and thirty wagons.

January saw a return to March shed and No. 15004 remained allocated there until January 1957 when it was transferred to Woodford Halse, then a month later to New England, its final allocation until withdrawn from service in October 1962. At New England it was used mainly in the yards, but sometimes worked at Peterborough East and Fletton.

As with many of the early diesel electric shunting locomotives that BR owned, heavier maintenance was undertaken at Derby Works, but from January 1960 this was transferred to the Eastern Region, presumably as such facilities were built up in the area by then.

Upon withdrawal, the locomotive was sent to Doncaster Works for scrapping. It is thought that this was its first visit since its partial birth there. On 7th July 1963 it was noted as still lying in the yard at the works.

Early withdrawal was almost inevitable because by this time a standard shunting locomotive design had been proliferated and demand satisfied, so a non-standard unit would become a maintenance and spare parts irritation.

As a prototype it is questionable whether No. 15004 was successful in demonstrating that what Brush had to offer was a better alternative to the English Electric/LMS Railway design. Certainly the locomotive came on the scene too late

to do this, but at the time of its conception the future of such locomotives looked assured, and certainly Brush was well aware of the intention of the LMS to go into quantity production of its final design. What Brush was not to know for certain was that the railways would be nationalised in 1948, and that the LMS design would be virtually accepted as a BR standard, with only minor modifications.

In December 1944, late in the Second World War, Mr Good and a colleague visited neutral Eire on a fact-finding mission and to establish relations between potential customers and Brush and its associated companies. It was hoped that this would lead to orders for various products, including rail traction. It was known that Eire was experiencing considerable difficulties in obtaining coal from Britain for her steam locomotives and that most of her locomotives were aged.

The following month it was decided that an exploratory visit to Eire should take place by representatives of Brush and Associated Locomotive Equipment Co. Ltd, (another of Mr A P Good's interests, and a subsidiary of Messrs Heenan & Froude) in connection with prospective traction business. Among the Brush representatives was Mr W M Good (A P Good's brother) who helped cement a relationship with Mr A P Reynolds the Chairman of Coras Iompair Eireann (CIE). Correspondence, exchanged during February 1945, made Mr Reynolds aware that the Good brothers were Irish born and bred, and not without considerable associations in Eire. Brush and associated engineers visited Eire again to discuss detail matters, which included supplying design detail and equipment for assembly in CIE workshops in accordance with Irish Government policy.

Mr Reynolds visited Loughborough during May 1945. During his stay in England he and his wife were entertained well, including time at the races during which Mrs Reynold's filly won 'a very hot sprint'.

As a result of this intercourse an order was placed by CIE, the newly formed Irish state transport company. Five diesel electric shunting locomotives were ordered as the first part of a dieselisation pilot scheme initiated by CIE Chairman Mr A P Reynolds. Brush received the order for the design and supply of equipment through ALE Ltd. and the locomotives were to be erected at the CIE Inchicore Works, Dublin.

The diesel engine fitted was a Mirrlees industrial TLDT6 vertical six-cylinder direct-injection four stroke turbo-pressure-charge type with an 8½ins bore and 13¾ins stroke, developing 487bhp at 710rpm continuous rating, and 535bhp at one hour rating. Directly coupled to it was a Brush 290kW DC generator with a top-mounted 10kW auxiliary generator, multi-belt driven from a pulley on the main generator shaft. Nose suspended traction motors were fitted on the outer axles, each having a continuous rated output of 177bhp at 1,200 volts. The overall length was 29ft with an 11ft 9ins wheelbase; total weight in full working order 52 tons 19cwt.

In April 1946 Mr Reynolds announced that CIE was about to commence using diesel electric traction, the first examples being the five Brush-designed 0-6-0s. Construction at Inchicore commenced in May 1947 and the first one, No. 1000, was completed by the December. The five locomotives (Nos 1000-4) were intended for shunting and transfer duties

Coras Iompair Eireann No. 1000 (later D301) as running in 1948. Although not actually built by Brush, it was designed by the Company. This locomotive and its sisters had Brush electrical equipment and paved the way for the Brush Bagnall industrial shunting locomotives.

BRUSH A769

in and around Dublin. No. 1000 entered service in January 1948 and it soon became apparent, initial snags apart, that the new units would be very satisfactory. The remaining four locomotives were completed during 1948.

The service on which Nos 1000-4 were to be engaged was transfer rail-to-sea traffic between Kingsbridge (Heuston since 1966) and North Wall yards, six miles of steeply graded line, which included 1½ miles of 1 in 84. Load requirements here were thirty-five wagons of 400 tons gross maximum, to be hauled at speeds up to 25mph. Fifty wagons totalling 600 tons gross could be hauled at lower speeds in the yards. Tests also proved that even starting 400 ton loads on the steepest gradient, with greasy rails and adverse weather conditions, the locomotives had an ample margin with the power equipment operating within its continuous rating.

An unusual test was conducted on 21st March 1948 when No. 1000 hauled a 350 ton train non-stop from Dublin to Cork, a journey of 165 miles, in 8 hours 40 minutes. At that time steam locomotives required 11 hours 50 minutes for the same journey. The really outstanding achievement was that the locomotive successfully undertook the task of continuous main line work, a duty for which it had not been designed. Additionally, a fuel cost saving of 75 per cent was achieved over steam haulage on the same route. One presumes that the exercise was designed to obtain some advance diesel haulage

data for the impending main line diesel locomotives that CIE had on order, and No. 1000 provided the first opportunity to do this.

Once the locomotives settled down to their intended duties they could be seen at North Wall, shunting empty stock at Kingsbridge, or shunting around Inchicore. Their initial livery was a pleasing green, with yellow lining and black edging, yellow numerals and CIE emblem (often irreverently referred to as the 'flying snail'). In the mid-1950s they were renumbered D301-5 as part of a scheme to classify diesel locomotives by alpha-numerical means.

Over the years they gave trouble-free service and withdrawal from service started with D302 in August 1966.

All five were cut up at Inchicore as tabulated below:

D301 (1000)	out of use by 1973	cut up 3/1977 to 5/1977
D302 (1001)	withdrawn 8/1966	dismantled and cut up after 1978
D303 (1002)	out of use by 1973	cut up 3/1977 to 5/1977
D304 (1003)	withdrawn 5/1972	cut up 3/1977 to 5/1977
D305 (1004)	out of use by 1973	dismantled and cut up by early 1979

They served CIE well and had successful careers on mundane and unromantic railway operations, but much was learnt from them by the Railway, particularly in the early days when there were no proper diesel maintenance facilities and staff were all steam traction orientated. Conversion to the ways of the new diesels was notably swift among members of that staff. No Brush works numbers were ever allocated to these locomotives, and it is regrettable that the pioneer example was never preserved. Its place in Irish railway history has been largely overlooked.

By June 1945, within months of the CIE order, the Great Western Railway had placed an order for one diesel electric shunting locomotive. It was similar in concept to No. 15004, except that the outline followed the English Electric/LMS design and it had battery starting for the Petter two-stroke engine, rather than compressed air. This move came as a result of approaches by Brush and allied engineers to the the Railway. The GWR was already embarking upon the new mode of traction for shunting purposes and had limited operational experience with the use of a single English Electric/Hawthorn Leslie 0-6-0 diesel electric locomotive since before the war.

On 1st March 1945 Captain R C Petter, representing the Brush/Petter interest, and Mr J H R Nixon of Brush visited Mr F W Hawksworth, the GWR CME, at Swindon. In attendance were Mr Hawksworth's Mechanical Assistant (Mr Hall) and Electrical Assistant (Mr MacDonald). It was a meeting considered to be most satisfactory in every way by Captain Petter and Mr Hawksworth was most interested in what Brush had to offer, requesting that detailed drawings be sent to enable GWR people to examine them to see how a set of Brush/Petter equipment could be incorporated into 'their chassis'. They were duly sent, and included general arrangement drawings.

By the end of March the GWR was sufficiently interested to request more details, including prices, to which Brush replied 'For One Complete Equipment to suit a 350 hp Shunting Locomotive, and generally in accordance with the attached specification, our price would be approximately £8,850'. Delivery was expected to be within twelve months of receipt of order.

The post-war moves were for the Railway's Swindon Works to produce a batch of six units similar to the final LMS design including English Electric equipment under Lot No. 364, and one unit also similar to the EE/LMS design, but equipped by Brush as described above, under Lot No. 363.

An official form of tender for equipment was received by Brush from the GWR on 18th April 1945 and matters were being put through official channels. The order was placed on Brush during the first week of June 1945.

The GWR planned to renumber the solitary prewar locomotive in 1946, from existing No. 2 to 500; the Brush unit was to become 501, and the remainder 502-7. The latter units came into service in 1948, within months of nationalisation and were given BR numbers 15101-6 in the diesel series. Number 2 became 15100, and the Brush locomotive on completion in November 1949 became 15107. Whereas 15101-6 entered service in green livery, 15107 did not. It was finished in the recently introduced BR black livery, complete with the new BR lion and wheel emblem. What was non-standard was the fitting of GWR style number plates instead of either painted or transfer numerals on the cabsides. Presumably they had been cast at the same time as those fitted to the previous locomotives, before any decision on standard liveries had been made. Equally, existing GWR steam locomotives did retain their number plates and new ones already ordered and being delivered after nationalisation received the GWR style from new. Whatever the reason No. 15107 did have its running number applied to the buffer beam in GWR style.

The main details of No. 15107 were as follows:

Engine	Petter SS4 two-stroke, 360bhp at 600rpm
Cylinders (bore and stroke)	8½ins x 13ins
Wheel diameter	4ft 0½ins
Main generator	190kW
Auxiliary generator	9kW
Traction motors (2)	116bhp, each
Main fuel tank capacity	584 gallons
Auxiliary fuel tank capacity	75 gallons
Starting tractive effort	35,000lbs
Weight in full working order	46 tons 2cwt
Wheelbase	11ft 6ins, equally divided

On completion No. 15107 was set to work at Bristol St. Philip's Marsh, where it spent its whole working life. Its career was very brief, being withdrawn from service in June 1958 and cut up at Swindon Works. The non-standard nature of the locomotive compared with the more numerous English Electric-equipped version probably was its downfall, but as with No. 15004, it may have attracted attention from potential industrial users. Indeed, it was to be from industrial sources that orders emanated, proving that there was an alternative to the English Electric-equipped 0-6-0 diesel electric shunting locomotive.

The two locomotives which went into BR service and the five that worked in Ireland represented the initial entry of Brush into the diesel electric locomotive market. It was a good start in difficult post-war conditions, and notably Brush achieved it without a locomotive building capacity. This would change within a few years.

At times the mixture of associations that A P Good had created caused concern among the people involved in gaining the new business. He was always keen to develop new avenues and associations, some including overtures to Metropolitan-Vickers Electrical Co. Ltd of Trafford Park, Manchester, but as these moves were of a personal nature they highlighted the necessity to establish a proper organisation to deal with enquiries. In April 1945 Messrs W M Good, F S Mitman (Brush Director) and Marten considered that a separate sales entity be formed, with the title Brush Locomotive Traction Ltd. (or similar name) and operate from the same offices in London as Associated Locomotive Equipment Ltd (ALE), a sister firm in the A P Good complex of companies. It was suggested that the company would deal with sales and general design of locomotives and would make the decision in appropriate cases as to what engine from the ABE group (Associated British Engineering Ltd, the new name taken by Petters Ltd in 1939) was most suitable for the particular job and thus avoid duplication of effort which would otherwise occur. An enquiry from New Zealand had already produced such duplication, involving both Mirrlees and Petters.

The engagement of suitable staff (whether from ALE, Brush, Mirrlees or otherwise) was considered to be essential. W M Good put the collective suggestions to his brother, who replied that efforts should be concentrated under Mr Marten in ALE and that Brush and British Oil Engines Ltd. should

Brush supplied the traction equipment for BR 15107, but it was built at Swindon Works in 1949. It carried a Great Western type brass numberplate. As a non-standard design it only had a short working life, being withdrawn in 1958.

BRUSH A1630

acquire a proportion of the shares that Heenan & Froude held in ALE. It was a typical move by him. He expected that this arrangement would result in an independent concern with few overheads, and would be able to carry the initial overheads during the first few, formative, years. Not everyone agreed with these suggestions, particularly Brush Director Mr Hoseason. In the event Brush and ALE collaborated with CIE for producing the five shunting locomotives in Eire.

In 1949 Brush produced its first locomotive brochure, publication No. 71101 entitled BRUSH DIESEL-ELECTRIC LOCOMOTIVES. It featured the prototype, that Bob Dilley had escorted to London, on the front cover and CIE No. 1000 on page 2. These illustrations and others that included equipment, were derived from actual photographs and extended to eight pages. The remainder of the brochure, pages 8 to 12 inclusive, detailed a range of eight locomotives in outline available for ordering to suit various applications. It consisted of three wheel arrangements, 0-6-0, Bo-Bo and A1A-A1A and offered engines of Mirrlees and Petters manufacture.

There were two 0-6-0 designs. First, to diagram TR15792/D19, was a standard gauge shunting locomotive fitted with

a 400bhp Petter SS4 engine, weighing 51 tons and having a maximum line speed of 20mph. This design was basically that of No. 15004.

Second was to diagram TR27027/D15 and depicted another shunting locomotive, this time fitted with a Mirrlees TLST6 engine of 487-535bhp. Its weight was 53 tons in working order and it had a maximum line speed of 25mph. With a track gauge of 5ft 3ins this approximated to the CIE locomotives.

The first Bo-Bo illustrated was to diagram TR27449/D12 and depicted a 48-ton design powered with a Mirrlees TLST6 engine rated at 400bhp. With a maximum axle load of 12 tons, a track gauge of 3ft 6ins, small cow catchers, centre coupler and no side buffers, this locomotive was clearly aimed at the export market. The bogies were truly massive and of fabricated steel construction. Its appearance would have been that of a stretched version of the 0-6-0s, mounted on bogies.

The second Bo-Bo, diagram No. TR27025/D17, offered a 'switcher'/transfer locomotive with an outline clearly inspired by contemporary American practice. It was a single cab bonnet design, with a railed running board around the bonnet and the cab at one end. The bogies were smaller-framed and there was a choice of coupling and buffing gear to suit customer requirements. With a track gauge of 5ft 6ins it was clearly for export. The engine fitted was the Mirrlees TVT12, rated at 700bhp. Overall weight was 64 tons and the maximum line speed was 35mph.

Diagram TR27108/D18 catered for the 1,000mm gauge, then commonly called 'metre gauge'. It was for a single cab, bonnet type Bo-Bo of 648bhp, fitted with a Petter SS6 engine. The cab was at one end and the underframe was trussed centrally in the manner of many railway coaches common in Britain at the time. This arrangement supported an underslung fuel tank. Weight in working order was 56 tons and maximum line speed was 25mph.

Diagram TR27046/D16 offered a locomotive of 800bhp, with a cab placed between two bonnets about two-thirds along the deck. A Mirrlees TVT12 engine was specified and total weight in working order was 70 tons, track gauge was 5ft 6ins and the maximum line speed was 35mph. Again, the exterior outline was very 'American', and reminiscent of some of the streamlined locomotives of the era, as on this occasion both ends of the locomotive formed gentle curves which reached from the top of the bonnets to a blended cow catcher. The buffer beam was horizontally curved and complimented that of the bonnets. The effect would have been attractive, but alas, none was ever built.

The fifth and final Bo-Bo design was somewhat of a composite idea based upon two 0-6-0 bonnets separated by a centre cab. Designated TR27450/D14, it was indeed a twin-engined locomotive mounted upon massive plate-framed bogies. The two engines were of the Mirrlees TLST6 type with a combined rating of 700bhp. Overall weight was 69tons, track gauge 3ft 6ins, with specified maximum line speed of 44mph.

The range of eight locomotives was completed by the solitary two-cab, full body width, A1A-A1A design to diagram TR27470/D13. Rated at 910bhp and equipped with a Mirrlees TVT12 engine, its total weight would have been 70 tons, with a maximum line speed of 30mph. It offered a maximum axle load of only 12 tons, not surprising when one realises that it was designed to run on a track gauge of 1,000mm, on railways of minimal facilities. This would also account for the low maximum line speed. In many ways it would have been akin to some of the first main line diesel locomotives that were supplied to CIE during the 1950s, peppered with decidedly ugly grilles and sporting four 'porthole' windows along each bodyside.

The articulated designs passed into history, but perhaps it would be interesting to see something three dimensional if only someone could take the trouble to model them. It was a brave projection by Brush at a time when mainline locomotive design and building experience was severely limited, not only at Loughborough but elsewhere in Britain.

Despite the fact that most of the designs remained on paper it could be that some may have translated from proposals arising from enquiries received by the Company.

It is known that Brush tendered for the twenty-five proposed LNER main line diesel electric locomotives for the East Coast Main Line between London and Edinburgh. The LNER Finance Committee authorised the seeking of quotations for these at an estimated cost of £1,390,000, on 29th July 1947. The quotations had to be received by 10th November, but alas, with nationalisation of the railways only months away, the whole concept was just too embryonic and it was cancelled during the early BR period.

The LMSR was better placed, having acted earlier and more quickly, and had one main line diesel electric, No. 10000, completed in December 1947. Its sister (10001) was completed by BR the following year. Brush actually received an enquiry for diesel electric locomotives from the 'London Mid. & Scottish Rly' on 5th August 1948. Quite what the details were is not known, but it makes an interesting point to ponder over.

Other enquiries were received, few of which ever materialised into orders for Brush locomotives. They are interesting nevertheless. John Fowler of Leeds, for some years builders of small diesel mechanical shunting locomotives, was one enquirer for at least two 150bhp diesel electric locomotives in 1948, and during the same year Head, Wrightson & Co. enquired regarding the supply of two trolley locomotives for Thornaby on Tees. No quotations were sent out for these. Among the larger outputs came an enquiry from Industrial Exports Ltd for twenty diesel electric locomotives of 800/1,200bhp for South America. Another interesting enquiry came from Polygon AB for one locomotive (steam driven) and then there was an enquiry from the London Transport Executive for seven battery locomotives.

In 1949 Mackmurdie Sanders Ltd were keen to supply Diesel Tractors (Agricultural) to India and approached Brush on the subject and Berry Wiggins & Co. Ltd sought axle boxes for a steam locomotive. The latter was not surprising as the firm owned a Brush steam locomotive, which is now preserved at Snibston Discovery Park at Coalville, Leicestershire.

Perhaps the most intriguing entry in the book concerns an enquiry from the India Supply Commission for 'Alcohol Locomotives' received on 11th October 1949! Brush decided not to enter into the spirit of things and did not tender.

A few enquiries came from W G Bagnall, the locomotive builders of Stafford, and some bore fruit, as did others received directly from industrial firms. These are described in Chapter 3.

3 – The Brush Bagnall Era

As previously described, the dynamic character of Mr A P Good had enabled experience to be gained with 0-6-0 diesel electric shunting locomotives through his interests in Associated Locomotive Equipment Ltd and oil engine manufacturers associated with or owned by Brush Electrical Engineering Co. Ltd (Petters and Mirrlees, Bickerton & Day, both part of Associated British Engineering Ltd.). Nevertheless, some of the seven locomotives ordered had been built by a company not under Mr Good's control.

Since 1938 it had been Mr Good's intention to dominate the oil engine industry and he used his professional skill as a solicitor to gain control of companies, despite attempts by some of them to evade this. His sound business mind, combined with financial backing, grouped together a number of companies, in which he was the key link, into associated but still individual companies.

In 1947 there came the opportunity to gain control of a locomotive building facility in the form of W G Bagnall Ltd. of Stafford. Originally, W G Bagnall was formed as a company under this title in 1876, continuing an engineering business established during the 1860s. Locomotives were first produced circa 1876 and it was also about this time that the Castle Engine Works came into use for locomotive building purposes. It became W G Bagnall Ltd. in 1887 and remained so until 1961.

The firm had an excellent reputation for good workmanship and produced a whole array of different locomotive designs from the most diminutive to main line locomotives for home and abroad. Most were steam locomotives but there were some petrol and diesel powered examples produced during the twentieth century.

In 1946 the company was still a private concern with ownership largely in the hands of James Cadman, a North Staffordshire industrialist, his family, and Managing Director William Sydney Edwards. Whilst Cadman, the financier, had the less active role, Edwards was the driving force. Latterly, Edwards had suffered ill health which had been exacerbated by the strain of the war period, and this led to his death in December 1946. Having no heir his shares passed to his widow who wished to sell. There was little interest from the Cadman family to continue with the business, so it soon became known that there was a willingness to sell. In July 1947 W G Bagnall came on the market and Mr Good moved quickly to have Messrs Heenan & Froude Ltd buy up the company. A P Good himself became Chairman of the new Bagnall Board of Directors in January 1948. The Board was formed partly by others holding high positions in Brush and other associated companies. The die was now cast to start producing diesel electric locomotives from within the various companies under the control and influence of A P Good.

With the locomotive building part firmly secured Mr Good had an initial stock order placed on the works for six 0-6-0 diesel electric shunting locomotives in July 1948. Further consolidation occurred in 1949 when the engine

Dynamic Alan P Good, the architect of bringing diverse interests together to achieve specific tasks. His vision of diesel electric locomotive production led to the setting up of Brush Bagnall Traction Ltd.

BRUSH, G TOMS COLLECTION

companies reformed as the Associated British Oil Engines Ltd (ABOE) and the Brush Group was created. For the next few years a myriad of company names intertwined and subtly changed with circumstances under the umbrella of Brush, and at least for the earlier part, that of Mr Good also. When one considers that Good himself held 28 directorships and held the position of chairman in 22 of them only then may the complexity be appreciated. For the purpose of diesel electric and electric locomotive production, control of all the essential requirements was now achieved, and Good was the common link. In many ways it was a strong link but, as events transpired, it had one flaw in that human beings are not permanent. Overall it was now possible to go ahead with diesel electric locomotive production and seek orders because with a common Chairman single control over engines, electrical and mechanical parts, and locomotive erection had been gained.

An order for six stock locomotives placed on Bagnall's Castle Engine Works at Stafford was in anticipation of speedy delivery in the event of an outside order being received. Works numbers were allocated within the existing and long-standing Bagnall works list, these being Nos 2971 to 2976. Brush was the main contractor and invoicing was directed to Loughborough. Provision was made to manufacture the mechanical parts and build the locomotives at Stafford with the electrical equipment coming from Brush and the engines from Mirrlees. Construction was to be under the supervision of Brush engineers. Although the previous seven locomotives had been ordered for ordinary railway use, and were partial offshoots of the already established English Electric concept, the future trend was towards industrial use.

As stock locomotives, it was envisaged that they would have Mirrlees TLT6 engines of 355bhp and in most respects continue the established pattern of the initial seven 0-6-0s, with a tendency to favour the outward appearance of the CIE examples and the fitting of a Mirrlees engine. As with most stock locomotives it was accepted that it might be necessary to alter the design in some respects to satisfy the individual needs of the eventual customer. Of course, some customers might prefer 'off the shelf' locomotives.

The frames were planned to be laid during the late 1949/ early 1950 time, and it does appear that the frames were laid in the latter part of that period.

In the event, only four out of the six were completed, these being Nos 2971-4. Additionally, it may well be that parts of the uncompleted pair may have been diverted to locomotives actually ordered by customers, the need for stock locomotives having evaporated at an early stage of design and manufacture.

Soon after the stock locomotives were initiated an order for four locomotives was received from the Steel Company of Wales Ltd (SCoW), Brush records dating this to 18th December 1948. They were allotted numbers from within the Bagnall works list, 3000-3, and it was natural that these locomotives received preference over the stock examples and production overtook the latter.

The Steel Company of Wales Ltd was incorporated on 1st May 1947 to acquire certain iron, steel and tinplate works with a view to rationalising the manufacture of tinplate in South Wales. Among the acquisitions were two large steel manufacturing plants near Swansea, the Margam Works and the Port Talbot Works, but soon after the formation of the company it started to construct another works adjacent to them, the Abbey Works. When the latter was eventually completed the three combined formed the largest steelworks complex in the country. When the Steel Company was formed it inherited a fleet of relatively modern steam locomotives, but made a bold decision for the times to work the rail facilities at Abbey by diesel power from the start. 600bhp locomotives were required and due to there being no suitable British design available at the time locomotives were ordered from the United States. Alco (the American Locomotive Company) was able to supply five 660bhp Bo-Bo examples quickly and at a reasonable price. Delivery took place in 1950, the locomotives being numbered 801-5 by SCoW. Smaller diesel locomotives were delivered from British sources fairly quickly, being almost standard products of the time. For the intermediate power range three of the aforementioned

Number 701 (Brush Bagnall 3000) is seen at work with the Steel Company of Wales in July 1955.

BRUSH A3800

locomotives were ordered for use in Abbey Works and the fourth, to the same design, was allocated to the newly-built Trostre Works at Llanelli.

In 1948 the decision was taken to retain steam traction at the other Port Talbot works for the time being and the opportunity to obtain the most modern locomotives was not missed. Refinements in the latest steam practice were incorporated into three 0-6-0 outside cylinder saddle tank locomotives ordered from W G Bagnall Ltd. in November 1948. There was a dual intention in having the latest features inasmuch that improvements would be made over and above existing steam locomotives and comparisons with the new diesels could be made to ascertain the better mode of traction for future use. The three ultra modern steam locomotives were allocated Bagnall works Nos. 2994-2996 and delivered in late 1950/early 1951 and received SCoW Nos. 401-3. Mr F H Wood, later to become a familiar personality at the Falcon Works, was largely responsible for their design.

The Brush locomotives were under assembly at Stafford concurrently with the steam locomotives, but obviously took more time to complete due to the less familiar work involved. Nonetheless, the four were completed by early 1951, three being numbered 701-3 by SCoW (the fourth receiving its number 704 in 1952, after an initial loan period). An official photograph shows No. 701 prior to despatch, fitted with a worksplate bearing the year 1950 and BRUSH BAGNALL, the curious feature being the title, in use before the official company came into being.

The main details of the locomotives were as follows:

Engine model	Mirrlees TLST6, supercharged
Engine rating	480bhp at 720rpm for 12 hours
	528bhp at 720rpm for one hour
Length over buffers	29ft 8½ins
Total wheelbase	11ft 6ins
Wheel diameter	4ft 0ins
Weight in working order	55 tons
Maximum speed	20mph
Maximum starting tractive effort	32,000lbs
One hour tractive effort	18,600lbs at 7.2mph
Continuous tractive effort	15,100lbs at 8.3mph
Track gauge	4ft 8½ins

Delivery took place commencing April 1951, Nos 3000/1/2 to Abbey Works and No. 3003 to Trostre Works, where it was allocated the number 'Trostre No. 1'. In July 1952 No. 3003 was replaced by No. 2972, which became the second 'Trostre No. 1'. No. 3003 then took up its intended role at the Abbey Works and was renumbered 704. From this time on three of the four spent their entire lives at Abbey Works until 1970, working under extremely arduous conditions.

Their external appearance was generally similar to existing practice, except that they had flat, asbestos-lined radiator fronts and deeper, wider, buffer beams to afford better protection within the steelworks environment. The effects of excessive heat encountered when engaged on duties concerning molten steel or white hot ingot operations made the radiator arrangement necessary. The lower portion of the deeper buffer beams was made detachable for running over BR lines when required. Heavier frames not only increased adhesive weight, but also provided additional strength by means of more rugged construction. Yellow and black warning stripes were later applied to the pleasing maroon livery in selected areas to make the locomotives more noticeable. Loads during the early period were usually ingots and ladles of molten metal, but when such loads subsequently became too heavy they were relegated to yard duties and interchange siding duties. At least two of them were scrapped in 1974, but No. 701 underwent a curious conversion, into what was termed a 'braked runner', after its withdrawal. The British Steel Corporation (successor to the Steel Company of Wales) removed the power unit, superstructure, traction motors and the centre pair of wheels. To the remaining chassis was added a box filled with 28 tons of concrete above footplate level. An additional feature was automatic air braking, which could be controlled by a propelling locomotive. The overall weight of the resultant four-wheeler was 50 tons, and its purpose was to provide locomotives with additional braking power when handling heavy trains on steep gradients. At some time No. 703 lost its coupling rods and ran as a six-wheeled uncoupled diesel electric, losing adhesive weight in the process on the centre pair of wheels. Number 704 also became a braked runner and by 1982 was numbered 19, but reported as in a dismantled condition. It was still in this condition in April 1998.

It is of interest to note that the works plates bore the title BRUSH BAGNALL. Brush Bagnall Traction Ltd. was registered in February 1951, just after No. 701 was completed. Obviously the plates recorded the planned title, albeit in truncated form, before wider intentions were made official. The new company was formed as a wholly-owned subsidiary of Brush, and was set up as a joint Brush and Bagnall effort operating as a selling and marketing organisation for electric and diesel electric locomotives. The executive office was located at the Falcon Works, and the new company set about consolidating and further co-ordinating the locomotive activities of Brush, Bagnall and Mirrlees, using the well-known name of Bagnall to good effect.

In the meantime, more orders had been received. The Brush register of locomotives records one locomotive being ordered on 3rd January 1950 by Lever Brothers Ltd. of Port Sunlight. The well-known manufacturers of soap had a large and complex establishment on the Wirral peninsula, just south of Birkenhead. It was served by an equally large and complex internal railway system at the time operated by a fleet of predominantly steam locomotives. Two small diesel locomotives had been added to stock in 1948 and more were planned. They were mainly confined to shunting work, inter-yard and transfer duties, but something more powerful was required for the 'Rout', the service that connected Port Sunlight to Bromborough Port.

Lever Brothers therefore ordered one locomotive of 480bhp. This was satisfied by utilising one of the stock locomotives then under construction at Stafford, No. 2971. This was a matter of convenience because very little alteration to the stock design was required, unlike the Welsh quartet which

Brush Bagnall 2971 was supplied to Lever Brothers Ltd in 1951 for use at their Port Sunlight Works. No running number was allotted, but in keeping with the Company's normal practice of naming its locomotives after national figures, this one was named **MONTGOMERY OF ALAMEIN.**

BRUSH

Below, a fine study of Brush Bagnall No. 3020 of 1951, supplied to the Consett Iron Company as their No.5.

TDA Civil

had heavier frames suitable for the more arduous work. Indeed, No. 2971 had standard buffer beams and the most noticeable difference at each end were the large diameter buffers. Otherwise, it followed closely the standard design, but with the engine rating increased by supercharging, the designation becoming TLST6.

The locomotive arrived at Port Sunlight in October 1951 and was named MONTGOMERY OF ALAMEIN, in keeping with the traditional policy of Lever Brothers of naming locomotives after national personalities. Needless to say, it was affectionately referred to as 'Monty'! The name was painted on the side of the battery boxes in shaded block letters. An official naming ceremony took place on 30th November 1951, with Lieutenant General Sir Cameron G G Nicholson, GOC in C, Western Command. No running number was allotted.

'Monty' worked diligently for a number of years on his intended duties, but ceased on 30th July 1961. Rail traffic was on the decline, some being lost to road traffic, and although the locomotive was stored rather than disposed, the Beeching cuts on BR decided 'Monty's' future at Port Sunlight. Storage was unusual whereby the whole locomotive was wrapped inside a plastic cocoon by Tropical Packers Ltd. Eventually the locomotive was sold to Stanley Davies Plant Hire of Middlesex in March 1967, and soon afterwards it arrived on a low loader at the Falcon Works for repair. With one traction motor removed and some rewiring undertaken No. 2971 was used on railway dismantling duties in Central Wales during 1968, but by June 1969 it had returned to the Castleford plant yard in Middlesex, where it was scrapped after 1970.

The next locomotive order to be received was on 27th January 1950, according to the Brush locomotive register. It was for two locomotives and the customer was the Consett Iron Company Ltd of County Durham. Due to the heavier duties required they were not met by the stock order, but by new construction. Works Nos. 3020/1 were allocated and the locomotives were delivered from Stafford in March 1952 and on 16th May 1952 respectively. They were numbered 5 and 6 by the customer. The Mirrlees TLT6 engine was fitted, naturally aspirated and rated at 355bhp. The locomotives were to the same 'steelworks' design and each weighed 56 tons in full working order. The pair worked at the Consett Works until September 1969, when No. 5 was scrapped on site. Number 6 was sold to the British Steel Corporation for use in South Wales at the Trostre Tinplate Works, Llanelli, in August 1971, being transported there by road soon afterwards. By the late 1970s it was the standby locomotive and it remained there until July 1991, when it passed into preservation in the keeping of the Llanelli and District Railway Society. Its stay there proved to be an unhappy one. During the autumn of 1992 it nearly met its fate in the hands of the scrapman, but escaped by a narrow margin by the concerted efforts of a former society member and other industrial railway enthusiasts alerted to what might happen. The end result was a benevolent purchase and the locomotive was moved to the Shropshire Locomotive Collection, near Wellington, on 23rd November 1992, in the company of two other Brush locomotives also similarly endangered. Number 3021 was then sold to McLaren's Antiques, Oswestry, at the end of 2001.

The remaining stock locomotives that were eventually completed were Brush Bagnall Nos 2972 to 2974 inclusive. The outstanding pair, 2975 and 2976, were cancelled, so were never completed but it is probable that some of the parts already manufactured were incorporated in 3020/1. By the end of 1951 Abbey Works found itself short of locomotive power, so, by arrangement between the Steel Division and the Tinplate Division, an order was placed on 10th January 1952 by the Steel Division for one stock, 350bhp, locomotive (No. 2972) to be delivered to Trostre Works. This became the second 'Trostre No. 1' (as mentioned previously) and when it was delivered, in July 1952, and as already related, No. 3003 was transferred to Abbey Works and numbered 704.

The engine fitted was the Mirrlees TLT6 as originally intended as a stock locomotive. This locomotive was, itself, displaced in 1957 by yet a third 'Trostre No. 1' (an 0-4-0 locomotive) and it was transferred to the Abbey Works to become 713, continuing its career until the mid-1970s when it was observed out of use. It ran at Abbey with the buffer beams modified to make them deeper and with a protective steel cover over the radiator grille. By 1982 it had been converted to a braked runner in company with the aforementioned example, receiving the number 20 in the process. By 1989 it was still in existence, although reported to be in a dismantled condition, a condition in which it was still reported to be in by the end of 1993. In 1997 it was not seen, understandable because it had been buried under a pile of coke, a state of affairs which continued to be the case the following year.

Numbers 2973 and 2974 were finally allocated to a customer order when the Steel Company of Wales placed its order for two 0-6-0s on 10th December 1952. The pair were required for the Abbey Works and were rated at 350bhp, being fitted with the same type of engine as No. 2972. They were completed in April 1953 and thus again delivery was quick from Stafford. At Abbey they were numbered 711 and 712 respectively. Because their duties were general, stock locomotives were provided, so, unlike some of their predecessors, no bonnet protection nor deep buffer beams were required when new, although No. 711 was modified later with extended buffer beams and a protective sheet over the radiator front. No. 712 was transferred from Abbey Works to the Velindre tinplate works, at Llangyfelach, near Swansea, in 1959, but underwent a modification, which converted it to a four-wheeler. The centre pair of wheels was removed thus reducing the unladen weight and enabling the locomotive to negotiate the curves at Velindre, which were generally of a smaller radius than those at Abbey. By April 1976 it had become the reserve locomotive and by 1987 was reported as out of use and was still so two years later, but passed into preservation in the winter of 1990-91 with the Swansea Vale Railway Preservation Society at Llamsamlet. Unfortunately, its life in preservation was short and 2974 went to Staffordshire Locomotives at Shawbury, Shropshire, and was scrapped during May 1996.

Number 711 remained at Abbey Works for many years, working alongside 701-4 and 713, initially on slag and coil train duties in the output yards, but latterly in the yards on general duties, until withdrawal from service in 1970. Like No. 701, mentioned previously, it was converted to a braked runner. Reported as dismantled in 1976, by 1982 it had gone.

In all, between 1951 and 1970 the six locomotives quoted above accumulated a total of 385,035 hours worked, a very creditable record.

The year 1950 brought a new development to the Brush and Bagnall association in the form of an order for 25 1,000bhp main line diesel electric locomotives for the Ceylon Government Railways. This came about as a direct result of a visit to North America, by the Technical Director of Brush, Mr J H R Nixon, two years previously in which he studied the development, operation and building of diesel electric traction. The findings of his visit were most encouraging and led to a successful outcome, because the £1,000,000 order placed through the Crown Agents for the Colonies was won virtually straight from the drawing board, and gained in the face of competition from other companies with previous experience in the field.

The association was fortunate in having experienced railway engineers and railwaymen among its personnel, quite apart from the long-standing Bagnall team. Mr W A Smyth had joined the Bagnall Board in July 1949, bringing with him expertise ranging from an apprenticeship at the Irish railway works at Inchicore, time served on the LNER and as a former Chief Mechanical Engineer of the Ceylon Government Railways. A P Good selected him as Managing Director of W G Bagnall Ltd in March 1950 and he was to be appointed to the Brush Bagnall Board on its inception in February 1951.

The Ceylon Government Railways were not without diesel traction experience, as limited involvement had taken place since 1933 when an Armstrong Whitworth 0-4-0 diesel electric locomotive came to the railway. Some diesel railcars were delivered after the war and other diesel locomotives were supplied also.

Mr B D Rampala, Chief Mechanical Engineer of Ceylon Government Railways had visited Britain to select a suitable type of unit that would satisfy the requirements of the railway. Discussions on final design were held between himself, the Crown Agents and Brush, resulting in the order finally being placed on 14th March 1950. Total value of the order was £1,038,500.

For such an order to be placed with a British firm was no mean achievement at this time bearing in mind the advantages of an already established diesel locomotive industry in the USA. The context was that although other firms had entered the overseas main line diesel locomotive market and had experienced some degree of success, Brush and Bagnall did so without the existence of a prototype or previous design and were to build not just a few examples, but a quantity not small by the standards of the times. Furthermore, only two main line diesel electric locomotives were operating in regular service in Britain at that time (the LMS/English Electric units, Nos 10000 and 10001) and the newly-nationalised British Railways was still committed to steam traction, so the order was something to be proud of.

A panoramic view of the new erecting shop taken from the roof of the Turbine Shop in February 1951. Notice the electric truck in the right foreground, an in-house product.

BRUSH A2209

The Ruston **SPRITE**, constant companion to **ACE** throughout the 1950s until scrapped in the early 1960s.

G TOMS COLLECTION

For its own works use Brush continued to use very much smaller locomotives. Here we see the Ruston & Hornsby **SPRITE**, complete with driver Anderson and James Morrow, aged 11, son of the Brush Group Managing Director. Photograph taken in 1957.

BRUSH A4830

Because of the importance of the contract and the arduous operating conditions in Ceylon, it was decided that two engineers should be sent out there to evaluate the railway system in detail. Gradients as steep as 1 in 40, altitudes of 6,000 feet, short radius curves, saline and humid tropical conditions all had to be provided for in the design. Much of the detail design was completed during 1950.

New facilities at Stafford and Loughborough were put in hand to cope with the increased workload and for future work. On the formation of Brush-Bagnall Traction Ltd in February 1951 the declared intention was that the shunting locomotives would be built at Stafford and the main line locomotives at Loughborough, with the former manufacturing the mechanical parts and the latter electrical components.

At the Castle Engine Works a shop was provided for the necessary work and the frames for the Ceylon locomotives were produced there prior to transfer to Loughborough. At the Falcon Works an existing shop was enlarged and extended to form the new Locomotive Erecting Shop and soon proved its worth when the Ceylon locomotives were erected in it. From this shop mixed gauge track crossed a roadway to brand new locomotive test facilities and then beyond to a test track which curved, then straightened to penetrate the Loughborough Meadow on an embankment to avoid the annual floods there. It terminated at a buffer stop and sand drag. This track was also joined by a new link that connected it through the yards to the rail access of the works behind the Loughborough Midland station.

The work was in progress by early 1951 and was completed the following year, prior to the completion of the first Ceylon locomotive. The annual production capacity of the new shop was for a rate of 36 main line locomotives, but this was not achieved for some years and only then with the aid of further facilities.

By this time another works shunting locomotive had arrived to join ACE. The date of arrival is not certain but, the locomotive inherited the name SPRITE, utilising the original nameplates of the original works locomotive. It was a four-wheeled locomotive built by Ruston & Hornsby of Lincoln in mid-1943, their works number 218049. The type designation was 48DS, having a Ruston type 4VRO engine of 48bhp, four 2ft 6ins diameter wheels and roller chain drives to each axle. Overall weight was 7½ tons – hardly likely to produce anything spectacular and certainly not designed to undertake some of the tasks given to it at the Falcon Works.

It had seen service at the War Department depot at Harlech, then it went to Mirrlees, Bickerton & Day at Stockport before next coming to Loughborough. Some time after arrival at the Falcon Works it was given the plain green livery that ACE carried.

SPRITE and ACE were to become almost like twins, constant companions for at least ten years. The SPRITE nameplates were bolted to the cab side sheets and overall this locomotive was more attractive to the eye than ACE. SPRITE was a very short locomotive with a small bonnet and comparatively roomy cab. The cab had small square windows, two front and two rear, but it had large openings to the sides to which the driver often added wooden sheets in

inclement weather – the north wind that sweeps in from the Loughborough Meadows has a keen edge to it!

SPRITE and ACE would often work in tandem when heavy loads were to be moved, but otherwise they worked individually on incoming and outgoing wagons plus boiler house duties delivering coal and removing the internal-user wagons of ash. For the first time in many decades the Falcon Works was equipped for locomotive-building.

The first Ceylon locomotive was completed by October 1952. It was Brush-Bagnall No. 3025 and Ceylon Government Railways No. 539, being designated Class M1 by the latter. The remainder of the class was consecutively numbered up to and including 3049, and Ceylon 563. The locomotives were erected at Loughborough with mechanical parts and the underframes manufactured at Stafford. The Mirrlees engines that powered them were produced at Stockport. The engine type was a V-type twelve-cylinder, turbo-charged, four-stroke diesel engine with a normal condition rating of 1,250bhp, but rated for Ceylon conditions at 1,000bhp. Its previous application had been as a marine engine. It was directly coupled to a Brush DC main generator of 652kW, 630/750V, 1035/870A continuous rating. Four Brush traction motors were fitted, being of the nose-suspended type of 196bhp continuous rating and 226bhp one hour rating each. The centre axle of each bogie was merely there for weight carrying purposes to reduce individual axle loading on the lightweight track of Ceylon Government Railways. Air braking equipment was supplied by Westinghouse Brake & Signal Company Ltd.

The main details are listed below:

Wheel arrangement	A1A-A1A
Track gauge	5ft 6ins
Engine model	Mirrlees JS12VT
Engine rating	1,000bhp at 850rpm
Length over buffers	50ft 9ins
Overall width	10ft 3 7/8ins
Overall height	13ft 3½ins
Wheel diameter	3ft 7ins (motored)
	3ft 0ins (carrier)
Bogie wheelbase	10ft 6ins
Bogie centres	27ft 0ins
Maximum speed	55mph
Maximum tractive effort (starting)	33,700lbs
One hour tractive effort	30,000lbs at 9.2mph
Continuous tractive effort	24,600lbs at 11.7mph
Fuel capacity	775 gallons (main)
	75 gallons (service)
Weight in working order	87 tons

All locomotives were fitted for multiple working.

The exterior appearance of the design was more functional than elegant, but during the early 1950s the attention to clean and uncluttered exterior lines was not generally considered

to be essential. That the locomotives looked impressive cannot be denied. With a short nose at each end and two widely-spaced front windows above, forward vision must have been restricted in some instances. 'Porthole' windows and three sets of air intake louvres were set in the body sides, with the 'portholes' next to the cabs protected by heavy wire grilles to prevent damage occurring when collecting single-line tablets. The railway running numbers were set centrally in raised metal. This was the standard method of affixing the running numbers on the Ceylon Government Railways. The style of numerals was very much akin to Gill Sans Serif and reminiscent of the style of running numbers affixed in raised metal to the cab sides of the famous LNER A4 streamlined Pacific locomotives. In raised metal also was a long waist line on each body side, reaching horizontally from cab to cab, almost in the style of the aforementioned LMS/English Electric main line diesels. One also wonders if there was direct influence on body styling by H G Ivatt, formerly the Chief Mechanical Engineer of the LMS and who came to Brush-Bagnall in mid-1951 as a director and consultant (later becoming General Manager). He was heavily involved in the design and production of the LMS main line diesels, but it is possible that the outline of these alone influenced the Brush Bagnall designers before Ivatt arrived on the scene at Loughborough. Certainly the 'porthole' windows were derived from contemporary fashion of the day, if not from the LMS locomotives.

The Brush-Bagnall elliptical works plates were affixed below the body side running numbers. Livery in ex-works condition was a silver-grey, actually a protective aluminium paint specially applied to provide protection from the

Above top: A delightful study of the first two locomotives for Ceylon coupled together on the test track. Readers may note some similarity in appearance to the LMS diesel electric locomotives 10000 and 10001.

BRUSH

Above: The fourth of the Ceylon locomotives, No. 542 (BB 3028), ready for despatch by rail to Birkenhead in January 1953. Note the special accommodation bogies fitted for rail delivery in Britain and ACE, then one of the two works shunting locomotives. It was formerly at the Yeovil works of Petters Ltd.

BRUSH A2847

Facing page: The tradition of a group photograph taken in the company of a newly-completed locomotive dates to the Ceylon period. Here employees are assembled in front of No. 540.

BRUSH

adverse affects of the sea water during the voyage to Ceylon. Deck cargo was often the manner in which locomotives were transported in those days. On arrival in Ceylon they were given the attractive Gulf Red livery of the railway, tending towards a dark shade. On the noses, below the headlights, a rectangular plate displayed the class designation and running number.

The roof was divided into three sections, which were removable for heavy repair requirements, but they incorporated top hatches for engine maintenance access.

All ventilating and air inlet louvres were made waterproof and to meet the saline atmosphere along the coastal routes anti-corrosive materials were generally used throughout the superstructure and mechanical parts.

Delivery of the locomotives from the works was by road on low-loaders initially, the first two going by this method to ensure a quicker delivery to the docks to catch the respective ships. The first one was observed on a Pickford's low-loader travelling northwards through Nottingham at mid-day on 17th November 1952. The others appear to have travelled by rail as out of gauge loads on special adaptor bogies (sometimes referred to as accommodation bogies) which had been specially made for them. It is probable that the accommodation bogies would need to have traversing pivots, and probably be accompanied by adaptor wagons because of the coupling differences as well. They were despatched from Loughborough between the autumn of 1952 and October 1955.

An official handing-over ceremony was held at the Falcon Works, but No. 539 did not participate as intended because it had to be despatched to Birkenhead in time for loading on board the SS CLAN McQUEEN. Number 540 was used instead, and it was handed over officially to the High Commissioner of Ceylon by Brush Group Chairman, Sir Ronald Matthews, on 20th November 1952. At least the first two locomotives were completed in sufficient time to have them photographed together on the test track.

Before the end of January 1953 No. 540 had run trials and entered service, the first to do so because it had been the first to arrive in Ceylon despite being the second to leave the Falcon Works. The first five locomotives bore the year 1952 on the works plates, No. 3030 being the first to bear 1953.

The dates of entering service and of final withdrawal from service are listed below, courtesy of the Ceylon Government Railways:

B-B No.	CGR	Date to Service	Date Withdrawn
3025	539	07/02 1953	24/01 1980
3026	540	29/01 1953	14/10 1983
3027	541	16/02 1953	24/01 1980
3028	542	18/03 1953	24/01 1980
3029	543	02/05 1953	14/10 1983
3030	544	29/07 1954	24/01 1980
3031	545	01/06 1954	14/10 1983
3032	546	30/06 1954	24/01 1980
3033	547	29/08 1954	02/10 1983
3034	548	04/09 1954	14/10 1983
3035	549	22/10 1954	14/10 1983
3036	550	18/11 1954	24/01 1980
3037	551	23/11 1954	03/11 1984
3038	552	26/01 1955	14/10 1983
3039	553	22/03 1955	14/10 1983
3040	554	23/04 1955	14/10 1983
3041	555	28/04 1955	24/01 1980
3042	556	24/06 1955	24/01 1980
3043	557	09/07 1955	14/10 1983
3044	558	26/10 1955	24/01 1980
3045	559	28/09 1955	20/10 1983
3046	560	21/10 1955	20/10 1983
3047	561	02/11 1955	20/10 1983
3048	562	03/12 1955	07/11 1983
3049	563	13/02 1956	14/10 1983

The first two were operating the mail trains on a regular basis before the end of 1953, between Colombo and the north of the island. Meanwhile the Falcon Works continued production of the class and on 20th February 1955 No. 554 was noted at Stafford en route for Birkenhead, having travelled in a train by way of Wichnor Junction and Lichfield (Trent Valley).

Referring to the above table it is noticeable that there was a delay of some fourteen months between placing Nos 543 and 544 into service. During the extensive initial tests carried out by Ceylon Government Railways on the first five locomotives a number of teething problems were found. A report was sent to Brush from the Chief Mechanical Engineer of the Railway detailing the teething problems encountered with them and some modifications were decided upon for application on locomotives in service and under construction. This tended to slow down production for a time. By December 1953 Brush was already rectifying the problems and incorporating modifications in the locomotives under construction.

Among the problems were some concerned with the water system, troubles with the main bearings of the engine, electrical components, and underframes. By this time also, thirteen underframes had been delivered from Stafford. As a result of the experiences of 1953, Brush gained valuable experience in what was, to the Company, the virgin territory of producing main line diesel locomotives. The initial results may seem surprising to the railway enthusiast.

Losses were incurred on the first five locomotives and before 1953 was out there were doubts as to whether future profits could be hoped for in the manufacture of locomotives. It was considered that the main profit was to be better derived from the sale of diesel engines and electrical equipment, rather than locomotives. Fifty or so years on, these words still ring true and there must have been more than a few moments between when they were echoed by those endeavouring to win orders or sort out ongoing problems. It must be added that Brush was not alone in experiencing such feelings, indeed some of the firms building locomotives in the 1950s are no longer with us. They did not have the traction equipment manufacturing facility to sustain them during the lean times.

At some time in Ceylon Nos 542, 544, 556, 560 and 561 were de-rated to give an electrical output of 620kW at 825rpm. The class was a familiar sight along the 99 mile Indian Ocean coastal route between Colombo and Mataya. The route from Colombo to the tea plantation areas of Talawaskelle, Nanu-Oya and Pattipola was a tough one for the locomotives, with altitudes in excess of 6,000 feet above sea level; it is no wonder the Brush engineers considered it necessary to survey the conditions in 1950.

After the introduction of the Brush-Bagnall locomotives the railway tended to buy locomotives from other countries, notably Germany, Japan and Canada, but in the 1980s returned to Britain and Brush for more. These were the M7s, more of which later, and these helped to replace the ageing M1s. Ceylon reverted to its ancient name of Sri Lanka in 1973 and the title of the railway remained the same for a long time. There is evidence to suggest that the old name still continues.

A visitor to Sri Lanka in August 1980 noted the following locomotives at these locations:

539	Ratmalana Works
540	Maradana Shed
541	Ratmalana Works
542	Ratmalana Works
543	Maradana Shed
544	Ratmalana Works (overhaul)
545	Maradana Shed
546	Ratmalana Works
550	Ratmalana Works (stored)
551	Maradana Shed (in traffic)
554	Ratmalana Works (derelict)
555	Ratmalana Works (stored)
556	Ratmalana Works (stored)
557	Ratmalana Works (overhaul)
559	Maradana (in traffic)
560	Maradana (in traffic)
561	Ratmalana Works (overhaul)
562	Maradana Shed

It was reported in 1992 that several of the class still remained in store and that No. 560 (B-B 3046/1955) was earmarked for preservation as an externally-refurbished static exhibit that would be displayed outside the headquarters of the railway just north of Columbo. During the winter of 1993/4 the locomotive was noted as set aside at Dematagoda steam shed for preservation, in the company of other vintage diesels, one dating from 1934.

The class had a successful career, accumulating some 30 million miles of service. Not only were the Sri Lankans happy with them, but there was great pride in the 'Ceylons' at the Falcon Works among many employees, indeed when your author commenced his service there in 1960 they were still a much revered and fresh memory. By this time the works was well into producing the BR Type 2s, the direct descendant of the Ceylon locomotives, an era probably not foreseeable ten years earlier.

The period through which the design and construction of the Ceylon locomotives passed, saw some changes in the company organisation. The aforementioned registration of Brush Bagnall Traction Ltd in February 1951 was an important step and of course the execution of the Ceylon contract was another, but there was further change, which had far-reaching effects.

In 1950 A P Good became ill and it became apparent that his immense capacity for work was having a serious effect upon his health. As a result, Miles Beevor (formerly the last General Manager of the LNER) was appointed Deputy Managing Director of Brush and in October 1952 became Managing Director when A P Good resigned that position. Good remained Deputy Chairman and continued to take an active interest in the affairs of the various companies, although he relinquished his day-to-day responsibilities. He was also Chairman of Heenan & Froude Ltd, the owners of W G Bagnall Ltd. He left for South Africa at the beginning of January 1953, where he died the following month.

As stated previously, Mr Good was the link between many associated companies; it was a strong link, but it had one fatal flaw in that should he become unable to undertake his wide-ranging duties the link would be broken. His tragic death broke that link.

Typical locos of the Brush Bagnall era. This 1955 view shows Ceylon Government Railways No. 559, a Steel Company of Wales Bo-Bo and No. 506 also for the steel company.

BRUSH A3782

The policy of Brush Bagnall Traction Ltd. was to co-ordinate the diesel electric traction activities of Mirrlees, Brush and Bagnall; it was a selling and marketing organisation, and a wholly-owned Brush subsidiary. Mirrlees was part of the Brush Group, but Bagnall was owned by Heenan & Froude and continued to exist as a company separate from the Brush Group. Its owners were not interested in locomotive matters and this led to a cooling in relations and the eventual parting from the selling company at the very end of 1955.

Those at W G Bagnall realised what was likely to happen and made provision for the future. Steam locomotives had continued to be built at Stafford and there was an urgent need to enter the diesel market on its own account by building diesel mechanical locomotives. It also intended to continue supplying mechanical parts to Brush for as long as possible, should Brush continue to build diesel electric locomotives. From 1953, therefore, Bagnall actively pursued orders for diesel mechanical locomotives. Its efforts were to be to no avail, despite good orders and good designs. Stafford based engine company W H Dorman Ltd., looking for a railway outlet for its products, took control of Bagnall in January 1959. This new owner had a very short tenure, being itself taken over by English Electric in July 1961. Locomotive work was soon transferred away from the Castle Engine Works and a proud locomotive concern was no more. If only Mr Good had used Brush money in 1947 when the business was acquired, history may have been very different.

Meanwhile, in 1951, following a tour by Mr Good of the USA and Commonwealth countries, an order was received from the Queensland Government Railways for a full bodywidth locomotive powered by a 1,300bhp Mirrlees J12T engine. It was dated 7th June 1951 and the works number allocated to it, 3057, was never used because despite work starting on it the order was subsequently cancelled on 29th

August 1952, surprisingly because Brush-Bagnall requested to be released from the contract. It was allotted running number 1220. This locomotive was never included in the Brush register of locomotives, when it came to be compiled, although other cancellations were included. It is assumed that the design was similar to that of the Ceylon contract and that manufactured parts were scrapped.

Later in 1951 the National Gas & Oil Engine Company came completely into Mr Good's control through Brush. Brush-Bagnall then offered four basic designs of shunting locomotive for general railway and industrial use. The range was as follows:-

0-4-0	with 375bhp National supercharged M4AAU6 engine
0-6-0	with 400bhp National normal R4AA6 engine or 540bhp Mirrlees normal J6 engine
Bo-Bo	with 540bhp Mirrlees normal J6 engine or 750bhp Mirrlees supercharged JS6 engine
Bo-Bo	centre cab, with two 375bhp supercharged National M4AU6 engines

Of this range only the last basic design was never built.

During April 1953 further industrial orders for locomotives were received, not only for 0-6-0s but 0-4-0s and Bo-Bos also, representing three of the four ranges listed above.

Not just a view of a locomotive about to leave the Falcon Works, but a works scene frozen by the camera for all time. As No. 901 waits, SPRITE can be seen in one of its favourite parking spots, having brought 901 to the southern exchange sidings. Note also the Midland Railway swivel signal (far right), otherwise known as a 'stop, blast' signal, usually found on lines adjacent to more violent quarry activities.

BRUSH A3728

The driver's view of the southern exchange sidings at the Falcon Works, taken in 1955 from the cab of one of the SCoW Bo-Bo locomotives. Note the Ruston SPRITE and the cab of ACE beyond the adjacent coal wagons. Also worthy of note are the copper-domed tower and the Brush Falcon (aggressively threatening an LMS 4F standing on the BR southbound goods line).

BRUSH

The first order was dated 1st April 1953 and was for three 515bhp Bo-Bos for the Steel Company of Wales. They were allotted works Nos 3063 to 3065 (SCoW Nos 901 to 903 respectively) and were destined for use at the Abbey Works to join the American locomotives of 1950 which had given such a good performance and the experience of which had determined that there would be a future preference for Bo-Bo types on heavier duties.

The heavier duties required included haulage of steel ingot cars, and marshalling trains of finished steel and slag ladle cars. Experience with the American and Brush-Bagnall diesel electrics of SCoW showed various points that could be improved with future locomotives and these were incorporated into the new locomotives in conjunction with the customer's engineers. One special attention was given to the visibility from the cab in which the bonnet section adjacent to the cab was significantly lowered to afford a much better cross vision. This lowering introduced a 'whale-back' appearance to the locomotive outline. Other details entailed making the cabs more spacious and comfortable for the crews. The bogies featured a unique type of hemispherical centre pivot, which could produce a rolling motion under certain conditions. The locomotives were of massive proportions, so robust as to withstand the rigours of the steelworks for over 35 years with good maintenance. At the time of delivery they were reputedly the most powerful diesel electric steel works shunting locomotives of standard track gauge in Britain.

The diesel engine was supplied by Mirrlees, being a six-cylinder normally-aspirated JT6 type, developing 515bhp at 875rpm. It was coupled to a Brush self ventilated compound wound main generator and a self ventilated shunt wound auxiliary generator producing 10kW at 90V. All axles were driven by Brush axle-hung, nose-suspended, force-ventilated, double reduction geared traction motors. The latter were series wound and operated in series parallel connection across the main generator output, each being rated at 78hp, 295V, 220A.

Very impressive lines graced these 515bhp shunting locomotives and certain features combined to bear very obvious family resemblance to the 0-4-0 and 0-6-0 locomotives on offer from Brush-Bagnall, with their bonnet and radiator design, lowered rear power compartment roof of the bonnet and excellent cab, as fitted to the 0-4-0s.

A very striking feature at the time was the bold wasp-stripe warning panels covering extensive areas to aid their visibility in not only the yards but more so in some of the gloomier indoor areas.

These impressive machines emerged from the Falcon Works between March and June 1955, noticeably wearing large advertisement sheets en route. They went by rail, being mounted on special accommodation bogies.

The main details were as follows:

Steel Company of Wales Bo-Bo No. 902 hauling one of the special wagons for carrying molten steel.

Wheel arrangement	Bo-Bo
Track gauge	4ft 8½ins
Engine model	Mirrlees normally aspirated JT6
Engine rating	515bhp at 875rpm
Length over buffers	38ft 5½ins
Overall width	9ft 8ins
Overall height	13ft 3ins
Wheel diameter	3ft 6ins
Bogie wheelbase	8ft 0ins
Bogie centres	18ft 6ins
Minimum curve negotiable	80ft radius running light
Minimum curve negotiable	150ft radius loaded
Maximum speed	28mph
Maximum tractive effort	47,000lbs
Fuel capacity	350 gallons
Weight in working order	70 tons 0cwt

A small bonnet to the rear of the cab housed blower equipment and ducting for the force ventilated traction motors on the rear bogie. The bogies themselves were of fabricated steel plate construction, the side frames being 2½ins thick slab, and the main frames lying on the coil spring suspension. Clasp type air brakes were fitted, with double acting cylinders. As with the 0-4-0s radio telephone equipment

Steel Company of Wales Bo-Bo No. 902 hauling one of the special wagons for carrying molten steel.

BRITISH STEEL CORPORATION

was later mounted centrally between the front windows, inside the cab. Experience in service soon indicated that the heaviest requirement for loading had been underestimated and the locomotives were slightly underpowered as a result. To make amends three more-powerful locomotives were ordered to rectify the situation for the heaviest loading conditions. Nevertheless these three original locomotives were in use continuously, other than during maintenance periods, for over three decades at the Abbey Works. They were eventually re-engined with 600bhp Rolls Royce units and all were noted still in service in mid-1998.

The second contract placed on 1st April 1953 was also for the Steel Company of Wales and was for the supply of seven 0-4-0 diesel electric shunting locomotives for use at the Abbey Works also. They were allotted works numbers 3066 to 3072 inclusively and carried SCoW numbers 501 to 507 respectively. They were the first examples of the new design to be built, being sturdy and attractive machines. They were ordered as a direct result of the steel company's policy of expansion, which included the standardisation of the Brush-Bagnall 0-4-0 of 300bhp for lighter and general steelworks duties, as well as the 515bhp design for heavier duties. The latter cost more to build, but some of the resultant savings in service operation were advantageous, particularly from the reduced wheel wear on the severe track curvatures at the steel works. Likewise the 0-4-0s had a short wheelbase, better able to negotiate these curves, and with an engine output that fell little short of that of the 0-6-0s.

Each locomotive was fitted with a National M4AAU6 6-cylinder engine developing 300bhp at 1,200rpm. Directly coupled to it was a Brush direct current main generator, mounted on a common bedplate. It supplied power to two Brush double-reduction geared, nose-suspended traction motors, one to each axle.

As all railway clearances within the Abbey Works were generous, to accommodate the ALCO locomotives supplied in 1950, the opportunity was taken to fit a generously proportioned cab to these locomotives.

Indeed the cab arrangement was very good, with a centrally positioned rear access door, and excellent all-round vision as a result of the numerous windows. The side windows were the horizontally sliding type to enable the drivers to lean out of to obtain an even better view or to communicate with shunters close by. An additional door in the front of the cab gave access to the railed in running board, which was provided around the sides and front of the power compartment bonnet. As with the Bo-Bos the fuel tank was situated below the cab floor.

On this initial batch the bonnet front was plain, the radiator air louvres being on the bonnet top and sides. This arrangement was for the occasions when the locomotives were working in the vicinity of hot metal. Large circular type buffers were mounted on deep, heavy buffer beams, which in turn were welded on to the equally robust plate frames and deck. Straight air braking was fitted, operating on all wheels, with one brake shoe per wheel. Additionally, there

was a handbrake located inside the cab, this acting upon all wheels. The single-stage twin-cylinder air compressor was belt driven from the engine. Radio telephone equipment was fitted, as on the Bo-Bos, inside the cab centrally between the front windows. The main details of these locomotives are detailed below:

Wheel arrangement	0-4-0
Track gauge	4ft 8½ins
Engine model	National supercharged M4AAU6
Engine rating	300bhp at 1,200rpm
Length over buffers	25ft 5½ins
Overall width	9ft 8ins
Overall height	13ft 2ins
Wheel diameter	3ft 6ins
Rigid wheelbase	8ft 0ins
Maximum speed	20mph
Maximum tractive effort	24,000lbs
Fuel capacity	275 gallons
Weight in working order	43 tons 5cwt

Delivery took place between December 1954 and June 1955 from Stafford, where they were built. All these locomotives remained in service at the Abbey Works in 1977, but following the phasing out of the 0-6-0 locomotives some of them were converted for working in tandem during 1971/2. No. 501 became a 'master' unit and No. 502 became a 'slave' unit, that is when coupled both units were controlled from the former. They were also used in conjunction with units delivered later on, but similarly dealt with at the same time. The slave units

The massive proportions of No.501 are clearly visible in this view of it at rest between duties at the steelworks. The commodious cabs were much-appreciated by the crews.

S CHRISTIE COLLECTION

were instantly recognisable by the absence of cabs, these being rendered unnecessary by the conversion. Numbers 503/6/7 were re-engined by the British Steel Corporation (successors to SCoW) with 335bhp Rolls Royce engines.

In November 1985, Nos 503/6/7 were publicly offered for sale by the British Steel Corporation, together with other locomotives, but this met with little response. By 1987 Nos 501-5 were still at Abbey, although 501-3 were in store in the Refractories Engineering Department, two years later 503 had been returned to traffic and 505 had taken its place in store. Numbers 506 and 507 were transferred by BSC to its Trostre Works, Llanelli, between September 1988 and November 1989 and remained in late 1993 the only working locomotives at the works. Number 507 was in service there during 1996, but both locomotives were out of use by the end of 1997, being replaced by two Sentinel locomotives transferred from the by then closed Ravenscraig Works. Both were still there in April 1998, but out of use. One was seen five months later, and both were still out of use in October 2003.

Late 1993 saw 501/3/4/5 still at Abbey, although out of use. Missing 502 had been removed earlier that year and was reported as being at the Nottingham Sleeper Company's site at Elkesley, near Retford, on 9th July. In fact, it had been purchased by a railway enthusiast as part of Staffordshire Locomotives and left Port Talbot on the 6th of that month. By 25th November it had been moved to Coopers (Metals) Ltd of Sheffield for scrapping, the useful parts having been

Number 2 at Cwm displaying the neat outline and purposeful looks of the second generation Brush Bagnall 0-6-0 design, otherwise known as 'Standard Specification No.2'. Photographed late 1955.

BRUSH

removed to provide spare parts for his sister locomotive No. 510. This latter locomotive was purchased for preservation at the same time as 502 and a third locomotive, No. 508, which also underwent the same treatment to benefit No. 510.

During 1997 No. 501 (with later build No. 512) was donated to the West Somerset Railway by British Steel plc and arrived there on 22nd August, being noted at Williton during the Autumn Gala of 12-14th September and was still on the railway until mid-2000. During August 1997 a visitor to Port Talbot noted that No. 503 had been converted with raised cab for use as a coke car. It was scrapped in July 2006. At the time of the visit Nos 504/5 were noted out of use. All three locomotives held the same status in May 1998.

The third order received in April 1953 was placed on the second day of that month and came from the National Coal Board for use at Cwm Colliery, Llantwit Fardre, Glamorganshire (Mid Glamorgan from 1974). It was for two 0-6-0 diesel electric shunting locomotives, of 400bhp each, Brush-Bagnall Nos 3073 and 3074. They were built at Stafford and were delivered in September 1955, bearing running numbers 1 and 2 respectively. The basic design was as previous, but with some emerging differences. For example, there was the considerably lowered roof section on the generator compartment immediately in front of the cab, as on the Bo-Bos, to facilitate better cross vision for drivers when running forward. This limited forward vision had been an undesirable operating feature of all the previous Brush-Bagnall 0-6-0s, which had featured end cabs and high power unit compartments. An additional centrally placed front cab window was fitted to further improve vision. Instead of the previously fitted Mirrlees engine there was a National Gas & Oil Engine Company type R4AA6, a four-stroke, six-cylinder design developing 400bhp at 750rpm.

The main details of 3073 and 3074 were:

Wheel arrangement	0-6-0
Track gauge	4ft 8½ins
Engine model	National naturally aspirated R4AA6
Engine rating	400bhp at 750rpm maximum
	375bhp at 750rpm continuous
Length over buffers	30ft 9½ins
Overall width	8ft 8ins
Overall height	12ft 7½ins
Wheel diameter	4ft 0ins
Rigid wheelbase	12ft 0ins
Maximum speed	20mph
Maximum tractive effort	32,000lbs
Fuel capacity	400 gallons
Weight in working order	51 tons

At the time of ordering Cwm Colliery was part of the South Wales Division of the NCB and the two locomotives were required for heavy shunting and the marshalling of wagons around the colliery, particularly in and around the reception and departure lines alongside the BR Western Region line. Each locomotive was expected to deal with trains of up to 1,000 tons in weight when necessary.

The main generator was Brush self-ventilated, compound-wound, with a continuous rating of 213kW, 425V, 500A at 750rpm and a one-hour rating of 250kW, 425V, 590A at 750rpm. A Brush shunt-wound auxiliary generator was belt-driven from the main generator and mounted on top of it. Electric engine starting was fitted, a feature which had been the standard method of operation since the late 1940s on Brush locomotives. Braking equipment was by Westinghouse and of the straight air type, backed up by a hand brake used primarily for parking.

By the mid-1970s they were officially allocated to the coking plant at Cwm, and in 1982 were still working. By 1985, however, they were observed as out of use and by the July of that year partly cut up. They had gone completely by October 1987, being cut up on site by Taff Metal & Chemical Industries Ltd.

Two more basically similar 0-6-0s were ordered by Stewarts & Lloyds for its steelworks at Corby, Northamptonshire. The Brush register of locomotives lists the date as 28th November 1956, but the year is believed to be in error for the original ordering, which was 1954. The explanation is that they were built as stock initially; the register recording the date of ordering by Stewarts & Lloyds. Certainly, the frames were welded in 1955. Instead of the National engine there was a reversion to the Mirrlees TL6, six-cylinder engine rated at 400bhp. They outwardly had the outline of the Cwm

Two 0-6-0s were supplied to Stewart & Lloyds for use at their Corby steelworks (BT 3094/5 of 1956).
Once at Corby the two locomotives gained wasp striping as a safety measure to aid visibility among the shunting staff. The pair worked there until scrapped in the early 1970s.

BRUSH

locomotives, but the later heavily-striped (presumably yellow and black) livery was as striking as the latter's was plain. They were allocated Brush-Bagnall Nos 3094 and 3095. Delivery was in March 1956 and 3094 went on various demonstrations after completion and was observed at Moor Green Colliery, Eastwood, Nottinghamshire 18th July 1956. It went to Coppice Green Colliery, Derbyshire, that same month. Number 3095 was also on demonstration and between them demonstrations also took place in Newcastle and Yorkshire.

The pair was numbered D5 and D6 respectively on the Stewarts & Lloyds locomotive list at Corby. These numbers were abbreviated to 5 and 6 in later years. One of the pair underwent a trial which took place between 20th April and 16th May 1959, initiated by Stewarts & Lloyds. The object of the trial was to compare costs with steam traction on all the major duties normally carried out on mineral trains from surrounding quarries to the North Bank ore reception sidings on the northern fringes of the steelworks complex. The quarries involved were Cowthick, Park Lodge North, Earlstrees, Martin's, Priors Hall (South), Brookfield Cottage and Park Lodge. Additional work was done in the BR sidings. Maintenance was undertaken at weekends in the steel works locomotive shed. Some steam locomotive trials had taken place in 1958 and comparison was made with these, with the changes in fuel prices taken into consideration. A considerable saving in fuel costs was shown from the diesel trial and at its continuous rating the Brush locomotive tended to have a haulage capacity lying between that of the 16ins and 18ins cylinder steam locomotives on an average length of haul, but had a superior performance with a long and heavy haul because the 18ins steam locomotives tended to lose boiler pressure. Further advantages also showed in mileages run per shift, due to the greater availability of the diesel during each shift to run continuously. Steam locomotives had to have fires remade and boiler pressure brought up again immediately after each haulage run, whereas the diesel

was immediately ready for more work. In retrospect, these findings may appear obvious, but at the time engineers had to prove that diesel traction had definite advantages before improvements could be implemented.

Strange as it may seem, the two Brush-Bagnall locomotives outlived steam traction at Corby by only a short space of time. The latter had ceased by February 1970 and the two diesels, although still working in 1973, had also ceased operating by 1976. Indeed No. 5 was in a dismantled condition that year and No. 6 out of use. Both appear to have been scrapped in 1976.

According to the Brush register of locomotives, two more 0-4-0s were ordered on 28th September 1956. Again, the year appears to be an error and should be 1954 as they were originally ordered as demonstration locomotives. On the latter date two locomotives were ordered by the Steel Company of Wales, one for the Trostre Works, Llanelli, and the other for the Velindre tinplate works, Llangyfelach, in Glamorgan (West Glamorgan after 1973). The demonstration locomotives were utilised for the contract and were allocated Brush-Bagnall works numbers 3096 and 3097 respectively and both were equipped with the National M4AAU6 engine rated at 300bhp as fitted to the previous locomotives 3066-72. They were completed at Loughborough in March 1956, the works plates bearing the title BRUSH TRACTION, but retaining the numbers from the Bagnall list.

The former became the third No. 1 at Trostre and was later renumbered 3. It had a long and active life at the works being used mainly on hauling loads of steel coils from BR sidings to the works, returning with loaded 'Shocvans', each carrying two tons of bulk tinplate. It was available for duty on a 24-hour basis, but Brush-Bagnall 3021 was its standby during maintenance periods. It was still in full use in 1989, but by April 1991 was acting as a standby. By July 1991 it had gone to the Great Mountain Railway at Cynhcidre, Dyfed, to start a life in preservation. Its stay there was one

Sister locomotive to 3096 was LD1 (BT3097/1956) of the Velindre Works, by this time in the ownership of the British Steel Corporation. Photograph dated March 1976.

BRITISH STEEL

The 0-4-0 shunting locomotives were far too large for the BR loading gauge, so they were delivered to South Wales by road. Number 508, first of a second batch (508-513) for the Abbey Works, is being winched onto a low loader outside the Central Laboratories at the Falcon Works in 1956.

BRUSH A4363

Below: number 501 (master) paired this time with slave No. 502 at rest at Margam on 16th April 1976.

A J BOOTH

of controversy, in company with Brush-Bagnalls 3097 and 3021, just escaping the attentions of the scrap merchants to continue preservation from November 1992 at the Shropshire Locomotive Collection, near Wellington, where it remained at the end of 1996. It passed to the Somerset & Dorset Locomotive Co. and at the end of 2001 3096 had passed to McLaren's Antiques of Oswestry.

Number 3097 became No. LD1 at the Velindre tinplate works and was employed on similar shunting duties to the Trostre locomotive for many years, some of them in the company of No. 712 (Brush-Bagnall 2974), and was still active in 1987. It was out of use by 1989 and on closure of the works soon after this time, passed to the Great Mountain Railway. This occurred about January 1991, but the stay was short, lasting until November 1992 when it was sold, and with the aforementioned locomotives, passed to the Shropshire Locomotive Collection. It was still there in late 1996. It then passed to the Somerset & Dorset Locomotive Co., was on the Chasewater Railway at the end of 2003 and was then loaned to Snibson Discovery Park, Coalville, Leics by December 2004.

The next order in the locomotive register is dated 30th June 1955. It was received from the Steel Company of Wales and was for six further 0-4-0s, each of 300bhp, and fitted with National M4AAU6 engines. They were destined for the Abbey Works at Port Talbot and were allocated Brush-Bagnall works Nos 3098 to 3103, receiving running Nos 508 to 513 respectively. One further 0-4-0 locomotive was ordered on 2nd November 1955 for use at the Abbey Works. This was allotted works No. 3120 and SCoW No. 514. The seven locomotives were delivered by road from Loughborough during 1956 and 1957.

They worked with the previous 0-4-0 locomotives at the Abbey Works as normal locomotives until circa 1971/72 when multiple working was introduced. This has already been mentioned in connection with the previous locomotives and indeed both batches were similarly modified. Numbers 512-4 were converted to slave units and operated under the control of others (Nos 508-11) adapted as master units. Initially, No. 512 was the slave to No. 508.

All remained in use until about 1986, by which time some had been put into store in the Refractories Engineering Department (Nos 512-4). Two years later No. 511 had been added to their ranks. The slave units had their cabs removed during conversion. The works plates bore the title BRUSH TRACTION as delivery was during that period. By late 1993 509 was noted as the only one still active, whereas the others (511-4) remained on the site out of use. Numbers 508 and 510 had been seen at the Nottingham Sleeper Company's site at Elkesley (with previously mentioned No. 502) on 9th July 1993. They had been purchased by the same railway enthusiast and had left Port Talbot on 9th and 21st June respectively. Numbers 502 and 508 were in poor condition and all useful parts were removed for eventual use on No. 510. By 25th November 502/8 had gone to Coopers (Metals) Ltd of Sheffield for scrap. Number 510, the best of the three, was retained for preservation by the end of the year as part of 'Staffordshire Locomotives' and although listed as being at an undisclosed location in Staffordshire, it still remained at the Nottingham Sleeper Company site (actually at the Alpine Industrial Park Elkesley) in February 1995. Sadly, it was reported later in the year as being scrapped between early June and 12th August.

By August 1997 Nos 509/11/13/14 were in store at the Port Talbot Works and slave locomotive No. 512 had been donated to the West Somerset Railway (with master locomotive No. 501 of the previous batch). 501 was noted during the preserved railway's Autumn Gala of 12-14th September 1997 at Williton. No. 512 and its companion were still on the railway in the mid-2000s. During mid-1998 No. 509 was noted in the workshops, but Nos 511/13/14 were still stored. Number 511 was scrapped circa November 2005.

Prior to the order for the single 0-4-0 No. 3120, there had been an order placed on 15th August 1955 for three heavy duty Bo-Bo locomotives, again by the Steel Company of Wales. As related previously, the output of the previous bogie locomotives was found to be insufficient for the heaviest duties – it had been underestimated, so these locomotives were ordered to rectify the situation.

They were heavier at 88½ tons and 660bhp each and delivery was in 1957 from Loughborough to the Abbey Works. They received works Nos 3111-3, and SCoW Nos 951-3 respectively. The Mirrlees JS6 type four-stroke, six-cylinder engine was fitted, and it had a 660bhp rating at 875rpm. Drop bar equalising beams were fitted to the bogies of these heavier locomotives and it is of further interest to note that these locomotives were among the last to be produced from the official Brush-Bagnall orders. The last Brush-Bagnall order was for the aforementioned 0-4-0 No. 3120; the highest-numbered joint number in the Bagnall locomotive list. It was not, however, the last Brush locomotive to receive a Bagnall number.

The main details of the three Bo-Bos were as follows:

Wheel arrangement	Bo-Bo
Track gauge	4ft 8½ins
Engine model	Mirrlees supercharged JS6
Engine rating	660bhp at 875rpm maximum
Engine rating	600bhp at 850rpm
Traction motors (4)	Double reduction, nose-suspended, axle hung
Length over buffers	38ft 5½ins
Overall width	9ft 8ins
Overall height	13ft 3ins
Wheel diameter	3ft 6ins
Bogie wheelbase	8ft 0ins
Bogie centre	18ft 6ins
Maximum speed	28mph
Maximum tractive effort at starting	50,000lbs
Fuel capacity	560 gallons
Weight in full working order	90 tons nominal

It should be noted that there was an increase in weight of 20 tons from the previous Bo-Bo design. The extra weight was achieved by considerably thickening up of various components, amongst them the buffer beams were increased from 2ins to 3ins thickness and the bogie side plates from 2½ins to 4ins thickness. The resultant locomotive was truly massive to British eyes and easily the heaviest industrial diesel electric design to emerge from a British builder. They were duly delivered to the Abbey Works in 1957 in service on the heaviest duties, although by late 1993 No. 952 was recorded as out of use. Its status remained the same when the works was visited in August 1997, but Nos 951/3 were still in use. The situation in May 1998 was that Nos 951/2 were dismantled, barely more than just frames, and loaded on wagons, whereas No. 953 was still in use. Numbers 951/2 were scrapped during 2006/7.

The final Brush-Bagnall design to appear was the modified Bo-Bo version of the original 70 ton design, weighing 75 tons. Seven locomotives were ordered by the Steel Company of Wales from Brush Traction Ltd on 18th December 1956, again for use in the Abbey Works. They received works numbers 3137 to 3143 and SCoW running numbers 904 to 910 respectively. Two points should be made. First is that the order was placed almost a year after the demise of Brush Bagnall Traction Ltd. and the second is that they received works numbers from within the Bagnall list, despite being allocated Brush Traction works Nos 92 to 98 respectively. They did of course bear the title BRUSH TRACTION on the works plates, but your author believes that because they were actually built at Stafford the Bagnall numbers necessary for production purposes were actually translated onto the worksplates as a matter of convenience. One might almost say that it was a convenient anomaly! Only the Brush works numbers appear in the Brush register of locomotives. The locomotives were built at Stafford and represented the final chapter of the Brush and Bagnall liaison, albeit with the latter playing the part of subcontractor in producing the locomotives. Although the works plates bore the year 1957, it is believed that delivery extended into 1958.

The main details of these 75 ton locomotives were:

Wheel arrangement	Bo-Bo
Track gauge	4ft 8½ins
Engine model	Mirrlees normally aspirated JT6
Engine rating	515bhp at 875rpm
Traction motors (4)	Double reduction, nose-suspended, axle hung
Length over buffers	38ft 5½ins
Overall width	9ft 8ins
Overall height	13ft 3ins
Wheel diameter	3ft 6ins
Bogie wheelbase	8ft 0ins
Bogie centre	18ft 6ins
Maximum speed	28mph
Maximum tractive effort at starting	50,000lbs
Fuel capacity	560 gallons
Weight in full working order	75 tons nominal

These locomotives have formed part of the mainstay at the Abbey Works (better known collectively as the Port Talbot works) of SCoW and its successors British Steel. They still continue to operate in service and are still regarded as an essential part of operations there, undergoing refurbishment on occasions as necessary, latterly at Hunslet-Barclay of Kilmarnock, where No. 908 was noted in September 1992.

The work on 907 and 908 was completed during the early part of 1994 and on their return to South Wales they were renumbered 07 and 08 respectively. Number 909 followed later that year and was returned to Port Talbot on 4th January 1995, and then renumbered 09. These three locomotives and the four un-rebuilt examples were still in service in mid-1998. They were a lasting tribute to the Brush-Bagnall era and are still fondly remembered by those people concerned with their design and building.

The association that existed between Brush and Bagnall had a reign of ten years, formally cemented for five of them by Brush Bagnall Traction Ltd. Over this period Bagnall produced the mechanical parts and the locomotives were erected at either Stafford or Loughborough as capacity allowed. Except for the aforementioned locomotives, Bagnall was a subcontractor to Brush Traction Ltd for the supply of mechanical parts. It was not the only subcontractor and it continued to pursue its own locomotive building activities at Stafford until 1962. There was some overlap between the two eras and for this reason it is necessary to partly segregate the locomotive building narrative.

At the end of 2005 the Corus works at Port Talbot had the following locomotives still working:

Numbers 504 BBT 3069, 506 BBT 3071, 509 BBT 3099, but 505/BT 1 BBT 3070, 513/BT 2 BBT 3103, 514/BT 3 BBT 3120, were noted converted to brake tenders for use with 504, 506, 509.

Out of use as a source of spares were 507 (BBT 3072), 511 (BBT 3101) and 503 (BBT 3068). The last was converted to a coke oven locomotive for use at Grange Coke Ovens and had been out of use for some years. Seven Bo-Bo locomotives were also in use at this time.

An unusual move took place, following a visit to the West Somerset Railway by a Corus engineer. Number 512, BBT 3066/1954, duly left preservation on the West Somerset Railway and arrived at Corus, Strip Products Division, Port Talbot Works on 29th June 2006. It was to be converted to a brake tender, BT 04. In effect it had arrived home again, together with sister locomotive 501 (BBT 3102/1956) which had preceded it by a day and was due to be overhauled for a return to work in industry again.

Number 501 returned to traffic on 16th January 2007 and was used with BT4, working from South Sidings to the various mills and to Margam Knuckle Yard exchange sidings on coil and slab steel traffic.

On 16th February 2007 visitors to the complex noted 504, 509, 903, 905 and 906 in the locomotive shop, with 09 (909) and 953 on hot metal workings.

On 14th August 2007 visitors observed and were informed of various Brush locomotives of the Margam Works as shown overleaf (with the term 'in use' indicating part of the operational fleet):

Brush Locomotives at Margam, 14th August 2007.

501	in use with BT-4 (ex 512) formerly preserved on the West Somerset Railway
503	scrapped 07.1996
504	in use with BT-1 (ex 514)
506	in use with BT-3 (ex 513)
507	out of use as a source of spare parts
509	spare loco used with BT-2 (ex 505)
511	scrapped c11.2005
901 to 906	in use (906 undergoing 500 hr examination)
07 to 09	in use (07 undergoing 3000 hr examination)
910	out of use as a source of spare parts
951	scrapped c2006/7
952	scrapped c2006/7
953	in use (under repair)

NB Corus records used for the locomotives listed in the table alongside indicate differing previous identities of Brake Tenders to previous reports.

The requirements were for ten out of fourteen operational locomotives to be available for service, with four of the original Bo-Bo locomotives required for working the two blast furnaces, with one of the Hunslet Barclay rebuilt Bo-Bo locomotives shunting at the steel plant. The remainder were for general use around the complex.

The veteran Brush locomotives were not expected to continue in service for much longer as Corus had three Corus-designed B-B diesel hydraulic locomotives on order to initially replace the 0-4-0 locomotives and brake tenders. If successful, further examples would be ordered to replace the un-rebuilt Bo-Bo locomotives.

*   *   *   *   *

The Mirrlees JVS12T 12-cylinder turbo-charged 1,250bhp power unit, coupled to its Brush generator producing 823kW at 686v and 1,200 amps for the Type 2 locomotives described in the next chapter (facing) as illustrated in a sales brochure published c1956

BRUSH

4 – The Brush Traction Era of the Type 2s

Brush Traction Ltd was formed in January 1956. Brush Bagnall Traction Ltd provided the operational basis and continuity for the new company and the changeover from a joint company representation to a single one involved the mutual withdrawal of some of the personalities to their parent Boards. The relations between Brush and Bagnall nevertheless remained cordial, the drifting apart had occurred between Bagnall's owners, Heenan & Froude, and Brush.

Brush sought another locomotive builder for its mechanical parts, and indeed for subcontracting the erection of shunting locomotives when the Falcon Works was short of capacity to erect its own. Beyer-Peacock Ltd of Manchester was to admirably fulfil this role for a number of years.

The history of Brush Traction has several concurrent and intertwined themes of locomotive building activity, some easily separated, others not so easily separated, so in describing the Brush Type 2 era of 1956 to 1962 it is necessary to include in the account some of the industrial shunting locomotives with the main line locomotives.

As a company in its own right, within the Brush Group, Brush Traction Ltd had a short life. During mid-1957 Brush and its group of companies were taken over by Hawker Siddeley and became part of the Hawker Siddeley Group. In 1958 Brush Traction Ltd became a division of the Brush Electrical Engineering Company Ltd under the management of Mr F H Wood, who originally had come to Loughborough under secondment. To those outside the works the change went almost unnoticed, to those within perhaps a little less, but certainly there were no great changes. To the staff the activity was always known as 'Traction'. The date of acquisition of The Brush Group by Hawker Siddeley was 31st July 1957, and the price of the Hawker Siddeley offer was £22 million.

One of the benefits to Brush was to be the provision of greatly-needed funds to expand facilities, particularly in the sphere of rail traction. Prior to the take-over capital had been in severely short supply. Indeed, doubts about the future of Brush Traction had been expressed within the works in an address to the whole of the traction staff in December 1956. They were told that locomotive building was to cease on completion of the twenty Type 2s ordered a year previously for the British Railways Modernisation pilot scheme. This included any other outstanding locomotive orders.

Due to the limited erection facilities and finance to provide them, Brush was going to link up with a large locomotive builder and cease to be a main contractor for main line locomotives for overseas and British Railways. Instead, the company would manufacture and sell electrical equipment for diesel electric locomotives to railways and locomotive builders. It would only be the main contractor for diesel electric shunting locomotives, and then only where prepared designs existed, and that the mechanical design staff would be reduced accordingly.

It was not the best outlook that one could have wished to hear, but the Brush company was operating at a loss and there was no capital available for expansion. In retrospect, this all may seem very surprising but it must be remembered that there was no immediate intention at the time for BR to acquire further diesel electric locomotives while those supplied to them under the pilot scheme were being evaluated. Only a surprise change in BR policy together with the Hawker Siddeley backing altered the course of events.

As alluded to above, the BR modernisation plan was the key to the success of Brush Traction. This was published by the British Transport Commission (BTC) on 25th January 1955 and was submitted to the Government for approval.

A summary of its intentions was that no new steam traction for express passenger or suburban use would be built after the 1956 programme of locomotive building and construction of all steam locomotives was to cease within a few years. Diesel traction was to replace that of steam and act as an interim provision on main routes where electrification was the ultimate intention. There would be a diesel locomotive pilot scheme whereby manufacturers would submit designs and the best available would be selected in small quantities for evaluation in service.

BR had already some seven prototypes in operation, experience of which was valuable but limited. A total of 171 (later 174) locomotives was considered to be desirable for a main line use, and a speedy delivery was an essential factor of the programme.

It was considered, quite correctly, that these locomotives would provide some valuable experience, but it was stressed that these new diesels would not necessarily be the future standard types to be adopted. Here we see the uncertainty of the situation at the time, reflected in the outlook of Brush as outlined above.

The modernisation scheme resulted in orders as listed below and overleaf:

Heavy Duty, 2,000bhp and over, Type C
10 locomotives of 2,000bhp from English Electric
5 locomotives of 2,000bhp from the North British Locomotive Company
10 locomotives of 2,300bhp from BR workshops, Derby

Mixed Traffic, 1,000-1,250bhp, Type B
10 locomotives of 1,100bhp from English Electric
20 locomotives of 1,160bhp from Birmingham Carriage & Wagon Ltd
20 locomotives of 1,250bhp from Brush Traction
10 locomotives of 1,000bhp from the North British Locomotive Company
6 locomotives of 1,000bhp from the North British Locomotive Company
20 locomotives of 1,200bhp from Metropolitan-Vickers
20 locomotives of 1,160bhp from BR workshops, Derby
Freight, 800-1,000bhp, Type A
20 locomotives of 1,000bhp from English Electric
10 locomotives of 800bhp from British Thomson-Houston
10 locomotives of 900bhp from the North British Locomotive Company

The above represented a variety of designs, diesel engines and transmissions in combination. The latter was divided between hydraulic transmission (the six North British Locomotive Company (NBL) mixed traffic locomotives and the five NBL heavy duty locomotives) and electric, for the remaining 160. It may appear as somewhat surprising that no examples from the USA were ordered. There had been some consideration, but it is believed that the hand of political expediency was the reason for no such order being placed. Conversely, Eire chose to order its main line diesel locomotives from the USA after troubles with its initial orders from British firms, but there also existed differing political expediences, which may have influenced events.

As alluded to above, Brush, therefore, had received an order for twenty diesel electric locomotives for BR during late 1955, the locomotive register states 22nd November 1955, just within the closing weeks of Brush Bagnall Traction Ltd. It was valued at nearly £1.5 million. The design was based upon that supplied to Ceylon and it was this design which led to the order for BR being placed by the British Transport Commission (BTC). Initial artist's impressions developed the Ceylon outline slightly by removing the nose sections and substituting a flat cab front reaching downwards to

encompass the buffer beam and extend nearly to rail level. This was the initial approach to cleaner lines, but above the intended inter-locomotive connection doors two very uninspiring windows were placed. The doors section projected forward prominently, but was recessed behind the flush front of the locomotive in the next artist's impression. In both impressions the side windows of the mid-body area remained circular, but the porthole fashion was discarded in a further impression and never reinstated. The bodyside louvre layout was tidied but initial views presented a fairly depressing aspect. Fortunately, as things progressed, the BTC design consultants Wilkes and Ashmore of Horsham modified it to the now familiar outlines, which vary only in detail. A wooden mock-up cab was produced in 1957 bearing these familiar lines, for workshop and later exhibition purposes. It bore the number D505 and the new BRUSH TRACTION works plates, together with the intended livery of Brunswick green with two horizontal lines and the cab window area picked out in a light colour, probably either a very light green or light cream. It then received the number D5500 and later still was fitted with an imitation roof-mounted indicator box. It was noted in this condition, sans works plates, at the Falcon Works in late 1959. The livery was also chosen with the benefit of the advice of Wilkes and Ashmore and although their impact on the pilot scheme diesels was minimal, what limited involvement did occur was effective in the short time available. Events led to the setting up of the BR Design Panel in August 1956, and it was this panel which rejected the original Brush proposals. It has been suggested that it was the Brush outline submission, in the shape of the

An artist's impression of the Brush Type 2, of November 1955, before the British Transport Commission Design Panel re-styled it. This re-styling undoubtedly enhanced the locomotive's appearance and paved the way for the now familiar outline of the Brush Type 4.

BRUSH A3912

Wheel arrangement	A1A-A1A
Track gauge	4ft 8½ins
Engine model	Mirrlees turbocharged JVS12T, 12-cylinder, four-stroke, V-type
Engine rating	1,250bhp at 850rpm
Main generator	Brush, 823kW, 686V, 1,200A
	820kW, 820V, 1,000A
Auxiliary generator	Brush, 450/850rpm, 30kW, 110V, 273A, continuous rating
Traction motors (4)	Brush, 250bhp, 343V, 600A, 485rpm, continuous rating. 247bhp, 312V, 660A, 420rpm, one hour rating. Force ventilated, nose-suspended, axle hung.
Length over buffers	56ft 9ins
Overall width	8ft 9ins
Overall height	12ft 7ins
Wheel diameter	3ft 7ins motored 3ft 3ins non-motored
Bogie wheelbase	14ft 0ins
Bogie centres	28ft 10ins
Minimum curve neg'able	4½ chains
Maximum speed	75mph
Maximum tractive effort	42,000lbs
Continuous tractive effort	22,400lbs
Fuel capacity	500 gallons
Weight in working order	104 tons

Once a decision had been reached about the general external form of the Type 2, a wooden mock-up was made in November 1956, for evaluation purposes. Why the number D505 was chosen is not known, but it was given a more relevant one when exhibited in 1958.

BRUSH A4384

artist's impression, which gave weight to the argument for BR to set up its own design panel for ensuring good aesthetic design appearances for the future. If this is so, then Brush unwittingly encouraged the changes that were still in the embryo stage.

The Type B specification called for double cab arrangement, provision for train heating equipment, inter-locomotive connections at each end, multiple operation and the facility to remove the power unit sideways. The Brush design was the only one to comply with this last-named requirement, hence a much heavier locomotive than the competitors' designs, needing the A1A-A1A wheel arrangement. This provoked some criticism from the press, but was much appreciated by the drivers as it gave better braking power to control the unbraked coal trains as well as a better ride. The robustness has proved its worth over the years. Naturally, Brush chose the Ceylon design as its starting point in most respects and it adapted well to BR requirements. The main details and dimensions of the Brush Type 2 (re-designated from Type B during construction) are given in the following table:

Straight Westinghouse brake equipment was fitted, with vacuum for the train and compressed air for the locomotive. The locomotive brakes could be applied directly by the driver via the 'straight' air brake when working light locomotive or unfitted trains, or indirectly via a vacuum/air proportional valve when working vacuum-fitted trains, plus of course the legally required emergency action if a fault occurred down the train. The underframe was of conventional design stiffened up to meet the requirement for changing power units. It was comprised of four rolled steel longitudinal girders welded to cross members and drag boxes. The body was steel-panelled and welded to a frame of formers and stiffeners, with hatches and access doors. Roof sections were readily removable for maintenance purposes, as were some body side panels. The bogies were made from one-piece steel castings of the Commonwealth type (rather than the plate type fitted to the Ceylon locomotives) with only the outer axles powered. The specification for the Type 2 design required an axle load not exceeding 18 tons, so because of the heavy nature of the electrical equipment and frame, and the sideways removal of power equipment stipulation, the A1A-A1A wheel arrangement was adopted, rather than Bo-Bo. No lightweight materials were used. Flexible gangways were provided for inter-locomotive transfer of personnel, but in practice these were little used and a source of unwelcome draughts.

The final livery chosen was Brunswick green, relieved by two light blue/grey or blue/green horizontal bands at mid-waist and lower bodyside levels and similarly shaded cab window surround. The roof section was pale grey. The running numbers were applied in the same shade as the lines, in a neat condensed style with the D prefix sans serif. Eventually serifs were officially specified for the prefixes to avoid the letters being read as zero! This post-dated the delivery of the first twenty Brush Type 2s. The running number was placed initially above the works plate at the No. 1 end, that nearest to the largest body side air intake louvres. The then new BR heraldic crest was applied in transfer form to the body sides as near to the centre-line as interruptions would allow. Control of the locomotives was by electro-magnetic means with two stages of traction motor field weakening. The train heating system in use at that time was by steam and the locomotives were fitted with Spanner 'Swirlyflow' boilers fed from independent fuel and water tanks.

Existing practice also dictated that train description indicating discs should be fitted, four mounted on each nose in the manner of three in a horizontal row, with the fourth mounted higher up above the centre disc. These positions corresponded with those established for steam traction many years before. Each disc was in two sections, being hinged horizontally across the centre, each half displaying its white-painted surface when opened out, but with a hole in the lower half allowing a marker light behind to shine through. When not in use the upper half was folded down to reveal its green-painted surface to provide no indication and to blank off the marker light if it was inadvertently left on. Two red marker lights were also fitted as well as the standard lamp irons, to take the traditional oil lamps.

Running numbers D5500 to D5519 were allocated by BR to these Brush Type 2s and Brush allocated works numbers 71 to 90 respectively. The former were part of a new series of running numbers selected especially for diesel locomotives, thus they were prefixed D to avoid confusion with steam locomotives of the same number. Brush felt obliged to have its own series of works numbers after the demise of Brush Bagnall Ltd and was no doubt inspired by the works numbers used by Bagnall. The lowest Brush Traction number issued was 71 and was derived in theory by being the sum total of Brush and Brush Bagnall production plus one. Strangely, this omitted SPRITE in diesel form, but did include other locomotives not built under the Brush Bagnall association (stock cancellations) and omitted the cancelled Queensland locomotive. The claims for some of the early locomotives were a little tenuous, some were built by the users, but counted because Brush was the main contractor. Regardless of the ethics involved in the summation it was the first time since before the First World War that Brush had consciously used its very own locomotive works numbers. Some interesting asides were to emerge in following years – indeed, the use of Bagnall numbers on locomotives built at Stafford, but subcontracted from Brush Traction has been considered in Chapter 3.

It is worth recording that mechanical parts for the Brush Type 2s were manufactured by Beyer Peacock Ltd. of Gorton, Manchester as well as by W G Bagnall, the latter certainly using its own works number series for the mainframes supplied to Loughborough from Stafford. Of the first twenty locomotives Nos D5515-19 had underframes made at Stafford, numbered 3127-31.

The first Type 2, No. D5500, nearing completion at the Falcon Works in the late summer of 1957. The second and third are well advanced, while the frame of the future D5505 can be seen on the extreme right. Note the boards hung on each locomotive, showing target dates for test.

BRUSH A4815

The Type 2 personnel group photograph of 1957, posed in front of one of the first of the pilot batch. Some of the faces were still familiar at Brush in the early 1990s.

BRUSH A4947

Work progressed at Loughborough on the pilot scheme locomotives and although there was some delay concerned with engine delivery, it progressed well. The underframe had a camber built into it and dummy power units were used to take up this camber and enable the body sides to be fitted. One story has it that the engine delay led to resort being made to fit a dummy power unit for longer than envisaged, to enable work to continue on the first one. When the time came to fit the proper power unit, removal of the dummy resulted in some buckling of the side panels as the frame flexed upwards. The cantrails had not been fitted by this time, so the non-load bearing sides bore the strain unintentionally. Some dismay was caused at the time because the handing-over ceremony was not too far off. If there was any buckling it was because the joints were not uncoupled, but it is unlikely that the foreman, 'Tag' Allen, would have allowed this to occur. If the story is true, then the situation was soon rectified, because D5500 was actually completed early in recognisable form, despite engine delays, in the first week of September 1957. It was ready for static testing towards the end of the month. The scheduled delivery to the Eastern Region of BR was to be within two years of the order being placed. In the event it was five weeks early.

Once mechanically and electrically complete D5500 underwent running tests at the Falcon Works and ventured out onto the Midland Main Line between Loughborough and Chinley at speed. It appeared with most of the body in workshop brown primer finish, complete with its running number, the waist stripe picked out in white and the BR crest applied.

The date of this first trial run out on the main line was 8th October. The times of the departure and return of D5500 leaked out and such was the interest that the boundary between the Falcon Works and the BR lines was lined with Brush personnel. It was the first of three arranged between that date and 11th October. That of 10th October was from Loughborough to Chinley, in the Derbyshire Peak District, via Trent Junction. Strictly, the trial proper was between Derby and Chinley because empty coaching stock had to be attached before D5500 set out from Derby, but any running light was a valuable experience beforehand and some brief driver training was done from Derby to Trent and back. The test train consisted of thirteen coaches giving a total weight of 393 tons. The maximum gradient offered en route was 1 in 90. The main line through Derbyshire provided a favourite test run for engineers for some years and so far as Brush was concerned the Chinley triangle and station provided a convenient stopping venue for photographic purposes as well as a convenient turn-round point. Once back in the Falcon Works D5500 was prepared for the handing over ceremony and painted in the aforementioned BR green livery.

Handing over ceremonies always offer the opportunity for a brief pause for the people involved to reflect upon the effort expended to reach that point and to project that success into the future. It was held on Thursday 31st October 1957 and was attended by the press, both local and national, and of course the technical press, all suitably armed with handout literature to describe the new product. Also in attendance were BBC radio and television and Commercial television.

The dignitaries of Brush, the British Transport Commission and British Railways Eastern Region naturally attended. Sir Reginald Wilson accepted D5500 on behalf of the Eastern Region from Mr Geoffrey Eley, Chairman of the Brush Group.

D5500 in primer coat at the head of its test train standing at Chinley station 10th October 1957.

BRUSH A4909

Also present were Mr R C Bond (Chief Mechanical Engineer, BR), Mr Maurice Tattersfield (Brush Loughborough Managing Director), Mr F H Wood (Manager of Brush Traction), Mr E S Cox (Mechanical Engineer, BR Development) and others. Special mention must be made that the occasion gathered together some personalities well known within railway circles for their historic contributions to the industry. Mr H G Ivatt, then a director of Brush Traction, but formerly the last Chief Mechanical Engineer of the London Midland &

Scottish Railway, had much involvement in the birth of the Brush Type 2, ably backing it with his immense experience in launching that railway's two main line diesel electric locomotives during the 1946-8 period. Also of note was the presence of two of his colleagues from LMS days, Messrs Bond and Cox. Brush was fortunate in having the influence of Ivatt combined with that of Sir Ronald Matthews and Mr Miles Beevor, both formerly of the London & North Eastern Railway and equally well-respected men. Although not all the influential men attended, it must not be forgotten that their contribution over the years led to this successful beginning.

After welcoming everyone to the ceremony, Mr Geoffrey Eley delivered his address and officially handed over D5500. Sir Reginald Wilson replied and accepted the locomotive, but amid all the pleasantries of the occasion he delivered a veiled implication that more orders might not be forthcoming. Certainly more orders were not expected immediately, and only then if BR was satisfied with the pilot locomotives, but people were well aware of the situation and the hints did not bode well for the future of Brush Traction.

Before the end of the year Brush officials were pessimistically viewing the future privately, considering that to enter the main line locomotive field proper some sort of licensing or liaison would be necessary. It is very probable that the pessimistic view emanated from a recommendation of August 1957,

D5500 following delivery to BR Doncaster Locomotive Works in the autumn of 1957.

BR 57/294 via BRUSH

stemming from a report by a BTC joint committee of Chief mechanical and electrical engineers. The recommendation was that the standard Type 2 would be built by BR and would include a Sulzer engine and British Thomson-Houston electrical equipment. Luckily, changes were to occur within BR and after Mr B L Goodlet became Managing Director at Brush in December 1957 a more optimistic and aggressive approach was initiated.

After the handing over ceremony Sir Reginald, accompanied by a number of senior executives, entered the leading cab of D5500 and after a quick examination of the controls, drove the locomotive along the quarter mile of test track and back again into the Erecting Shop. Escorted by Mr Ivatt and Mr F H Wood, he then made a detailed inspection of the interior of D5500. Later the guests adjourned for lunch at the King's Head Hotel in Loughborough's High Street and on returning to the works rode in the cabs of the second locomotive, D5501, along the test track. All departed the occasion suitably impressed. Certainly, of all the handing over ceremonies that occurred this one was perhaps the most notable, not only because of the sense of occasion of the day, but, regarding what was to follow, in retrospect also.

D5500 left the Falcon Works bound for Doncaster Works of BR (ER) where it was submitted for acceptance tests by the Chief Mechanical & Electrical Engineer's department and the attentions of the BR photographer. Further photographs were taken, particularly near Grantham on 8th November, during a run on the East Coast Main Line during these acceptance trials. Subsequently, mid-day Thursday became the regular delivery time, a crew from Doncaster motive power depot travelling to Loughborough to collect. A passenger train to Peterborough and a 750 ton freight train to Spalding were the usual test runs. If the locomotive was deemed satisfactory on return, Brush would receive the acceptance certificate within a week and the locomotive would enter regular revenue earning service, which in 1957 and 1958 was on the Great Eastern lines out of London into East Anglia.

D5500 initially went to Stratford motive power depot in London after being accepted by BR. Nominally based on this depot, and having come up light engine from Doncaster the previous day, she made her first revenue earning run on passenger train duties on 13th November 1957 when she left Liverpool Street station at the head of the 10.36 bound for Clacton. This was a return trip. The first main line diesel locomotive for the Eastern Region had arrived – and it was Brush built! The following day she returned to Doncaster, bringing the 12.48pm parcels train from Stratford as far as Whitemoor. On 25th November D5500 began trials with passenger and fitted goods trains between Stratford and Southend (Victoria).

D5501 soon followed on after D5500, in November 1957, but went on exhibition at the Mirrlees Hazel Grove Works, Stockport, as part of the celebrations commemorating fifty years of diesel engine production there. Following these celebrations it also went to Doncaster to undergo acceptance and further trials.

The Great Eastern section of the Eastern Region was where the first twenty Brush Type 2s were destined to operate. Being mixed traffic locomotives they were equally at home on a variety of duties but freight work was expected to predominate at the time. All twenty were based at Stratford and deliveries from Loughborough were scheduled at the rate of one every three weeks. Appendix 2 lists the dates to traffic.

During mid-January 1958 D5502 and D5503 were noted at Doncaster and then working in multiple at the head of empty coaching stock through Newark in both directions on the 14th, presumably on acceptance trials.

On 20th January the Brush Type 2s began a spell of passenger duty on the Great Eastern main lines. D5502 worked the 10.30am Liverpool Street to Norwich, returning with the 3.45pm and on the 23rd D5503 worked the 8.50pm Liverpool Street to Ely, returning from there on the 11.42 freight back to Stratford. Meanwhile, D5500 had been working passenger services and D5501 had been undertaking freight duties. The former had reached Sheffield during the month on Harwich - Liverpool boat trains.

D5507 went into service with its engine uprated to 1,450bhp, it was stated, so that it could act as standby to newly-delivered 2,000bhp English Electric Type 4s on the Norwich services. The difference in horse power was considerable and it is questionable whether this move was a practical one. What in practical terms was the most likely move for uprating this locomotive was to undertake trials to establish the engine capabilities and couple this move to establish a permissible increase in the top speed of the Brush Type 2 to 85mph. This was expected to provide information which could be used to determine whether or not the second order for Brush Type 2s could consist of locomotives of increased output and a top speed of 90mph. In this respect the trial uprating was successful and the next order of locomotives was so treated. The standby question was probably one posed by the operating people. The locomotive was reset to 1,250bhp after the trial and operated as a standard locomotive.

D5511 was at Doncaster Works on acceptance trials on 14th June 1958, but during the early part of August was noted at Inverness on loan to the Scottish Region. On 5th August the locomotive was noted on the 1.45pm freight train to Wick. Several runs were made to Wick and over the West Highland and Oban lines. Trips on coal trains were undertaken into the Glasgow area and main line workings to Carlisle were included. On 2nd September she was noted back on the Eastern Region, but had gained running numbers on the previously blank cabside panels when she called into Doncaster Works en route south from Scotland to Stratford.

D5516 was the subject of performance and efficiency tests over the Great Eastern lines. A dynamometer car was used to measure aspects of the tests, such as drawbar tractive effort, and work done on a time and speed basis. Various types of test were conducted. The first were controlled road tests over the main line between London and Norwich, via Ipswich, over the full speed range up to 80mph. The next tests were on passenger trains in normal service conditions, in the down direction on the 08.30 from Liverpool Street station to Norwich, returning with the 14.45.

The third batch of tests involved working freight trains on Class 'E' unbraked trains between Temple Mills and Whitemoor. Bad weather made these tests less informative

Contrasting scenes depicting D5515 (BT85) on the test track at Loughborough in August 1958. and the departing view of the Falcon Works, taken from a new Brush Type 2. One of the new Brush/Beyer Peacock shunting locomotives is seen ahead, in charge of shunting wagons near the boiler house. To the right is the striped cab rear of the Ruston SPRITE.

BRUSH A5285 BRUSH A5740

than they might have been. The final tests were with freight trains also, with loads of 900, 1,000 and 1,100 tons on the rising gradients between Cambridge and Elsenham. These were undertaken to obtain information as to the maximum starting tractive efforts that could be exerted, and to obtain a record of the full power performance at lower speeds than possible on the previous tests.

All the tests found that the locomotive was closely in accordance with its rated characteristics. The tests also indicated that the 1,250bhp rating was somewhat modest for the exacting schedules expected of the locomotives on the Great Eastern lines, a fact realised early on by those operating the locomotives. This was not adverse criticism of the locomotive performance, but passing comment on the uncertainty of horsepower requirement by BR in 1955. Future uprating of the Mirrlees engine came in stages. By the end of the tests D5516 had run a total of 16,700 miles.

On 6th November 1958 D5517 hauled the 4.45pm from Cambridge complete with attached Royal Saloon conveying Princess Margaret, one of the first recorded royal journeys courtesy of a Brush Type 2.

By the end of the month all twenty of the Pilot Scheme Brush Type 2s had been delivered and were in service on the Great Eastern section of the Eastern Region and several months later were receiving scheduled overhauls by Brush personnel at Stratford. The pioneer D5500 had completed 70,000 miles by the end of January 1959.

In 1958 the twenty locomotives were classified by the Eastern Region as DML 61/1250, an explanation being Diesel Main Line with Mirrlees engine (6), Brush manufacture (1), and 1,250bhp rating. In 1960 this was changed to D12/2.

The Eastern Region personnel took to the Brush Type 2s immediately and a further forty similar locomotives were ordered in July 1958. That first batch of twenty proved to be a turning point for Brush and the services upon which they operated proved their capabilities without any doubt. It is nearly always the case that when prototype or pilot batches of locomotives (and other things) are repeated, improvements and differences are incorporated in the successors. It often makes the first-born non-standard, once the succeeding standard has been established, and this was so with D5500-D5519 because BR subsequently standardised on air control of engine speed. The first twenty had electric control, with a driver's control handle (distinctively shaped to earn the locomotives the name 'Toffee Apples'), and of course different multiple-unit jumpers. Thus they became the odd men out, as it were, and spent their working careers based on the Eastern Region, in particular the Great Eastern Section, although they could be seen working into other regions. This reduced any disadvantages that might exist by concentrating spare parts, maintenance facilities and train crews familiar with them in one area of the country. Furthermore, should they be required to work in multiple and because they were compatible only with each other in this respect, then there usually would be pairs readily available by employing such a concentration.

To some extent they were overshadowed by their sister successors, but when in later years their existence was threatened, railway enthusiasts singled them out for adulation. For most of the time they undertook their tasks without fame or much widespread recognition, but the men who drove them and maintained them recognised that they were good and respected their charges. There were engine troubles in the early and mid-1960s, which affected most of the class and led to a decision to re-engine them all with English Electric engines. This problem will be elaborated upon later in the account, but in the meantime it is sufficient to record that the first twenty received new engines during the 1967 to 1969 period. They changed little visibly over the years, except that the blue/green area surrounding the cab windows was changed to green during some of the first repaints and that the attractive green livery gave way to the dull and uninspiring BR Corporate blue from the mid-1960s onwards, although they did pass through an intermediate stage of green with corporate identity markings.

One of the batch did change both outwardly and inwardly as a result of being repaired drastically following an accident. D5518 suffered extensive damage to both cabs, some damage concerning the control equipment, and an opportunity was taken to bring the locomotive up to standard. The electro-magnetic control equipment was replaced by electro-pneumatic and cabs having roof-mounted, four-character roller blind train indicating equipment replaced the ones fitted with disc indicators. One cab was taken from stock, indeed there were no stocks of the latter type available.

D5658 of a later batch of Brush Type 2s was a source of immediate replacement parts, notably the other cab, thus perpetuating a long-established workshop practice of freely exchanging parts among locomotives in for repair or overhaul. The rebuilding also provided a costing exercise regarding the feasibility of converting the rest of the Pilot Scheme batch to the newly established BR standards, but it proved too expensive. With considerable running and maintenance experience BR was establishing new standard requirements. Nevertheless, despite being non-standard, their careers were extended considerably by the fact that they had fairly new replacement engines fitted. Surprisingly, D5518 was not repainted blue, but merely had its green livery re-touched and varnished.

Because of the more obvious external changes D5518 was instantly recognisable there-afterwards as being different from the rest of her batch, but only for several years, due to a wholescale renumbering of BR locomotives into a computer based system that incorporated classification and sub-classification numbers within the running number. The system had been laid down in 1968 as part of the computerised system known as Total Operations System (TOPS) in which the Mirrlees-engined Brush Type 2s became Class 30 and the re-engined examples became Class 31. By the time the renumbering was applied, all had received replacement engines and had numbers commencing with 31. D5501 to D5517 became 31 001 to 31 017 respectively, D5500 became 31 018 and D5519 became 31 019 (of Class 31/0). D5518, because of its newly-found standard status shifted to Class 31/1 and became 31 101. The general renumbering occurred in 1974.

During the week ending 9th May 1976 nine of the original batch were placed in store, these being Nos 31 001/7/9/10/11/12/14/16/18. Official withdrawal from normal service commenced in July 1976 with six of them, Nos 31 001/9/10/11/16 and the pioneer 31 018. Of these only 31 018 survived. As the pioneer locomotive, the former D5500 was set aside at Stratford pending removal for preservation at the National Railway Museum in York. Still bearing the TOPS number she arrived there on 8th January 1977 and was on exhibition until early March, when she left for Doncaster Works for restoration to her original green livery. Of course she retained an engine that was not original for 1957, but to all intents and purposes the point of preservation had been made; D5500 deserved recognition for her place in history and this had been fulfilled.

As a preserved locomotive she was not to have an immobile career as a static exhibit in the museum proper, but was destined to become a working exhibit on one of the best known preserved railways in Britain, the North Yorkshire Moors Railway. This enlightened policy enabled people to see a preserved diesel locomotive in a working environment, and apart from occasional returns to York she still continues to act out this policy. Arrival on the NYMR was on 7th April 1978, happily bearing her original number and under her own power hauling a brake van and a NRM steam locomotive North Eastern Railway Class T3 0-8-0 No. 63460, also for the NYMR. D5500 was used mainly on passenger trains, but other duties were not unknown.

Her stay on the preserved railway lasted for several years and she returned to York towards the end of 1980 after suffering bogie damage on the railway. During the rebuilding of the NRM some years later she was transferred for temporary storage to Steamtown, Carnforth. While there an agreement was reached to enable her to return to traffic, for the first time in years. March 14th 1992 was the day of the first Annual General Meeting of the A1A Group, set up in 1991 to promote interest in the Brush Type 2s, and it witnessed D5500 coupled to two coaches used to hold the meeting. The wheels were turning once again. The short run had a delayed start due to discharged batteries, but soon rides were underway.

Some months later, in the September, D5500 headed 'The Waverley' charter train to Edinburgh. After a repaint, again in original green livery, she took part in celebrations, held at Carnforth on 14th November 1992 to mark the 35th anniversary of her first revenue-earning run from Liverpool Street. She was based at Steamtown for some time, but had returned to York in 1997.

In 1977 four of the Pilot Scheme locomotives were earmarked for conversion to electric heating units for preheating coaching stock fitted with electric train heat.

The plan was to disconnect the traction motors from the main generator supply which was then to be used as a source of electric power for the purpose. Numbers 31 007/002/014/008 were selected and allocated new numbers in the Departmental vehicle series, ADB 968013 to ADB 968016 respectively. These conversions were made in 1977, 1980 and 1981, but 31 007 was substituted by 31 013 as ADB 968013, although at one stage previously ADB 968023 had been allocated. Green livery with white horizontal stripes was revived for her, whereas 31 014/ADB 968015 retained the rather shabby corporate blue.

They saw brief service at Great Yarmouth, Norwich, Stratford and Bounds Green depots, but were withdrawn within several years.

After the initial withdrawals, railway enthusiasts staged the 'Toffee Apple Farewell' rail tour on 15th October 1977. Although the locomotives were under threat of withdrawal, the tour was a little premature as events transpired. Nevertheless, it proved to be a great success with 31 005 and 31 019 touring the West of England, starting out from Paddington Station and continuing via Bristol, Bath and some byways before returning with happy passengers.

Those locomotives that remained as such were still active after 1976, but were picked off in twos and threes until October 1980 when the last three left in original electro-magnetic control condition (31 004/008/019) were withdrawn from service. Number 31 019 was the subject of a failed preservation attempt and was also offered to Brush for sale late in 1980! It is believed that Brush had no use for her at that time. Rebuilt 31 101, formerly D5518, actually lasted longer until May 1981 when it too was withdrawn. This withdrawal proved to be short-lived and re-instatement occurred the following year. A repetition of this recurred and after periods of storage the locomotive returned to traffic for what proved to be a very long stay of execution until January 1993 when final withdrawal occurred on the 11th of that month. Even then it was not the end of the line for the locomotive, because it was purchased by Pete Waterman in September 1993, for preservation.

The first Brush Type 2s were collectively not the longest-lived of the Pilot Scheme diesels, nor did they prove to be the most successful; they were prototypes, had electro-magnetic control and had experienced engine troubles. However, it is an inescapable fact that they ranked among the best and that they served BR very well indeed, the Eastern Region in particular because they were resident there throughout their working lives. They were well liked by crews and depot staff alike, despite some pet hates inherent in them. They have provided a lasting memory for Brush personnel over the years and are still talked about with reverence.

While construction of the first Brush Type 2s was underway, consideration of the industrial side of locomotive matters was not ignored by Brush. Indeed, the Company was prepared to act as main contractor for only shunting locomotives, where designs already existed, and locomotive building activities were to cease at Loughborough.

This was the position, which still prevailed in December 1957, and it is clear that this was partly the reason that SCoW Bo-Bos 3137 to 3143 were built at WG Bagnall's works in Stafford. The Brush Bagnall 0-4-0 shunting locomotive design was modified to suit a smaller loading gauge than SCoW and the first order for this was placed by the Steel Company on 25th July 1956. This order was for one locomotive, destined for the Orb Works at Newport, Monmouthshire (Gwent since 1973). It bore Brush Traction works number 91, was built in 1957/8 and delivered in 1958, not from Loughborough, but from the works of Beyer Peacock & Co. of Gorton, Manchester. It was allocated Beyer Peacock works number 7856, which did not appear on the fitted works plate, but more probably on component mechanical parts. Electrical equipment was supplied from Brush and the engine from The National Gas and Oil Engine Co. Ltd of Ashton-under-Lyne, a title often abbreviated to National. It was a Brush Group company.

The main details of this locomotive are believed to have conformed to the standard design which were nominally as follows:

Wheel arrangement	0-4-0
Track gauge	4ft 8½ins
Engine model	National M4AA5
Engine rating	220bhp
Single Traction motor to rear axle	160bhp for 1 hour
Length over buffers	21ft 9ins
Overall width	8ft 9ins
Overall height	11ft 3ins
Wheel diameter	3ft 6ins
Wheelbase	6ft 0ins
Minimum curve negotiable	60ft 0ins radius
Maximum speed	18mph
Maximum tractive effort	19,200lbs
Fuel capacity	200 gallons
Weight in working order	30 tons

In general appearance the new design was neater than that of the Brush Bagnall, and retained the use of rounded corners and edges of the radiator, bonnet and cab areas, but the cab windows had rounded corners. The front radiator grille layout was different, there was a reduction in footplate handrails and there were three neatly arranged side bonnet grilles on each side. Deep buffer beams were standard and each was manufactured in one slab of steel, with the lower corners cut away for clearance purposes.

The locomotive spent all of its steelworks career at the Orb Works, its duties being general movement of wagons within the works and it was still active in 1976, sharing work with a Hudswell Clarke diesel locomotive. By 1982 it was reported as out of use and it does appear that it remained so until 1987.

In the July of that year it was newly acquired by the Middleton Railway Trust on permanent loan from the British Steel Corporation (successors to SCoW). The locomotive was reported as having arrived on the 1758 Middleton Railway, Leeds, in West Yorkshire, by 12th September. It was still there in April 2005.

The locomotive was overhauled and restored to SCoW maroon livery, together with replacement Brush Traction works plates. No running number had ever been carried by No. 91 and she was outshopped in superb condition in April 1991. It is very satisfying to note that this first Brush-Beyer Peacock locomotive has been preserved when so many other notable locomotives have not. It is part of the British

The first Brush/Beyer Peacock 0-4-0 diesel shunting locomotive was Brush Traction No.91 of 1958. It was supplied to the Steel Company of Wales and is seen here at their Orb Works, Newport.

BRUSH A5197

industrial railway heritage, not only from the operational and manufacturing viewpoint, but also the technical, as the four-coupled diesel electric locomotive type is very much a minority product.

It was thought desirable to have some stock shunting locomotives available for sale and during 1957 quite a number were planned, they were to be not only 0-4-0s but also 0-6-0s. Brush works numbers 99 to 103 and 109 to 118 were allocated to the former and 104 to 108 to the latter. Beyer Peacock were to act as subcontractor for the manufacture of the mechanical parts and for erecting the locomotives. Beyer Peacock works numbers were allocated, though it is doubtful if they were ever carried by those locomotives built other than on manufactured parts. Numbers 7857 to 7861 covered BT 99 to 103, 7879 to 7883 covered BT 104 to 108 and 7869 to 7878 covered BT 109 to 118. Brush was to provide the electrical equipment and the 0-4-0s were to have McLaren LE6 engines of 200bhp, the 0-6-0s National NMHS6 engines of 400bhp.

The plans were in keeping with the 1956/7 Brush Traction policy and were initiated as part of a speculative attempt to gain orders from within industry at a time when many concerns were considering replacing steam traction by diesel.

The first order was for five 0-4-0 stock locomotives and was placed in 1957, the actual date is not stated in the Brush locomotive register. The Beyer Peacock order No. 4412 was allocated and the specification date was 30th December 1957, covering Nos 7857 to 7861 inclusive. They entered service in 1958/9 and although some of them did have Brush Traction works plates fitted, most ran in anonymous condition because customers were not immediately forthcoming and as they became increasingly less new the year quoted on Brush works plates was too revealing and would have led to some awkward questions being asked. As a result of this

the exact identities and cross identities of the locomotives are not always certain but the following is offered as a guide as to what may have been the Brush and Beyer Peacock cross identity situation.

Brush No.	Beyer Peacock No.	Delivered	bhp
99	7857	18 July 1958	200
100	7861	29 December 1959	200
101	7858	04 August 1958	230
102	7859	18 September 1958	230
103	7860	not known	230

Some sources quote the cross identities of 101 and 103 as being 7860 and 7858 respectively. Sources are at variance as to the actual identity of SPRITE.

The writer recalls seeing No. 99 within the confines of the Falcon Works circa 1961 bearing its Brush works plate, but it is perhaps more convenient to quote the BP works numbers. According to BP sources Nos 7857 to 7859 (BT 99, 101 and 102) went to Brush and No. 7859 (BT 103) was retained by BP, being based at the Company's Gorton Works as a works shunting locomotive and it is thought as demonstration locomotive when the opportunity arose. Indeed No. 7859 was used by Brush for demonstration purposes and travelled far and wide on such duties. Number 7861 (BT 100) was soon allocated to British Railways for trials.

These stock locomotives were often out engaged on demonstration and there is little indication that there was any restriction as to which ones were used for such purposes, although those employed at the two works on shunting duties would have been considered too useful to lose for any

Left: The test track, as seen from one of the 0-4-0s in early 1959. It ran from within the works complex, and then towards the boundary and the Loughborough meadows in a northerly direction, finishing in a sand-drag (inhabited by a colony of rabbits) and a buffer stop just visible in this picture. Note the former Great Central line on the embankment in the background.

BRUSH A5626

Below: Another demonstration was undertaken at Gloucester docks during the winter of 1962/3. Again the locomotive is anonymous.

B J ASHWORTH via BRUSH

Facing page: One of the stock locomotives propelling a Brush Type 2 into the test house in 1960.

BRUSH A5807

length of time. They spent some years on these duties as they themselves did not readily find customers, although orders were later received for similar units. Livery was a pale shade of orange with light green bonnet roofs. Brush monograms usually appeared on the cab sides in transfer or plated form and also below the front radiator grille (usually in transfer form). It sometimes appeared on the cab door at the rear, particularly on No. 7861 (BT 100). One of the batch was later named SPRITE and received cabside BRUSH monograms in plated form. Of the three allocated to the Falcon Works two were regular works shunting locomotives, one being regarded as the Traction Division locomotive (probably No. 101) and the other as the general usage locomotive. Traction duties included moving dead locomotives or locomotive body shells from shop to shop or around the yards.

Number 7857 (BT 99) was at the Falcon Works from 1958 until 1963 when it was sent to Beyer Peacock for refurbishment prior to being despatched, complete with a new engine, to the Skopje steelworks in Yugoslavia as part of an order for six locomotives.

Number 7861 (BT 100) was reported as being used on demonstration at a quarry near Gravesend, but was detailed late in 1959 to receive modifications, required to enable it to operate on BR Eastern Region. These included a modified cab, cut down slightly to clear an over bridge, and smaller diameter buffer heads.

It was on trial at the BR Mile End Goods Yard, being allocated on loan to Stratford depot in 1960. At this location an observer noted that the wheels were stamped with the number and date 7861 1/60. BR bought the locomotive in September 1960 and initially superimposed their insignia and the running number D2999 on the existing livery. Subsequently, in early March 1961, it was repainted in BR Brunswick green livery at Stratford Works, and classified D2/11. Being a non-standard locomotive its BR service only lasted until April 1967, the majority of time being spent at Stratford. It was despatched to C&F Booth Ltd. of Rotherham, for scrap. It may have been used there on occasions, before being cut up. One report indicates that this took place during October 1967, but this may be incorrect as another states that the locomotive was first reported as being there on 2nd March 1968. Confirming the latter, another report states that it was still being used as a shunting locomotive in the yard on 6th September 1970.

Number 7858 (BT 101) spent most of its working life at Loughborough, probably on Traction Division duties, although it may have been out on demonstration for very brief periods occasionally. It was disposed of in 1969, when it became surplus to requirements at the end of large scale locomotive construction, and was sold to C F Booth Ltd of Rotherham for scrap. It made the journey from Loughborough to Rotherham on 21st November 1969.

One of the stock locomotives decked in all-over wasp stripes and named SPRITE, as seen on 25th August 1965. The nameplates were the originals of 1899 and the locomotive was the third to bear them. It also bears the Brush monogram, but in the form of a plate rather than a transfer.

BRUSH

Number 7859 was most probably named SPRITE from 1961 onwards, but from 1958 until 1970 was the works shunting locomotive at Loughborough, although BP records suggest otherwise. It was used on general duties, which included shunting the boiler house ash wagons and miscellaneous wagons brought into the works sidings. It also assisted with Traction Division duties and received overall black and yellow wasp stripes in 1965, when it was registered by the British Transport Commission for running on BR lines, to collect wagons. It carried BTC registration plates. It featured as a wasp caricature, complete with wings and a sting, which appeared in a cartoon on the BRUSH BROADSIDE works notice board news sheets of the period. SPRITE had a period on loan to Stanley Davies Plant Ltd. (of Castleford, Yorkshire) from August 1968 until about May of the following year, being used on track lifting operations on the Ruabon to Barmouth line in Wales. It was loaned to the contractor while their own locomotive, none other than Brush Bagnall No. 2971 and formerly Lever Brothers' MONTGOMERY OF ALAMEIN, was being overhauled at the Falcon Works. Dismantling of the line started on 25th June 1968 near Llandrillo and headed east, reaching Ruabon Junction in May 1969. Work also started on 2nd July 1968 at Llandderfel, heading west to Dolgellau and continuing to Barmouth Junction, which was reached on 26th February the following year.

With the end of locomotive building and the end of rail-borne traffic in and out of the Falcon Works SPRITE was disposed of in 1970 to the Lancashire Fuel Company, of Cheshire, departing on a low loader. It departed minus its name and BTC plates, but retained its distinctive livery. It was reported in 1973 as being at the company's Rathbone Road depot in Liverpool and at Bidston, Merseyside, in 1976. The former SPRITE survived until 1977, being reported as scrapped about May of that year. The nameplates were set aside at the Falcon Works in trust, as it were, in different locations, and although one is known to survive the other disappeared from what had been considered a safe place. The survival of this plate enabled glass-fibre replicas to be

manufactured in later years for placing on the works shunting locomotive acquired in the mid-1980s.

Number 7860 (BT 103) was the Gorton based locomotive used as the works shunting locomotive there. Its reign lasted from 1958 until about 1965 with a possible break on demonstration after January 1962. It was sold, together with 7857 (BT 99) to the Skopje Steel Works in Yugoslavia, before the closure of the Gorton Works. It also had a new 275bhp engine fitted and was refurbished before leaving for Skopje, probably from the Falcon Works. A curious sighting of what may have been this locomotive occurred at the Falcon Works, where it was noted on site on 2nd July 1966, a surprisingly late date. It was seen in the yard near the paint shop, bearing the works plates marked 605 of 1964 and appeared to be in an unused condition and 'had obviously been stored for some time'. What is certain is that the locomotive was destined for Skopje, but had been held due to problems being experienced in Yugoslavia. The Skopje locomotives are described further in Chapter 9.

Some reservation is held, therefore, regarding the exact identities of the locomotives concerned, but it is believed that the foregoing are as near as is possible without further and positive proof. More uncertain are the identities of those which underwent demonstrations around the country. While it is known that No. 7859 (BT 102) was intended to be the demonstrator and probably undertook its intended duties, some of the remainder were chosen for demonstration purposes when it was otherwise engaged or under repair. Demonstrations were undertaken at a number of sites, including the Pilkington Glass Company at St. Helen's, another near Doncaster in 1958 and Swansea South and Prince of Wales Docks during October 1962. One period of loan was made to British Railways' Mile End Goods Yard by 7861 (BT100), in 1959/60. In this instance the locomotive was recognisable by its cut-down cab roof. Late 1959 saw another locomotive visit Eastwood, Nottinghamshire.

Another loan was recorded in September 1959 to the Longmoor Military Railway. One locomotive was also used in Gloucester docks during 1962 and until 7th January 1963, when a Sentinel locomotive took over for similar evaluation trials. Here the object was to find a suitable replacement for the elderly ex-

In 1960 BR was sufficiently interested to purchase the stock locomotive loaned to it. It became D2999 and was repainted in Brunswick green livery. Its days were numbered when this view was taken in the Rotherham scrapyard of C F Booth Ltd on 2nd March 1968.

A J BOOTH

Midland Railway 0-4-0 tank locomotives used there. In 1961 one Brush 0-4-0 diesel shunting locomotive was reported to have been on loan to British Railways for a trial period, allegedly numbered D9998 temporarily, and latterly working at Danygraig in South Wales, possibly until after November 1962. No proof of this numbering has emerged over the ensuing years and there has been some doubt held as to the authenticity of this identity. Conversely, some identification would have been necessary for accountancy and reporting purposes, and some reports do indicate that it was identified as D9998 in some way. In particular, in The Railway Observer of January 1963, D9998 was reported as returned to the Falcon Works from BR ex-loan in November 1962.

Certainly the 0-4-0 shunting locomotives were very welcome additions to the facilities at the Falcon Works, because whilst the existing works shunting locomotives hitherto had been adequate up to that time, they were no longer because of the heavier work required by the Type 2 production. These existing locomotives were the aforementioned SPRITE and ACE, the Ruston and Fowler diesels. Neither was a very powerful machine and the advent of the Type 2 work meant that both locomotives were often required to be used in tandem for moving dead locomotives around the works, and even then a road tractor would sometimes be called upon to start the load moving for them! They were soon relegated to boiler house duties, shunting wagons of coal and ash, but by 1961 could be seen out of use on the end of one of the northern sidings at the Meadow Lane end of the works, adjacent to the British Railways freight lines. In January 1962 they were sold for scrap to F. Berry Ltd., of Leicester. The SPRITE nameplates had been transferred to one of the new 0-4-0s, as related previously.

Of the remaining plans for stock locomotives, some work was put in hand. The 0-4-0s BP7869 to 7878 (BT 109 to 118) progressed to the stage whereby some were partly built and others were manufactured parts. The work was halted when the order was cancelled. The Brush works numbers were never re-used, but the Beyer Peacock ones were retained. This retention was logical since many of the parts would bear the numbers stamped upon them. Incidentally, BP called them progressive numbers. The parts were used up on other orders received later.

The batch of five 0-6-0s 7879 to 7883 (BT 104 to 108), equipped with National NMHS6 engines rated at 400bhp, was also cancelled. In this instance it is not clear whether or not any parts were manufactured, but several years later 7879 was built in experimental form and either one or two more were intended to follow in this modified form. These developments are described in Chapter 9.

One further industrial locomotive was ordered before the 1950s ended. This was on 10th February 1959, according to the Brush register of locomotives, and it was for an 0-6-0 diesel electric shunting locomotive of 400bhp for the National Coal Board who wanted it for use at their Eastwood Colliery at Moor Green in Nottinghamshire. A National R4AA6 engine was fitted and, unusually, the locomotive was built by Hudswell Clarke & Company Ltd, of Leeds, in 1959/1960. That it was built by Hudswell was mainly due to the insistence of the NCB Area CME whose custom it was to order Hudswell locomotives for collieries under his care.

The design was basically Brush, as indeed was the electrical equipment, and the outline closely followed a pair of Brush-equipped Hudswell 0-6-0 diesel electric shunting locomotives supplied to the Manchester Ship Canal Railway in 1959. These were also equipped with the National R4AA6 engine and in some ways were reminiscent of the later Brush Bagnall designs with the lowered bonnet roof section immediately ahead of the cab. Indeed, they were designed in conjunction with Brush Traction and carried the traditional Hudswell steam outline 'chimney' which disguised the exhaust. The locomotive destined for the NCB did not have this decorative device, but shared the tastefully shaped bonnet complete with sloping upper sides and rear. It did appear rather the less attractive for having no 'chimney'. To all intents and purposes the three locomotives were of the same class, but one had a different main contractor. The Brush monogram was displayed on a plate affixed to the bonnet front above the radiator grille, much in the same fashion favoured by

More of interest and rarity rather than quality, this photograph shows DE 6 at work at Eastwood Colliery. The Brush monogram plate was affixed Hudswell-fashion to the top of the bonnet front.

BRUSH

Hudswell and other manufacturers. The main details of No. 179 are as follows:

Wheel arrangement	0-6-0
Track gauge	4ft 8½ins
Engine model	National R4AA6, six-cylinder
Engine rating	400bhp at 750rpm continuous 440bhp at 750rpm two hour
Traction motors, two	Brush, 135hp, 429V, 260A, 910rpm 150hp, 429V, 290A, 873rpm
Length over buffers	30ft 10ins
Overall width	8ft 8ins
Overall height	12ft 8ins
Wheel diameter	4ft 6ins
Wheelbase	11ft 6ins
Minimum curve negotiable	211ft 0ins
Maximum speed	20mph
Maximum tractive effort	34,000lbs
One hour tractive effort	16,300lbs
Continuous tractive effort	14,000lbs
Fuel capacity	450 gallons
Weight in working order	52½ tons

Delivery of the NCB locomotive was in 1960. It was fitted with rectangular NCB number plates bearing the running number DE6 and Brush Traction works plates bearing the number 179. Hudswell Clarke allocated their works number D1176 to this locomotive.

DE6 was in the service of the colliery until 1975, transporting coal three miles to the British Railways Midland sidings at Langley Mill, and waste material from the colliery washery to the dirt disposal site some two miles away. Its working life came to an abrupt end when the connecting rod of number two-cylinder of the engine fractured, forcing the piston through the side of the engine. The estimated cost of spare parts and repairs was £14,000, a figure considered by the NCB to be prohibitive for an already obsolete engine. The alternative of fitting a Lister engine was considered, but this would have cost £15,000. The NCB was not prepared to spend such sums for the repair of the locomotive and it was condemned and sold as scrap to J Bush Ltd of Leabrooks, who cut it up soon afterwards in November 1975.

This locomotive closed the first era of conventional 0-6-0 diesel electric shunting locomotives and none, as such, was produced for another thirteen years or so. The 0-4-0 was to have an extended lease of life, described in Chapter 9. Apart from seeing those examples working around the works, the involvement of Brush personnel on test duties at Beyer Peacock, and on demonstrations around the country, few people at the Falcon Works were aware of the shunting locomotive side of Brush Traction. The production of Brush Type 2s for British Railways focused the attention of most

D5520 (BT119) first of the follow-up contract, negotiates its way into the southern exchange sidings prior to its delivery journey. Note the change to Brunswick green for the cab window surround and two running numbers each side.

BRUSH

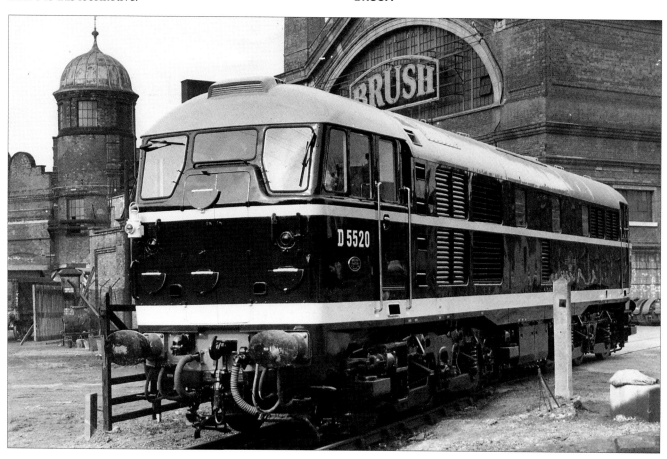

because of the scale of the whole effort. Work penetrated many shops and corners of the works and a production line approach to matters developed, particularly in the sphere of electrical machines.

Despite the declared policy of Brush Traction to concentrate on shunting locomotive work, just the opposite occurred after December 1957. It was soon apparent that a notable success had been achieved with the first twenty Type 2s; the Eastern Region of BR was eager to have more of them, despite the previously declared intention of BR to build its own Type 2s, and not a little persuasion was directed at Loughborough to achieve this end. Furthermore, during 1958 it became evident to BR that the workshop capacity to build the BR Type 2s was quite inadequate and Brush was approached for the supply

D5531, fitted with roof-mounted four-character headcode display, on the Falcon Works test track makes an interesting comparison with D5551 (BT150/1959) on the facing page demonstrating the inter-connecting doorway for inter-locomotive access.

BRUSH A5676 BRUSH

of more Brush Type 2s. Mr B L Goodlet, after becoming Managing Director at Brush in December 1957, considered it very necessary to make profits and it appeared to him 'crazy to withdraw from the only field in which a considerable expansion of our profits could be achieved'. He continued, 'I therefore decided to take on as much Traction work as we could get – and during 1958 we got a lot. At the end of 1958 it was clear that instead of getting out of locomotive building we should get into it and it became desirable to formulate a policy'. Some measure of the way BR was thinking must have come as a surprise to Brush; one enquiry concerned 400 Type 2s!

The large amount of work that came in during 1958 included the first repeat order for Brush Type 2s which,

according to the Brush Register of Locomotives, was placed on 3rd July 1958 and was for forty locomotives. These were destined to become BR Nos D5520 to D5559, and were given Brush works numbers 119 to 158. There were changes made in the light of experience gained from the first twenty Type 2s, limited though that experience was by that time. The outward appearance of the design remained little altered, although an extra grille appeared on the body side, in the access door mid-way along the body. Alterations to the layout of cab front grab rails were made and the cab window surround was painted Brunswick green to match the rest of the body paint scheme, which in turn had the stripes painted white. The electro-magnetic engine speed control equipment of D5500-19 was discarded for these production Type 2s which had electro-pneumatic control instead. For multiple working of Brush Type 2s, therefore, the former and latter systems were incompatible. The top speed for the latest locomotives was 90mph, and the Mirrlees engine was uprated to 1,365bhp as a result of the temporary uprating of D5507.

Production of the batch commenced in 1958 and the first locomotive, D5520, emerged from the Falcon Works in February 1959, within months of the last of the Pilot Scheme locomotives. As production continued differences started to appear. Most noticeable of these was the introduction of a roof-mounted, roller blind route and train description panel with four alpha-numerical displays. This dominated the area above the front cab windows and replaced the hinged white headcode discs mounted below window level. This in turn necessitated alteration of the front of the cab with the provision of four footstep recesses. Already, two of these footstep recesses had appeared on from D5520. Again, the grab handles were rearranged to suit. The changeover to the new arrangement was initiated early in the contract, but due to erratic deliveries of the original pattern of cab roof from subcontractors it was not a clean changeover so application of the new indicators was gradual over the series D5530 to D5565 range. This, of course, overran into the following contract.

There is some discrepancy in reports as to which locomotives were fitted with what when in new condition, and this is confused by later alterations when locomotives exchanged cabs during BR repairs and overhauls, but it is probable that the details listed in Appendices 2 and 3 reflect the position at the time of building.

A further change was introduced on D5545 with its engine uprated to 1,600bhp to evaluate the future potential of the Mirrlees engine. This was achieved by increasing the engine speed to 950rpm and the fitting of oil-cooled pistons. This brought the locomotive within the BR Type 3 range, but it was still regarded as Type 2.

The Duchess of Kent paid an official visit to the Falcon Works on 2nd June 1959. She was made most welcome aboard brand new D5532 (BT131/1959) in the Erecting Shop.

Facing page: Although captioned as 'attached for multiple operation', D5532 and D5533 were actually coupled for the demonstration runs during the visit of the Duchess of Kent. The late Bob Dilley is at the ready in the cab of D5532.

BRUSH BRUSH A5677

The order was completed in October 1959, by which time more Type 2s had been ordered. The Brush register of locomotives records that on 3rd December 1958 another twenty were ordered (D5560 to D5579, Brush 159 to 178). These locomotives were rated at 1,365bhp and were delivered between October 1959 and January 1960 to the Eastern Region and were allocated to various depots, including Ipswich and Hornsey. The last two locomotives of this order were of particular interest, because they bore startling new and experimental liveries. Hitherto, Brunswick green had been the standard livery, but operating experience had indicated that the diesels were far less conspicuous to the permanent way and depot staffs, because of their sombre colours and comparative quietness, compared with steam locomotives. A decision was taken to experiment with different liveries designed to make diesel locomotives more conspicuous, so to this end D5578 was painted an unrelieved light shade of blue called 'electric blue' due to its application on the new electric locomotives being introduced for the West Coast Main Line, and D5579 a vivid bronze gold with off-white bands. To some eyes they may have appeared excessively bright, at least to maintenance staff, as the least trace of dirt was very apparent. Conversely, it could be said with some justification that with so much unimaginative colour on the railway the changes concerning these two locomotives, were most welcome. Several decades on, these changes may seem tame after the spate (or flood) of liveries applied to railway rolling stock in recent years. No permanent livery changes resulted, but the yellow front warning patch of later years was probably derived from the experiment. D5578 kept its blue livery for several years, being repainted green some eighteen months before the 1966 general introduction of BR Corporate Rail Blue.

The year 1959 witnessed regular deliveries of Type 2 locomotives from the Falcon Works, usually two per week and usually on a Thursday. To cope with this unprecedented rate of work extra building space was obtained by using part of the former Turbine Shop. This shop, dating from the early 1920s, was being rundown as turbine production had been transferred to elsewhere in the Hawker Siddeley Group. On an inquisitive visit to the Falcon Works by your author on 24th August 1959, D5546 to D5561 were noted in the shops and yards to the rear of the works. It was likely that there were others to be seen, but one could not probe too deeply! On the very last day of 1959 D5576 and D5577 were noted heading north at Kegworth, six miles out from the Falcon Works, sparklingly brand new and ex-works by only minutes, and on 7th January 1960 D5578 and D5579 were noted ex-works at the same location – history in the making indeed.

The old Turbine Shop was not the only extra space to be required, so new buildings were erected between September 1959 and January 1960 on reclaimed land to the rear of the works, adjoining the meadows. These new buildings, built for the manufacture of locomotive superstructures, covered 48,000 square feet and came into use during January 1960 and were officially opened on the 25th of that month.

In 1959 two more orders were received for Brush Type 2s. The first dated 21st April was for seventy five locomotives (D5580 to D5654, Brush 180 to 254) and the second, dated 14th August, was for twenty-five (D5655 to D5679, Brush 255 to 279). Deliveries again averaged two locomotives per week and the first order commenced delivery in January 1960 and was completed in September 1960. The second order continued the deliveries unbroken from the latter month and continued until December 1960. Within this latter order a further uprating occurred, this time to 1,600bhp following the experience gained from D5545, which by March 1960 had proved capable of meeting the Type 3 requirements in East Anglia. Some anxiety within Brush circles was expressed over the camshaft gears as a result of the uprating.

Sixteen locomotives, D5655 to D5670, were so treated, but all the remainder were rated at the by then normal 1,350bhp. This batch was allocated to March depot to enable the Liverpool Street - King's Lynn trains to be timed to faster schedules and therefore fit into the new electric services at the London end. With D5671 came a new allocation to the Sheffield area of the Eastern Region, Darnall initially, but Tinsley soon afterwards, the depot code 41A being transferred from the former to the latter.

This latest uprating was part of a Brush initiative, dating from January 1959, to continually uprate the Mirrlees JVS12T engine, first to 1,600bhp on more locomotives and then if possible to 2,000bhp, by considered modifications backed by a 1,000 hour test, to enable the company to offer and sell Type 3 locomotives to BR. Trials with an engine uprated to 1,950bhp were due to start in March 1960, and it was recognised that some development in the electrical systems of the locomotive would be required with this uprating. The co-operation of BR was always forthcoming and relations cordial in such matters.

The works photographer captured the very last Type 2 of all, D5862 (BT398/1962) as it left the works. The locomotive is seen negotiating the diamond crossing of the southern exchange sidings on 25th October 1962. Note the Turbine Shop in the background.

BRUSH

On 26th January 1960 forty six more Type 2s were ordered (D5680 to D5699 and D5800 to D5825, Brush 281 to 326). The gap in the BR number series was due to D5700 to D5719 being occupied by the Metrovick Co-Bos, so therefore the whole block was avoided. Incorrect works numbers were applied to several of the locomotives due to the application of the wrong plates at the Falcon Works; in at least one instance the mistake was rectified before despatch. All the locomotives were rated at 1,350bhp. Deliveries were continuous and followed on from the previous batch without a break in production, from January 1961 to December 1961. So busy were the workshops that at any one time as many as twenty or more locomotives would be on site in various stages of assembly, testing, painting or awaiting delivery. D5681 to D5683 joined D5671 at Darnall and were later joined by most of the remainder of the order.

Part II of the Sheffield modernisation scheme also required more Brush Type 2s and to this end a further ten were ordered in late 1961, this order being announced in the November issues of the railway press. They were numbered D5826 to D5835 and were allocated Brush works numbers 362 to 371 respectively.

Within months a further and final order was placed for the Sheffield area for twenty-seven locomotives, this being reported in the December 1961 and January 1962 railway press. The BR numbers were D5836 to D5862 and the Brush numbers were 372 to 398 respectively. Delivery of the two orders spanned the period from December 1961 to October 1962. Production was continuous, although it had slowed down in 1961 due to a reduction of BR expenditure on

modernisation. The final orders were placed despite this and the last examples were delivered several weeks after the first Brush Type 4 locomotives had emerged from the Falcon Works. This brought the total of Brush Type 2s to 263.

All but one of the locomotives were rated at 1,350bhp, the odd one out being D5835 which was rated at 2,000bhp, and which went into service in April 1962. As related above, Brush had set its sights upon possible Type 3 orders, and possible overseas orders, and targeted 2,000bhp as an ideal rating to gain further experience to eventually win such orders. As events transpired it was English Electric that gained the Type 3 orders with the D6700 class, now more familiar as Class 37.

The uprated engine had oil-cooled pistons and had a rotational speed of 1,000rpm. This represented an increase of twice the output from the original application on the Ceylon locomotives, but an increase of a sea level rating from 1,250bhp to 2,000bhp. It was impressive, but was soon to be overshadowed by problems with the JVS12T engine in service rated at 1,350bhp. In the meantime D5835 went to Sheffield and saw initial service on Kings Cross-Hull trains. It was also used on Deltic diagrams from Kings Cross to Doncaster and later went to the Great Eastern lines. By October 1962 it was reported to have travelled 30,000 miles and performing entirely satisfactorily. The aforementioned engine troubles caused D5835 to be derated before long.

Producing the Type 2s occupied the works over a period lasting from 1955 to 1962, from design to D5862, and it was a period that changed Brush Traction from a concern with an uncertain future to one ranking with the best and one with a confidence to beat all-comers in the diesel electric locomotive field. A certain amount of sub-contracted work was undertaken on behalf of Brush, notably by W G Bagnall and Beyer Peacock. The former supplied underframes and other mechanical parts for some fifty two Type 2s, but the latter supplied over two hundred, and the bogie sets for most if not all of the 263 locomotives.

The Bagnall numbers of the underframes were allocated from within the locomotive register series. These are summarised as follows:

Bagnall Nos.	Year	BR Nos.
3127 to 3131	1957	D5515-19
3155 to 3159	1959	D5520-29 batch
3163 to 3187	1961	-
3192 to 3203	1962	-
3214 to 3217	1962	-
3218	1962	D5845

With the delivery of 263 locomotives by the end of 1962 Brush could concentrate on other orders, but for a few years the company did not ignore the service history of them, indeed it was essential to follow up delivery with contractual arrangements to ensure that any snags were ironed out and that they functioned properly. Within these pages it is of interest to plot the course of the Brush Type 2 on BR as an historical summary, albeit with some limit set to the degree of depth due to the fact that to course a detailed history would require a book in its own right. That of the Pilot Scheme examples has been dealt with earlier in this chapter, but some details will by necessity be included below.

In 1962 BR Eastern Region reclassified the Brush Type 2s. D5500-19 became 12/2, those rated at 1,350bhp 13/2 and the 1,600bhp examples 16/2. D5835, the 2,000bhp example, appears to have not been coded.

The fact that the world is not ideal is obvious; things do go wrong. When there are troubles there is a tendency for people to concentrate upon the troubles, sometimes to the extent that sense of proportion or gravity is exaggerated. People forget the good things, putting them aside as the accepted norm, without mention or praise; and so it was with the Brush Type 2 in 1961 when the news media highlighted the failure of D5667 on 11th January of that year when hauling the down 'Fenman' near Audley End, south of Cambridge. On this particular occasion the train included a special saloon conveying Her Majesty the Queen and the unfortunate event attracted unwelcome and inaccurate reporting. The cause of failure was loss of sump oil in the Mirrlees engine. Embarrassing to Brush it was, as the main contractor, but with two Brush personnel to hand it was even more embarrassing because the failure was not one that could be dealt with on the spot. Perhaps the most embarrassing was the publicity, which ensued, in which the newspapers, The Daily Telegraph in particular, portrayed the incident as typical of the still infant new mode of transport.

The 'Royal Train' failure was a godsend to those seeking 'headlines', but in reality it was not typical, indeed it was the first failure of this nature. The train was delayed by 56 minutes and rescued by a standby steam locomotive, which came fourteen miles, from Cambridge.

During these early diesel days failures on all types and makes occurred, due to a variety of reasons of which unfamiliarity of BR staff and poor servicing conditions on steam depots were not the least and which received little news attention. Not until the big freeze of 1962/3 did the diesel failures generally receive attention. Brush had very little option, but to let time pass and the publicity die down, despite the unfairness of the situation.

Of course, when things went right on 15th February 1962 on the occasion of D5695 hauling a Royal train on the London, Tilbury & Southend lines without adverse incident there were no headlines to be seen in the press. In some ways it was perhaps fortunate that it was so – one can imagine the headline reading in the vein of more luck than judgement.

Of a more serious nature were the events of 1962, which had far-reaching consequences for the Brush Type 2s themselves and the development of the Mirrlees J engine in its rail traction application. By mid-1962 the JVS12T engine had been uprated successively from 1,250bhp at 850rpm, through 1,365bhp at 900rpm, 1,600bhp at 950rpm (the locomotives often working the 'Master Cutler') to 2,000bhp at 1,000rpm.

They usually left the works in pairs, but sometimes there were three. D5596, D5597 and D5592 are formed up as a trio on the test track.

BRUSH A6216

Not all the uprating had consisted solely of rotational speed increases, far from it, but the increases did have an effect.

The J range engine was produced in two forms, the vee form being developed for marine use with the particular feature of being able to withstand detonation shocks from mines in Admiralty service. This version was designated the JVDM and from the design was derived the JVST for rail traction purposes. Both applications were offered with twelve cylinders, the M or T suffix denoting the respective application. The traction application had the type of usage that diesel engine manufacturers disliked at the time, some periods of operation at variable loads and speeds, together with being installed in a machine that flexed with the track profile and provided a less than ideal firm foundation upon which to mount an engine. Marine and industrial applications more often than not relied upon solid foundations of one form or another.

The JVST also had a fabricated engine crankcase and bedplate, rather than cast. Fabricated components had not been without troubles with other manufacturers, but Mirrlees by the late 1950s had confidence in such an engine in a rail traction application, bearing in mind the comparatively short time that it had been in main line service. By May 1962 it became apparent that some of the Brush Type 2s with over 500,000 miles accumulated were experiencing engine fatigue problems, and that these were going cause further problems of multiplication and deterioration as time went by. Initially, an investigation into thirty four engines of all four ratings was instigated to ascertain what the nature and cause of the problems were exactly. The fatigue problems concerned the crankcases, in particular due to the cracking of fillet welds at the foot of the cylinder housings, caused by firing loads and rotational speeds, the latter affecting the centre housings. The bearing housings themselves also suffered from fractures caused by inertia forces due to rotational speeds.

With 268 engines allotted to the class, something had to be done to prevent disruption to services on a region by the time almost totally converted to diesel traction. The resultant report advised that some remedial work could be done as the nature of the fatigue had nothing to do with bad workmanship, but the reaching of the limit of fatigue strengths in service. Re-design rather than remedy, was the long-term answer to the problem. Short-term remedial work was advised, together with a general de-rating to the basic 1,250bhp. D5835 was reduced from 2,000bhp to 1,000bhp.

For the long-term solution, the Mk3 version of the JVST 12 engine as fitted to the Brush locomotives then being produced and supplied to Rhodesia Railways was offered to BR. The latter found this solution to be not acceptable, it is thought, on financial grounds, and contacted the English Electric Company to provide an alternative engine. The only engine applicable then was the 12CSVT, still entering service in the English Electric Type 3s of the D6700 series, later better known as Class 37. The engine was already de-rated at 1,750bhp in this application and had seen good service since the end of 1960. Furthermore, in being fitted to the Brush Type 2 a further de-rating would be necessary to match the maximum acceptable output from the Brush main generator. As the power required was, in common with most electrical

machines of the time, well within the maximum rating, an increase in the nominal power output to the traction motors could be obtained. The resultant rating of the English Electric engine for the Brush Type 2 became 1,470bhp. Obviously an engine working well within its maximum potential had advantages over the Mirrlees engine modified to work within an increased rating, and was an attraction that BR found hard to ignore. That the incidence of fatigue was hardly likely to occur and the standard base horsepower of the production members of the class was increased also, with minimal risk, made re-engining attractive.

Number D5677 emerged from Doncaster Works in March 1964 fitted with the English Electric engine and performed satisfactorily. In June of that year fifty more engines were ordered, followed by two more orders of fifty each in April and December 1965, and a final order for 113 in March 1966 to complete the re-engining of the class altogether. The whole programme took some five years to complete, and by some curious fate it was the pioneer D5500 that was the last to be so treated in March 1969. The re-engined locomotives were initially classified 14/2, but by 1969 this and the classifications of 1962 had been replaced by the general reclassification of diesel and electric locomotives introduced in 1968. This classification system (Total Operations Processing System, TOPS for short) was based upon a computerised scheme which took several years to introduce in full and involved the renumbering of most of the locomotive stock of British Rail. A class number and individual unit number were combined to produce a five digit running number for each locomotive. The sub-division of the last three digits indicated certain major locomotive fittings. Locomotives fitted with Mirrlees engines became Class 30 and those fitted with English Electric engines, Class 31. Class 30 as such soon became extinct when the last replacement engine was fitted the following year. The cost of replacing the Mirrlees engines was £6 million.

The original Mirrlees engines were sold for marine use, trawlers being the main recipients. I was informed of this by a very senior person, once of Bagnall, various Brush companies and by the late 1970s elevated to Hawker Siddeley management.

The whole episode was a disappointment to Brush, and perhaps more so to Mirrlees, but the fact that these engines continued their lives successfully in the marine application, further underlined the fact that diesel engine manufacturers of the 1950s, and indeed the early 1960s, were extending the range of use of their products into virtually uncharted areas and experience was to show that for traction use a cast crankcase was superior to a fabricated one. The engines installed in the Rhodesia Railways locomotives appear to have been successful initially, but soon afterwards suffered somewhat from failures combined with the political situation of the country, which had sanctions imposed upon it for a number of years. As a result of the latter the railway experienced a variety of difficulties in obtaining spare parts for a whole range of industrial goods, including locomotives.

In 1961 BR introduced a code system to aid the coupling of diesel locomotives. A red disc indicating diesel-electric transmission with electromagnetic control was painted on the locomotive ends, just above the buffers, of D5500-19, and on the remainder a blue star was affixed signifying electro-pneumatic control.

In 1965 D5671-5 were fitted with tablet catchers mounted within recesses in the cabside doors. This was to aid single line working on the Highdyke-Stainby branch.

In 1964 BR initiated an experimental scheme which had some far-reaching consequences. A special train was assembled, in which various new ideas were tried out. New and improved design features were evident as were standards of comfort and convenience for the passenger. Perhaps more evident was the use of a new livery of blue and grey for the coaching stock and overall blue for the locomotive, which incidentally was Brush Type 4 No. D1733. A new BR symbol, the now-familiar double arrow symbol, made its first public appearance on D1733. The train travelled around the system for evaluation purposes. So far as locomotive livery matters were concerned the new symbol and a darker shade of blue were adopted generally, together with running numbers in a new style also. The blue was called Rail Blue and was part of the new and more up to date image being promoted by BR to try to rid itself of the steam traction image and all that was associated with it. It was comprehensive and took some years to complete, the locomotive part being especially prolonged in some cases.

The Brush Type 2s were included in the scheme. The new era dawned in 1965, but for Brush Type 2s, and not in isolation, there began a period of hybrid liveries whereby the new Rail Alphabet, BR symbol and running number positions were applied on the green livery. As instructions became more clear or correctly followed, as supplies of green paint became exhausted and blue paint became more plentiful, the situation settled down to a more uniform appearance for locomotives. In 1968 the deletion of the D prefix to the running numbers and the general renumbering of the locomotive stock tended to make the changeover to the new livery less tidy. Combined

with the yellow warning areas of the ends the livery was attractive when new, but the lack of lining to relieve it was more pronounced when the newness wore off; indeed the whole effect could become rather drab.

Changing traffic requirements affected the Brush Type 2s. A changeover to air brakes on trains was initiated to gradually replace the hitherto standard vacuum braking system. In March 1968 D5641 was equipped with train air braking during its visit to Doncaster Works to be re-engined. In due course this practice continued through the class as required, with most being in dual braked condition for some years. Early examples were coded 14/2 (A) by the Eastern Region.

Another change was the isolation or removal of the steam heating equipment, troublesome at the best of times on most classes so fitted. During the late 1960s those locomotives with the equipment removed bore the stencilled letters NB indicating no boiler.

Until 1968 all the class was allocated to the Eastern Region, other than when on loan. Towards the end of that year the first transfers away were directed towards the Western Region, at that time about to withdraw many of its diesel hydraulic locomotives as a result of a general BR rationalisation plan to reduce the number of different types of diesel locomotives. The troublesome North British Locomotive Co. Class 22s of the D6300 series were scheduled to be withdrawn and Brush Type 2s, made redundant by service cuts in East Anglia, were drafted in to replace them. During the winter of 1968/9 D5528/30/35/36/39 were transferred for crew training purposes, before the general transfer when mass withdrawals

The type 2s were regular performers on the Kings Cross outer suburban service which was amongst the last in the country to use BR Mk I suburban compartment stock as in this c1968 view at Kings Cross with a lightweight DMU.

JOHN A SENIOR

of diesel hydraulic locomotives took place in earnest. Even so, some three years were to pass before the ER could spare any more locomotives.

The winds of change continued into the 1970s when in late 1971 D5692/5,5809/12 were transferred to the Western Region, followed by D5554, 5655/68/82/88, 5803/14/18/23/24/26/27/28/37/42/43 in January 1972. By 1977 the region had 40. The WR was not the only region to receive Brush Type 2s at this time because the North Eastern and London Midland regions were also recipients. Changes in traffic patterns and levels, in addition to replacement of other diesel locomotive classes, were the cause of such transfers. The transfers to the WR continued in 1972 and after, until a sizeable allocation was built up. Old Oak Common depot, also in London, was the main recipient.

By May the Southern Region had started crew training on D5843 with empty van trains between Eastleigh and Weymouth, presumably as a result of the usual WR locomotives working into the region having become all but extinct.

March 1972 saw the introduction of a new Brush Type 2 variant with the fitting of several examples with electric train heat equipment. Dual wound brushless alternators of Brush manufacture enabled them to be compatible with the new rolling stock which was being introduced fitted with electric heating and air conditioning. At last BR was starting to replace steam heating generally and conversions such as this were to become commonplace during the 1970s and 1980s, not only on the Brush Type 2s but also the Brush Type 4s and other classes. Twenty-four Brush Type 2s were selected, the first eight appearing that year, the last during 1975. These conversions spanned a period of renumbering which started in earnest during the latter half of 1973, and they became Class 31/4, receiving numbers 31 401 to 31 424 either after conversion (those dealt with before the implementation of the TOPS renumbering scheme) or during conversion. They were destined for Eastern Region service.

The remaining Brush Type 2s, other than the aforementioned Pilot Scheme examples (Class 31/0 from 1972), were designated Class 31/1 and ran in a series from 31 101 to 31 327 with gaps created by conversions to 31/4.

By early 1975 all the Class 31s were reported as being in blue livery, although not necessarily with standard insignia layout. The process of change had taken almost eight years.

Another change taking place was the abandonment of the four character indication panel headcodes on the ends of locomotives, in favour of two indicator lights. The indication numbers continued to be used internally on BR as part of the national train timetable, but it was thought unnecessary to have them displayed.

After some variations of displaying four zeros or no characters at all, the usual change was to blank out most of the display and to leave two clear circles on the glass front through which the lamps could shine. There were variations of this theme, but this became the general principle of intention. Long term, many of the glass fronts were replaced by sheet metal.

Number 5685, now minus the D prefix, hauling a rake of soda ash hopper wagons on the four track section of the Midland main line near Chesterfield in 1971.

JOHN A SENIOR

The first accident, sufficiently severe to cause the first withdrawal from service of a Class 31, occurred in 1975. Number 31 150, of March depot and formerly D5568, was wrecked in September at Corby Tunnel, near Gretton, Northamptonshire, when a brake van and 38 coke wagons ran loose and out of control from near the British Steel Corporation sidings at Corby. With no possible means of either diverting or stopping them the signalman watched helplessly as they gathered momentum. They entered the tunnel, two miles on, at some considerable speed. Unfortunately, 31 150 approaching the tunnel from the opposite direction and was struck head on by the runaway wagons just as they emerged from the tunnel. The cab of the locomotive was crushed and the Leicester driver killed. It took some fourteen hours to cut him free from the wrecked cab. When the locomotive was recovered from beneath the pile of wagons the damage was found to be so extensive as to prevent economic repair. It was withdrawn during October 1975, sent to Doncaster Works and cut up in February 1976.

A further withdrawal occurred in December 1979, that of 31 254 (ex D5682). It was soon cut up at Old Oak Common depot and provided a much-needed supply of spare parts for other locomotives. Number 31 136, formerly D5554, soon followed. Considered to be one of the troublesome locomotives, this locomotive was due for heavy overhaul in August 1980. Instead of overhaul it was put into storage as unserviceable, withdrawn officially and was sent to Swindon Works to be cut up and provide more spare parts. By the end of October it was stripped – cutting up took place in the November.

More Class 31s went into store from late 1980, pending a decision on their fate, most being in an unserviceable condition. They were brought to Swindon.

Times were changing; a Conservative Government had been returned in the 1979 General Election and as part of its economic policies to fight inflation and improve the economic state of the nation, curbs on public spending were implemented. Of course this affected the nationalised industries, including British Rail. The resultant lack of investment which precluded replacing any Class 31s, the youngest of which were nearly twenty years old, instead led to a programme of refurbishment to extend the lives of certain locomotives by at least ten years. The decision to refurbish was taken in 1981, following a policy statement by BR in the March of that year. There was an ER reorganisation taking place and some Class 31/1s, particularly those from the north east with high mileages and vacuum brake fitted, were threatened with withdrawal. In 1981 a collection of unserviceable Class 31s, together with other classes, was assembled at Swindon, joining those which had arrived in late 1980. Most were stored pending a decision on their future, not so much as to whether they would ever run again, but more as to what form they would take when refurbished. Nearly twenty 31s were at Swindon by the end of 1981. From time to time others arrived for scrapping, these being mainly accident victims.

D5549 (BT148/1959) on a train of mixed stock at Ipswich station. The horsebox next to the locomotive is a reminder of a once extensive traffic which has long-since deserted rail for road.

BRUSH A6182

John Draycott took some fine photographs during his long tenure as works photographer. No exception is this pleasing study of D5531 (BT130/1959), which shows the new application of a roof-mounted route indicator, introduced on D5530. Note the revised style of the letter D for the running number.

BRUSH A5675

The Class 31s were a better prospect to refurbish than the BR Sulzer Class 25 and members of the class were taken out of store and moved to Doncaster Works to receive, in some instances, a treatment more thorough than anything before.

Some of the first to go had the minimum of attention and found their way to the LMR, being allocated to Toton in January and February 1982, but those which followed went to Doncaster Works to supply spare parts. Then a batch of five went into the works in the October for overhaul. Two months later BR intimated that sixteen or more Class 31s would be converted to Class 31/4 by the fitting of electric train heat (ETH) equipment, together with other improvements. It was expected that the conversions would take until early 1984 to complete and the locomotives would replace diesel multiple units on the trans-Pennine routes.

Number 31 101 was the first of a programme of rebuilding some twenty-four Class 31s at Doncaster Works, including the sixteen aforementioned destined to have ETH equipment. In November 1982 it was in the works having been stripped down and in the early stages of rebuilding, which included being fitted with dual brakes. It is of further interest to note that this locomotive had undergone a previous rebuild following an accident and was originally D5518 of the Pilot Scheme batch. On 24 August 1983 the former 31 274 was due for release to traffic as 31 425, the first of the latest ETH conversions. It actually appeared the following month. Both locomotives had resided on the dump at Swindon Works North Yard; their transformation was complete. The rebuilding included renovation of the bodywork, which in many cases was badly corroded and involved the removal of the waistline strip of steel. It also involved the plating over of the disused nose end gangways, for a long time the source of unwanted draughts into the cabs. Where appropriate steam heating equipment was removed and concrete ballast substituted to ensure even

weight distribution, the diesel engines were overhauled and the electrical machines and control gear were updated. In the case of conversion to ETH the main generator was replaced. The writer recalls seeing some of these locomotives being rebuilt at Doncaster and reflected that at some stages there was very little of the original locomotive remaining, other than the bedplate and some of the bodyshell.

The 31/4s were for use on cross-country services between Birmingham and East Anglia and also from Liverpool to Yorkshire and Humberside. They were replacements for elderly diesel multiple units. The conversions to ETH continued well beyond the initial phase and locomotives due for overhaul were chosen for conversion. The refurbishment programme ended in 1988, by which time 176 locomotives had been dealt with and the ETH examples had totalled a further 44 bringing the series to 31 469. Included in the programme were some of the earlier Class 31/4s. Two additional ETH conversions were authorised to replace 31 401 and 31 436, both of which had been withdrawn from service due to accident damage. These replacements were numbered 31 469 and 31 400 and appeared in 1986 and 1988 respectively. The latter was an exceptional TOPS numbering because it went against the convention of commencing a sub classification series with XX X01. The logic was exceptional because the locomotive chosen for conversion was being equipped with the same electrical equipment as that fitted to the first conversions and it assisted personnel in identifying the locomotive with its

The first Class 31 to be repainted in the Railfreight Coal livery by Vic Berry of Leicester. Photographed in Vic Berry's yard on 9th October 1988.

M J STRETTON

compatible sisters. For clerical and administrative reasons it avoided breaking the rules of the system by having a second 31 401. Another conversion to ETH was contemplated in 1987 to replace another accident victim, 31 440, but this never took place. It would have been numbered 31 470. Many of the Class 31/1s refurbished were painted grey and the 31/4 conversions received standard blue.

The grey livery was introduced late in 1982 with the introduction of the first Class 58 locomotive from Doncaster Works, No. 58 001. It was the first livery of the fledgling Railfreight operations of BR, and the basic grey of the bodysides and roof was relieved by red buffer beams and side frames immediately to the rear of the buffer beams, an area revealed by the removal of the lower end skirting during refurbishing. The cabs were attractively picked out in yellow to behind the side doors, but relieved in black around the windows. Somehow the very large version of the BR double arrow logo, in white, was fitted in among the bodyside apertures and windows. The running numbers were placed on the left cabsides in black and in BR corporate style Rail Alphabet. If the livery was correctly applied the Railfreight title was placed on the cabside at the opposite end to the running numbers in white lettering on a red rectangle edged in white. The general introduction of this livery on other classes started with Class 31/1 and took place during mid-1985, 31 252 being the first to appear in the new colours. When new it was very attractive, but less so once the locomotives had been in service when it appeared dull and flat. Its period of application was to be brief and was replaced from late 1987, but not before the red solebar band had been introduced belatedly. The 1980s were times of many changes and these often reflected the aspirations of the newly created business sectors of British Rail, liveries being one of the most noticeable of all. By the end of the decade there was

a bewildering array of liveries, all competing and probably confusing all but the most dedicated of railway enthusiasts. The Class 31s had some variety, but nothing like some other classes on the railway. As for the customer, much probably counted for little unless the goods were delivered or the passengers arrived on time.

By 1983 there was some indication as to what the course of events would take for Class 31 and certain other classes. Class 56 locomotives were still being delivered and their successors, Class 58, would provide new motive power for heavy freight services, older classes would be subject to some refurbishing to extend their lives in a similar manner to that of Class 31, and the ageing diesel multiple unit fleet could expect partial replacement by new modern units. Those locomotives and units beyond economic repair or refurbishment would provide spare parts to keep the remainder running.

In 1982 more 31s were involved in collisions and the victims found their way to Doncaster Works for attention. Nos 31 244 and 31 313 were just two such locomotives and by August 1982 the works had seven. In addition to this total there were three other 31s, all stored. Not all the victims were dismantled; the better ones were made serviceable again.

In March 1982 March depot received some of the ETH Class 31/4s for the Norwich - Birmingham services which were routed via Peterborough and Leicester. This sort of working typified the cross-country duties that the 31/4s were to be used upon for the next few years. They were sometimes referred to as provincial services. 31s were becoming a

An unusual study of D5500 on a turntable on 10th October 1957. Eventually turntables were rendered obsolete by the displacement of steam traction by diesel.

BRUSH A4910

familiar sight on the Midland Main Line ever since Toton depot had been allocated examples, the first, 31 149, arriving in 1981. Class 56s replaced others in the north-east and Class 47s replaced 31/4s on WR empty coaching stock duties out of Paddington station. Those displaced were transferred out of the region. Sister locomotives could be seen on similar duties out of Kings Cross on the ER. During 1982 ten 31s were reinstated to traffic and five withdrawn.

The following year 31 111 suffered an engine explosion and further accidents claimed 31 214 and 31 262. On a happier note further conversions to ETH commenced when the former 31 274 emerged from Doncaster Works as 31 425 in September. This series continued at regular intervals and many conversions emerged during 1984. By mid-1983 31s were replacing Class 25 locomotives on the LMR at an increasing rate at Toton. At this time also, of the original grand total of 242 production Type 2s seven had been withdrawn, and of the remainder 24 had been fitted with ETH.

Two years later the ETH programme was completed when 31 468 emerged from Doncaster Works, other than the two aforementioned replacements of accident victims 31 401 and 31 436. By January 1986 the class total was 232, of which 68 were ETH conversions. The 31/1s were allocated to WR depots Bristol Bath Road and Old Oak Common, LMR depots Bescot, Cricklewood, Carlisle (Kingmoor) and Toton, and ER depots Immingham, March, Stratford and Thornaby. The 31/4s were allocated to Immingham, March and Old Oak Common.

Number 31 252 was the first 31/1 to receive the original Railfreight livery in 1985 and was succeeded by more as they left Doncaster Works and by the following year the 31/4 duties on cross country duties were under threat from the new generation of diesel multiple units coming into service, particularly those of Class 150.

Nearly twenty-nine years after the first Brush Type 2 had been introduced advance publicity declared that one was to be named in September 1986. After some speculation as to which locomotive would be chosen, 31 296 (formerly D5829 of 1962) was officially named 'Amlwch Freighter/Tren Nwy ddau Amlwch'. The locomotive bore two different nameplates, the English version on one side and the Welsh on the other. The ceremony was held in brilliant sunshine at Amlwch, in Anglesey, on Wednesday 3rd September and the naming was in recognition of forty years of business between BR (latterly BR Railfreight) and Associated Octel Company, the former transporting chemicals from the latter's plant at Amlwch to its plant at Ellesmere Port, and between Mostyn Dock and Amlwch. The locomotive was in the original Railfreight livery, complete with large BR logo, and the nameplates were fitted below the two bodyside grills nearest to No. 1 cab. Happily, more namings of Class 31s were to take place over the next several years.

Another collision, head on this time, at Maryland in December 1986 led to the withdrawal of the victims 31 261 and 31 245 in January 1987 due to extensive end damage on both locomotives. This was soon followed by 31 440 which collided with 47 089 at Chinley, in Derbyshire, on 20th February 1988. The estimated £140,000+ cost of repair of the badly damaged locomotive was considered not to be economic and thus it was withdrawn the following month.

At the time it was thought that equipment from 31 440 would be transferred to another locomotive and the conversion numbered 31 470, but this did not occur.

One Brush Type 2, transferred to British Rail Research, and based at the Railway Technical Centre, Derby, was renumbered 97 203 and repainted in a special livery. This livery featured red upper bodyside panelling and white lower, separated by horizontal black and white waistbands with white uppermost.

The cabs, including roof, were painted yellow and the main roof areas were given dark grey. Part of the bodyside red extended to below the cabside windows, which received a black surround extending from the front windows. A small BR double arrow logo was placed on the upper panel of the mid-bodyside access door to the engine compartment. It was very attractive, but short lived. Within weeks of receiving this new, customised livery 97 203 suffered severe fire damage and was withdrawn from service. Almost immediately a successor was selected, 31 326, then in Doncaster Works under light repair to damage sustained in a collision at Ipswich. This locomotive was originally the penultimate Brush Type 2, D5861 of 1962. On re-entry to service it became 97 204, and was noted on 4th September outside the works still in blue.

It was continued for some months before being repainted by February 1988 in a livery similar to that applied to 97 203, though not exactly so.

Next to be named was 31 309 on 14th May 1987, when it became 'Cricklewood' to mark the demise of the BR depot there. The locomotive was painted in blue livery with white waist stripe red buffer beam cowlings and larger than standard cabside numbers. On the 27th of the month 31 327 was named 'Phillips-Imperial' at the Phillips-Imperial Petroleum road and rail terminal at Port Clarence, Teesside. Below the nameplates was fitted the Phillips Petroleum company's logo and below that the logo of ICI, the reason for this being that Phillips-Imperial was jointly owned by the two companies on an equally divided basis. The naming marked 21 years of BR involvement in moving oil by train.

During the autumn of 1987 BR Railfreight unveiled its new liveries, but not before hinting at what was to come by displaying the theme on the proposed Class 60 mockups. BR made the official announcement on 15th October at Ripple Lane Freight Depot, Barking, Essex during a public Open Day there. Because of progressive changes in British manufacturing industry Railfreight had witnessed the erosion of its traditional markets and as a result it reacted by initiating a reshaping of the Railfreight business, a process which was expected to take two years to accomplish. It was hoped that this would halt the progressive decline, which threatened the organisation's operating surplus. Among other changes, the Railfreight livery was to be changed to reflect the new order of things. The Railfreight business sector was to be divided into six subsectors known as Railfreight General, Railfreight Coal, Railfreight Petroleum, Railfreight Construction, Railfreight Metals & Automotive, and Speedlink Distribution. The basic livery was devised by the Roundel Design Group who were commissioned by the transportation division of Jones Garrard, the company which prepared the initial analysis of the railfreight situation on behalf of BR.

A two-tone grey scheme was developed, the darker shade uppermost on the locomotive bodysides. Yellow warning panels were retained on the cab fronts as was the orange warning strip applied at roof gutter level around locomotives to remind staff of live overhead electrical equipment on electrified lines.

A black cab window surround reached back to just inwards of the cab doors. The running numbers appeared in standard Rail Alphabet and size in transfer form and in black below the cabside windows of the left hand cab when viewed from the side. Below the running number was positioned the

BR double arrow logo rendered in bright metal. The cab side of the other end was the position reserved for the new-style depot plaques, large, diamond-shaped and bearing the depot symbol, with this and the raised edge in bright metal set against a black background. Perhaps the most striking part of the insignia was that of the sub-sector business identity symbol. Each one was contained within a square, the top left quarter being bounded by a right angle representing part of the F of 'Freight'. Petroleum was a blue F with blue and yellow waves in the square portion; Construction was a blue F with blue and yellow chequered squares; Metals & Automotive was also a blue F with blue and yellow chevrons.

General and Speedlink Distribution had red Fs, the former with a yellow and red chequered pattern and the latter with two large red diamonds set on a yellow background. Coal appropriately had a black F and four black diamonds set on a yellow background. It was all very colourful, if expensive. The depot plaques surely were the most expensive and certainly the largest 'shed plates' ever to be fitted to British locomotives. Miniature versions of the subsector insignia, similar though not exact, edged doorways. So far as the Class 31s allocated to Railfreight were concerned Coal and Petroleum predominated, although there is some evidence that there were some running without any insignia at all.

Early 1988 marked the start of a rundown of Class 31 with the advent of new locomotives and diesel multiple units making inroads into their workings. It was estimated at the beginning of the year that as many as 35 of the remaining un-refurbished examples could be withdrawn. Heavy repairs had continued and the class total stood at 223 in September 1987, a slight reduction from the total of 237 of mid-1983. The last heavy general repair occurred in March 1988 with 31 106, and the reduction in demand for Class 31 meant further withdrawals and transfer to departmental use. The last 31/4 to undergo rebuilding was 31 403, which entered Doncaster Works in November 1988. Further withdrawals reduced the total to 215 in September 1988, 191 in November 1989 and 186 in March 1990, some of these being the seemingly inevitable accident victims. Departmental use brought about a new classification of 31/5, which denoted readily a former Class 31/4 with its ETH isolated. Originally, some examples were expected to be drawn from Class 31/1, but this did not occur. Those 31/4s so treated had their running numbers increased by one hundred, for example 31 407 became 31 507. When required as a 31/4 again, it reverted to its former identity. By the end of 1992 there were 28 Class 31/5s.

The fashion of the times was perpetuated by introducing new liveries for these departmental locomotives, 31 412 being the first of the class to receive one in February 1989; not all departmental locomotives were in Class 31/5. Grey was the basic colour. For those locomotives on general duties this was relieved by black cab window surrounds and cab doors, yellow warning panels on the cab ends and a darker shade of grey for the roof. Standard size white numerals for the running numbers were transferred to the left cabsides and raised, bright metal BR double arrow symbols were fitted to the right hand cabsides. In its own way it was attractive when in mint condition, but somewhat dull when weathered.

Number 31 541 was the first Class 31 to receive the second new grey livery, in mid-June 1990. The livery differed from the one above by having a broad yellow band on the upper bodysides and metal double arrow symbol below the running number. Furthermore, depot plaques graced the cabside of the opposite end, in the manner of the Railfreight locomotives. This livery was dubbed the 'Dutch Livery' by railway enthusiasts because of its striking similarity to the livery of the Dutch Railways. It was applied on those locomotives under the jurisdiction of the Civil Engineer's department. Your writer believes that the yellow band was more of a safety feature when the basic livery was applied

to the wagons of this department. Soon afterwards the livery was adopted officially and the intention was made clear to apply the yellow band retrospectively to the plain grey examples when it was convenient to do so.

In 1988 two further namings occurred, that of 31 413 (Severn Valley Railway) on 22nd April and 31 428 (North Yorkshire Moors Railway) the following day. Number 31 413 was named at a ceremony held at Bewdley, on the SVR, and 31 428 at Grosmont on the NYMR. Both are famous preserved railways with extremely fascinating locomotives and rolling stock, the NYMR of course was the home of D5500 for a number of years.

Before the year was out another preserved railway was honoured when 31 444 was named 'Keighley & Worth Valley Railway' on 17th August at Keighley station.

From 16th May 1988 Class 31/4s were displaced from the southern cross-Pennine passenger services by new Sprinter diesel multiple units. They had been employed on these services since 1984, when they took over from diesel multiple units of classes 123 and 124.

Perhaps the most spectacular accident to involve Class 31s happened on 28th October 1988 at Cricklewood sidings, when two of the class parked 400 yards from the end of a siding started to move and rolled out of control unmanned.

Number 31 202 coupled to and leading 31 226 broke through the buffer stop at the end of the siding and plunged 50 feet onto the road below, at Staples Corner, where the M1 Motorway and A406 meet. The coupling broke as 31 202 leapt into the air whilst 31 226 followed, the No. 1 end landing on top of 31 202. The combination of landing in the road and the impact of the second locomotive broke the back of 31 202. Number 31 226 never completely left the end of the siding and came to a stand supported by this and 31 202. Road traffic was delayed for three days as the wreckage was cleared. It took a Class 47 and three Class 31s aided by cranes to haul 31 226 back onto the rails during the following night. It was the end of the line in more ways than one; both locomotives were damaged beyond any useful repair, indeed 31 202 was cut into two sections on site to ease transport away from the scene.

On 9th October 31 430 was named 'Sister Dora' at the Bescot depot Open Day. This name commemorated a celebrated Walsall nurse of Victorian times. It had been borne previously by London & North Western Railway locomotive No. 2158 from 1895. The BR intention had been to revive it by placing it on a Class 86 electric locomotive, but Bescot based 31 430 was chosen instead. Small brass numberplates and commemorative plaques were also affixed.

Number 31 276 was named 'Calder Hall Power Station' during the same month, and a further naming occurred in 1989. This was in March, when 31 201 received the name 'Fina Energy' from Class 56 locomotive No. 56 132 at Immingham Traction Maintenance Depot.

Livery changes during the 1980s meant that there were many different colour schemes on BR. Early in 1989 in an attempt to regularise the situation, four main liveries were made official; InterCity, Railfreight, BR Main Line and BR General. Class 31 qualified for all except InterCity, depending upon duties undertaken.

BR General and Railfreight have already been described and Main Line was first applied to the class on 31 423 at the end of the year. The livery was the former InterCity livery and consisted of a dark grey band uppermost on the bodysides and white on the lower bodysides, a red stripe being applied near the top of the white portion to give the effect of white and red stripes separating the two. Black cab window surround and yellow warning panel completed the effect.

Those Class 31s which remained unrefurbished by early 1989 were members of Class 31/1. There were thirty-one of them, and they remained in the standard blue finish, so were readily recognised from the others.

The year 1989 saw at least twenty one Class 31s withdrawn from service, for one reason or another. Some were in rundown condition, others accident victims, but heavy inroads were being made and the pace was starting to quicken. Scheduled overhauls ceased on the 31/1s, but of course unclassified work was undertaken and overhauls continued at Doncaster Works on the 31/4s.

For a class supposedly entering its twilight years, the Brush Type 2 was attracting more attention for naming purposes. There was no adulation, such as that witnessed in previous years on other classes, but more of a growing appreciation of these venerable machines. Thus the 1990s dawned on the 31s, being given more names and bearing some of the latest liveries.

The next naming concerned 31 102 when it was named 'Cricklewood' at Tinsley Traction Maintenance Depot in January 1990. Number 31 309 had previously borne this name. By this time 31 296 was running without its 'Amlwch Freighter/Tren Nwyddau Amlwch' and 31 327 had lost its name 'Phillips-Imperial' to 31 233, an Immingham based locomotive on Petroleum duties. Mercifully, the 31s suffered less than other classes with regard to name swapping but it served to confuse if nothing else.

Next to be named was 31 568, newly renumbered from 31 468, which became 'The Enginemen's Fund' at the Bescot Open Day on Sunday 6th May to commemorate the 125th year of the fund which provides reassurance for railway staff whose livelihood is adversely affected by illness or accident. The locomotive was smartly presented in the grey livery of the Civil Engineer's Department. At the same event that day 31 423, in Main Line livery, was named 'Jerome K Jerome' after the famous author from Walsall who wrote the delightful book 'Three Men in a Boat'. The ceremony was attended by members of the Jerome K Jerome Society.

On 31st March 1991 Stratford Diesel Repair Shop closed. To commemorate this 31 165 was named 'Stratford Major Depot' and painted as close as was possible to its original green livery complete with its first running No. D5583. The depot had been the major repair centre for diesel locomotives allocated to duties in East Anglia since the mid-1950s. Considering the official line that locomotives should conform to the proscribed official liveries, this was some creditable achievement of livery application.

May 5th 1991 saw 31 405 receive the name 'Mappa Mundi' at the Hereford Rail Festival. The naming was performed by the Dean of Hereford, the name of the locomotive serving to remind people of the ancient map and to encourage people to donate money to ensure that it remained in Hereford Cathedral. The proceeds of the festival were donated to the fund. As is often the case more than two plates were cast; additional ones being presented to organisations, companies or individuals concerned. The locomotive was finished in Main Line livery.

The remarkable railway enthusiast magazine RAIL was celebrated in a naming ceremony on 26th October 1991 at Doncaster Works, when newly overhauled 31 116 was named 'RAIL 1981-1991'. The magazine was celebrating its first ten years of publication and originally had appeared under the title of Rail Enthusiast. Few magazines had such a start as this one. It was the original idea of Peter Kelly and it was he who risked more than a little to launch it. He was editor for some years, before moving to the editorship of the long-established Railway Magazine. The unique design of nameplate bore the title RAIL with 1981-1991 below. No additional plaques were required, the magazine is so well-known. Later, EMAP APEX, the owning company of the magazine, did have plaques fitted bearing its logo. Incidentally, the nameplates were produced by Newton Replicas and were the 400th set supplied to British Rail.

Number 31 410, sparkling in the attractive livery of Regional Railways, was named 'Granada Telethon' on 17th June 1992 by television personality Paul Nicholas at a ceremony held at Manchester Victoria Station. The naming was undertaken in connection with fund raising events for the bi-annual television marathon appeal sponsored by Granada Television and the locomotive was to haul the fund raising train around the north west of England, pausing at selected stops to collect money. The plates had a blue background, most unusual, bore the logo of the television company and were to be carried by 31 410 for two years, then removed for auctioning as part of the 1994 Granada Telethon events.

Number 31 130 was named 'Calder Hall Power Station' at Crewe Traction Maintenance Depot in July 1992. At about the same time 31 411 received the unauthorised name 'Our Eli' by attractive self adhesive labels applied by rail staff in memory of Bill Baildon a former driver based at Blackpool North who died earlier in the year aged 55. He was highly regarded by his colleagues and they felt that he should be remembered. In fact, because their feelings were so strong the affectionate name was made official and Regional Railways North West decided to have proper cast nameplates fitted instead. A ceremony was held at Blackpool, at which the locomotive was named by the Mayor of Blackpool, Councillor Mrs Dorothy Preston. (This was the second class 31 to carry the name; it was previously held by 31 276.)

Bescot then swung into action and named 31 146 'Brush Veteran' to mark 35 years of service of the Brush Type 2. Although not the oldest member of the class 31 146 was expected to be one of the more durable members. This naming occurred on 27th August 1992 at the Traction Maintenance Depot. The nameplates were funded by the Class 31 Preservation Group whose idea it was in the first instance and was only the second occasion that Brush had been included in a BR locomotive naming. The first was the naming of brand new Class 60 No. 60 098 'Charles Francis Brush' earlier in the year.

Three days after this latest Bescot naming three more 31s were named there during the Open Day. Number 31 105 was named 'Bescot TMD' at the depot and 31 106 was named 'The Blackcountryman' in the yard. The latter was commemorating the 25th anniversary of the Blackcountry Society of Dudley. A small oval commemorative plaque was affixed below the nameplates. Also named in the yard was 31 107, which became 'John H Carless V.C.' after the man who served on HMS Caledon and who was awarded the Victoria Cross. A rectangular plaque was fitted below the nameplates, depicting the ship and bearing its name, and an oval plaque was fitted above briefly setting out the circumstances of the naming. Each locomotive was smartly painted in the 'Dutch' livery.

When 31 428 was withdrawn from service after catching fire, its 'North Yorkshire Moors Railway' nameplates were transferred to 31 439. The new recipient, resplendent in Regional Railways livery was officially so-named on 19th September 1992 at the preserved railway's Grosmont station. New plates were cast; the original ones were too large to fit in the Regional Railways livery layout.

Number 31 413 had its 'Severn Valley Railway' nameplates removed in April 1993, but they were transferred to 31 233, formerly 'Phillips-Imperial', soon afterwards. Number 31 233 was officially named after the preserved railway at a ceremony on 6th May. This was part of the railway's celebrations during the Spring Diesel Gala events.

The new sub class 31/5 was introduced in 1990. The ETH was isolated, but the jumper cables remained, parked in the retaining socket set into the cab front above the right hand buffer. The only external clue as to such isolation was the new number series, which effectively made easy recognition of status in its own right. Thirty one 31/4s were converted to 31/5 during the year, some of which later reverted to ETH operation and original numbers. Despite having been replaced on most of the cross-country routes by diesel multiple units, they often came back as substitutes for failed units. By the end of the year there were still fourteen un-refurbished Class 31/1s in service. The application of Mainline livery has been mentioned above and two locomotives, 31 423 and 31 464 received it in 1990. By the end of the year the class totalled about 180, still in service.

On 29th June 1990 the BR Board announced that a series of structure changes would eliminate the existing business sectors, which were based upon the Regions. The regional basis had a long history reaching back to 1948 but it was considered to be out of date in a railway organisation that was developing its business-led strategies. Indeed, the changes had been developing gradually since the early 1980s and in many ways were moving towards eventual privatisation. The Government had declared its long term intention to privatise BR, but had not really stated the exact manner in which this would take place, nor when. One certain fact was that the railway must be business led.

The new structure to be introduced over the 1990-2 period was to see the Railfreight divide into two basic business parts, Trainload and Distribution. The former retained the Coal, Steel, Construction and Petroleum basic titles so there was no need to alter the large logos affixed to locomotives.

This was a rare economical happening. Regional Railways, a new sector, was divided into five areas, responsible for many cross-country route services.

Early in 1991 31 400, the final locomotive to undergo ETH conversion, was placed in store following a collision with 31 514 at St. Pancras on 17th January. The Class 31s had their accidents, perhaps no more than some other classes, but at this stage of their life it did not require much damage to cause withdrawal. Official withdrawal from service came on 1st October that year. It languished at Crewe Works (by this time under ownership of ABB) until December 1992 when it was despatched to Booth Roe Metals of Rotherham for scrap.

With the advent of new Class 60 locomotives and a decline in business as the recession bit deeper, older and less powerful locomotives in the BR fleet were rendered surplus to requirements. During 1991 some seventeen 31s, including eight 31/4s, were withdrawn from service. By mid-1992 there were 152 of the class left in service. A year earlier at least twelve 31/1s were still in traffic in the old standard blue livery and the oldest class member, 31 101, the venerable former D5518 of 1958, was still in service. At least four 31s had been repainted in Mainline livery, a very attractive scheme which suited the class despite the multiplicity of body side windows and grilles.

Regional Railways applied its own livery to 31 410 in 1992. This was based upon that applied to Class 153 and older diesel multiple units. A dark shade of blue graced the upper two thirds of the body-sides and off white the remaining portion, this being relieved by a mid blue stripe carried to the outermost cab door pillars from where three narrower stripes continued the line to the yellow warning panels on the cab ends. Black surrounded the cab windows and grey was applied to the roof areas. Running numbers were placed on the left cab sides and on the body sides towards the opposite end REGIONAL RAILWAYS and a minute BR double arrow symbol was applied. The end result was a very attractive livery with minimal interruption to the stripe by body side grilles. As related previously, 31 410 received the name 'Granada Telethon' for two years. Another locomotive, 31 439, also received the livery, and the pair coupled together and to Regional Railways liveried coaching stock made an extremely attractive ensemble.

With the introduction of the May 1992 timetable the Parcels sector and Trainload Petroleum released their 31s for other work. The latter displaced other members of the class on Trainload Coal duties, which in turn moved into Regional Railways care. Only three serviceable 31/1s remained in standard blue by the end of the year, but were soon afterwards withdrawn. 1992 ended with 94 Class 31/1s on the books, together with 30 of 31/4 and 27 of 31/5.

InterCity had 26 31/1s, 13 31/4s and 23 31/5s, Regional Railways 34, twelve and four respectively. Central Services had eight 31/1s and five 31/4s. Network SouthEast had the use of fifteen 31/1s and Trainload Freight eleven.

On 11th January 1993 the oldest Brush Type 2 then in service, 31 101, was withdrawn leaving 31 102 as the senior citizen of the class.

On 30th May 1993 31 147, formerly D5565, was named 'Floreat Salopia' during a ceremony held at Shrewsbury.

The 'Dutch'-liveried locomotive was attending the joint Shrewsbury and Hereford Open Day at the former's Coton Hill Yard and the name was chosen through a Shropshire Star newspaper competition.

A transfer of name occurred earlier that month when 31 413 lost its 'Severn Valley Railway' name to sister locomotive 31 233. The recipient locomotive then worked on the preserved railway during the Diesel Gala of 7-9th May.

On 4th June 31 215, originally D5639, was withdrawn from service following accident damage sustained during a collision. Bescot-based 31 234 (ex-D5661) followed suit on the 11th, and 31 217 (ex-D5642) on 8th July following a traction motor fire which occurred on 30th June at Stockport.

The fourteenth Class 31/4 to be withdrawn was 31 442 (originally D5679 and 31 251) on 17th September, following an alternator failure which occurred at Edge Hill on 26th August. 31 460 (ex-D5696 and 31 266) soon followed, on 1st October.

As something of a contrast 31 116 underwent a visual transformation when it changed both its livery and its name during October 1993. Formerly named 'RAIL 1981-1991', it became 'RAIL Celebrity' and received an experimental yellow and grey livery, together with the branding 'Infrastructure' in large red lettering and red bodyside stripes to match. Cabside numerals were black and the raised metal BR double arrow insignia was retained. Certainly the effect was colourful, but must have been difficult to keep clean-looking. The locomotive was re-dedicated by Pete Waterman on 30th October at a ceremony at The Railway Age, Crewe, attended by the then Editor of Rail magazine, Mr Murray Brown.

On the preservation front 31 162 was discovered to contain no asbestos and during December 1993 its owners, the A1A Group, voted to base the locomotive at the Midland Railway Centre (MRC). Arriving on 14th January 1994, it was working by 30th April, when it headed an A1A Group special on that day. Another preserved Brush Type 2 found a new home when 31 101 (the former D5518) arrived on the East Lancashire Railway on 17th March 1994. Its first revenue-earning run on the ELR came on 10th June 1994. The pioneer D5500 was still to be found at Steamtown at Carnforth and although it was started and run regularly, it did not have secure, covered accommodation – surprisingly for a NRM-owned locomotive.

The generally poor condition of 31 296 (ex-D5829) led to its withdrawal on 1st December. Then on the 12th 31 544 and 31 556 had their ETH equipment made operable again and reverted to 31 444 and 31 456 respectively, whereas 31 438 had its isolated and became 31 538 on the 14th.

The new year saw the withdrawal of 31 282, formerly D5831, this occurring on 7th January. It was followed by the withdrawal of another Class 31/4, 31 457 (originally D5587), on 11th February.

1994 was noted for the first moves towards privatisation of BR, and Class 31 was part of a mass reallocation of locomotives, which took place in March. Trainload Freight South and Trainload Freight West both inherited Class 31s in quantity. The former took thirty-three Class 31/1s (Toton) and the latter seventy-eight (37 Bescot, 41 Crewe Diesel Depot) whereas the totals respectively for Class 31/4 were five (Toton) and twenty-four (14 Bescot, 10 Crewe Diesel Depot).

On 23rd March 31 558 was named 'Nene Valley Railway' at Orton Mere on the NVR. It had been specially repainted in a variation of the yellow and grey BR Infrastructure livery. The naming coincided with the opening of Platform 2 of the preserved railway's Orton Mere station.

Preserved 31 123 (originally D5541) was successfully started up at its new home on the Gloucestershire Warwickshire Railway on 11th June, within a fortnight of its arrival there on 25th May. Much body repair was required as some of the panels were missing, removed during its two-year stay at Bescot depot following withdrawal. Meanwhile at the MRC Butterley, restoration of 31 162 continued, with necessary servicing and repairs being undertaken to keep it in running condition for the summer season. Its first passenger run on the MRC occurred on Saturday 23rd July.

Withdrawn Class 31 locomotives, meanwhile, could be found at a number of locations by the end of June 1994, mainly the following: Basford Hall (Crewe), Bescot, Crewe Traction Maintenance Depot, Frodingham, Immingham and Thornaby.

Number 31 105 'Bescot TMD' attended the Crewe Rail Fair on 21st August and then proceeded to Cardiff Canton Depot to have the new Transrail markings applied. It reappeared so adorned on 2nd September before re-entering service. In doing so, it became the first of the class to receive a new 'company' branding.

In the original 'private' world of preservation 31 162 commenced its winter repair programme during which bodywork repairs and restoration of nose doors was undertaken. Meanwhile, 31 101 had been repainted into its original green livery as D5518 and re-entered service on the ELR appearing somewhat better in this splendid livery. Similarly, 31 123 was undergoing a repaint into green livery for its restoration on the Gloucestershire Warwickshire Railway as D5541. This was achieved by 11th November and a splendid appearance also resulted. It made its passenger debut at the line's Diesel Gala on 12/13th November. The only drawback which occurred was the discovery of a faulty traction motor, necessitating operation using the power of one bogie and requiring repair of the offending motor during the winter months.

Towards the end of 1994 there were around 140 Brush Type 2s still on the TOPS computer list. A few were stored, either in serviceable (31 209/252/263) or unserviceable condition (31 151/171/184/248/413). Soon, four more were added to this total, these being 31 125/174/230/408. Early in the new year the total reached twenty-two. Many of those still in service could be seen operating on Regional Railways passenger train duties in the North West and on a substantial amount of civil engineering freight duties generally.

During February 1995 31 116 had its 'RAIL Celebrity' nameplates removed at Toton Traction Maintenance Depot. Next to be de-named was 31 107 which lost its 'John H Carless VC' plates at Bescot TMD on 25th July, and 31 455 'Our Eli' the same month. As some measure of compensation, 31 112 was named 'Bescot Transrail' on 5th July.

Remaining Class 31s were still undertaking useful work, although passenger workings were dwindling. Among the last locomotives to haul passenger trains out of Blackpool were 31 439, 31 455 and 31 465. The final train of nuclear waste from Trawsfynydd power station in North Wales was provided with two Class 31s to haul it on 8th August. The pair used were 31 255 and 31 199, provided by Springs Branch depot. Withdrawals from service held off until 15th August, when 31 272 (D5659) succumbed.

The preservation scene improved considerably for Class 31 during 1995. Not only did examples already saved progress towards appealing running condition, but others joined the ranks. In the care of the A1A Group 31 162 progressed well during the winter of 1994/5 and this continued. Equipment was replaced and repaired, corroded bodyworks attended to and headcode mechanism reinstated.

Its livery of corporate blue, with full yellow ends was maintained in commendable condition and showed little sign of some of the major surgery of the previous months. The A1A Group secured their second Brush Type 2, No. 31 108 (D5526), during this period and once most of the work on 31 162 was completed, attention was expected to turn to the new acquisition. It had been stored in unserviceable condition at Scunthorpe since 1991, the year of withdrawal from service, and arrived at the Midland Railway Centre on 31st May, going into storage until the completion of work on 31 162. Essential maintenance commenced within months, followed by an expected two-year programme that included replacement of body and cabside sheeting, and reinstatement of steam heating equipment.

Pete Waterman's D5518, meanwhile, was externally renovated and prepared in an approximation of its original green livery in time for the Diesel Week of the East Lancashire Railway, held in June 1995. Its return to service in this condition occurred on the 15th – and it looked immaculate. It was soon in regular service following the Diesel Week, particularly when other diesel locomotives were despatched to the Crewe Railfair in late August.

Restored D5541 continued to show its paces on the Gloucestershire Warwickshire Railway, particularly during the railway's spring gala weekend in March.

Another Class 31 joined the preservation list in June 1995, when 31 210 (D5634) was acquired by the Colne Valley Diesel Group for the Colne Valley Railway in Essex. Although generally complete, it had been in open storage at Frodingham for a considerable time following withdrawal from service in February 1992. Work soon started with the eventual aim of restoring it to D5634, in its original livery.

Number 31 418 (D5522) was offered for sale and tender bids had to be in by 21st July 1995. Loughborough-based Type One Locomotive Association, owners of English Electric Class 20 No. D8098, were successful and announced as such on 14th August. Charnwood Borough Council provided a £2,500 grant towards the purchase, in recognising that local residents were among those who had originally built the locomotive. Initial hopes included restoration to original livery, despite much modification (notably ETH) since building, but mainly to conform to the Great Central Railway preserved railway's policy of running green diesel locomotives as part of an overall theme.

Further preservation interest in the Brush Type 2 occurred during 1995 when the Devon Diesel Society studied the feasibility of acquiring an example in south-west England.

First choice as a base was the Paignton & Dartmouth Railway.

With the disenchantment of Pete Waterman over privatisation matters, his involvement with the business side of Waterman Railways ceased and the separation of his preserved locomotives was sought. Included was 31 101.

Elsewhere, a Brush Type 2 was repainted in Mainline blue livery in February 1996. Toton unveiled freshly repainted 31 407 together with an LMS design saloon on the 27th of the month. This was to be the only member of the class to bear this attractive livery as Mainline Freight was sold to the consortium headed by Wisconsin Central three days previously. The new owners provided the opportunity to expend much speculation and comment as to what the fate of its inherited Class 31s would be. With thirteen Class 31s placed in store during March 1996, uncertainty was compounded further. Many of those lying at Toton were in a woebegone state, unmercifully vandalised. The fate of those still in service was still open to speculation while the new owners considered their acquisitions.

Wisconsin Central's newly-titled English Welsh & Scottish Railway (EWS) Ltd soon declared that their Class 31 fleet would be maintained for local workings in the short-term.

Whatever the immediate future held it was an indisputable fact that the Brush Type 2s had served their owners well and there were still duties available for them. How long they would survive remained to be seen.

The duties available to Class 31s were mainly local and EWS was expected to maintain them in the short term for these purposes, especially engineering duties. There were 89 stored examples and only 45 in service in mid-1996, so clearly some sorting out was required. Some twelve intact members of the class were moved to a secure building at Carlisle Upperby where they were held in reserve for an upturn in traffic. At least nine stored as unserviceable were withdrawn, eight of them being taken off the books during September.

The break up of the Waterman railway interests saw various locomotives offered for sale and happily 31 101 passed into preservation and was delivered to the Battlefield line at Shackerstone, Leicestershire.

Another preserved member of the class, 31 418, found its way to the Great Central Railway at Loughborough, still wearing its corporate blue livery. Pioneer D5500 was moved from Carnforth to the East Lancashire Railway early in June 1996 and operated some services there, before returning to the NRM at York in time to appear at the diesel weekend there on 7/8th September.

By the end of 1996 there were still around 150 Class 31s on the books, but at least two-thirds of them were not in working order, indeed many were in woebegone condition, dumped at Toton and Bescot. Thirty of those at Toton were earmarked for disposal of which twenty-two were to be offered for scrap and eight for preservation. By May 1997 only twenty-eight examples remained in operation following three withdrawals and another six placed in store.

Apart from a handful at Toton most of the active Class 31s were based at Crewe working infrastructure trains around the Crewe, Bescot and Warrington areas, with occasional trips along the North Wales coastal line and further afield. These light duties and occasional calls to assist on other trains, nevertheless displayed a usefulness which was still in demand.

Virgin Trains hired 31 420 to provide a source of power for the central door locking system on the 16.47 Reading-Liverpool train on 18th July, backing up the train locomotive 37 023. It was unusual, but satisfied the demand. Not so lucky was sister locomotive 31 413, which was moved to Booth-Roe scrapyard from Adtranz Doncaster a month earlier.

By the end of September 1997, with EWS reorganising its maintenance in line with combining the former trainload businesses into a single operation, twenty-seven Class 31s were maintained at Bescot. Seven Class 31/4s were included in this total and continued to be used on infrastructure trains and emergency duties described above. Although threatened by the impending introduction of the new Class 66 locomotives, their retention in traffic was extended beyond original expectations by traffic demands, with individual fates being dictated by cost of repair and upkeep.

Autumn 1997 saw the fortieth anniversary of the introduction of the Brush Type 2, and in Loughborough's Charnwood Theatre a special film show was staged by Rob Foxon's 'Railways Remembered' team to launch a superb video called 'A Tractive Effort'. This video not only celebrated the Brush Type 2 by making a vintage Brush publicity film available to the public, but it also featured other Brush motive power. Furthermore, the viewer was guided by Mr Neville Mays, retired Brush veteran from those days.

With ex-Anglia DBSO No. 9701 leading, a test train between Old Oak Common and Kettering (1Z16) runs through Wellingborough on 2nd September 2008, propelled by Class 31/4 No. 31 459 Cerberus.

BRIAN MORRISON

Happily, the A1A Group's preserved Type 2 31 162 at the Midland Railway Centre, Butterley, had appeared during mid-September 1997 in BR corporate blue livery and numbered 5580, in time to provide its own celebration.

By early November the serviceable survivors were 31 110/113/154/163/188/201/203/229/233/255/306/308/450/ 465/466/512/530, with 31 142/146/207/273/407/420/434/439 /467/554 awaiting repairs or maintenance. Some of these locomotives had their nameplates removed during late 1997. The remainder constituted a motley collection of around 120 stored locomotives awaiting their fate. A temporary reprieve appeared feasible for some stored at Carlisle Upperby, subject to the scrutiny of engineers, of course. On 5th December 31 229 was involved in a shunting collision at Warrington and a week later 31 146 'Brush Veteran' broke six months of inaction when it was returned to traffic.

On 3rd January 1998 the final charter train powered by Class 31s was the A1A Group's 'The Long Goodbye'. This saw 31 465 and 31 466 head ten coaches as a farewell to the class in main line service. As this was the last Class 31 charter to be allowed and because of the continued service of the surviving members, it became a premature event. The train left Blackpool at 06.37, calling at Manchester, traversing the Hope Valley line and visiting Doncaster, before reaching Barnetby. Passengers were taken to Cleethorpes by a pair of Class 37s while the Class 31s were serviced and upon their return the latter returned the train via Lincoln, Newark, Peterborough and later Derby, the Hope Valley line again then Blackpool. It was, indeed, a fitting tribute to the Brush Type 2.

Although the end of the Brush Type 2 in main line service appeared to be near, the scene was to change and commemorative efforts became somewhat premature. EWS continued to take Class 31s out of traffic, but did reinstate

them occasionally as conditions dictated. EWS sold 31 563 (D5830) to the Type 1 Locomotive Association and the locomotive was taken to the Great Central Railway in early 1998 to act as a source of spare parts for preserved 31 418 (D5522). Then, twelve locomotives were offered for sale in an effort to interest the preservation movement further. All were dumped at Toton and from this selection 31 271 (D5801) found its way into A1A Group ownership, 31 186 (D5609), 31 191 (D5614), 31 459 (D5684), 31 468 (D5855), 31 549 (D5840) and 31 552 (D5809) passed into Fragonset Railways ownership, and 31 165 (D5583), 31 461 (D5547), 31 551 (D5842) and 31 558 (D5836) were bought by Harry Needle. 31 461 and 31 558 were later resold to Fragonset Railways and the remains of 31 165 and 31 551 were scrapped at Adtranz Crewe by the end of September 1998. Meanwhile, EWS withdrawals continued with 31 462, retired due to fire damage and 31 563 in February 1998 and 31 541 in May.

In June 1998 the Rail Regulator, John Swift QC, intervened on behalf of smaller operators when it was learnt that EWS had started to call in scrap dealers to cut up locomotives, 44 Class 31s included, dumped at Bescot. EWS cancelled its plans and promised to review the situation and sell without detriment to the company. This led to regular advertisements in the railway press offering locomotives for sale and the creation of a centre at Wigan for stripping locomotives and recovering components for re-use. The smaller operators may have had a valid point as Fragonset Railways soon started to overhaul its Class 31s and had 31 452 (ex 31 552) and 31 468 well advanced by the late summer of 1998 sufficient to consider hiring out motive power to Silverlink on its Bedford-Bletchley services, an operation not in competition with EWS. Here older diesel multiple units were proving unreliable and the Class 31s were seen as a temporary solution to the motive power problems until new stock could be placed in service.

Number 31 452 was completed in time to attend the EWS/Rail Open Weekend of 29/30th August and was displayed in its new Fragonset black livery. Another Class 31 to be repainted and displayed was EWS's own 31 466, which bore the maroon and gold of that company, all the more remarkable, bearing in mind the intended early withdrawal of the company's twenty-seven strong Class 31 fleet. Early withdrawal or not, more had been re-instated and in addition to infrastructure trains longer distance freight workings were regularly being made.

Following a trial week of operation with 31 452 and 31 468 on the Bletchley-Bedford service 12-17th October 1998, the latter locomotive became the first Fragonset Class 31 to be used on a Virgin train. This occurred on 2nd November when the locomotive headed the 06.49 Shrewsbury-Euston as far as Wolverhampton.

With the continued arrival of Class 66s from North America EWS started to store its more elderly locomotives, including 31 116/146/273/434, hoping to reduce its fleet by the end of 1999 to seven for engineering trains on restricted loading gauge lines in the London area.

During the early part of 1999 the first of a series of advertisements appeared. With a closing date of 19th March five Class 31s were offered for sale publicly, these being 31 126/145/238/242/450. Throughout the year at monthly

intervals more followed and every one (except November) featured many Class 31s. Initially, a so-called working locomotive was expected to realise £20,000 or a scrap price of £5,000 per locomotive. Clearly EWS expectations were high.

More locomotives were taken out of traffic in January 1999, notably 31 163/166/190/201/255/530. By mid-March more had succumbed, leaving only seven in traffic, these being Nos 31 110/154/203/233/308/420/466.

Conversely, Fragonset was restoring more locomotives to traffic and when 31 186 appeared in March it sported a new number, 31 601. This new sub-classification was due to its fitting with ETH through wiring and control equipment to enable it to double head with ETH locomotives on trains requiring this facility. It was named BLETCHLEY PARK 'STATION X' on 22nd March at a special ceremony inaugurating at last the Bletchley-Bedford push-pull services. A few teething problems beset operations with 31 452/468 initially, but 31 601 operated without a hitch. Such operations ceased on a regular basis during the autumn of 1999.

Number 31 602 (formerly 31 191) became available for traffic in June, being named 'CHIMAERA' on the 16th of that month. More Fragonset namings occurred in June when 31 459 was named 'CEREBUS' and 31 468 was named 'HYDRA' when total of five Class 31s had been restored to main line working by this company. Continuing its naming practice the company then named 31 452 'MINOTAUR'. In July 1999 push-pull operations on a trial basis by Silverlink Trains commenced on the Gospel Oak - Barking line, using 31 468 and 31 601.

EWS made a surprise move when it repainted withdrawn 31 255 red and gold in late March. This was to test the new paint shop facility at Toton and the application was just sufficient to do this, the locomotive bearing a mottled side stripe but no insignia.

With the ebb and flow of availability and traffic demand the EWS Class 31 fleet in service changed with 31 110/154/203/306/308/420/466 being reported in action during May 1999. They were allocated to Old Oak Common depot, London, where in August staff repainted 31 110 in early BR green livery as D5528 in time for A1A Charters' 'Farewell to Arms II' railtour on the 21st, staged to mark the end of the EWS Class 31s. 31 154 also took part in this event. Then, in mid-August came the withdrawal of 31 306 and 31 308, leaving just five left in EWS service. On 16th September one of the survivors, 31 154 hauling a train with 31 420, caught fire after dragging brakes ignited the underside, necessitating fire services assistance. The damaged locomotive was placed in store and substituted by 31 207 ex-store from Old Oak Common.

Meanwhile, Fragonset Railways purchased another batch of locomotives from EWS, this time 31 105/415/462/524/526, then located at Bescot. The stated long term aim was to return all to traffic and have them available to secure new work, particularly rail tour business. Such expansion necessitated new maintenance facilities, which were secured in the former Railway Test Centre (RTC) Derby. The first Class 31 to arrive at Derby was 31 468. Before the year was out, 31 289 and 31 301 were purchased by Fragonset, followed by another pair 31 439 and 31 537. Also sold were 31 107 (to Howard Johnston Engineering), 31 130 (to the Battlefield Line, Leicestershire) and 31 128 which was acquired by a volunteer at the Birmingham Railway Museum at Tyseley.

Howard Johnston Engineering's 31 106 and 31 107, though long-term destined for preservation, were the subject of a deal with Fragonset Railways to return them to main line traffic for at least five years.

In one move Harry Needle Engineering then purchased eleven Class 31s from EWS, from the Bescot scrap line. These were 31 125/147/168/174/229/263/282/286/428/516/548; it was thought all were destined for scrap rather than restoration.

Further EWS sales saw 31 163/166/188/206 purchased by the Colne Valley Diesel Group with a view to hiring or loaning them to other groups. A fifth (31 255) soon followed in December 1999 for use on the preserved Colne Valley Railway. This locomotive was the one used as a guinea pig for testing the effectiveness of the new EWS Toton paint shop. More went to the preservation movement when Manchester-based Victor Korzeniewicz purchased 31 422 and the East Lancashire Railway, Bury, was destined to be the new home of Bescot-dumped 31 435 and 31 467.

With the preservation and further mainline use of former EWS locomotives it was good to know that the Brush Type 2 would be seen in action in the future. Proof of the new era came when Railtours North and A1A Charters jointly ran a Crewe-Edinburgh trip on 4th December 1999 via the Settle-Carlisle route, using Fragonset's 31 452 and 31 602 as motive power.

After the flurry of EWS sales, the company decided to dispose of some of its relics by awarding a contract to T J Thomson of Stockton on Tees to scrap twenty-three Class 31s. All were lying at Toton and had found no interested buyers for other purposes. The first deliveries, by rail, began in January 2000. Rail and road deliveries cleared the Toton dump by April. One remarkable event was the resale of 31 270 (D5800) already en route to Stockton on Tees. It was diverted to its new owners, the Colne Valley Railway Diesel Group.

EWS continued to dispose of its dumped locomotives at various locations, so further Class 31s were sold for scrap to Booth Roe Metals of Rotherham and some were cut up on site by other firms elsewhere. Number 31 252 met its fate at Peterborough, where it had lain for over five years. Curiously, 31 408 was advertised as for sale for a second time, in the advertisement which closed on 12th May 2000.

By mid-2000 the future of more than a few Brush Type 2 was assured. Less certain was the fate of the EWS residue of operating and reserve locomotives, but preserved locomotives and small operating companies operating former EWS examples virtually guaranteed continuation for some years to come.

The EWS working examples officially were down to four by the close of 2000, with 31 420 being taken out of traffic on 13th January 2001. Remaining trio 31 110 (by this time part of the unofficial EWS heritage fleet), 31 207 and 31 466 continued for some weeks more, working from Old Oak Common depot, often on engineering duties. Its members were finally stored on 12th February 2001, having seen their final workings three days earlier. On this occasion 31 207 and 31 466 worked the 09.36 Temple Mills to Hoo Junction engineering run, coming back on the 13.35 return working, following which the pair joined 31 110 at Old Oak Common.

Use of Class 31s was restricted to occasional shunting duties at the depot. EWS still retained forty-seven Class 31s at this time, whereas Harry Needle Railroad Company set about scrapping 31 196/207/283/320 at Stratford. EWS then advertised for sale twelve of its Class 31s, the closing date for bids being 13th April.

On the preserved East Lancashire Railway, the restoration of 31 435 to its original livery as D5600, was completed. More good news was the sale of the final Brush Type 2 31 327 (D5862) to George Littlejohn for eventual operation on the Keith & Dufftown Railway in Scotland. It had been in store at Carlisle Upperby and was despatched during November 2001 to the Bo'ness & Kinneil Railway to be prepared for its new life in preservation.

Fragonset continued to utilise its Class 31 fleet on a variety of duties, such as spot-hire, charter trains, empty stock movements, Railtrack work and longer term operation of public services. Following an overhaul and repaint into black livery 31 128 was added to its operational fleet and duly received the name 'CHARYBDIS' It also acquired five more locomotives from EWS for various purposes by September 2001 in a general sell-off and, concurrently, Cotswold Rail (CR) bought 31 203 from EWS and sent it to the Falcon Works where it could be found with two other CR locomotives 31 206/210. Number 31 210 left on 21st December 2001 bound for its owner's further storage at Moreton on the Marsh, eventual sale and transfer to the Dean Forest Railway seven months later. Another EWS sale saw 31 119 purchased by

Mike Darnell and moved to Newton Heath, Manchester and almost obscurity.

By the end of the year Harry Needle had scrapped eleven Class 31s and despite limited scrapping TJ Thomson of Stockton on Tees still had twenty-four in their yard awaiting disposal.

On 3rd May 2002 31 106, owned by Howard Johnston Engineering, was added to the operational fleet of Fragonset Railways following an overhaul at Derby. The following day it ran light to Carnforth and on 5th May it and 33 108 worked a Preston-Peterborough charter train. That weekend was the Spalding Flower Festival and as part of the festivities the newly-applied name SPALDING TOWN was unveiled by the Chairman of South Holland District Council Colin Fisher at Howard Johnston's home town of Spalding.

By contrast Fragonset's unrefurbished (but operational) 31 289 was transferred to the preserved Northampton & Lamport Railway on long-term loan on 2nd May 2002. It had been in store at Tyseley having been withdrawn from BR service ten years previously. Preserved 31 538 returned

to service on the Mid-Norfolk Railway during the summer and in June preserved 31 270 was started for the first time by the Colne Valley Diesel Group. June 2002 also saw the final clear out of Class 31s from Bescot when four members were transferred to Barrow Hill.

On the second day of the Battlefield Line's diesel gala of 21/22 September preserved D5518 was named 'Brush Veteran' by Martin Sargent of Fragonset Railways. He then drove the locomotive on the next train.

Wessex Trains ran an extra Westbury-Weymouth service on 14th October 2002 when a four-coach train leased from Fragonset Railways was topped and tailed by 31 459 and 31 602. The pair were working in multiple, by means of through wiring and demonstrated the concept as an alternative to using diesel multiple units.

At this time Fragonset sold two of its Class 31s to Railtrack for eventual use with its proposed ultrasonic test train. 31 105 and 31 285 were to be prepared by Fragonset for restoration to working order on behalf of Railtrack. One of Fragonset's own locomotives, 31 190 GRYPHON, was repainted in Railtrack blue and green and hired to Railtrack. This was a new move and it was a personal choice whether or not the new look was better than the Fragonset black livery. 31 601 BLETCHLEY PARK 'STATION X' followed suit. Two more Class 31s, 31 154 and 31 233 stored at Old Oak Common, were sold to Fragonset by EWS during October.

Another livery change involved pioneer locomotive D5500 when the National Railway Museum restored it as 31 018 in

Following failure of the Class 86 rostered for the 20.30 from Liverpool Street to Norwich on 4th August 2000, a pair of Fragonset Class 31/4s were substituted to power the train, which eventually departed from the London terminus at 21.30. Awaiting the departure are numbers 31 468 HYDRA and 31 459 CEREBUS.

BRIAN MORRISON

British Rail corporate blue as the centre piece of its 'British Rail – A Moving Story' at York. Although the locomotive remained serviceable, it was stressed that it would be no longer available for operational use.

Railtrack had become Network Rail and it added to stock 31 233, purchased from Fragonset, and 31 107 purchased from Howard Johnston Engineering for test train purposes. These locomotives were to appear, after overhaul by Fragonset, in yellow livery. Work started fairly quickly on these and the previous pair and was in progress in early 2003, with the Derby works being very busy overhauling them. Several months later Network Rail purchased 31 102/200/319 from Harry Needle Railroad Co. as a source of spare parts. Fragonset, meanwhile had 31 106/452/602 on hire to Wessex Trains with the Mk2 rake of coaches, operating extra traffic between Cardiff and Brighton.

The new year opened on a bright note when newly-restored D5581 (31 163) in original green livery made its first run on the Chinnor & Princes Risborough Railway on 12th January. It became the tenth working preserved Brush Type 2. Its entry into service came when the railway held its diesel gala on 23rd March 2003. At this time it was expected that Fragonset soon would be placing 31 454 into traffic, in InterCity livery to match a rake of HSBC-owned Mk2 coaching stock in these colours. In this role it was expected to be in the service of Wessex Trains for working Cardiff-Brighton and Westbury-Weymouth services. By mid-August the locomotive had been repainted and was nearly ready for service. It was out and about the country during September. One trip saw it make a weekend venture onto the Great Central North line. On 17th May Fragonset had Railtrack liveried 31 190 and black 31 468 double heading an FA Cup Final day train of supporters from Southampton to Cardiff.

Despite these happenings, the class total continued to dwindle as TJ Thomson restarted scrapping those remaining in its yard, which at this time totalled around eighteen examples, being reduced to ten by November 2003.

Fragonset's loaned 31 289 worked all the Northampton & Lamport Railway's services on 17th August, after much work on its engine. The locomotive still remained to be repainted. Happily, work was progressing at Fragonset Derby with 31 285 and by October 2003 it was already in Network Rail overall yellow livery and sporting end-fitted cameras and lights.

At the end of 2003 Fragonset had nine Class 31s registered for main line use (31 106/128/190/452/454/459/468/601/602 plus 31 289 loaned to Northampton & Lamport Railway), and Network Rail had one. In preservation hands operational Class 31s included 31 018/D5500 (NRM), 5580/31 130 (Battlefield Line) , 31 108 (Nene Valley Railway), 31 271 (Midland Railway), 5581 (Chinnor & Princes Risborough Railway), 31 255/270 (Colne Valley Railway), 31 235/538 (Mid-Norfolk Railway), 31 327 (Strathspey Railway), D5600 (East Lancashire Railway), D5830 (Great Central Railway).

Although none was in main line service and most out of use, EWS retained several (31 420/427/466) at Old Oak Common depot in London, for pre-heating ETS rolling stock purposes. At the other end of the spectrum, TJ Thomson's efforts in scrapping Class 31s had reduced the total remaining in its Stockton yard to just two examples, 31 155/237.

The year 2004 opened with the second Network Rail locomotive, 31 233, released from overhaul at Fragonset and returning to traffic on the 13th January. Fragonset, meanwhile, was preparing for a new operation with First North Western whereby two Class 31s were to top and tail Blackpool-Manchester and Chester-Blackpool trains. The new service, using InterCity liveried Mk2 coaches, commenced on 3rd February on a Monday to Friday basis. On the first day 31 468 and 31 602 were in charge.

An unusual task for 31 306 'SPALDING TOWN' was its use on an inspection tour of Scotland, during mid-April 2004. Leaving Derby on 19th April it made its way north hauling Network Rail's inspection saloon and it reached Fort William on 21st April. It returned to England on 22nd April, to Carnforth.

Fragonset then repainted 31 601 and five Mk2 coaches in Wessex Trains livery. In losing its Railtrack livery, the locomotive received a startling light purple/pink scheme. They went into service for the summer timetable, starting on 23rd May. Number 31 461 was expected to followed suit.

The nine-day York Railfest 2004 opened on 29th May and among some of its impressive visiting exhibits was the superbly restored 31 271, bearing Railfreight Trainload Construction livery. Unveiling the name 'Stratford 1840-2001' on 31st May revealed BR corporate plates with polished raised metal portions and a blue background. Truly, this locomotive was a delight to behold and a credit to all those who had restored her.

With a 27th August deadline, Fragonset offered some of its redundant locomotives for sale. Among those advertised were five Class 31s, 31 154/407/411/412/417. One of Fragonset's latest returnees, 31 454 in InterCity livery, was named 'HEART OF WESSEX' at Bristol Temple Meads station on 4th August 2004 by Bernard Lane, founder of the Heart of Wessex Rail Users Group. Then, on 18th October 31 601 was renamed 'THE MAYOR OF CASTERBRIDGE' by Mrs Pam Rayner of Pershore, Worcestershire, who won a newspaper competition organised by the Heart of Wessex Rail Partnership and Wessex Trains. The name recalled the title of Thomas Hardy's famous novel.

Back at Fragonset's workshops at Derby work had enabled Network Rail, by September, to place 31 105, its third Class 31, into traffic whereas in mid-September TJ Thomson scrapped its last two Class 31s at Stockton, being 31 155 and 31 237.

Work at Derby had also been in progress on 31 461, preparing it for a return to traffic for Wessex Trains use and livery. Indeed, this locomotive was intended to be named 'THE MAYOR OF CASTERBRIDGE' but it was not ready in time. Part of the work being done was the fitting of a long-range fuel tank in the former steam train heat boiler area.

The First North Western use of Class 31s between Blackpool and Manchester finished on 10th December 2004, with 31 459/468, and with the introduction of the winter timetable so did the Wessex Trains Class 31 service to Brighton.

From 7th January 2005 Fragonset Railways and train operator Merlin Rail merged under the title FM Rail, subtitled 'fragonset merlin railways'. The resultant logo incorporated a mythical beast that could be interpreted as being the beaked mouth, tongue and paw of the former

Fragonset dragon. Some sources quote the FM Rail beast as a gryphon. At this time the new organisation had the following operational Class 31s on its mainline books, shown in the table below:

Non-ETS	Through wired for ETS/multiple operation	ETS fitted
31 106	31 601	31 452
31 128	31 602	31 454
31 190	31 459	
	31 468	

On 15th February 2005 FM Rail's 31 106 'SPALDING TOWN' and 31 128 took the Network Rail structure gauging train between Craigentinny and Dundee, the former returning to Scotland some months after its inspection saloon foray.

Forever seeking new business, FM Rail ran an InterCity liveried test train headed by similarly attired 31 454 and Fragonset black 31 602. This occurred on 29th March 2005, the train running from Derby to Skegness and return.

On 12th April sister locomotive 31 190 was used to move Network Rail HST power car 43 014 from Derby to Craigentinny in Scotland, for servicing. It would not be long before the Railtrack liveried locomotive returned to Scotland, with 31 602. West Coast Railway Co. took over the contract to supply motive power for operating the luxury Royal Scotsman train for the 2005 season. The 31s were used from 30th April for the first week of the service, because WCRC motive power was in short supply and they were noted double heading the train on 2nd May. Although they operated for a week, a long-term hire arrangement for 31s for the service resulted in 31 190 being repainted in overall plum Royal Scotsman livery, and by 16th May she was back at the head of the train. WCRC similarly painted its own 47 854 in matching livery for the service.

It was thought that Network Rail might renovate two more of its Class 31s, 31 102 and 31 200, stored at Throckmorton airfield, although much work would be required to do this.

In May 2005 FM Rail returned to working the Wessex Trains again, with 31 601 prominent in its Wessex Trains livery, matching that of the coaching stock.

June 2005 saw the former Harry Needle 31 414 pass into preservation, being sent by road from Old Oak Common to Wirksworth, on the Ecclesbourne Railway, Derbyshire.

In July 2005, following a competition held in conjunction with Rail magazine, it became known what the winning FM

The 09.36 Bretts hoppers (6Y94) from Purley to Cliffe runs between Bexley and Crayford on the Dartford Loop line on 26th November 1999, headed by Class 31/4s No 31 466 in EWS livery and No 31 420 in Mainline colours.

BRIAN MORRISON

Rail livery was to be. Retaining Fragonset black, the FM Rail gryphons and company title (in red) appeared on a device reminiscent of BR's later Railfreight decals. Red and white bands relieved the solebar area and the wording 'fmrail.com' appeared on the body side.

Class 31, therefore, was holding out well on the main line and in preservation; by mid-2005 they appeared set to continue indefinitely. The youngest members were 43 years old.

Proof of continued longevity in preservation came very soon after the arrival of 31 514 at Wirksworth – its ETS alternator was reconnected and appropriately the locomotive was renumbered 31 414, before being started up on 3rd July. This enabled the railway's ex-Gatwick Express coaching stock air conditioning to be started up and heralded the retirement of the train heat van. The test run took place three days later and it hauled the Gatwick stock for the first time on 9th July. Repainting into a two-tone grey livery was well underway by the middle of the month.

Sometimes it is necessary to reduce the ranks of classes to ensure survival of the fittest. Over on the Gloucestershire & Warwickshire Railway preserved 31 123, returned to its original number D5541, had not worked since 1995 and was offered for sale on eBay. As a result, A1A Locomotives Ltd purchased the locomotive to provide a source of valuable spare parts for its collection of Class 31s, 31 108/162/271/418, the last one being the main recipient. Component recovery was swift and the locomotive left the preserved line on 24th November, bound for Booth's scrap yard at Rotherham where it was scrapped in February 2006. This scrapping added one more to the list of at least seven Class 31s so treated during the previous thirteen months.

On the main lines FM Rail Class 31s continued to find work around the country in various liveries. Wessex Trains pink was much in evidence west of Paddington, but in Scotland 31 190 GRYPHON wearing 'Royal Scotsman' plum to match the train's coaches, appeared on 31st August and 1st September 2005 working as far as Kyle. It had been hired by West Coast Railways and was still so several days later.

Not all the company's locomotives were so well presented, nor in main line use either. 31 289 wearing faded, drab and rusty BR blue livery and on loan to the Northampton and Lamport Railway was seen working trains on the line 19/20th November 2005 during the diesel gala. When it was named PHOENIX (complete with plaques), by 11-year old Jamie Squibbs the new plates enhanced its appearance.

Back on the main line, 31 602 CHIMAERA, still wearing the Fragonset black livery, and yellow Network Rail 31 105 reached Penzance on 15th January 2006, in charge of the ultrasonic test train from Paddington. This was a rare visit by members of the class to this extremity.

During the winter of 2005/6 FM Rail started a clearout of donor locomotives, selling them for scrap. One notable candidate was 31 407, still in Mainline Freight blue livery. Before its departure from Barrow Hill it had its exterior smartened for its last public appearance on 12th February, sufficiently to give the impression of a working locomotive. The interior would have revealed its true condition.

Number 31 190 GRYPHON left its usual haunts in the West Country in late February 2006 and undertook snow clearing duties in East Anglia, followed by crew-learning duties in the area the following month.

During March 2006 the Newton Heath Traction Group's newly restored 31 119 arrived on the Embsay & Bolton Abbey Railway. Prior to its public debut at the diesel gala on 25th/26th March, it underwent crew training runs at weekends. This was its first series of runs since withdrawal in 1995, storage and careful restoration – a credit to the preservation movement.

Old Oak Common depot in London finally gave up its long-term resident 31 465 when it was purchased and sent into preservation on the Dartmoor Railway where it was intended to make full use of its electric train supply.

Another long-term resident made a move in April 2006. This time Cotswold Rail's 31 206 left the Falcon Works on the 8th by low-loader for its owners base at Horton Road, Gloucester. With the increasing HST power car workload and resultant lack of space at Brush it clearly could not extend its long-term stay, already measured in years. Some relief was felt among the staff at Loughborough as over the years it had been shunted around countless times. Even so, it was frequently parked near the Paint Shop during the preceding six weeks before its departure.

Once at Gloucester it was advertised for sale and passed to CF Booth's in Rotherham for scrapping. It escaped this fate and was resold into preservation being moved to the Rushden Historical Transport Society for preservation and eventual use on the Rushden, Higham & Wellingborough Railway the following October.

The EWS 'heritage' locomotive fleet had one Class 31 within its ranks. 31 110, bearing green livery and residing at Barrow Hill, was advertised as for sale in April 2006, with other EWS locomotives in the small fleet. Contrary to the thoughts of many, the locomotive was not in the best of condition, having suffered frost damage to the engine and having only two traction motors fit for operation. Two months later it was sold to scrap dealers TJ Thomson, arriving at the yard in July.

The next Class 31s offered for sale were seven FM Rail examples during June. Numbers 31 154/407/412/424/426/433 /462 were scattered around the country in storage, without much prospect of being returned to traffic. Perhaps only retained 31 461, fitted with a new engine and additional fuel tank, stood any chance of revival, but work at Derby had stopped on this locomotive when attention was diverted to the overhaul of 56 125 (56 303) for Jarvis Fastline and coaching stock for the Blue Pullman train. The seven locomotives were sold to Rotherham scrap dealer R Hull Junior and had been cut up before the end of the year. For FM Rail it realised useful revenue.

Network Rail's stored 31 107 was chosen to star in a staged crash for television. The purpose of the crash was to highlight the dangerous consequences of the misuse of level crossings by road users. On 1st June, the battered looking candidate arrived at Barrow Hill, from FM Rail at Derby, to be made fit for the occasion. Three weeks later, a visual transformation had been made by replating and repainting its exterior. It was given a black livery, with full yellow ends extending around the cabside and cab door windows. The buffer beams were painted red, being prominent due to the shortening of cab front plating. It also carried the legend LEVEL CROSSINGS DON'T RUN THE RISK on its body sides, in addition to its running number on the cab sides.

On 21st August un-powered 31 107 was propelled along the Barnetby-Gainsborough branch in north Lincolnshire by sister Network Rail 31 233 and crashed into a Renault Espace people carrier car carefully placed on the line at Hibaldstow crossing on the B1206 near Brigg. Carefully filmed for showing on the BBC television programme Top Gear, the results were the main feature of a campaign to reduce the high incidence of deaths and injuries caused by road vehicle drivers who blatantly disregard safety signs and barriers and drive into moving trains. 31 107 was released and hurtled along the track at a release speed of 60 mph, to crash into the car and continue for another half a mile until it came to a standstill.

One of the more unusual main line sights was that of three Class 31s hauling a loaded coal train. FM Rail fielded 31 190 GRYPHON, 31 454 THE HEART OF WESSEX and 31 601 THE MAYOR OF CASTERBRIDGE to work the trial train on 25th July between Daw Mill Colliery and Rugely Power Station.

On 7th September the company's 31 601, still in its striking Wessex Trains light purple and pink livery, was renamed

GAUGE '0' GUILD and re-branded FM Rail in non-standard lettering. A promised repaint did not materialise.

The next month, following a B-Examination at Barrow Hill, sister locomotive 31 459 did receive a repaint into FM Rail black livery, albeit without the company's logo, and re-entered service. On 16th November 2006 it double headed with 31 128 the inaugural train of former Motorail vans carrying second-hand Mercedes and former hire vehicles between Gloucestershire and Mossend on behalf of Motorail Logistics and Cargo-D. Running twice a week, the train was monitored and evaluated for long term use.

Operated by FM Rail, but privately owned, 31 190 lost its 'Royal Scotsman' plum livery and GRYPHON name during a repaint at Barrow Hill into BR green. It also regained its pre-TOPS D5613 running number, all part of a filming exercise, which took place on Great Central Railway (North) on 15th November 2006. With yellow ends c1963 style, it looked neat and crisp.

Although the company's 31 468 HYDRA had been in store for some time, it was hoped to have it back in traffic, but despite declaring this publicly, FM Rail went into voluntary administration on 11th December 2006.

In the interim period Victa Railfreight, initially involved with the motor vehicle movement trains above, took over operating activities while matters were being sorted. It soon became apparent to those outside FM Rail that matters had been worsening in the wider spectrum of activities and despite shedding twenty jobs as part of a restructuring exercise during the previous summer, rationalising storage

of stock and selling off redundant locomotives, there were cash flow problems. It was a case of endeavouring to honour contracts while trying to reform or repackage elements of the company to produce something more effective.

Elsewhere, Martin Nixon offered his preserved 31 166 for sale to enable him to focus his attention to his other 31s maintained by Colne Valley Rail Enterprises. With 31 166 being based on the Wensleydale Railway and 31 188/235 based in East Anglia concentrating effort was not easy. The situation was further complicated by the requirements of other locomotives within his interests.

By the end of 2006 nine more Class 31s had been scrapped, leaving 60 survivors in various conditions, varying from empty hulks to splendidly restored machines and everyday workhorses.

By the first few days of the new year FM Rail's engineering portion was separated to become Rail Vehicle Engineering Ltd (RVEL) and the remainder was still in the hands of the administrator. The locomotives were for a while stopped at various places until some sorting could be undertaken. Some of the privately owned locomotives ceased to be part of the former FM Rail operational fleet, changing status to either private owner or preserved. Initially this concerned 31 190 and 31 422, the latter being intended to be used by Vintage

Naming of 31 601 at RTC Derby on 7th September 2006. as GAUGE 'O' GUILD recognising the dedication of modellers who work in that gauge - 7mm to the foot.

BRIAN MORRISON

Trains at Tyseley. Number 31 452 was authorised to work Serco trains by 4th January, but this was the only exception until 31 105/106/128/602 followed suit on various workings a few days later.

It emerged in due course that FM Rail had incurred heavy losses due to a combination of reduced income and increased costs and the gap had widened to the point of no recovery. It was apparent that the organisation had struggled for some time and may have laid plans for a future of some sort after the collapse. Furthermore, it was apparent also that the merger of Fragonset and Merlin had never been fully consummated and that the tangle of leasing, renting and owning had become beyond proper financial control. There was the impression that creditors' trust had been taken beyond the limit in some instances, because many stood to lose heavily. Keeping donor locomotives stored around the country incurred high rental costs, which accumulated steadily. Only the engineering side of the business presented a profitable and easily separated concern, as vouched for by the swiftness that it changed hands and continued to function successfully. Regarding operations, these were placed in the charge of Victa Westlink Rail.

Former FM Chairman Martin Sargent, was in contact with Cotswold Rail and several locomotives, including Class 31s (31 128/452/461), moved south to the latter's base in Gloucester. Privately owned 31 128, at least, in early February made the trip to Brush Traction as part of the MTU re-engineering programme contracted movements of HST power cars. Number 31 190, once operated by FM Rail but not owned by the company, returned to main line traffic with RVEL, as did 31 106 and 31 190. Offered for sale were 31 452/454/461/468/601/602. Number 31 602 was soon hired by RVEL from the FMR administrators rather than sold. In turn it was hired from RVEL to Network Rail, repainted all-over yellow. The exercise was to cover for the overhaul of its own 31 105, 31 233 and 31 285 in turn by RVEL, each estimated to cost £250,000 and thus enable the trio to continue operation until 2010 at least. A result of the overhauls would be the scrapping of NR donor locomotives 31 102, 31 200 and 31 319. NR continued to hire 31 106, 31 190 and 31 459 from RVEL.

Two, at the time mysterious, entities now appeared upon the scene, Nemesis Rail and Mainline Rail, into which various locomotives were assimilated, sometimes then transferring from the former to the latter. Each had operating and stored pools allocated. Included in the NR list was 31 128, its stay with Cotswold Rail ceasing before the end of February. The other two Class 31s briefly operated by Cotswold Rail, 31 452 and 31 461, went into store at Gloucester and passed to the Battlefield Line respectively. It emerged that Mainline Rail was headed by Martin Sargent formerly of FM Rail, and in due course his new company purchased 31 452, a somewhat full circle of sorts for the locomotive. It later emerged that Mainline Rail was owned by Ealing Community Transport and it may thus be assumed that Nemesis Rail was a 'transition stage' company.

As part of a clearout of locomotives by EWS, its last three Class 31s (31 420/427/466) were sold to CF Booth of Rotherham for scrap. Happily, 31 466 instead of moving to Rotherham, soon found its way into preservation on the Dean Forest Railway courtesy of its new owners the Dean Forest Diesel Association, arriving on the line on 14th March.

Early 2007 saw scrap metal prices at a high and Class 31s made their journeys to the scrapyards from various sources, either from the FM Rail fall out, the EWS clear out or the occasional gutted locomotive from elsewhere.

Starting from 20th July 2007 regular return through trains ran between Bristol and Minehead, utilising both the national system and the preserved West Somerset Railway to serve the Butlins holiday establishment at Minehead and also local people. Running on Mondays, Fridays and Saturdays until 27th August, Class 31s were used as motive power in top and tail manner. On 20th and 23rd July 31 452 and 31 454 were noted on these duties and, indeed for most of August. In the same region, the pair also worked on Sunday 22nd July on trains between Bristol and Weston Super Mare, in connection with a Pop Beach music concert at the latter. By this time 31 454 had had its branding changed from FRAGONSET INTER CITY to MAINLINE INTERCITY while retaining the cabside relief Fragonset emblems.

Another staged 'accident' occurred on 2nd July 2007 using 31 420, partly repainted green for the occasion. It took place at Tyersal Lane, Bradford, on the former Laisterdyke to Stanningley and Leeds route as part of a filming exercise. It had been moved from Booth's scrapyard in Rotherham. The former EWS locomotive was returned to Rotherham after filming and quickly cut up.

The filming was part of the production of a television drama 'The Royal', in which green-painted operational sister 31 190 provided the running scenes elsewhere. Non-discerning viewers would have the impression that only one locomotive was featured.

The fallout from the FM Rail administration continued, despite the fact that it had been reported that all its own locomotives had been sold. With regard to Class 31, re-selling, transfers and private owner transfers and re-hiring continued well into 2007. Number 31 602, for example, was hired by the FM Rail administrator to Rail Vehicle Engineering Ltd of Derby, which then re-hired it to Network Rail.

To mark the fiftieth anniversary of the introduction of the Brush Type 2, the Great Central Railway ran trains hauled by resident D5830 on 6th October 2007, between Loughborough Central and Leicester North. In particular the 2.15pm to Leicester carried current and former Brush employees as a result of an open invitation from the railway. Prior to this, a small display at Loughborough reminded those present of what Brush had been involved with during the past decades, sparking many to reminisce with each other. As one would expect their former activities varied and the event was enjoyed by all. People were invited to pencil in a similar slot for the fiftieth anniversary of the introduction of the Brush Type 4 in 2012!

On 1st October 2007 the situation regarding surviving Class 31 locomotives was believed to be as shown in the table which follows overleaf:-

FM RAIL ADMINISTRATION		
31 602	D5614	Hired to RVE and used by Network Rail
HNRC		
31 113	D5531	Chinnor & Princes Risborough Rly 07.04
MAINLINE RAIL		
31 452	D5809	Ex-Cotswold Rail 04.07
31 454	D5654	MRLO 03.07
31 468	D5855	MRLO 03.07
31 601	D5609	MRLO 03.07
NEMESIS RAIL		
31 128	D5546	NRLO
31 422	D5844	
31 437	D5603	Meldon Quarry 10.03, NRLS 03.07
31 439	D5666	Meldon Quarry 08.03, NRLS 03.07
31 461	D5547	Battlefield Line
NETWORK RAIL		
31 105	D5523	
31 107	D5525	Derby RTC, (2006 level crossing crash film loco.)
31 233	D5660	Derby, for stripping
31 285	D5817	
31 465	D5637	Derby
PRESERVATION		
31 018	D5500	National Railway Museum, York
31 101	D5518	Suburban Preservation – Battlefield Line
31 108	D5526	A1A Locomotives Ltd – South Devon Rly
31 119	D5537	Newton Heath Diesel Traction Group – Embsay & Bolton Abbey Rly
31 130	D5548	Suburban Preservation – Battlefield Line
31 144	D5562	Newton Heath Diesel Traction Group, Newton Heath
31 162	D5580	A1A Locomotives Ltd – North Norfolk Rly
31 163	D5581	PO – Chinnor & Princes Risborough Rly
31 166	D5584	Colne Valley Locomotive Enterprises – Wensleydale Rly
31 188	D5611	Colne Valley Locomotive Enterprises – Wensleydale Rly

31 203	D5627	PO – Chasewater Rly
31 206	D5630	PO – Rushden Station Transport Museum, Northants
31 207	D5631	M & GNJR Society – North Norfolk Rly
31 210	D5634	Dean Forest Diesel Association – Dean Forest Rly
31 235	D5662	Colne Valley Locomotive Enterprises – Mid-Norfolk Rly
31 255	D5683	Colne Valley Diesels – Colne Valley Railway
31 270	D5800	Colne Valley Locomotive Enterprises – Peak Rail, Derbyshire
31 271	D5801	A1A Locomotives Ltd – Nene Valley Rly
31 327	D5862	PO – Strathspey Rly
31 410	D5669	PO – Kirby Stephen
31 414	D5814	PO – Ecclesbourne Valley Rly, Derbyshire
31 418	D5522	A1A Locomotives Ltd – Midland Rly Centre, for spares then scrap
31 430	D5695	PO – Mid-Norfolk Rly
31 435	D5600	Newton Heath Diesel Traction Group – Newton Heath
31 438	D5557	PO – Mid-Norfolk Rly
31 456	D5823	Newton Heath Diesel Traction Group – East Lancs Rly, Bury
31 463	D5830	Type 1 Locomotive Co – Great Central Rly
31 466	D5533	PO – Dean Forest Rly
31 467	D5641	Newton Heath Diesel Traction Group – East Lancs Rly, for spares then scrap
PRIVATE OWNERS		
31 106	D5524	Howard Johnston – RVEL Derby
31 289	D5821	PO, on loan – Northampton & Lamport Ry, NRLS
31 301	D5834	PO – Meldon Quarry 08.03, NRLS
31 415	D5824	PO – Meldon Quarry 10.03, NRLS
31 423	D5621	PO – Meldon Quarry 08.03, MBDL, MRLS
RAILWAY VEHICLE ENGINEERING LTD		
31 190	D5613	RVLO
31 459	D5684	RVLO

RVLO/RVLS = Railway Vehicle Engineering, Derby, pools
NRLO/NRLS = Nemesis Rail pools
MRLO/MRLS= Mainline Rail pools
MBDL= private owner pool
PO= Private owner
O suffix= Operational
S suffix= Stored

During mid-2007 the Nemesis and Mainline pools consisted of the following:-

NRLO	31 128
NRLS	31 289, 31 301, 31 415, 31 423, 31 437, 31 439
MRLO	31 454, 31 468, 31 601
MRLS	--

With fifty two locomotives surviving out of an original total of 263 (nearly 20 percent) there existed a situation where a large core of locomotives could survive indefinitely, so the scope for further scrapping was minimal in the short term among the donors and woebegone examples. Earlier in the year eight Class 31s had been scrapped, leaving the scrap yards clear of the class.

The links between preserved lines and mainline operators increased when Nemesis Rail Class 31s were planned to be part of the Dartmoor Railway diesel gala in the autumn. What was not clear was the relationship among Nemesis, Mainline and Ealing Community Transport, where the last-named appeared to control, if not wholly own, Class 31s within the pools or groupings.

Clearer by far were the intentions of Network Rail which envisaged use of Class 31s until 2012. As if to emphasise this 31 602 was named DRIVER DAVE GREEN on 3rd November 2007, by Mr Green himself. It came as a surprise to the driver instructor, but he was sufficiently composed afterwards to drive the locomotive from the Railway Technical Centre at Derby to Leicester. The train consisted of 31 602, an inspection saloon and black-liveried 31 459 and returned to Derby later that day. Mr Green's family travelled in the saloon.

The nameplate design was most unusual for a diesel locomotive as it was in the shape and style of an LMS steam locomotive wheel splasher plate, in effect an arc. Even the cast lettering was in LMS sans serif style. Below each arced plate was affixed a steam locomotive style 19B shed plate, recalling the Sheffield Millhouses depot where Mr Green had started his railway career.

At this time Network Rail was still evaluating the condition of 31 465, brought up to Derby from the Dartmoor Railway as part of its efforts to continue with Class 31 use.

Various preserved Class 31s were also expected to be returned to traffic before the spring of 2008, including Colne Valley Diesel Enterprises' D5611 (31 188) on the Wensleydale Railway, still in EWS livery, 31 466 on the Dean Forest Railway and 31 235 on the Mid-Norfolk Railway. Elsewhere, at Newton Heath, the Newton Heath Diesel Traction Group named its 31 435 'Newton Heath TMD' on 16th September during the Northern Rail depot open day. Its stay there came to an end on 8th January 2008 when it was delivered to Embsay & Bolton Abbey Railway, rather than its previous location on the East Lancashire Railway.

The Class 31s on mainline duties continued to earn a living for their respective owners, but some of the former FM Rail stored examples were moved out of Meldon Quarry as part of a clear-out of rolling stock in general at the site. Owned by Nemesis Rail and Mainline Rail, 31 301, 31 423, 31 437 and 31 439 and some coaching stock were moved by Cotswold Rail 47 237 to Gloucester on 13th December 2007 and then to Long Marston, for further storage, the following day. Number 31 113, owned by HNRC, and on the Chinnor & Princes Risborough Railway, was due for the scrapman's torch by March 2008.

Anonymous black liveried 31 459 'CEREBUS' working under the Rail Vehicle Engineering Ltd could be seen out and about working on Network Rail test trains during February 2008. In March 2008 RVEL was seeking the use of 31 452/454/601 by hiring them as required, from Mainline Rail.

After fifty years, clearly there was some life in the 'old Brush Type 2' yet.

The 10.15 Dollands Moor-Trafford Park intermodal, via Temple Mills, is powered through Shortlands on 3rd January 2001 by EWS Class 66/0 No 66 142. In the consist are the two Class 31/1s that were despatched to Dollands Moor to haul the train as far as Temple Mills but were not needed as a Class 66 became available. Inside the '66' are No. 31 101 in green and No. 31 207 in 'Dutch' livery.

BRIAN MORRISON

5 – Falcon

Brush Traction No. 280 was allotted to an entirely new venture, the Company's 'Falcon' project. A very careful study had been made by Brush of the feasibility of producing a 2,800bhp lightweight Type 4 diesel electric locomotive.

The venture was launched during a period of development and evolution in diesel rail traction in Britain, particularly within the sphere of the BR Type 4 power range. The reasoning behind the move was to gain large orders for BR Type 4 locomotives.

British Railways had very limited experience with high-powered main line diesel locomotives by 1959. The LMSR/English Electric locomotives 10000 and 10001, together with the related Southern/English Electric trio 10201-3, provided the initial diesel electric experience to 1958 and during that year the first Modernisation Plan Type 4s went into service on the Great Eastern lines. These were built and equipped by the English Electric Co. and were a development of 10203. They were rated at 2,000bhp and were of the 1Co-Co1 wheel arrangement, being numbered by BR D200-9. The following year the first BR-built 1Co-Co1 locomotives were introduced. They were fitted with Sulzer engines rated at 2,300bhp and numbered D1-10 by BR. Initially, ten were built and the following year there appeared another batch rated at 2,500bhp. Crompton Parkinson supplied the electrical equipment. All these locomotives were heavy and employed non-powered axles which lacked adhesive weight. The 2,000bhp EE version weighed 133 tons and the BR-Sulzer design 136 tons. Both locomotive designs were long, too long as operational experience was to demonstrate on occasions and both were constructed by methods considered at the time to be traditional. The slow-running engines provided by English Electric and Sulzer were considered to be the most suitable then available for the Type 4 power range which commenced at 2,000bhp. Thus, by 1960 BR was already considering what form the ideal Type 4 diesel electric locomotive of the future should be – a lightweight Co-Co of 2,800bhp. The stakes were high because the requirement would be for some 500 examples.

Before the take-over of the Brush Group by the Hawker Siddeley Group in 1957 very little thought, if any at all, had been devoted to producing a prototype locomotive of such sort. Indeed, as related previously, it was intended that locomotive building activities should cease. Fortunately, this intention was reversed and by late 1958 thoughts within Brush had turned towards designing a Type 4 locomotive with a view to gaining orders. Several aspects were behind the change of direction. First was the considered opinion of the new Managing Director, Mr B L Goodlet. Then there was the Hawker Siddeley takeover, which made finance more readily available, and there were the financial benefits reaped or expected from the large and valuable orders for Brush Type 2s. Furthermore, the Brush Group had gained exclusive UK manufacturing rights for Maybach engines in 1956 and arrangements were made for them to be manufactured under sub-contract by Bristol Siddeley. With Brush and Bristol Siddeley both part of the Hawker Siddeley Group from 1957 a rail traction outlet for the high speed Maybach MD655 engine in the UK was very desirable. The Hawker Siddeley Group also offered experience of strong load-bearing, lightweight aircraft construction methods which could be applied to rail traction work.

Maybach Motorenbau GmbH had a long history of manufacturing diesel engines in Germany and by 1953 had two MD650 Vee type engines fitted to each of a pair of 78 tons, 2,000bhp locomotives with hydraulic transmission. The engines were rated at 1,000bhp and the V200 locomotive design of the German Railways (DB) was soon scaled down for a locomotive design for use on BR Western Region. This was the 'Warship' class B-B locomotive, built at BR Swindon Works and numbered from D800. The Brush Group was to supply the MD engines, but the first locomotives, new in 1958 and numbered D800-2, were fitted with engines built in Germany because the UK manufacturing facilities were not sufficiently advanced in time. In contemplating the use of the Maybach engines for rail traction purposes Brush was keen to take advantage of their lightweight qualities.

A Brush traction policy was formulated in January 1959, being built upon Mr Goodlet's 1958 platform of gaining as much work as possible. The policy intention was wide-ranging and imaginative, though not all of its contents came to fruition. Some did, and provided Brush Traction with much work over the ensuing years. The 'Falcon' project was one of the targets which did appear and was listed on a document dated 29th January 1959 as item 1b 'Design a Type 4 Locomotive based on twin Maybach engines and build a prototype'. The critical feature highlighted was the 1,500rpm DC generator design to accompany such each engine. Bristol Siddeley agreed to supply three engines on sale or return.

Each engine was to be rated at 1,400bhp and of the resultant 2,800bhp 300bhp was to be devoted to train heating purposes. The target date for completion of the prototype locomotive was 1960 and for resultant orders, 1961. Estimated cost was £100,000. In March 1960 consideration was given to designing a Type 4 locomotive for BR using a Sulzer engine, if specified, with orders envisaged for 1961. Considered problems were large generator design and the use of lightweight mechanical

The famous Brush prototype Type 4 locomotive 'Falcon' was built in 1961 as Brush Traction No. 280. It is seen on the facing page under construction in the Superstructure Shop, with the bodyside panels yet to be fitted to the load-bearing trusses. The works plates are already affixed.

BRUSH

'Falcon' was transferred to the former Turbine Shop for fitting out. This view, taken from the overhead travelling crane, shows it between two Type 2s in 1961. The sheer size and bulk of the power unit in the Type 2 is seen to good advantage in this view before the roof is fitted.

BRUSH A7031

parts. This latter consideration demonstrated Brush willingness to offer more than one option to BR and to commit itself to producing a prototype locomotive to demonstrate on the railway in everyday service and for test purposes. In some ways Brush Traction was ahead of its rivals and ahead of BR considerations, but produced the 'Falcon' design in conjunction with BR requirements and with BR consultation. The main disadvantage was that should BR change its opinions then the design could be out of line before it took to the rails. This was to happen, but BR never ceased to encourage Brush, and the Eastern Region in particular, welcomed 'Falcon' with open arms as the first private venture Type 4 to be built with a view to gaining its manufacturer second generation Type 4 orders. In this respect 'Falcon' did its job well. In achieving 2,800bhp two engines were necessary because at the time no single engine was available at this output for rail traction purposes. Additionally, an axle load target of 19 tons was set.

As the project was a private venture it was desirable to have as much equipment as possible manufactured by companies that were within the Hawker Siddeley Group. Another advantage gained by using two power units was that in the event of failure of one, the other unit could operate independently. The design was prepared in consultation with BR so that the locomotive would be a prototype for general requirements and would be able to undertake test runs on BR lines without the need for any major alterations.

After the order was placed in April 1959, design proceeded and continued throughout the year and into 1960. Construction commenced in October 1960 and proceeded until completion in September 1961. Externally 'Falcon' was a magnificent sight, being painted in a two tone scheme of light green, soon changed to lime green relieved by chestnut brown. The external appearance was produced in conjunction with Wilkes & Ashmore, who had altered the initial Brush Type 2 outline for the better. The cab design was evolved from that of the latter, but without the interconnecting cab front doors, and by reducing the number of front windows from the three of the Type 2 to two. A four-character train indication panel to the latest BR requirement was incorporated. The cab outline set the standard for years to come and was developed and imitated also. Class 56 of the mid-1970s was the last to adhere to the general principle of outline. A falcon motif was painted onto the bodysides centrally, and the name 'Falcon' was applied across it, being rendered in small, but neat, serif form letters. The running number D 0280 was painted on the cab sides in the contemporary BR style. A balanced and tasteful effect was achieved by specially grouping the louvres in the body sides and a few eeks later by linking some of them by means of a long horizontal panel painted brown. The lower body side skirt and cab window surrounds were also later picked out in the same shade. The tasteful grouping of the body side louvres was achieved despite the fact that they were plentiful, due to the duplication of power units, and because the time had not yet arrived when louvres could be placed entirely in the roof sections. It was still the case that the Railway required some measure of side access to the engine compartments.

Despite the need to retain some side access, the sides were built as an open lattice frame to assist the floor in load bearing, thus forming an integral framework with the floor, and enabling the overall weight to be lightened. This made use of the Hirondelle type of bridge girder construction, derived immediately from Hawker Siddeley experience of it with aircraft construction. The sheeting later applied to the bodysides was not stressed for load bearing purposes. BR made this solution possible by not stipulating sideways removal of the power units, as had been the case in previous specifications, therefore heavy weight-bearing underframes were avoided in this instance.

The main details and dimensions of 'Falcon' were as follows:

Wheel Arrangement	Co-Co
Track Gauge	4 ft 8½ins
Engine Model	Bristol Siddeley Maybach MD 655 Vee type, 12-cylinders, two fitted.

A very rare view of 'Falcon' undergoing works testing alongside the original resistance house.

Late BOB DILLEY

Engine Rating	1,440bhp at 1,500rpm, continuous rating, with pressure charging and intercooling. Bore 7.28ins. Stroke 7.88ins. Compression ratio 15.5:1
Main generator	Two, each of the 6-pole compensated type with three windings – separately excited and self excited shunts and a differential series winding. Self ventilated and mounted on extension arms from engine bed plate.
Continuous ratings	910kW, 493V, 1,845A, 915kW, 610V, 1,500A
Auxiliary Generators (two)	4-pole, self ventilated, shunt wound
Continuous rating	17.6kW, 110V, 160A, 1,286/3, 215rpm
Traction Motors (six)	4-pole, force ventilated, axle hung, nose-suspended type
Continuous rating	373hp, 493V, 615A at 704rpm
One hour rating	365hp, 455V, 660A at 630rpm
Length over buffers	68ft 10ins
Overall Width	8ft 9ins
Overall Height	12ft 9ins
Wheel Diameter	3ft 7ins
Bogie Wheelbase	14ft 11ins
Distance Between Bogie Pivots	42ft 0ins
Total Wheelbase	56ft 4½ins
Minimum Curve Negotiable	4 chains
Maximum Speed	100mph
Maximum Tractive Effort	60,000lbs
Continuous Tractive Effort	28,500lbs
Fuel Capacity	1,400 gallons
Weight in Working Order	115 tons
Axle Load	19¼ tons

No electric train heat facility was included in the design, but steam heating was. This equipment was provided in the form of a Spanner train heating boiler situated across the centre of the locomotive between the cooler groups of the two power units. Designated Spanner Swirlyflo Mark III, this boiler was a lightweight, horizontal type which produced 2,500lbs of steam per hour at a pressure of 75lbs per square inch. It was fully automatic, fitted with safety devices and fed with water from a tank of 800 gallons capacity, which could be refilled not only by gravity means but also by means of a retractable bidirectional water scoop for use on water troughs en route, which at the time were plentiful on the BR system. This scoop could be raised and lowered either electrically or pneumatically from controls located in the cabs. The relatively low water capacity of the water tank was a result of increasing the diesel fuel oil capacity to 1,400 gallons at an early stage of designing 'Falcon'. This emerged from discussions with BR Eastern Region personnel where it was suggested that sufficient fuel should be carried to ensure that a round trip between Kings Cross and Edinburgh could be run without refuelling.

The bogies were of the Commonwealth type, consisting of cast steel frames and swing bolsters, whose flat centre pivot plates carried the superstructure weight. Each bolster was mounted on four elliptical springs, which were carried on two spring planks between the axles, suspended from the bogie frame by swing links. The bogie frame was supported by four spring nests, mounted on overhung equalising beams. Conventional horn guides and stays located the roller bearing axle boxes.

Electrical power connection was simple. The three traction motors of each bogie were connected in parallel and supplied from one generator. This enabled one power source to be switched out in the event of an emergency and the locomotive to clear the line with the remaining 1,400bhp. Train braking equipment fitted was vacuum.

Aluminium cabs and some fibreglass roof panels further reduced the overall weight of 'Falcon'. In choosing the name 'Falcon', Brush Traction made use of the aggressive-sounding name first bestowed upon the Loughborough engineering concern way back in 1853. The Falcon Engine Works started in a small way in that year on the Derby Road, transferring to its present site during the 1864-67 period. Brush arrived on the scene in 1889 and, happily, kept the Falcon tradition using the falcon whenever the occasion suited.

Before considering the exploits of 'Falcon', once completed, some mention of events within BR and other manufacturers is pertinent. The changing requirements of BR have been alluded to above. These changes occurred in the light of experience and as equipment developments were made. In January 1960 the BR Technical Committee agreed to request tenders for a diesel electric Type 4 Co-Co locomotive design of about 2,750bhp with electric and/or steam train heating equipment. Three months later the British Transport Commission (British Railways Division) defined as Type 4 a locomotive rated at between 2,000bhp and 2,800bhp, fitted with either steam or electric train heating equipment. The specified locomotive was a Co-Co wheel arrangement, dispensing with the cumbersome 1Co-Co1configuration, within an axle load of 19 tons.

Wilkes & Ashmore produced an artist's impression of the proposed design for the British Transport Commission (BTC) based upon what they successfully proposed and had accepted for the Beyer Peacock 'Hymek' diesel hydraulic locomotive design for the Western Region. In general outline the cab matched the style of that used on 'Falcon'. Even the two-tone green livery was chosen at this time.

In producing a prototype Type 4 locomotive Brush was soon not to be alone, because two other locomotive manufacturers contemplated securing large orders for the new standard Type 4 for BR. These were the Birmingham Railway Carriage & Wagon Co. (BRCW) and the English Electric Co., and each set about building its own prototype locomotive with varying degrees of consultation with BR.

The former company produced a remarkable Co-Co that very closely resembled the outline appearance of the Wilkes & Ashmore artist's impression. It appeared early in 1962 after some delay and a hurried completion, named 'Lion', numbered D 0260 and painted in an attractive eye-catching (if impracticable) all white livery. 'Lion' was rated at 2,750bhp

and incorporated a single Sulzer 12LDA28C engine, the first one to be introduced into a locomotive destined to run on BR and the latest Sulzer development over that fitted to the Derby-built BR/Sulzer 1Co-Co1 Type 4s of 2,500bhp. Electrical equipment was supplied by Associated Electrical Industries (AEI).

Then the English Electric prototype appeared. It was rated at 2,700bhp, featured a single English Electric 16CSVT engine, with an increase in power of 700bhp above that fitted to the 1Co-Co1 Type 4s being supplied to BR since 1958 and numbered from D200. It was numbered DP2 (Diesel Prototype No. 2 – No. 1 being the Deltic prototype of 1955), but bore no name. Perhaps this was because to use the name of the EE Vulcan Works at Newton le Willows would result in a name that might be confused with the similar-sounding 'Falcon'. This is pure conjecture, of course, but it would be an almost certainty during discussions held behind closed doors.

DP2 further differed from 'Lion' and 'Falcon' inasmuch that it had the pronounced nose ends forward of the cabs proper, rather than the BR-preferred almost flat end specified. Indeed, it utilised the production Deltic bodyshell to house the equipment and there is no doubt that doing this cut production and design costs.

Brush, therefore, had two contestants join in the bid for gaining Type 4 orders, with BRCW appearing to be the strongest contender with 'Lion', the design closest to the BR specification. What exactly happened may never be revealed fully, but 'Falcon' as a design could now never be accepted wholly for adoption as standard because it employed the use of two engines. This was the eventual price paid for being a little too early and not being able to conform to a later and more ideal specification.

What does appear to have happened is that BR chose Brush and its second projected scheme of a Sulzer-engined Type 4 as proposed by Brush in January 1959. This may be an over-simplification of events, but it is an inescapable fact that the order for twenty Type 4s was placed upon Brush Traction in February 1961 as 'Falcon' was under construction and a further thirty were ordered in January 1962, shortly after it was completed. Fuller details appear in Chapter 6.

Disadvantages embodied within one competing company in one instance (BRCW) and within the 'Lion' and DP2 designs in the other probably steered BR towards Brush Traction and its capabilities, despite the fact that 'Falcon' eventually did not conform in the strictest sense. How BR persuaded BRCW and EE that there was hope for orders may only be speculated, but all three prototypes underwent trials on BR, those of 'Lion' going down with the demise of its builder into liquidation.

DP2 was an excellent machine, but essentially arrived upon the scene too late to influence BR, already committed to the Sulzer engine.

Thus, it was into this scenario that 'Falcon' entered service late in 1961. Upon completion in September thorough works testing was undertaken, followed by finish painting. Braking tests within the Falcon Works were conducted on the test track, which reached out towards the Loughborough Meadows, the rakish angle of the buffer stop at the end betraying the occasional failure or misjudgement!

Following painting 'Falcon' was positioned alongside the former Turbine Shop for its official photographs to be taken, on 18th September. Proving runs on BR metals then followed with the run to Chinley, Derbyshire being the favourite 'on the road' trip. On one return from Chinley with one power unit in operation, a 457 tons train of passenger stock was started from rest on a 1 in 90 rising gradient, this being equivalent to a tractive effort of 26,000lbs. Once the first snags had been ironed out it was possible to try more serious work and to implement a test programme proper.

'Falcon' was allocated to the Eastern Region in October 1961, being based on Finsbury Park depot after initial inspection by BR engineers. Indeed, the locomotive had already moved from Loughborough by 8th October, being observed in the Paint Shop of Doncaster Works on that day. 'Falcon' ran up to Finsbury Park depot on 13th October and was soon placed in service, being observed on Kings Cross to Cambridge passenger trains on the 16th and 17th. It was noted on the 06.52 departure from Kings Cross to Cambridge, 10.05 ex-Cambridge, 13.05 ex-Kings Cross and 15.15 ex-Cambridge. On 18th October 'Falcon' hauled the 08.15 Kings Cross to Hull, working as far as Doncaster, returning from there at 13.35. Later in the day it failed at Hatfield whilst working the 20.20 down mail train from Kings Cross. The cause of failure was not serious, a cab heater fire, but it necessitated a return to the Falcon Works for attention the following day, travelling light down the Midland main line. On 23rd October 'Falcon' returned to Eastern Region metals via the Erewash Valley main line and Doncaster. The following day 'Falcon' was engaged on dynamometer car trials from Doncaster, hauling sixty loaded coal wagons. Similar tests were undertaken between New Southgate and Doncaster on 24th October and the locomotive returned to Doncaster passenger train diagrams two days later. Trailing loads of 1,360 tons were hauled, but for passenger train timings 310 tons was the load. During the slow speed test a governor failure caused one

power unit to shut down, but the trial continued using the other power unit only until the fault was rectified at the next signal stop. For this period of single unit operation, about fifteen minutes, the three remaining traction motors each carried 800 amperes compared with the one hour rating of 660 amperes. 'Falcon' was noted on 27th October on the 08.15 Kings Cross to Hull working.

It was transferred to Stratford depot early in November 1961 and operated on Great Eastern lines, returning to the Falcon Works several times for routine checks. Then came a transfer to the Western Region the following month, with an official allocation to Swindon depot. The WR was eager to gain some diesel electric Type 4 experience, partly as a comparison for the new diesel hydraulic Type 4 'Western' Class with C-C wheel arrangement. Notably, this type was fitted with two engines identical to those fitted in 'Falcon', so some measure of performance to compare the same engines operating the different transmissions was desirable. 'Falcon' was noted newly-arrived at Swindon on 4th December 1961.

It was not until the new year that major tests were undertaken on the WR. Some of these were the first of the comparative performance tests between 'Falcon' and the 'Western' class diesel hydraulic locomotives. The exercise was somewhat academic for two years in this respect because the tests on D1029 of the latter class did not take place until June 1964. In reality the only direct comparisons undertaken in 1962 were between 'Falcon' and 'Lion', the former performing the better of the two.

On 2nd January 1962 the BR Chief Mechanical and Electrical Engineer's Department of the Research and Development

Gleaming in new two-tone green paint, 'Falcon' stands outside the former Turbine Shop, ready to make its first appearance on the main line. Photograph dated 18th September 1961.

BRUSH A7135

(Rolling Stock) Office, Swindon, under the direction of Mr S O Ell, proposed a programme of testing for 'Falcon' on the Western Region. The proposed performance and efficiency tests were scheduled on round trips from Swindon, which passed through Bath, Bristol, Didcot and Badminton, and included test stops and restarts. These were to take place 23rd to 26th January and 30th January to 2nd February inclusive. Trailing loads varied from 165 tons to 600 tons, the latter involving seventeen coaches plus dynamometer car. In general terms these tests were classified as high-speed tests.

The tests with maximum loads on steep rising gradients were to take place on the notorious Lickey Incline between Bromsgrove and Blackwell. Tuesday 6th February was detailed for passenger stock haulage with goods stock haulage the following day. The former included the 39 tons dynamometer car and about 600 tons of coaching stock (about eighteen coaches) and the latter made up of the dynamometer car, brake van (twenty tons), Class 1 mineral wagons (500-520 tons gross) and three brake vans (60 tons) which could be detached, if not required.

The next tests involved braking performance on steep falling gradients. The obvious choice for these was Blackwell to Bromsgrove and they were scheduled for 8th, 9th and 12th February, with vacuum braked stock.

On 13th February observational tests and maximum service load tests on steep rising gradients were to round off the test programme. These were undertaken hauling the dynamometer car and coaching stock (500-520 tons) of 15 to 16 coaches from Swindon to Plymouth and return. The test programme actually finished on 14th February with

In February 1962 trials were carried out on the Lickey Incline, with the Western Region dynamometer car and an eighteen coach train. 'Falcon' was able to restart this mammoth load from a dead stand on the notorious bank and clear the summit without difficulty.

BRUSH A7464

only minor alterations and 'Falcon' was tested over the full range of mph, tractive effort, and engine output. All tests were deemed completely satisfactory. Those undertaken up the Lickey Incline were the most dramatic and followed a schedule initiated during the previous year with a BR Sulzer Type 4 1Co-Co1 locomotive.

Before outlining the efforts of 'Falcon' on the Lickey Incline, some mention of the dynamometer car is appropriate. This test vehicle actually made its appearance several months before 'Falcon' in 1961. It was the newest large item of equipment of the Research and Development (Rolling Stock) Office at Swindon. It replaced the old former GWR clerestory-roofed dynamometer car dating from 1901 and was more up to date than either of the former LMSR cars or the Eastern Region car. More important, it was designed specifically for use during testing of diesel locomotives, whereas the others were obviously more akin to the testing of steam locomotives. The car was produced during times of change, both in motive power and testing methods. A relatively new system was being introduced known as the Controlled Road Testing System. The vehicle itself was not brand new, but had been built by the GWR in 1947 as a Corridor Third passenger coach to a Hawksworth design and it was thus made available for conversion into a new dynamometer car. Conversion took place at Swindon Carriage & Wagon Works, and the car was finished in the chocolate and cream livery of its parent region. After testing and calibration it was made ready for use. Its first proper and intended use was with 'Falcon'.

The Lickey Incline had long necessitated the banking of most trains up the gradient and indeed the Midland Railway had built a special 0-10-0 steam locomotive wholly for this purpose. The ascent of the 1 in 37.7 incline was first attempted by a steam locomotive and train prior to the tests on 'Falcon' on 6th February. It stalled amid clouds of smoke and steam. Then it was the turn of 'Falcon', with the dynamometer car recording details plus a van and eighteen coaches, a load of

628 tons in total. It successfully restarted from a dead stand at milepost 55, where all the train was on the incline, and continued until well clear of the summit. An 0-6-0 pannier tank locomotive trailed hopefully some distance behind the train, but was disappointed.

This test was repeated three times. The ascents with mineral wagons involved loads in excess of the 500 tons limit then in force on the incline. Indeed it was well in excess, 618 tons in total. The top limit for steam traction was 360 tons. During the restarting tests, wheel slips occurred on the trailing bogie on every start with the possible exception of the first one. This was contrary to expectation and was probably caused by unevenly-matched main generator outputs or a slight difference in engine speeds. The tests with mineral wagons included wet rail conditions due to heavy rain during them and sanding was resorted to, but the top rotational speed of the engines was not reached until the train was almost at the summit of the incline. Eight minutes was the time taken in ascending.

Overall, the tests proved very satisfactory and the electrical equipment came through with flying colours as it were, particularly with regard to standstill currents of 1,200 amperes across the commutators of the traction motors when 'Falcon' restarted on the incline. 'Lion' was later subjected to these tests, and although it performed fairly well, it did sustain some commutator damage.

The following week 'Falcon' moved into the South-west, again with the dynamometer car recording results, on the Swindon to Plymouth run. West of Newton Abbot it tackled inclines of 1 in 36 and 1 in 47 with loads of 500 tons. On 13th February Dainton Bank was surmounted with 571 tons trailing. Restarts were also performed on Dainton Bank. 'Lion' later failed to restart under identical conditions on the bank.

By the end of the test programme 'Falcon' had made a deep and lasting favourable impression among BR engineers with its prodigious feats of performance. The locomotive had achieved 100mph on the level with 273 tons trailing and 75mph with eighteen coaches (600 tons) during running tests. One may imagine the elation of Brush personnel back in Loughborough, indeed the exploits of 'Falcon' are still remembered well by people, not the least by the works photographer, John Draycott, who recorded the events on film for the Company.

'Falcon' was back at the Falcon Works during March 1962 for its inspection and routine maintenance, prior to returning to the Great Northern line of the Eastern Region to accrue mileage on regular passenger train duties. While at the works the opportunity was taken to replace the painted falcon motifs on the body sides with a new relief cast aluminium falcon motif, a far more imaginative embellishment. A special nameplate was affixed directly below bearing the name FALCON in upper case letters in serif form. On occasions over the years this same design has appeared at the Falcon Works, even down to 2007. Photographs were taken of the locomotive standing on the test track, bearing the train headboard of the 'Master Cutler'. This was a neat and simple publicity exercise prior to 'Falcon' actually operating this Sheffield Pullman service on a regular basis. 'Falcon' was still at Loughborough during the early part of April.

During that same month 'Falcon' moved to Sheffield Darnall depot and commenced regular working of the 'Master Cutler' between Sheffield Victoria and Kings Cross via Retford, normally making two round trips every 24 hours, totalling 670 miles. Weekly mileage was 3,400 miles and all 'in a trial of its suitability for future Eastern Region requirements' as one contemporary description commented. With the expected arrival of the first Brush Type 4s later in the year on the region, these words appear somewhat 'tongue in cheek'. At the time the statement perhaps conveyed the intended message more easily, considering that 'Lion' and DP2 were about to make their respective debuts.

'Falcon' returned to Loughborough following its exploits whilst on test. During this period the original painted falcon motif gave way to handsome polished aluminium falcons, cast in high relief, with raised metal nameplates below. This fine view was taken on 3rd April 1962.

After a lengthy trial period on various lines and duties, 'Falcon' returned to Loughborough for renovation and repainting in BR two-tone green livery, as seen below . It was then hired to BR Western Region which used it for several years under this arrangement, before purchasing it and running it until 1975. Photograph taken on 27th January 1965, prior to being hired.

BRUSH A7754   BRUSH A11662

The 'Master Cutler' consisted of six or eight Pullman cars of 240 or 320 tons, loads well within the capacity of 'Falcon', but nevertheless this helped build up mileage which reached just under 120,000 in sixteen months. Not all this mileage was on passenger duties. In the autumn of 1962 'Falcon' transferred to freight train haulage on the Eastern Region. This entailed working unfitted coal trains of between 800 and 1,000 tons, two double trips between Langwith Junction and March or New England yards. Attempts at hauling loads of up to 1,800 tons were made, but because the resultant trains were too long for the reception sidings at March they had to be divided on arrival, thus blocking the main line during the division. Because of this the attempts were brief. 36,000 miles of slow speed working were accumulated on Eastern Region freight working.

'Falcon' remained on the ER until late 1963 when it was returned to Loughborough for inspection and classified overhaul. It was found to be in good condition and had not suffered adversely, other than from the expected effects of wear and tear. Proper care and maintenance also played their part of course, but this would have been ineffective had 'Falcon' not been of fundamentally sound design and construction. One Brush service engineer was employed on a close watch during the ER period of operation.

By the end of 1963 it was generally accepted that none of the three prototypes was to become the new standard Type 4, indeed 'Lion' was no more as a complete locomotive and its builder not trading. Thoughts as to what to do with 'Falcon' turned towards the Western Region where maintenance facilities and staff familiarity were directly concerned with maintaining the Bristol Siddeley Maybach engines of the diesel hydraulic locomotives in its care and operation. It would also provide a useful comparison with these locomotives. It was time for 'Falcon' to start earning its keep and a period of hire

to the WR was contemplated after its overhaul. The work was delayed because of the heavy pressure of work building Brush Type 4 locomotives and for the most part of the 1963/4 period of stay at the Falcon Works the locomotive was parked out of the way, often at the end of the test track.

Later in 1964 it was brought into the shops and the delayed overhaul commenced, so by the end of the year it was completed. Brush offered 'Falcon' to the WR on a hire basis. The loan of the locomotive was under a joint agreement dated 1st January 1965, whereby the Railway would run it and carry out light repairs, while Brush would undertake any major electrical repairs or maintenance at its own expense of £8,750 per annum provided that it attained 80,000 miles each year.

'Falcon' emerged in a new livery of Brunswick Green relieved by Sherwood Green louvre panels, skirting and cab window surrounds. It was a more conservative scheme than previous, but it was still very attractive and still enhanced by the cast metal falcon motifs and nameplates. For Brush it was economical; there was a plentiful supply of both colours, used continually for painting the seemingly endless stream of Brush Type 4s being built at the Falcon Works. A small yellow warning panel was painted on each cab front below window level.

Its trials days were now over and although the design was not proliferated, 'Falcon' had already helped pave the way for the large Type 4 orders. Eventually, 512 units were built at both the Falcon Works and the Crewe Works of BR, with all the electrical equipment coming from Brush. Not yet life-expired, 'Falcon' was destined to work on the Western Region for the rest of its existence.

Upon leaving Loughborough in January 1965 'Falcon' went to Swindon Works of BR for acceptance tests and the fitting of automatic warning system equipment. The following month it was allocated to Bristol, Bath Road, depot and a period of crew training and familiarisation was commenced. February saw 'Falcon' go into service in company with WR diesel hydraulic locomotives. Among the services worked were the following:-

09.15	Bristol-Paddington
13.45	Paddington-Bristol
17.15	Bristol-Paddington
22.20	Paddington-Bristol (Penzance Postal train)

By April 1965 'Falcon' had encountered engine troubles similar to those already being experienced on the Bristol Siddeley Maybach engines fitted to the WR diesel hydraulic locomotives. Two engine failures were caused by water jacket fractures necessitating a return to Swindon Works for attention. Overhaul of the engine top parts and the cooling system were undertaken and the opportunity was taken to turn the tyres and overhaul the train heating boiler, compressors and exhausters. The water scoop was removed. 'Falcon' returned to service the following August.

Its return was not trouble-free due to No. 2 engine suffering two further failures, caused by fractured cylinder blocks, the following month. In December three cracked cylinder heads occurred. Total mileage for 1965 was only 29,400 miles – far below the expected 80,000 miles.

In 1966 'Falcon' still experienced troubles, spending further time in Swindon Works over three periods of repair. The first was due to water entering No. 3 cylinder of No. 1 engine, through a cracked head, and fracturing a connecting rod. Mileage that year was slightly improved, at 57,500 miles, despite a loss of 92 days in works.

A loss of 144 days occurred in 1967 when 'Falcon' was again under repair in Swindon Works. Sixty one days were due to the controls of the boiler panel burning out. Mileage achieved that year was 46,000.

1968 was a good year and the mileage increased dramatically to 90,400, considerably more than the average 85,000 for the 'Warship' Class diesel hydraulic locomotives, later known as Class 42. The only serious failure that year occurred in mid-December when a turbocharger bearing failed.

The end of steam traction on BR finally came in August 1968 and this was followed by a rationalisation plan to reduce the number of classes of locomotives operating on the Railway. Troublesome and non-standard locomotives were targetted and perhaps 'Falcon' only escaped withdrawal because it was still privately owned.

Engine maintenance on the WR did have its advantages, as outlined previously, but some aspects of it were not quite as simple as one might expect. The MD655 engines installed in 'Falcon' were not interchangeable with those installed in the 'Western' diesel hydraulic locomotives of Class 52. They were fitted with special mounting plates and couplings for mating with the main generators, and had Woodward governors with speed and torque control, whereas the latter engines were fitted with a Maybach governor with speed control only. The problems experienced were common to both applications, but the latter involved the convenient and quick expedient of power unit exchange to reduce locomotive time spent in works receiving attention. Despite the above disadvantages and an ideal candidate for withdrawal, 'Falcon' was retained. BR indeed wished to take matters a stage further, and negotiations with Brush took place in 1970 with a view to terminating the hiring agreement and purchasing 'Falcon' at its scrap value. Certainly Brush had no wish, nor reason, to retain the prototype because locomotive building had ceased at the Falcon Works, the expensive and long-running 'Hawk' project had also ceased and the newest prototype, the 4,000 metric horsepower 'Kestrel' was the subject of attention and expense. In short, 'Falcon' was an expensive luxury.

The cost of 'Falcon' to Brush eventually totalled £144,000.

Purchase was agreed at a price of £20,000 with Brush stipulating that as 'Falcon' was purchased at scrap value then when its useful life was over it would be scrapped, rather than sold for re-use. BR must have considered 'Falcon' as a bargain, because removal of vacuum brake equipment was planned as part of a scheme to overhaul the locomotive and also equip it with dual braking capability (compressed air and vacuum) at a cost of £43,000. BR authorisation for overhaul was granted in April 1970. 'Falcon' was noted in Swindon Works on 22nd August being fitted with air-brake equipment and the locomotive emerged the following December fitted for train air-braking only, not dual, a curious outcome that became a limiting factor in its subsequent operations. About this time BR allocated Class 53 to 'Falcon' under the 1968 locomotive classification scheme. This scheme was devised several years before full implementation of TOPS, the computerised information network for rolling stock.

As 'Falcon' was now BR property it was finished in Rail Blue with full yellow ends and the BR double arrow symbols on the right hand cabsides. On the opposite cabsides a new running number appeared, 1200. There had been some indecision at Swindon as to what the number should be. First the D prefix had been omitted, in common with other BR diesel locomotives and 'Falcon' bore just 0280 and was observed so in the testing bay at Swindon on 13th December.

On release to traffic 'Falcon' was allocated to Bristol, Bath Road, and during December 1970 and January 1971 undertook a series of trials between Swindon, Old Oak Common (London) and Didcot, and some high-speed trials between Bristol and Taunton. An eight-coach train was provided for these runs and 36 minutes were allowed for each 45 miles run. It was later noted on Paddington to Bristol expresses formed of Mark 2 coaching stock, but it soon returned to Swindon Works after another boiler fire, again in the controls. This fire occurred in February. More delay was caused by this, and 'Falcon' was not back in traffic again until May. The trials were resumed.

On its return to Bristol it went back to passenger duties, which it continued to operate until July 1972, albeit punctuated by returns to Swindon. On 13th October 1971 it was noted there with one engine removed.

One reason for the removal of 'Falcon' from passenger train haulage in 1972 was the advent of air-conditioned Mark 2 coaches, because it was not equipped for supplying the necessary electrical power. In October 1972, with its troublesome boiler isolated, it was allocated to Cardiff (Canton) depot and was observed several times at Ebbw Junction, Newport, during crew training duties. It then worked Newport Docks to Llanwern iron ore goods trips, being reallocated to Ebbw Junction depot in May 1973 while still employed on these and coal train duties.

'Falcon' was officially withdrawn from service in May 1974 and put into storage. This was to be brief, because reinstatement followed within the next two months. During the summer of 1974 'Falcon' mysteriously arrived at Loughborough, settling on a siding at the rear of Loughborough Midland station. At a first glance it appeared that a failed Class 47 had been sided, but no, it was 'Falcon'. Its arrival caused much local speculation and consternation as to its intended future. Apparently, it had arrived, months after a national power crisis, with BR hoping to resell it to Brush for use as a standby generating plant! Certainly it could not enter the Falcon Works without difficulty because the rail links had been severed following damage caused by mineral train derailments, but after a stay of several days

BR realised its error (probably after the Station Master had informed higher authority of the true situation) and 'Falcon' returned to its former duties in South Wales. It was back at Ebbw Junction by 14th July.

The annual mileage at this time averaged about 40,000 miles and 'Falcon' continued in service during 1975 on the Llanwern trips at least until July.

It appears that 'Falcon' was then stored. Certainly, its final withdrawal occurred on 5th October 1975, following a traction motor bearing failure.

Rather than scrap 'Falcon' itself BR sold the locomotive to Messrs J Cashmore Ltd for scrapping in March 1976 at a price of £5,125. It was taken into their yard at Newport on 26th March and scrapping, well underway on 2nd April, was completed within two weeks – a swift and decisive end to a remarkable locomotive that changed locomotive history in an indirect way.

Preservation appeals were made after the withdrawal of 'Falcon', but contractual agreements made this impossible. These facts were not widely known at the time and events must have perplexed preservationists more than a little. One thought does come to mind, that of the National Railway Museum's vested powers to select locomotives for preservation, one wonders if these were sufficient to have saved 'Falcon'.

For many years the fate of the falcons and the nameplates, which adorned the locomotive, were known only to a few. After removal they spent years in a storeroom at Swindon Works and in June 1995 one set was advertised as up for sale. It was offered for sale by tender at Collectors' Corner, which was seeking bids in excess of £1,800, plus VAT at 17.5%. The other set was donated to the National Railway Museum at York. Years later, in 2004, the former set was purchased for £22,500 at Sheffield Railwayana Auction. This astonishing sum proved the investment in such railwayana and the faith of the purchaser in such a continuance.

The total mileage of 'Falcon' from 1961 to 1975 was 635,000 miles, of which 515,000 were run on BR's Western Region.

Some writers have dismissed 'Falcon' as an expensive project that did not achieve much for its maker, but this view is a rather narrow one. Considering the early debut of the locomotive and the rapidly changing situation between 1959 and 1961, which rendered the design non-preferred before it took to the rails, one must take a wider view. Consider the foresight of Brush Traction, its splendid engineers and craftsmen, its flexible attitudes towards the customer, its ability to deliver a good product in good time and its resources available from within the Hawker Siddeley Group – these then were what 'Falcon' represented, and they counted a lot. As one Brush and Hawker Siddeley director once summed up the winning of the Class 47 orders, 'It was Brush willingness to fulfil the customer's requirement that won the day'. Of course Brush backed its words with results. Yes, 'Falcon' was a success in a most subtle way.

6 – The Type 4 Era

Genesis

Over the years speculation has existed as to how the Brush Type 4 became the standard BR Type 4 locomotive design. There was no grand design or plan, nor were any logical steps thought out in advance. It was more the case that events evolved, often in a haphazard way that was more to do with opportunism on the part of Brush and other firms. The art of the possible was very much to the fore, more than anything else. BR thinking was not always in unison; the Regions had different ideas and all were learning as the light of experience evolved. The engine manufacturers were developing their products all the time and the locomotive industry was always alert to new events and progress. In some ways that industry was learning as it progressed.

At the onset of the Modernisation Plan the BTC approached the private locomotive manufacturers to obtain tenders for Types A B C D (later Types 1 to 4). Brush offered Type B, (later Type 2) as described in Chapter 4. At the same time the various BR workshops produced designs in competition. The LMR, whose design office was at Derby under the direction of Mr J F Harrison, Chief Mechanical and Electrical Engineer, put forward a Type B and a Type D design (later Types 2 and 4) using Sulzer engines. The former used a six-cylinder engine and the latter a twelve-cylinder, double bank engine. It was Harrison's view that these two designs should become the backbone of the diesel electric fleet of BR locomotives. Matters turned out differently, and he was very much involved with these changes.

While Falcon was under construction an important engine development had taken place; the Sulzer 12LDA28 twelve-cylinder engine had been successfully uprated to 2,750bhp, by April 1960. The first BR application of the 12LDA28 engine had been to the Peak Class 1Co-Co1 diesel electric locomotives in the form of the 12LDA28A version rated at 2,300bhp. These locomotives were completed at Derby Locomotive Works in 1959 and 1960 as D1 to D10, were equipped with Crompton Parkinson electrical equipment and were named after peaks of England and Wales. Crompton Parkinson was a rarity among the electrical firms inasmuch that, one shunting locomotive apart, it did not aspire to be a locomotive builder, but had worked with Sulzer previously on rail traction matters.

The second engine application was the 12LDA28B fitted into the production batches rated at 2,500bhp and which followed on from 1960, being numbered from D11 to D193 inclusive and built until 1963 at both Derby and Crewe Works. Difficulties with the Crompton Parkinson main generator deliveries, despite some parts of the contracts being sub-contracted to Laurence Scott & Electromotors Ltd, led to Crompton Parkinson opting out of this aspect of its traction business and Brush providing sets of electrical equipment instead for D138 to D193, after the order had been reduced

from 76 to 56. The awarding of this contract to Brush was a major success for the Brush Traction team. The reputation for reliable electrical equipment and deliveries as well as keen prices all played a part, and the quotation for the 76 sets was fought out between all the major electrical manufacturers except Crompton Parkinson. All the locomotives were fitted with steam train heating equipment only. It will be noted from the above that it takes time for an uprated engine to be included in production runs, partly due to the design factor and partly due to the fact that the main generator may not be capable of a similar up-rating without the need for redesign in some way.

Sulzer Brothers, of Switzerland, for its part had continually developed its LDA range of engines since 1935. In 1939 the 12LDA31 (twelve-cylinders, each 31cms diameter) twin bank engine had reached 2,200bhp. The 12LDA28 was first used in some SNCF Co-Co locomotives in 1955, rated at 2,000bhp. Thirty-five were built. It was soon uprated to 2,200bhp and fitted into some twin-engined locomotives built for the Romanian State Railways. Further up-rating saw more single-engined locomotives supplied to that railway.

To facilitate engine production for BR Sulzer Bros selected a British manufacturer, Vickers-Armstrong of Barrow-in-Furness, Lancashire, to build Sulzer engines under licence. By 1964 they were producing thirty engines each month.

Collectively known as the Peaks, the BR/Sulzer Type 4 locomotives belonged to one of two types selected by BR in 1958 as suitable for production, following the re-appraisal of the 1955 Modernisation Plan. The other type was the English Electric 2,000bhp 1Co-Co1 introduced in 1958 and numbered from D200 onwards. This design was mostly English Electric equipped and fitted with their sixteen-cylinder 16SVT engine. Unlike the BR/Sulzer follow-on batches, the repeat orders for the EE Type 4 did not incorporate any output up-rating. The series continued up to D399 and was complete when this locomotive appeared in October 1962. The English Electric Type 4 had a proven pedigree ranging from the LMS 10000 and 10001 Co-Co twins of 1947/8, each rated at 1,600bhp, through the Southern Region 1Co-Co1 locomotives 10201-3 of the early 1950s which were rated at 1,750bhp (10201 and 10202) and 2,000bhp (10203) of 1954. All were equipped with the EE 16SVT engines (Mk2 in 10203) and EE electrical equipment, but were built in BR workshops. Nos 10000 and 10001 had noses ahead of the cabs, the remainder were flat-fronted. Both the EE D200 series and the BR Sulzer/Peaks had noses.

Both types were also ponderously heavy, with the English Electric examples weighing 133 tons and the Peaks reaching 138 tons. This weight required extra non-powered carrying axles to bring down axle loadings to within limits acceptable to the Civil Engineer who was responsible for track and bridge maintenance. It was when the use of some of these locomotives spread to other Regions and areas that their shortcomings were found to be unacceptable. The heavy bogies were long and resulted in long locomotives. Neither were desirable features, particularly when negotiating marshalling yard humps where it was not unknown for the outer carrying only wheels to leave the track momentarily as the locomotive passed over the hump. Similar experiences had occurred on the LMSR some thirty years previously when the Beyer Garratt locomotives had negotiated the same humps. There was also the view that 2,000bhp was a little on the low side for operations, and that 2,500 or 2,750bhp was required to replace some of the main line steam services.

The extra weight was partly due to several factors. BR stipulated some side access for engine maintenance and repair purposes, because some of their workshops did not have the height of lift on their cranes to lift a power unit out of a locomotive, so the sides were not weight bearing. The weight of the power unit and associated equipment was borne by a traditional heavy bedplate construction upon which the superstructure and equipment was mounted. Another reason for retaining a heavy locomotive was that goods trains were rarely fitted with a braking system that could be activated and controlled from the locomotive. Unfitted, loose-coupled trains relied upon the braking power of a locomotive, limited by its own weight bearing on the six driving axles, and a brake van. A heavy locomotive in this respect did prove to be useful, but it did not always haul such trains and its heaviness proved to be a disadvantage in such circumstances. Its extra weight was a burden equivalent to another two unbraked wagons. Another factor which added weight was that of the use of steel for most components when newer and lighter components were available and could be used for cab and roof areas.

If it were not for the aforementioned weaknesses there is little doubt that the production of the BR/Sulzer Type 4 would have continued for longer than it did, but the two Type 4s soon became regarded as interim types, until a new lightweight, single-engined standard Type 4 could be designed and go into quantity production. At least 400 examples were required according to some sources. The Modernisation Officer of the Eastern Region (the late R Somersall) foresaw the need for a higher-powered Type 4 on six axles, and with no more than a 20 ton axle load. The Deltics were regarded as a very special case and being too fanciful to provide a solid workhorse for all types of service.

Brush had anticipated some of this requirement already and had set about producing a prototype, Falcon, but as we have seen, the locomotive design was produced just before BR had evolved a specification for what it considered to be the ideal locomotive.

It would appear that what component parts were thought of as desirable by BR, were combined early in 1960. The Technical Committee agreed in the January to request tenders for a diesel electric Type 4 of Co-Co wheel arrangement with electric, or electric and steam train heating equipment. In the April the BTC (British Railways Division) issued a technical specification covering Types 1 to 4. The Type 4 specification called for an engine output ranging from 2,000bhp to 2,800bhp with a steam train heating rate of 2,500lbs/hr, or electric train heating output of 320kW at 800 volts. The wheel arrangement

was to be Co-Co and the axle load to be within 19 tons. The cab front was to be almost flat, and side access stipulation for the body was waived. An artist's impression of what the general outline should be was issued by Wilkes & Ashmore and an outline drawing to match was also issued.

Brush already had realised that Falcon did not fit the specification entirely, notably because it had two engines, and was aware that the Sulzer 12LDA28 engine recently had been offered at a new output of 2,750bhp by the provision of more aftercooling and an increase of rotational speed from 750 to 800rpm. In March 1960 the Managing Director of Brush, Mr B L Goodlet, had listed as a project the design of a 'Type 4 locomotive for BTC using Sulzer engine (if specified)'. The target date for orders was 1961 and considered problems were the large generator design and lightweight mechanical parts. The listing of this project was most probably the result of collective thoughts within Brush Traction.

Brush, among other locomotive manufacturers, was invited to produce a design and tender for the new Type 4 standard locomotive. This Brush did, offering alternative designs incorporating Sulzer or English Electric engines, in particular with a willingness to fit any other suitable engine or even electrical equipment of non-Brush design should BR so desire. On paper, therefore, the new design was offered to BR. It should be noted that Brush was aware of the EE intention to increase the output of its 16SVT engine (by fitting after-coolers to create the CSVT range, starting with the twelve-cylinder model).

Two other locomotive manufacturers also responded and each prepared to build a prototype. These prototypes, 'Lion' and DP2, from BRCW and English Electric have been outlined in Chapter 5.

There is little doubt that BR had considerable favour for the Sulzer engine. It was giving good service and had been progressively uprated to 2,750bhp, whereas the EE engine had not. The contemplated up-rating of the latter may have been considered by BR as too large a step to take from 2,000 to 2,750.

BR had also gained a favourable impression from the lightweight body design and construction of some of its diesel hydraulic locomotives operating on the Western Region and made this known. Falcon had incorporated into its design load bearing body sides and this demonstrated that Brush was moving in the right direction in this respect.

'Lion' was a joint venture of BRCW, Sulzer and AEI (the latter firm being the result of a merger of Metropolitan-Vickers and British Thomson-Houston). Naturally, Sulzer wished to install its latest 12LDA28 twin bank engine of 2,750bhp and this was done. One disadvantage lay within the joint venture. This was that BRCW was a subsidiary of BSA Ltd, which was experiencing financial difficulties at the time and indeed went into liquidation during late 1962. What was uncanny was that the outline of 'Lion' looked almost identical to the Wilkes & Ashmore artist's impression.

DP2 was purely an English Electric venture and combined the expediency of utilising the production Deltic body, complete with noses, with the up-rated 16CSVT engine. Its main disadvantages in BR eyes were considered to be its late arrival on the scene, the reticence of EE to offer much non-

EE alternative equipment and the reluctance to adopt the flat front. EE was also very much occupied on other work at the time. Of the three prototypes the one nearest to fulfilling the BR specification was 'Lion', as yet not completed. All three were designed with some degree of collaboration with BR.

More pressure was brought to bear on BR headquarters by the Regions to change and up-rate the current Type 4 designs and eventually Mr F H Wood of Brush Traction was called to BR and told that the Railway wished to cancel the last twenty Type 4 Peak Class locomotives D194-99, D1500-13 on order from BR workshops, and to replace them with twenty locomotives of a new Co-Co design with up-rated engine as being devised by BRCW, in conjunction with Sulzer, in the form of 'Lion'.

It would appear that BR favoured the design of 'Lion', then still being built, and saw it as a suitable replacement Type 4. Brush were asked to tender to BRCW for the twenty sets of equipment, but BRCW did not want to be the main contractor, so BR then asked Brush to tender for complete locomotives with BRCW mechanical parts and with erection at the Smethwick works of the latter, in Birmingham. When Brush assembled a quote on this basis the price was higher than expected due mainly to the high price quoted by BRCW for their parts. It is believed that the banks who then owned BRCW were not anxious to continue locomotive building; the site was much more valuable than the potential profits of continuing in the business.

Brush were invited to put forward a complete locomotive offer and they subsequently obtained a contract for these twenty locomotives, not only replacing the sets of equipment that should have been supplied to Derby, but also the locomotives as well. Brush tendered for complete locomotives on 11th July 1960. Anticipating that this might be the start of a large fleet of Type 4s BR had asked for certain undertakings and Brush agreed. BR wanted to be able to obtain competitive quotes from all locomotive manufacturers and also to build in their own workshops. Brush agreed to grant a licence to build the mechanical parts on the condition that Brush would always be allowed to quote in competition. Agreement was reached between Brush and BR, resulting in the pilot order being placed on 28th February 1961.

Once again BR made a move before the options had materialised when a further thirty Brush Type 4s were ordered on 1st January 1962, nine months before the very first Brush Type 4 was even completed.

Brush was in a strong position. It favoured a one-piece cast steel bogie, supplied by English Steel (Castings) Corporation. The bogie design was particularly advanced with little weight penalty over fabricated designs, and the new locomotive design generally was superior. Brush willingness to offer various versions with different power plants and install whatever electrical equipment BR required had a profound effect also. It should not be overlooked that Brush equipment was regarded in high esteem and had a very high reputation for reliability. The monocoque stressed skin body shell of the new design was superior to that of 'Lion', and was devised with the help of the Gloster Aircraft Co., thus utilising expertise from within the aircraft side of the Hawker Siddeley Group.

BRCW hurried its prototype 'Lion' along and DP2 appeared in the same year, 1962, but both were too late to have any influence upon BR thinking and the latter had the expensive mechanical construction of the Deltic body shell. There was a certain urgency during the final days of completing 'Lion', despite the restrictive atmosphere that prevailed within the organisation. There was a sense of commitment on the part of the team involved on the project and the firm was so committed anyway to the point that the project continued to completion, despite restrictions imposed by financial constraints. BRCW went out of business later that year and English Electric went on to build Type 3s in considerable quantity from 1960, notably without flat ends.

The twenty new locomotives were allotted running numbers D1500-19 (Brush 342-61). Construction proceeded swiftly and, with the new type of body construction, traditional methods of body-building virtually ceased, so a certain amount of re-education into the new methods took place at Loughborough. The first locomotive took shape in the workshops during the first half of 1962 and emerged complete in the September, just as the last Type 2s were nearing completion.

The main strength of the new locomotive lay in the integral construction of the body. The body sides were connected by cross stretchers, deck plate, bulkheads and roof sections, and were terminated at each end by dragboxes and end trusses. With the exception of the roof section over the power unit and minor brackets and support rails, all the structure members and panels were load bearing. Vertical and end loads were accommodated by the body sides, which were fabricated from rolled steel sections and panelled with sheet steel. These members were so designed that the panelling, suitably stiffened with folded steel sections to prevent buckling, took all the shear load. Traction and vertical loads were transferred from the bogie pivots and power unit mountings to the body sides by box section cross stretchers fabricated from steel plates. These cross stretchers also incorporated lifting and jacking points. A proportion of the horizontal differential loading was taken by the steel deck plate, which extended the full length of the locomotive and was suitably stiffened by folded steel sections. This deck plate also formed a sump under the engine and was drained by pipes discharging to the track.

Buffing and drawing loads were distributed to the body sides by drag boxes and end trusses which were fabricated from steel plates and hollow, rectangular steel sections. Buffing loads of 200 tons recorded on strain gauges, proved the structure to be successful during tests on D1500's body shell during construction. The triangular shapes of this structure lay hidden from outside view, obscured by the cab side sheeting below and to the rear of the windows. Diagonal end loads were accommodated by the roof sections over the radiator and boiler compartments, together with the adjacent bulkheads.

The bulkheads and the roof sections were constructed of folded steel sections and sheet metal, and were made readily detachable to facilitate installation and removal of equipment in the compartments. The radiator mountings, ducting, fan cowls and motor supports were incorporated in the radiator

roof section. The only openings in each body side were two small rectangular windows and a centrally positioned door. Near this door were three recesses for hand and foot holds for external roof access. Also on the body side was a circular aperture of the water filler situated between the door and the recesses. Well covered and disguised, this is one of the most elusive features to see on photographs of Brush Type 4s.

The whole structure represented the final stage in locomotive body construction, which had moved from the load-bearing deck of the Type 2s, through the sides and deck lattice framework load-bearing structure of 'Falcon'. At this stage the majority of the body shell was load bearing, including the sheet steel body side cladding. Much weight saving was achieved with this concept, and credit for much of the technology goes to the aircraft side of Hawker Siddeley in this matter.

More weight saving was achieved by fitting aluminium alloy cabs and a cab roof canopy made of fibreglass. Aluminium and fibreglass was used for the non load-bearing, removable roof section over the power unit. This was fitted with four hinged inspection doors for engine top maintenance, and removable panels for access to the turbocharger and heat exchanger. The fibreglass panels were translucent and increased the amount of natural illumination within the power compartment. The heat-insulated engine silencer box was built into this roof section and had an insulated removable cover shaped to the general roof profile. All louvres were fitted into the roof sections to retain the qualities of the new body design, and in doing so gave the flat body sides a clean look unequalled at the time by any other BR locomotive type.

The floors of the cabs were made of wood, covered with linoleum. The internal cab layout was the BR standard of the time with the equipment common to other diesel classes, complete with a left-hand driving position and a second man position to the right of the driver. The main controls and instruments were fitted into a desk/console in front of the driver and numbered somewhat fewer than usual today. The styling of the cab was the two front-windows theme derived from 'Falcon' and finalised with the guidance of design consultants Wilkes & Ashmore who clearly utilised some fine-tuning inspired by that of the 'Hymek' diesel

The body shell of D1500 (BT 342) begins to take shape. It is seen mounted on transporter bogies for transfer between shops. The former Great Central main line forms part of the background. April 1962.

BRUSH A7949

hydraulic locomotives and 'Lion', both of which had features benefiting from advice from the same consultants. The style still remains classically timeless, even in the late-2000s.

The engine fitted was the twin-bank, in-line, four-stroke, Sulzer 12LDA28C. It was a medium speed, four-stroke type, delivering 2,750bhp at 800rpm, being pressure charged, inter-cooled and had direct injection.

The main generator was driven from the engine through step-up gears linking the two crankshafts with the output shaft, to which it was coupled. This shaft had a speed of 1,150rpm. The engine cylinder block and the crankcase were formed into rigid structures by the use of steel castings and steel plates welded together to result in a stiff frame in both lateral and transverse directions. The pistons were forged in special high duty aluminium alloy and were machined all over and inside the crowns to ensure reliability and long life. The piston rings were cooled by lubricating oil, which was designed to flow from the force-lubricated piston pin through passages in the pistons before discharging.

Cast iron cylinder covers were provided, these having aerodynamically designed inlet and outlet passages, which were intended to give a high efficiency, and enable a two-valve configuration to be adopted without causing any restriction on the flow of gases. The single fuel injector was centrally placed and was fed through a special drilled stud to avoid the danger of oil dilution through breakage and joint leakage. The pressure charger was an exhaust gas turbine type developed specially for the engine.

The engine and generator were combined on a common lightweight bedplate and were lifted in and out of locomotives as complete power units. The engines were manufactured under licence by Vickers-Armstrong of Barrow in Furness, under a sub-contract arrangement from Sulzer Bros. The engine building programme was managed by the Traction Division of Sulzer Bros. (London) who acted as agents for the parent company of Switzerland.

Another view in the Turbine Shop as the 2,750bhp Sulzer engine is lowered into the body of D1500 in April 1962. Some of the year's final Type 2 production can also be seen.

BRUSH A795I

The DC main generator was not exactly the same as that fitted to the final Derby-built 'Peak' class, mainly because it was dual wound to incorporate the electric train heating facility and was of a higher output. Class F insulation was adopted generally, with some Class H materials in certain parts such as the armature and shunt field conductor insulation. In all, three generators were mounted within one common assembly, the main, train heating and auxiliary generators with the first-named being sandwiched between the other two. Your author remembers them well when they were being wound in one of the older shops adapted specially for their production. Their proportions were massive when compared with other electrical machines in production for traction purposes. The armatures were certainly heavy objects to revolve by hand on the special greased pedestal type stands used in the winding shops.

The traction motors were the TM 64-68 frame size, each rated at 368hp. The auxiliary machines consisted of traction motor blowers, braking system exhauster motors, compressor motors and pump motors, all being supplied from the auxiliary generator.

Automatic voltage regulation was provided by Newton (Derby) air-cooled, carbon pile regulators. Battery starting for the engine was provided for by the use of a 48-cell battery charged from the auxiliary generator. Two radiator fan motors were fitted, with switching controlled by a thermostatic switch in the cooling water circuit.

The two bogies were the 'Commonwealth' type, a one-piece cast manganese steel frame, manufactured by the English Steel (Castings) Corporation. Each was fitted with three motorised axles. Sprung swing bolsters, with coil spring primary and secondary suspension, were fitted. The main superstructure load was carried by large area, flat centre, bolster plates of 'H' form fitted with antifriction wear pads. Loading was transferred to the bogie frame by double coil springs at each leg of the bolster, and these springs were supported by cast steel spring planks suspended from the bogie frames by swing links. Hydraulic dampers for secondary springing were fitted between the bolsters and spring planks at each bolster spring nest. The bogie frames were supported by four nests of double coil springs mounted on under-slung equalising beams made from forged steel. Their suspension was by means of pins and rubber bushes at the outer axle boxes of the bogies and stirrups with rubber sandwiches at the inner axle boxes. These beams formed a visually prominent feature of the bogies on the Brush Type 4s and differed from those fitted to the Type 2s and 'Falcon' by being under-slung. Traction and braking loads were

113

Inside the original Locomotive Erecting Shop one of the first Type 4s is lowered onto its bogies on 3rd September 1962.

BRUSH A8407

The main details and dimensions of D1500 to D1519 were as follows:

Wheel Arrangement	Co-Co
Track Gauge	4ft 8½ins
Engine Model	Sulzer twin-bank 12-cylinder, model 12 LDA 28C
Engine Rating	2,750bhp at 800rpm
Main Generator	8-pole compensated type with three windings of separately excited and self excited shunt and a series wound decompounding winding
Continuous Ratings	1,798kW, 844V, 2,130A at 1,150rpm,1,805kW, 970V, 1,860A at 1,150rpm
Auxiliary Generator	6-pole shunt wound type
Continuous Rating	26.4kW, 110V, 240A at 1,150rpm
Train Heat Generator	8-pole shunt wound
Continuous Rating	320kW, 800V, 400A at 690/1,150rpm
Traction Motors (six)	4-pole, force ventilated, axle hung, nose-suspended type
Continuous Rating	368hp, 422V, 710A at 776rpm
One Hour Rating	362hp, 391V, 762A at 698rpm
Length over buffers	63ft 6ins
Overall width over body	8ft 9 ins
Overall width over handrails	9ft 2ins
Overall height from rail	12ft 9 3/8ins
Wheel Diameter	3ft 9ins
Bogie Wheelbase	14ft 6ins
Total Wheelbase	51ft 6ins
Distance between Bogie Pivots	37ft 0ins
Minimum Curve Negotiable	4 chains
Maximum Speed	95mph
Maximum Tractive Effort	55,000lbs
Continuous Tractive Effort	30,000lbs
One Hour Tractive Effort	33,000lbs
Fuel Capacity	850 gallons
Weight in Working Order (intended)	114 tons
Weight in Working Order (quoted actual)	117 tons
Axle load (intended)	19 tons
Axle load (actual)	19½ tons

transferred from the axles to the bogie frames by the axle box guides and the horn guides on the frame. Vertical rubbing faces on the bogie frames carried these forces to the bogie pivots, which in turn transferred the loads to the locomotive superstructure.

The traction motors were nose-suspended and axle-hung in the normal manner of the time.

In addition to the electric train heating equipment, steam heating equipment was provided. Indeed this was to prove to be the main source of train heating over the first years because BR had not yet decided on a definite policy change and the vast majority of its coaching stock was equipped with steam heaters. A Spanner horizontal type train heating boiler was fitted to provide a source of steam and water was fed to it from two tanks, of 1,250 gallons total capacity, suspended from the floor below the engine sump and in the space between the bogies.

The superstructure housed equipment in the following order, starting from behind No. 1 cab: 'Serck' roof-mounted radiators, cooled by two roof-mounted fans, were placed in a compartment above the brake equipment cubicle, the air compressor, compressor after-cooler, toilet and washbasin, a traction motor blower unit, exhauster units and air reservoirs. In the next compartment was housed the Sulzer engine, the generator and fuel tanks. The electrical control cubicle came next, forming a sandwich partition reaching from floor to ceiling and wall to wall, and pierced centrally by a door leading to the next compartment housing the 'Spanner' train heating boiler, traction motor blower and air reservoirs. This compartment was immediately behind No. 2 cab. The batteries were slung beneath the body, between the bogies.

The electrical connection of the six traction motors was series-parallel and the overall weight discrepancy was due largely to the dual train heating equipment provision. The resultant locomotive often has been described as plain or monotonous in appearance, but for a mixed traffic, no nonsense machine, the outcome was very impressive and stylish, though by necessity, functional. The livery was two-tone green, with horizontal olive bands, applied completely around the body, and separated by a central Sherwood Green band on the sides and by yellow warning panels on the cab fronts. The running number was applied in the standard style of the period to all four cab sides on the central green band. The BR lion and wheel emblem, of 1956 introduction, was placed centrally on this band in the vertical plane, but was off centre on the horizontal plane towards the right. The roof was olive green (but often appears grey in photographs) and all undergear black, although the former soon became dark grey through deposits of exhaust material and traffic dirt not being removed during cleaning operations. Buffer beams were red. It was a simple and effective arrangement and outstandingly befitting, relieving the plain body sides most successfully. The oval Brush Traction works plates were fitted to the No. 1 cab sides, just below the running numbers.

When D1500 was first photographed it bore the running number on a temporary label affixed to the cab sides. Since the locomotive was in unvarnished condition and without any proper markings, this may have been a temporary expedient to satisfy BR recognition requirements during initial runs on the main lines. It was once said that BR disapproved of this embellishment, but it is unlikely that this was so, because the painting specification was already in place and being conformed to.

The outline of the new design was neat and had an almost timeless appearance. The hand of Wilkes & Ashmore once more bore fruit, particularly in the cab and front end design. The interconnection hoses and cables were unobtrusively tucked away around the buffer beam areas and the electric train heat socket was conveniently located to the right of the right hand buffer. It was perhaps mainly due to the cowl design in this location which made the equipment almost unobtrusive. The four-character display was neatly located centrally on the cab front, below the front handrail, an obvious location but one which could have suffered from a less sensitive design consideration. Of course the lack of doors for inter-locomotive access helped matters enormously. The domed roof of each cab was relieved by a neatly designed cowl, which housed the warning horns. Another thoughtful inclusion was the provision of kick plates to the lowest portions of the cab doors, an omission on other classes, which resulted in some unsightly areas of damaged paintwork.

Although the body shell of D1500 was fabricated in the new Locomotive Superstructure Shop, the majority of assembly took place in the former Turbine Shop, which supplemented the locomotive erecting shop on a regular basis, and had done so for a little while on Type 2 work. It was in the Turbine Shop that the body shell was stress-tested. The Locomotive Superstructure Shop was to prove a most useful facility for producing Type 4 body shells. Its construction was started on the Meadows side of the Falcon Works during September 1959 and it was completed on 25th January 1960.

D1500 was completed during August 1962, news of its impending completion being noted in the September 1962 edition of 'Modern Railways'. The first official photograph of D1500 complete, though not varnished and with the temporary 'number plate', was taken on 3rd September. On 6th September it ran to Crewe Locomotive Works for weighing and returned to the Falcon Works the same day. Initial test running was undertaken between Syston and Cheadle Heath, hauling loads of up to fifteen bogie coaches. Then came its arrival at Cricklewood (London) in mid-September for inspection by BTC officials. The official photographs of D1500 in correct BR livery were taken on 19th September. On the 27th it was at Marylebone and then went to its allocated depot in London, Finsbury Park, being noted there in the Clarence Yard. At least one magazine published a photograph of D1500 before the official ones were published.

On 3rd September the first Type 4 has moved to the departure siding for its official photograph and first trip out of the works. Note that the running number is carried temporarily on a small white panel attached to the cabside. Within a few days it had been removed and the number painted on the side in the usual style. The locomotive has not been varnished.

BRUSH A8402

Upper: D5858 and D1500 pose together on the approach lines to the test track on 20th September 1962. This was a fairly rare occurrence as Type 2 production was ending at the time when that of Type 4 was commencing.

Above: By 19th September 1962 D1500 had received the standard BR livery and numbering. It is seen here under the loading gauge of the departure siding.

BRUSH A8495   BRUSH A8497

Indeed there was some delay and apparent reticence before official descriptions appeared. 'Modern Railways' carried its description in the February 1963 edition, complete with a three-quarter view of D1500 on the southern exchange sidings. Curiously, it was headed 'The Hawker Siddeley 2,750bhp Type 4 diesel-electric for BR', the title of Brush not appearing in the heading. For some months this was the

preferred description, but eventually Brush Type 4 became commonplace until 1968 when Class 47 started to be used in conjunction with the new classification system. In 1961 BR classified the new locomotive design ML4, but the Eastern Region classified it 27/2. The same issue featured the front cover colour advertisement for Sulzer, in which D1500 was seen hauling a passenger train on the ER.

On 8th October D1500 headed the 8.10am King's Cross to Hull, piloted from Grantham by B1 4-6-0 No. 61389. On the 10th and 11th of October what appeared to be comparative trials with 'Deltic' No. D9018 'Ballymoss' took place. D1500 was involved with high-speed dynamometer trials from London to Doncaster and back on the second day, D9018 being run the previous day. The train represented about 385 tons and a schedule of 2hrs 20mins was specified for the Down journey and 2hrs 14mins for the Up, which terminated at Finsbury Park.

Number D1500 went to the Western Region during February 1963 for trials. It is seen here on the 19th on Dainton Bank with the new Hawksworth dynamometer car, which was designed and built specifically for testing diesel locomotives.

BRUSH A9352

On 2nd November D1500 was transferred on loan to the Western Region for further dynamometer trials and was noted on the normal Swindon Works running-in turn from Swindon with the 6.55am Cheltenham to Paddington and the 1.30pm parcels train back to Swindon during the first week of the month. It also reached Plymouth.

December saw a return to Finsbury Park, but on 5th January 1963 the locomotive was back on loan to the WR for further dynamometer trials. While on loan D1500 was allocated to Swindon, where the test facilities were based. These trials with the WR Hawksworth dynamometer car and a seventeen-coach test train took place on 20th February 1963, between Swindon and Plymouth. Two test stops and restarts were undertaken on Dainton Bank in each direction. During the same month D1500 was tested on the famous Lickey Incline with nineteen coaches and the dynamometer car, totalling 690 tons. Two stops and restarts were successfully made and the resident Bromsgrove steam banking locomotive 9F 2-10-0 No. 92079, had a disappointing day, trailing hopefully some distance behind the train. On completion of the performance testing D1500 returned to the ER before the end of the month. It was then based at Finsbury Park and was noted on goods trains by 12th March. During May 1963 D1500 and sister locomotives were involved with Roadrailer train trials on the

East Coast Main Line and on the 20th was seen hauling the Up 'West Riding' express, probably for the first time that a member of the class had undertaken this working. By the end of the year D1500 had settled down to mixed traffic duties on the main line.

D1500-19 Enter Service

D1501 was completed by the beginning of November 1962 and on the second day of that month arrived at Crewe Works for weighing, returning to the Falcon Works during the same afternoon. Later in the month it was allocated to Finsbury Park depot and on 24th November was noted working the 8.10am King's Cross to Hull, returning twenty minutes late into Peterborough with the 12.45pm departure from Hull aided by V2 steam locomotive No. 60881. A similar occurrence on the same train happened on 30th November, but this time No. 60880 came to the rescue. D1502 also arrived at Finsbury Park during November, but went light Down to Doncaster Works on 17th December for the fitting of Automatic Warning System (AWS) equipment.

In late December seventeen Brush Type 4s were noted in various stages of construction at the Falcon Works and six were complete mechanically, with D1503-7 expected to be ready for service during the first part of January 1963. Official returns record D1503 as being allocated to Finsbury Park in December 1962. The delay into service of the above locomotives was due to modifications being made in the light of teething troubles occurring with D1500 once it had entered service. Some of the above locomotives under construction were probably part of the second order (D1520 onwards), and just being started.

Numbers D1504-8 duly entered service in January 1963, again the allocation being to Finsbury Park. The first of these deliveries went light to Doncaster for AWS fitting on 9th January and was noted working the 8.10am King's Cross-Hull on the 15th and 17th.

During the same month D1502 was employed on crew-training duties, operating from Gateshead depot, on parcels trains. D1503, meanwhile, was similarly employed between Doncaster and Leeds. By April 1963 it became clear that all twenty Brush Type 4s were to be allocated to Finsbury Park depot for main line passenger and freight services, the latter including Ferme Park (London) - New England and King's Cross - Doncaster runs. These were the new Class 7* Freight trains, high speed and heavily loaded services designed to give an improved service with improved quality and increased line capacity. D1501 was involved in crew training duties at New England in preparation for these services.

Numbers D1509-11 were delivered during February, the first two being noted in Doncaster Works paint shop on 3rd March. Soon afterwards D1510 was transferred to the Scottish Region on loan to Haymarket depot in Edinburgh, for crew training purposes. It arrived on 6th March and by 30th March these duties had been completed, the locomotive hauling the Up 'Flying Scotsman' through to King's Cross

that day. Deliveries from Brush were usually to Doncaster, for acceptance, and from there they usually ran light to Finsbury Park, but it became practice to despatch them from Doncaster on a train. D1511 worked Up on the 12.45pm ex-Hull on 7th March.

Numbers D1512-15 reached Finsbury Park during March 1963, D1512 working to the depot on the Up 'White Rose' express on 14th March. D1515 was soon despatched to Neville Hill depot in Leeds early in April for crew training purposes. On 28th March D1513 undertook dynamometer car runs on the Scunthorpe line. April saw the delivery of D1516/7/9 and on 18th April D1516 was employed on hauling a trial train of 41 new Roadrailer wagons, a load totalling 520 tons. It ran from Enfield Chase via Hertford North and Langley Junction,

Below: During the big freeze of January 1963 BR crews prepare to take over D1506 and D1507 at the southern exchange sidings outside the Falcon Works.

Facing page: Number D1520 (BT414/1963) just prior to leaving the Falcon Works in sunshine during June 1963. This was the first Brush Type 4 not to be fitted with electric train heating facilities.

BRUSH A8869   BRUSH A9229

Stevenage, to Doncaster St. James. The return journey was to Ferme Park and finally to Enfield Chase via Palace Gates. The working of the new Class 7* Freight trains by Brush Type 4s commenced on 1st April, when sufficient locomotives became available, the required number being ten.

Number D1518 was the last to be delivered. It travelled south from Doncaster on 17th May hauling the 4.28pm Doncaster - King's Cross passenger train. Thus ended the first Brush Type 4 deliveries. The majority of these locomotives were mostly employed on Class 4 and Class 7* freight workings running between Ferme Park and New England and between King's Cross and Doncaster, but new passenger workings evolved by early May. By mid-June they started to displace the 2,000bhp English Electric Type 4s from Class 1 duties, their numbers now being bolstered by the arrival of D1520 onwards of the second order. By the end of 1963 the first twenty had already helped to cause the first withdrawals of the famous Gresley A4 'Pacific' locomotives.

The Second Brush Batch – D1520-49

Occasional reference has been made to the second order which Brush received on 1st January 1962. This order was for a further thirty Brush Type 4s to be numbered D1520-49, nominally Brush Traction works numbers 413 to 442 but actually plated somewhat differently (see Appendices 3-1 / 8-1).

In retrospect it may not be clear why BR made such a move when it did, because if one believes what was appearing in the railway press at the time the Standard Type 4 design was still to be decided upon. The two rival contenders, the prototypes 'Lion' and DP2, had not been completed and were still worthy of consideration and evaluation – that was the impression. The obvious conclusion that can be drawn is that in reality BR wished to accelerate the introduction of Type 4s and only Brush could supply what BR wanted in general terms. BRCW was in a very uncertain position, despite an excellent previous record, and DP2 did not fit the specification (although it did

prove to be an extremely reliable locomotive during its brief career). Furthermore, English Electric was committed to Type 3 production for BR and had other distractions ongoing both in production and development. Nevertheless, it does appear that BR was content to allow continuation of the impression that nothing had been decided upon. It was not until the last months of 1963 that it generally became known that matters had been settled by the choice of the Brush Type 4 design.

Times were changing on BR by 1962 and indeed greater changes were to come over the next few years. Although these changes were largely unforeseen at the time, many of them affected the large-scale production of Brush Type 4s both at the Falcon Works and Crewe Locomotive Works because they were coincidental.

The decision to equip the first twenty Brush Type 4s with electric train heating equipment was commendable, and really should have coincided with a general plan to equip existing passenger coaching stock with electric heaters, but it unfortunately did not . Only the LMR had a plan to have electric heaters fitted, to existing and new coaches. This was made necessary by the intended introduction of electric traction on that region between Euston, Crewe and Manchester. There existed a long term notion of replacing steam heating generally on BR, mainly because one day there would be no steam locomotives left running on the system. Nothing concrete was done at the time generally, such was the state of flux during the changeover from steam traction.

Once in service D1500-19 were in a paradoxical situation operating on a Region that had rolling stock fitted with steam heating equipment. The ETH generators fitted in them worked lightly loaded (supplying the traction motor blower motors) for most of the time, a situation which was not ideal as it did not make proper use of the equipment provided, and resulted in glazing of the commutator surface under the brush tracks. Glazing caused the brushes to chatter as the commutator rotated beneath them. Glazing is a phenomenon which occurs in such situations when electrical current passes through the point of contact between commutator bars and

D1522 (BT417/1963) at the buffer stops of Kings Cross station shortly after entering service.
The traditional whitewashed platform-edge contrasts with the modern form of traction.

BRUSH

Work-stained D1529
(BT423/1963) stands on New
England depot on 1st December
1963. Note the different pattern
of the nearest three roof-
shoulder grilles.
The normal pattern was for
horizontal slots.

M J STRETTON

brushes in minimal amounts. It is sometimes referred to as a patina, along with the more ideal coatings that occur under proper load conditions. Perhaps foreseeing that problems would occur, the following Brush Type 4 batches were not fitted with electric train heating equipment. In retrospect, always the best view of all, what happened was for the best, because when conversion to electric train heating came as the sole heating system, the brushless AC generator was already a proven alternative.

The arrival of Dr Richard Beeching on the BR scene, fresh from ICI, ensured that the BR system would never be the same again. Many results of his arrival were regrettable, some were disastrous, but many others were of lasting good. Which ones fitted into which category was often hotly disputed, it depended (and still does) upon one's viewpoint. To some people he was the man who eliminated steam, which is not entirely true; that process was already underway when he arrived. His remit, mainly a financial one, was laid down by the Government, and he suffered from being the executioner, rather than the judge, such were the passions unleashed. He came to the Railway in 1961 as Chairman of the British Transport Commission. On the dissolution of that body and division of its former areas of responsibility, he became Chairman of the British Railways Board, which came into being on 1st January 1963. His notorious plan to reshape BR was formulated over a year or so, being published in March 1963. Together with a drastic planned pruning of the railway system many services were withdrawn, uneconomic practices were either stopped or the ways in which they operated changed dramatically. In fairness to Dr Beeching his task to make the railways pay was well nigh an impossible one, but he made it worse when he approached it in a far too literal manner. Branch line services were often examined in isolation, rather than as part of a system, for example. Where he did succeed in achieving something positive was in the field of introducing liner trains, merry-go-round trains and the change in attitude with regard to the modernisation plan. The original plan of 1955 grafted modern equipment onto a system which was prewar in its outlook and operations. During the Beeching era the way things were done were examined and a positive attempt to improve or change matters was made generally.

At the time, the negative side of the Beeching era attracted most of the attention and much of this predominates in the memory of those days. The Brush Type 4s contributed much to the more positive aspects of the Beeching years and were often tailored to meet them. Of course, some changes stemmed from other sources, but the main point to be made is that the term 'Standard Type 4' became something of a misnomer as production of the class continued.

The batch D1520-49 differed from the pilot batch mainly in that no electric train heating equipment was fitted, but there were various other differences.

Omission of this facility involved changing the main generator design to TG 160-60 Mk4 and its associated control gear. The original 26.4kW TG 69-16 Mk1 auxiliary generator type fitted to D1500-19, disappeared in favour of the TG 69-28 Mk3 with a higher output of 55kW, at 110V, 500A at 1,150rpm because it now had to supply the traction motor

blower motors.

The steam train heating equipment was retained, this taking the form of the Spanner Swirlyflow Mk3B boiler, powered from the locomotive batteries.

The braking equipment was changed from Westinghouse to Davies & Metcalfe/Oerlikon driven by Brush motors, but no significant change was made to the system or arrangement of the brake equipment. Control of the train brakes was through the driver's vacuum brake-valve, giving also a proportional air-brake application on the locomotive.

A completely different system of driving and controlling the radiator cooling fans was introduced from D1520, whereby the electric motors driving the fans of the pilot batch were replaced by a hydrostatic system in which motors of this configuration were used, being powered direct from the engine-driven pump. Serck Behr was the manufacturer and this system was used for the rest of the class. The traction motors were the TM 64-68 Mk1 type, with the armature core sleeved onto the shaft.

A rather subtle external change occurred with D1520 and was continued on all the Brush-built Type 4s. This concerned the metal sheeting which covered the gap between the buffer beam and the lower edge of the cab front. The gap was bridged by a pair of small brackets on D1500-19, and these were covered resulting in two protrusions. On D1520 one long protrusion, linking the two brackets, was substituted. Crewe-built Type 4s did not have this modification and continued with the two smaller ones.

Number D1520 was completed in May 1963 and left the Falcon Works on 5th June, entering traffic soon afterwards, being based on Finsbury Park depot in London. There was no noticeable gap in time between the despatch of D1519 and D1520, such was the speed that the building programme had gathered. Official records are at variance regarding what actually happened with regard to deliveries in some instances, but D1520-9 were all credited with entering service during June 1963. However, the Brush despatch dates extended into July for the last three of this batch. D1527 was soon transferred to Scotland arriving at Haymarket depot, in Edinburgh, on 19th July for crew training purposes. D1530-2 were also despatched during July, and entered service that month. D1533-6 were all August deliveries, but D1537 was recorded as entering service in August, with Brush recording the ex-works date as 2nd September. Finsbury Park took all deliveries to D1533, and these locomotives eliminated steam operation between King's Cross and Peterborough. From D1534 deliveries went to Darnall depot in Sheffield, reverting to Finsbury Park for D1547 and continuing with Darnall for the last two locomotives of the order. English Electric Type 3s and Brush Type 2s were among the locomotive types displaced by these higher-powered locomotives. Some reallocation of these locomotives took place and by the autumn of 1963 D1530-42 were based on Wath depot working a round diagram daily, starting from Wath and travelling to Frodingham on a Class 7* coal train. They continued on iron ore tipplers and Tipfit empties to Barnetby and on to Highdyke, from which they returned either on loaded tippler trains to Barnetby or worked to Colwick and back on loaded or empty wagon duties.

A scene in the Paint Shop during June 1963 with the first locomotives of the second batch being finished off.

BRUSH A9232

Numbers D1538-43 were recorded as entering service in September 1963, and the remainder concluding with D1549 in the October.

In one year Brush had delivered fifty Type 4 locomotives in two variants, all to the Eastern Region and in doing so had transformed workings on the former Great Northern lines, the southern section of the East Coast Main Line.

Crewe Works Enters the Scene

True to the agreement with Brush, BR workshops started to build Brush Type 4s, in an effort to further accelerate deliveries. The world famous, long-established Crewe Locomotive Works was charged with the task of building up a second production line to supplement that of Brush.

Crewe had a long tradition of locomotive building reaching back to 1843, from the early days of the Grand Junction Railway. By reason of amalgamation of railways the ownership of the works passed to the newly formed London & North Western Railway in 1846 and the London Midland & Scottish Railway in 1923. Nationalisation brought the works

into BR ownership, a state which still existed during the 1960s. The works was no stranger to quantity production of locomotives, and settled into the job well.

The first Brush Type 4 to be built at Crewe was D1550, and construction of it was already discernable in April 1963. The works was comparatively slower off the mark than Brush for two reasons. First was that its first order was later than that of Brush and second, work was in progress building Type 4 diesel hydraulic locomotives of the 'Western Class' for the WR. This class was built in the railway workshops of Swindon and Crewe and was numbered D1000-1073, with the former building D1000-29 in 1961-4, and the latter D1030-73 over the period 1962 until April 1964. As the 'Westerns' were phased out at Crewe, so the Brush Type 4s were phased in. These diesel hydraulic locomotives were the last such Type 4s to be produced for BR, and the Brush Type 4 was partly responsible for this. Originally, there had been a seemingly bright future for them and their predecessors, and the WR was particularly attracted to them during the earlier years because they offered a lower initial cost and an advantageous power to weight ratio when compared with earlier diesel electric Type 4 locomotives. This situation changed when the Brush Type 4 appeared, supplanting the latter, by virtue of its lighter weight and greater power together with its six axles replacing the former eight. Furthermore, increased building costs of the 'Westerns' and engine troubles started to plague the diesel hydraulic locomotives. The 'Westerns', therefore, became non-standard during the period of their building, an indication of how quickly events were changing in 1962/3.

At this point it is necessary to outline the total production of Brush Type 4s, by running number, ahead of the outline chronological sequence of events concerning the individual batches of locomotives. Production at the two works was concurrent for several years and modifications were made to locomotives as soon as it was practicable, so some cross-referencing is necessary.

| Brush built | D1500-49, D1682-1841, D1862-1961 (310 locomotives) |
| Crewe built | D1550-1681, D1842-61, D1962-99, D1100-11 (202 locomotives) |

The orders for locomotives, not mentioned previously, were as follows:

Order date	Locomotives	Delivered
December 1961	Crewe D1550-82	1/64 - 5/64
June 1962	Crewe D1583-1681	5/64 - 5/65
September 1962	Brush D1682-1706	10/63 - 1/64 (a)
September 1962	Brush D1707-1781	1/64 - 11/64
July 1963	Brush D1782-1841	11/64 - 4/65
circa July 1963	Crewe D1842-61	5/65 - 9/65
March 1964	Brush D1862-1961	5/65 - 5/67 (a)
circa June 1964	Crewe D1962-91	9/65 - 4/66
circa Sept.1964	Crewe D1992-99, 1100-1111	1966-5/67
(a) some specially modified locomotives delayed beyond these periods		

The background to these orders was formed basically as a desire by BR to replace steam traction, either directly or indirectly, by displaced diesel traction. Requirements were thought out in advance and by July 1962 tenders had closed for more Type 4s, scant details being made public, together with some suggestion that only the 'Lion' and DP2 designs were being considered for adoption. The Brush Type 4 was still regarded in public as something not for consideration. BR did not actually state this, but the suggestion was not challenged. The reality was more Brush Type 4 orders. Unlike the British Transport Commission, the British Railways Board was not so forthcoming regarding the automatic release of information for public consumption. Details filtered through in the railway press and it was known that the WR was interested in having Brush Type 4s as soon as the ER requirement was fulfilled. By mid-1963 BR admitted to Brush Type 4 orders reaching D1681 and in the August 1963 MODERN RAILWAYS there was speculation that the orders had reached D1861, some 362 locomotives in total. The speculation was accurate. Provisional allocation of these locomotives was said to be 124 for the Great Northern line of the ER, 13 to the North Eastern Region (NER), 75 to the LMR and 150 to the WR. This unofficial report was corrected in the following month's issue to the effect that the WR was to receive 42 in 1963 and that the first examples would be allocated to freight haulage between the North, the Midlands and South Wales.

Other details appeared with a more specific listing thus:

D1500-69	ER	70
D1570-82	NER	13
D1583-1732	WR	150
D1733-61	ER	29
D1762-81	LMR	20

Brush employees often remarked that you could recognise a Crewe locomotive by the rippled sides it bore. In this photograph, dated 9th February 1964, the ripples are very evident. D1553 on test on the Eastern Region.

BRUSH A10424

Crewe Locomotive Works started production of Brush Type 4s with D1550. Here, its fourth locomotive is seen on test with the ER dynamometer car during February 1964. Runs were made between Barnetby and Frodingham with 1,500 tons.

Below a rare photograph showing the scene at the Falcon Works whilst D1702-6 were on test. The number series had otherwise reached D1889, also seen coupled to D1702. Photograph dated 13th July 1965.

BRUSH BOTH

Crewe sent its locomotives out on test northwards along the West Coast Main Line. Here D1586, in pink primer, skims through the Lune Gorge near Dillicar on 14th May 1964.

BRUSH A11291

D1782-1806	ER	25
D1807-61	LMR	55

By the autumn of 1963 the standard Type 4 was considered to be the general design as represented from D1520, although variations were to make the word standard somewhat stretched in meaning. Parts of the plans changed and it was understood that D1682-1701 would be allocated to Old Oak Common depot on the WR. D1702-6 would be fitted with Sulzer twelve-cylinder V form engines of 2,650bhp, but it was not clear whether they would all go to the ER, or whether two would go the LMR and three to the ER for evaluation. The WR was to receive D1707-37 and D1762-81 and the NER was to have D1570-82 and D1738-61. Of D1583-1681 it was understood that the WR would take 79 and the LMR 20. A pause in ordering appeared to be the case for the time being, with consideration for future developments to be borne in the planners' minds. By mid 1964 the final orders had been placed, although it is fair to point out that further orders were considered possible, particularly for services north of Crewe should the proposed electrification of that section of the West Coast Main Line not materialise. Events were to deal with that particular issue in due course, in a very different manner.

With Crewe entering into the scene and Brush in full production it is pertinent to outline some of the effort required to sustain this production. The engines came from Vickers-Armstrong of Barrow-in-Furness, the electrical machines and control gear from Brush and of course the two firms had to provide new facilities (often from existing buildings).

The former firm was committed to supplying more than one Sulzer engine type to BR directly and indirectly for Types 2, 3 and 4 locomotives, and the arrangements under which it manufactured the engines under licence have been mentioned previously. To cope with the extra demand of the Brush Type 4 production Vickers-Armstrong provided special facilities in buildings specially set aside for producing the various Sulzer engines to the degree that in 1963/4 a peak of one fully finished engine was being completed each working day. The engines destined for the Brush Type 4s formed part of this production and with over 500 of them supplied in five years it was an impressive effort.

At Loughborough various shops were used all around the Falcon Works to produce the necessary mechanical and electrical parts as well as actually build, paint and test the locomotives. Crewe also had to be supplied with electrical equipment concurrently from 1963. The Superstructure shops on the Meadows side of the works were fully utilised fabricating the bodyshells and the former Turbine Shop provided superb erecting facilities, the capacity of the original Erecting Shop being outstripped. Shops producing control gear and auxiliary machines were kept busy continually, as were those producing the main generators and traction motors. It seemed almost impossible to go inside a shop and not see traction work in progress. Out in the yards and on the test track there were always locomotives in various stages of completion and on delivery day people would pause to see one, two and often three gleaming locomotives making their way through to the exchange sidings past the main offices. Design offices were kept busy dealing with modifications, which were introduced during the production run. The Brush/Beyer Peacock 0-4-0 diesel electric shunting locomotives provided ideal motive power for moving dead Type 4s around the site between the various shops. They were unique and interesting times.

Brush D1682-1706

The third Brush order was placed on 4th September 1962 and was for twenty-five locomotives. Intended Brush works numbers were 444 to 468 inclusive. Because Crewe Works was still preparing for production and because Brush was already in production, delivery of this batch commenced some months before the first Crewe deliveries.

More modifications were introduced into this batch of locomotives and applied to Crewe built locomotives soon afterwards, so it is doubly pertinent to describe it ahead of the Crewe deliveries. D1682 introduced a new design for wheel and axle sets because the original axles showed a tendency to crack under the wheel seat. This was due to incipient stress raisers built in during the forcing of the wheel onto the axle. This problem was not confined to Brush Type 4s; the standard arrangement of the time had been followed and they started to show the same general trends with regard to cracking. A new code of practice had been laid down and at the first opportunity the Brush Type 4 was modified to suit. It was desirable that a completely interchangeable traction motor should be retained and in order to do this it became necessary to re-design the traction motor suspension tube and introduce an arrangement using a split tube and larger diameter axle. The original design had a solid tube threaded onto the axle. In due course troubles were experienced with the new arrangement. The armature cores of the traction

motors were fitted directly onto the shaft rather than the previous method of sleeving them.

Because some of the locomotives were destined for the WR the AWS of that Region should have been fitted where relevant, but because there was some pooling of duties of the WR and LMR allocations this was not fitted until some months of service had elapsed. Similarly, the two lamp holder brackets affixed to the buffer tubes at each end should have been to the WR pattern, again where relevant. With regard to the latter, the portion inserted into the lamp presented its edge to the front whereas the BR standard presented the flat face. This was a legacy of the old Great Western Railway days and although it is by no means certain whether or not all the WR allocation was so fitted, most were eventually. The recessed footstep below each cabside door was continued until the D169X series, D1696 certainly featured them when new, whereas D1700 did not.

The last five of the batch (D1702-6) were experimentally fitted with a different type of Sulzer engine. This was the twelve-cylinder Sulzer LVA24 Vee-form engine which for BR requirements was rated at 2,650bhp at 1,050rpm. Some modification of the main generator was necessary, the TG160-60 Mk4 being replaced by the Mk5 version with the rotational speed decreased by 100rpm. The rotation was opposite to that of the twin-bank engine (which had gears between the crankshaft and output shaft) and the weight was six tons lighter. D1703 was fitted with a static load regulator.

Plans to fit the Vee engine were announced during mid 1962, the locomotives so fitted being regarded as mobile test beds. Certainly better comparison with the twin-bank engines was made with five examples in service, and of course a better idea of the success or otherwise of the Vee engine. For Sulzer the Vee engine concept was a resurrection dating from the mid 1950s after a lapse of thirty years. The new range

Number D1696 (BT458/1963) entering Loughborough Midland station with a Liverpool-London express on 20th December 1963.

BRUSH A10099

offered various models and outputs and the most powerful being developed in the mid 1960s was the 16-cylinder version fitted to 'Kestrel'. All five twelve-cylinder engines were built in France at the Sulzer works at Mantes. The nominal rating of the engine was 3,000bhp at 1,100rpm, and in this condition was already in use in France, but for BR use it was de-rated. The engine had a relatively light bedplate and crankcase combination built up from welded steel plate. Unlike the twin-bank design there were no gears. There was a Sulzer designed governor and exhaust gas turbo-charger.

Number D1682 was completed in October 1963, following on without a break in production from D1549. The locomotive bore a new type of works plate. The basic dimensions remained the same, but gone was the word TRACTION and in its place was SULZER. Gone also was the word ENGLAND. The new inscription read top BRUSH, centre line SULZER, and the bottom line the works number and the year.

This design remained standard for all the Brush-built Type 4s thereafter. It is believed that the change was instigated at the wish of Sulzer who wanted their name on the locomotives and who stood the cost of the plates. Why should Brush refuse such an offer!

The first locomotives were expected at Old Oak Common depot in London on 18th October 1963, initially for crew training purposes, but they were intended to take over the Paddington - Wolverhampton service, upon which the LMR had disfavoured the 'Western' class locomotives. Number D1682 received its works inspection certificate on 26th September and was despatched from the Falcon Works on 31st October together with D1683; D1685 and D1686 followed on 8th November and went to Oxley depot, north west of Wolverhampton (this was a former GWR depot, by this time transferred to the LMR); D1684 was ex-works on 11th November and was allocated to Old Oak Common. Oxley received D1687/8 later in the month.

WR depot, Bristol Bath Road, received D1689/92 at the end of November and D1693 during December, while D1690/1 went to Cardiff (Canton) depot at the end of November. D1693 went south from Loughborough on 6th December to Old Oak Common via the Midland Main Line, Welsh Harp Junction, Dudding Hill and Acton Wells Junction. Those at Bristol were initially involved with crew training. Number D1694 went to Old Oak Common in December, but D1695 went to Oxley, almost immediately being reallocated on loan to Derby depot (more familiarly Derby shed). Then D1696 followed, together with reallocated D1685 and D1688. Problems concerning locomotives not fitted with WR AWS running on WR lines occurred when the BRB banned their use on passenger trains until they were so fitted. This resulted in their introduction being delayed during December 1963 and afterwards. They eventually made their debut on the Paddington - Birmingham main line on January 13th 1964 and the locomotives loaned to the LMR made their way back to their intended areas of working. D1697 went to Cardiff (Canton) in December 1963 and D1698-1701 completed the WR allocation, going to Old Oak Common during that and the following month.

Production of Type 4s at the Falcon Works outstripped the capacity of the paint shop and soon locomotives were observed at Derby Locomotive Works where they had been finish painted, before returning to Loughborough for final completion. The original intention was for alternate locomotives to go to Derby, but this did not occur, instead immediate circumstances dictating events. Number D1696 was the first to be painted at Derby, followed by D1698 and D1701. The works plates were fitted after return to Loughborough. To comply with BR requirements running numbers were affixed in a temporary manner for the short journey from Loughborough to Derby, often in wood! The order of works numbers in relation to running numbers, not sacrosanct by any means before, started to deteriorate further from this time on.

The remainder of the order, D1702-6, were somewhat delayed by the very nature of the experimental fitting of the Sulzer Vee engines. This was to be expected, and the first examples (D1702/4) passed their Works Inspections on 28th July 1964, at least insofar as their Brush equipment was concerned. The remaining three followed the next month. Number D1702 was noted in base paint finish at Derby Locomotive Works on 27th September 1964 and again on 25th October. It was finish painted in time for display at an exhibition staged at Marylebone goods yard by the BRB and the Locomotive and Allied Manufacturers' Association (LAMA) on 30th April and 1st May 1965. Crewe-built D1678 was also on display. The five locomotives went to Tinsley, Sheffield, on the ER, although they operated from Shirebrook on freight duties and occasional passenger workings. D1703 went in September 1965, D1702/5 two months later, with D1706 being allocated in the December and D1704 not being allocated until July 1966. Despite some of the five being completed in 1964 all the works plates were dated 1965.

Mass Production 1964-7

The real flooding of the BR system with Brush Type 4s came when Crewe added its contribution to the already impressive production rate of the Falcon Works. Mention already has been made to D1550-82, of the first Crewe order dating from December 1961.

The first signs of construction came early in 1963 and by 10th November D1550-69 were under construction. During the beginning of January 1964 the whole contract and the first of the next contract (D1583) were under construction, with D1550-7 receiving their final coats of paint. Test trains were noted working to Penrith and back on the West Coast Main Line, one of the favourite test runs for Crewe Works. The first ones noted on test were D1550/1/2/4/6.

Runs were often made with the locomotives in base paint, as was the case with those ex-Falcon Works. With the latter the test run involved picking up the empty coaching stock from Queniborough, just north of Leicester, and working northwards on the Midland Main Line through Derbyshire to Cheadle Heath, south of Manchester. The test locomotive then returned southwards. The run involved going through Dove Holes tunnel and on one occasion the locomotive developed an unchecked wheel slip. The locomotive speedometer was registering about 60mph, but the actual speed was a very slow creep with a standstill at one point, verified later by the discovery of burnt rails, which had to be replaced!

A close-up of D1702 (BT444/1965) and D1889 (BT651/1965) at the Falcon Works on 13th July 1965.

BRUSH A12164

During the 'busy time' of the Brush Type 4 period many locomotive trials were conducted with locomotives double heading trains. It was difficult to keep speed down to 90mph with a combined horsepower of 5,500, so one locomotive was used on the northward stage and the other on the return. Maximum speed was the normal procedure when passing the Brush works, often with the 'horns ablaze'.

Numbers D1550-54 were all delivered to Darnall depot on the ER in January 1964, continuing the Brush Type 4 deliveries which had ceased temporarily with D1549 ex-Loughborough. Numbers D1555-8 went to Darnall during February. On 15th February Crewe had D1572-98 under construction in the workshops, D1564 in the yard and D1559/60/1/3 outside the paint shop. On 5th March D1560 was noted on the Crewe test train, D1559 and D1562 coupled together took their turn on 6th March, D1564 on the 7th, D1559 on the 9th, D1566 on the 11th and D1565 on 12th March.

On 25th March Crewe Works held D1563/71/2/3 in the yards and D1580-D1606 in the Erecting Shop.

One small change which came with the Crewe-built

locomotives was the omission of the recessed footstep just below the cab side doors.

The livery was unchanged, as one might expect, but rectangular Crewe cast works plates were fitted in the same positions as on the Brush-built examples. No works numbers were allocated to the locomotives.

The works plates bore the legend:

BRITISH RAILWAYS
CREWE BUILT
196X
POWER EQUIPMENT BY
BRUSH ELECTRICAL ENGINEERING COMPANY LTD
AND SULZER

During March D1559-62 and D1564-9 were added to the total at Darnall depot. D1563 was delayed in its delivery to Darnall until April 1964, but the first delivery to Leeds (Holbeck) on the NER (D1570) was at the end of March. The remainder of the contract went to Leeds (D1571-3, replacing BR/Sulzer Type 4s D1689-92 on various services to Kings Cross) and Gateshead (D1574-82) depots during April and May. The latter allocation was intended to eliminate steam traction on the East Coast Main Line express passenger services north of Peterborough. Crewe was quick off the mark and delivered thirty-three locomotives in four and a half months.

The basic design followed that established with the Brush-built batches built from D1520 and onwards, but commencing with D1575 the traction motor connections were arranged in all-parallel. This locomotive was not the first to appear with this arrangement because the change had been initiated on Brush-built D1715, completed in December 1963 and which appeared in service in February 1964. D1575 went into service during April 1964.

Noticeable external differences were small when comparing the Crewe-built examples with those which were Brush-built. The former continued the two aforementioned bracket covers above the buffer beams (featured on D1500-19), whereas the latter introduced a single version to cover the brackets from D1520 onwards. The two tail lights set into each cab front had differences. Those fitted to the Brush locomotives had lenses hinged horizontally whereas the Crewe locomotives hinged vertically. These differences remained so throughout the building programme, but in later years the exchange of the light components would eliminate this ready recognition sign of who was the builder.

During the period that Crewe was delivering its first batch, Brush had started to deliver locomotives of its fourth contract. This was the order for 75 locomotives numbered D1707 to D1781, placed 28th September 1962 and allocated works numbers 469 to 543 respectively. As before, the works numbers were not carried in the intended order, indeed far from it. Construction continued unbroken from D1701 of the previous contract.

Number D1707 was completed in December 1963 leaving the works on the 31st with D1708, bound for the WR. The former was finish painted at Derby Works and both were destined for Old Oak Common depot. D1709 followed with D1711 on 3rd January 1964, the latter also finish painted at Derby. As previously noted, deliveries were divided between the LMR and WR, D1709 going to Oxley and D1711 Old Oak Common, basically covering the area between both extremities as before.

Many of the locomotives were driven from Loughborough to Derby, either for finish painting or acceptance by BR and during January D1707 to D1713 were accepted for traffic.

Numbers D1714 and D1715 left the Falcon Works on 14th and 22nd January respectively for Derby Works and final painting, the latter being noted in the paint shop on 2nd February. As related above, D1715 was the first Brush Type 4 to be fitted with the traction motors electrically connected all in parallel rather than in series parallel. The decision to make this change was made late in 1963 and the primary reasons for the change were to reduce the voltage of the main generator to lessen the possibilities of flashover and to improve the electrical conditions immediately following wheel slip by avoiding sharp rises in voltage on the traction motor. This approach was preferred because controlled wheel slip technology was not particularly well-advanced at the time. The generator output voltage was reduced by half, from the previous 844 volts to 422, and this of course resulted in a doubling of the current from 2,130 amperes to 4,260, the rotational speed remaining unchanged at 1,150rpm. The advantage of this change was that the traction motor design, both mechanically and electrically, remained unchanged and the motors were still interchangeable. The disadvantage was that the main generator had to be redesigned with more copper content with the prospects of becoming much heavier and bulkier because of the increased current rating. There was also the need to install more bulky and costly control gear to control six electrical circuits and, of course, it followed that there was additional cabling required between the control cubicle and the traction motors together with associated cable ducting alterations. By designing the main generator as a twelve-pole instead of an eight-pole machine the anticipated weight increase was largely offset. The opportunity was

Number D1901 (BT663/1965) was the 250th Brush Type 4 to be supplied to BR by Brush. Photograph taken 10th September 1964. Note the Western Region type lamp brackets.

BRUSH A12286

The classic view of Type 4 mass production at Brush. No less than ten Type 4 members in varying stages of construction in the former Turbine Shop. The right-hand locomotive on the farthest row is one of the Rhodesia Railways Co-Cos. Photographed mid-1964.

BRUSH A11010

taken to change the method of controlling the separate field excitation of the main generator.

This initial design incorporated a field regulator and resistors energised from the voltage-controlled auxiliary generator and since these handled the full generator excitation current both the regulator and resistors were of substantial proportions. From the 109th Brush-built locomotive (D1740) a modified arrangement was applied in the form of a small inductor alternator, with two stator windings, affixed to the auxiliary generator. One of the windings was permanently connected through a silicon diode rectifier to the main generator field winding. The output of the main winding was controlled by a proportional change in the current in the DC control winding which dealt with very small currents up to a maximum of only one ampere. The whole unit worked very well and required minimum maintenance, there being no commutators or brushgear involved. The toroidal-wound load regulator, mounted directly onto the engine adjacent to the governor, proved troublesome and, despite being modified successfully, it was superseded by a better arrangement using electronic load regulation.

The new main generator was designated TG 172-50 Mk1, the new auxiliary generator was TG 69-20 either Mk1 or Mk1A.

There is some indication that the all-parallel arrangement should have been introduced on D1707 ex-Brush and D1583 ex-Crewe, but in the event there was a late introduction of eight on the former and a corresponding early application on the latter (D1575). This was probably an indication of a slight delay in phasing it in at the Falcon Works, and the balance of the first machines order going to Crewe. D1715 was completed during December 1963 and D1575 during April 1964.

More noticeable externally on this batch of locomotives were the WR pattern lower lamp brackets and the WR red spot route restriction transfers on the cab sides below the running numbers. D1715 was sent to Old Oak Common depot in February 1964, but was soon transferred to Oxley where it was joined by D1716 the same month. Number D1717 went to Old Oak Common, but D1718/9, the latter finish painted at Derby, went to Cardiff (Canton) depot. Bristol (Bath Road) took delivery of D1720 in March and Landore depot took delivery of Derby finish painted D1721. Deliveries to the WR continued with D1757, which went into traffic during September 1964. WR AWS was fitted to the locomotives on arrival and they conformed to the BRB edict. The area between London, Bristol and Birmingham became dominated by the Brush Type 4s as they displaced the 'Western' Type 4s, this process becoming almost total on the former GWR routes north of Birmingham by the spring of 1964. The new locomotives started to spread on various workings, including

A BR crew climbs aboard D1731 to take delivery on 14th May 1964. This locomotive was about the last one to be fitted with a single overhead electrification warning notice.

BRUSH A10747

excursions and football trains. D1722 penetrated into Devon on 26th March when the 11.50 York - Bristol was extended to Paignton. D1718/9 of Cardiff (Canton) depot were noted on Cardiff - Swansea semi-fast trains. Of course, as they spread across the system, crew training and familiarisation preceded the bulk allocations, D1697 of the previous Brush contract being loaned to Landore for these purposes for a while early in 1964, operating to and from Carmarthen.

Number D1731 was the one hundredth Type 4 to be built by Brush and went into traffic in April 1964, some eighteen months after deliveries had started at Loughborough.

However, D1733 was a special locomotive, not by being differently equipped but by being painted in a special livery, which in modified form was to have a lasting visual impact on the BR scene for many years to come.

This livery formed part of an interesting project, the XP64 train, designed to evaluate numerous ideas and assess new design features incorporated into it. There were improvements in internal equipment and decor and new door designs and a new livery to make the external appearance more attractive to the travelling public. It was one of the projects of the period which was being promoted by the BR Design Panel, and had the backing of Dr Beeching.

Eight new coaches were built at BR Carriage & Wagon Works, Derby, being completed in May 1964. Four further vehicles were adapted slightly to add to the set for regular traffic, once trial running had been completed. The external livery of the train was mainly a turquoise blue shade (described as Rail Blue at the time), relieved by a pale grey portion along the window areas. Number D1733 was painted in the blue shade to match, but received no grey. The bogies

and drawgear were painted dark brown and the yellow warning panel at each end was enlarged from the standard version applied to the other Type 4s and was taken around the cab corners to meet a square red panel under each cabside window. This red square bore a new double arrow symbol in white, representing a pair of railway tracks with the arrows representing the Up and Down directions fused in the centre. It was soon adopted as the modern BR symbol and has been familiar for over forty years (and remained as fresh as the day it was introduced until privatisation of the railways). The positioning of the new symbol necessitated siting the works plates and running numbers elsewhere, and these migrated to the bodysides, just to the rear of the cab doors. Instead of one overhead electrification warning label sited centrally below the four-character headcode display of each cab front, there appeared two, one each above the tail lights. Number D1731 displayed the single version and it may be that D1733 was the first Brush-built Type 4 to have the revised version. Those emerging from Crewe started to have two at about this time, D1570 being one of the earliest examples noted.

Number D1733 was despatched from the Falcon Works on 10th April 1964 in primer paint, to Derby Locomotive Works, where it was finish painted. It was noted in the paint shop on 26th April already being painted blue. On the adjacent Derby shed were sister Brush Type 4s D1730/2/5, all newly-delivered, the last one only the day previous. Most of the locomotives of this contract painted by Brush went to Derby for acceptance by BR before delivery to the WR.

On 28th May D1733 and the XP64 train were unveiled to the public gaze as 'the train of tomorrow' when a demonstration run was made from Marylebone to High Wycombe and back.

The train was due to tour the country to test public reaction and started on the 'Talisman' service between King's Cross and Edinburgh on 15th June and for the following winter it was due to be transferred to the King's Cross - West Riding services. Planned also were workings between Euston and Heysham from January 1965 and Paddington to Swansea three months later. Number D1733 soon parted from the train and was allocated to the WR in June 1964 based at Old Oak Common. Because the new symbol had not been approved by the BRB at the time and was applied for the initial publicity of the XP64 train the red squares were removed and the locomotive ran without any symbol of BR ownership. The train ran mostly with green locomotives, a practice which did not bother BR since the whole idea was to test reaction to the coaching stock. Number D1733 was busy on duties from Birmingham and was noted in South Wales. Crew training at Worcester had been utilising D1749 since July 1964, but D1733 replaced it on 21st September. Three years later D1733 still bore the special livery, but it had been patched with the later 'Rail Blue' paint and looked decidedly unkempt, but somehow the experimental shade of blue looked better than the one eventually adopted as a result of the experiment. The allocation of Brush Type 4s to the WR and LMR resulted in the Paddington - Birmingham - Wolverhampton express services being entirely powered by them early in 1964. Those in South Wales together with diesel locomotives supplied from other builders made inroads into the steam locomotive operations in the region, including inter Regional trains via

Not all trainspotters deserted the railway when the diesels came. The crew of D1742 chat with two boys taking an interest in their locomotive at Paddington station. One of the Western Region's Western class diesel hydraulic locomotives stands alongside. Photograph taken in June 1964.

BRUSH A10965

Hereford.

Commencing with D1730, spray painting was introduced to facilitate increased production because brush painting was proving too long a process, but nevertheless locomotives continued to be sent to Derby for finish painting. For the remainder of the contract (D1758-81) deliveries were to Tinsley depot near Sheffield on the ER, and all but one were over the period from August to November 1964, the exception being D1758 which was delivered in May. In May 1964 Darnall depot relinquished its allocation of locomotives (and its code 41A) to the brand new depot at Tinsley, which took over from it. Number D1758 was the first Brush Type 4 to be dual brake fitted, equipped for both vacuum and air-braking equipment for trains. This was a direct result of a decision by BR to introduce Liner trains fitted with air-brakes rather than the hitherto standard vacuum brake system for trains fitted with a braking system controlled from locomotives. The concept of using Liner trains as a means of providing a fast and acceptable freight service was established the previous year, another of the features of the new railway, which Dr Beeching supported wholeheartedly to replace the old-fashioned freight train concept. The scheme was much delayed for other reasons, but the compatible locomotives to work the trains were soon provided.

The introduction of air-brake equipment was made as quickly as possible and involved the fitting of an additional electric motor driven air compressor unit and the modification of the existing one, together with approximately 30 cubic feet reservoir capacity and all the associated brake equipment. Existing vacuum equipment had to be retained to enable the locomotives to operate on existing vacuum-fitted trains also. Much modification was necessary within the brake equipment and radiator cubicles. New controls in the cab and additional hose connections on the buffer beams had to be provided. Most of the problems occurred in fitting all the additional equipment in an already confined space within the locomotive body and at the same time maintaining good accessibility for maintenance purposes. In this respect the efforts were not particularly successful. The equipment fitted was the Metcalfe-Oerlikon system, soon to be designated Mark 1 when modification of the layout was made to improve

One of the earliest Type 4 crash victims was D1775 (BT537/1964), although thankfully not sufficiently serious to warrant withdrawal from service.

BRUSH A12689A

accessibility, commencing with D1807 of the next Brush contract. Number D1631 was the first Crewe-built example to be dual brake fitted, some months later.

At about this time BR also required that certain locomotives should be fitted with a slow speed control facility to enable them to haul coal trains at a precise 0.5mph over weighbridges, under loading chutes at collieries and over discharge chutes at power stations. This was connected with the introduction of merry-go-round trains, another of the systems advocated by Dr Beeching which revolutionised such operations and certainly allowed the BR wagon fleet to

D1772 in its original two-tone green livery awaits its next turn of duty at
Liverpool Street station, London, in 1970.

A Hook Continental Boat Train from Liverpool Street arrives at Harwich
Parkeston Quay hauled by a somewhat less pristine member of the class in
the summer of 1971.

JOHN A SENIOR BOTH

A southbound Liner train passing through the Cumbrian fells on the WCML around 1969, before the paraphernalia of electrification had arrived.

JOHN A SENIOR

be much reduced once agreement had been reached among the three parties concerned, BR, the National Coal Board and the Central Electricity Generating Board.

Number D1758 was the first Brush Type 4 to be fitted with this slow-speed control, which was developed by the Electric Control Group of Hawker Siddeley Dynamics.

Initial trials of the system were undertaken once a satisfactory method of indicating 0.5mph had been found. Initially, the system relied upon the driver manipulating the control, but because this operation was not easy an automatic electronic system was devised. Actually, speeds up to 3mph were selectable, upon which the system locked. The additional speedometer catered for indicating these speeds and was prominently mounted on the left hand corner pillar inside the cab. Signals were generated from an electronic probe unit mounted on the outer end of one of the axles. The slow-speed control was applied to D1842 ex-Crewe the following year.

Crewe Works continued its production of Brush Type 4s with no break between contracts. The second contract, placed in June 1962, was for 99 locomotives numbered D1583 to D1681 inclusive. Construction of the first one was under way early in 1964, with locomotives up to D1598 evident by 15th February and up to D1606 on 25th March. On this latter day D1583 was nearing completion and by 10th May it was in the Paint Shop yard prior to delivery later that month to Cardiff (Canton) depot. Construction at Crewe included embryo D1616 on 18th April and a month later eighteen locomotives were being assembled in the Erecting Shop, with others under fabrication elsewhere on the works.

Deliveries of Brush Type 4s escalated as both works supplied the WR, particularly in South Wales. Numbers D1584/5 went to Landore, near Swansea, ex-Crewe during May, but D1586-98 were allocated to Canton during the same month and June. Then D1599-1612 went to Landore, continuing deliveries well into August and D1613-5 went to Canton before the month was out.

The deliveries to the latter depot led to an extension of Brush Type 4 duties in South Wales and also on services connecting the area with the Midlands and the North of England. Some were also employed on steel-carrying trains, including the shuttle trains to Llanwern steelworks.

Crewe Works was making impressive progress. On 14th June in the Paint Shop D1594/5 were noted, final painted, together with D1596 in undercoat and D1597, D1601-3 in primer whilst D1598 was outside the shop in primer; D1599 was also in primer on the diesel test line and D1600 was in the Erecting Shop yard. Inside the Erecting Shop were D1604/5 in primer, with D1606 nearly complete and D1607-22 as bodyshells in various stages of being fitted out. Also in the yards were body shells for D1623-7. Being fabricated in the shops were D1628/9. The visible total was 36 Type 4s. By the end of July production on the works was D1606-32.

By the end of the summer Brush Type 4s had taken over through freight workings between South Wales and Scunthorpe via the Lickey Incline. Crewe Works was engaged on building D1614-44 during August and the Falcon Works had over 70 Type 4s under construction.

The annual open day at Derby Locomotive Works, held on 30th August, featured D1756 ex-Brush on display with other locomotives. Also brand new, D1757/60/1/2 were noted on Derby shed the same day. With these locomotives to choose from the staff were guaranteed no cleaning prior to displaying a Brush Type 4!

On the same day at Crewe Works D1615/6 were in the Paint Shop painted, with D1617/9-21 in primer. The missing D1618 was in primer on the diesel test lines area and inside the Erecting Shop were D1622-4 in primer, D1625 nearly complete and D1626-42 under construction. D1643-51 were body frames in the Fabrication Shop still being fabricated.

During September Crewe started to deliver Type 4s to the LMR, commencing with D1616, which went to Toton depot. The LMR had in the meantime altered its calendar of accounting to the four-weekly period system, so D1616 arrived in Period 9, which ended 5th September 1964. This locomotive was equipped with Stones-Vapor train heating boiler and equipment, whereas those supplied to the WR had been fitted with the Spanner Swirlyflo Mk3. Both types were powered from batteries. D1617-30 were also supplied to Toton soon afterwards; during periods 9 to 11. Early deliveries were noted around the Midland Lines, D1616/8 being reported as working from Nottingham, probably on crew-training duties. Four others, D1622/6-8, were around Kirkby-in-Ashfield on revenue earning duties, hauling freight trains from Toton. D1624 ventured further afield when on 15th October it worked from Euston through to Barrow-in-Furness on a special train, with a BR official party on board, visiting the works of Vickers-Armstrong. The following day BRB Chairman, Dr Beeching, formally took delivery of the one thousandth Sulzer engine for BR from Vickers-Armstrong. The main reason for allocating the batch of Brush Type 4s to Toton was to eliminate steam traction from freight trains in the Nottingham Division.

On 27th September D1619 was seen at Derby Works coupled to dynamometer car M45050.

On 4th October Crewe Paint Shop yard held D1624 in painted condition, and the Paint Shop itself contained D1626/30 in primer and D1627 painted. Numbers D1628/9 were in primer in the test area yard and inside the Erecting Shop were D1631 in primer, D1632/3 nearly complete, D1634 partly equipped and bodyshells D1635-45 being fitted out at lesser stages and the body frames of D1646-8. Meanwhile D1649-56 were still being fabricated in the appropriate shop. By the end of October construction of D1659 had already commenced and D1630 was seen on Derby shed on the 25th. Two of the Toton allocation (D1618/20) were noted in December working from Westhouses depot, employed on coal train block workings to Willington and Staythorpe power stations.

On 1st November the situation at Crewe Works was that D1631/3/4 were to be found in the Paint Shop fully painted, together with D1635 in primer coat. Number D1632 in painted condition was in the test area and D1636/7/9 were in the Erecting Shop in primer. Nearly complete in the same shop were D1638/41 and D1642-57 bodyshells in various stages of assembly, together with the body frame of D1658. Omitted from the foregoing was D1640, to be found in primer inside the Electric Traction Shop.

Number D1631 finally emerged from the works just before the end of October, but it did not have to travel far to its allocated depot, which was Crewe North, situated just across

The Western Region made wide use of its Type 4s, and block oil trains such as this example passing through Chippenham were one example of frequent usage.

JOHN A SENIOR

Number D1758 (BT520/1964), complete with headboard and flags, sets out from Stratford (East London) Freightliner Terminal with the inaugural train of the London-Paris freightliner service on 22nd April 1968.

BR via BRUSH

the lines to Chester. Before the end of period 12 D1632-5 had followed. All these locomotives were intended as replacements for steam traction north and west of Crewe.

Deliveries then returned to the WR for the rest of the contract (D1636-81), with D1636-55 and D1668/70-81 going to Canton depot and D1656-67 and D1669 going to Landore - another flood of diesel electric motive power for South Wales over the period from December 1964 to May 1965. Forty-six locomotives were delivered to eliminate steam in the area.

Crewe Works was certainly kept busy. On 20th December 1964 D1643/4/7 were to be found already painted inside the Paint Shop, together with D1650-2 in primer. In the adjacent yard were D1645/6 in finish painted condition and in the test area yard were D1648/9 in primer. In the Erecting Shop were D1653-5 finished, but in primer, and D1656-70 under construction. Also present as an unfinished bodyframe was the ill-fated D1671, more of which later. The bodyframes of D1672 and D1673 were outside in the yard with the next in line bodyframes of D1674-7 in the Fabrication Shop. Brand new D1642 was already ex-works on Crewe North shed, prior to despatch to the WR.

Two months later, on 21st February 1965, D1662-4 were inside the Paint Shop in painted condition and D1665/7 were in primer. Outside in the yard was D1666 also painted, and in the Erecting Shop were D1668-71 in primer and D1672 nearly complete. Numbers D1673 and D1674 were not far behind together with D1675-81 still under assembly. There were other earlier Brush Type 4s of both builds in the Erecting Shop for attention, including several from the D1500-19 batch.

A start had been made on the next Crewe contract (D1842-61) and the first three were also in the shop.

On 14th March Crewe had progressed to the stage where D1668 was to be found in the Paint Shop finish painted and D1670-2 in primer, with D1669 outside in finish painted

condition also. D1673/4 were complete in the Erecting Shop in primer finish and D1675/6 nearly complete. Also under construction were D1677-81. During April D1675/6 were inside the Paint Shop already painted in the company of D1677/9 in primer. Missing D1678 was in primer in the test area yard, and the last two locomotives of the contract were in the Erecting Shop, D1680 completed, but in primer and D1681 nearly complete. By 16th May all were gone.

Number D1631 was the first Crewe-built Brush Type 4 to receive the dual braking equipment as fitted to D1758 ex-Brush whilst D1639 was the first Crewe example to have the Universal Boiler Compartment, following the pattern established with Brush-built D1782, first of the contract of sixty locomotives which appeared from November 1964 (yet to be described). Numbers D1639-81 were equipped with the Clayton Mk2 train heating boiler. The completion of D1681 closed the long-standing gap between in the number series; D1682 had appeared in October 1963.

Soon after entering service D1666, D1661 and D1662 were named, the first Brush Type 4s to be so treated. Number D1666 was named 'ODIN' at Cardiff on 12th March 1965 and on 20th March 1965 D1661 was named 'NORTH STAR' in true Great Western fashion, by Mr Ray Gunter, the Minister of Labour at the time, at a ceremony held at Paddington station. The locomotive then worked a ten-coach special train non-stop to Bristol, where the second locomotive, D1662, was named 'ISAMBARD KINGDOM BRUNEL' by the Lord Mayor of Bristol. One comment of the day was that "the nameplate looking a little odd next to a Crewe works plate!". Further namings took place early in the careers of locomotives of this batch until the number block D1660-76 had been completed. All were of a Great Western theme, either recalling old locomotive names mostly of beings (mythical or otherwise) of great strength, or famous GWR characters. All were names good and true, unlike some later names of the 1980/90s

Concurrent with these locomotives emerging from Crewe Works was the batch of sixty Type 4s being delivered by Brush, D1782-D1841 and nominally Brush works numbers 544 to 603. They were ordered on 22nd July 1963 and were delivered during the period November 1964 to April 1965.

The first locomotive incorporated changes. Because BR had decided to standardise certain makes of train heating boilers for certain Regions the compartment housing such equipment was redesigned to accept any one of the three choices available, according to the Regional destination, thus was born the universal boiler compartment. As most of these locomotives were not required for passenger train working in the first instance, steam train heating equipment was not fitted until D1837, which received Stone Vapor.

There was no break in production between contracts and D1782 emerged from the Falcon Works on 29th October 1964 in the company of D1784, two days before D1781 of the previous contract. They were allocated to Tinsley depot, Sheffield, in continuation. Deliveries to this depot ceased with D1806 and some examples were stabled in the area at Shirebrook and Wath working slow-speed merry-go-round trains and air-braked freight trains in the Sheffield area. Not all the locomotives left the Falcon Works finish painted, some still went to Derby for this, D1783 being the first of the batch to do so, leaving for painting on 23rd October. D1782-91,93/4 went into service in November and December 1964, with D1792 following the next month. Derby often had an assembly of brand new Brush Type 4s visible on shed, D1791/3/4 being noted there on 29th November. On the same day D1790 was noted inside the Paint Shop of the adjacent works.

On 3rd January 1965 D1802 was inside the Paint Shop and D1792,5-8,1800/1/5 on shed. Numbers D1795-D1806, with the exception of D1804, went into service during January and the odd one the next month.

Numbers D1807 to D1841, the remainder of the contract, were destined for the LMR. Deliveries up to D1836 initially went to the Nottingham Division (Code D16), being based at Toton depot. The remainder went to Crewe North depot.

The first of these, D1807, introduced further change, being equipped with Mk2 automatic air train brake equipment, following difficulties in obtaining proper access to various important parts of the Mk1 brake equipment. More space was required and to obtain this the radiator drain tanks were eliminated together with other small items of equipment. With the new space thus made available the revised and considerably improved layout was installed. Elimination of the radiator drain tank necessitated the provision of

some alternative arrangement to minimise the possibility of radiators freezing up in icy weather conditions during the operation of locomotives at high speed. Various alternative methods were investigated and it was decided that hydrostatically operated shutters should be fitted on the air intakes. Two conspicuously large panels of shutters replaced the three plain grilles at the roof shoulder of the radiator compartment and contrary to other reports, D1807 was the first to have these twin panels. Crewe followed suit with locomotives numbered in the D1670s after D1671. Many of the brand new locomotives of this Crewe-built batch, which appeared prior to the application, were re-equipped within months.

The LMR by early 1965 was working to a four-week monthly period system, which increasingly became out of step with the calendar months as the year progressed.

Numbers D1807-9 went into service during the first period of 1965 and D1810-29 during Period 2, with the remainder of the contract to D1841 during Periods 4, 5 and 6. Period 6 concluded the four weeks ending 19th June, the final delivery from Brush being D1838 and D1840 on 26th April, the latter being sent to Derby for final painting. On 25th April D1828/31/33/35/37/41 were noted on Derby shed. D1826 was used for crew training purposes, and while on such duties was on loan to Leicester depot working to and from Saltley. Locomotives of the Crewe North allocation (D1837-41) were soon noted working through Rugby on Carlisle to Camden parcels trains, so displacing English Electric Type 4s.

Meanwhile, during the last weekend in April, D1820 made a test run hauling a Liner train of 15 cars and a dynamometer car from Derby to Eastleigh, via Acton, Feltham and Woking. The trailing load was 900 tons and the outward journey was made on 24th April with the ensemble returning three days later.

More test runs, using other Brush Type 4s, continued during the following month between Rugby and Manchester.

Deliveries to Crewe North depot continued, but this time with Crewe Works-built machines. Twenty locomotives, D1842-61, ordered in late 1963, were delivered to the depot from Period 5 to Period 9 (week ending 11th September 1965). The building of the first one continued production at Crewe and followed on from D1681 without a break.

As usual production was quick. On 21st February D1842-5 were in the Erecting Shop in the form of body shells, outside in the yard were D1846-8 and in the Fabrication Shop were the future D1849-58. On 14th March D1842-9 were in the Erecting Shop, D1850-2 in the yard and D1853-8 in the Fabrication Shop. About one month later D1842/3 were nearly complete in the Erecting Shop in company with D1844-54. D1855-7 were in the yard and D1856-61 in the Fabrication Shop. On 16th May the first locomotives were ex-works and D1843 was in the Paint Shop finish painted. D1844 had been placed in the yard in primer, but D1845-8 were already in the Paint Shop in primer condition. The Erecting Shop held D1849-61 in the various stages of erection. By 27th June D1853/5-7 were in the Paint Shop and D1858-61 in the Erecting Shop. On 25th July D1855 was in the yard finish painted and in the same condition in the Paint Shop were D1856 and D1858 together with D1859/60 in primer. In the test area was fully-painted

Class 47/0 & 47/3 Nos. 47284 & 47327 round the Dartford Loop between Bexley and Crayford on 2nd August 1979, hauling the 23.50 merry-go-round coal from Welbeck Colliery (Nottinghamshire) to Northfleet in Kent.

BRIAN MORRISON

D1857 and in the Erecting Shop nearly completed D1861.

From the beginning of the summer timetable the locomotives based at Crewe took over some of the North Wales coast trains from English Electric Type 4s and they included most of the London - Holyhead services, but not the 'Irish Mail'.

Locomotives of the D1844-55 batch were soon noted working deep into the Scottish Region on Edinburgh - Stirling trains and on the Callander and Oban line continuing an old tradition of unofficially borrowing visiting locomotives rather than sending them back promptly! Other duties which they operated on were the Birkenhead - Stoke on Trent air-braked freight services, air-braked passenger services north of Crewe and air-braked slow-speed merry-go-round duties to Rugeley and Fiddlers Ferry power stations.

Numbers D1842-56 were fitted with slow speed control, but the remainder were not, being fully wired only. All had the modified axle design, initiated on Brush-built D1682.

The last Brush Type 4 orders were placed in 1964. Brush received its final order, for 100 locomotives, on 24th March (D1862-1961) and Crewe two orders, the first for thirty locomotives (D1962-91) by June and the final order for twenty locomotives (D1992-9, D1100-1111) by September. Rumours at Brush circulated that more were to come, but in the end they proved unfounded and many employees later grudgingly complained that "English Electric's got the last order". They were referring to the fifty Type 4s built by that

company for use north of Crewe until electrification of the route was completed. These were numbered D400-449 and became better known as Class 50. They were developed from the prototype DP2 and were packed with new and novel electronic equipment and rheostatic braking, proving a headache to the manufacturer and operators alike, and although Brush would have liked more orders the retrospective view of your author is that it was well let off without. Brush management, closer to BR intentions, made provision for alternative work – overseas orders and BR locomotive repair and refurbishment work. The latter was cemented early in 1965 with a contract for Brush to repair various locomotives of Types 2, 3 and 4, and refurbish BR Sulzer Type 4s. It was scheduled to last for four years, but much of the work was done earlier rather than later during the period of the contract.

Deliveries of the Brush and Crewe locomotives remained concurrent, the bulk of production reaching BR from mid 1965 to February 1967. Numbers D1862 and D1863 were despatched on 2nd May 1965, but the first of the contract to be despatched was D1864 on 30th April, four days after the last deliveries of the previous contract (D1838 and D1840).

Number D1842 continued the universal boiler compartment as standard and was fitted with Stones-Vapor equipment, as were locomotives up to and including D1874. Manual slow speed control was fitted also, and this was continued up to and including D1920. May 1965 saw D1862-68 and D1873 enter service on the ER, all being allocated to Tinsley depot, Sheffield, itself by this time no stranger to Brush Type 4s. Derby received many of the locomotives from Brush, including some of the last final painting work. D1870 was noted in the Paint Shop on 30th May and on shed were other locomotives fresh from Loughborough, including D1865-9,72/3/7/8. On 4th July D1888 was noted in the Paint Shop and on shed were D1867/75/9/82-7 whilst D1870-2/74,76-8,81 entered service during June, all allocated to Tinsley. However, D1875 was allocated to Immingham, and as it was intended for freight duties was not fitted with any train heating equipment, the boiler compartment being fitted with 35cwt ballast instead. This arrangement ceased with D1900.

Visits by railway enthusiasts to the Falcon Works were comparatively rare. At Crewe they were very regular. One such visit was made to Loughborough on 7th August 1965 and new locomotives noted were D1880 in the test area, together with D1894-8 in finish painted condition and D1910/2/6-8, presumably in primer paint finish – D1899 was noted in one of the shops together with D1903, the latter destined for finish painting at Derby. The Paint Shop held D1900/4/5 and the Erecting Shop (presumably the former Turbine Shop) held D1909/10 and the future D1911-9. The next body shells for D1920-7 were in the yard and those for D1928-34 were under construction in the Superstructure Shop.

Number D1880 at this time was already held on the works, some weeks after its immediate sisters, presumably because it was fitted with a static governor and load regulator. It was noted still at the Falcon Works, as 'under repair' on 20th November, but a more likely reason is that it was undergoing special tests. It was noted in the yard adjacent to the Paint Shop on 4th December. It was despatched from the works on 24th January 1966 and was noted at Derby shed on 6th February. It entered service proper that month operating from Tinsley depot, eight months after being built. Derby shed was host to brand new D1886/94/5 on 15th August 1965.

A decidedly faded class 47 at the head of a rake of blue and grey Mark I coaches leaves Bristol, passing a newly repainted example in Rail Blue livery, around 1969. Between the two class 47s a Western diesel hydraulic loco can just be seen – the Brush machines would replace these in due course.

JOHN A SENIOR

Deliveries to D1900 were to Tinsley and Immingham, the last-named being delivered during September. Another delivery exception was D1894, delayed until December, probably due to being the first one fitted with automatic slow speed control equipment – D1895-7 were also fitted with this equipment. The batch D1862-1900 worked air-braked freight duties around the Sheffield and Scunthorpe areas, including slow speed merry-go-round services from Shirebrook and Knottingley. They also hauled bulk oil trains from Humberside. Early members were often pressed into service at short notice on the 'Talisman' when Deltic locomotives were not available during July and August.

Brush now started to deliver to the WR once more, commencing with D1901 and finishing with D1938, these locomotives entering service over the period October 1965 to April 1966. Most were initially allocated to Cardiff (Canton) depot in south Wales (D1901-26/36-8) and the remainder to Bristol Bath Road.

Those of the former depot worked air-braked passenger services from south Wales to Paddington and air-braked, slow speed merry-go-round services to Aberthaw power station, but D1921-6 were loaned to the Southern Region soon after delivery to work Waterloo - Bournemouth services until Class 74 locomotives arrived in 1968 as part of the 1967 Bournemouth electrification scheme. The Bristol allocation was put to work on air-braked passenger services from there and Weston-super-Mare to Paddington.

Clayton Mk2 steam heating equipment was fitted to these locomotives up to and including D1947, and D1913 became the first to be fitted with static automatic voltage regulation, the rest of the batch to D1951 being so fitted. D1921 onwards were not fitted for slow speed operation.

Number D1901 left the Falcon Works on 10th September 1965, but was preceded by D1904 and D1903 on the 2nd and 3rd respectively. D1906 was spotted on 17th October at Crewe

North depot, having been despatched from Loughborough on 30th September. Derby shed sported brand new D1911-3 on 24th October.

A visit to the Falcon Works on 20th November revealed new Type 4s at various stages thus:- D1920/1 painted and D1922-4 (presumably being painted) in the Paint Shop; D1925-35 under construction and D1936-47 body shells. D1880 and D1894, the two stragglers, were also noted in the yard near the Paint Shop.

Another visit, on 4th December revealed D1923/4 in the Paint Shop, D1925/6 in the Test House and D1927-35 in the Erecting Shop. The situation inside the Superstructure Shops was not reported but D1923 had reached Crewe diesel depot by 2nd January 1966. The first out of the Falcon Works in the new year was D1927, despatched on 12th January. Noted at Derby shed on 6th February were D1929/30 in company with the long-awaited D1880. The same location on 13th March revealed D1934/5. D1938, the last of the WR allocation from Loughborough, left the works on 19th April.

Before outlining the outstanding Loughborough-built locomotives, D1939-61, the output from Crewe (D1962-91) for the WR, Scottish and North Eastern Regions over the similar period as for D1862-1938 should be described, followed by the remainder for the NER from Crewe (D1992-9, D1100-11).

The embryonic D1962 was already evident at Crewe Works by 16th May 1965, when its frames were noted in the yard with those of D1963/4. Inside the Fabrication Shop were D1965-9. By 27th June D1962-7 were already under erection in the Erecting Shop, still being there on 25th July, together with D1968-70. On this latter date D1971/2 were awaiting entry into the shop and D1973-8 were in the Fabrication Shop. By 19th September D1962/3 had gone and D1964-6 were already finish painted, in the Paint Shop with D1968/9 in primer. Number D1967 was also in primer, but in the yard, and D1971-80 were in the Erecting Shop. The Fabrication Shop held D1981-4.

On 17th October the Paint Shop held D1967/9/71 (painted) and D1972-4 in primer, the missing D1968 located already ex-works on Crewe North depot. Elsewhere D1970 was in the test area, the Erecting Shop held D1975-84 and the Fabrication Shop D1985-7. Nearly a month later (14th November) D1974/5/7-9 were being painted, D1976 was in the test area and D1980-9 being erected. Numbers D1972-4 were painted by 17th November.

D1977 was involved in an accident while undergoing running tests north of Crewe, at Southwaite in November, but its entry into service was not noticeably delayed.

Although D1962-7 all went to the WR during September and October 1965, being allocated to Cardiff (Canton), they were soon transferred to the LMR at Crewe. However, D1968-76 were allocated to the Scottish Region, to Haymarket depot in Edinburgh. Their duties were working air-braked passenger trains on the East Coast Main Line between Aberdeen and Newcastle-on-Tyne, in doing so they replaced English Electric Type 4 locomotives. They were not restricted to these duties, of course. From Gushetfaulds, Glasgow, one of the first regular liner trains was hauled by D1971 on 15th November. At the time the locomotive was still operating

from Crewe, prior to its intended allocation.

Haymarket's new Type 4s started to appear daily on runs between Edinburgh (Waverley) and Carlisle, D1968/9/71 being among the first of these locomotives to be noted there.

Numbers D1962-76 were fitted with Stone Vapor train heating equipment and from D1962 and through to the very last Crewe-built locomotive (D1111) static automatic voltage regulators were fitted, the first application being the aforementioned D1913 ex-Brush.

Numbers D1977-89 all went to Gateshead depot on the North Eastern Region (NER) and D1990/1 went to the NER depot at York, all during the period December 1965 to March 1966. They were fitted with Clayton Mk2 train heating equipment and slow speed control. Crewe production by 2nd January 1966 was such that the newest locomotive, D1983, was noted on Crewe diesel depot. D1984 was still in the Paint Shop in painted condition, with D1986/7 in primer. D1985 was in the diesel test area, also in primer. In the Erecting Shop D1988/9 were nearly complete and in the company of the body shells of D1990/1, under assembly.

However, D1988 was noted out on the line on running tests before the month was out. It was back in the works again by 30th January, being noted in the Paint Shop in prior to being delivered to Gateshead early in February.

The same day D1987 was noted in the yard at Crewe Works in painted condition. D1991 was in the Paint Shop on 27th February and reached its York allocation the following month. These NER locomotives were introduced to work the ECML services between Leeds, Newcastle-on-Tyne, and King's Cross.

Crewe continued its production of Brush Type 4s and was engaged on the final contract by early 1966. On 2nd January D1992-7 were already being assembled in the Erecting Shop, D1998 was in the yard awaiting entry and D1999 was in the Fabrication Shop. By 16th January these two and D1100 had joined those in the shop. The situation on 30th January was that D1992 had already reached the Paint Shop but was in primer finish – D1993/4 were almost complete and already D1101/2 had entered the shop for building whilst D1103 was awaiting its entry into the shop. During February D1992-5 were noted in the Paint Shop, but it was evident that production had started to slow down when on 24th April D1995-8 were noted finish painted. That same day D1999, D1100-7 were in the Erecting Shop and D1108-11 in the Fabrication Shop. Production of the last Crewe-built example was already underway. By 8th May D1996/8/9 were already in the Paint Shop and were noted there on the 29th in painted condition. D1992-9 reached the NER during March, April and May 1966.

During the last-named month D1995 was noted on the up 'Yorkshire Pullman' and D1996 on the down train. The latter was noted on some unusual duties during June 1966 in Standedge Tunnel, between Manchester and Huddersfield. Under the direction of the Channel Tunnel Company a special train of nine coaches, including Mobile Laboratory Coach No. 1 (DM395001, a former Lancashire & Yorkshire Railway saloon), was allowed complete possession of both bores for eight hours on 13th June. With ventilation shafts sealed off air pressure and wind speeds through the tunnel bores were

The up Tees-Tyne Pullman descending Stoke Bank at speed in the early '70s, with a mixed rake of traditional and later Metro-Cammell Pullman stock. Some 40 years earlier Mallard had established its world speed record for a steam locomotive on this same stretch of the ECML.

NOEL INGRAM

measured to assist in determining the size of locomotive required for the proposed Channel Tunnel. Tests lasted until the 16th, but D1766 was used as motive power subsequently. One wonders if the results gained were ever used when the 'real' tunnel was started in the late 1980s!

On 29th May 1966 D1100 was noted in the Paint Shop at Crewe in primer coat. D1110-19 were in the Erecting Shop and D1110/1 in the Fabricating Shop. Progress had been made by 7th August in the paint where D1100 had gone into service during the previous month, D1101 was in the Paint Shop and D1103-11 in the Erecting Shop. One further body shell was reported and presumed to be a spare. This was the only report of such, so no further comment can be made at this distance of time. Missing was D1102, which had failed on test the previous week in North Lancashire.

Three weeks later, on the 24th, D1101 was still in primer in the Paint Shop and there was some progress noted with the remainder. Curiously, D1100 was noted as 'ex-works' on Crewe North sidings!

The situation on 11th September 1966 was that D1101 had already gone (August), D1102 was in Crewe North sidings ex-works, D1103 was in the Paint Shop in undercoat and in the Erecting Shop was D1104-11 (D1104 almost complete). Soon D1100 and D1101 were to become frequent visitors to King's Cross. By 9th October D1103/4 were finish

painted, D1105 was in primer and the remainder still under construction. Notably, D1500, the pioneer locomotive from Brush in 1962, was also in the Erecting Shop for attention at the same time as the last Crewe-built example, both offering a comparison regarding development of the design in over four years. Number D1106 was the lowest numbered brand new locomotive to be seen fully painted by 20th November, although returned D1102 and D1104 were present in the New Erecting Shop. D1108 was inside the Paint Shop bearing its primer coat and D1107 was in the yard similarly attired. The by now 'old' Erecting Shop held D1109-11 – D1500 had also ventured into the Paint Shop.

Completion of the contract did not come before the end of the year, but it was close to doing so. On 18th December the Paint Shop held D1107 final painted and D1108-10 in primer whilst D1111 was nearly complete in the Erecting Shop. Over a month later, on 22nd January 1967, D1110 was finish painted and D1111 in primer. D1107 had migrated back to Crewe after leaving the works in December and was noted in the arrival sidings and returned D1102 was in the Electric Traction Shop. On 5th February D1111 was noted in Derby station being hauled through by BR/Sulzer Type 2 No. D5208, having been seen previously at Burton on Trent shed. Number D1111 joined its companions at York during that month and was seen at King's Cross on the 22nd, having come in at the head of a train from Leeds. It returned the same day and was seen on the 27th hauling the up 'Yorkshire Pullman'.

In a change of equipment D1101-11 were fitted with Stone Vapor train heating equipment, rather than the Clayton of their immediate predecessors. They did not have slow speed equipment. No Crewe-built Brush Type 4 received the new BR corporate blue livery when built, although they did later.

The lengthy Type 4 construction run was almost over when the Rail Blue livery was introduced. Consequently, not many new locomotives were turned out in blue from Loughborough. Although not the first one, D1958 provided the first opportunity to photograph the livery at the works on 14th January 1967.

BRUSH A13743

All were painted in two-tone green; they just missed the changeover to blue. Significantly, D1100-11 actually went into service with second-hand engines. This was as a result of the rectification programme of the Sulzer engines at Vickers in Barrow in Furness, a consequence itself of fatigue problems, which had manifested during day to day operation of the Brush Type 4 fleet – more of this later.

The Falcon Works, meanwhile, had continued production of its last contract. D1938, has been noted as the final locomotive to be sent to the WR, entering service in April 1966. Once delivered, it was soon fitted with push-pull equipment. The remainder of the contract, D1939-61 was destined for the LMR. The first of these, D1939, was despatched from the Falcon Works on 7th April 1966 and entered service on the Western Lines of the LMR during Period 4 (four weeks ending 23rd April), being seen on Crewe diesel depot on 24th April. It soon returned to the Falcon Works and was there on 7th May. BR officially accepted D1939 on 15th May.

Other Brush Type 4s in production at the Falcon Works on 7th May 1966 were D1940-1961, the balance of the contract for 100 locomotives. They were noted as follows:- D1940-3/47/55 in the yards; D1944/5 in the Paint Shop; D1946/8 in the Test Area; D1949-54 the Main Erecting Shop (presumably the former Turbine Shop); D1956-61 in the Superstructure

Shops. Number D1940 was despatched on 20th May, the only new locomotive to leave that month. Noted on 30th May were:- D1941-5 in the Paint Shop, D1946-8 in the Test House, D1949-56 in the Main Erecting Shop and D1957-61 in the Superstructure Shop. There were more locomotives in the works undergoing repair or refurbishing, one probable reason for the slowing down of production.

The situation changed when D1941-5 and D1947 were despatched in June 1966 and D1946 in July. D1941-4 went to the Western Lines of the LMR and D1945-7 went to D16, the Nottingham District of the LMR Midland Lines. D1941/3/4/5 were all on Derby shed on 26th June and D1942 was noted at Toton. The latter was probably on a brief loan to D16. Weeks later it was hauling a test train from Cricklewood, on the Midland Main Line. Numbers D1945-61 all officially went into service on the Western Lines, once accepted by BR.

The next new despatch was D1948 (fitted with Stone Vapor train heating boiler) on 1st August according to official sources, but it had been noted at Derby with D1946 during the previous day whilst D1949 left on 18th August and D1950 on the 26th, the latter being noted on Derby shed on 4th September – D1951 followed on 23rd September, the only one to leave that month, and was noted on Derby shed on 9th October. The output for October 1966 was just D1952, which left the works on the 19th.

Next to leave the works was D1953, on 3rd November 1966, later being observed on Derby shed on the 13th. This locomotive was the first Brush Type 4 to receive the new BR corporate blue livery. It is assumed that the stocks of green paint had finally run out – just under two years from the announcement that BR was to have a new corporate image, one more suitable for the age. It must be remembered that D1953 was not the first to receive blue livery when new; D1733 received the experimental livery for publicity purposes in 1964 as part of the XP64 train. The shade of blue was lighter and the livery proved to be the prototype for that applied to D1953. Certainly, the new livery was a contrast to the old two-tone green, attractive when new, but dull after some months in service.

The blue was applied to most of the body sides and the roof area. It was a polyurethane enamel, a two-coat process manufactured by Kearsleys and applied by airless cold spray. The yellow warning panel was replaced by a full yellow cab front, which reached back through to the hinged edges of the cab doors. Under each of the cabside windows was a large version of the new BR double arrow motif. This displaced the running numbers, which migrated to the main bodysides just beyond the cab doors, on the horizontal centre line of the motif. The Brush Sulzer works plates were in an unusual position, on the cab doors. Buffer beams and shanks were black as was the equipment below floor level, including the bogies. Brown was the official colour for the latter undergear.

This basic livery was to become widespread from this time onwards – a familiar feature of the BR scene, even into the 1990s, albeit with detail differences and somewhat displaced by the time that decade had dawned. However, D1953 was no livery prototype, nor was it the first application in the BR fleet. It simply was the first new Brush Type 4 to appear wearing it. Brush first recorded the livery on film when D1958 was photographed on the southern exchange sidings. Indeed, it was D1958, much modified on paper, which featured in the advance publicity for 56 001 during 1975!

Number D1954 was despatched on 7th November and D1955 on the 18th, and both were noted on Derby shed on 18th December. They were followed by D1956 on 12th December, the only new despatch that month, and D1957-9 on 5th, 17th and 30th January 1967. On 22nd January D1954 and D1957 were seen at Crewe, the former bringing D1509 into the works and hauling D1925 and English Electric Type 1 No. D8017 out of the works. On 5th February D1958/9 were seen on Derby shed. D1947 was soon in action on the Midland Main Line hauling the 'The Tartan Arrow' trial train. This was a Company Train of Tartan Arrow Service Ltd, which transferred its Glasgow-London traffic from road to rail, using terminals at Bridgeton and Kentish Town. The train carried its special company livery.

The only locomotives outstanding with regards to being delivered to BR were the final two, D1960 and D1961. To all intents and purposes production of Brush Type 4s was complete, certainly all were built, but some delay with the finishing touches for this last pair was necessary because they incorporated experimental electric train heating equipment, the electrical power source being an alternator attached to the main generator. Some delay therefore was necessary due to the testing and evaluation of this equipment, not only at the Falcon Works, but also at the Railway Technical Centre at Derby and on the main line.

The arrangement involved fitting a brushless AC generator (alternator), which was secured to the free end of the main generator on a common shaft, without extensive alteration to it. It had two power outputs, one of 110 volts and the other 800 volts, both of which were rectified to DC. The former supplied the auxiliary equipment with an output of 55kW and the latter 320kW for train heating purposes. The control and rectifier equipment was fitted neatly between the AC generator and the engine compartment bulkhead, and was cooled by the flow of air drawn into the generator. It was possible to fit this new equipment without engine removal and without disposing of the steam heating equipment still necessary on BR.

It was another practical application of AC generation, as opposed to DC, a trend in which Brush played such an important part. The influence of 'Hawk' and 'Kestrel' technology (see Chapters 7 and 8) was spreading and the resultant conversion of many other diesel electric locomotives to electric train heating (notably Brush Type 2s, Brush Type 4s and some English Electric Type 3s) was to stand Brush in good stead for orders of the relevant equipment.

It may have been the intention to allocate D1960/1 to the Western Region, because the WR red spot route indication transfers were affixed, but in the event they spent much of their early days on the LMR Midland Lines, ostensibly allocated to the Western Lines! The red spot was part of a route restriction system of GWR origin, which graded axle loads by coloured spots where a deeper colour indicated a higher axle load and therefore a greater restriction. This was designed to protect branch lines and routes with a weight restriction from damage to track and bridges. A red spot indicated an axle load in excess of 17 tons 12cwt.

Whatever the original intention, D1960 left the Falcon Works on 5th May 1967 and was noted in the sidings of Crewe Works on the 21st. By 25th June the locomotive was back at the Falcon Works, and at the same time D1961 was noted in the yard, complete in undercoat condition. Number D1960 was added to BR stock officially during Period 12 of 1967 (4 weeks ending 2nd December 1967) and was allocated to the Western Lines of the LMR, being officially accepted on 6th December.

Officially D1961 left the Falcon Works on 8th January 1968 and it was noted at the Railway Technical Centre at Derby on the 20th. It was again noted there on 11th February, but was added to BR stock during Period 5 (4 weeks ending 11th May), officially to the Western Lines of the LMR. The official acceptance date was 5th May 1968.

Considerable running was noted in the Nottingham, Derby and Leicester areas as the equipment was evaluated. The successful outcome of the new form of electric train heating equipment resulted in orders being placed in 1970 for the conversion of Brush Type 4s to electric train heating. Accordingly, D1961 was used on the Midland lines to Cricklewood during 1971, in conjunction with electric train heating tests scheduled by the Research Department of the Railway Technical Centre at Derby. On this occasion it was not the locomotive which was being tested, but the experimental electric train heating equipment and coach air conditioning. Some measure of the degree of compatibility between the locomotive supplying the system and the system itself was also required. This was the period prior to the general introduction of Mk2d coaching stock, fitted with Brush motor-alternator sets.

A total of 512 Brush Type 4 locomotives was built from 1962 to 1967, the Falcon Works producing 310 and Crewe Works 202, but there were never more than 510 in operating stock due to two examples being withdrawn from service when almost new and before all the class had been constructed. The whole effort was unique and controversial because of the variations incorporated during the building programme and the sheer effort by the various firms concerned. Further controversy followed when engine problems manifested themselves after locomotives had run in service for some time. The subject of works numbers of the Brush-built examples is a study in itself and the attention of readers is directed to Appendices 1-1, 3-1 and 8-1, and their accompanying notes.

An Outline of Service History from 1963

The first few Brush Type 4s to enter service made very little impact as the year 1963 dawned; only four had been delivered and there was a need to use the new locomotives for test and crew-familiarisation purposes. The situation soon changed when more had been delivered and the other needs satisfied. By May the first twenty were delivered, but already the ER was making good use of them and they were proving a valuable asset on the East Coast Main Line between London and Peterborough hauling freight trains. They were capable of handling loads equivalent to 75 wagons, an increase of ten from the previous limit using steam or diesel traction of a lower power output. One result of this was a reduction in the number of scheduled trains. It was an instance of the new design altering operating patterns. The fact that the first duties were not passenger mattered not to the ER or Brush, the real truth lay in the immediate advantages to be gained in applying the new power where it was needed. It must be remembered that the ER had been the most critical of the regions over the heavy and underpowered Type 4 predecessors and was the region most advanced in the great effort to eliminate steam traction, and in doing so, became the first contender for the Brush Type 4 allocations. The arrival of the Brush Type 4 coincided with planned changes in freight services. Being a mixed traffic locomotive it was equally at home on both freight and passenger duties. The limitation of most mixed traffic locomotives is that they rarely excel on the extreme duties; usually they are good on most others. The Brush Type 4 was subject to this limitation and it was demonstrated later when they substituted for failed Type 5 'Deltic' locomotives. It was perhaps too much to expect over a sustained period, bearing in mind the power difference between the two types. Their use was not restricted to freight traffic in 1963, they were used on passenger duties also. They became very common on the ECML that year – by November the number delivered had reached fifty.

Change on BR was not restricted to introducing new motive power to replace steam traction. Already moves were afoot to change operating methods and practices, as mentioned above. For years the advantages of having trains marshalled in blocks, rather than a string of individually and variously-loaded wagons were well-known. Indeed, limited applications had run for years. One disadvantage to general change had been the sheer weight of numbers of small, loose-coupled wagons

equipped with only handbrakes – an expensive programme would be required to replace or re-equip with either vacuum or air-brakes where necessary. Finance had been scarce for many years for such programmes, but where wagons so equipped (fitted, in railway parlance) were in operation real savings could be made. The application was particularly appropriate to the business of conveying perishable goods quickly. The old unfitted trains were notoriously slow and the partially fitted ones a compromise.

Another type of block train was the fixed formation involving high capacity wagons dedicated to a specific type of traffic. One such operation had existed for some time in the north-east of England with bulk iron ore traffic between Tyne Dock and Consett iron works. Steam traction had operated on this working for some years, and although an improvement over previous methods was evident it was clear that the system was capable of application elsewhere and could be further refined by the use of diesel traction.

One glaring problem existed with regard to supplying coal to power stations. The collieries tended to hoard thousands of BR mineral wagons, often loaded with coal. This denied BR the revenue-earning use of them and kept excessive numbers of them in stock, an unnecessary expense in provision, repair and upkeep. It was the source of much animosity between BR and the National Coal Board. The problem was being investigated as Dr Beeching arrived on the railway scene; the late G F Fiennes, Chief Operating Officer of BR at the time had been formulating his ideas regarding the way ahead on such matters during this time and concluded with his recommendations during 1962. The so called term 'Merry-go-Round', mgr for short, was coined. Nor was the system restricted to coal traffic; the bulk haulage of the fly ash waste from power stations, of oil traffic and other minerals were all potential applications. The basic concept was one of automatic loading or unloading 'on-the-move' at very low speeds, thus allowing the complete train to remain in operational service.

The bulk haulage of containers was also another traffic in the embryo stage, at least in its modern form. The use of either detachable bodies or containers predated the steam railway, early users being the horse traction Little Eaton Gangway and Nanpantan to Loughborough tramway, to quote just two examples. The most memorable container train of the early 1960s was the 'Condor' a container door to door (hence the condensed title) service which operated between Glasgow and London. This fast link was the precursor of the Liner train, later better known as the Freightliner. The roadrailer concept appeared around this time, but never became a serious contender, although it did some experimental service. The real key to the Liner train concept was the International Standards Organisation (ISO) container – Dr Beeching gave the system his backing. The bulk carriage of goods, freight and minerals was the way ahead, but progress was slower than BR preferred – there was much to be done not only in providing the material but also in convincing others that the preferred way ahead was the correct one. There were other obstacles. Coupled to these ideas was the application of fully fitted braking to the relevant vehicles, fed by and controllable from the locomotive. The Brush Type 4 entered into this changing world and proved to be a capable part of it.

Before the end of 1963 the Type4s were hauling high speed fish traffic from Aberdeen and steel traffic between Scunthorpe and South Wales, the latter offering next-day arrival.

The prototype vehicles for the impending Liner trains were exhibited by BR in April 1964 in the Marylebone Goods Yard in London. Among the improvements incorporated was the air-operated braking system. Indeed the BRB decided to equip other block trains with air-brakes, thus a start was made in the gradual abandonment of the loose-coupled wagon and vacuum braked trains. In taking this decision to standardise on air braking it became necessary to equip locomotives with suitable equipment to supply and control the system. New Brush Type 4s started to emerge suitably equipped, but at the same time retained the vacuum braking equipment. The provision of what is popularly termed dual braking was to remain a feature for many years until the older rolling stock had been withdrawn from service. It was always known that the changeover would be prolonged, the economics dictated this as also did the practicality of it.

The spread of the Brush Type 4 into various parts of the country continued, firstly on inter-regional services and then with regional allocations. The WR started to receive them late in 1963 ex-Brush and during the early part of 1964 the trickle became a steady flow. Meanwhile, Crewe added its contribution to the ER. The increased numbers on the latter led to them appearing on the Great Eastern lines in East Anglia, initially on freight duties once the necessary crew training had been done. By the end of 1964 Stratford, Norwich and March depots had received allocations totalling seven locomotives. There was a significant improvement in services and timekeeping, particularly during the following year when more allocations and re-allocations were made.

January 1964 saw the long term agreement between BR and the CEGB on coal movement to power stations in line with the Beeching Report of the previous year, which had endorsed the mgr principle. This further reinforced the changeover to the air-braking system. It also required slow-speed control for passage of trains through power station facilities, such as weighbridges and over discharge hoppers, at 0.5mph. Some of the Brush Type 4s were suitably equipped with electronic equipment produced by Hawker Siddeley Dynamics.

The more visual aspect of BR presenting a corporate identity appeared in experimental form during 1964, and it has been related how D1733 received an experimental blue livery to match a special XP64 train. This was only part of the slowly emerging modern railway. Similar experimental colour schemes for the new Liner trains appeared at the Marylebone exhibition. The mgr trains never received such attention insofar as the power station services went. Perhaps the operations were too dirty to keep an attractive livery looking so. The fly ash trains remained a plain bauxite colour for years to come.

Number D1773 was often used as a test locomotive for various reasons. Completed during September 1964, it was first reported on the 27th of that month at Derby in base paint ex-Brush. On 26th November it worked a Liner Train on test from Derby to Leicester and following this test remained in

Number 47 242 (D1919) in the corporate blue livery, still with train reporting indicators, parked at Hereford station on 18th April 1976.

A J BOOTH

the Research Department yard at Derby over the following weekend. Months later, it was still not officially taken into BR stock and was still operating on test trains out of Derby in March 1965. On 25th April it was observed in the yard at Derby coupled to Mobile Laboratory Coach No. 1 and in the same area on 30th May. It was based at Derby and had been involved with further testing. On 26th April it ran a special test train of fourteen coaches and the laboratory coach to Trafford Park, Manchester, and back. It was seen on 6th May repeating the run. The tests were being undertaken as part of the efforts to resolve the increasing Sulzer engine problems.

Early in 1964 two of the WR Type 4s developed fractured cylinder liners in the Sulzer engines and while the problem was being investigated a close watch was kept on the other locomotives of the class. The problem was caused by stress points, in machined grooves in the liners, and the fractures started to appear after about 1,000 engine hours. Extra grooves to accommodate rubber sealing rings had been incorporated when the engine had been uprated to 2,750bhp several years previously and a reversion from two to one per liner, the original arrangement, was made. Teams from the manufacturer carried out modifications at BR depots, at the rate of four engines a week. Each modification took three days, including a running test on the engine lasting 15 hours, after which the locomotive was returned to service. Engines under production were modified or incorporated the new arrangement as required.

Early in 1965 the WR began to experience further problems with the Sulzer engines after some time in service. The problems became political when, eventually on 25th July, a national Sunday newspaper reported them somewhat inaccurately and the issue then became clouded for some time. The press had scoured the railway journals for a 'good story'. Compared with the efforts of the press in more modern times the issue was rather tame, but at the time it was embarrassing for the manufacturers and BR. The problems with the engines were further fractures, caused by vibration stresses.

The problems had not been foreseen because of the limited prototype work, which the up-rated engine had done in service initially. The locomotives had been ordered straight from the drawing board in quantity without several years of prototype or initial batch experience preceding mass building. Furthermore, despite considerable test running of the 12LDA 28C engine and the uprated 12LD 28B engine already in service in BR Sulzer Type 4 No. D57 nothing untoward had emerged.

Under these conditions, therefore, it had not been foreseen that stresses caused by vibration would in turn cause fractures in certain areas. It is interesting to note that some were in areas which had been lightened after the original uprating of the 12LDA 28B version of the engine, to bring the locomotive weight to within the Type 4 specification. This action had followed concern by BR that their locomotive weight limit was being exceeded.

Basically, the engine was a fabricated structure with cast steel cross members and steel plate welded together. The close twin crankshaft arrangement also had special problems with regard to rotating balance. The fitting of weights to the affected areas was a compromise. Balancing is not always a finite art. After lengthy investigations the root cause was found to be imbalance, which in turn caused stresses and fractures elsewhere.

When they came, the problems were not confined to the 12LDA 28C engines, but some appeared in the 12LDA 28B version fitted in the 'Peaks'. Some of the problems were related to some sub-standard welding and some concerned corrosion probably due to the use of untreated cooling water. These produced cracks in the welds between the cylinder block top

Perhaps amongst the most impressive workings were the articulated car carrying trains using specially-built double-deck cartic stock as seen here on a very frosty morning at Iver, Buckinghamshire, during 1970.

JOHN A SENIOR

and side walls. Next came cracks in the steel castings, caused by the incidence of sharp corners. Modification of all the 12LDA 28B engines and 184 crankcases for the 12LDA 28C engines ensued, and all new engines were then produced with the alterations built-in.

Most of the cracking problems had been overcome and it appeared that some lesser cracks would take just a little more time to resolve and would not pose a major problem. These were located in the cross girder sections located between the thrust bearings of the two crank shafts and eventually it became clear that resonant vibration was the cause. A resonant frequency is one which is natural within a material and will appear in sympathy with an identical frequency source from without. That source lay in the actions of the cylinders and pistons at certain speeds and piston loadings.

To remedy the causes and effects took time, but following tests with D1773 and in conjunction with the BR Research Department of the Railway Technical Centre it was decided to increase clearances and allow more float for the crankshafts in their bearings. Over the period of July to December 1965 D1821 was used for test purposes connected with these and other faults. It was possible to effect the remedies in the BR workshops without excessive loss of revenue-earning service.

During the winter of 1965/6 two more faults were discovered; cracks in the lubricating oil sump sides and also in the cooling water feed pipe, the latter being an integral and central part of the cylinder block. Although the problems could be detected before locomotives failed in service the relatively inaccessible positions required either engine or major component removal to effect repairs, so in consequence unscheduled attention was necessary in the BR workshops or at Barrow-in-Furness.

Taking the problems as a whole a programme of rectification was necessary with the full agreement and co-operation of Sulzer, Vickers-Armstrong and BR. It took four months to formulate proposals and reach agreement upon a modification programme, which at the same time would minimise the disruption to traffic while the locomotives were receiving attention. Number D1773 went to Crewe Works and was there by 25th July 1965. It was officially added to BR stock on 15th September and allocated to Tinsley depot, but immediately placed on loan to BR Research Department and based at Toton. Tests using suitably modified D1773 and the BR Mobile Testing Units took place on 3/4th January 1966 between Stratford and Norwich, after which the locomotive was sent to Barrow-in-Furness for engine removal and examination. Removal took place early in February and by March a programme of rebalancing 727 engines (201 of the 'Peaks' and 526 of the Brush Type 4s) was formulated. Agreement was reached among the parties and the programme, therefore, commenced in April 1966. At the same time it was agreed that there should be some restriction to further the prevention of stresses occurring. It was decided, therefore, that there should be a temporary reduction in the crankshaft rotational speed to 750rpm, a move that reduced engine output to 2,585bhp and which eventually became permanent. The modification programme was scheduled to have the 12LDA 28C engines of the Brush

locomotives modified by September 1967, and those of the 'Peaks' by the middle of the following year. An average of eight locomotives a week was expected to be withdrawn from service during the modification period and although the losses were to be kept to a minimum some locomotives did not return to their original allocations. The start of the programme coincided with the rundown in production of engines at Barrow-in-Furness and, therefore, the facilities for modifying the engines was that much more readily available than previously, although temporary lifting facilities and buildings had to be provided for engine removal and re-installation. Although the programme was curtailed slightly and some of the problems eased because of preventive measures, it was necessary to continue to monitor the engines and in the long term problems continued to occur. Following D1773, the next locomotives to be modified were D1992, D1937, D1993, D1898, D1933 and D1974.

The whole incident was most unfortunate and some of the earlier criticisms of 1965 appear to have originated from a letter to a newspaper from a "discontented motive power officer on the LMR" on the theme "that BR eggs should not have been concentrated in the Sulzer-engined Type 4 basket to the total exclusion of a production series based on the English Electric DP2". One background to this matter, which may have prompted such a letter was that the BRB had requested tenders from manufacturers for more Type 4 locomotives in at least three combinations, Brush Type 4s with Sulzer engines, Brush Type 4s with English Electric engines and English Electric Type 4s with English Electric engines of 2,700bhp. The Regions are believed to have pressed for the latter and the tendering period expired in July of 1965. A batch of either 50 or 110 locomotives was required and of course the former total was chosen for what became the all-English Electric D400 series, later Class 50. More cautious on this occasion, BR leased the locomotives for the first few years – their troubles (mostly of BR origin in requested design features) caused some headaches in service. Ignoring the 10 to 1 numerical superiority of the Brush Type 4, the Class 50 has had a somewhat shorter operational life; its demise has been more deliberate. By the late 1970s the events of the previous decade were being seen in a different light, but as early as January 1966 a spirited and timely defence of the Brush Type 4 was being made by Mr F H Wood, then Chairman and Managing Director of Brush Electrical Engineering Ltd, against published criticisms of the design and suggestions that it was rushed. As main contractor for the locomotives, Brush soon came into the line of fire, so his reply is as true today as it was then, reminding readers to consider the way the class was introduced and altered whilst in production, mostly at the request of BR. There was very little retrospect available to him in 1966, just practical engineering commonsense. During late 1966 Sulzer and English Electric agreed to collaborate in further development of the then new LVA engine. Against a background of the problems with the LDA engines and the decline in locomotive requirement in Britain it was an economical move. Over the years the Brush Type 4 has been one of the most versatile machines on BR metals, but nevertheless BR never again had Sulzer engines included in a new design. This is fact, not criticism.

It has been stated previously that the maximum number of Brush Type 4s in stock at one time was 510, rather than the 512 total built during the period 1962-7. This was due to two locomotives being involved in accidents during 1965, causing them to sustain damage beyond repair. Although it had been proved beyond doubt that the structural design was extremely rigid and capable of withstanding considerable impact, there were obviously conditions in which a locomotive could be virtually destroyed.

The first casualty was Brush-built D1734 of Bristol (Bath Road) depot when barely eight months in service. On 11th January 1965 it was working the 03.56am Saltney to Pontypool Road partially fitted freight train, consisting of 46 loaded wagons and a brake van totalling 775 tons. It was a clear morning and before first light. The driver failed to stop at a stop board, which was situated at the top of the 1 in 100 Hencote Incline, approaching Coton Hill South yard, near Shrewsbury. Here he was required to stop to allow the guard to pin down hand brakes on some of the wagons – only the first 22 of the 45 wagons were fitted with vacuum brakes. The train ran away out of control down the gradient and it ran into the Up goods loop at 45mph, three times the limit permitted, and overran the loop exit signals. The driver had made a full brake application and the train went through the trap points at 20mph, despite this late brake application. The locomotive and the first eleven wagons were derailed and continued for 72 yards beyond the trap points, demolishing Coton Hill South signal box and killing the signalman in the process. Facing points were opened by this collision and another 24 wagons piled into the buffer stop at the end of the siding. Trapped in the cab the driver was seriously injured and the second man slightly so, but the locomotive sustained extensive damage to its No. 1 cab, including an embedded beam from the wrecked signal box and was so badly damaged that an economic repair could not be effected. Damage to the No. 2 cab from trailing wagons was less extensive. The wreck was taken to Crewe Works and was officially withdrawn from stock in March 1965. It was noted in the Stripping Shop on 14th March and had migrated into the nearby yard soon afterwards. Its remains were cut up in April 1965.

The second casualty that year was Crewe-built D1671 'THOR', of Cardiff depot. During the early morning of 17th December 1965 this locomotive was hauling the 04.00 Carmarthen empty coaching stock train (intended for Christmas shoppers' special trains that week) when it ran into a landslip, caused by heavy rain. The accident occurred as the train approached the cutting east of Bridgend, South Wales. In this cutting, near Coity Junction, D1671 ploughed into the debris and fell over onto the other track and almost immediately the 15.35 (of the previous day) Newton Abbot to Margam fast train of empty mineral wagons double-headed by a pair of English Electric Type 3s, and running four hours late, crashed into it, causing severe damage. The collision was head on and tragically the driver and second man of D1671 were killed, and the damage extended to well behind the cab. The poor crew never stood a chance. The South Wales main line was blocked for three days. Following the accident the locomotive was towed to Bridgend station sidings where it was stored for a while, covered by a tarpaulin. During May or

June 1966 it was sold as scrap to Birds Commercial Motors of Bridgend together with the other victim of the crash, English Electric Type 3 D6983. Both locomotives were almost new, the Brush Type 4 entering service in March 1965. It was scrapped at Bridgend by R S Hayes & Co. by August 1966, having been noted in Hayes' yard until that time. The official withdrawal date from BR stock was August 1966. By late August D1677 was noted bearing the 'THOR' nameplates from D1671, see picture on page 164.

From early 1965 the new corporate blue livery and abbreviated British Rail title came into use, together with the new double arrow motif so familiar to most people until the days of privatisation. The new livery took some time to take effect, but hybrid partial repaints apart, the Brush Type 4s assumed the new livery during works visits and were perhaps later than most classes in first applications.

Block train working was on the increase, but some of the earlier ones were made up from older wagons. At least the decision had been taken during the year to construct no more vacuum braked rolling stock, only air-braked stock.

The beginning of the end for vacuum or hand braked stock had arrived. The Brush Type 4s were well equipped for vacuum and air-braking – a prolonged changeover was expected. Unfortunately, the progress with regard to introducing Liner trains was prolonged, mainly due to detail objections from the railway unions regarding the proposed unrestricted use of the terminals and single-manning on the trains. Meanwhile, the Scottish Region was making preparations for the first BR merry-go-round trains, the automated trains incorporating new high-capacity coal wagons equipped with bottom-discharge doors and two-pipe air-brakes. The first working was scheduled to be the Cockenzie power station near Edinburgh, in 1966. The ER also was making its preparations for mgr introduction at the West Burton power station, then under construction. The fly ash from the power station was to be transported by mgr to Fletton, near Peterborough, where old clay pits were to be filled with the waste. Up to 24 trains a week were planned to carry the fly ash, hauled by Brush Type 4s. Ratcliffe on Soar power station, adjacent to the Midland main line south of Trent, was destined also to add its contribution to traffic.

Brush Type 4s in the number series D1631-81, D1758-1999 and D1100-11 were fitted with the two-pipe air-braking equipment necessary for the new trains. Test runs with new Liner train vehicles were made during April 1965 with D1820 hauling a 900 ton, 15 car train plus dynamometer car from Derby to Eastleigh.

The new Freightliner containers looked smart, with their horizontal broad, flame red bands set against a pearl grey background. On this band was applied the BR double arrow symbol and the legend 'Freightliner'. The first commercial train hauled by a Brush Type 4 set out from Maiden Lane depot, London, to the West Coast Main Line destined for Glasgow on 15th November. On the same day D1971 left Gushetfaulds at 20.17 with the Up Freightliner. It was more symbolic than anything else, the type was to become the primary motive power for such trains for many years.

A Liverpool to London service commenced on 13th June 1966 and a week later a second London - Glasgow train was introduced, then Liverpool - Glasgow and Manchester - Glasgow services in September. This expanding service became so popular that a shortage of containers occurred, though, certainly, there was no shortage of Brush Type 4s to haul these trains.

Progress with the mgr trains was delayed in 1966 and rows of new high-capacity wagons could be seen in storage awaiting the completion of power stations and their facilities for receiving them. Some of the mgr trains were in operation, in particular those serving Ferrybridge power station on the North Eastern Region in South Yorkshire. Again, the Brush Type 4s were there. Oil trains working on the block principle were becoming very common and a staple traffic for them.

It has been mentioned previously that Brush changed to the new blue livery with the painting of D1953, during late 1966. At the same time the previous yellow warning patch applied to the cab fronts was enlarged to include all the cab front and side window surrounds as an extra visual safety aid. This application concerned a variety of BR diesel classes and at the time of introduction was experimental. It was soon adopted as standard and applied to many Brush Type 4s still in green livery, without resort to complete repaints. Examples of the latter noted during the following year were D1588, D1719/38/86, D1843/9/64/71 and D1978.

During 1967 many more freightliner terminals opened and the network of routes developed. On electrified lines electric locomotives were usual motive power for the Liner trains, but elsewhere it was the Brush Type 4. On 9th July the last 'Bournemouth Belle' was hauled by D1924, on loan to the SR from the WR. Despite it being a Pullman service and the last day of operation the locomotive was in unkempt condition.

On 27th November the ER introduced the first passenger trains totally formed from air-braked Mk2a coaching stock. The original series D1500-19 were displaced to secondary East Coast Main Line duties as a result, with D1500-9 going from Finsbury Park depot to Immingham and the remainder to Tinsley depot. Their duties often became east-west in direction, rather than north-south, sometimes reaching the WR on some workings.

Standard gauge BR steam traction ceased in August 1968, the last enclave being in the north-west culminating with a special commemorative run. The Brush Type 4 had done much to displace steam traction, either directly or indirectly. The end meant that no longer would diesel locomotives have to share facilities that were contaminated by the dirt of steam locomotives. Modernisation was to continue and BR prepared for the future. In ten years BR had learnt much regarding diesel traction and prepared to adapt to new requirements and weed out the less successful or non-standard locomotives within its fleet. As soon as steam traction had gone BR dropped the use of the D prefix to the running numbers of its diesel locomotives. The vast majority of diesel locomotives had borne such numbers, the exceptions being only a few pre-nationalisation designs with numbers from 10000 and above. The result in theory was a fleet numbered from 1 to 15236. In reality it took some time for the D prefix to disappear from locomotives. Electric locomotives remained numbered in their own series, many with an E prefix, though not all.

A new locomotive classification scheme was introduced at this time. Class numbers ranged from 1 to 55 for diesel locomotives and from 70 to 86 for electric locomotives. With regard to the former, the higher the class number the higher the output was the general theme, although there were some anomalies. The Brush Type 4 became Class 47, with the exception of the five fitted with Vee engines (D1702-6), which became Class 48.

At the time the most it achieved was to establish a national scheme and abolish all the Regional classifications in all their diverse forms, the ER being the one which constantly revised its classifications. Long term it was the prelude to a computerised classification scheme, TOPS, which has been described in Chapter 4. During the same year a start was made in fitting air-braking equipment to those Class 47s not built with it and this increased the versatility of the class. Such locomotives were more commonly known as dual-braked locomotives, for that is what they became. At least eight examples were so treated in the first year and 37 in 1969. The programme continued well into the 1970s.

Steam and diesel locomotives were never going to make good bedfellows and servicing and maintaining the sophisticated new machines in old fashioned and dirty steam sheds must have been a nightmare.

NOEL INGRAM

By late 1967 the five Class 48s originally based at Tinsley, and fitted experimentally with the Sulzer 12LVA 24 engine rated at 2,650bhp, had amassed 8,000 to 9,000 hours running and 115,000 miles (three of them accumulated 8,000 operating hours and 100,000 miles each in two years). By 1969 some had been reallocated away to Norwich and Stratford depots, but a decision was made to convert them to Class 47 as soon as was convenient. There had been bearing problems, but it is more probable that the reason was due more to make them standard with the rest of the Brush Type 4s (as was possible, considering all the variations in existence). Their popularity had never been high, small quantities of non-standard locomotives rarely are, but they did spend quite a lot of time in Crewe Works for attention, so no great advantage was gained. In February 1968 three of them, D1702/3/6 were there, May two (D1702/5), June one (D1702) and July two (D1702/4). Number D1702 disappeared after this time, but mid-September saw D1705/6 in the works. Before the end of the month D1702 was noted in the arrival sidings of the works and D1704/5 were in the test area. None was reported as on Crewe during November, although it is believed that D1702 was actually there. It was next noted out of use in the departure area in mid-December and remained out of use until July 1969 at least awaiting a decision on the possible conversion to Class 47. This decision was made in April 1969, D1702 was in the Repair Shop by 2nd August, the Erecting Shop by 12th October. It was observed in the Paint Shop on 14th December resplendent in blue livery and bearing the number 1702 and the locomotive emerged duly converted later in the month. During its time in the Erecting Shop it had the legend 'conv. to 1908' written on it. Quite what this meant is uncertain, but D1908 had arrived in the works for stripping following an accident which had rendered it beyond repair. It is probable that D1908 donated some components to 1702. During December all five were in Crewe Works, the following month just D1703/4 were noted, the former remaining there until it too emerged as a Class 47 during November 1970 together with D1706. D1705 followed in April 1971 and D1704 in June 1971. At the end of 1970 the official allocations were D1702, Imminham, and the remainder, Tinsley. The redundant Vee engines eventually found their way to France viaSulzer Bros. to be fitted in French locomotives and the generators were returned to Brush to be made compatible for use with the twin-bank engines.

On the West Coast Main Line the Class 47s were a common sight on the Freightliner trains and some of the named trains such as the 'Royal Scot' and the 'Midday Scot', the former particularly so since January 1966, but their use on the premier passenger work declined rapidly north of Crewe when the English Electric Class 50s (D400-49) entered service from late 1967 onwards. Despite their 2,700bhp rating these new locomotives were commonly used in pairs to enable rapid accelerations away from speed restrictions resulting from electrification work on the route.

The pioneer batch of Class 47s, D1500-19 was converted to dual braking in 1969/70 at Crewe Works, each locomotive gaining the blue livery in the process. They returned to the ECML, being allocated to Finsbury Park and York depots.

On 8th April 1969 at about 14.26 Brush-built D1908, of Cardiff (Canton) depot, was severely damaged in an accident and subsequent fire at Monmore Green, Wolverhampton, on the Stour Valley line of the LMR. A four-car Class AM10 electric multiple unit, the 14.15 from Wolverhampton to Coventry, ran through signals set at danger and crossed from the Up to the Down line at about 45mph. It collided head-on with D1908, which was standing with the 06.30 Class 7 special freight from Chesterfield to Wolverhampton, consisting of thirty two loaded steel wagons. The leading vehicle of the multiple unit rode up through the No. 1 cab of D1908 and into the auxiliary compartment behind, where it ruptured the 500 gallon fuel tank, following which it rode up and over the main engine compartment and fouled the 25kV overhead.

A fierce fire broke out, which further damaged the locomotive before the local fire service could arrive. The drivers of both trains were killed, their trapped bodies not being released until the following day. The second man of D1908 managed to jump clear. The Stour Valley line was blocked for 48 hours. D1908 was taken to Crewe Works, being noted there by 28th May and in the yards there on 22nd June. On 27th July it was in the Erecting Shop, but by 12th October was in the nearby yard, just a body shell completely stripped of equipment. These remains were cut up soon afterwards. Official withdrawal from operating stock was August 1969.

Crewe-built D1617 was lucky to avoid withdrawal in 1969 after being involved in an accident on 9th July of that year. It was hauling the 02.25 Birkenhead to Etruria iron ore train of 1,000 tons which ran out of control when approaching Chester. It was diverted into the diesel depot to avoid the station and the locomotive and train ploughed into other locomotives within causing much damage, the worst of which resulted in the withdrawal and scrapping of four Class 24s (5043/93/138/9). On 2nd August D1617 was noted in Crewe Works yard with damage to both ends. On 9th November it was on the departure siding and returned to traffic soon afterwards.

Towards the end of the 1960s BR, and in particular the LMR, had become very concerned about the high incidence of accidents and collisions which had reached 700 during a six-month period of one year alone. Most were minor, but the severe were devastating in terms of written-off locomotives.

By 1970 the layout of the insignia of the corporate blue livery had changed slightly. The double arrow symbol now appeared once only on each bodyside, adjacent to the centre door. The running numbers migrated to the bodysides rearwards of each cab door. Despite the fact that Class 47s had first worn the livery in 1966 there were many still in two-tone green livery, mainly with full yellow ends (for safety reasons). The running numbers sometimes were the originals with the D prefix deleted or replacements in the corporate style. Most of the green Class 47s were gaining a work-worn appearance. Anyone modelling this class should consult a dated photograph for the correct details. In later years the situation, from the modeller's point of view, became much worse! D1733, the blue XP64 locomotive, eventually gained corporate blue (in the above style). It emerged from Crewe Works, probably in January 1970 being seen in service soon afterwards with this livery. The Brush-Sulzer works plates remained in the unique position to the rear of the cab doors.

In 1970 also, Brush received its first orders for electric train heating equipment to convert Class 47s to ETH, in the same manner as D1960/1 – with train heat alternators. Orders for 134 sets of such equipment were then received for the class.

In the absence of data for the ETH alternators fitted to D1960/1, the rating for some of the conversions is given below from a machine rating plate dated 1973:

Frame size	BL100-30
Output	328kVA eth, 73kVA auxiliary
Power factor	0.91
Voltages	700/88V
Currents	270/480A
Phases	3
Rotational speed	470/1,500rpm
Frequency	62.6/153.3Hz
Excitation voltage	50V
Excitation current	130A

The dual-wound alternators provided power for train heating and auxiliary services. The first conversions (1101-11) probably appeared during 1971, the last of this batch being noted so-fitted in the December and in blue livery. Until this time only 22 Class 47s had been ETH equipped (D1500-19, D1960/1). Some sources have stated that D1101-11 were built with ETH equipment, but this is not so – photographic evidence proves that they were not. During the winter of 1970/1 through to the following winter all this batch had visited Crewe Works and while not all the work was necessarily concerned with the fitting of ETH equipment, there was a definite concentration of work undertaken and they were the last Class 47s to be built at Crewe Works. Behind the conversion move was the BR decision to equip Mark 2 coaching stock with air-conditioning and electric train heating, these coaches being designated Mark 2d and for which Brush received the orders to supply them with motor-alternator sets. Number 1111 was noted hauling Mk2d coaching stock, and fitted with the ETH connections above the buffer beams early in December 1971 on the ECML. Meanwhile, 1109 had worked a test train of Mk2d new coaching stock on the Midland Main Line from Derby to Cricklewood and back on 1st December. From 10th January 1972 the 10.30 Aberdeen - Kings Cross was formed of Mk2d coaches and during the first week it was noted that 1104, 1108 and 1111 had been the motive power.

Further test trains composed of the new coaching stock were noted on the LMR hauled by 1110 on 1st March and 1961 on the 22nd. The latter was a run from Derby to Cricklewood, and this was repeated on 18th April with 1111.

On 23rd May 1970 Stephenson's Britannia Bridge carrying the Chester - Holyhead main line across the Menai Straits was severely damaged by fire. The twin tubes carrying the lines across were distorted beyond repair and a new road and rail deck was designed to replace them. The supporting piers were retained. Apart from the disruption of over 1½ years when a linking shuttle service by road was provided, an immediate problem of main line locomotives isolated at Holyhead had to be solved. Among those isolated were Class 47s D1724, D1940 (both Brush-built) and D1851 (Crewe-built). During

June these had the unusual distinction of being transported by sea between two home destinations, Holyhead and Barrow-in-Furness, so that they could continue in revenue-earning service on the mainland. Seven marooned EE Class 40s also made this unusual journey. Although it took several years to rebuild the bridge it was made passable for rail traffic at the earliest moment; on 18th January 1972 a Class 47 and five bogie tank wagons formed a test train through the temporarily supported Up tube, prior to re-opening on the 30th.

On 13th March 1971 1562 (Crewe-built and still in green livery) of Stratford depot, caught fire when it was hauling the 19.43 Norwich - Liverpool St. service. As it approached a speed restriction at Haughley Junction, near Stowmarket, sparks from the brake application ignited accumulated oil and dirt on one of the bogies. The resultant fire in turn overheated one of the fuel tanks, which exploded, spraying the engine compartment with burning diesel fuel. With the aid of Brush Type 2 No. 5523 the locomotive was disconnected from the train. As 1562 was drawn clear of its train and over Haughley level crossing there was an explosion in the engine compartment. The Ipswich crew gave such valuable assistance with their action that they later received a letter of commendation from the Area Manager. Unfortunately, they were unable to extinguish the fire. The local fire services efforts were also unsuccessful, and the blaze completely burned out the engine compartment of the locomotive, leaving the cabs untouched, at least externally. The leading cab was badly damaged by smoke and the door between the cab and the engine compartment was blown off its hinges and came to rest against the seat of the second man. The engine compartment was completely wrecked and a mass of twisted and buckled metal. Molten metal, particularly alloy from the rocker cover boxes, was as one viewer of the resultant destruction commented "clinging to the engine blocks like lava from a volcano". After the fire 1562 was towed to Ipswich station, where the affected area was sheeted over.

The un-sheeted area of the locomotive appeared undamaged, but the distortion of the body beneath the engine must have been tremendous. 1562 was then taken by special freight train to Crewe Works on 24th March, leaving at 05.35 and limited to a maximum speed of 25mph. Crewe salvaged what it could and on 27th June the remains were noted in the Flag Lane part of the works. That same month was the official withdrawal date, the locomotive being beyond repair. It was gone by September.

Accidents continued to afflict Class 47s, although the class was not the most frequent victim of this trend. On 26th November 1971 1623 was involved in a collision with Class 25 No. 5250 at Sharnbrook on the Midland Main Line. Brake failure on one of the locomotives was the cause and both locomotives were noted a month later near Bedford station. In January 1972 1623, damaged at both ends, was noted in the Erecting Shop at Crewe Works. It was still there in late February, but left repaired within a month.

Also in the works on 30th January awaiting repair was 1836, severely damaged in a collision on Beattock Bank on the Scottish Region portion of the WCML. Running away out of control, 1836 had hit the rear of a preceding freight train at something like 100mph near Wamphray Station, on the night of 6/7th October 1971. The wreckage was extensive because of the speed of impact and the train that 1836 had been hauling consisted of new bogie wagons heavily loaded with steel. The train ran into the rear of a preceding steel train and all the wagons of both trains were derailed. The guard of the preceding train never stood a chance and was killed, but remarkably the crew of 1836 escaped death in what was described as one of the most destructive accidents in Scotland, probably only second to Quintinshill. Both cabs of 1836 were destroyed, and all that was left was the engine compartment and the main frame structure. Amazingly, Crewe Works repaired the badly-damaged victim, which received parts from the deceased D1562, but it was in the Erecting Shops for many months and left before the end of the year.

During 1972 other damaged Class 47s were noted inside Crewe Works; D1638 and D1971 with fire damage, and D1630, D1736, D1813 and D1912 with collision damage. Number D1630 was the victim of a derailment, which occurred during the evening of 11th June, when it was hauling a seaside excursion train, chartered by Kentish Town Railwaymen's Club, returning from Margate. The accident occurred near Eltham Well Hall station. The locomotive jumped the rails on a 20mph restricted curve and continued for 100 yards across a coal yard, coming to rest on its side, sustaining a badly damaged cab. Among those killed was the driver.

Towards the end of 1971 a tentative start was made, with electric locomotives, on the TOPS renumbering of locomotives, following approximately the classification scheme introduced in 1968. Some time was to pass before the Class 47s became involved, but in the meantime a start was made on renumbering BR Sulzer Type 4s early in 1973. This was followed by more details being released on the classification and renumbering of other classes. Class 47 was to be subdivided into three parts. Class 47/1 (47 001-298) was allocated to those locomotives fitted with steam train heating only; 47/2 (47 301-381) was allocated to those with no train heating equipment; and 47/3 (47 401-441) was allocated to those equipped, or to be equipped with electric/dual heating equipment. The total fell far short of the number of Class 47s involved, but the number batches were soon amended to 47 001-298, 47 301-381 and 47 401-529 respectively as more ETH conversions were expected. The situation was fluid. General renumbering started in earnest from around August 1972 and continued well into the following year, with a peak of activity during the winter and spring. During the January a reclassification occurred whereby 47/1 became 47/0, 47/2 became 47/3 and 47/3 became 47/4 in order that they should correspond to a greater degree with the third digit of the new five digit numbers. With more than 100 locomotives to each sub-classification the system could not comply with total visual completeness, but railwaymen know their charges. These classifications remained as such thereafter, being added to as new variants were introduced. Perhaps that it was an extension of the system to conform with Continental numbering is the only speculation available. The vast majority of renumbering was completed before the end of 1974 and there is no doubt that the odd straggler remained.

The renumbering was introduced at a time when numerous Class 47s were continually being converted to ETH, and whilst 47/4 numbers were allocated to those either converted or earmarked for conversion, there were instances where some had two TOPS numbers within a short space of time, before and after conversion. A small handful, two or three perhaps, reverted to the pre-TOPS numbers as a temporary convenience! Locomotives converted to ETH before the renumbering retained their existing numbers as they emerged from Crewe Works, until September 1973, when the renumbering commenced. By this time over seventy examples had been converted.

The ETH number series allocation was 47 401 to 528 with all the conversions being renumbered in ascending order from within the series 1500-1999 and then 1101-11. 47 529 (ex 1551) was added just after the series details had been finalised. Conversion allocations continued thereafter, although there was a period when some conversions numbered above and below 47 529 were appearing concurrently, mainly during mid-1974. The position of the TOPS numbers on the blue livery was to the left on the body side, adjacent to the cab side door, and it appeared once only on each side. This may have been a matter of expediency, since the vast majority of renumbering was done at the depots. Those locomotives which still bore the old green livery had their TOPS numbers applied to the left cab sides, often in a somewhat crude fashion. Of course, there were exceptions in both cases. To those interested bystanders or those working on the railway it was a period of flux and possible confusion.

One renumbering aspect was that it was no longer easy in most cases to readily recognise whether a locomotive was a Brush or Crewe-built example, particularly where works plates were missing. An examination of the type of plating bridging the gap above the buffer beam would provide one clue and to a lesser degree the hinging arrangement of the tail light lenses on the cab fronts. Some Brush employees would have said that the smoothness of the body sides would have indicated a Brush-built locomotive! The ETH conversions continued into 1974 and then ceased temporarily at 47 555.

During September 1974 BR ordered sixty Type 5 heavy freight locomotives of a new design, Class 56. That same month BR decided to equip a Class 47 with a Ruston Paxman 3,520bhp 16RK3CT engine. The engine manufacturer preferred to install its new 12RKC engine, then completing its development, and recommended such, but BR preferred the 16RK3CT due to the perceived urgency of the Class 56 deliveries and the requirement to have worthwhile pre-production engine service. Then, on 29th September 1974, 47 046 (formerly Crewe-built 1628) at the head of a fly-ash train, was derailed north of Peterborough and sustained severe damage. More damage was sustained to the body during re-railing. The first two decisions were connected and the third incident decided for BR engineers which locomotive should serve as a mobile test bed for the engine, electrical and control equipment. At first it was thought that 1715 was the locomotive selected. It was in Crewe Works during the Autumn of 1974 for conversion to ETH as 47 548 and the rumour was to the effect that it would undergo conversion at the Derby Research Centre. This was no more than speculation. In losing 47 046, a valuable 47/0 locomotive, BR decided to retain 1715 (47 125) as such, rather than for its

earmarked conversion to eth as 47 548. It re-entered traffic as 47 125 at the end of the year and the number 47 548 was never reallocated to another locomotive – it was replaced by 47 555 (47 126, originally 1717) converted to eth several months previous. The locomotive to be fitted with the new engine was to receive the new classification 47/6 and the running number 47 601.

The newly-refined 16RK3CT engine was selected as the engine type for Class 56 and it was thought that the duly converted 47 601 would provide valuable experience for the Class 56 designers and help smooth entry into service, a necessity borne of urgency due to the precipitated reversion to coal rather than oil as the principal fuel for firing Britain's power stations. This precipitation was the result of the escalating price of imported oil, itself a political result of the Arab-Israeli war of 1973. Higher-powered freight locomotives were required to haul the anticipated increased coal traffic between the collieries and the power stations. In the event 47 601 had a protracted conversion and was later than anticipated in re-entering service, only a matter of months before the first Class 56 was completed. The story of Class 56 is dealt with in Chapter 11.

Number 47 046 entered Crewe Works and by 26th January 1975 was in the Fabricating Shop being reconstructed. This entailed much replacement of the damaged superstructure and were it not for the authorised expenditure on radically converting a Class 47 it is open to speculation as to whether a repair would otherwise have taken place. Once the fabrication of the body shell was complete it was transferred to the Electric Traction Shop, being noted in there on 23rd February and reported regularly as there until 20th September. On 7th December it was noted in pink primer in the test area. A report appeared stating that "47 601 entered traffic from IM (Immingham depot) at the end of December (1975) following its re-engining and renumbering, and was transferred to Tinsley in the early part of January". If this happened the locomotive must have remained in primer paint condition

and must have been under test to prove equipment prior to being finished. On 25th January the locomotive was noted in Crewe Works, inside the Paint Shop and on 1st April it was in the yard in pink primer, complete with full yellow ends and its new number in position on the body side adjacent to the left cab door. The yellow ends and numbers would be essential for any runs out on the main line, so it may have been out of the works previously. By 4th April it was back in the Electric Traction Shop in the same condition. Shortly after 47 601 went to Tinsley depot and on 28th July it was already at work on an mgr coal working, being noted passing through Retford. It was based at Tinsley depot because this was where the first Class 56s were due to be based, indeed the first example had already been completed in Romania two months previously and was to arrive at Tinsley in August. It did give the depot staff some experience with the new equipment as well as providing a slightly early trial of the haulage powers and reliability of the new equipment. Its duties were the very heavy mgr coal trains.

The new equipment which was fitted in 47 601 required substantial alteration to the Class 47 design. Most of the internal equipment was replaced and the basic body shell required considerable alteration to accept it. It did provide the answer to one of the considerations which engineers must have made during the early 1970s, that of rebuilding Class 47s to a higher output. It was too expensive an exercise.

As with the Class 56s proper, 47 601 was an amalgam of the latest developments in British rail traction. The engine was a development of the English Electric 16CSVT fitted to the Class 50s but refined, updated, uprated to 3,520bhp and re-designated since the late 1960s. By 1974, when the engine was chosen, even English Electric had ceased to exist as a separate company. In 1968 it became part of the General Electric Company (GEC) when an amalgamation of various companies took place. As the name of the Ruston Paxman 16RK3CT engine implies, other absorbed companies' influences had been brought in. Nevertheless, it had a good pedigree, the

EE range of engines had a good traction reputation of many decades of development. The engine was coupled to a Brush three-phase alternator rather than a DC generator and the auxiliary generator was a three-phase alternator also. As it was regarded primarily as a freight locomotive no ETH was provided. In producing alternators the research of the 1960s with 'Hawk' and 'Kestrel' was providing further work for Brush. Engine starting was accomplished by two Bosch starter motors, mounted one each side of the engine. The new engine entailed a completely different cooling system of two circuits and two radiator banks. The radiator fans were driven by a Serck-Behr hydrostatic system similar to that fitted to the majority of the Class 47s. The double panel arrangement of thermostatically controlled shutters of the radiator air intake was retained. The space formerly allocated for use as a boiler compartment was reduced in size and housed the main rectifier for supplying the DC traction motors. The auxiliary alternator fed AC motor driven compressors and traction motor blowers. Electronic control gear replaced much of the electromagnetic control gear, and the power output of the locomotive was controlled by a Woodward engine governor and a thyristor based load regulator unit, subject to driver requirements. Slow speed control equipment was a necessary provision for the mgr duties, but it incorporated the latest improvements. A brake control unit with centralised electronic control was introduced.

The bogies were essentially almost the same as the standard type fitted to Class 47s, and the traction motors and 95mph gearing remained as before. The Class 56 gearing was to be 80mph. Although the traction motors retained their 710 amperes continuous rating their external electrical connection was to be series-parallel. The four-character head codes were sealed off and two electric marker lights installed in each one instead, in keeping with the new policy to discontinue the

use of the former, consequent of the spread of power signal boxes from which staff plotted the course of trains from electric indicator panels and had no provision for observing the trains themselves.

Rated at 3,250bhp, 47 601 was really placed in the Type 5 bracket, but retained the Class 47 classification. This anomaly bothered no-one except the drivers who wished to have a full week of driver familiarisation for each driver. In doing so this caused trouble for the ER Operating Department, which would only pay Tinsley drivers for such training. Obviously, this resulted in a restricted operating schedule of Tinsley and return runs. 47 601 thus radiated from Tinsley hauling coal trains from the South Yorkshire coalfield and the Nottinghamshire and Derbyshire coalfields from the summer of 1976.

47 601 was exhibited with the first Class 56, 56 001, at Tinsley on 9th November for the benefit of railway union representatives. The belated and limited running experience ran parallel with the introduction of the first two batches of Class 56s from Romania and Crewe and lasted just over two years when it went back into Crewe Works in September 1978 for a repeat process as a mobile test bed for the proposed Class 58 locomotive power equipment, the engine of which was the 12RKC, by this time ready for line operation.

By the mid-1970s most of the green Class 47s had been repainted blue, with insignia layouts of one variation or

Blue painted number 1682 passes through Bletchley station whilst giving the stock of the Royal Train an outing from its base at Wolverton Works on a trip round the triangle to turn the train prior to its next regal working.

JOHN A SENIOR

another, depending upon what was in vogue at the time of repainting. About thirty green examples remained during mid-1975, but this total was reduced to about a dozen a year later. One of those still running in green in 1975 was 47 091 'THOR', by this time a very unkempt green and minus its nameplates. The pride of the 1960s WR was wearing thin – literally.

On 31st May 1975 47 206 caught fire at Killiecrankie on the Scottish Region, while hauling the 18.30 Inverness - Kensington (Olympia) Motorail train. It suffered considerable damage. It had reached Crewe Works for attention by 8th June and duly emerged none the worse for its mishap.

A very unusual but practical event took place in January 1976 when Stratford based 47 155 (ex D1748) was separated from its bogies and transported by road on a low loader to West Thurrock Power Station, in Essex. It was installed there as a temporary excitation source for a turbo-alternator after the failure of the usual exciter. It was hired by the Central Electricity Generating Board, at very short notice and delivered power to the equivalent of a sustained 60mph in running service. The loan was brief and by the end of March 47 155 was back in normal BR service.

During 1976 the whole class finally became dual braked after a long and protracted conversion programme lasting some years. 1976 also saw the start of another protracted programme, that of the replacement of the four character head code panels, when the final abandonment of these was officially announced. Class 47s went through numerous combinations of displays of noughts and twin lights over the ensuing years. Another programme commenced, that of the five-year refurbishing routine, the aim of which was to prolong locomotive lives and increase availability. This was the Heavy General Repair programme and Crewe Works was committed to completing two locomotives every working week to enable the class to be fit for operation into the 1990s. The work was centred on improvement and updating equipment and the tackling of some of the weaker points that had emerged over the years. Each locomotive was to be brought up to the standard of being as new as possible. With ten or more years of Class 47 service completed BR by this time knew its locomotives well.

1977 was the Silver Jubilee of the accession of HM Queen Elizabeth II. With Sandringham within Great Eastern territory and a long tradition of 'royal' locomotives Stratford depot decided to celebrate events in a simple but highly effective manner. Two Class 47s, 47 163 and 47 164, were adorned with large Union Flags painted on the body sides, utilising the whole height of the bodyside. The choice of decoration was spot on and very much in keeping with all manner of Union Flag-adorned articles which appeared that year. Officialdom kept a discreet distance from all of this unauthorised adornment and the two locomotives also received red buffer beams and casings, silver buffer faces and silver roofs. The 08.30 Liverpool St.-Norwich and the 15.48 return services ran as 'The Jubilee' from 8th June to 2nd July, being equipped with a special headboard, complete with Union Flag, of course. Following this special effort, the two locomotives were once more placed in normal service and roamed far and wide, reaching such places as Blackpool and York during July. Other

Stratford Class 47s received 'silver' roofs which were actually light grey. This style became a Stratford hallmark for some time hence. The proportions of parts of the Union Flags were not quite correct initially, but they soon received corrective measures. The locomotives were good publicity and worked some special trains, but 47 164 was transferred to York depot and the flags and silver roof were painted out by Stratford before the transfer. On Christmas Eve of that year 47 163 was involved in a serious collision with two electric locomotives at Willesden and suffered fire damage also. This meant a stay in Crewe Works until mid 1979, and the disappearance of the special livery, but it was all good fun while it lasted.

By late 1977 47 367 (Brush-built D1886) became the last Class 47 to run in the old two-tone green livery. This situation occurred when 47 256 was repainted from two-tone green to overall green, rather than blue, with double arrow symbols by Cardiff (Canton) depot following fire damage to the locomotive. The latter soon became the only green member of the class, albeit an exceptional one, when 47 367 was repainted standard blue.

In 1977/8 Crewe Works repaired 47 510 after the fire services dowsed it on the morning of 2nd September 1977. It was piloting 25 155 and caught fire when hauling a bulk clay container train through Follaton, near Totnes in Devon. Flames leapt roof high, but the local fire services saved the day, gaining access through an adjacent field.

After some years of having very little interest in the naming of locomotives BR had a change of heart in 1977. That year witnessed the mass allocation of names to the Class 50 diesel electric locomotives and the new Class 87 electric locomotives. The former were operating on the WR and the latter on the LMR. The ER appeared not to be in favour of following suit, but Stratford decided otherwise, unofficially. 47 460 acquired the name 'GREAT EASTERN' and duly appeared so-named on 3rd April 1978. The 'nameplates' were actually made from black-painted wood with vehicle licence plate lettering. Unofficially they went on and officially they came off – on 20th April. Public response to the naming actually convinced higher authority that something should be done to change matters and the following month approval was granted for six locomotives, all Class 47s due for conversion to eth, to be named after the five counties served by the so-called Great Eastern lines. In 1979 47 169/184/180/172/167/170 received the names 'Great Eastern', 'County of Cambridgeshire', 'County of Suffolk', 'County of Hertfordshire', 'County of Essex' and 'County of Norfolk'. Those ending with 'shire' were not in the strict grammatical sense correct because the shire or county was named after the county town, but it was all a commendable gesture nonetheless. At the time there existed differing opinions on this aspect. It should be noted that they received their names before conversion to eth and indeed 47 170 was not in the best mechanical condition, despite its glossy coat.

One of the former WR named Class 47s, 47 085, by this time on the Great Eastern, had its name 'MAMMOTH' restored (in October 1978) and provided the first example of putting the theory into practice.

47 601, it has been related, went into Crewe Works during September 1978 to be fitted with a new engine. By this time

Ruston-Paxman was able to offer the RK3CT Mk3 engine in twelve-cylinder form instead of sixteen, while still retaining a 3,500bhp output, as a result of progressive development. Clearly, there were advantages to be gained not only in reduced maintenance but lower fuel consumption. BR thinking was already turning towards the design that should supersede Class 56 for its heavy freight locomotive and also provide an export version for the railway workshops of BREL to build. It was a step towards railway designed and built locomotives, rather than buying from the private sector. There was some mutual convenience, therefore, in providing a mobile test bed to evaluate the new engine development prior to entering production with a locomotive design, later to become Class 58, using this engine. The electrical equipment was by this time evaluated, but the engine was nearing the end of its development testing at Ruston Diesels Ltd, Newton-le-Willows, towards the end of 1978. The next stage was to have it fitted into a locomotive.

Number 47 601 was noted in the test area of Crewe Works on 24th September awaiting its turn for attention. By 29th April 1979 it could be found in the Electric Shop with its new engine already installed, and over the next five months remained there receiving attention. In November 1979 it was officially reclassified Class 47/9, given the number 47 901 and reallocated from Tinsley to Cardiff (Canton) depot – all without leaving the works. As with most prototypes one expects problems to arise and they must be met and rectified – 47 901 was no exception in this respect and delays in its release to traffic occurred during works testing. These were caused by the incidence of high engine room temperatures and the resultant need to provide covered louvres in the roof at both ends of the engine. An additional modification was the provision of a headlight to each cab front to make the locomotive more visible at night and in poor visibility conditions, a fitting common by the 1990s. The official completion date was 31st December and 47 901 then spent two weeks at the Railway Technical Centre at Derby early in January 1980. The service rating of the engine was set at 3,300bhp. Its foray out of Crewe Works was short-lived because it was out of traffic on the 21st, due to the engine suffering a camshaft cover failure. Back to Crewe Works went 47 901 for repair, but the engine had to be removed for return to Ruston-Paxman and modification. In the meantime the locomotive rested quietly in the test area awaiting the return of its engine, it was seen in this location on 10th February. Two months later it could be seen in the Electric Shop, there waiting in anticipation for the return due before the end of the month. A return to traffic by early June was expected and on 30th May 47 901 came out of the shops. Its release from the works was on 13th June, but it mysteriously appeared at Mollington Street depot, Birkenhead. By the 19th it was at its intended depot of Cardiff (Canton) and then went to Margam for crew training purposes and to cover runs to Trostre and Velindre on steel traffic. When the patterns of this traffic changed 47 901 moved to Ebbw Junction on 1st July to work trains of imported coal from Cardiff Tidal Sidings and Newport Docks bound for Didcot power station. It took its turn on these duties with the regular Class 56s and its first trials were made in conjunction with 47 205, hauling

45 wagons, each weighing 46 tonnes gross. Trouble was experienced going through the power station facilities at slow speed, but the problem was soon solved. Four trains per day were the normal routine. Whilst at Ebbw Junction, its engine was 'uprated' to 3,500bhp, almost to the true design rating. It was not set on a load bank, but by 'static' governor adjustment. This exercise was done to accelerate 'wear and tear' and, therefore, highlight any developing weaknesses.

The 30th August 1980 was the first Open Day to be held at the Landore depot and 47 901 was an obvious choice for display. It was viewed by many visitors, outside in the yard.

Driver training at Swindon was in progress by mid-January 1981 and this widened its scope of operations a little, but the imported coal traffic came to an end and from 24th August 47 901 reverted to steel traffic, from Llanwern and Pengam to Ebbw Vale. When this traffic was lost by February 1982 it moved to the ARC stone traffic from Stoke Gifford to Wolverton. On 3rd October 1982 47 901 went to Bristol (Bath Road) depot and while outstationed at Westbury it worked stone traffic from Merehead quarry and was not displaced until November 1987, when it was reallocated to Cardiff (Canton) and hauled stone trains from ARC Whatley quarry.

As a test locomotive it had many smaller experimental fittings, including different types of sanding arrangements, but the main interest was always the engine. Strange as it may appear the prototype engine led a relatively trouble-free life compared with the production version in the Class 58s. There were differences as one might expect, the most notable was the fitting of two turbochargers to the prototype and one to each Class 58 engine, but the latter were plagued with piston failures whereas the former was not. In May 1986 47 901 was towed to Toton (the depot for all the Class 58s) and Ruston Paxman engineers removed them for examination. They were replaced by another set and the locomotive was sent to Doncaster Works for running in. Exhaust problems beset the locomotive in 1985/6 and some time was spent out of traffic on occasions.

Remarkably, 47 901 was released from Doncaster Works in February 1988 in the two-tone grey Railfreight Construction livery. Its availability declined in the later years and what was to be its last run came on 11th January 1990 from Theale to Whatley Quarry, after which it ran light locomotive to Westbury where it was held with brake controller problems. It was officially withdrawn from service on 23rd March, ending two years of troubled service. It went to Crewe Works and then transferred to Doncaster Works where components that could be re-used were salvaged. After languishing there for quite some period of time its remains were disposed of to MC Metals of Glasgow, where it went on 17/18th February 1992, being cut up there by 2nd March. Thus ended the career of 47 901, alias D1628, 47 046 and 47 601, which commenced in October 1964.

Class 47 locomotives have proved to be ideal for various experiments over the years. Many of these received little publicity and not all were adopted for further use. By 1971, green-liveried No. 1979 of Knottingley was sporting a warning light on its cab roofs, ahead of the horn grilles. This fitting was in connection with remote control experiments conducted on mgr trains operating through power stations. The Railway

Number 47 601 underwent further rebuilding as the mobile test bed for the Class 58 power equipment. Bearing its final number and the later Railfreight livery, 47 901 rests at Doncaster Works on 26th October 1991.

A J BOOTH

Tecnical Centre (RTC) experiment DL/605 covered the project, which continued for some years and affected Eggborough power station facilities. Two Class 47s were involved, 47 277 (renumbered from 1979) and 47 373. An inductive loop system was developed to enable an automatic operation through the power station, involving an interaction between fixed facilities and the train passing through, to the extent that it was envisaged that the driver could leave his train at the start of operations and regain the cab when the inductive loop system halted it at the finish. Over the years the system was tried and improved, and eventually transferred to Class 56 operation when the locomotive equipment was removed and fitted to 56 073/4.

During the 1970s 47 370/9 were fitted with multiple working equipment whilst allocated to Immingham Depot for working iron ore trains to the Appleby-Frodingham complex at Scunthorpe. It was envisaged that they might operate in a push-pull mode, one locomotive at each end. Two jumper cables were provided on each cab front, adjacent to the route indicator panels, but it is believed that little use was made of the equipment. During this period they became affectionately known as 'Pinky and Perky'.

In 1966 Brush-built D1938 (47 258) had been fitted with 27-way remote control equipment for push-pull working on a proposed Paddington - Birmingham high speed service, but apart from some test running nothing materialised from the exercise and remnants of the extra fittings remained on the locomotive for some years after. The idea of push-pull operations for Class 47 was revived in the 1970s for a much needed improvement in the Glasgow - Edinburgh services.

These services were prestigious and a vital link between the two cities and had already received two boosts since the BR Modernisation Plan of 1955.

The 47½ mile Edinburgh-Glasgow route was re-equipped and provided with inter-city diesel multiple units in 1957. These increased standards of comfort, increased frequency of trains and reduced journey times, at the same time as replacing steam traction on the service. This increased business, much of it new, and the scheme proved successful. The years passed, road competition increased and the dmus became out-dated and less reliable. By the end of the 1960s the time was ripe for another improvement.

After studying various alternatives, including the use of specially adapted Class 47s, it was decided to use a push-pull service utilising two Class 27 Bo-Bos, each of 1,250bhp, and Mark 2 coaching stock for each high speed set, the coaches being sandwiched between the locomotives. All the stock was cascaded from other services and refurbished. A six-coach formation and speeds up to 90mph were set, controlled from either locomotive through a single multi-core cable linking the two locomotives. The new services commenced in May 1971 and these latest improvements lifted the standards once again to a new high level. Time and wear took its toll again, but not to the degree that there was a serious deterioration in the quality of the service available – indeed the 1971 update was expected to be an interim measure. Perhaps this was not a bad idea, for the Class 27s did not take too kindly to the punishing schedules of 700-800 miles per day at high speeds and with quick accelerations. Two to three years of this kind of intensive work led to failures and maintenance difficulties.

Proposals for further upgrading of the services were completed in mid-1977 and received approval by the BRB and the Department of Transport. This time there would be Mark 3 air-conditioned coaching stock and higher-powered locomotives to replace the Class 27s, providing an improved service and reducing maintenance costs. Instead of two locomotives providing a push-pull arrangement at both ends of each trainset, there was to be one which could be driven from either the outermost locomotive cab or from a specially-adapted Mark 2 coach (known as a driving trailer or driving brake open second – DBSO for short) at the other end of the train, depending upon which end was leading.

The locomotive type chosen was the Class 47. An RTC experiment was initiated under No. DL/820 Twelve locomotives were required to operate five regularly diagrammed push-pull sets of coaches. A sixth set was provided to allow for regular scheduled maintenance and twelve locomotives provided a comfortable margin over the regular requirement. If the margin was favourable with few of the batch in Crewe Works for overhaul, then the spare locomotives were quite at home on normal services – indeed they often ranged far and wide, well away from the Scottish Region. The twelve Class 47s were selected from within the 47/4 eth series and all were from among the last few to be built by Brush, ranging from the former D1932 to D1957. They were taken into Crewe Works for a thorough refurbish and overhaul, together with the fitting of a new 'two-wire' control system. Modifications included the replacement of the former boiler water tank by an additional diesel fuel tank of 575 gallons capacity to make re-fuelling less frequent during the high mileage operations.

The 'two-wire' system of control was a Brush-patented scheme developed to allow the implementation of push-pull or multiple unit operation without the need for expensive multi-way jumper cables. Digital techniques were used to enable the two-wire interconnections between the driving position (wherever it may be located) and the locomotive power unit. The two-wire transmission line was capable of being used for simultaneous use for on-train public address purposes, driver-to-guard communication and DC control functions. Each electronic module was designed for a twenty-channel system. The two lines used for the system were the train lighting circuit. The new system used only 300 watts of power and the system was quite ingenious and relatively simple to install. It was a tribute to Brush electronics engineers. The locomotives so converted were designated Class 47/7 and were numbered 47 701-712.

Conversion commenced by mid-1978 and the first locomotive (47 701, ex-47 493, originally D1932) emerged from the workshop at Crewe during the middle of January 1979, named 'Saint Andrew'. On the 26th it was working the Crewe test train from Crewe southwards through Shrewsbury to Church Stretton and back. It then worked north on the 30th heading a freight train from Crewe to Glasgow. It reached its allocated depot of Haymarket, Edinburgh by 2nd February. The decision to name the locomotives was made towards the middle of 1978 and the names allocated all had a Scottish association, but the last two were quickly cancelled in favour of having a public competition to select alternatives. This had the added benefit of generating more publicity for the new services. The livery was standard blue and each cab front sported a spotlight and two jumper cables for the coach lighting circuit connections, one each side of the former head code panel.

Number 47 701 spent some time in the Edinburgh area on empty coaching stock workings and made occasional trips to Carstairs and Aberdeen, but because of the delayed deliveries of the other locomotives it was pressed into service on the ECML, often crossing the border into England. 47 704 was released from Crewe during February, then went to the Railway Technical Centre at Derby, but 47 702/3/5 emerged during March. It had been hoped to start the new service in May 1979, but delays in delivering the coaching stock and locomotives, (particularly the former) deferred this until the start of the winter timetable.

On 2nd May 1979 47 701 was used to haul the 08.00 Edinburgh - Glasgow, high speed service, probably the first occasion that a Class 47/7 had done this albeit because a pair of Class 27s was not available. That month also saw 47 707 enter service, with 47 706 and 47 708 the following month. Deliveries faltered, but the remainder were delivered in September (47 709/11/12) and October (47 710) in time for the introduction of the winter timetable, which was not the case for the rolling stock. Numbers 47 711 and 47 712 entered service unnamed. It is of interest to note that as 47 708 was released for traffic 47 496/8 arrived at Crewe Works for conversion to 47 710/1 respectively. 47 707 'Holyrood' and 47 703 'Saint Mungo' were used on the Stirling - Perth line early in June and 47 702 'Saint Cuthbert' was noted on 25th June on the Settle-Carlisle route at the head of the afternoon Nottingham to Carlisle working. During July the 47/7s were a common sight on the Highland main line. Trial running and driver training with the new rolling stock commenced from 6th August hauled by 47 704 'Dunedin'. 47 704 had previously been used by the Railway Technical Centre operating out of Derby on test runs with a push-pull set of coaches. It had travelled north with the set on 3rd August.

Some of the locomotives acquired grey roofs soon after reaching Scotland, in the fashion of their Great Eastern sisters, relieving the otherwise plain livery. On 22nd September 47 709 'The Lord Provost' reached WR lines when it hauled the 21.56 Stirling - Newton Abbot Motorail service. On 22nd October the inauguration of the new service took place when one train set was brought into revenue-earning service powered by 47 709. 47 706 'Strathclyde' provided the motive power for the rest of the week. The 47/7s did not supplant the Class 27s immediately, but gradually. During November 1979 the 47/7s extended their takeover of the new services, with two sets in operation, sharing duties with the Class 27s operating with two of the older sets.

Generally, the new service settled to an almost trouble-free existence, although teething troubles were experienced. 47 704 continued to operate with one set engaged on driver training duties. By February 1980 all the services were 47/7 operated and some of the displaced Class 27s and their trainsets were used elsewhere in the area, but were disbanded soon afterwards. 47 707 'Holyrood' undertook a rare duty as haulage power for the Royal Train on 5th May 1980, when it was seen passing through Blair Atholl. On 29th July 47 710 'Sir Walter Scott' hauled the Royal Train, bound for Wick, from Mossend to Inverness. There was disruption to the high-speed services when Falkirk Tunnel was closed temporarily, but in general terms the services operated well and were a great improvement. After the tunnel was re-opened they functioned as intended and it was found possible to extend operations to Aberdeen from 2nd February 1981. This came about as a result of a long midday layover in one diagram which allowed two round trips between Glasgow and Aberdeen instead. A buffet car was added to this extension service. The only long term concern with the new services was the adverse effect that the intensive operations might have upon the locomotives, which in fairness were designed for top speeds of 90mph (later 95mph) for short periods, rather than the 100mph maximum sustained speed which was now common practice.

The last two 47/7s received their names on 30th April 1981, following contests to choose them. The names were chosen by listeners of Radio Clyde and Radio Forth in contests organised in conjunction with BR and the winners, assisted by Sir Peter Parker, Chairman of the BRB, unveiled the nameplates at separate ceremonies. 47 711 became 'Greyfriars Bobby' at Edinburgh Waverley station and 47 712 'Lady Diana Spencer' at Glasgow Queen Street station. The latter name was topically popular nationally at the time and the former was in commemoration of the Skye terrier which remained faithful after the death of his master, to the point where he would not leave his grave in Greyfriars Cemetary in Edinburgh for fourteen years. 47 711 was in the new 'large logo' blue livery pioneered by Class 56 No. 56 036 several years previously.

Number 47 701 was involved in a collision with a freight train on 27th October 1982 while hauling the 09.00 Glasgow - Edinburgh push-pull through Winchburgh Junction. The freight train, from Ayr, was in the act of reversing and the impact crushed the cab of 47 701. Happily there were no serious injuries and the locomotive was repaired at Crewe during the following months, receiving a new cab.

On 30th July 1984 the 17.30 Edinburgh-Glasgow push-pull express, accelerating at about 85mph, hit a cow, which had strayed on the line between Polmont and Falkirk High.

The train had just cleared Polmont station when the driver saw the cow and made an emergency brake application, but within seconds the train collided with the unfortunate animal. The train was in push mode, with 47 707 at the rear, and the cow appears to have lifted the wheels and caused the driving trailer to derail. When the various vehicles came to rest, some having ridden up trackside earthworks and some having overtaken others before colliding with each other or trackside obstructions, thirteen passengers had been killed and a further fourteen and three railway staff seriously injured. It was a tragic incident and for once the Class 47 came out of it virtually unscathed. It placed the whole question of high speed push-pull services into the limelight for a while, but the subsequent report found that they were safe, but could be made safer. Whilst prevention of animals straying onto the track was an important factor, the provision of a suitable deflector plate on locomotives and driving trailers was deemed worthy as an early application. For the future of push-pull services of 100mph and above, the accident raised important principles regarding the consequences of such collisions in terms of damage and derailment, as they become progressively greater as speeds increase. Clearly,

the incident did not prevent BR introducing such services elsewhere (electric push-pull trains have operated on the East Coast Main Line since the late 1980s), but improved safety measures resulted from it.

During the mid-1980s the push-pull operations were extended further to Aberdeen, which previously had only the single daily service, and included Perth. This extension required four more Class 47/7s, so during 1984 47 511 'Thames' was earmarked as the first conversion with the intention of appearing as 47 713. Due to the non-arrival of the necessary equipment, it left Crewe Works and returned to traffic for a short period and found its way back in again when the equipment did arrive. By this time 47 713 had been earmarked for conversion from 47 510, so 47 511 became 47 714 instead. 47 715 and 47 716 were formerly 47 502 and 47 507 respectively. All of the batch 47 713-16 were originally among the last Brush-built examples, D1954/55/45/51 respectively.

They appeared from Crewe Works early in 1985 unnamed, but received names over the following months. 47 713 became 'Tayside Region', 47 714 'Grampian Region', 47 715 'Haymarket' and 47 716 'Duke of Edinburgh's Award'. With the additional four locomotives a pool of sixteen locomotives was available to cover all the push-pull services, by this time marketed as 'ScotRail Express'. Diagrammed workings for the Class 47/7s ranged from eleven to seventeen runs each day, averaging 800 miles. This involved twelve locomotives in service and four under maintenance each day to maintain a reliable service. From 1987 the allocation changed when Eastfield depot, in Glasgow took charge. Some of the locomotives and rolling stock were already repainted in the cream, dark grey and light blue livery and presented a complementary appearance. ScotRail in general had already made considerable efforts to brighten its stations and make them attractive also. Conversely, 47 706 had its 'Strathclyde' nameplates removed in April 1986.

Bad luck befell 47 713 when it was damaged by fire in late June 1988, It was stored unserviceable, condemned and then taken into Doncaster Works for stripping of parts. At the same time two other 47/7s were in the works for attention, 47 707 and 47 716. A replacement locomotive, 47 497 (originally D1940) was converted to become 47 717, taking the name 'Tayside Region' from the stricken 47 713. Conversion was completed in September 1988.

By this time ScotRail plans for replacing the push-pull mode of operation were well advanced as part of a further upgrading of the services, this time with the introduction of Class 158 'Express' diesel multiple units. Displaced Class 47/7 locomotives were scheduled to move to the south of England to replace troublesome Class 50s. The changeover to the new 'Express' units was scheduled to take place by the end of 1989, but the delivery of the units was protracted and the revised service did not commence until a year later and in the meantime efforts were made to maintain the services generally with 'Sprinter' and 'Super Sprinter' railcars to relieve the pressure on the Class 47/7s which by this time were suffering from the constant and intensive use and were failing regularly. The transfer of two 47/7s to Network SouthEast in anticipation did not help matters and caused additional problems. 47 714 was already in Stratford Works under overhaul early in 1989 pending its move to Laira depot. Upon release it was actually allocated to Old Oak Common depot. 47 701/5/8/10 were scheduled for overhaul and repaint at Stratford during 1989/90. The second loss came when nameless 47 705 was towed south to Stratford on 5th May 1989 and re-entered service on 11th July working from Old Oak Common. The new timetable commenced on 14th May 1990 without many of the Class 158 trains and the overhaul and transfer southwards of 47/7s was deferred, indeed 47 701 was overhauled and repainted in ScotRail livery at Doncaster Works early in 1990. As the new rolling stock filtered into service 47/7s together with 47/4s started to work northwards to Inverness hauling Mark 2 stock and during the summer of 1990 47 702/7/15/16 were transferred to Old Oak Common. The full Class 158 service came into operation on 5th November 1990 and the remaining examples in Scotland, 47 703/4/6/12/17, filtered southwards to be based at Crewe on parcels train duties. The intensive service that the 47/7s maintained in Scotland over the years from 1979 to 1990 was unparalleled on BR. They amassed the highest mileage of any BR class and achieved the punishing schedules as a result of being a good basic design and being well maintained by Haymarket and Eastfield depot staffs.

At the time the original conversions to 47/7 commenced the WR decided to name some of its 47/4s from the same last Brush-built series. Names chosen were 'Great Western', 'Great Britain', 'Albion', 'Fair Rosamund', 'Thames' and 'Severn' and were applied to 47 500/8/9/10/11/13.

Further conversions to Class 47/4 were authorised in 1979. Thirty were to become 47 556 to 47 585 inclusive, and they were intended for working services on the trans-Pennine route and in East Anglia. The conversions took place during the period 1979 to 1981, the renumbering details are to be found in Appendix 3-2.

On 9th April 1979 the BRB Chairman Sir Peter Parker named 47 555 'Commonwealth Spirit' at St. Pancras station to honour the return to Great Britain of the Ninth Commonwealth Expedition after a rail trip of twelve weeks across India performing the musical 'Kenaki' at places en route. Expedition members were then conveyed on the 14.40 to Derby, hauled by 47 555.

As the decade closed the scene was becoming more colourful and the naming of locomotives was officially back in favour and there was more to come during the ensuing years with Class 47 in the forefront.

The decade ended with the withdrawal of a Class 47 due to an accident. For some years the class had escaped withdrawals, indeed 47 402 had received a new cab after an accident on 5th September 1977 when it was in collision with a dmu at Farnley Junction, two miles west of Leeds City station. Tragically, both drivers died, but the locomotive was repaired. Not so lucky was Haymarket depot's 47 208, formerly D1858 and Crewe-built, on 22nd October 1979. The locomotive was hauling the 09.35 Glasgow-Aberdeen, a train of seven Mark 1 coaches, and ran at a speed of about 60mph into the rear of the 08.44 Glasgow-Dundee near Invergowrie, west of Dundee. At the time, the Dundee train was stationary and the force of the impact pushed the rear three coaches down an embankment onto the northern shore of the Tay estuary. Four people died and eleven were seriously injured. Number 47 208 was severely damaged having suffered damage at both ends. Of those who died were the driver and second man of the Class 47. A Sheriff's inquiry decided that the cause of the accident was driver error, but there was some controversy over the angle at which the semaphore signal was positioned from the horizontal when the train passed. The locomotive was stored unserviceable after the collision, but on 2nd February 1980 it was officially withdrawn from service, the fifth Class 47 victim. It lay at Dundee for four months and was cut up there by BR in April 1980.

On a brighter note, by the end of the decade progress had continued with scheduled overhauls and over half of the class had been refurbished and brought up to date under the Heavy General Repair programme. The namings increased and in November 1979 47 480 was named 'Robin Hood'. The Great Eastern lines sported more Class 47s in special liveries and during May 1980 47 581 'Great Eastern' in immaculate condition, sporting its 'Stratford' grey roof and red buffer beams, headed a formation of modern freight rolling stock past crowds at the 'Rocket 150' celebrations. A companion on the GE, 47 170 was already wearing the large logo livery.

By the end of the 1970s also, Gateshead depot had on its allocation all the former D1500-19 batch (by this time numbered 47 401-20) under its care and some of these received names from 1980, usually with a theme relating to the North-East of England. 47 402 was named very appropriately 'Gateshead' in November 1980, 47 403 became 'The Geordie' the following year. Others were named 'Hadrian', 'Aycliffe', 'Northumbria' and 'North Eastern'. One exception was 47 406 which was named 'Rail Riders' in December 1981 to celebrate the BR club of the same name organised for young travellers. Club member 47 406, nine-year-old David Atkins, unveiled the name at a ceremony at Newcastle Central station.

The plain corporate blue livery was becoming diluted; the winds of change were already upon the locomotives. The large logo theme and the Union Flag efforts of Stratford were largely instrument at initiating the trends.

In 1981 another Class 47 received a special livery in celebration of the Royal Wedding of Prince Charles and Lady Diana Spencer, which took place that year. Number 47 583 'County of Hertfordshire' was given two broad horizontal white stripes, virtually extensions of the large BR logo, along each body side. For some of the time at least, the double arrow logo itself was subject to being embellished with red, white and blue stripes on both its horizontal and angled components. This feature together with the large size running numbers, red-backed nameplate topped with county arms, Stratford roof and overall yellow cab relieved only by black window surrounds, presented a unique and colourful arrangement. There was one thing that Stratford could not be accused of, and that was dullness.

Further namings in 1981 produced 'University of Nottingham' (47 444), 'Benjamin Gimbert G.C.' (47 577) and 'James Nightall G.C.' (47 579). The last two were named at March on 28th September 1981 in honour of the memory of two brave LNER railwaymen who, in the early hours of 2nd June 1944, detached a blazing wagon loaded with forty 500lb bombs from their ammunition train in an attempt to clear the station and town of Soham, Cambridgeshire. The ammunition train consisted of 51 wagons, all laden with bombs for the US Air Force in East Anglia. The threat of all the train exploding was, therefore, in the minds of the crew when they ignored their own safety and hauled the wagon away. As they were doing so the bombs on the blazing wagon exploded, destroying Soham station and nearby houses and leaving a crater 66 feet in diameter and fifteen feet deep. The town of 5,000 inhabitants was saved. Driver Gimbert, 41, was badly injured but Fireman Nightall, 22, was killed. The nearby signalman, Frank Bridges, was also killed, but in separating the wagon from the train a much worse disaster was avoided. Both the driver and fireman were awarded the George Cross, but despite returning to railway service, Mr Gimbert never really recovered from his arm and back injuries. He died in 1976, shortly before his golden wedding anniversary. His widow and the 86-year old uncle of Mr Nightall performed the respective namings.

A curious occurrence took place on 2nd December 1981 when Immingham-based 47 216 was renumbered 47 299,

Class 47/3 No 47 344 approaches Shrewsbury on 14th September 1981, hauling a down engineers train.

BRIAN MORRISON

without any apparent operating, mechanical or electrical reason. Apparently, the staff at the depot were sworn to secrecy and it became extremely difficult to extract information at the time. Even today an air of mystery surrounds the act, but the story which gained the most ascendancy was that some evil fate awaited locomotive 47 216, already supposedly a rogue.

All classes of locomotive have their 'bad' members, those that seem to be always in trouble for one reason or another. 47 216 had its troubles, all easily overcome, but gained a bad reputation wherever it went, or so the story relates. It is said that a clairvoyant telephoned BR and enquired as to whether they had a Class 47 locomotive. The affirmative reply revealed the fact that there were many, but which one did she have in mind? "47 216" she replied, adding that this particular locomotive would suffer a fatal crash. Another version has the clairvoyant actually identifying 47 216 in her initial enquiry. Nonetheless, the news was unusual and unnerving, and shortly afterwards the same office received a warning letter.

Not normally superstitious, but probably trying to allay any possible fears, BR discussed the matter and decided to renumber the locomotive, presumably in the belief that it was the identity that was under threat rather than the locomotive no matter what it was numbered. On the other hand to be

rid of a jinxed identity (these quickly gather reputations regardless) might prove fruitful in the long term.

Whatever was the truth of the matter, 47 299 continued in service and on 9th December 1983 was indeed involved in a fatal accident. It was hauling an oil train through Wrawby Junction near Barnetby when it was involved in a collision with a Cleethorpes-Sheffield dmu. A 19 year-old girl passenger in the dmu was killed and the dmu itself was damaged beyond repair. 47 299 suffered damage to both cabs. At the subsequent inquiry held at Doncaster, it was alleged that a set of points moved on their own after being manually set on site following an indicated 'Track Failure' on the monitoring equipment. After cranking the points, the signalman checked the setting and, satisfied, he and the accompanying flag man retired from the scene. Shortly afterwards the collision occurred, with 47 299 on the wrong line and the dmu being manually flagged past a faulty signal at danger. In engineering terms it was revealed at the inquiry that if a public electricity power supply failure had occurred then it was possible for the points to reset on their own accord. What actually happened is uncertain, but to many the prediction had come true. The reader should draw his or her own conclusion.

There was considerable activity on the naming of Class 47s during 1982, some of which have received mention above. Others included 'Charles Rennie Mackintosh' (47 461), 'Mayflower' (47 558), 'Sir Joshua Reynolds' (47 559), 'University of Leicester' (47 535), 'University of Dundee' (47 550) and 'The Queen Mother' (47 541). This last-named unveiling was performed by The Queen Mother herself, and it was the first occasion that a member of the Royal Family had done this. A replica of her own crest was affixed above each nameplate. 47 539 was named 'Rochdale Pioneers' at Rochdale to commemorate the 28 men who founded the modern Co-operative movement in 1844. So far reasonable names had been selected and names removed, and some, such as 'Thor' and 'Python', had been re-instated.

Accidents continued to happen. On 4th May 1982 47 522 (originally D1105) collided with a tractor at 90mph and left the track at Forteviot, near Perth, while hauling the 11.35 Glasgow-Aberdeen express. Six of the seven coaches also left the track and 58 passengers were injured, four of them seriously. 47 522 careered down a 35ft. embankment and came to rest on its side in water. Damage was considerable, with the cabs and roof badly affected and both bogies sheared off. The tractor disintegrated and badly damaged the cab of the locomotive. By 6th June the locomotive had been removed to Perth. The estimated cost of repair was in excess of £200,000 but it was considered a better option than withdrawal and replacement with an eth-converted 47/0. The monocoque body was relatively undamaged. Crewe Works received it soon afterwards, performed the usual engineering miracles and returned it to traffic during the October of the following year.

Accidents still caused concern for BR, and at one stage during the middle of 1983 seven Class 47s were out of traffic because of accident damage, six of them in Crewe Works. The works was busy with other work, so the accident victims had to be programmed into the system.

Some of this work concerned further conversions of Class 47 to ETH following the announcement of 24 in November 1982. This total was extended by a further 18, and the conversions eventually emerged renumbered 47 586-600, 602-28, omitting 47 601 which had been used for 47 046, converted as a mobile test bed for the Class 56 power equipment. First out of Crewe Works in mid-1983 was 47 586, formerly 47 042, with 47 628 being completed early in 1985.

Namings continued and in 1983 some of the Class 47 examples chosen included 'Wilton Endeavour' for 47 361, bestowed on 22nd July by ICI Chairman Thomas Hutchinson at the ICI Petrochemical & Plastics Division, Wilton-on-Teeside. Another was 'University of Edinburgh' which was given to 47 470 by David Steel MP on 6th July. Number 47 593 received the delightful name 'The Galloway Princess' on 16th September and was followed by 47 562 'Sir William Burrell' on the 19th and 47 592 'County of Avon' on the 30th, the latter being named at a ceremony conducted at Bristol Temple Meads station. The great engineer Thomas Telford was commemorated by the naming of 47 590 at Wellington station on 21st October and on 4th November the ample bodyside space of 47 595 received 'Confederation of British Industry'. This rather long, though unexciting name was unveiled at a ceremony held at Glasgow Central station on 4th November on the occasion of the first CBI conference to be held in that city.

Somewhat late in its life 47 408, one of the original Brush Type 4s dating from 1963, was named 'Finsbury Park' on 10th March 1984 at Bounds Green depot to commemorate the by then closed Finsbury Park motive power depot and 47 596 was named 'Aldeburgh Festival' on 8th June 1984 at Liverpool Street station. 47 574 then received the name 'Lloyd's List' at the same station on 11th December in celebration of the 250th anniversary of Lloyd's List and the three million copies of the list carried annually at the time by BR from Colchester, where it had been published since 1973.

On 24th June 1984 47 452 was derailed on a curve at Morpeth while hauling the 19.50 Aberdeen - Kings Cross at speed. The locomotive came to rest on its side as did some of the coaches, and it was very fortunate that no-one was killed. The tarpaulin-covered locomotive was observed being hauled through York by Brush Type 2 31 277 on 18th July, en route for Crewe Works. Next, on 30th September at about 15.00, 47 331 hauling the 11.40 Manchester - Gatwick was derailed after passing Bentley Heath Crossing, between Solihull and Dorridge. The train had been diverted due to engineering work. The locomotive and all the coaches left the rails but were prevented from falling over by Cartic wagons on an adjacent track. Number 47 452 was despatched to Crewe Works for repair. It proved to be a lengthy task, the locomotive eventually emerged in October 1986.

As the winter of 1984/5 approached, ScotRail introduced its own livery for locomotives and coaching stock, an adaptation of the Advanced Passenger Train livery, but with blue stripe replacing the red. This was introduced at about the same time that the APT livery was extended to locomotives elsewhere on BR. The ScotRail version was for use on services within Scotland. ScotRail also utilised the APT livery for services across the border, but both versions bore the ScotRail

Modified for ScotRail's Glasgow-Edinburgh service, push-pull
Class 47 No. 47 717 pauses at Leeds Holbeck en route to
Crewe Works for a repaint, 14th April 1991.

M J STRETTON

branching on locomotives. Number 47 614, originally D1733
and the unique XP64 locomotive, was earmarked as the
first to receive the internal ScotRail livery, but it was 47 708
'Waverley' which actually was the first to be repainted so. It
made its debut in November 1984 and the ScotRail branding
appeared as two separate words for the first time. It was a
most attractive livery.

As the year drew to a close, it was announced that 52 more
Class 47s were to be converted to ETH and numbered 47 629 to
47 680 inclusive. In actual fact only 38 were converted, during
the period late 1985 to March 1987, bringing the series to an
end with 47 665, despite various permutations regarding the
number series prior to finishing the conversions. These were
to be the last ETH conversions for Class 47 and they speeded
up the final elimination of steam heating on BR passenger
services. No doubt the maintenance staff were pleased about
this event, having struggled with indifferent steam heating
boilers and controls for many years.

As 1985 dawned Class 47 was noticeably entering into a
new era. Firstly there were the new liveries and a growing
interest among railway enthusiasts in the original twenty
members, by now numbered 47 401-20 and giving cause
for concern to BR as their availability declined. Despite
this BR continued to give some of them names and railway
enthusiasts nicknamed them 'Generators' because of their
electric train heating generators, which it may be remembered,
were DC. Talk of 47 401, the pioneer D1500, being preserved
by the National Railway Museum upon withdrawal from
service was very much on the lips of the railway press and
enthusiasts, but when this did occur the NRM was not
interested. The museum people had their reasons, but how
could such an historic locomotive be passed over? It was
left to railway enthusiasts to secure it eventually, and it was

perhaps the reminder of the fate of the pioneer LMS/English
Electric main line diesel electric locomotive No. 10000 which
provided the impetus to avoid the scrapping of 47 401 and
the reminder that official bodies could not always be relied
upon to save a locomotive.

The decline of the BR Corporate blue livery of 1965/6
continued, although Crewe Works still outshopped
locomotives bearing it during 1984/5. The WR saw fit to
repaint some of its Class 47s in green livery, in suitably
modified form. First to receive the livery was 47 484 'Isambard
Kingdom Brunel' which was noted during late November
1984 being repainted. This was in connection with the pending
events for the GWR 150 celebrations commemorating the
150th anniversary of the Great Western Railway in 1985.
Initially, the livery was rendered in too light a shade of green
for GWR green, so the first examples were repainted in the
correct shade. Initially also, they had the running numbers
in transfer form, but within months they were carried on cast
brass cab side number plates in true GWR fashion and new
cast brass nameplates were also provided. The orange black
orange lining was applied around the main body side area in
a simple and effective manner. It is pleasing to note that the
temptation to apply complicated lining was avoided; it rarely
is effective on diesel locomotives. Numbers 47 628 'Sir Daniel
Gooch', 47 500 'Great Western' and 47 079 'G.J. Churchward'
then followed suit, although the latter was not fitted with
ETH and was thus restricted to passenger work during the
summer months. The BR double arrow emblem was fitted in
polished raised metal.

It fell to Stratford to repaint 47 487 into InterCity livery
during 1985 and in doing so it became the first of the class
to receive it. This livery had, by this time, a prolonged
acceptance. It originated with the Advanced Passenger
Train and in modified form was applied tentatively to some
AC electric locomotives and coaching stock in the form of
a so-called 'Executive' livery. As related above, ScotRail
adopted it, but replaced the red stripe with a blue one. By
1985 this scheme had been adopted by InterCity. Crewe
Works, meanwhile, increased its output of large logo blue for

Intercity liveried 47 846 THOR (D1677) in ex-works condition at Doncaster Works on 23rd March 1991. This was the second Type 4 to carry this name; the first, D1671, was scrapped following a serious accident described on page 148.

A J BOOTH

repainted locomotives. The livery situation was changing and the corporate image fading as the new business sectors of BR attempted to make their visual impact. Railfreight grey was introduced to Class 47 when 47 050 was repainted by Crewe Works during August 1985. The cab side numerals were somewhat larger than standard and were black, rather than standard white, to contrast with the yellow cab background. It was then exhibited at the Open Day at Coalville.

In 1985 BR unveiled plans for its future motive power requirements until the turn of the century. It was ambitious and envisaged a combination of new and refurbished motive power together with the withdrawal of older and less reliable units. Changing circumstances and the ever-impending privatisation of the railways led to the modification of the plans during the early years and some projected locomotive designs were never built. The future of Class 47 was to entail imposing some speed restriction in the operation of 47/0 and 47/3 and withdraw them over the 1992-5 period. Being Railfreight locomotives those without boilers would receive the grey/red Railfreight livery and would be replaced in due time by new locomotives. 47/4 was to continue without being allowed to run down unduly, with withdrawals commencing in 1992 and continuing indefinitely. No decision regarding their livery was made at the time. The 47/4s were scheduled for replacement by a proposed Class 48 design of 3,200bhp and the Railfreight locomotives were to be replaced by a proposed Class 38 design of 1,800 to 2,000bhp. Neither new design was built and external developments, mainly from the USA, changed the plans. Instead, Railfreight ordered 100 Type 5 Co-Co diesel electric locomotives of Class 60 in 1988

and delivery of these, combined with a general recession and decline in the coal industry, altered the course of events further. The planned introduction of new electric locomotives did take place and displaced HSTs were cascaded onto previously locomotive-hauled passenger services. The 47/4s were affected by these changes. It must be also remembered that most Class 47s would be approaching the end of their economic working lives during the mid 1990s, the railway 'one score years and ten' as it were, so it was against this background that the class soldiered on.

In 1985 much of this was not in the minds of those who promoted the names for locomotives. It was the year of prolific naming ceremonies and the GWR 150 celebrations played no mean part of it. New names were traditional and regional to the old GWR, with some being regionally topical. There was 'Sant Dewi/Saint David' (47 600), 'Y Draig/The Red Dragon' (47 616), 'Windsor Castle' (47 620), 'Glorious Devon' (47 602), 'County of Somerset' (47 603), 'Fire Fly' (47 609 and involving the fitting of unique divided nameplates). The amendment of 47 508 'Great Britain' to 'S.S. Great Britain' directed attention to Bristol and the return there of the old steamship from the Falkland Islands. 'Red Star' (47 567) of Cardiff depot celebrated a yacht of the same name and large red stars were affixed to the body sides, mercifully one each side. Somewhat belatedly, 47 409 became 'David Lloyd George' at Kings Cross station and 47 517 became 'Andrew Carnegie' at Edinburgh. 47 421 was named collectively 'The Brontës of Haworth' at Haworth on 8th August, with the co-operation of the preservation movement on the Keighley & Worth Valley Railway.

Not all the events were happy. 47 324 of Bescot depot was severely damaged on 12th April 1985 after suffering brake failure at Oxley near Wolverhampton. The locomotive was hauling an mgr train of thirty hopper wagons, weighing 1,400 tons at the time, and following the brake failure it was propelled by the train, derailed and nearly pushed from a bridge into an adjacent canal. Number 47 324 was sent to Crewe Works for attention, eventually emerging fully repaired during February 1986.

Few technical advances had been made with Class 47s for several years, but in 1985 one experiment did appear. This was the so-called Sepex experiment in better control of wheel slip and the development of high adhesion. It had particularly useful application for wet rail operating conditions. Colliery railway systems often had the rails submerged beneath coal slurry, so any improvement in adhesive capabilities was most desirable. The term Sepex is an abbreviation for separately excited traction motor fields. Normally, traction motors were series wound and thus had self-excitation and the same current was applied to both the rotating armature and the static field coils. With separate excitation the current in the field coils is supplied from a separate source and controlled independently, hence the term 'separately excited'. The motors were normally connected together electrically in parallel, but under the new arrangement each one was separately excited on an individual basis. Number 47 543 was chosen as the guinea pig locomotive and Brush Electrical Machines Ltd, Traction Division, undertook the design and modification which was carried out at Derby. The torque/speed characteristic of the new arrangement was very steep with a constant armature voltage and this resulted in a self-corrective arrangement whenever wheelslip commenced because the increase in rotative speed resulted in a rapid decrease in tractive effort. In addition to this the external control of the motor characteristics by electronic regulation provided another advantage with a wide range of possibilities. At the time the experiment demonstrated that there was a British alternative to the US built high adhesion locomotives of Class 59, which had recently been delivered to the Foster Yeoman company.

Trials took place on specially prepared rusty track, wet and coated with a paste-like substance to reduce adhesion. Number 47 543 was loaded with twenty loaded stone wagons, a brake van and Class 47 47 064, a train of 950 tonnes. It not only started this test train successfully on a 1 in 100 rising gradient but also maintained a sure grip on the rails thereafter. In the long term it was one feature which contributed to the Class 60 contract being placed with a British locomotive builder, and happily for Loughborough, in particular Brush.

One of the most unusual mgr concept train services was initiated on 15th November 1985 when 47 592 'County of Avon' hauled an inaugural train of containerised rubbish from Bristol Barrow Road waste compaction plant to re-fill brick-clay pits at Calvert in North Bucks. It was not the first such waste transfer train, but at the time the longest distance yet attempted, involving a round trip of 300 miles. Normal haulage for the regular runs was by 47/0 locomotives.

A new Class 47 feature proposed during 1985 was the fitting of extra fuel tanks to some of the latest ETH conversions to increase their operating range. By the end of 1985 it became clearer as to what the policy was with regard to livery. The 47/0 and 47/3 locomotives without operational boilers were to receive Railfreight grey and those with operational boilers the standard corporate blue. 47/4s were to receive the so-called large logo blue livery, but in special cases, where the

The pioneer Brush Type 4 47 401 (originally D1500) preparing to leave Oxford Station with a Cowley-Bathgate car train on 20th July 1989. Note the side screens to prevent damage to the motor vehicles caused by flying ballast, often happening when trains passed at high speed. Compare with the earlier photograph on page 146.

M J STRETTON

Number 47 218 'United Transport Europe' hauling two tank wagons on the up line of the Midland Main Line at Cossington, between Loughborough and Leicester on 16th July 1991.

M J STRETTON

operating region required it, the InterCity livery of dark grey and cream with red stripe was to be applied. There was little evidence of the changes before the year was out, but 1986 saw a considerable increase.

The new year was still young when Class 47 withdrawals from service started in a more deliberate manner. The pioneer batch 47 401-20 was proving troublesome and accident victims were treated in a less benevolent manner. Hitherto, an accident victim had to be in a very bad state to warrant withdrawal and from this time onwards such locomotives became a handy source of spare parts that kept other Class 47s in service. This was to be so with those withdrawn from within the pioneer batch, the popularly styled 'Generators'. Number 47 401 just escaped withdrawal and emerged from Crewe Works fresh from overhaul in large logo livery.

Not so fortunate was 47 111 (originally D1699). This locomotive sustained a wrecked cab in a high-speed collision at Preston with a runaway two-car diesel multiple unit at about 18.45 on 19th January 1986. At the time 47 111 was standing before a signal showing red, and almost as soon as it had stopped at the signal its driver saw the dmu approaching. He and another driver in the cab had time only to jump from the cab, but nothing else. This certainly saved their lives. After the collision he ensured that other traffic was stopped, alerted the rescue services and then climbed into the dmu to calm the passengers and determine what injuries they had sustained. He was not injured, but was drenched with diesel fuel from a

burst fuel tank and received hospital treatment for this. The Class 47 was moved to Lostock Hall depot for storage and then went to Crewe Works for an assessment and costing of remedial repairs. It appears that although the damage was restricted to the cab area the estimated £60,000 expense of repairing the locomotive was considered not worthwhile and it was withdrawn from service in February 1986. Certainly, the equipment thus released as a source of spare parts was an attractive prospect. Number 47 111 marked a turning point in Class 47 history in this respect. The locomotive was then towed to Cardiff (Canton) depot and arrived there on 29th March. It stayed for many months, being stripped of useful equipment, the remains being cut up on site in March 1987.

Following a BRB request to select three of the 'Generators' for withdrawal to provide spare parts for the other seventeen, 47 405, 47 414 and 47 416 were taken out of traffic in March 1986. The demise of two of them marked another turning point in the Class 47 history – withdrawal without accident damage. 47 414 had damage caused by collision with a concrete beam. The aim was to lift the low availability of the 'Generators' from 50% to 58.8%. Equipment was to be donated to 47 420. The remaining total of seventeen was soon reduced by one when 47 408 was withdrawn in the July and further when 47 409 went in August and 47 403 in September. Stratford Works received 47 414 and Doncaster Works received 47 405/16, this last pair appearing as part of the locomotive display during the works open day on 4th May. By July 47 414 joined them and the trio was despatched to Crewe Works for stripping, arriving there on 22nd July.

There had been some possibility that the body shells of 47 405/14/6 would be retained for re-use as part of a programme which included re-engining, but this did not occur and indeed the programme itself did not materialise. About this time Brush had presented proposals for the remanufacture and progressive modernisation of selected Class 47 locomotives, and this included the provision of 95mph mixed traffic units of 3,000bhp, 100mph passenger/parcels units of 3,000bhp and 60mph freight only units of 2,000bhp. Among the re-equipping proposals the Sulzer engines were to be replaced by 3,000bhp Mirrlees Blackstone ELS 12 II engines or 2,000bhp Mirrlees Blackstone 6MB275 engines. The proposals did not materialise, although some limited comparative re-equipping of Class 37 locomotives did soon afterwards.

Of these locomotives perhaps the remains of 47 403 had the most bizarre disposal. It went to the Ministry of Defence establishment at Moreton-on-Lugg, north of Hereford, arriving on 13th October 1986. Here, it is believed to have provided the SAS regiment with suitable training facilities together with some ex-BR coaching stock.

During mid-1986 Crewe Works was host to five Class 47s in for repair following collision damage, these being 47 150/334/452/73/589. Another member of the class was soon to be involved in a collision. On 23rd September of that year 47 464 failed at Elgin whilst hauling the 09.35 Aberdeen - Inverness train. 37 416, at the head of the 10.25 from Inverness standing at Elgin, was detached and went to rescue it, but collided with it instead. Six passengers were injured and the cab of 47 464 was extensively damaged. Withdrawal of the Class 47 soon followed, on 2nd October, and after a standing at Polmadie depot for a while it was sent to Crewe Works and the remains were finally cut up in November 1987.

September 1986 saw the withdrawal of 47 275 (due to a main generator explosion) and 47 282 (following a collision near Micheldever, Hampshire, on 27th April 1986) and in November 47 001 followed. 47 001 was originally D1520, the first of the so-called standard series. The withdrawals for the year totalled eleven, and marked the start of culling of the class on a regular basis.

Namings continued unabated during 1986. On 27th January 47 280 was named 'Pedigree' at the Pedigree Petfoods depot in Melton Mowbray, Leicestershire. This marked the start of a major contract to move petfood from the depot by rail. On 13th February 47 457 was named 'Ben Line' at Southampton Central station. Of course, the name commemorated the shipping line, but perhaps passengers could mistake it for a celebrity or (north of the Border) a remote Scottish mountain!

April was a good month for naming. First was on the 8th when 47 379 was named 'Total Energy' at Leeds station, by Robert Judin, Managing Director of Total Oil (GB) Ltd, to celebrate a relationship of 21 years between the company and BR. Then at the same location came 'Holbeck' on the 15th, bestowed upon 47 425 by retired driver Fred Whatmough. Following this came 'Herbert Austin' for 47 337 in a naming ceremony at Longbridge on the 24th. This celebrated the relationship of 80 years standing between the railways and Austin Rover (and its predecessors). Named after the founder of the firm, 47 337 then hauled a trainload of new cars out of the company's car plant. North of the Border, at the opening ceremony of the new Falkirk Grahamston station on the 28th, 47 636 was named 'Sir John de Graeme'. The name recalled the knight who fought alongside Sir William Wallace and who was killed at the battle of Falkirk in 1298.

47 645 was named 'Robert F. Fairlie' on 1st May at a ceremony held at Blaenau Ffestiniog. The nameplates bore the footnote 'Locomotive Engineer 1831-1885' and below each one was affixed a plaque bearing a special 150th anniversary crest of the Ffestiniog Railway. Robert Fairlie played an important part in the development of the locomotives of the Railway and his patent articulated steam locomotives are widely known around the world by railway engineers and enthusiasts alike.

Number 47 573 was named 'The London Standard' at Liverpool Street station on 9th June after the famous newspaper. The locomotive was the first Class 47 to be repainted in the new Network SouthEast livery. This expensively applied, but colourful, livery consisted of a mid-blue body side background with a combined arrangement of broad white, red, thin white and grey stripes on the lower portion, angled upwards across the cab areas. White window surrounds and yellow cab front and corner areas finished off the effect, together with a red background to the nameplates, and the bodyside running number, double arrow and the NSE title all applied in white. The roof area was dark grey.

One of the less inspiring names of the year was 'Industry Year 1986' officially bestowed upon 47 639 at Euston station by the then Trade & Industry Secretary, Paul Channon. Number 47 366 gained the name 'The Institution of Civil Engineers' at Liverpool Street station in London and on 8th June 47 644 was named 'The Permanent Way Institution' at Perth. By this time 47 572 had become 'Ely Cathedral', 47 374 was to become 'Petrolea' and 47 638 'County of Kent'. 47 526 gained the name 'Northumbria' from 47 405 when the latter was withdrawn from service. 47 647 regained its nameplates after running without them for some years. The name 'Finsbury Park' was transferred from the withdrawn 47 408 to 47 654, and on 5th September 47 492 received the name 'The Enterprising Scot'. On the 25th and 26th September 47 515 and 47 549 were named 'Night Mail' and 'Royal Mail' respectively. The name 'Colossus' was removed from 47 641 in favour of 'Fife Region' and 47 007 became 'Stratford'. Not all the namings and denamings are included here, but the foregoing serves to illustrate just how much that events had turned around within ten years, perhaps too much when one considers how obscure some of the names were to the travelling public.

A change in BR maintenance policy came before the end of 1986, but its implementation was not felt until the following year. The BREL workshops underwent a contraction in size and workload when some of their work was undertaken elsewhere, or reduced due to modern rolling stock requiring less maintenance at less frequent intervals. Work being undertaken elsewhere came with the introduction of the Cost Effective Maintenance (CEM) scheme, whereby work was devolved from main workshops to depots, suitably trained and equipped. BREL workshops already had experienced considerable reductions in their staffing levels since 1980; 30,000 down to around 21,000 in early 1987, with further reductions to an estimated 17,500 by early 1989. With Class 47 scheduled to conform to the CEM scheme in April 1987 some 281 jobs were to go from Crewe Works, the main (though not exclusive) repair centre of the class.

One advantage to be gained from the new system was that if a locomotive required major maintenance or remedial work on equipment such as, for example, the power unit, it was unnecessary to wait its turn for several weeks at main workshops but could have its unit removed and exchanged on depot using a replacement from a central store, thus saving valuable time. Depots were classified on an ascending scale of levels of work done from 1 to 5. The latter included major component changes. Cost effectiveness combined with a stricter philosophy with regard to incurring expense were to adversely affect Class 47 withdrawals over the next few years.

On 14th January 1987 fire-damaged 47 162 of Bristol Bath Road depot and 47 230 of Cardiff, suffering from a defective main generator, were withdrawn from service rather than be repaired. Both were to provide urgently required spare parts for other Class 47s. The Cardiff locomotive had never been allocated elsewhere since its delivery in October 1965 as D1906, a remarkable occurrence. Later that month 47 429 of Inverness was withdrawn.

47 131 was derailed at Dorrington, between Hereford and Shrewsbury, on 19th February. It came to rest on its side and sustained damage sufficient to cause its withdrawal. The next day 47 089 'Amazon' was involved in a collision with 31 440 at Chinley, in Derbyshire. The Class 47 was tipped onto its side and after re-railing was taken to Buxton for damage repair assessment. Its condition on withdrawal in June 1987 made it too expensive to repair. Also withdrawn during February were 'Generator' 47 419 of Gateshead depot, 47 013 of Crewe, 47 486 of Bescot and 47 529 of Bristol, the latter mainly as a source of spare parts.

47 031 of Tinsley had been badly damaged in a collision at Conington, south of Peterborough on 22nd February, whilst on ballasting duties. Having sustained cab damage, it was condemned on the spot four days later. The class was now numbering about 487 locomotives, some 25 examples having been withdrawn over the years.

During February 47 576 was named 'Kings Lynn' and 47 564 received the name 'Colossus' from 47 641. The following month 47 291 was named 'The Port of Felixstowe' and 47 202 was withdrawn from service following an accident at Frome on the 24th. 47 202, hauling thirty empty stone wagons on the 07.08 Westbury Yard to Whatley Quarry, collided head on with 33 032 hauling the 06.55 Yeovil to Cardiff passenger train. The unfortunate driver of the Class 47 was trapped in his wrecked cab and seriously injured to the extent that it was several months before he could officially give evidence regarding the accident, and admit that it was his error in passing a signal at danger that caused the collision. The Railway Inspectorate's report summed up with the comment that there was a need to design stronger locomotive cabs and to either improve or eliminate existing locomotives with unsatisfactory cabs, "again shown up in this accident". The remains of 47 202 were eventually cut up in September 1991. Number 47 484, damaged in a collision at Preston, was repaired at Crewe Works, the work including straightening out of the cab, realigning of the drag box and the replacement of the cracked trusses inside the cab.

Class 47s were not only being withdrawn from service, some were being stored unserviceable. Such were 47 437 and 47 478, both treated as such in February 1987 and some measure of the new era. Withdrawal soon followed for the former. It is of note that at about this time the final Class 47 conversions to eth were being completed at Crewe Works. From this time onwards 47/4s would increasingly rely on spare parts from other locomotives, indeed 47 429 was the first of the class to be withdrawn in full working order to provide spares for CEM, and 47 529 a close runner up. By order of the BRB 47 429 was sent south from Inverness to Crewe Works to be there for 26th January, but although it arrived in the area in good time it was borrowed on the 25th to work what was to be its last duty, to Holyhead and back!

Numbers 47 011, 47 437 and 'Generator' 47 415 were withdrawn during April, but on a happier note several Class 47s were named (47 016 'The Toleman Group'; 47 348 'St. Christopher's Home'; 47 350 'British Petroleum'; 47 563 'Women's Guild'; 47 622 'The Institution of Mechanical Engineers' and 47 635 'Jimmy Milne'.

A surprising example of a locomotive placed into store was 47 713, converted to push-pull mode only two years before, but proving troublesome. Crewe Works held it as stored unserviceable until immediate financial restraints were past. At the time Crewe was holding twelve withdrawn Class 47s, 47 001/162/230/75/82/ 405/9/14/16/29/64/529. During the early part of 1987 Class 47s were being placed in store at regular intervals, but some remained so only for a short period of time, being called out when problems occurred on other members of the class. The months of March and April were particularly active. May saw 47 015 of Bescot and 'Generator' 47 404 'Hadrian' of Gateshead withdrawn from service. 'Hadrian' was not the only 'Generator' to go; 47 410, 47 412 and 47 420 were also withdrawn during the same month.

47 637 was named 'Springburn' the following month, which also saw 47 191 of Crewe withdrawn from service.

The traction plan of 1985 was two years old when revisions due to greatly altered traffic plans were made. Most of the plans for new locomotives disappeared (Class 60 being one of the few survivors) and Class 47 was targeted for extensive withdrawals from service to the point where about half of the original 512 members would survive by mid-1992. Included were many of the ETH-fitted members, and so soon after the completion of the ETH programme.

July 1987 saw more Class 47s withdrawn, 47 103, 47 148, 47 199 and 47 486, the last due to fire damage. The following month it was the turn of 47 109, 47 122 and 47 137. July saw the name 'Benjamin Gimbert G.C.' transferred from 47 577 to 47 574, and in September 47 214 named 'Tinsley Traction Depot' and 47 380 named 'Immingham'.

On 3rd October 47 522 was named 'Doncaster Enterprise' as part of the Doncaster Works Open Day celebrations. The locomotive had been specially painted in an approximation of LNER green, with white/black/white horizontal lining at cab doorstep level stretching along the body sides from door to door. The running number appeared in large numerals on the body side left and the BR double arrow symbol and the legend 'Parcels' on the right. The cabs were painted yellow overall (with black window surrounds) to the junction with the body sides and the roof was painted light grey. Buffer beam areas were red, running gear and underslung equipment black. Buffer faces were silver. The special treatment marked the occasion of the launch of Doncaster Works as a Level 5 Depot under the new maintenance scheme.

47 079 'George Jackson Churchward' lost its green livery and name during its preparation for the new Railfreight livery launch in the autumn of 1987. This livery has been described in Chapter 4. The preparation was undertaken at Stratford Works during September and 47 079 was presented at the works with 37 673 for the making of a special publicity film. The Class 47 bore the Metals and Automotive sub-sector markings and the Ripple Lane depot torch symbol. Both locomotives went into normal service on 16th September. The pioneer Class 56, No. 56 001, went into service within days also bearing the new livery, so it was strange to find Railfreight officially announcing the new livery on 15th October! Whatever the reason for this is of little consequence, the fact was that a little more colour was being added to the railway scene, albeit when the locomotives were new and clean.

The threatened 47 120 'RAF Kinloss' was not withdrawn in 1987 despite being a troublesome locomotive. Doncaster Works had been unable to remedy a hot axle box problem and the locomotive was transferred to Crewe Works on 3rd October 1986 losing in the process the name it had carried since June 1985. It soldiered on until placed in store in 1990.

A different renumbering of Class 47 locomotives was contemplated for December 1987, in connection with the idea of transferring two locomotives to the RTC at Derby. The intention was to number them 97 414 and 97 415 in an existing special departmental series. Nothing materialised for almost a year, then 47 472 and 47 480 'Robin Hood' became 97 472 and 97 480 respectively.

In January 1988 47 093 of Tinsley and 47 113 of Crewe were withdrawn from service, but on a happier note 47 531 was named 'The Silcock Express' at Liverpool Lime Street station to mark the relationship between BR and the railborne delivery of cars by the car delivery firm. Number 47 319 was named 'Norsk Hydro' to mark the firm's first company train on 3rd March and 47 106/30/40 were withdrawn from service that month. The withdrawal of 47 130 was officially acknowledged during the following September. 47 106 and 47 140 were collision victims, both coming into mutual contact at Carlisle. Tinsley then withdrew its 47 104 during March, re-instated it in May and finally withdrew it in June!

Gateshead motive power depot closed in May 1988 and the remaining eight 'Generators' (47 401/2/6/7/11/13/17/18) were transferred away from the depot and their duties across the northern Pennines. They went to Immingham depot where some were to operate on Provincial Sector services, which took them along the Settle-Carlisle route on passenger duties, while others operated parcels services and departmental duties. The named examples lost their titles in this transfer, some being transferred to other Class 47s as soon as possible. Number 47 443 became 'North Eastern' (ex-47 401), 47 448 became 'Gateshead' (ex-47 402) and 47 488 became 'Rail Riders' (ex-47 406) the very same month.

A plan to provide three more 47/7s (47 717-9), but for Leeds-Harrogate services rather than for Scotland, did not materialise in 1988, but one more conversion to 47 717 was required due to the misfortune of 47 713. In late June 1988,

previously troublesome 47 713 was badly damaged by fire and was stored unserviceable. It was towed to Doncaster Works on 28th June and was soon officially withdrawn from service, on 11th July, and its power unit was transferred to 47 707. Number 47 497 was earmarked as its replacement and received the push-pull equipment from the victim before emerging from Doncaster as 47 717 and bearing the name 'Tayside Region' removed from 47 713. It arrived on the Scottish Region on 21st September.

Number 47 001 was earmarked for preservation as D1521 and on 18th April was moved to the Crewe Heritage Centre, but its stay was to be a short one. On 17th December it moved out of the Centre and found its way to nearby Basford Hall sidings. 47 192, withdrawn in the May and in better condition, had been selected instead. It was restored to two-tone green livery in 1989 and was given its original D1842 running number.

In addition to 47 192, 47 145/59/89 were also withdrawn during May. The following month 47 311 was named 'Warrington Yard', 47 317 'Willesden Yard' and 47 434 'Pride in Huddersfield'. The significance of the purely railway names would no doubt be lost without explanation on an observant passenger with a few moments to spare.

For Class 47s involved on Shell oil traffic there were to be appropriate names. These were the Latin names for shells, and a seemingly endless supply was available. August witnessed 47 085 with the name 'Conidae', 47 119 'Arcidae' and 47 194 'Bullidae'. Others named at about this time were 47 010 'Xancidae', 47 233 'Strombidae', 47 196 'Haliotidae' and 47 278 'Vasidae'. Each nameplate had a shell emblem incorporated into it at one end. As locomotives were transferred away and back into the oil traffic pool the names were liable to removal and refitting, a practice understandable, but perhaps too frequent for retaining any credibility for individual locomotive identity. By 1988 naming a locomotive served several causes, the least being permanent individuality. October saw 47 060 become 'Halewood Silver Jubilee 1988'.

During the middle of the year railway enthusiasts of The Class 47 Locomotive Society launched their '47 401 Project' with the object of preserving D1500 upon withdrawal from BR service. The apparent lack of National Railway Museum interest in the locomotive was one of the reasons for the move, but the historical importance of the locomotive was foremost in their minds, and correctly they considered that the locomotive must be saved.

By July 47 131, originally D1722, became the first of the class to be scrapped at the Leicester scrapyard of Vic Berry, only a few miles south of its birthplace. Despite heavy withdrawals, only five of the class had been scrapped during the previous two year period, 47 111/62/464/529 being the other four.

Almost no-one could be mistaken regarding the name given to 47 283 on 11th September. On that day the plates 'Johnnie Walker' were unveiled at Kilmarnock to mark the transportation association between the whisky firm John Walker & Son Ltd and BR Speedlink and Railfreight. At least one additional nameplate was presented to the firm. No doubt those who attended entered into the spirit of the occasion!

During the winter of 1988/9 the Departmental Class 47s totalled four, 97 414-7 formerly 47 472/480/545/561. They were soon allocated numbers 97 472/480/545/561, but they were not readily recognised as Class 47s, on paper at least. The three still in Departmental stock were renumbered 47 971-3 (97 480/545/561) in July 1989. 97 472 reverted to 47 472 in June 1989. Their working lives were rather fluid due to the fact that when not required for departmental duties concerned with the Research Department of the RTC, Derby, they were loaned elsewhere for revenue-earning duties.

In January 1989 47 097 of Tinsley depot and 47 428 of Crewe were withdrawn, and almost immediately the former was reinstated. Tinsley then withdrew 47 235 the following month and 47 203 during March. March also saw 47 101/89 of Crewe and 47 469 of Inverness withdrawn from service.

At last the sub-classification 47/8 became a reality in 1989. Already 47 551-3/91/650-65 were fitted with long-range fuel tanks giving a total capacity of 1,295 gallons. The intention was to increase the operating range of locomotives without the need to refuel so often. These locomotives were allocated the series 47 801-20 and further conversions were to be numbered from 47 821 – indeed, some of the latter were renumbered before the long-standing conversions over the ensuing months. Eventually, the series reached 47 853.

Number 47 475 became the first main line locomotive to receive the Provincial Trans-Pennine livery normally applied to coaching stock and Sprinter units. It was one of nine Class 47s selected to work Newcastle-Liverpool Trans-Pennine services until such time as Class 158 Express Sprinters arrived. The livery consisted of all yellow cab, blue upper body with light blue/white waist stripes and off-white lower body.

In May 47 098 and 47 110 of Tinsley were withdrawn, as was 47 198 of Cardiff. The following month Tinsley withdrew 47 124. In May 97 561 was painted in a special maroon livery and named 'Midland Counties Railway 150 1839-1989' in connection with the Midland Counties Railway 150 celebrations. The body sides were painted maroon with yellow border lining edged with black. The cabs were yellow with black running number affixed below the left cab side windows. The BR double arrow motif, in black, was correspondingly affixed to the right cab sides. Roof areas were painted a mid shade of grey. Official dispensation was given for the extremely attractive scheme and it was applied at weekends, out of working hours, by Derby, Etches Park painters. The scheme was sponsored by Joseph Mason Paints of Derby. 97 561 made appearances at the various events connected with the celebration and was named on 23rd May at Derby station. It had pride of place at the Coalville Open Day on 11th June.

On 9th June 47 831 (formerly 47 563) was named 'Bolton Wanderer' at Bolton station by the Mayor of Bolton, Councillor Ken MacIvor. The naming was intended to draw attention to the new services from Birmingham and Manchester to Bolton and Scotland. Among those who attended were members of the local football club, who perhaps may have preferred the title to be in the plural! The locomotive was finished in Mainline livery, the newly-introduced version of the InterCity livery, complete with miniscule running numbers.

Withdrawals continued and in June they included 47 124 and 'Generator' No. 47 411. The latter left just seven examples left in service.

On 22nd July 1989 47 971 'Robin Hood' quietly propelled 89 001 'Avocet' into the Falcon Works via the new Meadow Lane rail access, provided that year for the Class 60 deliveries. It was the first time that a Class 47 had been in the works since the late 1960s, twenty years at least. It was an event which went almost un-noticed, but it was significant nonetheless. The electric locomotive was propelled through the yards to the Traction area adjacent to Loughborough Meadows. The entry of a Class 47 was repeated when 47 152 attended the Falcon Works Open Day on 12th August as part of the array of displays. The locomotive had originally left the works brand new as D1745 in July 1964, so it celebrated its silver jubilee in its own way.

Number 47 586 was named 'Northamptonshire' and 47 836 lost its 'Fair Rosamund' name in September. On 10th November 47 528 received 'The Queen's Own Mercian Yeomanry' on attractive two-line nameplates, above which were mounted small plaques depicting the Regimental Coats of Arms. Her Majesty The Queen, as Colonel-in-Chief of the Regiment, unveiled the nameplate at a special ceremony at Worcester Shrub Hill station. The Royal Train conveying HM The Queen was hauled overnight from London to Worcester by 47 821 'Royal Worcester'.

Another naming took place in December, that of 47 210 which was named 'Blue Circle Cement' at Eastfield Traction Maintenance Depot. The same month saw 47 012/143/298 withdrawn from service. With reinstated members of the class taken into account the total was reduced by about a dozen over the year. A few Class 47s were de-named during 1989 and towards the close 47 010 lost its 'Xancidae' plates, 47 119 its 'Arcidae' plates and the names 'North Star' and 'Springburn' were removed from 47 613 and 47 826 respectively.

On 4th December 47 434 caught fire near Guildford whilst it was hauling the 19.25 Portsmouth-Waterloo postal train. The locomotive was badly burned and the efforts of six fire appliances was to no avail and when their water supplies were exhausted, four more appliances were required to extinguish the blaze.

The new year opened with the remains of 'Generators' 47 404/10/5/9 going to the Leicester scrapyard of Vic Berry for scrapping. Withdrawals continued and namings were still frequent as were the removals and transfers of names. To plot all the exchanges is to weave a tangled web – some were transferred between various classes. For example, 47 330 was named 'Amlwch Freighter/Trên Nwyddau Amlwch' during 1990, a name originally carried by Class 31 No. 31 296 and relinquished a few months before the transfer. Number 47 214 was named 'Tinsley Traction Depot', lost it to 47 375, but gained 'Distillers MG' later in the year. The original names allocated to the WR Class 47s in the mid-1960s did not always stay put, indeed it is probable that some were removed illegally. Sometimes they were located and refitted years later, sometimes they were replaced by different names. Number D1661 was named 'North Star' and was reunited with its name in late 1990 after the locomotive was numbered 47 840 and a year after its removal whilst 47 210 was named 'Blue Circle Cement', receiving the name from donor Class 56 No. 56 124. Of the renamings that of 47 973 was one of the most prominent. It had carried 'Midland Counties Railway

150 1839-1989' for less than a year – it was a topical naming. It lost its nameplates and maroon livery in April 1990 when it was repainted in Mainline livery. During September 1990 it was renamed 'Derby Evening Telegraph'.

By this time three more Class 47s had been renumbered into the 47/9 departmental series. 47 531 became 47 974 in the June, taking the name 'The Permanent Way Institution' from 47 644. The same month 47 546 became 47 976 and 'Aviemore Castle' and two months later 47 540 became 47 975 and gained the name 'The Institution of Civil Engineers' from 47 366.

Long names tend to attract attention and, perhaps, some degree of bemusement as to the meaning of it all. Such names usually recall an association with a body or an event somewhat specialised and localised. Number 47 568 was named 'Royal Engineers Postal and Courier Services'. Unless one has military leanings or interests the name requires some explanation. The Ministry of Defence, like all organisations, received and generated mail and relied upon the Royal Mail to deliver it in part by rail. The locomotive was named on 20th March at Long Marston MoD establishment, which served as the Royal Engineers Resources Depot, and then hauled a charter mail train to Paddington. The locomotive, although belonging to the Parcels Sector, was in InterCity/Mainline livery, but with no sector markings, and the train in the new Royal Mail travelling post office red livery.

The first locomotive to receive Parcels Sector livery was 47 474 during April 1990. It was a simple livery of dark grey for roof and upper body sides, black for cab window surrounds,

and below the window line was a pleasing red of a shade akin to post office red. The BR double arrow symbol in raised metal was affixed to the right hand cab sides and the running number transferred in white to the left hand cabsides. The naming took place on 1st May at Kidderminster Severn Valley Railway (SVR) station and it celebrated the 150th anniversary of the postage stamp. The name of the postal services pioneer, 'Sir Rowland Hill' was appropriately bestowed upon the locomotive.

Another new livery to mark another new organisation change entered the scene during May 1990. Number 47 333 was named 'Civil Link' on 2nd May during the official launching of a network of train services to transport civil engineering materials between depots, sites and suppliers around the system. In all BR had forty terminals around the system. The network had actually started operations five months previously. The Civil Engineering Department at the time had 39 Class 47s on its books and it was the intention to paint all its locomotives in an overall grey livery, relieved only by black window surrounds and roof areas, and yellow ends. In new condition the finish was attractive, though functional. The plainness of the livery was apparent and it

Now sporting Network SouthEast livery after transfer from former duties in Scotland, push-pull Class 47 No. 47 714 waits to leave Paddington Station on 7th March 1990.

M J STRETTON

was soon modified for following applications by the addition of a yellow upper body side portion at cab window level.

A name with a bureaucratic ring to it befell 47 218 when it was named 'United Transport Europe' on 5th July at the Cowley Railfreight Terminal, near Oxford. The occasion was an international gathering of businessmen at the United Transport building there and the naming drew attention to the importance of the rail transport system as an attractive means of distribution over long distances and the need for such an organisation as United Transport Europe to take full advantage of the Channel Tunnel.

In August 47 209 received the name 'Herbert Austin' from 47 337 and the following month Railfreight Distribution locomotive No. 47 309 became 'The Halewood Transmission'. The naming ceremony of the latter took place on the 19th at the Ford Motor Company Halewood Transmission Plant to commemorate its silver jubilee and the relationship between the company and BR. A plaque of the Ford logo was mounted above each nameplate. Though an obvious and meaningful name at the time, it may have gained an air of mystery as time passed and as the locomotive strayed afar.

During October 47 547 became 'University of Oxford' and 47 587 became 'Ruskin College Oxford' to mark the opening of the rebuilt Oxford railway station.

On 27th July 47 479 was named 'Track 29' to mark the launching of the Parcels Sector's new heavy-haulage operation of that name. The service was to provide the movement of parcels in excess of 50kg, the upper limit of the Red Star service. The locomotive was wearing the new Parcels Sector grey/red livery and was named at the Peter Allen building of the National Railway Museum at York.

'Transmark' was another name to ponder over. Number 47 314 was named thus on 20th December at Paddington station to commemorate the 21st birthday of the BR international transport consultancy of the same name and the placing of contracts worth £2.2 million. One wonders if such names would be better explained with sub-titles to gain better effect or appreciation. A large Transmark logo was affixed above each nameplate. The full title of Transmark was Transport Systems & Market Research Limited.

Perhaps the most significant withdrawals of 1990 were those of 'Generators' 47 406 and 47 407 in August, further reducing their total to five survivors (47 401/2/12/7/8) left in service. At this time 47 401 was running in 'large logo' blue livery with the addition of its original number D1500 on the bodysides, adjacent to the right hand cabs. Elsewhere, the declining availability of the 85 InterCity Sector Class 47s during 1989 caused concern when it hit an all-time low. Thirty-five recommendations to improve the situation were put forward by engineer Mr Clive Burrows during 1990, after he had been appointed to solve the problem. Among his recommendations were the fitting of long-life R5 brake blocks, bogie bedplate seals to lessen or prevent underframe fires resulting from the accumulation of dirt and oil, and the reduction of time between bogie examinations and servicing.

On Sunday 14th October the preserved D1842 hauled three restored LNER coaches on the Severn Valley Railway during the Diesel Gala Weekend on the preserved line. It presented a heart-warming sight in its two-tone green livery, but was soon to be complemented by other Class 47s similarly painted.

Before the year was out the Parcels Sector took over six of the former Glasgow-Edinburgh Class 47/7s, by this time redundant from their push-pull role. These were 47 702/3/4/6/912. The move south of the 47/7s to replace increasingly unreliable Class 50s on Waterloo/Salisbury/ Exeter duties never really materialised properly, the 47s also proving unreliable.

As the BR business sectors moved towards privatisation various reorganisations took effect to adapt to new situations and cost effectiveness. Over the years since 1979 government policy had changed BR and this was reflected in the locomotive fleet, among other things. Matters steadily became lined up behind sectors and it ever more appeared that perhaps the sectors would undergo a metamorphosis and eventually become private companies. Uncertainty prevailed in many minds as to what form privatisation would take, and it appeared that the government also wasn't sure, indeed it now appeared that the sectors might not form the basis for future companies.

On 9th January 1991 47 844 was named 'Derby & Derbyshire Chamber of Commerce & Industry' at Derby station. The nameplates were of a changed pattern of thin etched metal rather than the previous cast type. One descriptive variation applied to these recently introduced plates was 'tinplate'. Number 47 844 was soon to be involved in a shunting collision with a SR de-icing unit and suffered cab damage, but was later repaired.

By 19th January the first of the 47/7s of the Parcels Sector to wear the red livery entered service. It was 47 703 and was outshopped from Springburn Works in Glasgow. Hard on its heels from BRML Doncaster was 47 712 on the 22nd. Eleven Class 47/7s moved from ScotRail were a common sight between Paddington and Oxford, with occasional trips to the South West and South Wales, but changes were afoot. About now 47 702/8/10 were all noted on Class 50 substitution duties, the latter pair being noted on Waterloo - Exeter trains.

From December 1990 to February 1991 'Generator' 47 402 was withdrawn from service, but during the latter month it was reinstated. Meanwhile, 47 418 was out of action at Immingham depot, awaiting a repair that never came – it was withdrawn during February. The two locomotives were a direct exchange. Another withdrawal, that of 47 233 'Strombidae', occurred during February as a result of fire damage suffered the previous month. Withdrawals began to increase in number as business declined and the new Class 60s entered traffic. Some were directly due to this and some were indirect, a result of Class 60s displacing Class 56s, which in turn unseated Class 47s. The decline in business included the rundown of the Speedlink network. Railfreight in particular planned to reorganise and rationalise its fleet of Class 47s to meet the new situation. At least eight Class 47s were withdrawn during March, two in April, one in May and in June, another eight.

Happier circumstances involved 47 249 on 11th April when it hauled the first load of 180-metre length rails for the Channel Tunnel. The locomotive was in remarkably clean condition, although still bearing the original Railfreight grey livery, complete with red stripe.

In May 47 401, formerly 'North Eastern' when it was allocated to Gateshead, was unofficially named 'Star of the East'. It was no amateurish naming; the nameplates were the standard cast metal pattern and your author remembers first sighting the locomotive bearing them at the 1991 Coalville Open Day. During the latter part of June the locomotive was repainted from its 'large logo' blue into near original two-tone green livery, together with its original number D1500 and replica Brush Traction works plates, a pleasing move in every sense. During August fellow 'Generator' 47 413 was withdrawn, leaving just 47 401/2/17 still in service.

A new sub-class was created during the summer of 1991, Class 47/6; a somewhat obscure classification because the number series was partly occupied by the final eth 47/4s. The number series created was 47 671-77 and it was entirely composed of higher-rated eth locomotives allocated to Inverness and previously numbered 47 562/86/93/5/604/16/7 respectively. No details were released of the modifications required to achieve this higher rating. Concurrently, the locomotives had their maximum speed reduced to 75mph. Renumbering was undertaken at the depot as the locomotives came in for repair or maintenance.

During July a further eight Class 47s were withdrawn, although at least one was to be reinstated several months later. The fate of 47 801 hung in the balance for a while, being withdrawn in August, reinstated in September and withdrawn again before that month was out. This was one of the locomotives that placed pressure on tight budgets. October and November continued the reduction in the active fleet with the loss of five each month, and December rounded the year off with twelve. At least three of the more recent victims were returned to traffic and the class finished the year about fifty members down. The class total in service was down to around 375, from the original 512 built.

Some highly professional repainting work resulted in a number of the Class 47s looking like new locomotives. Such was 47 701, which emerged in Network Southeast livery and newly renamed 'Old Oak Common Traction & Rolling Stock Depot' during August 1991. Officially named at the depot's Open Day on 18th August, the locomotive took pride of place at the event.

A plan to equip Class 47s with 1,300 gallons capacity fuel tanks and fit Plessey TDM (Time Division Multiplex) emerged during the year. At the time 47 582 was earmarked for fitting of the equipment and renumbering to 47 750. This placed it in the same push-pull classification series 47/7 hitherto only allotted to the Brush TDM-fitted examples and created a sub division within it to avoid confusion between the two types. Over two years were to pass before the system was extended.

On 19th October 1991 an unusual naming occurred. Number 47 222 was named 'W A Camwell' for the day in honour of the eminent railway photographer and Stephenson Locomotive Society member on the occasion of his 85th birthday. Affectionately known as 'Cam' he was most surprised by the naming, which took place at Kidderminster. It was one of those days when railway enthusiasts and BR conspired to honour a mutually respected personality – a warm, touching event.

By September 1991 47 500, still wearing its Great Western green, was looking decidedly shabby. Its paintwork was faded and very patchy touching in of damaged areas added nothing but protection. Gone were its 'Great Western' nameplates and the cast number plates, the latter replaced by standard white transfer numerals.

Conversely, 47 594 was resplendent in a new livery (pun intended). This was a preview of the new grey and red scheme of Rail Express Systems, and was unveiled during July, two months ahead of the official launch of the new specialist division of the British Rail Parcels Group. This new organisation was set up to provide a fast and efficient service for the bulk movement of letters and parcels, combined with better utilisation of overnight capacity of the railway system. The branding took the form of 'Rail Express Systems', Res for short, and soon introduced names beginning with Res, quite a novel move. The livery was a development of the Parcels livery, but the upper body side grey portion teminated short of the left cabs in a corporate identity logo that defied explanation by the observer and cried out for a sub-title. According to the system's newspaper 'Response' the symbol (logo) "is designed to be integral to the base livery...... The wing device or 'blue flashes' within the symbol denote speed and quick

Number 47 597 'Resilient' at Leicester in new Rail Express Systems (Res) livery fourteen days after naming. Photograph taken 25th October 1991.

M J STRETTON

response. The 'plus sign' has a positive proactive connotation. The interlocking shapes allude to interacting systems and the box shapes are appropriate for an organisation specialising in the movement of light freight." There, then, is the official explanation. Roundel Design Group were responsible for it and the livery, which was applied to rolling stock and road vehicles also. A new typestyle named Frutiger was introduced for all numbers and lettering. 47 594 was painted at the Midland Railway Centre (MRC), Swanwick Junction, and took part in a publicity photographic session with six matching vans at St. Pancras station on 28th July. In the October 47 594 was named 'Resourceful'. The same month saw the names 'Resilient' and 'Resplendent' applied to 47 597 and 47 625 respectively.

The next year, 1992, dawned with Network Southeast experiencing continued problems with its Classes 47/4s, 47/7s and 50s, all due to poor availability. The 47/7s were all high mileage machines, and despite works attention before re-entering service in the south of England, were proving problematic. During the latter half of 1991 47 704 went elsewhere after suffering a main generator failure and 47 711 was *hors de combat* after being involved in a collision at Yeovil, then in February 1992 several were under repair, these locomotives being 47 710/4/5/7.

An accident led to 47 801 reverting to its previous identity of 47 551 early in the new year. Rather than repair one of its damaged fuel tanks, it was isolated and reclassified back to 47/4 – all very logical indeed.

In February 1992 'Generator' 47 418 was withdrawn and in the summer the remaining pair, 47 401/2 followed, in June to be exact. Waiting in the wings was the Class 47 Locomotive Society, who were busily gathering funds to purchase pioneer 47 401/D1500. By January 1991 £27,000 had already been raised. Unfortunately for the society, BR decided not to offer 47 401/2 for sale by tender due to the uncertainty surrounding the sale of assets prior to the forthcoming White Paper on the Privatisation of BR. The decision was soon reversed and both locomotives awaited their fate whilst being held in store at Immingham depot. The closing date for the receipt of tenders was 9th March 1993 and happily it was the Class 47 Locomotive Society that became the new owners of 47 401/D1500, the second of the class to enter preservation. The society was formed in 1983 to attempt to save at least one Class 47, but the decision taken by the National Railway Museum not to claim the locomotive, changed their plans, following a membership ballot, into saving the pioneer locomotive. The society's '47 401 Fund' was then initiated to achieve this aim. Initially, the locomotive was expected to move to the Great Central Railway at Loughborough, but the Midland Railway Centre, with its direct rail link and purpose-built diesel depot became more in favour and during July 1993 it arrived there. No time was lost in showing off the new arrival and it was one of the star attractions of the Midland Railway Centre Diesel Gala, held at Butterley on 17/18th July. It was hauling trains during the event, two return trips each day.

The efforts and success of the society inspired others. The Class 47 Preservation Group was formed, the intention being to purchase, restore and maintain 47 054 (originally D1638 and withdrawn in July 1992), and a fund was started for its

rescue – with an initial target sum of £20,000 to be raised.

47 974 left departmental stock in June 1992 and became 47 531 again. Two months later after a period in store, 47 468 was reclassified to 47/3 and renumbered 47 300, an unusual move but one prompted by necessity. 47 343 had been involved in a collision and it was thought that only a cab renewal was required to effect a repair, but it was discovered that the end bracing was fractured. The withdrawn line of locomotives at Crewe was examined and 47 468 hauled into the works for resurrection. The power unit and bogies from 47 343 were fitted and the ensemble renumbered 47 300. The only number it had ever had prior to the 47/4 TOPS number was D1594, so a new TOPS number had to be found. The reclassification was the first of its kind whereby an eth locomotive reverted to non-eth condition. The grey and yellow so-called 'Dutch' livery was applied. 47 343 was despatched by road on a low-loader, bound for MC Metals of Glasgow – and scrapping.

Nearly thirty Class 47s were withdrawn from service in 1992, leaving 350 in service by the end of the year. By this time the 'Inverness 7' (47 671-7) had been displaced by Class 37s and had moved south.

In January 1993 47 833 was repainted in two-tone green livery, an approximation of its original livery when new as D1962. The locomotive was at the time part of the InterCity Special Trains Unit and the special repainting was undertaken at Landore depot. The TOPS running number appeared on the lower dark green portion of the left hand cabsides and the old D1962 was applied in black transfers to below the right hand cab side windows. The locomotive was also named 'Captain Peter Manisty RN' and bore a plaque as below bearing the following legend:

> CAPTAIN PETER MANISTY MBE DSC RN
> WAS A FOUNDING MEMBER OF THE
> BRITISH RAILWAY PRESERVATION MOVEMENT
> HAVING SHARED IN THE SETTING UP OF THE
> ASSOCIATION OF RAILWAY PRESERVATION SOCIETIES
> OF WHICH HE WAS CHAIRMAN FOR MANY YEARS

It was officially named by Dame Margaret Weston DBE, President of the Association of Railway Preservation Societies, at King's Cross station on 27th January. Captain Manisty had died on 15th June 1992, aged 76 years.

In the wake of the previous two Class 47 preservation groups, there followed the founding of another, the Class 47 Preservation Trust, with the aim of preserving a Class 47/7 or any other Class 47 that might become available. A target fund of £20,000 was launched, and it was hoped that the resultant Class 47 saved would be kept initially on the East Kent Light Railway, Shepherds Well.

In February BR hired two Class 47/9s to Balfour Beatty for the purpose of providing motive power for high speed testing of the overhead catenary through the Channel Tunnel. The test train consisted of five test coaches and speeds up to the 160kph (100mph) maximum were to be undertaken. The locomotives were to be worked at their maximum permitted speed and gradients preceding any such speed were as steep as 1 in 90 for fifteen miles, so some extremely hard work was involved before they emerged from the tunnel at 100mph!

The locomotives sent down to the Channel Tunnel initially were 47 971 and 47 975, but the former was found to have electrical faults that prevented starting. Because two locomotives were required for the tests 47 973 was sent from Derby, arriving early in the morning of the day of the tests, 24th February. Unfortunately, it was discovered that it had wheel flats, probably caused by skidding at some time.

Slow speed tests were undertaken while attempts to restart 47 971 were made. Using the original pair, 47 975 under power and the still dead 47 971, an attempt at the high speed run was made from the centre of the tunnel towards England, but the speed fell short of the required amount by 13mph. To achieve the required 100mph the test was then undertaken on the same section, but in the opposite direction to gain the advantage of the falling gradient, and without the errant 47 971, which was detached for more starting attempts to be made separately. All three locomotives and rolling stock returned to Derby on the 25th.

Number 47 972 was unavailable for the tests because different duties were allotted to this locomotive. It was scheduled to have its newly-fitted nameplates unveiled at a ceremony at the Central Ammunition Depot, Kineton on Friday 26th February. There it was named 'The Royal Army Ordnance Corps' by Major General DFE Botting CB, CBE in his capacity of Director General of Supply of the RAOC organisation which was being dissolved during the following April. The locomotive was specially repainted in its owner's (BR Technical Services) new livery of maroon and grey, being the first locomotive to receive it.

An unusual name was given to 47 186 on 20th April when 'Catcliffe Demon' was unveiled at the Tinsley Traction Maintenance Depot by two schoolchildren from the local Catcliffe Junior School. Following a local schools art competition, to design a railway poster emphasising the dangers of playing on the railway the two Catcliffe schoolchildren were given the naming performance honours, hence the 'Catcliffe' part of the name. The 'demon' part originated from the fitting of Diesel Engine Monitoring System (DEMON) equipment to 47 186. Whether anyone outside the area appreciated this or not, locally it served its purpose.

Over the years some remarkable liveries appeared, most of which diluted the BR Corporate Image of the mid 1960s to a residue. By early 1993 nearly every specific project or aim had its own corporate image, producing an array of liveries with directly opposite effects. One of the most garish was the mostly yellow Infrastructure livery applied in experimental form to 47 803 in April of that year. Thankfully, the roof was dark grey, but the side appearance was relieved by a broad red stripe above an off-white lower band. The upper yellow body portion bore the title INFRASTRUCTURE in large red letters and cab side running numbers also in red, but of the common smaller sized numerals.

An early victim of the livery was the loss of the INFRASTRUCTURE legend. Of course, it was the proposed infrastructure (track, signalling and associated civil engineering) organisation making its bid for an identity, pending the privatisation, then only a year ahead.

Several Class 47/7s passed into Res stock and moved to Crewe during May 1993, these being 47 706/8/15. They brought the total in Res ownership to seven and reduced Network Southeast's problems in doing so. The final locomotive working on Waterloo-Exeter services came on Saturday 10th July when 47 716 returned from Exeter hauling the 13.46. Number 47 702 headed the final locomotive-hauled Waterloo-Yeovil and return trains. This was prior to Monday 12th July, when the full Class 159 'South West Turbo' service was introduced. The remaining Class 47/7s of Network South East (47 701/2/15/6) then moved away to Crewe, to join the others.

Preserved 'Generator' 47 402 (the former D1501) started the first part of its journey from Immingham to the East Lancashire Railway on Tuesday 1st June. It went to Longsight to receive minor repairs courtesy of Trainload Petroleum. Once on the preserved railway, it was named 'Gateshead' again. The ceremony took place at Bury, on Saturday 5th June, by Don McNab and Pete Waterman. Mr McNab was from Immingham depot, the last BR home of the locomotive. Pete Waterman, the well-known record producer and railway enthusiast, was its new owner. The locomotive made its first runs in preservation that day, a day which also saw the launch of the latter's company 'Waterman Railways North West', an organisation responsible for the operation of his collection of modern traction locomotives and preserved rolling stock.

Number 47 403 (originally D1502), meanwhile, had been moved to the scrapyard of Booth Roe Metals in Rotherham. Its stay there was brief. On 28th June it was moved by 47 379 to the 'Railway Age' at Crewe to start its life of preservation, saved by Pete Waterman. Likewise, 47 449 (originally D 1566) entered preservation during August 1993 under the ownership of Pete Waterman whilst in store at Old Oak Common, having been withdrawn during May. It was moved to Crewe on 21st October for restoration and intended move to the Weardale Railway. Subsequently, 47 403 was stripped of re-useable parts and was scrapped – its condition was found to be inferior to other Class 47s becoming available for preservation.

Pete Waterman's company merged with Sir William McAlpine's Flying Scotsman Enterprises on 21st September to form Flying Scotsman Railways, and between them they owned twenty four diesel and electric locomotives. Also campaigning to preserve a Class 47 locomotive at this time was the North Star Preservation Group, which set its aim on preserving 47 840 (originally D1661 'NORTH STAR') as 47 077 or D1661 – it was offered a home by the East Kent Railway.

During the early hours of 6th September 1993 47 288 was derailed near Maidstone East station while hauling the 01.20 Dover-Willesden Railfreight Distribution (RfD) train carrying steel and general freight. The locomotive and the first five wagons mounted the platforms, created havoc in the station and left 47 288 on its side detached from the train as it left the station. The driver failed a breath test and was subsequently arrested.

Yet another new livery was introduced in 1993, Railfreight Distribution International; a modified version of Railfreight grey with blue roof and the title 'Railfreight Distribution' in large black letters applied to the lower bodysides. Intended recipients were Classes 47, 86 and 90 working the RfD International feeder services consequent from the impending opening of the Channel Tunnel. 47 217 was the first of the class to receive the new livery variation.

47 443 'North Eastern' (originally D1559) was withdrawn on 1st October and was one of the last of Class 47s fitted with series parallel connected traction motors to be taken out of traffic.

As intimated earlier, the classification 47/7 was to be extended. After a delay, Rail Express Systems (Res) decided to renumber its fleet of 62 Class 47s into a series 47 721-82. The original proposal had suggested commencing the series at 47 750, but there was insufficient space within the classification series. Commencing with 47 721 also made the new series discernible from the original ScotRail 47/7s. Design features of the new series were the fitting of long-range fuel tanks and the eventual fitting of RCH push-pull equipment for working in conjunction with new Propelling Control Vehicles (PCVs). It should be noted that the term driving van trailer had disappeared. Many of the locomotives were renumbered before the RCH equipment was fitted, and some with long-range fuel tanks already installed. Locomotives were renumbered from Class 47/4 and at least one from 47/8. The new push-pull system differed from the original Brush system, by then outdated technology with fewer facilities available. Early in 1994 there was only one 47/7 which had the new push-pull communications equipment for two prototype PCVs and that was paradoxically one of the former Scotrail examples, 47 704!

Res had inherited some rather work-worn locomotives and it was necessary to undertake some extensive and cannibalistic work before reasonably efficient locomotives could be made ready. ABB Transportation, the new owners of Crewe Works, were by the Autumn of 1993 in the process of making good locomotives from others heavily stripped of parts when withdrawn from service. It was work of an extensive nature and involved 47 641 and 47 644 which were to become 47 767 and 47 756 respectively.

It does appear to be a paradox that in the times of 'Quality Assured' and strict procedures of maintenance, it was found necessary to have designated 'rescue' locomotives (and publicise the fact). Obviously there is a sensible reason, in that a crippled train causing an obstruction to other traffic needs to be cleared as quickly as possible. By late 1993 Intercity had four Class 47s (47 520/671/3/5) forming a special fleet of rescue locomotives for the East Coast Main Line and which were manned and on continuous standby at King's Cross, Doncaster, Newcastle and Carstairs. The quartet were within one hour's reach of any failed train along the whole of the Anglo-Scottish route and the locomotives were nicknamed 'Thunderbirds' by BR staff, after the 'Thunderbirds' television series dating from the 1960s and receiving renewed media attention at the time. On 24th November 47 520 was officially named 'Thunderbird' at King's Cross station. Present was Mr Gerry Anderson, creator of the series. All four were to receive the name, rather than 'Thunderbird 1' and 'Thunderbird 2' and so on, so the names were more of a branding or functional indication nature. Nonetheless, the name sat happily upon one locomotive and would have made a very appropriate name for a steam locomotive in years gone by.

On 11th November Res locomotive 47 562 'Restless', hauling the 06.17 Leeds-Penzance postal train collided with a Class 156 multiple unit in Leeds station. The cab of the Class 47 was extensively damaged, particularly on the side and corner. Repairs were expected to take some time to effect. The locomotive was allocated the number 47 760.

On 16th November 47 364 (originally D1883) was renumbered into the Central Services series as 47 981 and based at Bescot depot which made use of its 100mph facility as an additional provision for the Infrastructure Research Pool of locomotives. 47 981 was in operation on test trains, which included a new National Power wagon, during January 1994. Number 47 976 was similarly occupied over the same period.

About nineteen Class 47s were withdrawn from service during 1993, a reduced rate compared with the more recent years, but one to escape the attention of the accountants was 47 004, the oldest member of the class remaining in BR service, originally D1524 and Brush Traction No. 419 of 1963. It was repainted in two-tone green, an approximation of its original livery, and named 'Old Oak Common Traction & Rolling Stock Depot'. Repainting was undertaken by depot staff, mostly in their own time, during January 1994. The official naming took place on 5th February. Its TOPS number was applied to the right hand cab sides in matching style to the D1524 and replica Brush Traction works plates were also fitted. 47 004 became the fourth of the class to bear two-tone green livery during the early 1990s, renaissance style. That of preserved D1500 was soon to be replaced by 'large logo' blue, following a members' ballot on preferred livery.

More good news for the new year came when Pete Waterman purchased his fourth Brush Type 4 No. 47 488 (originally D1713). Hard on the heels of this move came the news that he had secured 47 117, the former Class 48 D1705. He was eager to preserve one of these historical locomotives and had commissioned a survey as to which one was the best of the remnants of the batch. Surprisingly, 47 117 was found to be in good condition and order despite over two years of disuse.

The Brush Type 4 Fund, a small group of private investors, secured 47 105 (originally D1693) in full working order after it had been placed in store in October 1993 and withdrawn on 13th December. It was purchased for use on the Gloucestershire Warwickshire Railway at Toddington, where it arrived by road haulage on 8th April the following year.

Yet another Class 47 was saved at this time, 'Generator' 47 417 (formerly D1516). The owners of D1500 made this move to provide a source of spare parts for the former. Of course, as is sometimes the case, the future of the donor locomotive is likely to become a contentious issue among railway enthusiasts who disregard the practical intentions of the original purchase. To preserve the donor locomotive requires the spares equivalent of another locomotive and more, because one doubles the commitment. Such a situation was the case among railway enthusiasts concerned with steam locomotive 45699 'Galatea', the former LMS 'Jubilee' 4-6-0. Wisely, its owners adhered to their original intentions. 47 417 was taken to the Midland Railway Centre.

By March 1994 nine Brush Type 4s had been secured by the preservation groups or individuals, as follows:- 47 105 (D1693), 47 117 (D1705), 47 192 (D1842), 47 401 (D1500), 47 402 (D1501), 47 403 (stripped, then scrapped), 47 417 (D1516), 47 449 (D1566) and 47 488 (D1713).

Away from all this activity a pool of eight Class 47s was formed to haul freight trains from the Channel Tunnel. Railfreight Distribution and its RfD 'European'-liveried locomotives were thus prepared for the impending, though delayed, opening of the tunnel for freight traffic. Crew training trips with various Class 47s, not necessarily those from within the pool, were also ongoing.

March 1994 dawned with just four weeks left in the life of British Rail early 1990s style, Privatisation commencement day being 1st April, a date thought by some to be of relevance with regard to government policy on railways. For Railfreight locomotives the changes were to be gradual with three companies emerging temporarily as subsidiaries of the British Railways Board. These were to trade as Trainload Freight West, Trainload Freight North East and Trainload Freight South East. New identities on locomotives were expected, together with the omission of decals and retention of the basic triple grey Railfreight livery. September 1994 was the intended start of something more permanent. The livery scene of Class 47 represented more changes than anything permanent. The wholesale transfer of Class 47s to their respective interim companies occurred during March, all three new freight companies taking some into stock. With the privatisation in mind the BR Charter Train Unit was offered for sale, together with at least six Class 47/8s. The sale was finalised on 11th May 1994, when Waterman Railways became the new owner of these locomotives and over 200 coaches. As a prelude to privatisation many of the withdrawn and unwanted locomotives on BR books were put out to tender for scrap. This move included twenty Class 47s. The whole process of privatisation was to be prolonged and some of the initial arrangements were very short-lived.

RfD set about introducing double-headed Class 47 freightliner trains from Felixstowe in early 1994 to replace double-headed Class 37s. As a preliminary move 47 150 and 47 152 were modified with multiple working equipment at Tinsley depot for undergoing trials in March. The trials commenced on the 14th and proved successful. Two more Class 47s were so-treated (47 303/328) and another sub-classification became necessary. Because no completely vacant block of 100 numbers below 1,000 remained renumbering ran from 47 399 downwards. The new identities were as follows:

| 47 399 (47 150) |
| 47 398 (47 152) |
| 47 397 (47 303) |
| 47 396 (47 328) |

Others followed until the series had reached 47 384 before the end of the year.

By 1994 it had become commonplace to do something different. Old Oak Common depot repainted 47 016 (originally D1546) into original Railfreight grey livery, complete with large BR double arrow logo, and had the name ATLAS transferred to it from Res-owned 47 626. Someone had taken the trouble to ensure that the latter had been re-united with this name, which had been bestowed upon it in the mid-1960s, in the days when it was almost new and plain D1667!

February 1994 saw 47 323 named 'Rover Group Quality Assured' at Rover, Swindon. This took place on the 23rd and was occasioned by the signing of a new five-year contract with Rover for the movement by rail for body pressing panels and components between the two Rover plants at Swindon and Longbridge. That same month the name 'Saint Cuthbert' was removed from 47 702, one of the Scottish push-pull exiles, in favour of a more geographical (and appropriate) name, 'County of Suffolk'. Res Class 47 No. 47 738 was named 'Bristol Barton Hill' in celebration of the depot's achievement in securing the British Standard 5750 quality award on the 3rd of the month. A small square plaque bearing the depot's new unicorn symbol was affixed above each nameplate.

The slow renumbering of the Res fleet of parcels traffic-dedicated Class 47s into the 47/7 series continued throughout the year, and was usually accompanied with the overhaul and repaint of each locomotive.

Bestowing the name 'Capital Radio's Help a London Child' on 47 366 might have been an opportune move at the time, during March 1994, but it did highlight the extreme nature of namings that was becoming commonplace. The honour and sincerity is not doubted, merely that with the passage of time the names of such locomotives sit rather uneasily upon locomotives, sometimes until they are discreetly removed.

Perhaps less extreme, but more remote of public under-standing was the name given to 47 673 during March. This locomotive became 'York InterCity Control' and soon lost its name when transferred to the 47/7 fleet later in the year! It had been delightfully named 'Galloway Princess'. Open to considerable risk of adverse criticism is to opine that the name 'The Morris Dancer' is totally inappropriate to any railway locomotive, unless of course it rides as the name suggests. Whether or not this is true matters little because 47 206 was given this name during April 1994 at Manchester Piccadilly station.

Pioneer D1500 became 47 401 again during the same month, following the wishes of the shareholders of the 47 401 Project, its owners. In doing so, it regained its 'large logo' blue livery, complete with large numerals and generously painted yellow cabs. The work was undertaken on the MRC where the preserved locomotive was based.

The dividing line between a revenue-earning BR locomotive and a preserved locomotive became almost indistinguishable by this time, extremely thin and somewhat distorted. One could observe BR Class 47 No. D1524 in two-tone green livery, looking for all of the world preserved, and at the same time observe 47 401 conversely appearing to be not preserved, but a BR restoration. Clearly, each locomotive was the object of people deriving great satisfaction from nostalgic repainting of their charges. As an aside, not a few Class 47 locomotives surely must have the best-protected exteriors of any railway vehicles to be found in Britain!

One imagines that to the casual observer, taking less than usual disinterest in passing locomotives, the name 'Southampton WRD, Quality Approved' would cause some bemusement. 47 095 was named after the wagon repair depot at Southampton on 19th April by RfD Managing Director Ian Brown on the occasion of his visit to inspect the newly qualified BS5750 facilities there.

The notorious curve on the ECML at Morpeth was the scene of another spectacular derailment on 28th June 1994, ten years after 47 452 had left the rails there and twenty-five years after ten people died in a previous accident. This time it was the turn of 47 783 and its train which churned up the track and track bed and left a familiar scene of dereliction. The northbound locomotive came to rest on its side between lineside bushes and the mangled remains of its mail train, 'The Capitals Mail'. Miraculously, the 35-year old driver Mr Gerald Brown of Glasgow, escaped with only minor injuries, but it did take thirty-five minutes for the emergency services to cut him free.

The six Waterman Railways Class 47s purchased as part of the Special Trains Charter Unit deal were soon identified as 47 701/3/5/9/10/12, all originally part of the Scottish push-pull group of locomotives. 47 710 was despatched to The Railway Age at Crewe for repainting into the Waterman Railways livery of pseudo-LNWR lined black, an attractive, if somewhat unusual, application if there ever was one. Fortunately for Mr Waterman, the clean lines of the Brush Type 4 presented ample chance to make a neat presentation. The name 'LADY GODIVA' was given to this locomotive, when it was officially named at Coventry station on 28th June by the Lord Mayor of Coventry. Inspiration for the design of the nameplates was derived from those fitted to the 'Peaks' of thirty-five years previous and the earlier Bulleid 4-6-2s of the Southern Railway. The upper portion bore the title Waterman Railways and the lower portion Heritage Class. The Waterman Railways crests affixed to the right hand cab sides in turn were of LNWR inspiration. The design of crest incorporated indications of England, Scotland, Crewe and the City of London.

Proudly bearing its name 'Dollands Moor International', 47 053 headed the first of two special trains from the RfD Wembley terminal on 27th June during the inaugural celebrations of the first official Channel Tunnel freight trains. 47 375 'Tinsley Traction Depot – Quality Approved' headed the second train to Dollands Moor. Both locomotives were in immaculate RfD livery and bore the Railfreight Distribution legend in large body side lettering applied to the lower, light grey portion.

On 8th July 47 245 'The Institute of Export', similarly-liveried and newly-named that day left Mossend with the first container train from the new Eurocentral terminal there, bound for the Channel Tunnel. This inaugurated the first Scottish link of the new order of international freight flows.

A poignant reminder of the frailty of life came on 22nd July when 47 786 was named 'Roy Castle OBE'. It was a surprise event staged at Waterloo International Station for Roy Castle as he arrived at the conclusion of his four day fund-raising tour of Britain. His wife Fiona unveiled the nameplate, as part of the surprise. Roy Castle was terminally ill, suffering from cancer which he contracted as a result of his years spent as an entertainer in smoky clubs. The world was soon to be deprived of this remarkable man, an inspiration to the end.

The first nameplates to be cast in Braille script were applied to 47 745 when it was named 'Royal London Society For The Blind'. The official naming ceremony was staged on 24th September to mark the fundraising events organised by the society; the unveiling was performed by the actor Brian Blessed. Each special plate was affixed below the usual Res nameplate.

An unusual renumbering and duty for withdrawn 47 538 came in September when as ADB 968035 it commenced use as an un-powered carrier for Class 47 power units transported between Crewe Diesel Depot and ABB Crewe Works. The usual movements by road ceased temporarily due to road works en route.

The following month, one of the Class 47s earmarked for preservation (47 403) was cut up due to its poor condition, but not before useful equipment had been removed. Some parts were destined for preserved sister locomotive 47 402, on the East Lancs Railway. In some ways this should not have been surprising – the locomotive was used by the army for exercises of a special nature at Moreton-on-Lugg and had suffered fire damage and vandalism after this. It had gone by 6th November.

Withdrawals of Brush Type 4s in 1994 had been negligible by the autumn, just 47 196, but November brought three more in the shape of 47 050 (D1632), 47 190 (D1840) and 47 214 (D1864) – all on the 11th. Balance was restored when four (47 096/102/539/585) were reinstated. The class was still very numerous by this time with over 325 locomotives still on the various official books, twenty-eight of them officially stored in unserviceable condition.

On 13th December Res-owned 47 791 was officially named 'VENICE SIMPLON ORIENT-EXPRESS' at a ceremony at London Victoria station. The nameplate design was unique to a British diesel locomotive, being the circular styled and intricately detailed device of the Venice Simplon Orient-Express company. The naming was performed by the retiring UK General Manager of the VSOE, Mr John Glover Rennie.

A very late reinstatement was 47 488, officially on 16th December. This locomotive had been considered as a preservation acquisition by Pete Waterman when withdrawn from service, but his dual purpose approach to purchasing in this case led to a grey area into which a locomotive could slip and filter through to revenue-earning status. When 47 488 did emerge from overhaul at Crewe the following month it was in the same livery as 47 710 'LADY GODIVA', but with the name 'DAVIES THE OCEAN', after the founder of Cardiff Docks.

Other Brush Type 4s that were preserved continued to make good progress under their new owners. 'Generator' 1501 re-entered service on the East Lancs Railway hauling dual-heated stock on 7th January 1995, and D1842 continued its storage at Basford Hall Yard, Crewe, but underwent preventative maintenance to avoid unnecessary deterioration. 47 117 still wore a dowdy appearance, but had completed its part in filming for a television programme and had been placed in store at Bury in serviceable condition for the winter. 47 449 was moved back to Crewe on 11th January, following its exhibition at Tyseley.

Perhaps one of the more unusual reinstatements was that of 47 019, which did not return to traffic, but more probably, became a convenient means of transporting two bogies to Brush Traction for renovation. The bogie project was an exercise in evaluating the work done by an alternative private company and no doubt reaped information of use to both the operator and renovator alike. It did emphasise the fallibility sometimes involved in interpreting official information. The locomotive itself sat on wooden blocks for many months, a grey and rusting monument to the state of some parts of the railway.

Naming locomotives continued. Reprieved 47 488 rose from the ashes to become Waterman Railways' 'DAVIES THE OCEAN' in a naming ceremony at The Railway Age, Crewe, on 18th January 1995. 47 789 was named 'Lindisfarne' on 23rd February at Newcastle station and 47 790 was named 'Saint David/Dewi Sant' on 1st March at Swansea station. The Welsh naming produced a different locomotive to bear the saint's name, still bi-lingual, the two versions being reversed from previous application! Perhaps this broke the monotony of seemingly endless renamings.

Number 47 744 followed on 8th March by becoming 'Saint Edwin' at Leeds station, Waterman Railways' 47 703 (formerly 'The Queen Mother') was named 'LEWIS CAROLL' and 47 743 became 'The Bobby' honouring the close working relationship between Res and the British Transport Police. 47 743, newly outshopped in pristine Res livery, was named at a ceremony held at Bristol Temple Meads station on 30th March. Sadly, its new-found celebrity status was short-lived when the locomotive was involved in a dramatic derailment and rolled down an embankment at Skelton, north of York, on 24th July. Its young driver had to be cut free from the wreckage, losing a leg in the process, and the locomotive was swiftly condemned as un-repairable.

A twinkle may have been in the eye of Pete Waterman when he decided to name one of his locomotives 'GUY FAWKES'. Despite some political appeals not to do so, 47 705 was so-named during the weekend of 27/8th August during the Crewe Railfair event.

More namings occurred, but among the more noteworthy were three in particular. The first is more of a personal choice. Number 47 146 (originally Brush-built D1739) was named 'Loughborough Grammar School' in a damp ceremony held in the Falcon Works yard on 17th May to commemorate the 500th anniversary of the school's founding by Thomas Burton. The locomotive was fitted with the school's badge, a shield bearing three herons. Despite five years attendance at the school, the exact identity of these birds escaped your author and his fellow pupils! Perhaps some forgiveness might be in order, because as part of the Loughborough Endowed Schools, each of the three sections had different representations of the bird.

Immaculate 47 146 immediately after being named 'Loughborough Grammar School' at the Falcon Works on 17th May 1995. Note that unusually this locomotive has been fitted with oval buffers in place of the normal round type fitted to the class 47s. Oval buffers assist in preventing buffer lock on tight radius curves in sidings etc.

M J STRETTON

The second two namings were of a national celebration, connected with Royal Train duties and involved new numbers and liveries. Numbers 47 834 and 47 835 were renumbered 47 798 and 47 799, and named 'Prince William' and 'Prince Henry' respectively. To harmonise with the Royal Train, they received a Royal Claret version of the Res livery, complete with cast metal numerals and insignia, a very tasteful blend of modern and royal tradition. Wolverton Works undertook the application of this superb livery and its insignia and the locomotives were subject to a restricted photographic session on 10th May, their official roll-out day.

During March 47 805 lost its 'Bristol Bath Road' and 47 833 its 'Captain Peter Manisty RN' names. The latter regained its title a few months later! Further de-namings occurred, but such changes were only surpassed by the almost ritual renumberings. The appearance of 47 798 and 47 799 created yet another sub-section in the 47/7 series and highlighted the limitations of the numbering system, not created to deal with renumbering whims. Concurrently, the slow reclassification and renumbering of locomotives into the 47 721-92 series continued.

Various moves were afoot to preserve Class 47s, some being long-projected, some not so. One which proved successful was that by members of the Bo'ness and Kinneil Railway, when they secured 47 643 for their preserved Scottish railway in April 1995. Originally built at Crewe Works as D1979, the locomotive had spent its entire BR career based at depots in Scotland and the final four years in outdoor storage at Inverness. It had been extensively cannibalised.

After a lengthy time under repair the Morpeth accident victim, 47 783, finally returned to service, but not before being named 'Saint Peter' at the National Railway Museum at York on 29th June. Res commenced its 'saint' theme upon completion of the 'Res' theme, although 47 732 was named 'Restormel' on 21st August. Namings and renumberings continued at regular intervals when at least six locomotives were named in the September and the multiple-fitted batch 47 384-99 reverted to their previous numbers. The multiple fitted role disappeared when their Felixstowe freightliner duties went over to Class 56 haulage. More namings continued into the winter months, sometimes at the expense of other members of the class. One naming in particular was that of 47 301 which was named 'Freightliner Birmingham' at a ceremony held on 15th November to mark the thirty years of running freightliner trains. Another saw 47 746 receive 'The Bobby' plates from the ill-fated 47 743. 47 840 was re-united with its 'NORTH STAR' plates.

September 1995 proved to be a month heavy with withdrawals when five members of the class were taken off the books. From the end of the following month the pool of thirty Class 47s operated by Freightliner was moved from Tinsley to Crewe diesel depot to make operations more convenient. One result was the removal of some names deemed unsuitable.

With the Government making a third attempt to sell Freightliner these Class 47s hardly made a good advertisement, with many of the locomotives in need of overhaul. Of the thirty Class 47s on its books, only two had received recent overhauls. The least recent overhaul dated

back to 1985! Nonetheless, following reallocaction to Crewe, a start was made to paint and apply Freightliner markings to the locomotives before the end of 1995.

At this time 47 726 was named 'Progress' (24th November) and bore the title 'Manchester Airport' on separate plates above the nameplates proper. The ceremony took place at the airport station and the locomotive became the first to visit it.

Unusual nameplates were fitted to 47 584 when it was named 'The Locomotive & Carriage Institution 1911'. This took the shape of a locomotive wheel, complete with balance weight, with the name around the rim and the year in the centre. The ceremony took place at Bristol Temple Meads station on 14th December.

With the sale of Rail Express Systems (Res) to Wisconsin Central in December 1995 much attention was paid to the intentions of the new owners. Initially its President, Ed Burkhardt, was scathing in his comments on the Class 47s, stating that they were pretty poor locomotives and that replacement with new locomotives was the answer. For recently overhauled veterans, the Res Class 47s suddenly had a bleak future ahead of them. Doubt then crept in. With the acquisition of the three freight companies in February 1996, Ed Burkhardt then hinted that the Class 47s might be pooled and the state of the pool examined before a decision could be made. Certainly, the future for the Wisconsin business appeared encouraging.

Unhappily for Pete Waterman, his dealings with the mechanism of privatisation were quite the reverse. His decision to quit his involvement in running the business side of Waterman Railways came during the first few weeks of 1996. It was intended that his preservation activities should continue.

Elsewhere, Class 47s were being stored. January 1996 saw 47 221/38/41/72/481 placed aside, only slightly offset by the return from store of 47 830.

Like the Brush Type 2s, the Class 47s had served their masters well. They had proved extremely adaptable, far beyond the imagination of those who steered into uncharted waters in the first years of the 1960s. They kept pace with numerous developments over the years despite not seeming to be cured of some of their ills. As 1996 unfurled into another stage of privatisation, foreign eyes seemed to relax the uncompromising view first held. Wisconsin Central's newly-formed English Welsh & Scottish Railway Ltd was only a little less scathing in summation, seeking to either replace many of its Class 47s and re-engineer others, possibly installing new power units (including American engines).

After thirty years of hard work, and sometimes indifferent care, was it not more than a little unfair to berate those hard-working survivors? The only answer is that it was indeed unfair.

One result of the EW&S takeover was that the 47/7 conversion programme was halted, in the light of their placing the order for 250 new locomotives. In the meantime, active members of the class continued as ever to haul their varied traffics around the system and their owners continued to name and de-name them with regularity. Perhaps the most unusual renaming was that of 47 710 when Waterman Railways bestowed the name 'QUASIMODO' upon it during May 1996. This was in connection with a special train, which was prepared to publicise the new Walt Disney film, The Hunchback of Notre Dame. The naming was supposed to be temporary, but many months later the locomotive was still in service bearing the new name! At least ten others lost their names before the year was out.

With the reduced Waterman railway involvement came the disposal of locomotives. Number 1501 went to the Bury Hydraulic Group on the East Lancashire Railway and D1705 to the Great Central Railway and towards the end of the year the Rail Charter Services were left with 47 449/488/701/3/9 with sale pending and 47 705 just sold, but still at Crewe, and 47 710/12 retained for future RCS use. Number 47 712 was the only locomotive of the Class working the commuter trains between Rhymney and Cardiff.

When 47 701 was sold it was part of an exchange of Christmas and tenth wedding anniversary presents between husband and wife Alan and Tracey Lear of Cheltenham! The couple already owned other items of rolling stock, so neither was at a loss as to what presents to buy. Conversely, 47 705 was bought back by Pete Waterman during November 1996!

Three more were sold on 7th January 1997, 47 488 and 47 703 to Mr Martin Sargent of Fragonset Railways and 47 449 which was destined for the Llangollen Railway. Then came the further sale of 47 709 to Fragonset Railways towards the end of the month. This left 47 710/12, which were moved to Kidderminster, then to Tyseley at the end of July to join the Fragonset trio.

Meanwhile, 47 701 was named 'Waverley' at Crewe Electric Open Day on 3rd May 1997, the name formerly carried by 47 708. The locomotive moved to the Birmingham Railway Museum at Tyseley the following month to complement the Fragonset fleet, which was due to arrive soon afterwards as an operational base was established. During July 47 701/3 were given full Railtrack running certification and 47 710/12 were cleared soon afterwards.

The year 1996 had waned with eighteen Res Class 47s placed in store in serviceable condition at Crewe as a result of the reorganisation of postal services. Another four were sent to Immingham to join the Loadhaul contingency fleet and a further nine were transferred to the Transrail restricted use weekend fleet.

At the close of 1996 thirteen Class 47s were in preservation, although in some cases such a classification was nominal. There were thirteen Class 47s stored at Bescot, where seventy-five locomotives of various classes were gathered. In all, around the country there were sixty-one Class 47s out of service. Soon, twenty-four would go to MRJ Philips for scrap.

More speculation of a Class 47 rebuild exercise (on 47 347 and 47 156) came at this time, for English, Welsh & Scottish (EWS), and although nothing materialised, Freightliner-owned 47 356 arrived at Loughborough following the departure of 47 555, the previously-rumoured candidate. 47 356 lay at the works for some months and was taken into the Erecting Shop and had its power unit removed for inspection during a visit by Freightliner personnel on 14th August as part of a Brush Traction effort to secure a rebuild contract.

Number 47 270 arrived at the works on 15th May 1997 and soon became the subject of a cab refurbishing exercise, which included air-conditioning, for Freightliner. Within seven months the work was done and the locomotive returned to traffic.

On the cosmetic side of the locomotive scene 47 814 emerged from an overhaul at Adtranz's Crewe Works during early March 1997 repainted in Virgin CrossCountry livery of dark grey and red with white horizontal stripes. With the Virgin XC logo applied to the body sides adjacent to the cab side doors, another Class 47 livery variant had arrived, and one pleasing to the eye. It was unveiled on 17th March and the locomotive went into service the following day.

Only a short period of time passed before EWS had 47 785 and 47 786 repainted in maroon and gold. The latter retained its name 'Roy Castle', but in a specially prepared surprise his widow unveiled the name 'Fiona Castle' on 11th June – she thought that the name of 47 786 would be 'Tour of Hope'! The 1997 Tour of Hope that she was launching had an international flavour. Both locomotives powered the inaugural train from Waterloo Station in London to Liverpool Lime Street.

Following the return of a Labour Government the new Deputy Prime Minister Mr John Prescott waved the first train away from the new Hams Hall Freight Terminal in Warwickshire on 11th July 1997. At the head of the Milan-bound train was Railfreight Distribution 47 312, newly named 'Parsec of Europe' by Mr Prescott. The name honoured the American operator Parsec which operated forty terminals in North America and was intending to develop a European network. The locomotive looked smart and attractive in its three-tone grey livery and diamond 'sector' decals, the continued use of the mid-1980s freight livery, modified only in detail to suit the new situation.

Privatisation continued to produce various sales. During mid-1997 Freightliner purchased seven Class 47s from EWS to alleviate its motive power crisis. Prior to this EWS had 47 193/296/329/332/334/353/372 stored out of use in Bescot yard and by mid-August the new owners had returned 47 332 and 47 372 to traffic and had 47 296 and 47 329 under repair, Toton being charged with this task for the former pair and Crewe Diesel Maintenance Depot the latter. One locomotive was reserved as a source of spare parts for the others.

By this time the official withdrawal from service of 47 317 had taken place, a rare occurrence at this time. Better things were promised for this locomotive when Freightliner announced its long-awaited plans. Six of its Class 47s would be fitted with 2,500bhp General Motors GM645-12-E3 engines and 'Class 56' alternators. The first conversion would be 47 356, already at the Falcon Works awaiting its fate. This move created Class 57, with this locomotive becoming 57 001 and with 47 350/317/187/322/347 intended to become 57 002-6.

The official announcement of the £3 million order, placed with Brush Traction, came on 28th October 1997, with 57 001 expected to be completed in time for trial running in the following s pring. Benefits expected were better reliability, the ability to haul heavier trains of 1,600 tonnes, upgraded wheel slip control, sanding equipment and improved driver's cabs. Although the retention of the existing traction motors dictated the Type 4 diesel and alternator power output, the Type 5 classification probably indicated Type 5 haulage capability.

The success of such improvements hinted at a re-engineering of the entire Freightliner fleet of sixty Class 47 locomotives, involving a cost of up to £30 million. Such moves represented a radical and long-overdue change, following years of neglect by the railways. Many Class 47s were in pitiful condition, but despite this many drivers still held the past successes and potential capabilities in high regard.

In the meantime, the Class 47/7s gathered under the wing of Fragonset Railways became certified for main line use and started to appear in a new livery of black, relieved by a red bodyside band reaching arrowheads adjacent to each cabside door. First in this guise was 47 703, by this time nameless, with 47 701/09/10/12 due to follow. Number 47 488, retaining green livery, was to be added to those restored main line running condition whilst 47 703/12 were noted on Class 1 Virgin passenger trains during November 1997. Following the tragic death of Princess Diana, many hoped that 47 712 would have its Lady Diana Spencer name restored, having lost it in May 1995. A more apt name would have been Princess Diana.

As part of the arrangements of Princess Diana's funeral on 6th September 1997, the Royal Train carrying members of the Royal Family from London to Long Buckby, Northamptonshire, was appropriately hauled by Royal Train locomotives 47 798 'Prince William' and 47 799 'Prince Henry'. At the time of her death a week earlier, the train was undergoing scheduled overhaul and the locomotives being repainted into a revised livery. The base colour remained claret, but the cast Res logos were removed and a five-inch maroon, gold-edged, body side stripe was added. A cast EIIR monogram, surmounted with a crown, was added to each body side, in line with the stripe, and the EWS logo appeared under each right hand cabside window.

The appearance of preserved locomotive 47 643 on the Bo'ness & Kinneil Railway in InterCity livery and with ScotRail branding was a welcome change. Work on the locomotive was completed in time for it to star in the Diesel Gala of 30th/31st August 1997. Its previous guise had been the briefly worn XP64 livery.

The following month EWS had 47 627 repainted maroon, but with a gaudy advertisement promoting Mars confectionery. The word 'celebrations' appeared twice on each body side, with letters rendered in various typefaces associated with the various brand names. On 17th September a special promotional train carrying mostly Mars employees ran from St. Pancras to Bedford. There followed several weeks of wearing this livery, but removal of the advertising material was effected by mid-November.

Following an upturn in traffic EWS had found itself short of motive power and reinstated stored locomotives. Its variously acquired Class 47s were treated much the same as its Class 31s, but on a longer timescale. The former Trainload examples continued to operate so long as repair and maintenance costs were not excessive, whereas the fate of the former Res Class 47/7s operating Royal Mail and charter trains would be sealed when the new fleet of Class 67 high-speed locomotives came into service in 1999. With the purchase of RfD by EWS, completed on 22nd November 1997, the future of the latter's Class 47s, around seventy in number, depended upon which services would be better Type 5 loaded and hauled. Significant changes were expected, but in the

The 20.30 'Caledonian Sleeper' for London Euston awaits departure from Inverness on 19th May 2000, headed by Class 47/7 No. 47 790 Saint David/Dewi Sant.

BRIAN MORRISON

short term EWS returned 47 474/75/522/802 to traffic during November and December 1997, with four more locomotives being sent to Tinsley for assessment.

More Class 47 hulks were despatched from Doncaster Carr Depot on 19th January 1998, to the Booth Roe scrapyard in Rotherham. The locomotives concerned were 47 346/359/677. Contrasting with this was the repainting of 47 813 into Great Western Trains green livery at Adtranz Crewe. It emerged at the end of March sporting the name 'SS Great Britain', the company's name and 'roadrunner' logo. Thankfully, 47 710 lost its name 'QUASIMODO' upon repainting into Fragonset Railways livery.

Since the opening of Tinsley depot in 1965 Class 47s had been a familiar feature there and it was a sad time for the staff when closure came on 28th March. The depot's pride and joy 47 145 'Merddin Emrys', resplendent in newly-applied dark blue livery and bearing RfD diamond decals, was prominent and following closure Tinsley's operational allocation was transferred to Bescot, near Walsall. Mid-March also saw the total number of Class 47s in CF Booth's scrap yard near Rotherham increase to fifteen as two of Tinsley's derelict locomotives were disposed of.

During the early Summer of 1998 the twenty-seven strong Class 47/8 fleet operated by Virgin ran into difficulties due to failures and transfer to other duties at the worst time leaving only eleven available for one Saturday's traffic when eighteen were required. Fortunately, there was recourse to other locomotives, hired from elsewhere, and some 47/0s and 47/3s came to the rescue. Fragonset supplied 47 701/703/712 on occasions.

A curious case of clerical slowness saw 47 340 and 47 473 withdrawn on 1st June 1998, which was somewhat belated as both had been scrapped at Crewe months previously. Three weeks later the Rail Regulator prevented EWS from scrapping locomotives. John Swift was following up a complaint from one of the smaller railway operators that such concerns were being denied access to working assets.

EWS had intended quick disposal of locomotives once its new Class 66 locomotives arrived in sufficiently large numbers to replace them. Although Class 47 disposals had not been in large numbers, future efforts to dispose of them were seriously delayed. As it transpired, EWS chose to sort out its Class 31s among its initial disposals and advertised many for sale during 1999. Few Class 47s were featured in these lists. If the pitiful condition of some Class 47s was sufficient indication, then scrapping was perhaps the better option. August saw the withdrawal of six EWS Class 47s 47 144/222/291/378/520/543.

Meanwhile, Fragonset continued to maintain its locomotives. Its operational hire fleet in July 1998 consisted of 47 701/703/709/710/712, with 47 488 not far from being reinstated and 47 710 due for repair and maintenance. They continued to help alleviate Virgin's availability problem; indeed Virgin arranged to use EWS-owned 47 702 and 47 711, having them repainted in Virgin livery at the Falcon Works.

When Fragonset's 47 488 reappeared it was finished in 1960s two-tone green livery as near as possible. Instead of the old BR lion and wheel emblem there was a new version of the Fragonset dragon in the same theme.

During the autumn of 1998 EWS reclassified its codes for locomotives taken out of traffic. Gone were the days of a locomotive being withdrawn or stored, not that much credibility had surrounded these classifications for some time. In came WNXX denoting stored, WNYX for component recovery and WNZX for withdrawal.

Fifty-one Class 47 locomotives entered these categories, but unfortunately, the meaning of some of these became somewhat tenuous in practice and locomotives could be reinstated, albeit only sufficiently for towing along main lines to another location. EWS soon established a component recovery depot at Wigan (Springs Branch) and Class 47s trickled into it. Potential locomotives for the centre entered the scene when seven former RfD Class 47s were displaced by new Class 66s before the end of the year.

Mid-January saw 47 051 and 47 281 at the Wigan depot being stripped of components and a further eight members of the class taken out of traffic, with even more during February. This brought the total to around sixty for the winter months, leaving only thirty available for freight traffic. By early May twelve were at Wigan. The first Class 47s were offered for sale during March/April, six in all, as EWS started to advertise some of its relics. Three more followed the following month, and further withdrawals reduced those available for freight traffic to thirteen. In contrast to this, EWS hand painted Freightliner Class 47 No. 47 193 into the latter's new green livery, first applied to 57 001. The re-styled locomotive soon featured in celebrations at Felixstowe on 13th April 1999 to mark the completion of modernisation of the Felixstowe branch. Nine more such repaints were planned.

At Crewe the LNWR-owned 47 705 'GUY FAWKES' was ready for main line re-certification following its prolonged static use for providing electrical supplies for LNWR coaching stock being overhauled there. It was back in service during June and soon relieving the continuing Virgin Trains locomotive shortage. Surprisingly, it was sold during the following autumn to Riviera Trains to enable them to provide a facility to train operators for charter train operation. The locomotive was expected to remain based at Crewe.

Number 47 701, owned by Tracey Lear and operating under the Fragonset banner, was stopped because of an engine room fire as it arrived at Birmingham New Street station on 16th May 1999. The stricken locomotive brought the station to a standstill as overhead power was isolated and the fire services called in to deal with it. It was reported as back in traffic some weeks later, but by early September was in Fragonset's newly acquired facility at Derby undergoing repairs to its traction motors. Before the month was out it was back in traffic.

On 20th August the first EWS Res 47/7, 47 779, was placed in store following a main generator failure. It also required a bogie change. Its last working had been on 4th May on the 13.30 Mossend-Inverness train and was towed to Crewe two days later. Not having it repaired was no doubt influenced by the expected arrival of the first examples of thirty Class 67 locomotives from Spain. 47 769 was switched off on 29th October at Cardiff Canton and officially stored on 26th November.

The problems encountered with the first Class 67 arrival, 67 003, and the ensuing delays probably gave 47 765 a reprieve when it suffered a generator fault and entered the Falcon Works for a generator change during January 2000. It was expected that most of the Res 47/7s would be withdrawn from service, leaving sixteen with reliability modifications in service for a little longer.

The arrival on 1st December 1999 at the Falcon Works of derelict 47 221 caused some speculation that it was to become a Class 57. It had been earmarked some time previously by EWS for sale to Freightliner, but nothing came of it and the locomotive was sided. The reason for its arrival was to be used as a guinea pig for conducting Brush experiments with a different fire protection system. These tests were undertaken on 15/16th December using the Pyrogen fire suppression system using technology developed for the Russian 'Soyuz' space missions. The tests were conducted in the sections between cabs, particularly the engine room, and were successful when several fires were extinguished within seconds.

The new century dawned with the majority of operational Class 47s grouped as follows:- EWS, Freightliner, Porterbrook hire fleet and Fragonset. There were, of course, sundry survivors and the preserved locomotives also.

Losses, due to the EWS cull on former RfD locomotives, were particularly heavy during the previous year and the trend was completed during 2000. At Healey Mills alone, thirteen Class 47s awaited their fates.

EWS continued to advertise sales and started to dispose of its withdrawn Class 47s with examples continuing to be sent to the Springs Branch disposal centre. Withdrawals commenced within the ranks of the former Res 47/7 locomotives, although three (47 747/766/769) were transferred on long term loan to Virgin Trains from January 2000 to relieve that company's constant shortage of operational and reliable Class 47s. Meanwhile, Fragonset Railways returned 47 701 'Waverley' to traffic, following fire damage repairs effected at Derby.

A new lease of life was expected for Porterbrook Leasing's 47 825 'Thomas Telford' when it was driven into Brush Traction during the morning of 29th March 2000 for expected conversion into an electric train supply (ETS, formerly known as ETH) Class 57. It was by no means certain at this time what was to happen, but the locomotive was kept active and used for shunting on occasions, before being brought into the Erecting Shop and having its power unit removed on 25/26th May. This move was prompted by a letter of intent received from its owners. The resultant rebuild was expected to become 57 601 in 2001. In several ways there was life still to be squeezed from the Brush Type 4 yet.

EWS finally took 47 702 and 47 711 out of traffic following continued failures whilst hired to Virgin Trains. This left EWS operating three 47/4s and most of its former Res 47/7s, the latter being withdrawn whenever misfortune or impending costs dictated withdrawal. Number 47 745 went into store following a fire on 4th April and several of its sisters, displaced by new Class 67s, went into Virgin livery for extended lives

Porterbrook-liveried Class 57/6 No 57 601 approaches Bristol Temple Meads on 5th September 2001, hauling the 09.20 Plymouth-Paddington service. This was the locomotive's fifth running number, having previously been allocated D1759, 47 165, 47 590 & 47 825.

BRIAN MORRISON

on hire to Virgin. Likewise, more of Porterbrook's 47/8s on hire to Virgin were repainted into Virgin livery.

With continued deliveries of Class 66s, completion of the Class 57 deliveries and increasing problems with the Class 47s it operated, Freightliner reduced its operational fleet further. It also announced that it was bringing final withdrawal of the Class forward to the end of 2003.

Meanwhile, in January 2001, Fragonset Railways returned 47 712 to traffic in its black livery and named it 'ARTEMIS', following the naming theme of 47 703 'HERMES'. 'ARTEMIS' recalled the Greek goddess Diana, a well-researched link with the locomotive's former name 'Lady Diana'. First Great Western, meanwhile, was leasing 47 811/813/815/816/830/832 /846 from Porterbrook.

EWS continued to take its Class 47s out of traffic. 47 575 'City of Hereford' saw its last run on 1st February 2001, leaving 47 635 the sole remaining non-47/7 left in its front line fleet. With life left in the 47/7 ranks, even after official displacement by Class 67s on mail trains, EWS-liveried 47 744 was named 'Royal Mail Cheltenham' during February. Indeed, the company was to regard most of them as general purpose locomotives, with 47 798/799 specialising in Royal Train duties. At this time EWS had around fifty 47/7s in service. A trickle of withdrawn EWS Class 47s continued to

be cannibalised, offered for sale and scrapped. Freightliner also placed some of its fleet into store from time to time.

On 28th April 2001 47 828, in Virgin red and black livery, was named 'Severn Valley Railway, Kidderminster Bewdley Bridgnorth' by the railway's chairman, Paul Fathers, during the spring Diesel Gala. Virgin Trains also decided to commemorate the last months of Virgin Class 47 service (before replacing them with Class 220 Voyager trains) by more namings and running several in heritage liveries.

A happy event was the re-appearance in traffic of preserved 47 401, the pioneer Brush Type 4, after five years. It was painted in BR large logo blue and worked trains at the Midland Railway Centre's autumn Diesel Gala on 15th September.

By September 47 145 had been sold by EWS to GB Railfreight (GBRf), a surprising move amid a large batch of Class 47 purchases by Alstom Traincare (2), Fragonset Railways (14)

After the naming ceremony, the presentation plate of Virgin Class 47/4 No 47 828 is given to SVR Chairman, Paul Fathers (third from left), by Chris Green and Virgin Trains' staff at Kidderminster Town station on 28th April 2001.

BRIAN MORRISON

and others. GBRf required its locomotive for 'thunderbird' Anglia passenger duties as well as its own use and Alstom intended their pair (47 488 and 47 802) to undertake its own nationwide rolling stock movements. 47 145 was to stay with GBRf for only a few months after a change in plans – in March 2002 it was sold to Fragonset Railways.

The wait of some months to see Virgin Class 47/8s in heritage liveries came to an end, when 47 826 was released from Toton in InterCity 'swallow' livery and was re-united with its former name 'Springburn', and then in mid-November by 47 847 in BR style large logo blue livery. They were quickly followed by 47 853, which reappeared in XP64 livery and bearing its first number D1733 and retaining its TOPS number, and 47 851, which received as nearly original two-tone green with original number D1648. All four presented extremely attractive sights with their superb finishes.

Then came the namings in January 2002. First at Euston station on the 10th was 47 847, which received dual naming 'Railway World'/'Brian Morrison' and second was 47 851, which was unveiled 'Traction Magazine' at Derby on the 15th.

Virgin's next namings were unrelated to the above, being 47 805 'Pride of Eastleigh', 47 812 'Pride of Toton' and 47 839 'Pride of Saltley'. They were named after the depots that maintained them and the names commemorated them for their last months in traffic, expected in 2002. All were named on 6th February at their respective depots.

For the first time in many years locomotive hauled services returned to the Midland Main Line on 18th February 2002 when Fragonset Railways provided Class 47 haulage and a rake of HSBC-owned InterCity liveried Mk2 coaches to cover for extended HST repairs. Initial allocations included 47 703, 47 709 and 47 712, with green liveried 47 488 acting as standby locomotive. The St Pancras-Nottingham and Sheffield coverage was arranged on a renewable fortnightly period arrangement.

In February 2002 Fragonset Railways purchased another ten Class 47s from EWS. Although in varying condition, it was intended to return some to traffic as freight locomotives. All were former Railfreight Distribution examples (47 053/ 201/219/226/229/293/313/314/360/375).

The presentation nameplate is given to Brian Morrison after the surprise naming ceremony at Euston on 10th January 2002. He thought he was unveiling Railway World Magazine!

BRIAN MORRISON

As part of a nationwide campaign to reduce trespass and vandalism, repainted 47 829 was unveiled on 25th March wearing a 'police' livery of white with red horizontal band, relieved by a British Transport Police badge and POLICE branding. High profile launching and touring followed.

Virgin's heritage 47 853 in XP64 guise, finally received its name on 26th April when it was unveiled 'Rail Express' at Grosmont, on the North Yorkshire Moors Railway. About this time it was announced that Virgin CrossCountry Class 47 hauled trains were scheduled to cease on 19th August due to the further and earlier introduction of new Voyager diesel electric multiple units.

Virgin 47 840 'NORTH STAR' was repainted into BR corporate blue livery in May to make the fifth and final heritage livery Class 47 in its fleet. Its return in this livery was on 22nd May, when it powered the Derby-Plymouth return service.

Number 47 714 left the Falcon Works at 11.30 on 8th June and made its return to service under Cotswold Railway ownership soon afterwards, taking up 'thunderbird' duties at Norwich for Anglia Railways, albeit retaining its shabby Res livery. It had been at Loughborough since 28th December 2001. Its return represented the company's first main line locomotive hiring.

During the summer Direct Railway Services (DRS) acquired four Class 47s with 47 484 and 47 802 coming from Alstom and 47 194 and 47 501 coming from Bralesford Engineering. Though not fully operational, 47 802 was close returning to traffic during the late summer. During this period EWS offered another fifteen of the class for sale and this was soon followed by Freightliner and Porterbrook offering twelve of their Class 47s for sale jointly.

Virgin CrossCountry had its celebrations following the cessation of regular Class 47 haulage with 47 840 and 47 847 on 19th August with the Penzance-Manchester. The two locomotives then made their way to Derby, then onwards to Toton depot, where they joined a special line-up of Virgin Class 47s made up of the following:- 47 851, 47 853, 47 040 (disguised as 47 077, its original TOPS number), 47 847, 47 826 and 47 805, the last-named in Virgin red and black livery.

Virgin West Coast continued with its daily Class 47 haulage of trains between Crewe and Holyhead, along the North Wales coast, expected to continue until May 2003 at least.

By late summer EWS had started a life extension and reliability modification programme for seven of its 47/7 fleet, the first to be treated was 47 773, appearing from Toton on 29th August in newly applied EWS red livery.

August 2002 saw the fortieth anniversary of the completion of D1500 and the following month the same anniversary of its appearance on BR metals. Despite being long in the tooth and more than just a few being neglected and still in service the class survivors represented an overall successful career on many types of duty. It was a proud record, and a continuing one.

Another purchase of eight Class 47s from EWS by Fragonset during the early autumn brought its total to forty-two; it was a case of buy when you can. Although the company had not increased its operational total significantly, it did require a source of spare parts and sufficient to place non-ETS examples into service.

Considering some Class 47s to have longer futures than others, Freightliner repainted 47 279 and 47 292 in its standard green livery, while Virgin continued to use its Class 47s, and following the cessation of regular cross country duties it reorganised its fleet into two pools. First was the retained ILRA pool based at Crewe Diesel depot, serving the Holyhead workings along the North Wales coastal route and the Saturday Manchester-Paignton booking, using 47 812/839/840/847/851/853. Second was the ATLO pool based at Longsight, Polmadie and Willesden depots. In this pool nine vintage locomotives, 47 805/810/818/826/828/ 829/841/843/848, plus Thunderbirds 57 301/2 were detailed to cover diversionary towings of trains affected by the continued West Coast Main Line upgrading.

All these Virgin locomotives were owned by Porterbrook and represented a dwindling fleet as other examples had been sent to the Falcon Works for conversion into Class 57. Later, Porterbrook would sell further locomotives to other operators, and indeed 47 839 'Pride of Saltley' and 47 853 'Rail Express' were transferred to Riviera Trains before the year was out, in exchange for releasing 47 705 for incorporation into the Class 57 conversion programme at the Falcon Works. 47 839 appeared on 10th January 2003 in plain Oxford Blue in BR corporate style and without its name, to match the company's luxury charter train.

Cotswold Rail (CR) acquired another locomotive in the shape of 47 200. The former EWS locomotive soon emerged from overhaul at Wabtec Doncaster on 6th November bearing the attractive silver CR livery and the following day, the name 'Fosse Way'. It was the company's second main line locomotive to enter service and its first in CR livery. The locomotive was released from Doncaster on 5th December.

Fragonset saw the end of its Midland Main Line involvement in providing Class 47s and rolling stock when 47 703/712 worked the last locomotive-hauled trains on 11th October. The company also returned to traffic 47 355 on 13th November and named the locomotive 'AVOCET'. The livery remained black but with Fragonset placed along the body sides in large red lettering outlined in white and relief metal cab side Fragonset dragons rather than the usual livery. As a non-ETS locomotive, 47 355 sported what became to be known as Fragonset freight livery. At this time DRS repainted its first Class returnee 47 802 in its blue livery and returned to the main line in December, albeit briefly.

The autumn also saw Porterbrook select six of its Freightliner locomotives for sending to the Falcon Works for the Class 57 conversion programme. The batch consisted of 47 209/330/337/349/371/372 and arrived at the works during November 2002. Another three former Freightliner locomotives passed into preservation with 47 206, 47 367 and 47 376. The first went to an un-named private individual whereas the latter pair went to The Stratford 47 Group and Brush Type 4 Fund respectively. As it transpired, 47 206 did not survive long in this status and was sent to the Falcon Works as a Class 57 candidate becoming 57 605 in due course.

The next EWS sale of locomotives had a deadline date of 10th December 2002 and included twelve Class 47s, all ETS fitted and all but one were Class 47/4 examples. Slowly, the ranks of the 47/7s were being chipped away as storage beckoned various locomotives, notably 47 741/759 and the latest being 47 785 in January 2003.

During the early part of the new year it became known who had acquired former EWS locomotives. Purchasers included Harry Needle Railroad Company (HNRC) (47 462/492/535), Fragonset (47 471/547/574), Cotswold Rail (47 475/528), and into preservation (47 524/540/596). Number 47 596 was acquired by the Stratford Class 47 Group.

North Wales attracted more Class 47s in February to supplement First North Western services using EWS 47/7s, initially in February but more formally from 1st April. Services affected were Birmingham-Holyhead and Manchester-Holyhead and continuing problems saw further 47s drafted in when required.

First Great Western continued to use their four Class 47s (47 811/813/815/832) between London and the southwest aided by prototype 57 601.

DRS eventually took delivery of its first working Class 47 from the Alstom Railcare works at Springburn, Glasgow, on 1st March 2003. This was 47 237, and although it was the second to be completed, recurring problems with 47 802 led to its overtaking the ETS locomotive. The third locomotive, 47 298, left Springburn on 3rd May.

Mid-2003 saw six former Virgin-used Porterbrook locomotives transferred to Freightliner Heavy Haul use. Numbers 47 805/812/829/843/847/848 were moved to their new operator to cope with increased workings and the loss of older examples. In particular, the movement of new Pendolino units required ETS provision and the 47/8s fitted the bill. Further reducing its stock, Porterbrook transferred 47 854 ex-Virgin CrossCountry to Carnforth-based train

operator West Coast Railway Company (WCR) during May. This was followed by 47 818 transferring to Cotswold Rail and re-entering traffic in East Anglia during July, still in Virgin red and black livery. Cotswold Rail at this time was expecting 47 316 'Cam Peak' to enter service after overhaul at Wabtec Doncaster. It had emerged from the works in mid-June in CR silver livery. Number 47 714, meantime, still retained its shabby coat, though not for long.

On 26th June The Class 47 Preservation Project's newly acquired 47 771 arrived at its preservation site, the Colne Valley Railway, for restoration to full working order. It was one of the last few Brush Type 4s to be built at Loughborough, and a preservation rarity at the time of purchase.

Wabtec Doncaster celebrated 150 years of providing for the railway over the weekend of 26/27th July 2003 by opening its works to the public. On display were steam, diesel and electric locomotives dating from 1870. Among the visiting locomotives was 47 635, the lone survivor of Class 47/4 in EWS service, newly repainted in BR large logo livery (Highland Rail variant) and newly named 'The Lass O' Ballochmyle'. Toton paintshop had done a superb job on her repainting and transformed a once-shabby Parcels red and dark grey exterior

Class 47/4 No. 47 815 PORTERBROOK near Rhyl on 29th July 2004, hauling the 08.35 service from Euston to Holyhead. DVT No. 82124 is on the rear of the rake.

BRIAN MORRISON

into a delightful finish, with the locomotive emerging on 10th July. Fragonset Railways provided newly overhauled 47 715 'POSEIDON', but although not quite completed, it was sufficiently presentable for display. Also there was ex-works 47 316 'Cam Peak' representing Cotswold Rail.

Other Fragonset locomotives were working during August, noted were 47 355/488/701/703/709/712, with absent 47 710 still undergoing protracted overhaul at Derby.

With the deadline for fitting Train Protection and Warning System (TPWS) looming at the end of the year, Freightliner provisionally selected 47 150/270/289/303/309/358 to be so fitted, leaving 47 197/224/279/292 for storage, provided that no untoward incidents or traffic requirements deemed otherwise.

Completion of the overhaul of DRS 47 501 came at the end of August when Alstom Glasgow finished eleven months of work bringing the locomotive back to running order in DRS livery, fulfilling the task of bringing the Class 47 fleet to its intended four. It left the works on 6th September and entered traffic three days later. In contrast, EWS placed another five locomotives into the WNTR storage pool (the code adopted for stored locomotives), these being 47 758/772/781/782/785, leaving its operational fleet at a total of 29.

On 6th October Cotswold Rail 47 714 showed its new face at Norwich station. The locomotive had been repainted in Anglia Railways light blue livery, complete with Anglia branding and a horizontal white band around its waist and another below cantrail level. Concurrently, West Coast Railway repainted its 47 854 in maroon livery, relieved by a black band along the body sides. The pattern was almost the same as the Fragonset passenger livery, but with the colours reversed. Maroon was chosen to match Mk1 coaching stock used for charter work.

Fragonset's operational 47 716, loaned indefinitely to the preserved Dartmoor Railway, returned to use on the line and its ETS was made operable to haul heated trains during the winter period. It still bore faded Res livery.

New tour operator Garsdale Tours entered the charter market on 29th November when it ran a sell-out Sheffield-Edinburgh excursion using Fragonset's green 47 488. To provide his own motive power, owner Tony Gadd bought former EWS 47 492 from HNRC and moved it to Carnforth for long-term restoration to working order.

Before 2003 closed EWS was emitting warning signals that further fleet reductions were on the way for the start of its financial year in April 2004, with charter train operators being told not to accept any bookings for after this time. It was thought that the Class 47 fleet could be reduced to as few as nine.

Such a move was affected in part by the decision of Royal Mail to abandon the Travelling Post Office workings on 10th January, these being worked by EWS Class 47/7s and Class 67. Although the latter were largely employed on these duties, their displacement was certain to have a further knock-on effect. Already the active fleet was down to 26. Another trim in January 2004 reduced it further to 22 examples – 47 635/727/732-734/737/747/750/757/ 760/770/773/776/778/784/787/790-793/798/799.

By mid February the total had been reduced to nine. Not included was the royal pair 47 798/799, effectively replaced by Class 67. Last booked duties for EWS Class 47s were Arriva Trains Wales duties along the North Wales Coast and by mid-March only five remained. The Arriva contract expired on 31st March. By the end of April only two remained, as standby locomotives for Virgin.

As First Great Western (FGW) introduced its four Class 57s (57 602-5) the withdrawal of its four Class 47s beckoned. Numbers 47 811/832 were planned as the first to go, followed by 47 813 and finally 47 815 later in 2004 when delivery of 57 605 was expected. By April 2004 only 47 815 remained in theory, but the others were placed on standby. Number 47 815 was treated to a Porterbrook-sponsored repaint into BR two-tone green at Bristol St. Philip's Marsh to mark the final few months of FGW service. It was unveiled at the depot on 17th May. FGW also hoped to use it on special trains during the summer period.

Fragonset increased its operational fleet of non-ETS Class 47s to three when 47 145 and 47 375 were returned to traffic. The former was finished in April and appeared in its former French Blue livery with RfD sector markings and a new version of its Welsh name 'MYRDDIN EMRYS'. 47 375 was repainted in Fragonset freight livery as per 47 355 and returned to traffic some months later.

Promised by EWS for the National Railway Museum, 47 798 'Prince William' was taken from its storage at Ferrybridge on 3rd May and moved to Toton for a repaint, keeping its Royal Claret livery. It was destined to appear at the Railfest at York and on this occasion it was formally handed over to the museum.

It made its first journey in museum ownership on 22nd July, when it stood in for failed 4472 'Flying Scotsman' on a York-Scarborough return trip.

On 15th June 47 750, one of the surviving EWS operational locomotives, caught fire at Colwyn Bay. The damage saw it taken out of traffic and stored, leaving 47 787 to soldier on. The survivor lasted until 20th June, when the Virgin contract expired. It was a fading end to many years of faithful Class 47 service.

With a deadline of 22nd June 2004 EWS advertised nine more Class 47s for sale, all located at Wigan. Seven were 47/7s. This was soon followed by Freightliner offering locomotives for sale, including ten Class 47s. These were 47 114/157/193/258/339/353, dumped at Crewe Basford Hall, 47 205/207/334 at Southampton Maritime and 47 287 at Crewe Diesel Maintenance Depot. With scrapping in mind, metal recycling firm Booth's of Rotherham bought the lot. One, however, did not go to Rotherham, it found its way into preservation, moving from Southampton Maritime to the Northampton & Lamport Railway in early December.

News of Riviera Trains buying two more Class 47s came in July 2004, bringing its fleet to four. These were former EWS locomotives 47 575 and 47 769, which had been purchased by HNRC. Number 47 769 was collected from Toton on 5th July by 47 839 and taken to the East Lancashire Railway, where it was started up the following day. It arrived in time for the railway's Diesel Gala (7-11th July) and featured in the event. 47 575 remained stored at Motherwell in the meantime, moving south on 21st July. This locomotive was mooted at the time to be provided with long-range fuel tanks and a possible renumbering to 47 855 to reflect this status.

Cotswold Rail had its 47 818 repainted in early July, being out-shopped on the 10th. It appeared in the colourful livery of 'one' the controversial new name of the combined railways of East Anglia. The livery represented a combination of colours guaranteed to be eye-catching with its blues, whites, orange and yellow front warning panels – quite a fruit salad selection.

Fragonset Railways had quite a collection of Class 47s by mid-2004, scattered around the country on various sites. Many were purchased for spare parts and others were considered to be candidates for overhaul, but the company had not placed any more ETS Class 47s in service for some time. The busy workshops were concentrating on returning various Class 31s and three freight Class 47s to traffic, and had taken 47 701 and 47 703 out of traffic pending the fitting of TPWS. 47 715 had remained at York, its overhaul almost finished. In August the company offered 47 236/348/363/368/ 471/489/547/574/972 for sale. Most were destined for scrap.

The North Wales coast continued to see a variety of Class 47s during the summer months and Virgin even hired non-ETS examples from Freightliner on occasions. Freightliner at this time was operating a selection of Class 47s, some of its own and some hired from Porterbrook, including ETS examples bearing Virgin colours with small Railfreight stickers below the cab side windows. Such are the ways of privatisation that unusual hiring occurs. During August EWS hired Cotswold Rail's 47 200 and 47 316, albeit at short notice. This was a company that could not be rid of its Class 47 fleet quickly enough a few months previously. Even Fragonset had to hire Porterbrook 47 832 in the short term, pending

the return to traffic of 47 715. This locomotive was even sub-hired to Riviera Trains to work North Wales Coast services for Arriva Trains Wales! In BR days there was no middle man, just regions where one could 'borrow' a visiting locomotive. Months later, there was only one daily passenger working that was Class 47 hauled.

November 2004 brought the news that Riviera Trains had bought seven Class 47/8s from Porterbrook, at the time these were 47 805/812/815/829/843/847/848. They were officially handed over on 1st January 2005. Coming as a surprise to Freightliner who had six of them under hire, the company sought suitable replacements. Porterbrook provided 47 811 and 47 816, with the possibility of others to follow.

On 11th December 2004 First Great Western ran its farewell trip for its Class 47s, running Paddington-Penzance and back. Locomotives used were BR green 47 815, which on the outward journey developed an AWS fault and had to be piloted by 47 811. The return working retained the pair with only 47 815 working.

The year 2005 opened with the news that Fragonset Railways had merged with Merlin Rail on 7th January to form FM Rail, sub-titled 'fragonset merlin railways'. The company was reported to be assessing its far flung stored locomotives. A competition among Rail magazine readers produced a winning entry in July 2005 for the new livery

Formed of six Virgin-liveried Mk2s, the 18.14 'Footex' from Cardiff Central to Manchester Piccadilly passes Maes-Glas, near Newport, on 30th May 2005, 'topped and tailed' by Class 47/4s Nos. 47 853 Rail Express and 47 847 Brian Morrison/ Railway World Magazine.

BRIAN MORRISON

for the company's locomotives. Black livery was retained, but with decals reminiscent of the later BR Railfreight livery, bearing the company title in red and the stylised gryphons. Red and white bands relieved the solebar area and the wording 'fmrail.com' appeared on the bodyside.

Cotswold Rail acquired 47 828 from Porterbrook and sent it to the Falcon Works for attention. It arrived during the morning of 6th January 2005 and received a repaint into CR silver livery. On 4th February the locomotive was fitted with the nameplates 'Joe Strummer' in memory of the lead singer John Graham Mellor of punk band The Clash, who had died in 2002. The locomotive left the Falcon Works with sister CR locomotive 47 316 on 11th February and the following day its name was unveiled by Joe's widow Lucinda at Bristol Temple Meads station.

On 23rd February the locomotive undertook its first rescue when it assisted a Norwich-Liverpool Street train after its Class 87 failed.

Cotswold Rail also set up Heartland Rail to provide regular charter trips using its rake of ex-Virgin West Coast Mk3 coaches and pairs of CR Class 47s. Furthermore, CR wished to increase its Class 47 fleet to ten operational examples.

During February and March 2005 CF Booth of Rotherham completed the scrapping of 47 114/156/ 223/353, reducing the class even further.

DRS on the other hand, with four nominally operational Class 47s, found it difficult to keep its quartet occupied. Based at Crewe and Carlisle, 47 237/298/501 and 47 802 were rare sights in action. Indeed, 47 237 had been out of action since July 2004 and had been sent to the Falcon Works for attention to its engine. It arrived at the works on 17th January 2005. By June it had been repainted and was close to despatch. In contrast, in March Freightliner withdrew 47 358, one of its remaining Class 47s, as being beyond economic repair. Doubt about the future of FM Rail's 47 710, long officially under overhaul but actually well picked over for spare parts, was expressed by the company to the point whereby it was considering scrapping the locomotive to provide workshop space.

With the final Class 57s going to Virgin West Coast, use of its remaining Class 47s dwindled and owner, Porterbrook Leasing, gradually found either other work or buyers. Of the latter, West Coast Railway Co took on 47 826 and 47 851, with Cotswold Rail seeking two more. In April 2005 West Coast Railway Co also repainted one of its previous purchases, 47 854, into plum livery for use on the luxury train Royal Scotsman. The livery complemented that of the train.

After being withdrawn by Freightliner in 2001 and purchase for preservation in December 2004, 47 205 made its first movements under power on the Northampton & Lamport Railway. Other than air leaks the event was satisfactory.

Some more encouraging preservation news was the return to traffic, after nine years, of two-tone green liveried 47 192 (D1842). Restored by Staffordshire Type 4 Limited, the locomotive made its working debut on the Churnet Valley Railway on 22nd May.

The Mid Hants Diesel Gala was held in mid-May 2005 and Freightliner sent two Class 47s to feature in it. Number 47 358, resplendent in well-spruced two-tone grey and unofficially

named 'Ivanhoe', and 47 303 hauled trains during the event.

Increasingly active Cotswold Rail next leased 47 810 'Porterbrook' from Porterbrook to supplement its own fleet. It was intended to keep the name in CR service.

The 300th Class 47 to be scrapped was 47 574, by Ron Hull of Rotherham, in June 2005. The locomotive was delivered from Brush as D1769 in October 1964. Meanwhile, at Crewe Diesel Maintenance Depot, Harry Needle commenced scrapping of Class 47s stored there.

Mid-2005 saw a core of Class 47 with an assured future, albeit in a lesser role than in previous years and in much reduced numbers. More assured in the long term were the preserved examples, but until deemed wholly uneconomical those in main line service soldiered on. Sometimes controversial, sometimes superb, the Brush Type 4 served its various owners well and in particular, in 2005, DRS persevered steadfastly to return its 47 237 to traffic. The locomotive had suffered engine troubles in May 2004 and in 2005 it was despatched to the Falcon Works for attention, including a repaint. Much careful work was done to return it to the main line.

When 47 237, together with 37 607, was collected by 47 298 on 18th August 2005 it represented the exceptional quality and doggedness of Brush in solving difficult problems associated with old locomotives in well-worn condition being resurrected anew. As usual, the Brush painters proved their skills in the fine finish she displayed.

EWS disposed of more locomotives in July 2005, thirty eight in all, of which seventeen were Class 47s. 47 764/768/779 passed to Harry Needle Railroad, TJ Thomson of Stockton purchased 47 474 and 47 519, whereas 47 765 went into preservation via Mark Fowler, and the majority were purchased by CF Booth of Rotherham which took 47 146/217 /241/328/478/536/566/576/624/725/762.

In action during the summer were the Cotswold Rail, DRS, West Coast Railway and FM Rail Class 47s. Working a variety of trains, they could be seen the length and breadth of the country. Saloon haulage and moving empty rolling stock were popular, as well as rescue work. DRS 47 298 was hired by Virgin Trains as standby at Carstairs, on 26th June and 3rd July. On one of the occasions, at least, its patience was unrewarded. West Coast Railway in particular would be cheered by Network Rail giving clearance to Classes 47 and 57 for operating to Kyle of Lochalsh and Mallaig, albeit with certain speed restrictions over some bridges and no routine double heading of Class 47s. The 'Royal Scotsman' charter train which operated along these routes had previously relied upon Class 37s or Class 31s. On 6th August 47 826 'Springburn', in InterCity livery headed the 14.54 Mallaig-Dundee charter debut. On 13th October the 'Royal Scotsman', on private charter, was hauled by West Coast Railway's 47 854. The locomotive bearing the attractive WCR maroon livery, closely matched that of the coaching stock, which it hauled from Tain to Kyle of Lochalsh.

On 13th August Cotswold Rail 47 813 arrived at the Falcon Works for repairs and a repaint into CR silver livery. It also brought with it electric locomotive 90 003 for repairs. Initially, 47 813 was parked up against the headshunt buffer stops for several days and was in the paint shop by 1st September, then duly left the works in its new livery on the 13th. It was named 'John Peel', after the celebrated DJ who died in 2004. The ceremony took place on 8th October at Bury St Edmunds station, his widow Sheila Ravenscroft unveiling the plate.

Still in worn Res livery, newly-preserved 47 765 arrived at the Great Central Railway (North) from the EWS CRDC site at Wigan Springs Branch by early August. Number 47 832 emerged in the new FM Rail black livery, complete with prominent branding, owing much inspiration to the BR Railfreight logos of the mid 1980s. It sported the legend 'fmrail.com' on the bodysides and received the name DRIVER TOM CLARKE O.B.E. at the Crewe Works open weekend, on 11th September 2005. Tom Clarke was an LMS driver and the plate was unveiled by his great grand-daughter, Pam Brooks.

Towards the end of the year, West Coast Railway returned 47 245 to traffic in its maroon livery. The locomotive had been acquired from HNRC in April 2004, and was then overhauled. Likewise, DRS returned its 47 237 to traffic, following some eighteen months undergoing repairs, partly at Brush from where it left on 18th August 2005, being collected by sister DRS locomotive 47 298. With four operational Class 47s, DRS appeared to be undecided as to whether or not to keep them. Certainly, at times they were under utilised. Prominent duties were the nuclear fuels trains, working in pairs.

By the end of December 2005 the ranks of the class diminished by at least twenty-five Class 47s, which were scrapped during the year.

The new year started well for Class 47. On 5th January 2006 FM Rail launched its 'Blue Pullman' train, operated by its newly-acquired Hertfordshire Railtours, on a special inaugural run from Derby to Manchester Piccadilly, using specially repainted 47 709 'DIONYSOS' and 47 712 'ARTEMIS' in matching Nanking Blue livery. The train and two FM Rail locomotives matched the original diesel multiple unit train of 1960 as near as possible. Using mainly Mk2 air-conditioned coaches, sometimes up to eleven or twelve vehicles from an available fifteen, the train was an impressive sight and proved extremely popular during the ensuing months, and was said to have accrued £2 million worth of business for FM Rail during 2006. On occasions other FM Rail locomotives were used when 47 709 or 47 712 were unavailable.

FM Rail ran its first revenue-earning freight train on behalf of Fastline on 14th February 2006, using 47 145 'MYRDDIN EMRYS'. The 11.30 train left Doncaster for York and consisted of twelve new wagons.

Cotswold Rail took over the lease of Porterbrook 47 840 'NORTH STAR' in early May. The locomotive actually arrived at Brush on 1st March, for repairs. In due course the future of the locomotive was mapped out; it would have vacuum

Awaiting the 'Blue Pullman' headboard and departure time, the inaugural service is headed by Class 47/7 No. 47 712 ARTEMIS at King's Cross on 10th January 2006.

BRIAN MORRISON

brake equipment re-instated and would work for Cotswold Rail, before being donated by Porterbrook into preservation on the West Somerset Railway in 2007. Duly converted to dual brake, using salvaged vacuum equipment from 47 326, 47 840 departed 28th November, towed by 47 714. It was bound for Eastleigh requiring further work for which that works was specially equipped to undertake. Number 47 326 was sold to TJ Thomson for scrap, arriving at the Stockton yard on 25th July and being scrapped during late October 2006.

Cotswold Rail installed itself in the Horton Road depot at Gloucester earlier in 2006 and soon utilised the facilities as a base along the general route of hauling First Great Western HST power cars between the South West and Loughborough during the MTU re-power programme which started in earnest that year. The Class 47s became a regular feature in and out of the Falcon Works.

In May 2006 FM Rail offered ten locomotives for sale, including 47 236, 47 704 and 47 803. Ron Hull Junior, Rotherham scrap dealer, purchased them and by the end of the year had scrapped 47 704.

May also saw the storage of Freightliner's 47 197, which had been used as depot shunter at Crewe Basford Hall since being withdrawn from main line duties the previous October. This move left 47 150 as the final non-ETS Class 47 in Freightliner service; it soldiered on and was still hauling trains in 2007.

After being stored at the Alstom works of Springburn, Glasgow, for more than four years, 47 484 was sold by DRS. It went into preservation, being moved to a new storage location in Sutton Coldfield on behalf of Andrew Goodman, who also purchased 47 475 as a source of spare parts. Next to be preserved was Old Oak Common resident 47 004/D1524, part of the EWS 'Heritage Fleet', purchased by Mike Darnell of the Newton Heath Diesel Traction Group and moved to the Embsay Steam Railway on 6th August. It re-entered traffic on the preserved line on 29th October. In the same EWS sale another of the 'Heritage Fleet' went to Harry Needle Railroad Company. This was 47 306 'The Sapper', deposited at St. Blazey for some time.

July saw Cotswold Rail Class 47s hired to First Great Western to cover for poor availability of Class 57/6 locomotives. Numbers 47 813 and 47 828 made a variety of regular workings between London and Penzance.

In August Riviera Trains hired two Class 47s to DRS in preparation for use on 'Sandite' railhead treatment trains during the autumn leaf fall period. The first of seven locomotives, 47 815, in BR two-tone livery and 47 839 in Riviera Oxford Blue were despatched north from Crewe on 2nd August. The hire was of a temporary nature, partly due to the delayed delivery of seven new Class 66s for DRS and partly due to DRS locomotives being used on other duties. Initially, the pair was used on a variety of duties until 1st October when the trains started operation. In the meantime, Riviera Trains prepared the balance of Class 47s required.

First to follow in early September was 47 848 repainted Oxford Blue and newly-named 'TITAN STAR'. It was also fitted with a raised metal leaping cat emblem under each driver's cab side window. Next came 47 805 'Talisman' (Oxford Blue). Both were despatched north on 29th September. Next

were 47 843 'VULCAN' (Oxford Blue) and 47 839 'Pegasus' (already blue). October saw the arrival of 47 812 (already BR green), 47 847 (already BR large logo blue) and 47 853 'RAIL EXPRESS' (already XP64 blue), and the return of 47 815 to Riviera Trains.

For its own use Riviera Trains returned 47 769 to the main line, retaining its Virgin red livery and regaining its name 'Resolve' in the process.

The delivery and introduction of DRS's 66 414-419 prompted the return of the Riviera Trains Class 47s during November, the official date being the 8th for all seven locomotives.

The Mid-Norfolk Railway witnessed the arrival of 47 596 on 16th November from Tyesley Railway Museum. Owned by the Stratford 47 Group, the locomotive was operational, albeit a lack of cab fittings limited it to being driven from one end only. It had been withdrawn from EWS service in September 1999 and at the time of arrival at the preserved railway it was still in somewhat battered Res livery, with the hope of being repainted into BR blue, with 'Stratford' grey roof.

Number 47 345, long term resident on the storage park at Brush, was finally hauled off its track onto a low loader on 24th October, bound for R Hull Junior of Rotherham as scrap.

FM Rail also sold 47 053/229/707/717 to TJ Thomson of Stockton, for scrap, and on 1st November started two new freight operations between the Midlands and Scotland, working with Victa Railfreight.

Class 47s featured prominently on these runs. The operator was also expected to return more Class 47s to traffic, but as the company went into voluntary administration on 11th December 2006 such expectations were soon lost in the subsequent events, which are outlined in Chapter 4. The year 2006 saw at least sixteen Class 47s scrapped.

In a surprise move in early January 2007, EWS offered 39 locomotives for sale, including 23 Class 47s. The company quickly added a further 24 locomotives to the list, of which fourteen were Class 47s. In selecting these 37 Class 47s, 47 799 (one of the former Royal Train locomotives) became the only member of the class to be not offered for sale.

The combined list offered was as follows:-
47 635/721/722/726/727/732-4/736/737/739/741/742/746/747 /749/750/758-61/770/772/773/776/781-793.

The next advertised sale came from the administrators of FM Rail – 38 locomotives, of which 25 were Class 47s, as follows:-
47 053/145/186/201/219/226/228/280/293/307/313/314/335/3 55/360/375/488/703/709/710/712/715/717/ 780/832.

Concurrent was the start of the gradual sale of Freightliner Class 47s not fitted with train supply equipment.

With so many locomotives being released a combination of preservationists, smaller concerns operating and hiring locomotives and, inevitably, the scrap man (notably European Metal Recycling of Kingsbury) were buying. During the course of the year, some passed through more than one new owner. The scrapping of Class 47s continued and a new scenario started to emerge as the West Coast Railway Company returned former EWS locomotives to traffic in the attractive deep maroon livery, sometimes referred to as plum. Cotswold Rail continued the operation of former FM Rail 47

703 in particular, albeit de-named and still in Fragonset black.

It was fortuitous for sellers that the price of scrap metal was high, and rising, due mainly to demand in the Far East. For the creditors of FM Rail, not much would find its way to them because of the complex unravelling of its affairs, where some locomotives were not readily redeemable, being of doubtful value or ownership. A clearout of FM Rail locomotives at Derby saw Class 47s in reasonable condition taken to Barrow Hill and Carnforth for storage. By mid-2007 the illegal removal of copper cable on the railway network was causing some concern as scrap metal prices increased.

Cotswold Rail continued to repaint its Class 47s into the attractive silver livery. Number 47 810 became the first repaint for the new Oxley depot paint shop, appearing from there with the name 'Captain Sensible' on 5th February. The official naming ceremony came on 10th February at Brighton when the lead guitarist of The Damned punk rock group unveiled the name.

DRS purchased 47 790 from the EWS disposals and became a likely candidate to replace 47 298 which had suffered a major engine failure in October 2006 sufficient to warrant the withdrawal of the locomotive, followed by stripping and scrapping. By mid-March it had been gutted and finally met its end at Booth's in Rotherham during May 2007. The same fate befell the former Fragonset 47 710, which had been 'under repair' for such a long time at Derby, heavily stripped to keep other FM Rail locomotives in traffic, it met its end at EMR, Kingsbury, in March 2007. DRS proceeded to purchase two more ex-FM Rail locomotives, 47 709 and 47 712 (the 'Blue Pullman' pair), latterly stored at Carnforth.

Conversely, it was possible to see Class 47s still performing on the main line. Cotswold Rail provided a silver duo, 47 813 and 47 828, for the 'Northern Fells Express' on 24th March between Watford Junction and Carlisle. That same day a pair of Riviera Trains two-tone green members, 47 812 and 47 815, impressively headed the thirteen-coach charter train 'Yns Mon Express' (Carlisle-Holyhead return) between Crewe and Holyhead. The original two-tone green always suited the Brush Type 4 design and over the years since it had been officially supplanted by blue and a myriad of other colours it had quite a few retrospective-repaints by various owners and operators, both within or without preservation.

47 840 'NORTH STAR' came to the end of its main line career with Porterbrook on 30th April 2007 when it came into the Falcon Works for its intended repaint into two-tone green prior to entering preservation. By 16th May its old paintwork was being rubbed down in Bay 5 of the New Test House and had received its full repaint by 24th May, when its insignia was being applied. It received its original number D1661 as well as retaining its TOPS 47 840 number and also received oval Brush Traction works plates in the late 1950s/early 1960s fashion as well as its Crewe Works works plates, surely the only Class 47 to have both.

It left the following day in convoy headed by Cotswold Rail 47 813 and with newly re-engineered 43 171 on delivery. Once the delivery to Gloucester had been completed, D1661 made its way north again, to Derby. From there, on 28th May, it hauled the six-coach Heartland Rail charter train to Minehead on the West Somerset Railway, with Cotswold Rail

47 828 and 45 112 on the rear. On the preserved line D1661 was donated and handed over by Porterbrook Leasing to its new owners, The Diesel and Electric Preservation Group.

47 635 also passed into preservation several weeks earlier, when it had been purchased from Seco Rail and made its way to the Swanage Railway in Dorset.

Former Freightliner locomotives 47 270 and 47 292 also passed into preservation, both in green livery, The former passed to the Nene Valley Railway and was soon in traffic, and the latter to the Great Central Railway (North). Not so fortunate were sister Freightliner locomotives 47 197 and 47 302 which were delivered to the scrap yard of T J Thomson at Stockton on Tees late July and early August.

The final non-ETS fitted Class 47 to be withdrawn by Freightliner at this time was 47 150, which had been out of traffic for some months.

Riviera Trains 47 575 was one of the Class 47s which had been kept in running order on a preserved railway, on behalf of its owners. In this case the railway in question was the East Lancashire Railway. Unfortunately, the locomotive had suffered a persistently recurring electrical fault and it was decided to have a farewell trip on the line and then break it up for spare parts. The trip took place on 20th May and 47 575 was despatched to Crewe LNWR for stripping.

Meanwhile, West Coast Railway Company (WRCC) returned former EWS 47 792 to traffic with its previous number 47 804 and deep maroon WCRC livery. Apparently, 47/7s were not on the owner's safety case, hence the number reversion. The other WCRC Class 47s on the books at the time were one 47/1, two 47/4s and six 47/8s, with eight others in store for various reasons. 47 826 also received maroon livery shortly afterwards, in place of its InterCity livery. It re-entered service on 16th July. It was reported that the company expected to return 47 760/776/786/787 to traffic before the end of 2007, with 47 786 and 47 787 expected to revert to 47 821 and 47 823.

Although the plain, but attractive, maroon livery of WCRC was becoming a familiar sight, two new Class 47 liveries appeared in June 2007. DRS repainted 47 802 in its familiar blue, but with the large compass and stripes arrangement with DIRECT RAIL SERVICES emblazoned on the body sides. Although only used previously on its Class 66/4s, it proved to be a good move for advertising purposes. The locomotive was exhibited at the DRS Kingmoor open day 7th July, where it joined similarly liveried 57 011. Number 47 501 was also given this livery and was noted being admitted to the Falcon Works on 21st September for repairs.

Grand Central Railway was expected to start its HST operations in September 2007 and prior to this the company hired two DRS Class 47s and five DRS Mk 3 coaches for driver training trips between Sunderland and London King's Cross. Initially available for these duties were 47 237/501/802, but 47 501 dropped out when it failed on the first Grand Central training run on 13th August. Using the newly constituted DRS train the training runs continued, the original two-week plan being modified subsequent to the failure, but it was not until the end of September that the first HST power cars started to find their way north from overhaul in Devon.

An entirely new livery, that of Victa Westlink Rail, was

applied to former FM Rail 47 832. This was black body sides with light grey cabs and the company title and logo on the black portion. It was unveiled at Barrow Hill and exhibited on the West Somerset Railway during its Mixed Traffic Gala on 16/17th June. During late August it reached Scotland on the 'Highland Clansman' with Riviera Trains 47 839. Soon afterwards it was hired out to DRS.

Freightliner's stored 47 150 was re-activated and despatched from Crewe Basford Hall to attend an event at Ratcliffe Power station on 26th September. The power station, just inside the Nottinghamshire boundary with Leicestershire, was celebrating generator E.ON's 40th anniversary. It returned to store after the event.

Infrastructure company Colas Rail/Seco Rail received its two overhauled and repainted 47 727 and 47 749 from Eastleigh Works in its orange/yellow/black livery in late September and in doing so added more touches of colour to the main line. A test run from Eastleigh to Basingstoke and return was made by the pair on 21st September, prior to entry into service.

With a newly-won contract to operate railhead treatment trains in the South West during the leaf fall season the pair were topping and tailing such a train in Devon on the first day of operation on 30th September. 47 727 was named 'Rebecca' and 47 749 'Demelza' by Charles-Albert Giral, chief executive of Colas Rail at Eastleigh Works on 20th September 2007. Both names were taken from Daphne du Maurier and Winston Graham novels respectively.

The company also purchased 47 750 and 47 791 from the Kingsbury scrap yard of EMR. A further purchase from EMR, that of 47 739, made a protracted road journey south from the yard in October.

Cotswold Rail had a run of bad luck with its Class 47s during the late summer and early autumn of 2007. Various failures affected class members and although the preferred motive power for delivery and collection of HSTs to and from the Falcon Works, Classes 31 and 33 sometimes substituted. On one of these occasions 33 202 actually caught fire in the test yard and remained there for some time. 47 818 also failed, at the head of a railtour at Northallerton, and its passengers completed their journey by road. Conversely, Cotswold Rail's ubiquitous 47 703, still in Fragonset black livery complete with Fragonset logo, but minus Brush plates and nameplates, could be seen around the country on duties including rescue work in East Anglia to the HST run into the Falcon Works.

Former FM Rail 47 375 emerged from Barrow Hill depot in plain dark blue livery, without owner's markings, during late September. It was destined to work freight duties for Cotswold Rail's subsidiary Advenza, but initially it was put into service on general duties with the other Cotswold Rail Class 47s, including HST duties into the Falcon Works.

Sporting BR green livery, on 11th October 47 773, of Vintage Trains, emerged for a test run from Tyseley to Oxford and return, accompanied by West Coast Railway Company's 47 245 in case of failure. West Coast Railway Co. also returned 47 787 to traffic, adding another attractive maroon locomotive to the rails in time for it to haul the last 'Royal Scotsman' western tour train of 2007 on 5th October. On 19th October DRS 47 790 was moved to DRS Carlisle Kingmoor following

overhaul and repaint into 'Compass' livery at Crewe LNWR works. The former EWS 47/7 locomotives were proving to have life in them still, although 47 790 unfortunately failed on its first trip in revenue-earning service on 1st November.

A surprise exchange, that of DRS 47 237 for two Cotswold Rail Mk3 First Open coaches, occurred by early December and the latter was quick to utilise the locomotive on HST duties, bringing 43 306 into Brush Traction on 4th December. During the morning of 21st December 2007 47 237 arrived outside the Falcon Works with a barrier car, to collect HST power car 43 042, and paused. She was joined by 47 375, the pair was coupled, and the ensemble entered the works. 43 043 duly made its exit soon afterwards.

It was a year of heavy Class 47 scrapping due to the release of derelict locomotives and the high price of metals generally. This amounted to around thirty-six Class 47s, leaving some eleven others awaiting their fates at the end of December.

On 1st January 2008 the ruling came into force that On Train Monitoring and Recording (OTMR) had to be installed in relevant locomotives, resulting in a few Class 47s being placed in store, albeit until OTMR equipment could be fitted in some cases. One such locomotive stored was Cotswold Rail's 47 703, a busy locomotive during the run down to the end of 2007. Others belonged to Freightliner, DRS and West Coast Railway Company, but during December 2007 Cotswold Rail started to make more changes to its fleet of locomotives. Various moves took place and two Class 57s (57 005/6), released from Freightliner service, were purchased from Porterbrook Leasing in early January, with the intimation that two more might be purchased.

Number 47 715 was removed from the National Railway Museum and taken to the Wensleydale Railway, 47 316 was moved from Oxley to Gloucester to have its power unit replaced by that from 47 033 and 47 200 was sold for scrap to TJ Thomson of Stockton on Tees. Number 47 714, stored at Brush Traction, was to be disposed of, and then, despite previous intimations, 47 703 was offered for sale on eBay. One way or another, the locomotive was sold, to HNRC for component recovery.

It was reported at the end of January that Adrian Parcell, Managing Director of Cotswold Rail, had previously considered that there had been no prospect of acquiring Class 57s and for that reason bought more Class 47s in 2007. Four remaining Class 47s, he related, were to be based in the east of England, with the Class 57s and 47 237/375 being based at Gloucester for Advenza Freight operations. Before January was out 47 375 had received Advenza Freight branding and 57 005/6 were about to receive the same Advenza Freight livery. Clearly, more moves were to be expected with redundant locomotives being disposed of. Sure enough, before January was out, 47 033, 47 200 and 47 316 were taken north to Stockton on Tees for scrap, the first mentioned being scrapped in mid-March. By this time 47 237 had received its Advenza Freight markings and with its stablemates had appeared frequently at the Falcon Works on deliveries and collections.

The saga of the Freightliner Class 47s continued as their decline reduced them to lesser duties or withdrawal. It was announced in February 2008 that two would act as shunting locomotives at Crewe Basford Hall yard and Dagenham, being limited to 20mph. The remainder would be sold. At the time 47 841 was at Dagenham and 47 150/811/816/830 were at Basford Hall. The main prompt for these locomotives not seeing further main line work was the mandatory requirement for locomotives working on Network Rail to be fitted with OTMR equipment from 1st January 2008. The 47s in question had just about run their main line course and the expense of fitting OTMR was considered to be not really justified. Most had been replaced on infrastructure trains by Class 66s.

For the first time in eleven years and within two months of entering preservation the former FM Rail and Cotswold Rail 47 715 hauled a train, on the Wensleydale Railway. In February a new lease of life came to former Royal Train locomotive 47 799 when it was transferred to Old Oak Common depot for carriage heating duties.

Preserved 47 270 was repainted BR Rail Blue on the Nene Valley Railway and bearing the name 'Swift', a name borne previously, albeit unofficially, in BR days. The new guise was unveiled at the end of February. Naming was not restricted to preservation circles because earlier that month the 'Stobart Pullman' made its debut in co-ordination with DRS, which supplied two of its locomotives and rolling stock to operate

it. Numbers 47 712 and 47 802 were named 'Pride of Carlisle' and 'Pride of Cumbria' respectively and when the train was launched it fell to 47 712 to provide motive power. Stobart Rail planned to run 65 charter trains in 2008.

Languishing on a track panel at the Falcon Works in March 2008 was Cotswold Rail 47 714, resident since 24th August 2007, when it arrived for repairs after several years service in East Anglia. As had happened on previous occasions with Cotswold Rail locomotives, 47 714 was shunted dead around the test yard for some months before being taken out of the equation. With the works shunting locomotive fully occupied moving HST power cars some relief was afforded to test personnel. In March 2008 47 714 was sold to HNRC.

That same month it was reported that West Coast Railway Company was continuing to make more of its Class 47s ready for traffic, so in a mainly multiple unit railway scene it was satisfying to see Class 47s still earning a living for their respective owners. Certainly, the Brush Type 4 was a splendid example, nearly half a century later, of Brush foresight and determination.

The 10.43 'Stobart Pullman' from London Victoria to Fareham approaches Wimbledon West Junction on 12th February 2008, the newly-liveried coaching stock 'topped and tailed' by DRS Classes 47/7 and 47/8 Nos. 47 712 Pride of Carlisle and 47 802 Pride of Cumbria. Passing is the late-running 10.53 Waterloo-Alton service led by Class 450/0 Desiro EMU No. 450005.

BRIAN MORRISON

7 – The Hawk Project

With the passage of time one locomotive perhaps fades from the memory more than any other – the old prototype and mobile test bed, No. 10800. In its earlier days it was overshadowed by its more powerful and glamorous brethren Nos 10000 and 10001, the LMSR twin units which caught the limelight working prestigious trains such as the 'Royal Scot'. This is not surprising because 10800 was never intended for such duties, but rather for the more humble and mundane, though very necessary, light and short-haul duties. It was publicised quite deliberately on three occasions. The first was for its conception, the second for its birth and the third for its rebirth as a mobile test bed. Intertwined into the story of 10800 is an interesting project, which gave it a new lease of life as this mobile test bed.

10800 was originally conceived by the London, Midland & Scottish Railway in 1946 as a diesel electric locomotive capable of light and short-haul duties and was one of a group of three prototypes, mentioned above. The LMSR had already had initiated a programme of building diesel shunting locomotives and sought to gain prototype experience for main line and other duties. Number 10800 was intended to be a possible replacement for 2-6-2 tank locomotives on the LMSR system. Whereas Nos 10000 and 10001 were built in the workshops of the Railway at Derby in 1947 and 1948, 10800

(originally intended to be LMSR No. 800) was ordered from the North British Locomotive Company of Glasgow, being completed in May 1950. On completion it bore works number 24613 and the BR running number 10800. It was painted overall black with some white trimmings, notably handrails and fittings, bearing the BR lion and wheel totem (introduced in 1949). It did receive some silver embellishments for publicity purposes, notably bogies and roof. The locomotive was delivered to Polmadie shed on 29th May and undertook preliminary running there and ran trials in Scotland before being sent to Derby, where it arrived on 14th June. It undertook some test running between Derby and Leicester coupled to a dynamometer car. It was noted on such a test run on 30th June before being allocated to Bletchley in July

When this photograph was taken at the Falcon Works Open Day on 3rd June 1961, the former LMS prototype 10800 was a recent arrival from Derby locomotive works. It had been sent for experimental work to be carried out to develop commutatorless machines for traction purposes. It was a far-sighted experiment and the locomotive, soon known as 'Hawk', became a mobile test bed.

M J STRETTON

and Willesden motive power depot, in London, in December 1950. A demonstration run was staged between Euston and Watford on 14th November.

The original main details and dimensions of No. 10800 were as follows:-

Wheel Arrangement	Bo-Bo
Track Gauge	4ft 8½ins
Engine Model	Davey Paxman 16RPH, 16-cylinder
Engine Rating	827bhp at 1,250rpm
Main Generator	British Thomson-Houston 6-pole, 800kW, 326 V
Traction Motors (four)	BT-H force ventilated, 4-pole 155hp, continuous rating
Length Over Buffers	41ft 10½ins
Wheel Diameter	3ft 6ins
Bogie Wheelbase	8ft 6ins
Distance Between Bogie Pivots	22ft 6ins
Maximum Speed	70mph
Tractive Effort	34,500lbs
Fuel Capacity	330 gallons
Weight in Working Order	69 tons 16cwt

A Clarkson train heating boiler was fitted, and 10800 was equipped with vacuum locomotive and train braking equipment. The locomotive was a bonnet type with the single cab positioned between two unequal bonnet length sections. It passed its time being tried out on various London Midland Region lines and the impression gained is that the steam-orientated operating department really was not very interested in a one-off diesel locomotive that was prone to having an indifferent performance and engine troubles notably concerned with the cylinder head.

In July 1952 it was transferred to the Southern Region and based at Brighton, running trials over the Central Division, often on Victoria to Oxted duties, sharing them with 2-6-4 tank locomotives. It undertook further trials on the London, Tilbury and Southend line early in 1955 and then returned to the LMR, being allocated to Rugby. From this base it operated on Birmingham to Peterborough cross-country trains until withdrawal took place in August 1959.

By this time No. 10800 had covered about 160,000 miles, the best yearly mileage being 41,941 in 1951, followed by 38,382 in 1955. Its original power classification was 3MT (Mixed Traffic), being equivalent to the former LMSR Class 3 tank locomotives. No. 10800 remained in black livery, complete with the 1949 BR totem, throughout its original working career. It led to BR ordering ten similar locomotives as part of the 1955 Modernisation Pilot Scheme. These were built by the North British Locomotive Co. from 1958 and were numbered by BR D8400-9. They were not a success and lasted only ten years.

After withdrawal, No. 10800 was laid aside in the yard at the BR Derby Locomotive Works. It was noted in the Klondyke (arrival) sidings on 17th October 1959, together with another prototype diesel locomotive, the BR/Fell No. 10100. Both were still there in 1960, but 10800 was moved

to the Foundry Row, still in the works yard, by early August that year. Here it remained until at least two months later.

It was next noted on 9th January 1961 inside the Diesel Erecting Shop, but not noted anywhere at Derby thereafterwards. Its removal from the yards into the works was in connection with a unique, forward-looking and fascinating research experiment that was taking place with regard to developing and perfecting commutatorless alternating current traction motors, together with associated solid state controls.

The accepted manner of equipping electric locomotives in 1960 was to collect alternating current (AC) from the overhead power supply at 25,000 volts by means of a pantograph, feed it into the primary winding of a transformer which would step down the voltage to safer and more easily controlled voltages (by tap-changer) and feed the resultant output into mercury arc rectifiers. These in turn converted the AC into direct current (DC), which under electrical and mechanical control, supplied DC traction motors.

Diesel electric locomotives at that time were equipped with a diesel engine directly coupled to a DC generator, the output of which supplied DC traction motors.

Both systems worked well, but required mechanical and electrical components which required constant attention and maintenance. For example, DC generators and motors had commutators and brushgear which involved wear, care and attention. Control gear always relied upon electro-magnetic or electro-pneumatic systems for operation of contactors, the actual contact mechanisms of which required constant surveillance and maintenance.

If some of these items in the system could be replaced by more maintenance- free equipment the running of locomotives between examinations could be increased and maintenance schedules reduced. Parts requiring replacement could also be reduced in number. These were just a few of the advantages that were desirable.

Engineers sought to replace some of the DC equipment by AC by providing solid-state rectifiers in electric locomotives to feed DC traction motors, or more ideally, to have those rectifiers feed controlled inverters to provide variable frequency AC for AC traction motors. In diesel electric locomotives an AC generator (more commonly described as an alternator) and rectifier would replace the DC generator, feed rectified AC into a controlled inverter, which in turn would supply AC to the traction motors. The ultimate aim, of course, was to replace all the main DC equipment with AC.

The 'Hawk' project had its beginnings in the late 1950s, which were times of change in not only the rail traction world, but also the electrical world. Since 1956 the Battelle Research Institute of Geneva, Switzerland, had been engaged in research in the field of variable speed AC drives and had been working on a synchronous traction drive for the French National Railways (SNCF) since early 1957. The term synchronous drive refers to an AC motor which rotates in sympathy with its supply frequency without any reduction in shaft speed. An asynchronous drive refers to an AC motor which does not and usually runs at a slightly reduced speed.

BR had expressed a wish for a locomotive 'without control gear or a commutator' and Brush had been approached to

determine whether or not 'a system of this kind' could be developed. At about this time, certainly by November 1957, Brush was already experimentally working on single-phase rectified AC systems for application to traction purposes in its very forward-thinking Research Division.

In September 1958 Battelle offered to Brush two research proposals, one a synchronous drive for industrial application and the other an asynchronous drive for rail traction purposes. At the time Brush accepted neither proposal, but recognising the future potential of the static inverter which formed the basis of both schemes, placed a research contract for a comparative study of the systems on the understanding that one or the other could be selected for more detailed study at a later date.

Before the preliminary study was completed, Battelle approached the British Transport Commission (BTC) in November 1958 with a proposal for an asynchronous traction drive, which was almost identical to that made earlier to Brush. Brush in the meantime decided to pursue development of alternative AC transmissions together with Battelle. After some discussion the BTC decided in June 1959 that it should place a development contract with Brush Electrical Engineering Co. Brush was to employ Battelle as sub-contractor. By September 1959 the contract was signed. Costs were divided equally between Brush and the BTC, to a total limit of £120,000 which was subject to review. Number 10800 was made available and £7,500 allowed on the

Number 10800 inside the Falcon Works in November 1962. The AC generator and the Bristol-Siddeley Maybach engine can be seen quite clearly and have just been installed. The original works plates have been removed.

BRUSH A8665

locomotive as a BR contribution to half its estimated value of £15,000.

Much of the time had been taken up with theoretical work and discussions, which primarily concerned the suitability or otherwise of materials and equipment.

Furthermore, work had been centred on the equipping of electric locomotives, which may have stemmed from Battelle and their involvement with the French Railways. From this time onward, British work would be directed towards a 1,200bhp diesel electric locomotive, a more practical application when the time came to undertake running tests; no overhead electrified railway line was close to the Falcon Works, nor within the works complex. It appears that the withdrawal of 10800 was due to engine failure, and of coincidental good fortune for the experiment.

A programme was established between Brush, Battelle and the BTC, and work proceeded. Among considerations were the merits or otherwise of using slipring motors and squirrel cage induction motors, with some attention towards the latter because of developments in the field of static frequency

changers. The key to varying the speed of an induction motor is that of being able to vary the frequency of its AC supply. Work on switched silicon rectifiers also proceeded.

During 1960 some concern was expressed by Brush about the rate of progress by Battelle and the Company sought co-operation from other sources with more practical applications in the form of developing actual hardware, rather than mainly theory. In particular, the Westinghouse Brake and Signal Company of London, then among the early leaders in the field of semi-conductor power devices, were approached, and a course of co-operation was agreed on.

Brush then concentrated upon the traction side, including electrical machines and control systems, and Westinghouse upon the development of rectifiers and inverters. Battelle tended to slip away from the scene as matters became more concerned with practical implementation.

By mid-1960 preliminary work was completed and only three motor schemes warranted further investigation. These were synchronous motor drive, squirrel cage induction motor drive and hypersynchronous motor drive, the last-named remaining something of a mystery. ASEA of Sweden was also invited to advise upon progress so far. Concurrently, discussions were now centred upon installation of equipment in the 1,200bhp diesel electric locomotive, not always identified, but obviously No. 10800.

By the end of September 1960 motor design work was being concentrated upon the squirrel cage traction motor scheme and the traction motors from 10800 at Derby had recently arrived at the Falcon Works. Perhaps this explains the new location of the locomotive in the yards at Derby in the August and September of that year.

A study of one of the traction motors allowed design work to proceed to convert it from DC to an AC squirrel cage induction motor, the latter being inserted inside the original

Number 10800 undergoing static tests on the long Research Department siding within the Falcon Works. The locomotive is connected to the pedestal which provided the electrical link to research equipment. The Shell-BP tank wagon was used as a diesel fuel tender. Photograph taken June 1963.

G TOMS COLLECTION

cast steel frame after the DC field system and brushgear had been removed. The advantage gained in doing this was that there were no new problems in fitting the motors back into the bogies, although each motor had six cables instead of the original four. Work on solid state control equipment proceeded apace. Already, low output solid state equipment and induction motors had shown promise under laboratory conditions. Early experiments in the Research Laboratory involved the use of a method of producing very low frequency AC using machines only, and a mercury arc rectifier.

Before the end of 1960 some measure of grouping equipment together was happening. An engine, the third supplied to Brush as a spare for 'Falcon', was to be coupled to an alternator and rectifier and the DC output fed into the remaining two DC traction motors from 10800, as yet not altered. Regarding those undergoing conversion, a traction motor test rig with a generator for load purposes was being manufactured. The alternator was to be a three-phase brushless type, self-excited from its own automatic voltage regulator.

Number 10800 was brought into the Diesel Erecting Shop at Derby to be prepared for despatch to the Falcon Works, its last known report of being there being dated 9th January 1961. It left minus the troublesome Paxman engine, its DC generator, the Clarkson boiler and original control equipment. It had been repainted green, bearing the latest BR emblem

(originally introduced in 1956). The running number 10800 was reapplied to the cab sides in the latest style adopted for diesel locomotives, and the power classification '3' was painted above. The locomotive was seen by visitors attending the Falcon Works Open Day, on 3rd June 1961. By 1962 the rectangular BT-H plate had disappeared from the cabsides, the diamond shaped North British Locomotive Co. works plates having been removed at Derby.

The prototype traction motor was under construction during the spring of 1961 and at about this time, with the arrival of 10800 at Loughborough the title 'Hawk' started to be used. There is little doubt that the term was influenced by 'Falcon' and was introduced to distinguish work being done on the two projects at the Falcon Works. Reference was usually made to 'the Hawk locomotive' when under discussion.

The programme for 1961 was to build and test the alternator, then install the spare 1,400bhp Bristol Siddeley Maybach MD655 engine, together with the 950kW, three-phase, eight-pole, brushless alternator, in 10800. Concurrently, the first traction motor was to be tested in the laboratory of the Brush Research & Development Division. In the longer term, the newly installed power unit was to be loaded, through a rectifier, at the same laboratory within the works. A siding was installed alongside the Research building, being spurred from the line access from the Meadow Lane end of the Falcon Works, and which once fed timber sheds during coachworks days, but latterly fed the bar steel stores. The programme

A rear view of 10800 shortly after leaving the Paint Shop, late 1964. David Rowe is 'tweaking' the electronics. Although officially known as 'Hawk', the name never appeared on the locomotive, but the legend RESEARCH LOCOMOTIVE did.

BRUSH

then planned for all four AC traction motors to be rig-tested before being installed in 'Hawk'.

All these plans took time and equipment had to be developed, proven and be made to work together. During November 1962 the engine and alternator were already installed in 'Hawk', as was the rectifier, and by March 1963 they were almost ready for testing. Also at this time, design work on the final design of inverters was in progress. During 1962 the term SCAFI-Locomotive began to be used, an abbreviation of 'Locomotive with squirrel cage traction motors and Semi-Conductor Adjustable Frequency Inverters'.

By March 1963 'Hawk' was already alongside the Research building, coupled to a four wheeled SHELL-BP tank wagon, used as a diesel fuel tender. Electrically, 'Hawk' was connected to test gear inside and outside the Research building.

It appears that the British Railways Board, (successor to the BTC) was becoming concerned over delays in progress with 'Hawk' in 1964. It had been expected to have the locomotive ready for delivery to BR before the end of 1963 (October was the preferred month), but problems encountered resulted in delays. Indeed, two inverter designs were now being developed, one by Brush and the other by Westinghouse, such was the pioneering state of matters. Solid state equipment problems were to be the main causes of delay well into 1964. Computer problems associated with development work also caused some delay.

By September 1963 the plan was for 'Hawk' to go into the Traction Shops in November for fitting out. The BRB also added their contribution to delaying the progress of 'Hawk'. An urgent demand from BRB requesting modifications to some Brush Type 4 locomotives was received. They required their traction motors should have all parallel connection, rather than series parallel connection, so this modification and its resultant ramifications tied up the Traction Drawing Office and the special traction fitters who were able to work from initial drawings and sketches. Both groups of personnel were thus diverted away from 'Hawk' work. As a result, the Traction Division was unable to accept the locomotive until 4th June 1964. Fitting-out proceeded thereafterwards.

Four inverters were produced, one for feeding each motor, the first being delivered for test in January 1964. Failures in these and the thyristors caused further delays, but the fitting out of 'Hawk' continued with an expected delivery date to BR of November 1964. The inverters were all crammed into the short bonnet, together with their cooling fans. Although somewhat enlarged from the original, this space was not really large enough to allow adequate electrical creepage and clearance, and to provide wiring room. There were both design and production problems as a result of this. One of the design team, in retrospect, considered that it was probably too ambitious to attempt a four-inverter arrangement in such a small locomotive at this stage of the development. Each modification of an inverter had to be done four times. It was planned that the completion of any monitoring checks on inverters thereafter was to be undertaken at the BR Rugby Testing Station, where the locomotive was expected to go.

The completion of 'Hawk' now proceeded on an urgent basis and by 5th December it was completed sufficiently to be considered as a mobile locomotive, if only in theory and outline. Basically, it was tentatively possible for it to operate under the power of one of the four traction motors. 'Hawk' was finished in Sherwood Green overall, with black bogies. The shade of green was readily available as it was used for painting the centre band of the two-tone green livery of the Brush Type 4s. The BR emblem was re-applied, as was the running number 10800, the latter on the cab sides with the legend RESEARCH LOCOMOTIVE below. Above the running number was the standard Brush Traction works plate of the period bearing BRUSH TRACTION No. 710 and the year 1964. 'Hawk' was photographed in the shops and in the yards at the Falcon Works. One view in particular shows it in company with Type 4 No. D1806 and the newly refurbished 'Falcon'. Strangely, the name 'Hawk' was never actually carried.

It is now pertinent to review the scheme in outline as it existed at the time of its debut in December 1964.

The main generator, as outlined previously, was an AC brushless type with a built-in exciter of the rotating type, sharing the common rotor shaft with the main generator. Basically, in industrial applications, residual magnetism within the machine ensured that when rotation began there was sufficient available for the excitation system to develop as rotation increased speed. Electromagnetic energy was the operating principle. In rail traction applications separate excitation of the exciter was used. The exciter, as its name implies, was the direct or indirect energy source for the field of the main generator, depending upon the application as outlined above. The rotating exciter armature component was three-phase and fed an arrangement of diodes connected as a three-phase bridge rectifier which was mounted on an insulated carrier fixed to the common shaft. Three phases were chosen mainly because the alternator was basically a standard industrial machine, and therefore three-phase. The exciter output from the rectifier unit, a reasonably stable DC, was fed in turn to the rotating field of the main generator. The energy transfer from the rotating field to the main stator winding was magnetic, thus totally eliminating the need for brushgear for the transfer of energy. The energised main winding thus delivered the final output of the generator through three output cables. From this output, in industrial application, was derived a voltage signal for the exciter field to complete the almost self-contained circuit.

With a DC generator the field is stationary and the output winding rotates, which means that the full output has to be transferred physically through a commutator and brushgear pickup to the output cables.

Commutators and brushgear are a source of wear and therefore require maintenance; also carbon dust from the brushes is highly conductive to electricity and resultant deposits on insulators or in the air provide short-circuit paths not only between terminals of the opposite polarity but also to earth. The result at high voltage is a flashover and often, though not always, much damage follows, with a possible locomotive failure as the outcome. Obviously, the AC generator avoided all of this and had only two points of contact between the rotor and stator, the bearings. With due care and attention these could run with little trouble for years.

In common with all AC generators, the rotational speed and AC frequency of the generator were directly proportional and variation of the exciter output in turn changed the main generator output. Another advantage to be gained from the use of AC was the application of a smaller rotating machine for the same output of a DC generator. Equally advantageous was that for the same frame size an AC machine would deliver a greater output.

The generator output was fed into a Westinghouse three-phase silicon bridge rectifier of at least 900 volts, 600 amperes capacity, mounted immediately behind the alternator. It was cooled by electrically powered fans to dissipate the heat generated by the passage of current and was protected by a short-circuiting device across the generator output, should a fault occur. This was not detrimental because under normal conditions a short-circuited AC brushless generator will react very quickly with a collapse of output voltage, exciter reference voltage, exciter output and in turn, main field excitation. Without adequate protection, a DC generator would react to a short circuit by sustaining excess current damage.

A smoothing circuit of reactors and capacitors reduced ripple effects in the DC output of the rectifier and stabilised the DC voltage for the next stage of operation, the inverter switching.

Alternating current, as its name suggests, is electrical energy which alternates from a flow in one direction to a flow in the reverse direction, caused by the rise and fall of electrical energy in the winding conductors as they pass through magnetic fields of opposing polarities. Direct current is produced in a similar manner, but the commutator bars are connected to the windings in such a manner as to switch back the reverse flow so that all the current is uni-directional. With multiples of conductors, therefore, the output voltage is constant at the required voltage above zero. With AC the voltage starts at zero, reaches a peak, falls through zero and reaches an opposite peak to return once again to zero – one cycle of operation of one conductor which when plotted against time is sometimes expressed as cycles per second and more commonly by the symbol Hz, an abbreviation of Hertz. With three phases, the peaks closely spaced can maintain a reasonable level or stable voltage output as they gain ascendancy in turn, with a very tolerable ripple effect. This frequency is a very convenient property in supplying industrial AC motors because they lock onto the supply frequency and will run at a constant speed so long as the generator output frequency remains constant. Conversely, vary the frequency and the motor speed will vary accordingly.

It is with the next stage of the electrical circuit that 'Hawk' produced some innovative ideas. The adjustable frequency inverter, as its name suggests, was a device that allowed AC to be produced from DC at a controllable frequency for supplying the traction motors.

This controlled frequency was produced by the use of thyristors. A thyristor is similar to a diode except that whereas the former has an additional control connection which has to be energised before the one-way current flow will start, a diode will allow electrical flow only in one direction at all times. The thyristor can be thought of as a switch, but it is not sufficient to turn off the control supply; the flow of main current must have ceased also, and on 'Hawk' this was done by impressing a reverse voltage across the thyristor.

'Hawk' was designed to have four Brush inverters, one for each traction motor. Each was made up of 36 thyristors rated at 150 amperes, 500 volts, arranged in six banks to form a three-phase thyristor bridge. An additional sixteen thyristors, arranged in two banks of eight, were provided for the static commutation necessary for firing the main thyristors. Silicon diodes arranged as a three-phase bridge carried the return currents from the traction motors following each commutation. This equipment was activated by DC pulses, which were fed into the circuit under the control of the driver. They switched on the thyristors, but instead of being fed again in reverse polarity to switch the thyristors off, a new method was employed. In each inverter thyristor circuit a commutating capacitor was charged with a reverse polarity instead, and the inverter thyristor was fired, forcing a reverse voltage across the inverter thyristor and the bypassing of the motor current into the commutating capacitor. The motor current then passed from the capacitor and commutating thyristor to a return current diode, which allowed the commutating

thyristor to switch off. This method was applied to all six inverter thyristors in turn in a predetermined sequence. The operating range was between 0.5Hz and 100Hz, but at 13Hz there had to be a star/delta reconnecting switch in each traction motor supply to avoid the incidence of high current at low frequencies. The star/delta switches were conventional electro-pneumatic reversers, which had the right contact combination, and they were mounted under the second man's seat, in the cab.

Through the above switches, therefore, the four 225hp AC traction motors were to be supplied. Each motor was mounted in the then conventional nose-suspended, axle-hung method. The AC motors were induction motors of the squirrel cage type, which had rotors with low voltage bar conductors with end connecting rings, an assembly which since the early days of the industrial induction motor has been referred to as squirrel cage because of its similarity to cages once used for containing squirrels. The stators of the motors were wound with copper wire and insulated in conventional manner with the coil connections being grouped internally and the necessary main connection being cabled to the star/delta switches. In the case of 'Hawk' the old BT-H traction motor carcases were retained, but they were rewound as induction motors after the old windings had been discarded.

As mentioned previously, the motors would adapt their rotational speeds to the supply frequency, but one factor had to be taken into consideration, that of slip. An induction motor has a rotating magnetic field speed synchronous to the supply frequency with which it is supplied, the rotor tries to catch up but never does. The result is a slight speed difference, which is termed slip. The transfer of energy between the stator and rotor as in the case of a brushless generator, is magnetic – one induces into the other and in doing so prompted the term induction motor. Other than the bearings, no parts connect the stator to the rotor, greatly reducing maintenance costs over DC motors.

The inverter firing rate altered the frequency, which in turn altered the rotational speed of the traction motor and therefore the locomotive speed to a maximum of 75mph. It was a complicated and ingenious scheme, which had involved much laboratory work on individual pieces of equipment, even into 1965 and 1966, at a time when 10800 had re-emerged into the public eye. Much of the work was directed into successfully applying inverter principles already in use. It was a considerable task, because at the time it demanded the development of a twenty-fold increase of power for rail traction purposes.

The problems continued after 'Hawk' emerged as a reasonably complete locomotive, and were mainly inverter problems. There were also other problems of finance.

The original limit of £120,000 joint expenditure for the project, agreed in 1959, had been exceeded but agreement had been reached to increase this amount to £200,000 to allow work to continue. Early in 1964 this amount had been reached and the BRB indicated that their contribution would not exceed £100,000 to complete the 'Hawk' contract. To complete the requirements of the contract, Brush had to show that 'Hawk' had the ability to perform for 200 miles in service or the equivalent mileage at the Rugby Testing Station.

Brush was prepared to fund the difference to achieve the aim of 'Hawk'. Nevertheless, a sense of urgency was prompted by several factors, technical, financial and some degree of impatience by one of the participants.

'Hawk', as intimated above, was not fully completed. One inverter and motor were despatched to Rugby for commissioning tests, with the intention of matching all four sets in the locomotive at a later date. In short, mobile tests were to be attempted with first one set, then two. In publicity releases early in 1965, the incomplete nature of matters was freely admitted, logically explained and fully understood as a result. Grouping the equipment into the locomotive was one of the planned steps along the way of progress, but not the final one.

'Hawk' carried out some test running within the Falcon Works before venturing out onto BR lines. Time had to be taken to co-ordinate the operation of the newly installed equipment to provide a working locomotive and to iron out any problems that arose.

Originally, it had been planned that 'Hawk' should go to Rugby in January 1965, to follow tests on a BR railcar, but the railcar was delayed until mid-February and was expected to occupy the plant for around four weeks. 'Hawk' was inspected by BR engineers during March 1965, prior to accepting it for running on BR. After some tentative runs 'Hawk' then went into the Rugby Testing Station the following month. Provision was made for the locomotive to have a test route on the Great Central main line, between Leicester and Nottingham, and was allowed track occupation between 10.00 and 14.00 each day.

The Plaster Board (now British Gypsum) sidings adjacent to Rushcliffe Halt (north of East Leake) were offered as a refuge facility should the need arise, but it did not. This may have been connected with the plan to run 'Hawk' on the nearby Gotham branch, an arrangement which caused some concern as to whether it would be adversely affected by the rough track. Conversely, it was thought that the Gotham branch was suitably rough. Engineers discovered during actual running on the main line that the irregularities there were sufficient to test some aspects of the equipment. The electrical system coped on rough track, but every bump (even rail joints) showed on the UV oscillograph records of motor current.

By this time prospects of undertaking the 200 miles endurance run had receded to November 1965 or even April 1966. There was a feeling among the 'Hawk' technical staff that the BRB was becoming disenchanted with the project. Brush had borne the brunt of development effort and it was felt that the BRB interest shown in 'Hawk' was more academic than practical. Certainly some of the requests from BRB did upset test work and the prolonged uncertainty regarding future BRB funding was the cause of some concern, sufficient for Brush to seek a new partner at the end of the BR/Brush contract. Basically, the BRB wished not to overspend and have Brush complete the locomotive during 1965. Of course, completion included the 200 miles of trouble-free running on four motors, under BR driver control. It was a tall order, bearing in mind the nature of the problems, which were occurring in the circuitry. Brush considered a further year to be a possibility before this could be done.

Switching control circuits were regarded as complete by April 1965, but the control circuits for the operation of 'Hawk' as a locomotive were not. These were essential to optimise engine speed, alternator excitation and inverter frequency.

By July 1965 'Hawk' had returned to the Falcon Works and was running around the works under its own power and was scheduled to return to Rugby for running on the water-braked rollers.

Following a Brush/BR meeting Brush decided that it would be important to bring the contract to a close within the specification acceptable to BR, and it was thought to be just possible, though not ideal, to fit all four inverters into 'Hawk' and do the 200 miles test run on the rollers at Rugby. In the meantime, Brush would work on the control scheme so that the equipment could be fitted after the proposed Rugby tests. Following this, the track tests could commence using one motor to evaluate the effectiveness of the control scheme. It was estimated that this should be complete by mid-October 1965 to December 1965. If successful, it was further proposed that running with four motors should proceed up to a maximum speed of not less than 40mph.

'Hawk' returned to Rugby during 1965 and stayed until 3rd January 1966. On that day it left, for running trials on the Great Central main line, via Nuneaton, Market Bosworth, Burton, Derby (Friargate) and Nottingham. Test running then commenced between Loughborough Central station and East Leake. There was an additional intention of running on the Gotham branch, just north of Rushcliffe Halt, but it is believed that this was not fulfilled. Although it never went there, 'Hawk' was nominally based at Leicester. The trials continued until the 20th when they were halted by the failure of the flexible coupling between the gearbox/dynastarter and the engine. Ironically, this was conventional equipment, nothing connected with the experimental work, but it was an inconvenient disruption.

The trials had been conducted under hand control of voltage and frequency, a maximum of 30Hz being obtained under these conditions. Higher speeds were not possible under hand control and while work was being carried out on a closed-loop control system the trials had to be abandoned temporarily. The gearbox failure necessitated a return to the Falcon Works and 'Hawk' was noted being hauled dead by a Type 2 locomotive on 25th January 1966 en route for Loughborough via Nottingham Victoria, Netherfield Junction, Nottingham Midland and Trent Junction.

Very little additional evidence emerged from the Rugby and GCR tests, but it is clear that when all four motors, by now in the locomotive, were fed from a common oscillator they operated up to half speed (50Hz) on the rollers at Rugby. A top speed of 30mph had been achieved during track tests (presumably in January 1966). During the tests the power inverter circuits and control circuitry had proved reliable.

Back in the works further tests took place on the internal railway system and 'Hawk' was noted by visitors as still in the yard on 7th and 30th May. By July it was hoped possible to have track running tests undertaken up to 60mph and speeds of 50 to 55mph already had been achieved running light on one motor. A speed of 54mph was recorded in this condition as 'Hawk' passed the Falcon Works on an up test run along the Great Central embankment over the Loughborough Meadows.

Outstanding work included some redesign and proving on the control system to permit satisfactory control on an operational basis. Tests on more than one motor were required, but under what circumstances is not known, and control of all four motors from one large inverter was regarded as an essential consideration.

The main argument in favour of continuing with variable frequency inverters was seen to be the potential in breaking into the market for multiple unit trains and rapid transit systems. Without more work this potential would be missed. 'Hawk' was reaching a crossroads. Other schemes utilising some of the 'Hawk' technology were already under discussion, and there was some evidence that the final push with 'Hawk' would not take place, due to this situation, staffing levels and lack of finance. With regard to financial matters, Brush offered to buy out the BR share in 'Hawk' for £10,000, with the latter retaining certain rights to technology gained from the project. The BRB finally replied to the offer in September 1966 accepting it. The BRB was also to pay its outstanding contributions and before the end of the month an agreement was reached. During the following month matters were formalised and the 'Hawk' contract with the BRB was amicably ended in November 1966. 'Hawk' became wholly Brush property.

At this point the 'Hawk' project appears to have slowly run down with some vague notion of revival when solid state equipment development by other manufacturers reached a suitable stage. It is worth recalling that at the time control electronics were not very advanced and there were no integrated circuits, nor were microprocessors available. It was freely acknowledged that 'Hawk' was at least two years ahead of its time and the project was outstripping the capability of the solid state equipment available. Certainly insufficient funding was available – Brush was approaching other firms abroad with regard to further supplies, involvement or collaboration, and indeed firms in the USA had expressed interest of a practical nature. They all came to nought. Useful technology from the 'Hawk' project found its way into the last two Brush-built Type 4 locomotives (D1960 and D1961) and 'Kestrel'. There was even a proposal for a 'Peregrine' locomotive. This would have been a Brush Type 4 fitted with an alternator, equipped with electronics and all solid state with no relays and contactors. The traction motors would have been DC, but separately excited rather than series connected. The locomotive would have been one taken out of service rather than a specially built prototype.

'Peregrine' never went beyond the theoretical stage. The idea dated from late 1965 and faded after 1966, dying with the cuts in high level research activity at Brush, the demise of locomotive building during the late 1960s and the advent of 'Kestrel' which occupied company resources on prototype matters.

'Hawk' was moved to a place near the old diesel locomotive testing house and was used from time to time as a power source for other test purposes. One was the early testing of the motor-alternator control system for BR Mk2d coaching stock. Another was contactor testing. The final one was connected with the bogie testing rig. This was a test bed upon which rapid transit bogies were service-simulated and tested. Eventually, the rig went out of use and with it, went 'Hawk'.

'Hawk' stood forlornly on its track and became isolated, not only from any access to BR but also from other parts of the internal railway system. Weeds flourished around it, discarded objects collected on the spot, the paint faded on the locomotive and decay set in.

In 1972 the coal industry suffered a miners' strike and the power stations became short of fuel needed to produce electricity. Brush had limited capacity to generate its own electricity and was faced with rationing of the supply from the Electricity Board.

It was decided that extra emergency electrical power should be provided, so the Bristol Siddeley Maybach engine inside 'Hawk' was selected as an ideal prime mover for a standard Brush generator, diverted from production, coupled together on a common bedplate. The engine and radiator were duly removed and work on the proposed generating set began in the old boiler house at the front of the Falcon Works. By the time this arrangement nearing fruition the crisis passed and there was no longer any requirement for the set, so the generator was uncoupled and the remainder, including the radiator section from 'Hawk', was left in situ for a while.

Most of the remains of the locomotive itself were broken up on site in April 1972 by a local scrap firm, and other components were also disposed of. The bogies soon followed, during the following month. The few remnants to survive were the radiator section and the traction motors, the latter surviving until 1976 and the former until at least 1988, near the Research & Development building.

This was how 'Hawk' ended, but it was not the end of alternating current application for rail traction purposes. 'Kestrel' and D1960/1 have been mentioned, but the technology continued with Class 56, High Speed Train power cars, Class 58 and Class 60.

Additionally, there were the locomotive conversions for electric train heating facilities during the 1970s and 1980s and the hundreds of motor-alternator sets fitted to coaching stock, including the Royal Train. In brief, the brushless alternator became standard. It was to be many years before AC traction motors could be properly powered, and development proceeded on the Continent. Even so, it did not start to make any impact on production locomotives until the late 1980s. The successful all AC locomotive was generally a long time in the making.

The 'Hawk' project had cost over £226,000 when the books closed in late 1966 on the BRB/Brush contract, just over half of which was paid by Brush. Brush gained the locomotive body shell and much future business from BR, and BR gained better equipment and locomotives as a result of the project for many years thereafter.

8 – Kestrel

During the period when the Brush Type 4s were being produced, the next logical step in the development of diesel electric locomotive power was being considered.

Thoughts in more than one camp were turning towards locomotives with power in excess of not only the 2,750bhp of the Brush Type 4, but also the 3,300bhp 'Deltic' locomotives. The latter resulted from an order placed by BR Eastern Region in 1958 for 22 English Electric twin-engine locomotives. They were a development of the EE prototype introduced in 1955, but were ordered for specific passenger train services on the East Coast Main Line. Even so, obtaining the order was something of a regional triumph because opposition to such locomotives was experienced from within BR, and no further such locomotives were ordered. In several ways they were unsuitable for freight and other work, and very much against the general feeling of the time.

By 1963 BR was, in general terms, therefore, convinced that it was advantageous to have single-engine locomotives for the highest power outputs because they represented a more economical use of power, particularly if the unit operated well within its rated capacity. At the same time, it considered that it neither required nor foresaw a future requirement for locomotives in excess of 2,750bhp.

By 1964 Brush was considering the potential prospects of Type 5 requirements on BR, and saw a future for such locomotives. Further development of the Brush Type 4 concept was considered to be an ideal basis for the way forward to meet such a requirement. Consideration for the case of the '4,000bhp' locomotive was given in the August 1964 issue of 'Modern Railways' and the author of this submission also pressed home the point for the need to build a prototype.

The BR view on Type 5 locomotive requirements soon started to change because of growing internal airline competition from British European Airways (BEA), and road competition developing with the growing motorway network. Higher speeds for all services and heavier loads for freight in particular, to combat the expected competition, were considered essential. Radical changes in the way freight was handled were required, and bulk haulage of coal, steel and petroleum products together with the liner train principle, based upon the road/rail/sea containerisation, was expected to replace more traditional ways of rail transportation. The increasing and uneconomical double heading of trains, particularly on the Western Region of BR by Type 3s, certainly demonstrated that something better was needed. WR interest in a higher-powered locomotive became more active as a result. One further reason for the change concerned a requirement for providing high-powered diesel locomotives to work north of Crewe until the electrification of the West Coast Main Line to Glasgow was completed. At the time this was a prospect by no means certain to happen, but in the event the high-powered locomotive idea was eventually dropped for this purpose and in 1966 fifty Type 4 locomotives (later known as Class 50) were ordered from English Electric for use in coupled pairs. The double power unit aversion and the expected eventual transfer of the locomotives to the WR in replacement of diesel hydraulic locomotives was probably the cause of this particular change of requirement.

Sulzer Bros. also had a keen eye on the developing situation and saw possibilities for the company's Vee range of engines, newly-developed to 3,946bhp with the 16-cylinder 16LVA24 version. Sulzer had previously given up producing Vee type engines in 1927, but in 1958 had re-entered the field when it developed the new LVA range for the French Railways (SNCF). An eight-cylinder version of 1,750bhp and a twelve-cylinder version of 2,650bhp went into SNCF service. Five of the latter were soon fitted into Brush Type 4s D1702-6 in 1965. The 3,946bhp version made its debut in late 1964. Prior to this Sulzer had approached various locomotive manufacturers in Britain and elsewhere and discussed with them their ideas, and reached the point of producing an outline drawing of a single cab locomotive with one engine.

The first engine was built, as a prototype, in France by Mechanique Procede Sulzer (CCM), the French Sulzer licensee of Paris. It was one of three such engines and an extensive development test programme commenced at the Sulzer works at Winterthur in Switzerland. At the end of 1965 arrangements were made for UIC (Union Internationale des Chemins de Fer/International Union of Railways) 100 hours and 840 hours tests to be undertaken on one of the engines. As a result of the test bed runs, improvements and modifications were incorporated in time for the UIC runs. At the time, Sulzer was in an advantageous position, being the only engine manufacturer able to offer an engine of this output suitable for rail traction purposes.

Early in 1965 BR expressed an interest in a locomotive with an engine rating of 5,000bhp if possible. At least two responses are known. In 1966/7 English Electric proposed a 'super Deltic' Co-Co design in three versions, at 4,400 to 4,600bhp. The three versions, all twin-engine, offered a variety of engines, conventional EE, EE-Sulzer and the French AGO. At some time BR considered costs for batches of twenty and fifty, but no orders were placed.

The other response came from Brush, which had been preparing for such a possibility since early 1964. In 1965 Brush had been approached with the idea of providing a high-powered locomotive of around 5,000bhp for use north of Crewe, among other things. A meeting between the executives of BR and Brush was held on 21st July 1965. At this meeting both parties established that BR would foresee a future use for high-powered locomotives and that a twin power unit design was not practical at 4,000 to 5,000bhp, but that a single engine locomotive of 4,000bhp was practical. Obviously, all concerned had the engine developments by Sulzer in mind.

Flanked by the last two Brush Type 4s D1960/1, 'KESTREL' makes an interesting comparison of cabs in the former Turbine Shop. Photograph dated 23rd January 1967.

BRUSH A13790

The meeting closed with an agreement that Brush would finance, design and build a private venture prototype, single engine locomotive of around 4,000bhp and weighing no more than 126 tons, and BR would make available its technical resources and co-operation in the design. Brush also had an eye on potential overseas sales. Thus, the 'Kestrel' project was initiated and in doing so continued the Brush theme of using a name of a bird of prey. Works number 711 was allotted to 'Kestrel'.

As the design of 'Kestrel' was being prepared, BR involvement aimed to ensure that the eventual locomotive would suit its requirements and would be within the limits set for safe running. Brush based the body shell on the monocoque principle of the Brush Type 4. The main generator was to be an alternator (AC generator) and its rectified output was to feed six DC traction motors of an improved and up-rated version of those fitted to the Brush Type 4s. It became the first AC/DC locomotive to run on BR. The latest technology was incorporated into the design, much of it derived from the 'Hawk' project, but some from the Type 4s, particularly the electronic speed indication and control, field divert, and automatic voltage regulator systems. Most of the auxiliary motors were AC, and as with the main generator some weight saving was possible as a result. Using one engine also created weight saving and to meet the higher power output it was designed to run at a higher speed and mean effective pressure thus giving it a

comparatively low weight for that power. Also, it did not restrict the space available unduly within the locomotive. Braking was both vacuum and air, but there was the addition of dynamic braking, a system whereby air-cooled resistors dissipate current generated by the traction motors under braking conditions. Basically, the new locomotive differed from the Type 4 in respect of power generation and braking. There were many smaller innovations contained within the design. Electric train heating equipment was also provided, the generator being driven separately from a dynastarter gearbox powered from the diesel engine.

The new locomotive was scheduled for completion in early 1967. By February/March 1966 two of the traction motors had been tested at their full rating. Two main AC generators were also produced, one for 'Kestrel' and the other to be supplied to Winterthur to complete the tests on the first engine. The 100 hours test was completed in March 1967. By August 1966 'Kestrel' was in the early stages of construction and the body shell was finished during the autumn, being transferred by the Brush/Beyer-Peacock 'Sprite' to the former Turbine Shop where it was fitted with its engine and alternator. 'Kestrel' was still there undergoing fitting-out late in January 1967, flanked by two important Brush Type 4s, D1960 and D1961, the last Brush-built examples and both equipped with AC electric train heating generators.

The locomotive was complete by November 1967, a little overdue because the braking resistors were relocated from beneath to within the body to avoid the exhausting of hot air at platform level, instead exhausting it at roof level.

On completion 'Kestrel' was a magnificent sight, painted in a most attractive livery scheme of golden yellow for the upper bodywork and chocolate brown for the lower, separated by a thin white waistline which passed all the way around the locomotive and matched the white waistline of the then current blue and grey livery of BR coaching stock. The chocolate brown was most practical; to a degree it disguised the build up of brake dust on the body sides, although the writer remembers 'Kestrel' passing through Loughborough one day thoroughly caked in brake dust to roof level. The then fairly new Hawker Siddeley logo appeared on the cab sides with the title in full below rendered in sans serif upper case letters. The name was painted centrally on the body sides, on the yellow portion, in widely spaced, large serif letters. The running number HS4000 appeared four times, being located to the rear of the cab doors on the chocolate brown portion in sans serif form. All the insignia was white. On a more personal note, a kestrel motif would have made a fitting finishing touch, particularly if it were to have been in lifelike form. The roof was grey and the bogies black. The most startling visual difference from that of the Brush Type 4, livery apart, were the semi-streamlined cabs, shrouded buffer shanks and lower cowlings. 'Kestrel' was truly a magnificent sight and perhaps the best-looking diesel locomotive of its day. Certainly, it was a far cry from the Ceylon locomotives of the early 1950s. The works plates were of a new pattern, rectangular and mounted on all the cab doors. The recently introduced sans serif BRUSH logo was incorporated together with the Hawker Siddeley and Sulzer titles, the locomotive number 711 and the year 1967.

Some deep thought had gone into its appearance and aerodynamics. BR's Design Panel under George Williams began a study in future locomotive shapes using Wilkes & Ashmore as consultant designers. The study examined existing locomotive designs and then made proposals for the next generation of high-speed locomotives, suggesting possible shapes for a variety of designs, of which 'Kestrel' was one. A number of wind tunnel tests were made, with the help of Malcolm Sayer, who designed the famous E-Type Jaguar car.

Curiously, the first studies gave 'Kestrel' a single cab, with the driver placed centrally inside. The cab shape was originally a rounded Vee shape and this survived through to the double cab stage, to become a gentler rounded shape which settled midway between the almost flat front of the Brush Type 4 and the almost bullet shape originally conceived, the driver's position reverting to the side. Brush for its part, decided to appoint Anthony Hill to work on the ergonomics and external design. For the basic shape he followed the lines already suggested by Wilkes & Ashmore, and developed the final livery from that shape.

The main details and dimensions of 'Kestrel' were as listed in the table below:-

Wheel Arrangement	Co-Co
Track Gauge	4ft 8½ins
Engine Model	Sulzer 16-cylinder 16LVA24
Engine Rating	3,946bhp/4,000 metric hp at 1,050rpm
Main Generator	10-pole, 3-phase, salient pole alternator with integral AC brushless exciter
Continuous rating	2,520kW at 410V, 1,100rpm, 91.6Hz
Auxiliary/Trainheat	8-pole, 3-phase, with integral generator brushless AC brushless exciter
Continuous rating	534kVA, 680V AC at 2,750rpm. Driven from the dynastarter gearbox through a flexible coupling.Electronic voltage stabilizing fitted.
Dynastarter	DC generator-operated as a motor for engine-starting.
Continuous rating	47.6kW, 110V at 1,125rpm. Connected to engine via gearbox
Gearbox	Mounted on bedplate with dynastarter and auxiliary/train heat alternator. Line output shaft 2.5 times engine speed, right angle output shaft 1.6 times engine speed
Traction Motors (six)	DC series wound, parallel connected, axle mounted, nose suspended, force ventilated
Continuous rating	515hp, 504V, 830A at 681rpm
Length over buffers	66ft 6ins
Overall Width	9ft 2ins
Maximum Body Width	8ft 9ins
Overall Height	13ft 0½ins
Wheel Diameter	3ft 7ins
Bogie Wheelbase	14ft 11ins
Total Wheelbase	51ft 8½ins
Distance between bogie centres	37ft 2ins
Minimum radius curve negotiable	264ft
Maximum speed	125mph
Continuous speed	110mph
Maximum Tractive Effort	70,000lbs
Continuous Tractive Effort	42,000lbs at 27mph
Diesel Fuel Capacity	1,000 gallons
Weight in Working Order	126 tons (estimated) 133 tons 6cwt 1qr (actual with fuel tank full)
Brakes	Independent air braking on locomotive only. Vacuum or air for train braking. Dynamic braking integrated with mechanical braking under single control

The main generator was a three-phase AC generator (alternator) and this extended the use of AC output as demonstrated by 'Hawk'. This output was rectified integrally within the alternator with the use of silicon diode rectifiers, and the ensuing DC supply was fed into the traction motors as in previous practice. This demonstrated indirectly, by omission, the progress made with 'Hawk' at this time. Nevertheless, electronic control equipment was used extensively and a lot of the experimental work connected with 'Hawk' was put to further use. Additionally, most of the auxiliary equipment was made up of AC induction motors instead of the usual DC motors. Weight reduction achieved by such use helped limit the overall weight.

The bogie frame design was a cast-steel, one-piece Commonwealth-type supported on coil springs, mounted on forged-steel equalisers and with tie bars fitted to all pedestals. The equalising beams were overhung, as in the case of the Type 2s and 'Falcon', a departure from the underhung method used with the Type 4s. The gears were straight spur, single reduction. The interior of the locomotive was pressurised to resist the ingress of dirt, and inertia type self-cleaning filters and AC motor-driven radiator fans were fitted. Additional, and no doubt welcome, facilities were a wash basin and urinal fitted into No. 1 radiator compartment. The dynastarter had a double function. It was necessary for engine starting purposes, in the absence of being able to use the main AC generator as a motor for starting purposes, as one would in the case of a DC generator. In its auxiliary generator mode the dynastarter was used for supplying the DC auxiliary machines that were fitted.

'Kestrel' spent the last weeks of 1967 and early January 1968 at the Falcon Works under test and having the finishing touches and adjustments finalised. Although there had been considerable publicity concerning 'Kestrel' in the technical press, its completion was accompanied by further descriptions, backed by photographs. 'Modern Railways' carried a full front cover advertisement showing 'Kestrel' being lowered onto its bogies. This was backed by the statement, "'Kestrel' the most powerful diesel electric locomotive in Great Britain." There followed a brief description and the name and address of the Company, as one would expect. In those days the journal was

particularly fond of carrying such advertisements and the technical article within fully described the locomotive.

The future appeared bright for the prototype and Brush was convinced that there was a requirement for a number of 4,000hp locomotives on BR. The anticipated main duties were the acceleration of freight trains to improve line capacity and the high-speed operation of passenger trains. Demand from overseas was anticipated from developed areas of the world; Europe, Australia, the USA and Canada. The emergent nations of the period were not expected to order because 'Kestrel' was too powerful, and trains in those areas would be too heavy for the existing drawgear of the rolling stock and too long for the passing loops on single track lines. The locomotive would be too expensive also for many of these nations. Brush was prepared to negotiate licensing agreements either for mechanical parts or electrical equipment where appropriate.

'Kestrel' has often been described as revolutionary, but in most respects it combined the new equipment developed in the Type 4s with the successful elements developed in 'Hawk'. Perhaps it was better described as a combination of a number of evolutionary developments. The engine design, of course, was still in the process of development and the dynamic braking system was a new application. Much hope was pinned on 'Kestrel', which was expected to provide work in building locomotives in succession to the Type 4 production runs. With not only BR orders in mind 'Kestrel'

Newly-completed 'KESTREL' positioned for the works photographer on the southern exchange sidings in January 1968. Note the streamlined end arrangement, very similar to that of the steam-powered LMSR Princess Coronation Pacifics of the late 1930s.

BRUSH A14860

This close-up of the cab portion, taken in January 1968, gives a clear impression of the smooth curves evolved by the design consultants for the ends. A new rectangular style of works plate (BT711/1967) was also used for the first time.

BRUSH

On the facing page we see 'KESTREL' at the head of a twenty-coach test train that ran between Crewe and Carlisle in May 1968. This and other trials enabled a number of minor snags to be identified and corrected.

BRUSH

was designed as suitable for track gauges from 4ft 8½ins to 5ft 6ins. Above all, the locomotive was a first appearance in many respects and there was no other locomotive that could offer comparison.

'Kestrel' emerged from the Falcon Works later than expected for reasons related previously, running light to Derby on 22nd January 1968 for weighing on the Locomotive Works weighbridge.

To some, it came as a surprise that the locomotive was considerably overweight, with a total weight of 133 tons 6cwt 1qr.

The exact weights were recorded as detailed below:

Wheels	Left Hand	Right Hand	Total
	Tons/Cwt/Qrs	Tons/Cwt/Qrs	Tons/Cwt/Qrs
Leading bogie			
1	10/14/2	11/12/1	22/6/3
2	10/11/2	11/7/0	21/18/2
3	10/6/2	10/17/1	21/3/3
Total	31/12/2	33/16/2	65/9/0
Trailing bogie			
1	10/16/0	11/12/0	22/8/0
2	10/17/2	11/4/3	22/2/1
3	11/9/1	11/17/3	23/7/0
Total	33/2/3	34/14/2	67/17/1
Grand Total			**133/6/1**

The leading bogie was that at No. 1 end of the locomotive, the one containing the dynamic braking equipment. The diesel oil fuel tank was three-quarters full.

One of the problems concerning any prototype locomotive is the uncertainty of estimating weights of materials included.

Obviously, some components were easily weighed, but major items were not during construction. Railway history is littered with prototypes and first builds which were overweight, and various measures were taken to counteract the problem. With regard to steam locomotives there was some scope to do this, but with diesel locomotives it was not particularly easy. In the case of 'Kestrel' many measures had been taken to use weight-saving materials and equipment, so at the time there was little scope to effect any reduction. Nevertheless, the problem was to have its repercussions.

'Kestrel' was sent to London shortly afterwards for its official handing over ceremony to BR prior to its evaluation. Two days before the ceremony 'Kestrel' undertook a test run from Marylebone Station to Princes Risborough and return. The handing over was held at Marylebone Station on 29th January and there 'Kestrel' was handed over for service trials by Sir Arnold Hall, Chairman and Managing Director of Hawker Siddeley, and Mr F H Wood, Chairman and Managing Director of Brush Electrical Engineering Co. Ltd. Sir Henry Johnson, Chairman of the British Railways Board, accepted the locomotive on behalf of British Rail. After inspection by invited guests, including the press, 'Kestrel' hauled the guests on a special train to Princes Risborough. Arrival there was timed for 13.00, with thirty minutes allowed for photographic purposes during the running around procedure of 'Kestrel'. The train and its ensemble then returned to Marylebone.

Following the official handing over, 'Kestrel' was required to return to the Falcon Works to undergo a 30 hours running period, before returning to BR once again for dynamometer trials and passenger train duties. Certainly, there was little heard of it for the next two months and there is little doubt that modifications and routine checks were also undertaken.

On Monday 6th May 1968 'Kestrel' left the Falcon Works for Crewe, running light. During the run the dynamic brake control behaved erratically, but the journey was completed without further problems. The following day, again running light, 'Kestrel' left Crewe for Llandudno on dynamic brake

trials, returning later and experiencing further trouble with the fault still apparent.

On the Wednesday a test train of twenty Mark 1 coaches of 660 tons was assembled and a run northwards to Carlisle and then back was made. A minimum speed of 46mph was recorded on the notorious Shap Incline as the train surmounted the summit. On another ascent the train was stopped and restarted on the incline with no wheel slip being experienced. During the tests the dynamic brake control was still erratic, excessive heat at the rear of the engine was discovered and water hoses were found to be expanding under pressure. By this time mileage accrued was 610.

The following day the locomotive was taken into Crewe Works for attention and 300 gallons of fuel oil was taken on, and next day a solo run towards Chester as far as Tattenhall Junction was made to check the dynamic braking, apparently with only two problems being encountered. Engine hours to date were recorded as 314 and mileage was 834. On Saturday 11th May the locomotive was at Crewe for checks and rectification of any faults discovered during the check.

Behind the scenes the excess weight problem was the cause of some concern and 'Kestrel' was limited to non-passenger duties. Because of the 100mph and 20 tons axle load limits BR would not allow the locomotive on passenger train services. This is not to say that BR was not co-operative, it was fully, but within the limits of its established operating schedules and commitments. The notable exceptions were the runs between Crewe and Carlisle, and the later BR dynamometer car trials from Derby. The aforementioned 100mph/20 tons axle load limits were introduced at about the same time as 'Kestrel' was completed, a somewhat ironic coincidence indeed, but the rethink came at a time when the effects on the track of heavy unsprung weight of nose-suspended traction motors were becoming better understood. For a while the plans for future passenger services on the East Coast Main Line were held in abeyance.

One event had emphasised the traction motor weight problem more than any other. On 5th November 1967 a fractured rail joint had led to a derailment at Hither Green on the Southern Region of a 12-coach diesel electric multiple unit. The train was travelling at 70mph when it encountered the broken rail and the accident resulted in 49 passengers killed and 78 injured, 27 of them seriously. The resultant enquiry revealed that the general standard of track maintenance on the section of track where the accident occurred was inadequate for the speed at which the trains were being run. Prior to the accident BR had been concerned about the effects of intensive use over rail joints by modern rolling stock, particularly that fitted with traction motors. There was no clear indication that the high incidence of rail breakages at joints was caused by rolling stock, the state of the track or a combination of both, but the punishment effects of multiple units on track was surely a factor to be considered. The Hither Green accident therefore made BR more cautious and 'Kestrel' entered service with this caution being exercised.

The first proper evaluation runs, therefore, were freight turns, because the locomotive weight was above the 126 tons target, and the coincidental BR reconsideration of preferring a 20 tons axle load on 100mph schedules involving nose-suspended traction motors had been contravened.

The freight duties were to be undertaken on the Eastern Region between Shirebrook and Whitemoor(March), hauling coal trains. To this end 'Kestrel' left Crewe on Monday 13th May 1968 bound for Shirebrook, logging five engine hours and increasing the mileage from 869 to 960. Officially, the locomotive was allocated to 41A Tinsley depot. Next day was taken up with crew training to Lincoln and back and on the Wednesday 'Kestrel' was coupled to 64 mgr wagons of coal and undertook the first Whitemoor to Shirebrook run returning with 53 empty wagons without problems occurring.

These runs were to be undertaken on a regular basis, the diagrams being as shown in the table below:-

7*J31	SX	11.09	Mansfield Colliery Sidings - Whitemoor (Arr.14.20)
7*P31	SX	15.10	Whitemoor (Norwood Yard) - Mansfield Colliery Sidings (Arr. 18.23)
7*J07	SX	19.40	Mansfield Colliery Sidings - Whitemoor (Arr.22.53)
5P07	SX	23.45	Whitemoor(Down Yard) - Thoresby Colliery Junction

Typical workings were two round trips every weekday, covering 360 miles and logging 15 engine hours on them. The

Part of the 'Kestrel' concept was the heavy modern block freight train, as seen in this photograph, dated 7th August 1968. The prototype is hauling 52 loaded mgr hopper wagons totalling 2,028 tons between Mansfield and London.

BRUSH A15361

average load was 1,500 tons full, and 750 tons empty on the return journey, using approximately 75 percent of the available power, at a maximum of 35mph, a limitation determined by the wagons being hauled. The duties were normally in the charge of Brush Type 4s and it was unfortunate that the loads could not be increased due to problems concerning accommodation of longer trains in loops and sidings. Up to 30th June 1968, 8,290 miles had been covered by 'Kestrel' on these duties.

On Thursday 23rd May 'Kestrel' travelled light to Darlington Bank Top for bogie rotational tests on the calibrated turntable there. They were found to be rotationally stable when the tests were undertaken the following day. Saturday found 'Kestrel' back at Shirebrook receiving routine attention in readiness for resumption of the freight runs on the Monday. The resumption was short-lived because next day 'Kestrel' was taken out of service on account of excessive diesel fuel loss, investigation of which revealed a leak on the upper surface of the lower fuel tank. Only using this tank during running, investigation into the leak was continued for one week to locate the exact place.

During late June and early July a work to rule by BR staff disrupted the working pattern with 'Kestrel' being either confined to depot or restricted to shorter trips to Lincoln. A resumption of regular running was made on 9th July. On Saturday 20th July 'Kestrel' ran light to Manchester for what were described as high-speed trials the following day at Wilmslow. With track-holding performance being monitored by BR staff from Derby, five runs were undertaken at 2, 60, 80, 90 and 100mph respectively. The locomotive worked back to Tinsley later that day and returned to Shirebrook on the Monday, resuming the freight duties next day.

Friday 2nd August saw 'Kestrel' run light to Ratcliffe on Soar power station, a few miles north of Loughborough, on the Midland Main Line, for display at an exhibition for

'KESTREL' entering Loughborough Midland station with a test train consisting of LMS dynamometer car No.3 and the three mobile test units, affectionately known to engineers as 'Faith, Hope and Charity'. Photograph dated 5th September 1968.

BRUSH A15377

Locomotive and Allied Manufacturers Association personnel, after which the locomotive was sent to the Falcon Works for power tests and dynamic brake equipment checking. Running light on Monday saw a return to Shirebrook in preparation for special runs scheduled for Wednesday 7th August.

A train of fifty-two 32-ton loaded mgr hopper wagons was assembled in Mansfield Concentration Sidings, a load totalling 2,028 tons. Tests took place between Mansfield and Lincoln. One aim was to determine whether one locomotive could handle such a load instead of the usual two. On the outward journey the whole train was deliberately stopped on the rising 1 in 150 Broughton Bank and 'Kestrel' successfully restarted it under wet rail conditions, with the driver's controller in the three-quarters position. The train moved away at about 1mph, when wheel slip occurred on the leading bogie. This was corrected by the automatic detection and correction system, bringing the power down to a balancing point where slight continuous slipping occurred. Speed crept up to 5mph within four minutes, at which point the wheelslip stopped and the train accelerated normally to 15mph within a further three minutes. On the return journey another stop and restart was made on the 1 in 120 rising gradient of Marnham Bank, with a slight curve and in dry conditions, but the controller was used with more control at the one-quarter setting. The train accelerated smoothly without wheel slip up to a balancing speed of 20mph and 'Kestrel' was on full power for eight minutes. BR claimed that this was the heaviest load to have been hauled on its system by a single locomotive. Later that day it returned to its Shirebrook to Whitemoor duties.

Two days later, on Friday 9th August, 'Kestrel' ran light to the BR Rolling Stock Development Unit at Derby for a 'B' Examination and preparation for dynamometer car trials. On

'KESTREL' entered passenger train service during October 1969 and this view shows it about to leave Kings Cross station on 20th October with its first regular scheduled passenger service. Unfortunately, two months later, following a change of BR policy, the locomotive had to be returned to freight working.

BRUSH

24th August it was noted in the Research & Development yard and on Tuesday 27th August further tests were commenced. At this time it had logged 15,788 miles and 1,098.5 engine hours. 'Kestrel' was reported to be on trial runs to Nuneaton via Crewe, returning via Leicester on 27th, 28th and 29th. Class 86 electric locomotive No. E3132 was attached to the rear as ballast, but with its pantograph raised, when travelling over the electrified lines and probably using regenerative power for extra loading purposes. Saturday 31st August saw 'Kestrel' on display at the annual Derby Locomotive Works Open Day, where it was viewed by many visitors at close quarters.

Running trials continued during September, from 12th to 27th, with a variety of test vehicles. A circular route of Derby - Stoke on Trent - Crewe - Nuneaton - Leicester - Derby was used and on occasions a dead Class 86 was again added to the rear of the formation, E3132 being used on 20th September. The former London, Midland & Scottish Railway Mobile Test Unit (cars 1, 2 and 3 in various combinations) provided electrical load (by rheostatic means whereby the electrical output of the bogie-mounted generators was dissipated into electrical resistance banks) and test results were monitored by the former LMSR Dynamometer Car No. 3.

In steam days it was a most unusual sight to see a large and powerful steam locomotive working at full power, noisily emitting clouds of steam and smoke, but hauling only two or three vehicles. Engineers associated with the trio gave them the affectionate names 'Faith, Hope and Charity'. The same mobile test units were used with diesel locomotives and constant power and speed was possible by adjusting the load en route, ironing out as it were, gradients and curves.

No high speed running was undertaken because the purpose of the tests was to concentrate on locomotive performance related to normal BR service requirements. Nevertheless, a speed of 102mph was recorded, 2mph over the maximum permitted by BR and achieved with a comfortable margin of power.

The October 1968 issue of MODERN RAILWAYS carried the usual large illustrated advertisement, this time it was for Sulzer, featuring the engine type fitted in 'Kestrel'. The accompanying caption added "4000HP Not just 4000HP – But now a proven 4000HP from a compact medium speed engine after a successful 840 hour endurance test to U.I.C. rules under exclusive supervision of SNCF.".

'Kestrel' returned briefly to Loughborough for minor adjustments, inspection and further static testing and during October it undertook speed and brake trials on the Derby - Crewe - Nuneaton - Leicester - Derby circuit. On 10th October it was at Derby under repair and on Monday 21st October the dynamic braking system was being set up for brake trials the following day. On these trials the brakes faded at 70mph during the 100mph run and the test was somewhat unsatisfactory. Remedial work was carried out 'on shed', and during the following two days the trials continued without adverse incident. By Friday the brake blocks were sufficiently worn to justify the slack adjusters being taken up. The following Monday was spent on static tests, hand brake tests and de-cabling. This continued until Monday 4th November, on which day 'Kestrel' returned to the Falcon Works for booked repairs and further trials with the hand brake and further static tests. The next period was spent repairing and sorting out snags on the locomotive and on Friday 22nd November it returned running light to Shirebrook to resume its plodding existence on the freight turns the next week, once more being allocated officially to Tinsley depot.

On Sunday 8th December 'Kestrel' was prepared for further dynamic brake trials. These took place the following day, the locomotive being towed to Pyewipe, near Lincoln, and also being prepared for photographic purposes. Then the freight turns resumed once more. By the end of the year 'Kestrel' had accumulated 1,731 engine hours and 26,000 miles, of which some 22,000 miles were in revenue-earning service.

While the locomotive was on the Shirebrook - Whitemoor duties Brush was preparing new bogies in an effort to reduce weight to a level acceptable to the BR limits. Although BR thinking tended to shift on occasions, that concerning traction motors did not, so earlier in 1968 engineers had devised this move to overcome the problem. Some encouraging talk from within BR still gave cause for hope within Brush that there was a future for 'Kestrel'. On 23rd September, Mr A E Robson, General Manager of British Railways Workshops,

in his Presidential Address to the Institution of Locomotive Engineers, forecasted major developments concerning rolling stock on BR.

Among the various developments it was considered beneficial that by 1974 the number of main line diesel locomotives would be reduced considerably and future development should aim at the evolution of two or three basic types of diesel electric locomotive with Bo-Bo and Co-Co wheel arrangements. The former was intended to be exclusively for freight traffic and the latter was intended to introduce a divided role for a locomotive geared for either freight purposes at a maximum speed of 80mph or passenger duties at a maximum speed of 125mph. The Co-Co design envisaged 6,000bhp locomotive of 120 tons gross weight. Furthermore, there was an alternative mixed traffic variation, obtained by re-gearing, designed for mixed traffic use at speeds up to 100mph.

It was opined that if work started that year, prototype locomotives could be produced in two to three years and if successful during intensive running, further locomotives could be produced within five or six years. This sounded very fine and, power output apart, appeared very encouraging for 'Kestrel', but one assumes that more signals than these would require heeding to make positive moves. Whatever the case, Brush perceived that there was scope for promoting 'Kestrel' and prepared to re-bogie the prototype to make it more acceptable to BR for passenger work on a regular basis at speeds over 70mph.

'Kestrel' was scheduled to be withdrawn from its current service during the third week of February 1969 for the bogie change and static tests at the Falcon Works, for a re-appearance in service before the end of March 1969.

The replacement bogies were of the type fitted to the Brush Type 4, but modified to accept a hydraulic brake system. The change also introduced a gear ratio of 53:18, instead of 60:19, and traction motors with a lower continuous rating of 368hp each instead of 531hp.

Fractures appeared in No. 2 bogie during February 1969, but were relieved by drilling holes at the peaks and the locomotive was returned to traffic after three days. The routine was punctuated on Wednesday 5th March, when 'Kestrel' returned to the Falcon Works for viewing by visitors the next day. The visitors were the British/Soviet Diesel Locomotive sub-group, part of an arrangement newly-established by the USSR Ministry of Ways of Communication (MPS) whereby they and the British Railways Boardeach would organise exchanges of groups of experts, so that each side could study the most advanced experience of the other. Groups were formed according to specialist interest. It was as part of this arrangement that the visit to the Falcon Works was made. The visit was to have far-reaching consequences, as we shall see.

Brush continued to advertise 'Kestrel', and the front cover advertisement feature of the March 1969 edition of MODERN RAILWAYS showed an illustration of the locomotive at Greetwell Junction, south-east of Lincoln, hauling the Whitemoor - Shirebrook empty return run, probably on 9th December 1968. Inside the same issue was an article updating progress with the locomotive.

On Friday 28th March 1969 'Kestrel' went to Tinsley for a 'C' Examination and returned to the freight runs on the following Monday and Tuesday only. On Wednesday 2nd April, 'Kestrel' returned to the Falcon Works, mainly to be fitted with the new bogies. Other work was carried out and when completed, the locomotive underwent static and limited movement tests within the works.

'Kestrel' spent the rest of April and the first fortnight of June at Loughborough, leaving for Derby light locomotive for weighing. After fuelling to 1,000 gallons capacity 'Kestrel' weighed in at 124 tons 13cwt, resulting in an axle load of 20.78 tons. It was a creditable weight reduction attempt, but still over the BR maximum limit of 20 tons. Two days later 'Kestrel' returned to Shirebrook and on this day engine hours recorded was 2,801 and mileage 47,185.

The freight runs were resumed, broken by a brief visit to Cricklewood Depot, North London, on Friday 11th July for exhibition the next day at the open day jointly staged by BR and 7029 Clun Castle Ltd. As soon as the show was over 'Kestrel' returned light northwards on the Midland Main Line minus some minor fittings, presumably lifted as souvenirs. The freight runs resumed yet again on the following Monday, punctuated by a high speed run on the morning of 29th July. Two days after this 'Kestrel' was at Tinsley for an 'E' Examination. At this time the engine had logged 3,275 hours and 56,683 miles had been run.

The locomotive returned light to Shirebrook on 6th August – back to familiar duties, often with a driving instructor present in preparation for training BR personnel for East Coast Main Line passenger train operations.

The open day at Barrow Hill depot, north-east of Chesterfield, relieved the boredom on Sunday 14th September, 'Kestrel' travelling light from Tinsley the previous day. On Monday 6th October 'Kestrel' ran light to Finsbury Park depot, London, and was involved with driver training the next day. On the Wednesday a special run to Peterborough was aborted when an earth fault appeared on the main alternator. Next day 'Kestrel' went into Stratford Works for attention, having its alternator removed on the Friday. The following two days were taken up having another alternator fitted, presumably the second machine originally sent to Sulzer for engine testing purposes. On Tuesday 14th October 'Kestrel' ran light back to Finsbury Park. Mileage at this time was 67,615. Wednesday saw a test train hauled northwards from Kings Cross to Peterborough, returning later that day. The return was not without incident, No. 1 traction motor flashing over and its interpole securing bolts moving out of position. The offending motor was replaced at Stratford and within 24 hours 'Kestrel' was back at Finsbury Park depot ready to undertake a test run, with six coaches (including four catering vehicles), to Peterborough and back on the Saturday.

On Monday 20th October 1969 'Kestrel' headed the 07.55 Kings Cross to Newcastle upon Tyne express as far as York and, minor problems apart, the locomotive performed its first revenue-earning passenger duty successfully making the return journey next day. Some sources state that 'Kestrel' ran the full journey to Newcastle and returned the same day. 'Kestrel' certainly did the full return trip on the Wednesday, leaving Newcastle at the head of the 16.45.

This became the regular diagram and at some time during the year 'Kestrel' climbed the 1 in 178 gradient Stoke Bank, ten miles south of Grantham, at a speed of over 100mph, on this occasion hauling a train of Pullman coaches.

Another source tells of 99mph being attained on 10th November 1969 with the 16.20 King's Cross-York stopping train (334 tons) at Little Bytham, during the ascent of Stoke Bank.

The new duties with 'Kestrel' on passenger work were short-lived.

The BR Civil Engineer soon imposed a 75mph speed restriction on its operation on the East Coast Route and this meant that 'Kestrel' was unable to work to its full capacity in the passenger role. This prompted a reaction by Brush to change its operating policy and it was removed from the Kings Cross - Newcastle duties.

Quite when the removal was planned in not clear, but another incident happened.

This concerned engine troubles towards the end of November 1969, the locomotive returning to Shirebrook by the 25th. Within two days 'Kestrel' sadly returned to the old routine, trundling back and forth between Shirebrook and Whitemoor, accumulating mileage but not by any means reaching full potential on anything. It is most probable that after repair it was felt to be a safer choice to settle in the locomotive on these duties. On 8th December the mileage counter was removed (reading 083801) and replaced by another, reading zero.

'Kestrel' broke the routine on Saturday 20th December when it ran light to York and two days later hauled the 08.40 departure from there to Kings Cross, twelve coaches totalling 396 tons. At Kings Cross 1,017 engine hours total were noted together with a mileage of 2,671 (86,472 grand total). This run appears to have been staged for the benefit of visiting Australians, guests of Messrs F Beasant and FH Wood, both of Brush.

On Friday 2nd January 1970 'Kestrel' underwent a 'B' Examination at Shirebrook and was found to be in need of repairs, so was towed to Tinsley on the Monday. These were undertaken at Tinsley and lasted until 26th January. On the 27th the locomotive was transferred to Doncaster Works, entering the shops at 13.30. The power unit was removed the following day and coupling damage was revealed. On the 30th the alternator was separated from the engine and despatched to Loughborough.

After its return to Doncaster the alternator was refitted during 9-11th February, the power unit on the 12th and locomotive reassembly commenced on the 13th. 'Kestrel' returned to Shirebrook on Friday 27th February and managed one round freight trip on the regular run.

The old routine lasted until 6th March and three days later 'Kestrel' was transferred to Hull for working Freightliner trains between there and Stratford, in London. This move was the result of much discussion between Brush and BR, following the imposition of the 75mph restriction. A regular run was the 19.35 from Hull, returning with the 02.30 from Stratford. During weekdays 'Kestrel' was stabled at Hull Dairycotes, but each weekend had to visit Tinsley depot for maintenance, as the former was not a main line diesel depot.

Its first night run saw a failure at Bawtry when contactors tripped out on power, resulting in a tow back to Hull. The fault was soon rectified and regular workings followed, punctuated by a visit to the Crewe Electric Traction Depot open day on Sunday 19th April 1970.

Nine days later the intercooler water level was reported to be low and 'Kestrel' was taken out of traffic. The air section of the intercooler was found full of water and the locomotive was sent to Tinsley. Repairs were effected and on 20th May the running-in of the engine commenced. This was short-lived because next day Number three-cylinder big end bearing seized and the crankshaft pin was damaged. The day afterwards cabling was removed prior to sending the locomotive to Vickers Works at Barrow in Furness. The stay at Vickers was prolonged, from 22nd May until 7th September, and on the latter day 'Kestrel' returned to Tinsley for final repairs and sorting out of snags. Regular runs between Shirebrook and Whitemoor recommenced yet again and this time it was to be the last regular spell of working of 'Kestrel' on BR, and indeed, in this country. By the end of January 1971 the mileage counter read 38,955 (122,756 total) and if one adds uncounted, but otherwise recorded mileage the corrected total becomes 124,137 miles. On the same day engine hours accrued were 6,503.

This marked the end of logging 'Kestrel' on a daily basis by Brush personnel, and the locomotive was withdrawn from service officially during March 1971, with reports filtering into the railway press in April. Rumours had some limited circulation in late 1970 to the effect that 'Kestrel' was to be sold to the USSR, but it was not made public until several months of 1971 had passed.

As was the occasional custom of BR engineers, papers were presented to engineering institutions. The opening of the 1970/71 series of meetings of the Railway Division of the Institution of Mechanical Engineers was presented by Mr T C B Miller, BR Chief Mechanical and Electrical Engineer. The address dealt with various BR developments in progress or planned aimed at achieving higher speeds. It was obvious that a new era had been entered into whereby track and rolling stock were affected as never before. It was considered essential that track and locomotive design should be considered together as a single joint problem. This was just one consideration of course, but it was relevant interest to any locomotive builder, both public or private. Consideration to increasing the upper speed limit from its then current 100mph to 125mph was the next step. The emphasis of course was on passenger workings. A recent study of axle loads and suspensions had referred to the need to minimise track maintenance costs and to provide the necessary adhesive weight. Somewhere between the two lay a solution. This led to one being found, and a BR decision to build no more vehicles with nose-suspended, axle-hung traction motors. This ignores certain facts, and indeed was never fully implemented, but it was essential to keep wheel impact on the rail to a minimum. One attractive diesel locomotive proposal then under active consideration was the high-speed diesel train (HSDT), later abbreviated to the high-speed train (HST). This was planned to run at 125mph but with an axle load of only 16 tons and unsprung weight of 2½ tons. This presented a much gentler

treatment of the track and was partly achieved by dividing the locomotive role into two units, one at each end of a set train. The building of a prototype High Speed Train by BR was authorised in August 1970.

On the freight side, Mr Miller discussed the changing pattern of freight haulage towards high-capacity wagons and bulk trains at higher speeds. These were promising a combination of speed and load beyond the capacity of the Brush Type 4, and he saw the prudence in introducing a new design to cope with the future trend. There was plenty of time available to produce a prototype diesel electric locomotive Co-Co design of 4,500bhp and with a 90mph maximum speed. The proposed design was to have two power units, despite the inherent duplications incurred – there was no choice at the time, the engine fitted in 'Kestrel' was not at an uprated stage.

Clearly, there were obvious deductions to be made from the above. The role of passenger and freight locomotive design was to be separated and the role of a single high-speed passenger locomotive was to be dissolved, in favour of two power cars. 'Kestrel' fitted into no proposal in its existing condition. Furthermore, it was too heavy. Brush was in no doubt that it had a very slim chance of being proliferated on BR, nor did any sales overseas look like materialising. For speeds over 125mph BR was already considering the Advanced Passenger Train theory, with initially gas turbine propulsion and later electric propulsion.

The entry of the USSR into the scene was not unwelcome at Brush, therefore, and when it came it was at the right time. It also showed promise of more exacting testing than was possible in Britain.

The Soviet visit to the Falcon Works on 6th March 1969, during which 'Kestrel' was examined, left a lasting impression on the visitors. The delegation was led by Dr N A Fufrianskii, in his capacity as Deputy Director of the USSR Ministry of Ways of Communication (MPS) All-Union Scientific Research Institute of Railway Transport (VNIIZhT) and head of the VNIIZhT research centre. This centre, with its 6km closed-loop test track at Shcherbinka (about 30km south of Moscow), had been for many years the most advanced railway research establishment in the world.

A few days after the visit to Loughborough Dr Fufrianskii was walking in a London street with Mr Beasant (at the time Manager of Brush Traction Division), when the latter suggested the idea of the USSR buying 'Kestrel', presumably hoping to open up a new market for Brush locomotives. He received the cautious reply that he was putting his suggestion to a head of a scientific department, not the Minister of Transport, someone who did not have any powers to negotiate. Dr Fufrianskii, however, promised that he would report favourably to the MPS and the Ministry of Transport Machinebuilding, which produced locomotives for the SZD, the USSR national railway. The promise was fulfilled and a recommendation was made that negotiations be opened with Brush to purchase 'Kestrel'. The Soviet side expected that details of the scope of sale of locomotive or components could be decided once operating tests had been conducted on the locomotive on Soviet tracks and technical and economic comparisons made with home-produced locomotives.

It took time for these matters to proceed and as they approached the point whereby it was possible for something to be mutually agreeable another proposal in the Soviet Union was making progress. This concerned an international railway technical exhibition to be held at the Shcherbinka research centre, focussing on the present condition and future development of railway transport. The proposal was strongly supported by the President of the USSR Chamber of Trade and Industry. It was to be the first such exhibition staged by the Soviet Union and it took place 1-20th July, 1971 entitled 'Rolling Stock – 71'. Brush and Hawker Siddeley were invited to present 'Kestrel' as an operating exhibit. Brush was reluctant to incur the considerable expense of shipping 'Kestrel' to Moscow, bearing in mind the experiences on BR and with the knowledge of BR intentions with motive power, together with little prospect of selling overseas. The idea of selling 'Kestrel' to them was put to the Soviet side. To this they agreed early in 1971 and a deal was confirmed, with Brush making the locomotive ready for the exhibition and subsequent operation on the Soviet test track and railway system. This involved conversion to 1,520mm, the USSR track gauge. Negotiations with Brush were handled by the Director of the Railway Rolling Stock Office of the Mashinoimport foreign trade firm of A A Maksimov, assisted by the Deputy Minister of Ways of Communication, Dr P G Muratov. Messrs Checketts and Minkley of Hawker Siddeley International and Brush respectively represented the selling side.

An initial contract price of £205,820 was specified by Brush. In addition to the locomotive, which was valued at £158,750, Brush wanted £25,900 for the electrical equipment and Sulzer wanted £15,000 for the diesel engine and a further £7,070 were required for various spare parts. Eventually the contract price was reduced to £127,000, a reduction of about 37 percent. The negotiations were quite difficult and lasted for some months, not only over price, but more so because of the Soviet side familiarising themselves with the technical documentation. They started negotiations with little more than a description of the locomotive's parts and a copy of the operating manual, both of which were only available in English. Furthermore, the locomotive would only be guaranteed for not more than a few months, something that the Soviet side could not contemplate because it would take longer than this for their people to become familiar with it. Of course, the Soviets realised that Brush would suffer considerable expense if a sale could not be made and the locomotive had to return to Britain, although it is almost certain that Brush would not have exhibited the locomotive without a sale, nor would Sulzer be willing to incur further expense. A mutually-acceptable agreement was arrived at by a combination of producing an end to the expense of 'Kestrel' on the one hand and the gaining of up-to-date technical hardware and knowhow on the other. 'Kestrel' was ultimately acquired by the USSR Ministry of Transport and Energy Machinebuilding.

After the last Brush logging of 'Kestrel' on 29th January 1971 the locomotive remained at Shirebrook. It was noted there on 5th April and on the 22nd of that month went into Crewe Locomotive Works to be prepared for its transfer to Russia. It was credited with having accumulated a total of 136,646 miles at this time, which suggests that it continued on its freight runs through March 1971. Certainly, there has been some uncertainty as to when it was actually withdrawn. It was taken to Crewe because by this time locomotive building had actually ceased at the Falcon Works and the facilities and some of the traction personnel transferred to other work. Furthermore, the rail link was now broken with the BR system following a destructive and spectacular derailment of a southbound mineral train caused by a broken axle. The link was not replaced because at the time there was no need for it then or in the foreseeable future. The first financially viable occasion for such a link came with Class 60, in 1989!

'Kestrel' was made ready at Crewe and its original bogies had their wheel sets changed to 1,520mm track gauge. 'Kestrel' was noted at Crewe diesel depot on 5th June 1971, boarded up ready for shipment to Russia. Two days later it left Crewe for Cardiff Docks on Brush Type 4 bogies and hauled by BR/Sulzer Type 2 No. D5027. On the next day 'Kestrel' was loaded on board the Soviet vessel, KPACHOKAMCK. Some Brush records date this event as 11th June. It arrived at Leningrad (now St. Petersburg) and after unloading was immediately prepared for the rail journey to Shcherbinka. 'Kestrel' duly appeared to the railway world at the Rolling Stock Exhibition during July 1971. At this event 'Kestrel' was officially handed over by the Chairman of Brush, Mr F H Wood, on behalf of the Company. At the time he was also the Chairman of the Railway Industry Association of Great Britain.

A programme of operating tests was devised to evaluate the operating characteristics and the reliability of its systems. After familiarisation and crew training these tests were conducted on the October Railway between April and September 1972. Thirty trips were made in all, with a total of 15,304km being recorded. Of these runs, twenty-four were made on the Leningrad-Tallin and Leningrad-Pskov routes with passenger trains normally hauled by Soviet TEP-60 diesel locomotives. Train weights varied between 1,000 tonnes and 1,100 tonnes, with speeds reaching 100kph. Tests, hauling freight stock, normally the preserve of Soviet TE3 diesel locomotives, were made on runs between Leningrad and Narva, and also Leningrad and Veinmar. Train weights were from 2,450 to 2,760 tonnes with speeds of up to 80kph.

Runs between Leningrad and Tanmir and also between Brasov and Bucharest have been reported, though the accuracy of these reports cannot be confirmed.

Test results indicated that the Sulzer engine had a higher fuel consumption than that of the IID45 engine fitted in the TEP-60 locomotives normally used on these trains despite the fact that 'Kestrel' did not develop full power. Difficulties with the electronic control systems caused some periods of idleness awaiting engineers from Britain. The planned number of test trips had to be reduced because of these delays.

Dynamic tests and studies of the operation of 'Kestrel' were undertaken on the track of the Ozerskaia branch of the Moscow Railway, near the town of Kolomna. Speeds of 140-160kph were reached on the experimental high-speed section between Belorechenskaia and Maikop. It was proved that it met the requirements demanded for locomotives in series production and that it was able to run safely at high speeds.

Traction and thermal tests were conducted on the

Up, up and away and bound for the Soviet Union. On 11th June 1971 the lift of 'KESTREL' onto the MV KPACHOKAMCK at Cardiff Docks takes place, although Health & Safety regimes appear to have progressed since then. The angle of the shot makes the locomotive look much smaller than it actually was.

BRUSH

experimental closed-loop test track at Shcherbinka to examine the characteristics of the engine, cooling system, electrical machines and electronic control systems. While at Shcherbinka, 'Kestrel' was fitted with a large and prominent headlight on one cab roof. It appears that the Sulzer engine reached its full capacity successfully and that in general terms 'Kestrel' was up to its estimated specification and the Soviet engineers felt fully justified in having bought the locomotive and it enabled Soviet designers and operators to change their perspective and to see a new approach to high power locomotives. This latter, alone, was considered to be justification for buying it. Twenty years later careful study of 'Kestrel' and its technology was still very productive. There is no doubt that in Russia the locomotive was thoroughly tested. For decades most items of railway equipment had been through the examination and testing procedures at Shcherbinka, from the humblest nuts and bolts to complete locomotives. There they knew their work well and seized the opportunity to have 'Kestrel' in their charge.

Over the ensuing years speculation as to the eventual fate of 'Kestrel' has been varied. From the words of Dr Fufriarskii himself the actual fate has been revealed in recent years. In line with the Soviet research programme 'Kestrel' was dismantled in 1973/4 at the end of the series of experiments, and its main components were handed over to the relevant organisations of the Soviet locomotive-building industry for further study. The body shell survived intact for some years, but by mid-1993 had been cut into three sections, the cabs and central body portion. This occurred at Kolomna, south of Shcherbinka; soon they were gone.

Including test trips and operational service in the USSR 'Kestrel' travelled about 30,000km (18,642 miles) giving an approximate grand total mileage of 155,000.

Most aspects of the locomotive were examined and studied, as was the custom of any railway equipment brought to Shcherbinka. The knowledge gained for the USSR railway industry was valuable and comparisons were frequently made when new locomotives were designed. Some of the technology was incorporated into new designs, some of which found its way into Soviet locomotives supplied to Eastern Bloc countries and overseas countries allied to the former Soviet Union. Sadly, no expansion of the joint work done by British and Soviet railway specialists occurred. The memory of 'Kestrel' remains.

The tests in Britain, both static and running, revealed that 'Kestrel' was a good locomotive overall. It was discovered that the engine output fell short of the designed 3,945bhp by 170bhp. Its performance and specific consumption of fuel oil were satisfactory and engine speed for maximum efficiency appeared to be about 800rpm, approximately half power. When running at full power the cooling system was adequate and the pressurisation system was found to be unnecessary for service in Britain. Adhesion at low speeds was very good and tractive efforts up to 85,900lbs were measured without wheel slip on dry rails. On wet rails the highest tractive efforts were sustained by continuous use of the driver's anti-slip brake (air brake). The automatic wheel slip equipment was very responsive and efficiently arrested slipping due to local bad track conditions, provided that the adhesion demanded did not exceed the general level available.

It has often been remarked that very little word of the dynamic brake has been spoken. It could not be properly assessed, due to prolonged difficulties in matching the traction motor current signals, and associated damage to the brake set-up switches. What was apparent was that the maximum brake power was not quite adequate. The

hydraulic handbrake in Cab No. 1 was just adequate and that in No. 2 less so.

The electrical machines all produced reliable performances throughout the tests, and the use of AC power was convincingly demonstrated. One traction motor flashover was caused in part by a misunderstanding arising from the rather unusual procedure of dragging 'Kestrel' with its brakes applied for test purposes. The rectifier performance was spoilt by failures of the protecting fuses, but this problem was alleviated by improving the cooling air supply. The electronic control system provided a sensitive but stable control of engine and alternator output over the whole range of power and speed, although numerous power cuts suggested some lack of reliability in the connections and some of the components.

Riding qualities in the vertical plane were in need of improvement at speeds above 75mph and calculations suggested that the amount of secondary damping was excessive, but in the lateral plane riding characteristics were quite acceptable up to 100mph. The tests carried out at Darlington showed that the bogie rotational stiffness was lower than normal and the rotation was smooth. The running tests showed that the bogie was lively, but quite stable rotationally.

The cabs proved to be well insulated and not particularly noisy, except when the engine was idling and gearbox chatter became troublesome in No. 2 cab. The cab heating was not tested, but BR personnel were very favourable in their comments regarding cab comfort. The train heating systems were not tested, but Brush train heating equipment was generally excellent at the time and has been ever since.

The common factor of Brush prototype locomotives up to this time was that each design was not repeated, but the technology and equipment therein led to orders for locomotive designs that leaned heavily on the prototype. In the case of 'Kestrel' it was an excellent proving ground for the AC/DC electrical equipment and when BR hurriedly decided that it required a heavy freight locomotive in the 1970s, the resultant Class 56 leaned heavily on the experience and technology gained from 'Kestrel'. It also helped Brush win the first order for locomotives and of course Brush supplied the electrical equipment for the class, including all the subsequent examples built in BR workshops. The supply of electrical equipment continued when Class 58 succeeded Class 56 as the standard Type 5 diesel freight locomotive. Of course, after 'Kestrel' the main AC generator (alternator) became a standard item of equipment. In effect 'Kestrel' confirmed the experience of 'Hawk' in this respect. Its use was extended to the High Speed Train also, and with great success. The latest concept of electric train heating equipment also resulted in the experimental fitting of it in the last two Brush Type 4s to be built at Loughborough. This pair and 'Kestrel' proved the electrical reliability of the system and led to many conversions of locomotives during the 1970s and 1980s. The drive for the train heat generator differed on 'Kestrel' by being conducted through shafts and a gearbox, whereas all the other applications were by direct attachment to the main alternator as a complete assembly, rectifiers and all. More subtle spin-offs were the AC auxiliary machines

and the motor alternator sets supplied to BR for the new air-conditioned coaches built during the 1970s and early 1980s. Orders for wheel slip control equipment also resulted.

The rheostatic or dynamic braking slipped from view as it were. It does appear that it was a theoretical ideal of BR engineers during the late 1960s. The fifty Class 50 locomotives built by English Electric in 1967/8 all had this type of braking, much against the wishes of the builders it may be added. Much trouble was experienced with it and one concludes that it was one of those theoretical ideals which could not be matched in service. Certainly, electrical loading of machines in the generator mode can be effective; it depends upon the application and associated equipment.

The Sulzer engine went out of favour within BR circles, probably due to the experiences of those fitted into the Classes 47 and 48. Another factor was that English Electric had entered into an agreement with Sulzer in 1966 to collaborate in the further development of the Sulzer LVA24 series of engines, with the former having the exclusive UK manufacturing and selling rights. Subsequent history showed that engines powering locomotives and power cars for BR service mostly came from within the GEC group, of which English Electric was a constituent company.

'Kestrel' was well ahead of its time, probably some ten years as subsequent history has proved. Not all its features were repeated, but it placed Brush in good stead during the

After featuring at the Moscow Rolling Stock Exhibition in July 1971, 'KESTREL' underwent extensive testing at the Shcherbinka test centre (Soviet Railways Research Institute). This view of the exiled locomotive was probably taken in 1972 and it shows it on the circuitous test track. Note the cyclopean roof-mounted headlamp at one end only, fitted specifically for the test centre trials.

BRUSH

leaner years of the 1970s and 1980s, when locomotive orders received by the private sector were not as plentiful as before. The traction equipment side of business continued to prove a regular source of orders, and this is often largely unnoticed by many people.

Although 'Kestrel' is remembered well by older Brush personnel, the memory may not be so fond as that of 'Falcon'. This is perhaps because the latter led to the massive orders for Brush Type 4s – a most visible result if there ever was one – one which eluded the successful 'Kestrel', for its results were placed out of sight inside locomotives and power cars. People would stop and watch a locomotive leave the works, but how many would watch an alternator leave on the back of a lorry?

9 – Industrial and Overseas Locomotives of the 1960s

Stock locomotives are expensive items of equipment to have on the books for too long a period of time. To have them is very convenient for quick deliveries, but if not sold quickly, they may become a problem. In Chapter 4 the Brush/Beyer Peacock stock orders and locomotives were detailed to the effect that five complete 0-4-0 locomotives were built and some parts for another contract were manufactured.

This second contract for ten stock locomotives was cancelled so far as Brush was concerned (BT 109-118/BP 7869-78) but the parts were placed in abeyance should the need arise to progress them into locomotives. This need came on 10th December 1959 when Park Gate Iron & Steel Co. Ltd ordered twelve 230bhp 0-4-0 diesel electric shunting locomotives for use in its Park Gate steelworks, Rotherham, then in the West Riding of Yorkshire. They were similar to, if not exactly the same as, the stock locomotives.

Five sets of mechanical parts, completed or otherwise, under BP progressive numbers 7874-8 were taken out of abeyance and those parts suitable were transferred to this order. The remaining locomotives came from two new BP orders for four and three locomotives respectively. These were No. 1734 (BP 7939-42) and No. 1735 (BP 7943-5). The expected delivery of the locomotives was June/July 1960 for 7874-8, November/December 1960 for 7939-41, May/June 1961 for 7942 and April/May 1961 for 7943-5. They were allocated Brush Traction Works Nos 327-338 and Park Gate running numbers 81-92 in sequence with the ascending order of the BP numbers.

Each unit was fitted with a McLaren LES6 engine, rated at 230bhp at 1,800rpm and a Brush TM 50-50 Mk3 traction motor.

The twelve locomotives were among the first diesel locomotives to enter service with Park Gate Iron & Steel Co. Ltd as part of its modernisation programme. Until this time

Number 86 (BT 332) hard at work during British Steel Corporation days at Rotherham.
Photograph taken 25th November 1973.

A J BOOTH

the locomotive fleet consisted mainly of steam traction, some locomotives being Sentinel geared types, one a Barclay fireless locomotive, but the majority were conventional saddle tank locomotives built by Andrew Barclay of Kilmarnock.

The Brush locomotives had been ordered to replace fourteen 0-4-0 standard gauge steam locomotives, and then only after comparison trials and keen sales competition with other manufacturers' diesel locomotives. In these trials many factors were taken into account, such as operating in confined areas, shunting on tight curves and steep gradients, locomotive driver comfort, cab visibility, good access to and from the cab, and low engine noise levels. The Brush locomotives met the specifications and delivery of the locomotives was made during 1960 and 1961, the official ex-works dates from the BP Works at Gorton are as follows:-

7874	20 June 1960
7875	9 August 1960
7876	9 September 1960
7877	20 September 1960
7878	5 October 1960
7939	17 February 1961
7940	2 March 1961
7941	27 March 1961
7942	19 April 1961
7943	25 May 1961
7944	13 June 1961
7945	21 June 1961

During the transition period of changing from steam to diesel traction some mechanical problems were encountered because of harsh shunting at the steel works. All were overcome in due course and the locomotives worked regularly at Park Gate until the gradual shutdown of the works. They were then transferred to the Rotherham works and were replaced by higher output diesel hydraulic locomotives. Some were equipped for tandem operation in the manner used on BR and British Steel Corporation systems. There was an intention to re-engine single units with Rolls-Royce engines.

At the time of their introduction the quality newspaper/comic for boys, 'The Eagle' featured the Brush design in its educational section and it included a sectioned illustration of No. 81, based upon an official photograph taken at the BP works.

The batch of locomotives remained intact until 82 and 83 were scrapped in January 1972 after sustaining accident or fire damage. By 1976, and now under British Steel Corporation ownership, all but Nos 81 and 87 were in use at the Rotherham Works, Aldwarke. No. 81 was scrapped on site circa December 1979 and No. 90 in the May of that year.

In this scene, taken at the Beyer, Peacock works at Gorton, No.22 (BT 340) newly-built for the Renishaw Iron Company in 1961 is seen in the company of another of the 1958 stock batch. The latter was used as a demonstrator and one of the works shunting locomotives. A youthful Brush Traction engineer Ken Baker is in the foreground.

K BAKER COLLECTION

In 1982 Nos 85/6/7 were out of use. Nos 84 and 88 were fitted with equipment for tandem working, but 89-92 remained as single operating units. None was in use by 1987, and although one source reports that the eight survivors (84-9,91/2) were still on site another states that Nos 85/9/91 were scrapped about 1985. By this time ownership had passed to United Engineering Steels Ltd. and Nos 84 and 88 could be seen from the adjacent BR lines and by the early part of 1988 these two were the only survivors. A report dated 2nd July 1990 noted them in sidings at the north end of the works still in a state of disuse, but they were scrapped around April 1991.

On 25th April 1960 an order was placed for three more 0-4-0 diesel electric shunting locomotives by the Renishaw Iron Company of Renishaw, in North Derbyshire, seven miles south of Sheffield. Running numbers 21/2/3 were allocated by the company, and they were built under Brush Traction works numbers 339-41 and Beyer-Peacock 7946-8 respectively. Another locomotive was ordered by the company on 8th February 1962 as Renishaw No. 24, Brush Traction No. 443 and Beyer-Peacock No. 7873. The first three were composed of new parts and delivery was expected to be effected in May 1961, actual deliveries from BP being later in the year with 7946 13th September, 7947 3rd October and 7948 on 30th October. No. 24 was built utilising parts made for the fifth stock locomotive, some being modified as necessary. New components were required where major design changes differed from the original stock design. The locomotive was due to be delivered during in July 1962, but actually went later in the year. The Brush Traction works number was of interest because it was duplicated the following year by that fitted

incorrectly to Brush Type 4 D1549! The problem probably arose from the combined effects of this 0-4-0 shunting locomotive being placed between two Type 4 orders and the plates for the Type 4s probably being ordered incorrectly. It is most probable that by the time D1549 was delivered Renishaw No. 24 was not considered and there may have been one pair of plates too many. What is certain is that apart from the fact that No. 443 was duplicated, No. 361 (allocated to D1519) was never fitted! Furthermore, there was random fitting of works plates among the two Type 4 orders.

The locomotives for Renishaw had the McLaren LES6 engine rated at 230bhp at 1,800rpm and the TM 50-50 Mk3 traction motor. In utilising parts from the stock order, there remained four partly produced locomotives on this order, Nos 7869-72. No. 24 was named 'Sir William' and all four bore Brush Traction works plates.

They had a comparatively short stay with the Renishaw Iron Company, all being sold in either 1968 or 1969. No. 23 went to Italy in the service of a permanent way construction company, Attilio Rossi of Rome. This locomotive was last heard of as in need of overhaul and still with the firm in 1977.

Renishaw No.21 was resold in later years to Raine & Co. of Newcastle upon Tyne, where it ran as that company's No.1. It was photographed there on 15th July 1974. The larger of the two plates bolted to the cabside is the registration plate certifying the locomotive to run on BR lines.
AJ BOOTH

Nos 21/2/4 went to Park Gate Iron & Steel Co. Ltd where they joined their twelve sister locomotives. They were there in 1970, but had left by 1973. By 1976 they had migrated to the North East of England to Raine & Co., steel suppliers and re-rollers, of Blaydon, Newcastle-upon-Tyne. One locomotive, Brush No. 340, was stripped as a source of spare parts for its two sisters and was noted as out of use in 1976. By October 1977 the company was endeavouring to have the engine of No. 339 repaired, but was experiencing difficulties in obtaining spare parts. Only No. 443 was working, but in need of serious attention, so the company was considering replacement locomotives. When your author visited the site on 12th May 1981 No. 340 had already been scrapped on site earlier in the year and No. 443 was lying in a siding in derelict condition, bearing Railway Executive No. 1692 plates of 1953, but no works plates. No. 339 was very active indeed under the control of its youthful driver who drove it in the manner of a stock car with particular emphasis placed upon rapid acceleration and deceleration as required. It had gained mushroom-like red spots on two white-painted and prominent mushroom-shaped pipes protruding from the bonnet top. It had other decorations, better left not described! It also had Railway Executive plates (No. 1815 of 1953) and retained its Brush Traction works plates. At the time, it was powered by a Rolls-Royce engine. Both locomotives bore faded green livery. The situation was little changed by the following year, but No. 443 was scrapped in June 1984. No. 339 was used until rail traffic ceased in May 1984 and then sold in March 1985 to TJ Thompson & Son Ltd of Dunston-on-Tyne, who scrapped it there the following month. BT 339 and 340 were numbered 1 and 2 respectively by Raine & Co.

On 16th March 1962 Brush Traction then took delivery of an 0-6-0 diesel electric shunting locomotive from Beyer, Peacock. It was rated at 400bhp and was powered by a National NMH56 flat-type engine. The drive between the traction motors and axles was through experimental right angle gearboxes. The original idea was to provide an inexpensive alternative to the accepted method of drive prevalent at the time on diesel electric shunting locomotives, i.e. nose-suspended, axle-hung

motors, with double reduction in-line geared drive. Having the traction motors in this latter arrangement was a well-proven method, but Brush wished to explore the possibilities of alternative arrangements that would still retain high tractive effort. Considerable delay was experienced during the development testing of the right angle drives when work on more important projects took precedent over it. By the end of 1961 work on the locomotive was almost completed.

In outward appearance the locomotive resembled the stock 0-4-0 shunting locomotives. It was obviously longer, it wore the same orange livery relieved with green and it was anonymous, bearing no works plates. One main difference that was immediately noticeable was that the wheels were situated outside the plate frames. Another difference was the small bonnet to the rear of the cab, in which the fuel tank of 400 gallons capacity was housed. It was 28ft 4ins long over the buffer beams, 8ft 5ins wide, 11ft 6ins high and weighed 50 tons in working order. Its wheelbase was 10ft and wheel diameter was 3ft 5ins. An information leaflet gave further details of the design, which whilst describing a 300/400bhp type fitted with Cummins VT12-825, Vee form, twelve-cylinder engine, gave other details which were possibly pre-1960 in origin:

Main Generator Continuous Output	398kW
Auxiliary Generator Continuous Output	12.5kW
Traction Motor Continuous Output (two)	202bhp
Locomotive Maximum Tractive Effort	15,000kg
Locomotive One Hour Tractive Effort	7,500kg
Speed at One Hour Tractive Effort	15.2kph
Locomotive Continuous Tractive Effort	6,500kg
Speed at Continuous Tractive Effort	16.3kph
Locomotive Maximum Speed	34kph

The locomotive was No. 7879 on the Beyer Peacock works list, and originally had been allotted Brush Traction No. 104, the first of five stock locomotives (BT 104-8) of BP order No. 4413 of 1958. The order was cancelled, or at least placed in abeyance, and in the long term only No. 7879 ever materialised into locomotive form. It is probable that it only materialised because a locomotive was required to provide running experience with the experimental drive. Somewhat belatedly an addendum to the order covered the modification of two locomotives to right-angled drive gearboxes supplied by Brush. The date was 14th December 1964! Only one locomotive was built, although by the end of 1961 more than one were still envisaged, and it does appear as though someone was tidying the accounts.

The working life of No. 7879 was unspectacular to say the least. It was not altogether successful as there were frequent oil leaks from the fabricated gear case, and difficulty was experienced in negotiating the sharper curves on the Falcon Works internal railway system. Added to these difficulties was the cessation of National engine production, coupled with a fall in the demand for new shunting locomotives in Great Britain because British Railways was disposing of many of its redundant diesel shunting locomotives to industrial concerns. Certainly, it was not popular with personnel, mainly due to its 'track' record, mentioned above, but it did prove useful on occasions as a load vehicle, presumably on the straight portion of the test track. It was finally used for providing a load during Type 4 brake and wheelslip tests carried out on D1961 in 1967. Soon afterwards it was moved and stored out of use on a short stub siding, which terminated at the base of the Meadow Lane bridge. It was out of everyone's way there! Its final setting in this position was one of being almost enveloped in summertime by the adjacent trees and bushes that eventually took over the site. The site became home to numerous rabbits that skipped around quite happily, oblivious to the nearby traffic on the adjacent BR lines.

The locomotive was sold for scrap in 1968 to Slag Reductions Ltd, of Rotherham. It arrived at the Millmoor Works during the September and was noted during that month standing in the yard minus its buffers. It was scrapped by 1970.

Until 1961 Brush had received only one overseas order for locomotives, the Ceylon contract. Then, on 8th September of that year an order for fourteen 1,730bhp Co-Co locomotives was placed by Rhodesia Railways to deal with increasing traffic on its system and displace about twenty-seven steam locomotives. They were intended to operate on the 257 mile route between Bulawayo and Malvernia, on the Rhodesia/Moçambique border. On this line they had to contend with gradients of 1 in 80, reaching 4,500 feet above sea level, ambient temperatures reaching 116 degrees F and a relative humidity of 50 per cent. Freight train loads over the line were from 1,300 to 1,400 short tons, running up to the maximum permitted speed of 50mph.

They were also the first modern locomotives to be built by Brush for the 3ft 6ins track gauge, the design being to a maximum axle load of 15 tons, and an overall weight of 90 tons in working order. They were classified DE 4 and numbered 1400 to 1413 by Rhodesia Railways, and also bore Brush Traction works numbers 399 to 412 respectively. The locomotives were also required to run in multiple with the English Electric Class DE 3 (1300-15), thus ensuring good availability, whilst simultaneously reducing the number of

footplate staff formerly required for steam traction haulage. Rhodesia Railways ordered these locomotives as part of the same plan and originally intended to order only one class, but to facilitate a quicker delivery divided the orders between English Electric and Brush. This decision meant of course that two classes rather than one went into service.

It was an important export order for main line diesel electric locomotives and the ancestry of the locomotives could be traced back through the BR Type 2 to the original Ceylon locomotive order. It was mainly the influence of the highly successful Type 2, which led Rhodesia Railways to seek locomotives from Brush, partly to diversify its suppliers and not become too dependent on one particular builder. The order was based upon a ten year hiring arrangement, after which the locomotives might be retained on an annual charge.

The main details and dimensions were as follows:-

Wheel Arrangement	Co-Co
Track Gauge	3ft 6ins
Engine Model	Mirrlees-National JVSST 12
Engine Rating	1,730bhp
Main Generator	8-pole compensated type with separate and self-excited shunt windings and a series decompounding winding, also used for engine starting
Continuous Ratings	1,122kW, 680V, 1,650A: 1,112kW, 530V, 2,100A each at 1,000rpm
Auxiliary Generator	6-pole shunt wound
Continuous Rating	37.2kW, 110V, 338A
Traction Motors (six)	4-pole, series-wound, force ventilated, axle hung and nose-suspended
Continuous Rating	222hp, 265V, 700A at 556rpm
One Hour Rating	216hp, 239V, 770A at 477rpm
Length Over Buffer Couplings	54ft 5ins
Width Over Framing	9ft 9ins
Overall Height	13ft 4ins
Wheel Diameter	3ft 4ins
Bogie Wheelbase	13ft 0ins
Bogie Pivots	27ft 3ins
Minimum Curve Negotiable	275ft 0ins
Maximum Speed	60mph
Maximum Tractive Effort	57,800lbs
Continuous Tractive Effort @ 13mph	37,500lbs
Fuel Capacity	1,000 gallons
Weight in Working Order	90 tons

The external appearance of the locomotives bore a family resemblance to the Type 4 and 'Falcon', particularly with regard to the cabs, and like the former most grilles and louvres were confined to the roof area. The body followed that of the Type 4s, being of the integral monocoque type, basically consisting of bodysides connected by cross-stretchers, deck plates and roof sections. At each end were dragboxes fitted with a centre-buffing coupler, but no side buffers. Mounted centrally below the cab front windows at each end was a large headlight, and below this an encased coat of arms of Rhodesia Railways. The main livery was light green relieved by a broad cream band which ran completely around the locomotive body, tapering in 'whisker' curves to meet centrally below each coat of arms. A much narrower cream band positioned just below window level encircled the locomotive, subtly curving only below the front windows to follow their gentle curvature. On the large band, central to each end of the locomotive, were the raised metal letters R R in serif form and picked out in red. On the body sides, just inwards of each cab door was the standard RR oval number plate bearing the running number centrally, with RR above and DE4 below. The raised numerals, letters and border were picked out in cream against a red background. The standard Brush Traction works plates were similarly treated and affixed to the No. 1 end cab sides between the two cream bands. The lower front valance corresponding to the buffer beam in alternative practice was painted red. Below this was a black-painted cow catcher. The roof areas were painted a very light grey/white.

This livery applied to clean, uncluttered body sides was a far cry from the 'portholes' and heavy body side grilles of the Ceylon locomotives. The whole effect was very pleasing to the eye. For ease of maintenance there were two access doors, one in each body side. This arrangement allowed removal of and access to small components, without the need to pass through the cabs. There were removable roof sections for access to and removal of all large equipment, except the radiator roof section, which was load bearing. In contrast to the sheet steel body sides, the cab sections consisted of aluminium and glass-fibre.

The bogies were the cast steel 'Commonwealth' type supplied by the English Steel Castings Corporation Ltd, with three Brush nose-suspended, force-ventilated TM 73-42 Mk1 traction motors fitted to each one.

This new locomotive design brought together good features of both the Type 2 and the Type 4 designs; one might be correct to describe them in simple terms as the Type 2 equipment in a shortened Type 4 body.

Locomotive braking was operated by both air and vacuum. The latter system not only supplied the locomotive but also the train, although an independent air brake-valve operated the locomotive brakes only.

The diesel engine was the Mirrlees National twelve-cylinder, four-stroke, Vee-type, being pressure charged and inter-cooled. It was rated at 1,920bhp at 1,000rpm under normal conditions, but was only rated effectively at 1,730bhp in Rhodesia due to the altitude, ambient temperatures and relative humidity. The engine and main generator were mounted on a common bedplate, the former having stress-relieved steel plate fabrications on the cylinder housing and upper crankcase parts. The cylinder linings were made of cast iron with continuous bore, enabling free downward expansion. The batteries were prominently situated centrally below the deck level, in boxes located within the fuel tank assembly just above rail level.

Construction began in 1962 and the first one emerged in June of the following year, having been constructed alongside the Type 4 production lines, notably in the former Turbine Shop. By the end of July 1963 No. 1400 had been tested, painted and was ready for the official handing-over ceremony, which took place on Friday 9th August in the original Erecting Shop. The locomotive was officially handed over by the Managing Director of the Brush Electrical Engineering Co, Mr M C Clear, to Mr A M Hawkins, the Assistant General Manager of Rhodesia Railways. The latter drove the locomotive along the works test track after the ceremony.

Delivery from Loughborough commenced in December 1963 when No. 1400 left the works by rail on the 21st of the month, mounted on accommodation bogies. The sea journey ended at the port of Beira, in Moçambique, had witnessed the presence of Brush locomotives before, when in the 1890s a number of narrow gauge 4-4-0 steam locomotives had been supplied by the Company to the Beira Railway. After offloading, the locomotive was taken to Rhodesia via Umtali.

On 24th March 1964 there was another handing-over ceremony, this time at Bulawayo station, which was attended by Government and Civic officials, representatives of Brush and officers of Rhodesia Railways. Mr J Davison, local Chairman of Hawker Siddeley Brush (Pvt) Ltd, handed over No. 1400 to Mr T A Wright, General Manager of Rhodesia Railways. Later in the afternoon a short special train, complete with lounge car, was hauled by the locomotive on a demonstration run to Heany Junction and back. During the 21mile return trip the locomotive was deliberately given the chance to provide a speedy run and probably achieved a record run for this short section in the process, during which it performed faultlessly. En route refreshments were served. The second locomotive arrived in Beira during March. Each locomotive cost £83,606.

The locomotives entered service during 1964/5 (see Appendix 9-1), but even before the first one entered service RR started to change its mind as regards where the class should operate. Rather than operating in the southeast of Rhodesia to Malvernia, they were allocated to Lochinvar (Salisbury) Diesel Motive Power Depot instead, for working eastwards towards Machipanda six miles beyond Umtali. Machipanda was the interchange point with the Beira Railway. They also worked southwards from Salisbury to Gwelo and when more locomotives had been delivered the workings were extended further, southwest to Bulawayo. Lochinvar diesel depot was of recent construction, being completed at the end of 1962.

Tests were conducted with the DE4s working in tandem with the English Electric DE3s. These proved successful and such tandem working became common practice on the Salisbury-Umtali-Machipanda section, the Salisbury-Gwelo line and on branches out of Salisbury. Having two cabs was a popular feature of the DE4s with the locomotive crews. The English Electric locomotives had single cabs, and it was a rare sight for one of them to lead a DE4.

The class had a promising start, but soon clouds appeared on the horizon. The first of these were mechanical and the second were political. In the first year of service Nos 1401/4/6/9/10/11/12 were troublesome, whereas 1400/2/3/5/7/13 were not, each of the latter returning an average monthly mileage of 7,026 miles. Of the former, seven

On 21st December 1963 Rhodesia Railways No. 1400 was moved to the despatch siding. As the Rhodesian track gauge is only 3ft 6in, the locomotive had to be mounted on adaptor bogies for towing to the docks on the first stage of its journey to Africa.

BRUSH A10093

(No. 1412 excepted) collectively spent a total of 24 months in the workshops suffering from cracked engine crankcases, bogie defects and sundry other faults described later. Their average monthly mileage, including time spent in the workshops, was only 4,541 miles. Consequently, they were de-rated to 1,430bhp when they were returned to service. They remained so for five years, whilst modifications were being made to the engines. No. 1409 worked 9,452 miles during its first month in service, a most creditable performance. Then the troubles beset it, and mechanical engineers of RR had to rectify them with reduced assistance from the makers, due to economic sanctions imposed by the United Nations. After the engines were de-rated it was necessary to re-introduce steam traction back on the Umtali workings to a limited degree. Whenever possible the DE4s would always be worked in tandem to ensure a profitable load. As a result the railway was always desperately short of running staff and massive numbers were promoted from passed fireman to driver and main line driver. Later this then turned into a tide of running staff opting to move from Zambia to Rhodesia when the former gained independence, resulting in drivers working perhaps four or five trips in a month.

Number 1402 was involved in an accident at Battlefields in September 1964, and it was 22 months before it returned to service following repair. Then No. 1412 was damaged in a collision at Umniati in May 1965. This locomotive and Nos. 1408/11 were assigned to special duties and for 42 months they were not credited with any revenue-earning mileages.

Until 1963 Rhodesia had consisted of two parts, Northern Rhodesia and Southern Rhodesia, constituents of a federation. Upon the break up of this federation, Northern Rhodesia gained independence from Britain and became Zambia in 1964, but Southern Rhodesia (by this time, Rhodesia) pursued a different course in its efforts to gain independence.

The political situation in Rhodesia gradually worsened during the mid 1960s as the country unsuccessfully sought its independence from Great Britain. The issue that became a stumbling block was that of majority rule by free election.

Matters worsened further when the ruling minority white government, headed by Mr Ian Smith, issued its Unilateral Declaration of Independence, a term usually shortened to UDI. This self-proclaimed independence occurred on 11th November 1965, and was followed by international economic sanctions against Rhodesia initiated by the United Nations. Not all nations conformed to sanctions and indeed Rhodesia managed to purchase more diesel locomotives from abroad during this troubled period, but the situation was serious and caused endless problems for the country. It caused problems for Brush, which had to conform to the sanctions, but was required by contract to honour its after sales services. It proved to be a difficult task. In April 1966 a desultory guerrilla war commenced. It was poorly organised and it was not until 1972 that any serious threat was posed to the Smith government.

It is worthy of note that regardless of the rights or wrongs of the sanctions era, and despite the difficulties of isolation which Rhodesia endured, personal ties remained with people in Great Britain and eventually information was kindly made available by railway enthusiasts and engineers who recorded what they could during those troubled years. Certainly it has

Three new Rhodesia Railways DE4s lined up prior to going into traffic; nearest the camera is 1408 (BT407). Despite alterations to suit customers' requirements there was a pronounced 'family' resemblance between the Brush main-line diesel locomotive designs.

Below: Number 1400 during one of its trial runs in Rhodesia.

BRUSH A10757

NATIONAL RAILWAYS OF ZIMBABWE

Two DE4s meet out in open country, with one crew member preparing to exchange messages.

NATIONAL RAILWAYS OF ZIMBABWE

Rhodesia Railways No.1404 (BT403/1963) on a freight train in Rhodesia. Despite some damage above the cow catcher, the high standard of cleanliness is apparent.

NATIONAL RAILWAYS OF ZIMBABWE

made this account more complete than it otherwise would have been, and more complete than those of some other troubled, or differently cultured countries around the world. Not all countries have railway enthusiasts – indeed some actively discourage people interested in railways.

Rhodesia Railways hired various locomotive types from South Africa, both steam and diesel traction and kept what it could serviceable. The DE 4s were particularly hard to keep in service on account of their troubles and the difficulty in obtaining foreign currency to purchase spare parts or impossibility of finding spare parts. Accidents did not help matters either. In December 1972 Nos. 1409 and 1412 were derailed near Headlands due to being run too fast. Both locomotives were damaged and out of service for some time undergoing repairs at Umtali Diesel Workshops. Number 1409 was out of service for seven months. By December 1975 No. 1400 was the only one of the class to work over 800,000 miles and No. 1412 had not reached 500,000 miles.

The initial troubles concerned the fabricated steel crankcases, which failed at the welds, particularly in the area of the camshaft bearing mounting pads through to the water space. Strengthening of the pads proved to be of no value. The eventual replacement of these crankcases, by ones of cast steel, was undertaken by Rhodesia Railways, with Mirrlees supplying the parts. Cylinder head gaskets tended to blow because they were thin and the nuts that held them down tightened to low torque limits. The latter had to be re-torqued on a monthly basis. Engine lubrication suffered from high pressure on an intermittent basis.

Bogie frames were prone to persistent cracking either side of the centre wheel horns so strengthening ribs were fitted following advice from Brush, and a visit by a Commonwealth representative from the USA who went to Rhodesia, complete with over a ton of equipment, all by air freight. The cracks were not caused by fatigue, but contraction of the casing, so had to be chipped out and welded. When the axles and traction motor suspension tubes became life-expired, problems arose with the non-availability of replacements, so new axles of modified design were substituted, incorporating standard bearings. Latterly, there occurred a high percentage of engine crankshaft failures, which put the locomotives out of service one by one. They were afflicted by fractures and were also prone to throwing balance weights.

By August 1975 eight DE 4s were out of service and in two years all had been withdrawn. They were stored until such time that the political situation improved to allow the purchase of spare parts readily.

The cooling system initially suffered trouble with the centrifugal clutch to the fan burning out. A new and better grade of friction lining was substituted, together with new springs, under guarantee.

A fuel transfer pump fed into an overhead 40 gallon gravity feed to the fuel injector pump and this proved inadequate with the tank running dry when the engine was on full power for more than five or six minutes. Fuel dilution was no more troublesome than on other engines, but the fuel overflow pipe extended some nine inches into the fuel tank, resulting in about 200 gallons of fuel siphoning away after the tank had been filled. Until anti-vacuum valves were fitted tanks

were only three quarters filled. The cow-catchers caused problems because they allowed too much clearance above the rail tops. Some obstructions were missed by them and remained in situ until they fouled the fuel tanks. The lower portion was extended downwards by about two inches. The damaged aluminium fuel tanks proved difficult to repair.

Control wiring circuits posed constant problems with cable lugs breaking due to vibration. Brush devised a modification of rubber pads on the bolster pivot centres, but although this curbed the vibration to some degree it did not make any difference to the lugs breaking. The lightweight aluminium contactor cubicles and contactor mountings proved troublesome due to vibration and fractures became commonplace.

At first the DE4s had exceptionally powerful braking. It was not uncommon for someone sitting in the second man's seat to have to brace himself against the console during a full application of the straight air brake! Unfortunately, the pin on the brake hanger was slim, wore, and the brake blocks went off the wheels. A bracing stay had to be fitted between the two hangers. Once the bogies passed through the workshops this was replaced by a more robust pivot pin. The machines proved to be well suited to their duties electrically, and the cab layout was excellent, being well liked by the crews.

At some time during the sanctions period it is thought that at least four of the DE4s (including 1408,1411,1412 over the period March 1966 to October 1968) had power equipment removed and were used as mobile fuel carriers on trains from bordering countries willing to allow fuel through. The pseudo locomotive would be coupled to a powered locomotive and to all intents the train appeared to be double headed! On many occasions more locomotives headed a train. Although it was preferable (for reasons of braking) to use two fuel carriers at a time, three could be used. No raised eyebrows were caused as for years locomotives had been re-fuelled in neighbouring countries, for economic reasons, and was therefore not an unusual sight. One estimate places the fuel capacity of one of these conversions at about 10,000 gallons.

Neighbouring Moçambique gained its independence from Portugal in 1975 and guerrilla attacks increased. A so-called 'Internal Agreement' was reached in Rhodesia and in 1978 Ian Smith stepped down and Bishop Abel Muzorewa took his place under a curious arrangement which gave apparent power to the latter, who became the first, and last, African Premier of what was by then entitled Zimbabwe Rhodesia. Elections were held in April 1979 and as a result Ian Smith ended his rule as rebel Premier officially a few weeks later, on 31st May. Not all factions in Zimbabwe Rhodesia were satisfied with the situation, as many matters remained unresolved. The guerrilla war had continued and further negotiations resulted in a cease fire which took effect at 24.00 hours on 28th December 1979. Full and free elections were held during February 1980, which resulted in victory for Mr Robert Mugabe, a former principal leader in the guerrilla war. There followed a formal and internationally recognised Declaration of Independence on 18th April and the country became Zimbabwe and within it Salisbury became Harare.

The title Rhodesia Railways was replaced by the title National Railways of Zimbabwe (NRZ). A 1970s plan to electrify the Gweru-Harare line led to the consideration of converting the DE4s to straight electric transmission as an alternative to the obviously difficult task of buying new locomotives. Two of the class were selected for experimental preparatory work and No. 1404, at least, was stripped of much of its equipment in preparation for this. This was taking place about 1979, and the changing situation was still not making matters easier for purchasing new electric locomotives. The projected conversions work was put out to tender, but because of the high cost of conversion the project was then abandoned during the following year. It had been one option considered by the electrical engineers. All the DE4s were still out of service in 1979 awaiting their fate.

In 1981 a decision was made to retain the locomotives as diesel electrics, but fitted with some new power equipment. They were fitted with the new Ruston Diesels Ltd eight-cylinder 8 RK3CT after-cooled engine, rated at 1,780bhp at 900rpm, coupled by means of a cardan shaft to the retained Brush main generator which was fitted with separately excited and self-excited shunt windings, together with a decompounding series winding which was also used for engine starting. Its continuous rating was 1,122kW, 680V, 1,650A at 900rpm.

By the end of 1981 the first two chosen were already re-engined and rehabilitated at Rhodesian Engineering Steel Construction Company (RESCCO, later becoming ZECO, Zimbabwe Engineering Company) and were almost ready for engine-running tests. The first locomotive, No. 1408, was completed early in 1982 handed over to NRZ at RESCCO Bulawayo. In attendance for this were Mr B Sephton of Brush Electrical Machines Ltd, Mr N Lea-Cox, General Manager of NRZ and Messrs G Dale and B Wyness of RESCCO.

The locomotives emerged in the new livery of NRZ. This was bright yellow, with black undergear and roofs, the new title appearing only on the bodyside numberplates, which were finished in black. The locomotives were based at Lochinvar but went to Mutare workshops for repairs. By July 1982 three had re-entered service, 1400/2/8, and appeared to be a great success. At the time three (1402/3/4) were in the workshops with faults found on test and 1412 was due out. The renewal programme was completed in 1983.

Unfortunately, their new lease of life was not without problems and their performance was erratic. They were plagued by problems with the exhaust system and turbo blower on a number of engines, which were fitted with integral air chests and the manifolds required redesign work as a result. Testing was carried out on the test bed in Bulawayo workshops and theoretical modelling of the exhaust tuning at Manchester University took over a year for the Ruston engineers to be satisfied with the engine performance.

By July 1985 some of the DE4s had been set aside pending rectification work. Eleven months later the position was that four were in service, four out of service, one in the workshops and five awaiting workshops attention.

During the 1980s Moçambique was in the grips of a civil war and Zimbabwe endeavoured to keep its supply lines from that country open, indeed many thousands of Zimbabwean troops were guarding the various railway and fuel lines in Moçambique itself and running trains was a hazardous task.

In 1986/7 the fleet was fitted with armour-plating over the cabs and locomotives were detailed to work over the Mutare (formerly Umtali) to Gondola section of the Moçambique Railways. This section was being run by the National Railways of Zimbabwe, because of the shortage of motive power by MR. In 1987 problems were experienced with the exhausters, and the reciprocating units were replaced with rotary exhausters taken off DE5 locomotives. It appears that because of the different design of motor for this new exhauster the electrical circuit breaker was overloaded, which resulted in one locomotive (possibly 1412) having its control cubicle burnt out and the locomotive was set aside. Later in the same year one DE4, (probably No. 1402) came under attack from dissidents in Moçambique and in trying to escape entered a siding too fast, was derailed at the trailing points and set on fire. This locomotive was burnt out and had to be scrapped.

The remaining locomotives all suffered regularly from earth faults as a result of the rehabilitation work, when the end to end conduit was replaced by a cable duct fitted to the body side. Two factors caused the earth faults. One was that although the power wiring had been renewed the original control wiring was retained. The other was that during the manufacture of the ducts no de-burring was done, they were left in a rough state, so as the wires were pulled through the insulation was punctured in places. An exercise was set up to replace the control wiring on all the locomotives, but only one locomotive was completed before NRZ decided on a policy to standardise its locomotive fleet.

The 'Railways of Southern Africa, Locomotive Guide' in its 1990 edition listed that 1400/1/3-11/13 were in service at Lochinvar and that 1402 was withdrawn at Mutare workshops. It was still at Mutare Workshops in 1992 and the remaining thirteen were still allocated to Lochinvar depot in Harare. This total of locomotives in stock was reduced to nine by December 1992, by the withdrawal of No. 1412. The serviceable locomotives were 1400/1/3/4/7/8/10/11/13 and they were still allocated to Lochinvar operating on the Mutare-Machipanda route, branch lines to Chinhoyi (Sinoia) and Shamva and on intermediate traffic on the Dabuka sections. One source states that only three locomotives were left in service at this time. Those not listed were said to be permanently withdrawn.

The situation as of 31st March 1993 was reported to be that Nos 1404/7/8/10/11/3 were allocated to Lochinvar, while 1400 was in Mutare workshops under repair. Nos 1402/3/5/6/9/12 were listed as scrapped and 1401 listed as proposed for scrap, although the paperwork may not have reflected the situation on the rails regarding actual scrapping. Conflicting reports do occur, and the writer is of the opinion that the situation was less severe than the above might suggest.

The 1993 edition of the 'Locomotive Guide', correct to 15th May 1993, listed Nos 1400//1/3-8/10/11/13 as being still in service and allocated to Lochinvar, with Nos 1402 (at Mutare), 1409 (at Lochinvar) and 1412 (at Mutare) listed as withdrawn.

By the autumn of 1993 No. 1401 had been withdrawn and seven (1400/4/7/8/10/11/13) were still operating out from Lochinvar depot, albeit nominally. By December 1993 only one was left in service and it is understood from the Chief

Mechanical Engineer, Mr Kuzviwanza, that during 1994 all the DE4 locomotives would be withdrawn from service and scrapped.

Visitors to Zimbabwe on 20th February 1994 noted the presence of No. 1400 at Lochinvar depot. Its condition was not stated. Another visitor was told on 30th July 1994 that "all the DE4's have now been withdrawn from service and the last one left Lochinvar for Mutare Workshops for scrap 'about six months ago'".

Further enquiries supported this statement, but as convenience sometimes overrules paperwork, No. 1407 was retained as a shunting locomotive at Mutare Works. By early 1995 it was the only operational DE4, but in September 1996 Nos 1407 and 1410 were reported to be in use as shunting locomotives at Mutare Works, a situation which still prevailed in mid-1999. By this time No. 1411 was reported preserved. Similarly, on 18th November 2000 1407 was seen at Bulawayo Railway Museum restored to RR green with yellow waistband.

In 1995 some totalling of collective distances run by classes DE3 and DE4 was made, with interesting comparison. The former, based on fifteen of the sixteen locomotives delivered revealed that the Brush locomotives ran only 49% of that of the English Electric locomotives and appeared to bear out the opinion of former engineers of Rhodesia Railways that obtaining the Brush units was not a good decision and indeed recommended that the option to buy the locomotives be not taken up. Brief extracts from locomotive record cards summarise certain details of the DE4 locomotives in service, and are to be found in Appendix 9-1.

The aforementioned withdrawal situation appeared confusing at times, perhaps a symptom of African ways, but in 2001 a table was published to the following effect:-

TRZ No.	Withdrawn/Condemned
1400	05.1994
1401	01.1994, for sale by tender 10.1994
1402	1988, final month in service 11.1987
1403	02.1993, fire damage
1404	08.1993
1405	1991
1406	1991
1407	03.1994, Plant No. 3436, Mutare Works shunter (1994), dumped (02.1995), to NRZ museum
1408	03.1994, for sale by tender 10.1994
1409	02.1993
1410	01.1994, for sale by tender 10.1994
1411	01.1994, for sale by tender 10.1994
1412	04.1991, final month in service 08.1990
1413	08.1993

Politics, as practised by governments, are rarely as simple as first envisaged. Politicians, often well meaning with their intentions, set in motion matters less than ideal. Throughout the history of railways proper, governments have had their say on them, often to the good and often to the detriment. Frequently, the political leaning mattered little, the effects on the railway concerned railwaymen more and decisions taken on behalf or railways around the world were not always the best ones.

One country with a volatile political situation in modern times was Cuba. Under Fidel Castro and his Communist regime the country had had an uncertain future for over forty years. Relations between Cuba and the USA had been at a very low ebb since Castro came to power and gained the support of the former USSR. Matters came to a head during October 1962 when the 'Cuban Missile Crisis' occurred – a confrontation between the USSR and the USA over the siting of the former's missiles in Cuba. The USA did not take kindly to the missiles pointing in its direction and took steps to have them removed. Removal followed some direct political moves, but the whole affair left a situation whereby Cuba was further isolated from the so-called Western World, particularly in trade. Indeed, there was a trade embargo in place, with the hand of the USA firmly held on the reins. It is largely forgotten that this embargo has never been lifted officially. Countries friendly to the USA trod a cautious path, and so did firms trading worldwide.

During 1963 a Cuban trade delegation visited Great Britain and representatives of the Ferrocarriles de Cuba (Cuban National Railways) discussed with BR which modern design of diesel locomotive could be adapted suitably to their requirements.

It does appear that the Cuban engineers had to follow a budgetary and political remit laid down by their political masters, but in practical terms what was required was a type that was suitable for the railway's requirements and had extensive service experience. Later that year it became known that the Brush Type 4 had been selected and that an order for ten locomotives had been placed with the Clayton Equipment Company Ltd, to the value of £1.7 million. The locomotives were completed under licence at Hatton, near Derby, in the works of the International Combustion Company.

Clayton was no stranger to locomotive building, having produced its first main line diesel electric locomotives in 1952, in the form of mechanical parts for AEI Ltd. These were fourteen 39 ton Bo-Bo locomotives of 400bhp destined for Western Australian Government Railways. During the 1960s the firm was responsible for building 88 of the 117 ill-fated Bo-Bo Type 1 locomotives of the D8500 series for BR.

That the Brush Electrical Engineering Company was not the main contractor is significant. Such direct involvement was avoided in acknowledgement of the prevailing political situation and the possible adverse effects upon Hawker Siddeley interests in the North American continent. Brush acted as a subcontractor, providing the design work and producing the body shells and electrical equipment alongside the Type 4 production at the Falcon Works. This substantial role was not particularly emphasised, but it was acknowledged sufficiently to attract possible orders.

The resultant Brush Type 4 derivative was a curious combination. Rather than the Sulzer LDA engine, use was made of the Sulzer twelve-cylinder LVA24 Vee-type engine rated at 2,534bhp, the same model as fitted to the five Brush

The bodyshell of a 'Cuban Type 4', mounted on transporter bogies, seen on the Falcon Works test track on 11th December 1964.

BRUSH A11488

The Sulzer engine and Brush main generator are lowered into the body of one of the Cuban locomotives, at the Hatton works of The Clayton Equipment Company Ltd, during January 1966.

BRUSH A12644

Type 4s, D1702-6, which were classified as Class 48. This output was at 1,050rpm, the maximum design speed. Eleven engines were manufactured in France by Cie de Construction Méchanique Procédés Sulzer (CCM) for the ten locomotives. At an early stage of the proceedings it became clear that Vickers-Armstrong of Barrow in Furness were not going to supply 12LDA28C engines for locomotives destined for Cuba, for the same reasons that Hawker Siddeley had declined to supply locomotives directly.

Brush manufactured the basic body shells in the manner and pattern of the BR production shells and added at each end a drag box manufactured at Hatton in order to accommodate central buffing and draw gear, altering the appearance considerably in this area. The drag boxes were sent to Loughborough for fitting to the body shell. A cow catcher was fitted below each drag box. Much of the internal control and auxiliary equipment was common to the BR Type 4s, and as much as possible was fitted at Loughborough.

The outline of the parent Brush Type 4 was not lost, despite such alterations to suit Cuban requirements. A prominent headlight was affixed to the front of the cab roof at each end. Mounted on each cab corner was an illuminated number box each displaying the running number. This number was repeated twice on each body side beneath the body side windows, being applied either in transfer or painted form in a direct copy of the current BR style. The livery was BR two-tone green as applied to the Type 4s, complete with yellow warning panels on the cab fronts!

Rectangular Clayton works plates were affixed to each cab side beneath the window. The adoption of BR colours certainly did not draw undue attention to the locomotives during their delivery journey in Britain, but it did confuse some of the few railway enthusiasts who espied them into thinking that they were BR locomotives. Test runs were conducted with the locomotives in primer paint, and even then hardly anyone noticed the difference. Perhaps this was part of the intention to not draw undue attention to their existence at too early a stage of events.

The main details and dimensions were as follows:-

Wheel Arrangement	Co-Co
Track Gauge	4ft 8½ins
Engine Model	Sulzer 12LVA24
Engine Rating	2,534bhp at 1,050rpm
Main Generator	12-pole compensated, with a separately excited and self-excited shunt fields and a series decompounding winding. A series winding was provided for engine starting
Continuous Rating	380V 4,260A at 1,050rpm
Rating At Maximum Voltage	439V 3,720A at 1,050rpm
One Hour Rating	353V 4,570A at 1,050rpm
Auxiliary Generator	6-pole shunt-wound interpolar, rated at 50kW 455A 110V at 1,050rpm.
Traction Motors (six)	TM 64-68, 4-pole axle-hung, nose-suspended, force-ventilated. 336hp output. All connected in parallel across main generator.
Continuous Rating	380V 710A at 1,727rpm
One Hour Ratings	353V 762A 324hp at 625rpm 330hp at 1,505rpm
Length Over Buffers	64ft 0ins
Overall Height	13ft 0ins
Wheel Diameter	3ft 9ins
Bogie Wheelbase	14ft 6ins
Distance Between Bogie Pivots	37ft 0ins
Maximum Speed	65mph
Weight In Working Order	110 tons

Official works photograph of No.2507 supplied to the Cuban National Railways in 1965/6 by the Clayton Equipment Company Ltd. Clayton assembled the locomotives, with Brush acting as main supplier and subcontractor.

BRUSH A12642

A single-phase inductor alternator of 42 kVA output was fitted to provide, through rectifiers, the excitation for the separate field winding of the main generator. The continuous rating of this machine was 28A, 150V at 4,050rpm. Load control of the generator was by variation of the inductor alternator excitation, which in turn was supplied from the auxiliary generator. One compressor unit provided the compressed air for the locomotive and train braking systems. It was driven mechanically from the engine.

The fabrication of the ten body shells commenced before the end of 1964 and at least one was completed by the December. These and the ten sets of electrical equipment were despatched from the Falcon Works in primer coat, for final erection at Hatton. All movement of the body shells was undertaken with the use of accommodation bogies, and generally under the cover of darkness. To facilitate movement further because of the centre buffer/coupler it was necessary to provide wooden-bodied match wagons, as was the case for the Rhodesian locomotives.

Upon arrival at Hatton, adaptation of the body shells had to be made to accept the Vee engines and even then the engines sat higher than the LDA engine, sufficiently to cause problems with the silencing of the exhaust. The main

braking system was compressed air because Cuban practice had abandoned vacuum by this time. A four-cylinder Vee air compressor directly coupled to a shaft extension from the free end of the engine.

Twenty-two bogies, which had a different gear ratio to the BR version, were sent to Hatton for final completion, which included the fitting of sanding gear.

To meet the humid atmospheric conditions of Cuba the cooler group radiators had to be larger than on the standard Type 4 and this necessitated enlarging the air inlet roof grilles accordingly. This altered the roof profile and appearance.

To help the staff at Hatton, Brush provided a Type 4 as a physical guideline. Although not specifically identified, as it was in primer, it was probably one of the Vee-engined batch for BR. It sat in one corner of the erecting shop, almost unobtrusively, with the Cuban locomotives.

As would have been at the Falcon Works, the locomotives were statically tested, then load bank tested and undertook slow speed movement within the Hatton Works environment.

When completed except for final painting the locomotives were tested as light locomotives during quieter times on the Derby-Birmingham line and between Derby and Lichfield via Burton on Trent at higher speeds and then returned for completion. A BR man was always the driver, with a Clayton engineer present.

Following their returns to Hatton, the locomotives were then prepared for despatch by rail to Hull and then for the sea journey to Cuba.

Cuban National Railways No.2501 seen at an unidentified roundhouse in Cuba. The original British Railways style livery has given way to a more distinctive local design.

BRUSH A13221

The first two locomotives, 2501/2, were shipped from King George Dock, Hull on 30th July 1965 on the Jugoslavian ship 'Kolasin', followed by 2503/4 on 2nd September, 2505 on 18th October, 2506 on 26th October and the rest followed soon afterwards and into 1966. Numbers 2507/8 were noted heading for Tilbury as part of a Derby-Brent freight train later in 1965. Delivery to Cuba was completed early in 1966. Most of the understandably subdued publicity followed delivery. By February 1966 they had been introduced into service under the supervision of Brush service engineers and were giving satisfactory service.

The Cuban Railways classified them Class T. They were numbered 2501-2510, but no Brush works numbers were allocated because they were built under a sub-contract arrangement. Clayton works numbers were 4936/U1 to 4936/U10 respectively.

There has been some suggestion that the construction of BR Type 4s D1842-61 was diverted from Brush to Beyer-Peacock of Gorton, and then again to BR workshops at Crewe, to facilitate the construction of the Cuban Type 4s which did take place at the Falcon Works, but this was then strongly denied by Mr F H Wood, formerly of Brush. Certainly, D1842-61 were built at Crewe, but it is assured that this was the original intention. Furthermore, at this time Brush was actively seeking work to replace the expected completion of Type 4s for BR. Knowing of the determination of Mr Wood to provide work for Brush there is no reason to doubt otherwise.

It is the opinion of some of the former service engineers that these Type 4 locomotives were ordered for political reasons as well as for operating reasons. They were regarded as being too powerful and certainly too heavy for the poorly maintained track, the latter being the problem. The livery of the locomotives was modified soon after delivery to display in large, serif, upper case letters between and in line with the body side windows, the railway title in full, FERROCARRILES DE CUBA. Two horizontal lines were added to the two-tone green scheme at the junctions of the bands. These encircled the whole locomotive. 'wasp stripes' were added to the drag box portion around the centre buffer/coupler. Later a totally different livery of red with white stripes was applied.

It appears that by mid-1976 only about three locomotives were in running condition, the remainder being out of service awaiting spare parts and being cannibalised to keep the remainder running. This was due to lack of finance by the Cubans, although some limited work by Sulzer engineers was reported to be in progress at the time.

Very little information has emerged from Cuba over the years. This is understandable, but in recent times with the relaxation of political attitudes in both directions railway enthusiasts have visited Cuba. They have reported back their findings, which do not generate a happy story. It appears that by the early 1980s all the locomotives were out of service and at some time previous (probably the 1970s) had been renumbered into a national series, becoming 52501 to 52510. It is believed that the first digit indicated diesel electric, the second and third approximately 2,500bhp, and the final two the individual locomotive identity.

By February 1983 52502 and others were seen stored in sidings at the rear of Havana Zoo. In March 1985 the last active locomotive was reported at the time as a shunting locomotive at the docks in Havana, with the others said to have been derelict for some years.

Number 52510 and others were noted, dumped and derelict, at Cardenas scrap yard and on 6th March 1988 a visitor to Havana Cristina diesel depot found 52504 on site, but out of use.

Eight of them were noted in February 1992 dumped and gutted of most equipment, near a station in the town of Cardenas, near the tourist resort of Varadero on the north coast. They were little more than bodyshells on bogies, and rotting away. They did retain their engines, but the cabs and much electrical equipment had been stripped. They were still there the following year, but one more, 52504 was located dumped in the depot compound at the Camilo Cienfuegos sugar mill. This location was formerly known as Heshey and on the Heshey Railway, some 50km east of Havana. The other (52501) although not seen, was believed to be possibly inside the works at Cardenas.

In February 1993, the visitor of 1988 was at Havana Cristina again, but did not find 52504 – it had gone. Answers to enquiries suggested that it had gone to Cardenas, and a visit there a few days later found the following derelict in the yard there:- 52502/(52503) T977/52505/52506/52507/(52508) T982/52509/52510. 52504 was not there, nor was 52501. Both may have been in the works at Cardenas, but there was no positive proof. The T series numbers quoted above appear to have been part of a non-national series at some time or another, more probably connected with the locomotives' use as generator sets and predating the national 52xxx series. Some of the locomotives listed above still bore their Clayton works plates.

In March 1994 eight of the locomotives were seen together with the exception of T975 and 52504. The latter was reported as at a sugar mill elsewhere. A year later visitors noted the situation regarding these locomotives as follows. Numbers 52502/3/4(T977)/5/6/7/8/ 9/10, were still dumped at Cardenas, whereas 52504 was additionally noted as still at Camilo Cienfuegos. Number 52501 was not seen, but Cuban staff at Cardenas indicated that one Clayton locomotive was still running at Camaguey, 540km east of Havana and the location of one of the two Cuban Railways locomotive works. To the recipients of this information it appeared to be unlikely news. If it were correct, then 52501 would, by the process of elimination, be the one.

The derelict locomotives lay there for only a few months longer. A visitor in January 1996 witnessed that the scrapping of them had already commenced. Seven of the locomotives were at Cardenas Works, with the cabs of 52502 and the probable remains of T975 scattered on the ground. Number 52504 still survived during the summer of 1996, dumped and intact at the sugar mill at Hershey, east of Havana. The scrapping operation was reported as completed within a few months, it was thought, marking the end of an interesting piece of British locomotive history, but this was not the case.

In late 1998 52 504 was reported dumped at Camilo Cienfuegos and during mid-1999 reports came in that two of the class still survived. Bad news that followed a few months later reported that 52 504 had just been scrapped, leaving a question mark as to whether or not the class was extinct.

During March 1963 six standard gauge 0-4-0 diesel electric shunting locomotives were ordered for the Skopje Steelworks in Jugoslavia. They generally conformed to the basic Brush/Beyer Peacock design and were all built by Beyer Peacock utilising Brush electrical equipment and Cummins NT 335 engines rated at 275bhp at 1,900rpm. The engines were similar to those fitted in some of Skopje Steelworks' earthmoving equipment and presented a complementary addition to the plant maintained in the workshops.

The contract for these six locomotives was satisfied not by building completely new locomotives, but by refurbishing two stock locomotives and re-activating manufactured parts of another stock order. It should be recalled that some of the five stock locomotives completed in 1958 remained unsold (Chapter 4) and that four sets of stock mechanical parts remained on the books at Beyer Peacock, following the completion of the fourth Renishaw locomotive (BT 443/ BP 7873). The six locomotives therefore were BP 7857 and BP 7860 (stock locomotives) and BP 7869-72 (stock parts re-activated). BP 7857 was operating at the Falcon Works at the time and was then returned to Gorton for re-engining and renovation. BP 7860 was operating at Gorton as the Beyer Peacock works shunting locomotive and it was also similarly treated. Brush works numbers 604 to 609 were allotted. The contract required two locomotives for single unit working and four others for tandem operation for use on the heavier haulage duties at the steel works.

The single units were allocated BP order No. 17315 and the remainder, order No. 17316. During 1963 there was a change of plan regarding which locomotives should be equipped for single operation and which should be for tandem operation. The two plans are outlined as follows:-

ORIGINAL PLAN 9.1963			REVISED PLAN 11.1963		
BT No.	BP No.	BP Contract Number	BT No.	BP No.	BP Contract Number
604	7857	17315	604	7869	17315
605	7860	17315	605	7872	17315
606	7869	17316	606	7870	17316
607	7870	17316	607	7871	17316
608	7871	17316	608	7860	17316
609	7872	17316	609	7857	17316

Following the revised plan the expected delivery dates quoted in BP records were as follows:-

604/7869	31 January 1964
605/7872	30 April 1964
606/7870	28 February 1964
607/7871	27 March 1964
608/7860	29 May 1964
609/7857	26 June 1964

All the locomotives were due for completion before the end of 1963, but some were completed during early 1964. Some difficulties concerning this contract arose for various reasons. During the summer of 1963 an earthquake devastated the Skopje area and although its effects were wide-ranging, deliveries of the locomotives actually commenced in early 1964. The first was due in the February and two more due later in the year. One was fitted for single operation and the other two for tandem. The single unit (No. 604) was loaded onto the SS Brescia at Birkenhead Docks on 15th May 1964, bound for Thessaloniki in Greece. By June all three were reported as delivered, the first arriving in Skopje on 20th March and the other two were reported as arriving early in May. From Thessaloniki the locomotives were transported by

Two of the 275bhp 0-4-0 diesel electric shunting locomotives supplied to the Skopje Steelworks, Jugoslavia, at the Beyer Peacock works, Gorton, in 1964. These locomotives, and four others of the contract, were the last such locomotives to emerge from the works; it closed the following year.

BRUSH A11916

Brush Traction No.604, one of the standard gauge shunting locomotives for the Skopje Steelworks in Jugoslavia being lowered into the hold of the 'Brescia' at Birkenhead Docks on 15th May 1964, for shipment to Thessaloniki.

BRUSH A10758

One of the six Brush/Beyer Peacock 0-4-0s at the head of a ballast train at Skopje Steelworks.

BRUSH A14670D

road and rail, some of the latter with locomotives under their own power. When being towed there were incidences of hot axle boxes, caused by being continuously run too far in one direction, something that shunting locomotives usually are not designed to do.

All three were then reported to be working perfectly satisfactorily at Skopje 'despite somewhat adventurous journeys from Greece through mountains'. By the end of 1964 the remaining three locomotives had been completed, but were stored until delivery was required in mid-1965. Presumably this delay was due to the after-effects of the earthquake, but it has been related that there was some concern by the customer regarding the two refurbished locomotives. Whilst all bore 1964 on the new works plates, this pair originally dated from 1958. The work undertaken during the intervening period was not intensive by any means, so any concern must have been quickly allayed. In February 1966 a report quoted that the remaining three locomotives had been delivered four months previously. Allowing for some delay between such a report being written and appearing, then the latest delivery was September/October 1965. As sometimes occurs with the history of events concerning Brush locomotives (of the steam age as well as the more modern times) the element of mystery creeps in. Were it not for a curious subsequent sighting, the matter of the Skopje deliveries might rest at this point, but the reader's attention is drawn to the mention in Chapter 4 of the sighting of 0-4-0 diesel electric shunting locomotive BT605 of 1964 at the Falcon Works on 2nd July 1966. This report was published in a letter to the 'Railway Observer' of October 1966 and the relevant portion reads thus: "Also present in the yard, near the paint shop, was an 0-4-0DE industrial shunter of the standard Brush design, which was unused but had obviously been stored for some time. This carried works plate 605 of 1964". This indeed was one of the locomotives destined for Skopje, delayed because of problems in Jugoslavia. Brush was anxious to have it delivered and during early 1966 was making efforts to achieve this. What is certain is that the steelworks received its sixth locomotive. This probably occurred later that year.

They were put to work on heavy ore trains within the works complex, sometimes in pairs if heavier loadings were run. They were also fitted with train air braking. All were recorded as still in service in the late 1970s, but no report has been received subsequent to this time, which is not altogether surprising when one considers the political and uncertain nature of events since then in this region. The despatch of the Skopje locomotives marked the end of the Brush/Beyer Peacock 0-4-0 saga, other than service history. To this day no diesel electric locomotives of this wheel arrangement have been sold by Brush – the need for such locomotives disappeared as power demands and adhesive capabilities outstripped coupled four-wheeled locomotive design.

Uncertainty at the Falcon Works with regard to future rail traction business prospects was voiced as early as 1964 when it was realised that the locomotive requirements of BR would be fulfilled within two or three years. By 1965 it became apparent that the main part of the locomotive business would have to be won from overseas sources against the full weight of international competition.

The business to be found from British industrial users of locomotives had proved limited and was expected to become almost non-existent as changing patterns of BR operating reduced the need for shunting and released redundant diesel shunting locomotive onto the second-hand market. The Beeching Plan became a two-edged weapon and the locomotive-building industry as a whole was soon to feel the sharper one. In 1965 Beyer Peacock went out of business, with some of its main line locomotive work being transferred to BR workshops for completion. Indeed, these were sad times for the industry and the need to survive in a shrinking market was ever-present. Ideally, a strong home market suppored the export side of locomotive building, but it is a rarely experienced ideal in Britain.

In July 1964 Brush Traction set out the products for which the Division was in the market. These are outlined as follows:-

Complete locomotives
1. Main line diesel electric locomotives from 800 to 8,000bhp.
2. Diesel electric shunting locomotives from 200 to 700bhp.
Equipments
1. Complete power equipments for all sizes of diesel electric locomotives.
2. Control gear for all sizes of diesel electric locomotives.
3. Control gear and electrical machines for all sizes of diesel hydraulic locomotives.
Straight electric
By collaboration with GEC Brush was able to offer main line straight electric locomotives utilising either 1,500 volts DC, overhead 3,000 volts DC, or 6.25/25 kV AC overhead supplies.

In addition to the above, Brush was prepared to consider consultancy work in connection with all aspects of locomotive design and also to consider licensing agreements for the manufacture of Brush designed locomotives in Britain and overseas. Another consideration being fermented at about this time was the repair and refurbishment of locomotives. Concurrently, Brush esteem was at a high point. Mr F H Wood at this time was not only Chairman and Managing Director of Brush Electrical Engineering Co. Ltd, but also Chairman of the Locomotive and Allied Manufacturers' Association and a Council Member of the Institute of Locomotive Engineers. This not only reflected Brush esteem but also the shrewd judgement and ability of the people who directed the company in its traction matters.

Between 1964 and 1967 no order to build locomotives was received by Brush, but in 1965 a four-year contract was negotiated with BR for the repair of Type 2, 3 and 4 diesel locomotives. BR Sulzer locomotive D154 was the first locomotive to be dealt with during that year and on 7th August D138/54/5/6/65/8/88 were all present receiving attention. On 20th November D138/46/55/6/7/65/8/82/8/9 were present. On 4th December D146/55/6/7/65/76/88 were in the shops, D168 was in the test house and in the yard adjacent to the Paint Shop was D189. On 30th May 1966 D143/6/7/58/9/66/84/6/9 were in the Superstructure Shop and D176 and BR/Sulzer Type 2 No. D5006, in the Erecting Shop. Meanwhile, D138/41/57/88 were in the yards with BR/Sulzer Type 2s D5084/5283, and Brush Type 4 D1520. BR/Sulzer Type 4 D163 was in the Paint Shop.

A report, which appeared in September 1966, stated that in recent weeks as many as twenty BR/Sulzer Type 4s and about four BR/Sulzer Type 2s had been at the Falcon Works for overhaul. During the period between September 1967 and February 1968 D153/60/70/8/80 were in for attention, as was Brush Type 4 D1801. Over this period the cab of D1894 was noted in the works.

It is known that repair work concerned the Type 2s and the Brush Type 4s and that some of the latter were collision victims and included Crewe-built examples. In the main it was the 56 BR/Sulzer Type 4s that were brought in for extensive refurbishing (or remanufacture). These were at the time numbered in the series D138 to D193 (later classified as Class 46). In this programme improved filtration, revised wiring runs and repositioning of cable ducts were undertaken. The electrical machines were stripped down and rebuilt and structural modifications were made. The latter concerned body panelling, which had suffered corrosion problems due to moisture being held in cavities by insulation materials. The programme provided work in the Traction Division at a time when the Type 4 programme was running down and kept the workforce intact for that much longer.

An export drive developed during this period and a range of diesel electric locomotives was developed and advertised widely as being available for use at home or abroad, particularly the latter. They were suitable for building by Brush or under licence elsewhere. In some instances the engines available were either Cummins, up to 800bhp, or Caterpillar, up to 1,050bhp and 1,500bhp with speeds of 1,350rpm on the latter. They had originated in heavy commercial and earth-moving units and were also backed up by a world-wide spares and service organisation of long standing, so there were running and repair cost savings to be made by potential customers. Traditional engines were available for applications above 1,500bhp. The advertised range was a mixture of current and new locomotive designs and was as follows:-

FS1	0-6-0 shunting locomotives, rated at 650bhp. The first examples were built in 1967/8 by the Australian Tulloch Company for Western Australian Government Railways.
S1/B	B-B locomotives of 720bhp - 1,050bhp. The first examples were built by Brush in 1968/9 for the Cuban sugar railways and the Panay Island Railway (Philippines) respectively.
S2/FB	Co-Co locomotives of 1,500 - 2,000bhp (Rhodesia Railways type).
S3/FB	Co-Co locomotives of 2,000 - 3,000bhp (Cuban Type 4 pattern).
S4/FB	Locomotives of 4,000bhp of the 'Kestrel' type

For the lower range up to 1,500bhp it was the intention to combine the engines with a series of standard components, a narrow gauge traction motor, two sizes of DC generator and other electrical and mechanical parts, and to use the standard modules to produce a range of export locomotives which could be built cheaply and to short delivery times. Added to this was the intention to increase the use of electronics for the more powerful types, as developed in 'Hawk', 'Kestrel' and the final Type 4s built at Loughborough (D1960/1).

At the time there was little demand for electric locomotives, so no range of locomotives was projected.

Not widely advertised publicly, but made available to potential customers, was the fuller and more detailed version of the new range which was as follows:-

FS1	Shunting/Transfer Type 500/700bhp 0-6-0 diesel electric locomotives.30/40mph, axle load 13 tons.
S1/B/4-10	Bonnet Type 400-1,000bhp Bo-Bo Diesel electric locomotives. 45mph, axle load 10.5 tons minimum.
S2/B/10-20	Bonnet Type 1,000-2,000bhp Co-Co Diesel electric locomotives. 65mph, axle load 13.3 tons minimum.
S2/FB/10-20	Full Body Design - One or two cabs 1,000-2,000bhp Co-Co Diesel electric locomotives. 65mph, axle load 11.5 tons minimum.
S3/B/20-30	Bonnet Type 2,000-3,000bhp Co-Co Diesel electric locomotives. 65mph, axle load 15 tons minimum.
S3/FB/20-30	Full Body Design – Two cabs 2,000-3,000bhp Co-Co Diesel electric locomotives. 60 or 100mph, axle load 18 tons minimum.
S4/B/30-40	Bonnet Type 3,000-4,000bhp Co-Co Diesel electric locomotives. 60 or 100mph, axle load 21 tons.
S4/B/30-40	Full Body Design – Two cabs 3,000-4,000bhp Co-Co Diesel electric locomotives. 60 or 100mph, axle load 21 tons

The outcome of advertising this basic range of diesel electric locomotives was a mixed one. First was the almost immediate placing of orders for lower-powered units and, second, the belated orders from elsewhere in the 1970s for 0-6-0s (Chapter 10).

In 1966 the Brush Electrical Engineering Co. Ltd and Tulloch Ltd. of Rhodes, New South Wales, Australia entered into a joint agreement whereby the full range of diesel electric locomotives from 200 to 4,000bhp to Brush designs and using Brush electrical equipment would be offered to potential customers in Australia. It also provided for a full interchange of information between the companies with as much equipment as possible manufactured in Australia. This was known in Britain as the Brush-Tulloch agreement, but in Australia, predictably, the Tulloch-Brush agreement. Tulloch Ltd had been established as engineers for ninety years, fifty years of which involved the building of railway rolling stock. Hawker Siddeley Brush Pty. Ltd, the Australian representatives of Brush, were the direct associates for the arrangements in Australia, although there was much direct contact between Brush and Tulloch. It appears that the 0-4-0 concept was not abandoned, because the range covered by the agreement commenced at 200bhp.

The first order for locomotives under this agreement came during the same year and was for five FS1 0-6-0 diesel electric shunting locomotives of 660bhp for the 3ft 6ins track gauge Western Australian Government Railways (WAGR). Their intended use was for yard shunting and light transfer duties. The locomotives were powered by Cummins VT12 825 engines. The locomotive duty requested was that the continuous tractive effort should not be less than that required to haul a train of 850 tons up a gradient of 1 in 180, at a speed of 10mph. The locomotive outline consisted of a single cab and two bonnets arrangement. The larger bonnet housed the power unit and associated equipment and the smaller bonnet the diesel fuel tank of 400 gallons capacity. The cab was situated between the two. This combination was mounted on a conventional robust and rigid deck and underframe assembly. The running gear was conventional and employed the wheelset inside the frames and the fly-cranks outside. Two single gear reduction drive traction motors were fitted, one to each of the outer axles, the centre axle being driven through side rods. The cab layout was designed in close conjunction with the mechanical engineers of the Railway with the control desk mounted on one wall with the controls arranged such that the locomotive could be driven in both directions from either side. The floor of the cab was raised so that in conjunction with large windows an unrestricted view could be obtained. Above cab waist level the sides were angled inwards to afford better clearances when working in restricted dockside areas. For temperature extremes two heaters utilising hot water from the engine cooling system and two cooling fans were provided.

The main details and dimensions were as follows:-

Wheel Arrangement	0-6-0
Track Gauge	3ft 6ins
Engine Model	Cummins 12-cylinder, Vee-form, VT12-825
Engine Rating	660bhp at 2,100rpm
Main Generator	Brush single bearing, self ventilated, separately excited and self excited shunt windings and a series decompounding winding (also used for engine starting). 407kW output
Traction Motors (two), each	Brush, 243hp, axle hung, forced ventilated. Both connected in parallel across the main generator. Single reduction gear drive
Length over buffer beams	24ft 10ins
Overall Width	8ft 5ins
Overall Height	12ft 6ins
Wheel Diameter	3ft 4ins
Minimum Curve Negotiable	330ft radius
Wheelbase	10ft 0ins
Maximum Speed	30mph
Starting Tractive Effort	25,000lbs
Continuous Tractive Effort	15,500lbs at 11mph
Fuel Capacity	400 gallons
Weight in Working Order	39 tons

The original plan was to have all construction take place at the Osborne Park plant of Freighter Industries, but as the company had no heavy engineering facilities the mechanical portions, such as main frames and running gear, were all manufactured at the Tulloch Works at Rhodes and despatched by rail for final completion. Livery was green with red fly-cranks, coupling rods and buffer beams. Below running board level was painted black. A yellow or white warning panel, on each bonnet end, was relieved by a prominent red V. The running number was painted in yellow on the left of each buffer beam and appeared on oval brass cabside plates with red-painted backgrounds.

The five locomotives were given running numbers T1801 to T1805 and Tulloch works numbers 043 to 047 respectively.

No Brush numbers were allotted. Completion dates and to stock dates for the locomotives were as follows:-

Running No.	Completed	To Stock
T1801	06.1967	08.1967
T1802	09.1967	09.1967
T1803	11.1967	11.1967
T1804	12.1967	12.1967
T1805	02.1968	02.1968

Each locomotive was rated at 490bhp for WAGR use.

The first locomotive was actually completed at Tulloch's New South Wales plant to prove the manufacturing drawings and also be full load tested. Following this the cab was removed in order to allow delivery by rail through the various State railway systems of differing loading gauge clearances. At Parkeston (Kalgoorlie) the locomotive was reassembled and following preliminary trials around Kalgoorlie, it hauled a load over the 400 miles to Perth.

A further ten locomotives were built for WAGR, but with straight-sided cabs and a different Cummins engine, the VTA-1710L, of the same power output. They were one ton heavier. They had Tulloch works numbers 055 to 064 and had running numbers TA1806 to TA1815 respectively.

The completion and entry into service dates were as shown on the facing page:-

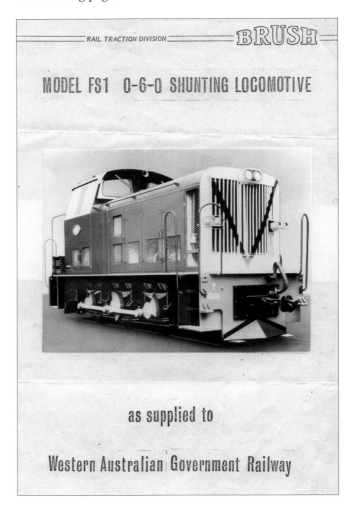

RAIL TRACTION DIVISION — BRUSH

MODEL FS1 0-6-0 SHUNTING LOCOMOTIVE

as supplied to

Western Australian Government Railway

Running No.	Completed	To Stock
TA1806	01.1970	02.1970
TA1807	02.1970	04.1970
TA1808	03.1970	04.1970
TA1809	05.1970	06.1970
TA1810	05.1970	07.1970
TA1811	07.1970	09.1970
TA1812	10.1970	10.1970
TA1813	10.1970	11.1970
TA1814	11.1970	12.1970
TA1815	11.1970	02.1971

Each locomotive was rated at 447bhp for WAGR service.

The last four were assembled at the Perth WA plant of Freighter Industries, from major mechanical components supplied from Tulloch Ltd. TA1815 was the last Tulloch locomotive to be built. Tulloch Ltd went out of business circa 1974.

The locomotives were allocated to North Fremantle and Avon Yard depots for shunting work locally and also worked on shunting duties in country districts such as Northam, Merredin, Narrogin, Bunbury, Albany and Geraldton, and proved successful in their duties in all of them. Due to changes in rail freight operations on the railway, the T and TA Classes became surplus to requirements and by early 1994 all the locomotives were written off the books of Wethe, the title of the railway by this time. Any shunting duties that remained were entrusted to main line locomotives.

The withdrawal and disposal of the T and TA locomotives is summarised below:

Running No.	Withdrawn	Scrap	Notes
T1801	12.90	03.94	
T1802	12.85	03.90	
T1803	?	03.94	
T1804	12.90		PRESERVED - Geraldtown
T1805	?	03.94	
TA1806	11.92	03.94	
TA1807	11.92		To State Energy Bunbury PRESERVED - Boyanup after 1966
TA1808	06.93		PRESERVED - Merredin Stn Mus
TA1809	11.92	03.94	
TA1810	11.92	03.94	
TA1811	11.92	03.94	
TA1812	06.93	03.94	
TA1813	?		To A Goninan, Bassendean
TA1814	06.93		PRESERVED - Ghan Preservation Society, Larrimah a Museum Tourist Rly NT
TA1815	11.92	03.94	

a At the time of acquisition TA1814 was said to be in excellent operating condition and was conveyed to Port Augusta by goods train on 20th May 1994.

The first order to be received by Brush Traction as a direct result of promoting the new range came on 15th April 1967. It was placed by Empressa Cubana Importardra de Vehiculos y Equipos de Transports on behalf of MINAZ (Ministerio de Azucar/ Ministry of Sugar) and was for seven S1 locomotives for use on Cuban 3ft track gauge sugar railways. These were allocated Brush Works Nos 712 to 718, but at the time of building, no running numbers. The second order was received on 24th May 1967 and was placed by the Development Bank of the Philippines on behalf of the Philippines Railway Company. One S1 locomotive was ordered for the 3ft 6ins railway on Panay Island. This was allocated Brush Works No. 719 and the running number 106. Empressa Cubana Importardra de Vehiculos y Equipos de Transports placed a second order, for a further eight S1 locomotives, for the sugar railways on 4th July 1968. These were Works Nos 720 to 727.

The Panay Island locomotive was a typical application for the new concept of offering inexpensive narrow gauge units for overseas service to countries with very slender financial resources and railways operating under difficult conditions – the railway there was actually owned by the Development Bank of the Philippines. The same concept applied with regard to the Cuban locomotives. Furthermore, Cuba was still experiencing political problems internationally, although not as acutely as when the Cuban Brush Type 4s were ordered, so the S1s provided an ideal way of obtaining motive power quickly, cheaply and with little chance of repercussions on the supplier. Nonetheless, the only markings visible were the Minaz logos and the packing details. No evidence is to hand to prove whether or not Brush works plates were fitted at Brush, but a works plate drawing was prepared specially for their manufacture and fitting to the locomotives. The works plate design was new. It was a rectangular plate, rather than the previous oval design and appeared concurrently with the S1s and 'Kestrel'. It was an engraved metal plate measuring 20cm X 5cm. The drawing called for it to be made from stainless steel. Whereas those fitted to 'Kestrel' and the Panay Island S1 had the Hawker Siddeley title and logo, it is significant that the markings for the Cuban locomotives omitted these, but retained the Brush logo and title, together with the locomotive number and year of manufacture. In later years such plates were observed fitted inside some cabs. By 1967 there had been some revision of the Brush and Hawker Siddeley logos. The former was now a non-serif version, still in a curved top enclosing frame, but somewhat flatter overall. It dated from circa 1966, certainly its use started during that year. The drawing office manual referred to it as the arch logo. The latter was in use by early 1964, having been selected following a competition within the Hawker Siddeley Group to design a new logo. At best it could be described as the distorted letters H S combined at complementary angles. At worst it was a decipherable 'squiggle', as one person was heard to remark at the time when it was chosen. It is also significant to note that the publicity for the S1s covered the locomotives for both countries, albeit in slightly differing ways, but there was a subtle introduction for the Cuban contracts. *Modern Railways* had a front cover feature advertisement in the June 1968 issue, with an illustration of one of the Cuban S1s, but with no reference to Cuba.

The first FS1 0-6-0 diesel electric shunting locomotives were built in Australia by Tulloch Ltd in 1967 for Western Australia Government Railways. Here the batch of five can be seen under construction in the Tulloch workshops.

The Panay Island locomotive was a 1,050bhp example fitted with a Caterpillar D398B engine. The locomotive outline was a basic 'no-frills' single bonnet, single cab design. Compound curves were avoided where possible affording a very utilitarian, box-like outline – the Fabricating Shop's dream locomotive. The frame was an all-welded structure, made up of two longitudinal channel sections, braced with cross members at the load bearing points, and at each end there was a box section housing the coupler and reinforcing the headstock. The bonnet doors were of the lift-off type, mounted on pin hinges for ease of maintenance. There was a large, spacious cab, with a rear entrance door, situated at one end and a running board round the bonnet with access from the cab front.

The most interesting departure from accepted Brush practice was the final drive arrangement, because although two traction motors were fitted they were not mounted on the bogies, but on the underframes instead. They were three-point mounted, centrally and under the deck, between the bogies and were highly accessible. They were series-wound, connected in parallel and force-ventilated. The drive from each motor to its respective bogie was through a cardan shaft to one axle, with an interconnecting shaft to a secondary gearbox on the other axle. The advantage of this arrangement in maintenance terms meant that no inspection pits were

BRUSH

necessary for traction motor renewal, or inspection, and a comparatively short bogie could be employed. The bogie design was the standard English Steel Corporation type with two axles. The S1 was intended to operate on light passenger, freight and shunting duties. Twin headlights were fitted on the bonnet front, at the top. Straight air braking equipment was fitted as standard for locomotive and train brake.

Number 106 was finished in an attractive livery of orange with a venetian red horizontal band, edged in lemon yellow, encircling the locomotive, but meeting in two downward curves centrally on the bonnet front. The numerals of the cab side running number were in white and the headstocks (a more appropriate alternative term to buffer beams for this application) were picked out with black and lemon yellow 'wasp-stripes'. The railway logo, a roundel device in cast metal relief, containing the letters PRC, was placed on the front headstock, above the central buffing/coupler. The raised border and letters were left in polished metal, whilst

the background was painted black, although the specification called for venetian red. This plate did not survive long in service.

The main details and dimensions of the Panay Island locomotive were as shown below:

Wheel Arrangement	B-B
Track Gauge	3ft 6ins
Engine Model	Caterpillar D398b
Main Generator	Brush compound-wound, with separately-excited fields, and a series winding to enable engine-starting
Continuous Ratings	686 kW, 520V, 1,320A, 1,300 rpm
CAV Alternator for main generator excitation	702kW, 836V, 840A, 1,300 rpm
Auxiliary Generator	7.5kW, 75V, 100A, 1,540/3,600rpm
Length over headstocks	35ft 0ins
Overall Width	8ft 6½ins
Overall Height	12ft 3ins
Wheel Diameter	2ft 9ins
Total Wheelbase	25ft 6ins
Distance between bogie pivots	19ft 0ins
Minimum Curve Negotiable	100ft 0ins radius
Maximum Speed	50mph
Fuel Capacity	500 gallons
Weight in Working Order	48 tons

Panay Island Railway No.106 (BT719) basks in the sun in this 1968 view taken at the Falcon Works.

BRUSH A15013

The locomotive was built in late 1967 and completed during March 1968. It was shipped from the Royal Albert Dock, London, on a Belships vessel during the following month. It led something of a charmed life on Panay Island, but no repeat order ever materialised. Perhaps the exceptionally poor financial situation made the chance of the latter unlikely.

The locomotive was reported in 1977 as still in service, running on the Phividec Railway. In May 1979 it was observed running satisfactorily, but each year it divided its time with eight months of working and four months under maintenance. Apparently the rough track, with little or no ballast under re-laid sleepers, was causing transmission problems through vibration. By this time the railway was reported to by owned by the Philippines Sugar Commission. It appears that the fate of No. 106 was linked with the fate of the railway. In December 1984 the 117 km railway (from Iloilo to Roxas) was closed, and a subsequent Australian attempt to reopen the line did not succeed. By April 1988 the railway was in a derelict condition, but some of the newer locomotives were under maintenance at Iliolo City. Number 106 was reported as 'potentially active'. In April 1993 the only item of rolling stock seen was a Japanese-built Bo-Bo diesel, No. 114. Quite what had become of No. 106 is uncertain.

The Cuban S1s were similar to, though not exactly the same as, the Panay Island locomotive. They were fitted with a Paxman 12 YH XL engine of 720bhp and gauged to 3ft 0ins. The livery consisted of a similar striped arrangement to that of the Panay Island locomotive, but the stripe had no edging to it. Above the stripe the superstructure was painted a light grey and below a light orange. Areas below the running board were painted black. Deliveries commenced early in 1968 and for the second contract, December 1968. The final delivery was during the following year.

Their careers in Cuba are obscure for the early years, but it is known that some problems occurred with transmission failures, caused by the rough, badly maintained track. Modifications made to the gearboxes proved successful and the locomotives have worked very well over the years.

As mentioned previously, relations with Cuba relaxed over the years, and although not perfect, were sufficiently well advanced to allow railway enthusiasts to make organised trips to the island. In March 1988 at least one was seen, by then numbered 2734, in use at the Hermanos Ameijeiras sugar mill (No. 435), near Santa Clara and about 300km east of Havana. A Brush Traction source quoted in January 1989 that of the fifteen locomotives, fourteen were still in service at Antonio Guiteras. The missing locomotive was rumoured scrapped, after falling into a ravine.

On 8th March 1991, at Hermanos Ameijeiras mill, two S1s were noted at the depot, and three others were lying dormant in the marshalling yard. At Heriberto Duquesne mill (No. 410) the fleet included three other S1s.

A visit report, dated 26th March 1993, listed Nos 2721/24/26/32/34 as being at Hermanos Ameijeiras, and that the Brush locomotives covered most of the main line work there. They were the only diesels at the mill, the rest were steam locomotives. Since 1989 2720-4,26-32,34 have all been seen. From the foregoing it would appear that Minaz numbers its S1s in a series 2720-34, assuming at the time that one had

been scrapped as indicated above. The first digit indicates diesel electric transmission, the second about 700bhp and the third and fourth the individual locomotive identity. It is believed that this series dates from circa 1975. The only Brush plates noted on this visit were affixed to the controls inside the cabs. They bore the date 1968.

In March 1995 visitors to Cuba noted Nos 2721/4/6/9/31/2 at Hermanos Ameijeiras, with 2734 said to be out on the line.

It was not until the latter half of 1996 that a visitor's report confirmed the survival of all fifteen locomotives and established the running number series to be 2720-2734. The locomotives were located as follows:

Mill 401	H. Duquesne 2720/2/3/5/8
Mill 435	H. Ameijeiras 2721/4/6/9/31/32/4
Mill 450	B. Jurez 2727/30/3

The allocations were the same early in 1998, except that Nos 2728/9 were not reported.

It was not until 2000 that news reached your author that visitors had discovered works numbers affixed to the cab interiors of some of the locomotives. Those noted were as follows:-

2722	714/1968
2725	717/1968
2730	723/1968
2733	726/1968

Of note is the year 1968 for those of the second batch. Nos 2723 and 2728 did not carry works numbers and other locomotive cabs were not accessible.

During the first half of 2001 visitors to Mill 435 Hermanos Ameijeiras found all its S1 locomotives in service, but during the sugar season of 2003 they were out of service, in the shed, and outside the track had been lifted.

After the last of the Cuban S1s was delivered in 1969, there was a gradual rundown of locomotive-building facilities at the Falcon Works. A lack of orders for locomotives not only affected Brush, but also several other well known companies. At home the BR main line diesel programme was complete and the home industrial market was dead, as by this time the selling-off of comparatively modern, but redundant, BR shunting locomotives had run into hundreds. The situation overseas was little better, as established foreign competition, particularly the American giant General Motors, had already pushed British locomotive builders out of most of their traditional markets. Japanese and European manufacturers were also very active, but with one advantage – the support of their respective governments.

Brush began to turn the erecting shops and other traction facilities over to other manufacturing purposes, and by the

end of 1970 had disposed of the works shunting locomotives. Some of the easily removable works railway track was also removed as were the rail accesses into the Falcon Works. The latter removal followed a spectacular derailment and an enforced relaying session of the southbound freight line, which had formerly provided access into the works.

The cause of the derailment was a broken axle on a mineral wagon in a southbound train. It caused considerable damage to a long stretch of the track, hundreds of yards, and the cost of renewing the points was prohibitive, particularly in the light of the limited usage they had experienced of late. Boiler house traffic, goods inwards and outgoing products were all by road transport, so the rail link, dating back over 105 years, disappeared.

Brush Traction started to concentrate on supplying electrical equipment to overseas railways, British Rail and locomotive builders which did not normally use electric transmission for their standard locomotives. Hunslet, in particular, was one of the latter, and built ten 1,124bhp Bo-Bos in 1972 for the British Steel Corporation Anchor Project at Scunthorpe, all having Brush electrical equipment. It was fortunate that company policy had always been one of supplying traction equipment concurrently with locomotives.

The equipment side was on more than one occasion able to keep the traction business successful when no locomotive work was in the offing. 1969 marked not only the end of a decade, but also the end of an era.

10 – Renaissance Under Brush Electrical Machines Ltd 1973

During August 1971 the main product divisions of The Brush Electrical Engineering Company Ltd at Loughborough were transformed into individual companies. The former Rotating Machines Division became Brush Electrical Machines Ltd (BEM) and incorporated the Rail Traction Division, much as it had been before August 1971. That the Traction Division remained so, reflected the low business activity with particular regard to locomotive building. The other new companies were Brush Transformers Ltd and Brush Switchgear Ltd. The Brush Electrical Engineering Co. Ltd was not dissolved but continued to be the effective 'landlord' of the Falcon Works site.

On 6th November 1972 there came the first locomotive order since 1968. It was placed through Crown Agents by the Nigerian Railway Corporation and was for the supply of twenty-two 400bhp 0-6-0 type FS1 diesel electric shunting locomotives. The order came at a time when there was limited workshop space generally, but a small decline in turbo-alternator business had left sufficient space to fulfil the contract. The limited space available was a side bay in one of the shops formerly used for erecting locomotive superstructures. It was now possible to build shunting locomotives at the Falcon Works without resort to sub-contracting as had been the case previously. The order meant that these locomotives were the first Model FS1s to be built in Britain, although as related in Chapter 9, not the first FS1s to be built.

Brush works numbers 728-749 and NRC running numbers 921-942 respectively were allocated to these locomotives.

The very first British-built FS1, Nigerian Railway Corporation No. 921 (BT728) stands on temporary track in the yard at the Falcon Works in 1973. By this time, the original facilities for locomotive building and testing had been dispersed or had fallen into disuse.

BRUSH B318G

The construction of the locomotives was robust and followed closely the arrangement of the WAGR locomotives. The frames were made up from steel plate and were welded to a plate deck, the combination being well able to withstand shunting shocks. The cab was situated between two bonnets of unequal length, the shorter housing the diesel fuel tank, and the longer housing the power unit and its associated equipment. Braking equipment was compressed air for the locomotive and vacuum for the train. The main details and dimensions were as follows:-

Wheel Arrangement	0-6-0
Track Gauge	3ft 6ins
Engine Model	Ruston Paxman 8 RPHXL Mk7, eight-cylinder, Vee-form, pressure charged
Engine Rating	400bhp at 1,250rpm
Main Generator	TG78-43 Mk3 compound DC three field type, with separately excited, self excited and series windings. The latter used for engine starting purposes and supplied from the batteries
Continuous Ratings	235kW, 178V, 1,320A, 1,250rpm
	240kW, 250V, 960A, 1,250rpm
One Hour Rating	234kW, 165V, 1,420A, 1,250rpm
Auxiliary Generator	TG28-16 Mk3 Shunt wound, 3.3kW, 75V, 44A, 1,710/3,290rpm
Traction Motors (two)	Each TM68-46 Mk4 series wound, nose-suspended, axle hung, force ventilated. 94kW, 178V, 660A, 241rpm
Length over Buffer Beams	24ft 0ins
Length over Couplers	28ft 1ins
Overall Width	9ft 8ins
Overall Height	13ft 0ins
Wheel Diameter	3ft 6ins
Wheelbase	10ft 0ins
Minimum Curve Negotiable	130ft radius
Maximum Speed	15mph
Starting Tractive Effort	30,000lbs
Continuous Tractive Effort	18,738lbs at 5mph
Fuel Capacity	400 gallons
Weight in Working Order	39.5 tons

Externally the locomotives were of impressive appearance and clearly bore a family resemblance to the WAGR locomotives. They were painted Brunswick green, with a horizontal yellow band around the bonnet sides and ends. The buffer beams were painted with yellow and black stripes, in inverted vee form, while the coupling rods and balance weights were finished in red. The cab side running numbers were affixed in raised stainless steel numerals, in line with the yellow bands and in line with the Nigerian Railway Corporation shield emblem transferred to the cab side. This shield portion of this emblem had a red band diagonally across it from upper left to lower right, and upon this band was a black silhouette representation of a steam locomotive. Above the band and on a yellow ground was a

representation of a palm tree, and on the lower portion was a camel. Three red scrolls below the shield each carried a word of the railway's title. It was attractive and colourful, but quite how accurately it represented the railway is a matter of consideration. The running numbers were affixed in transfer form to the right hand part of the buffer beams. The numerals were in sans serif form, being gold leaf shaded black to the right and below, and were applied to a dark green painted rectangular area. The rectangular works plates were affixed to the lower cab side area adjacent to the ventilation grilles. The first locomotive completed was despatched without these being fitted, and it was the intention upon discovering the error to fit them in Nigeria. Prominent on each bonnet end was a large single Stone-Platt cyclopean headlight. Each was 14ins diameter and rated at 250 watts. Before despatch the locomotives were tested on a short temporary test track within the works. It emerged from the erecting bay and headed in the direction of the Nottingham Road employees' car park and test house. At some time it was modified to include a point and related curves, thus adding more realism to running tests. The price per locomotive was £64,050.

The first locomotive was completed in May 1973 and delivery commenced during the following month. The official dates ex-works were as follows:-

NRC No.	Date	NRC No.	Date
921	05 June 1973	932	19 November 1973
922	19 June 1973	933	30 November 1973
923	04 July 1973	934	07 December 1973
924	31 July 1973	935	27 December 1973
925	28 August 1973	936	16 January 1974
926	11 September 1973	937	21 January 1974
927	03 October 1973	938	31 January 1974
928	10 October 1973	939	07 February 1974
929	22 October 1973	940	24 February 1974
930	01 November 1973	941	24 February 1974
931	19 November 1973	942	12 March 1974

A commissioning ceremony was held on 16th August 1973 at Lagos, with officials of the Nigerian Railway Corporation and BEM representatives Mr J M Durber and Mr D R Minkley present. After the initial speeches, Dr R A B Dikko, Federal Commissioner for Transport, performed the ceremony and this was followed by a parade of four locomotives on three parallel tracks.

The twenty-two locomotives worked from three major depots, Ebute Metta, Zaria and Kafanchan. Examinations were carried out at the smaller depots of Offa, Ibadan, Kano, Kaduna Bauchi and Maiduguri, from where the locomotives worked for 30-day periods. By October 1974 no repeated failures or defects had occurred. About this time trials were underway to test the suitability of the locomotives for main line working, hauling up to 260 tons. This necessitated the removal of the speed control device to lift the speed to a maximum of 40mph.

During the first few years they proved to be reliable units and were well liked by NRC personnel. This success led to a second order for another twenty locomotives being placed in April 1976, but delays in ordering resulted in another period when no locomotives were under construction at the Falcon Works. Once again the production of traction equipment for railways continued and proved to be the mainstay of traction business. One order for locomotives was received by BEM between the two NRC contracts, this being for thirty Class 56 heavy freight locomotives for BR. The size of the contract, insufficient building facilities at the Falcon Works, and short delivery time meant the construction was undertaken in Romania. These locomotives are described in Chapter 11.

The second NRC order was valued at £3.5 million and the locomotives were basically identical to those of the first order, except that they had a top speed of 30mph as a result of the trials undertaken in Nigeria. The order had been long anticipated and this date really marked the formal signing of the contract, because material orders had already taken place. They were allocated Brush works numbers 780 - 799, following on from those allocated to Class 56. NRC running numbers originally allocated were 943 to 962, but the series was changed when the Crown Agents informed BEM that they must be numbered 951 to 970 respectively to conform with the NRC system of numbering each of their batches of locomotives from xx1 onwards.

The frame of the first locomotive was completed and transferred to the former Turbine Shop for fitting out and erection in August 1976, and tested during the latter part of January 1977. It spent almost a month being lavishly prepared for final painting and emerged complete and ready for despatch early in March. On 10th March, 951 left the works on a low loader lorry of Wrekin Roadways bound for Liverpool Docks and shipment to Apapa. Deliveries continued at an average rate of two locomotives a month. The dates were noted as below:-

NRC No.	Date completed by	Date ex-works
951	early March 1977	10 March 1977
952	29 April 1977	02 May 1977
953	29 April 1977	03 May 1977
954	April 1977	c.24 May 1977
955	20 June 1977	28 June 1977
956	21 June 1977	28 June 1977
957	c.01 July 1977	07 July 1977
958	08 August 1977	c.22 September 1977
959	September 1977	c.22 September 1977
960	09 September 1977	c.14 September 1977
961	c.20 September 1977	08 October 1977
962	early October 1977	08 October 1977
963	27 September 1977	c.04-07 March 1978
964	01 November 1977	c.04-07 March 1978
965	08 December 1977	c.04-07 March 1978
966	c.06 December 1977	c.04-07 March 1978
967	c.20 January 1978	c.04-07 March 1978
968	c.01 February 1978	c.04-07 March 1978
969	c.22 February 1978	c.04-07 March 1978
970	c.10 March 1978	c.04 May 1978

The forty-two locomotives of both batches had working lives curtailed by dire shortage of money to maintain them properly. During the mid 1980s the NRC was seeking financial aid from the World Bank, but the latter regarded managerial reform, training and financial discipline as a greater immediate importance. Very little information has emerged regarding the fate of these locomotives, but it does appear that most, perhaps all, have ceased running. Indications are that cannibalisation of some units to keep others in service was commonplace for some time. When new batteries were required, but could not be purchased, starting the engines by other means was avoided by the simple and expensive expedient of keeping the engines turning for days on end! The inevitability of such practices was the rundown of the fleet, and reports and rumours of locomotive hulks stripped of equipment and with saplings growing through them appear to confirm this. By September 1995 no spare parts had been provided by Brush Traction, which also suggested that they were all out of service.

The fifth frame of the second NRC contract should have been Brush 784 and NRC 955. It started manufacture in 1976 as such, passing through the various stages of construction until nearly completed when it was diverted to another contract just before the test and paint stages, on 22nd March 1977. This new contract was for one locomotive to be supplied to Ashaka Cement Company of Nigeria, a member of the Blue Circle Cement Group, and had been placed in June 1976. Identical to the NRC locomotives in all but livery, it was required urgently by the customer and BEM obliged without uduly affecting the former contract. It was given the works number 800, this being entered into the register of locomotives on 27th January 1977, and at first was allocated Ashaka number 01, then 201, and finally 001. The basic livery was an overall rich blue, with the running numbers and Ashaka Cement emblem applied in transfer form, in orange. The locomotive left the Falcon Works on 24th May 1977, nine months after the order was placed. According to some sources, the facilities for which the locomotive was required, were not well-advanced and it went into storage on arrival in Nigeria. It was noted in this state of storage in the background of a Brush film describing its 0-6-0 diesel electric shunting locomotives. Its early life in Nigeria is not documented outside its operating circles. BEM did not have any further contact with the customer and the contract files were disposed of after the six-year warranty period expired.

It was employed as a shunting locomotive for transporting wagons of bagged and bulk cement in the Packing Plant rail loading area of Ashaka Cement. On the rare occasions that it did venture out of the Ashaka Works it would have been for the transportation of these wagons to Ashaka Cement area depots in Bajoga, Maiduguri and Jos. When maintenance was required it travelled to the Nigerian Railway Workshops in Kanfanchan. The maintenance undertaken in March 1990 proved to be its last. An inspection revealed that a major overhaul was required on both engine and transmission, the compressor was seized and the alkaline batteries required replacing. Although Ashaka did stock spare parts these proved insufficient for what was required and other sources would have been more expensive than replacement units.

The following year Ashaka Cement's Group Purchasing Department in Britain carried out a survey for replacement units and the total cost for the required refurbishment totalled £100,000. With the majority of the Company's despatches being transported by road and the extreme difficulty in obtaining foreign exchange, this was considered to be a costly exercise and the refurbishment was held in abeyance.

In 1994 the idea of refurbishment was revived, but as the locomotive had been out of action for several years in a Nigerian Railway Corporation workshop the belief was widely held that various other spare parts would have disappeared during its sojourn. The Company concluded that it was uneconomical to repair it and the exercise would not be repeated. Instead, consideration was given to recovering the locomotive at some time in the future and having it on view as an historical display only.

This seemingly simple consideration brought with it politics of frightening proportions. As soon as NRC personnel realised that the locomotive was valuable to its owners they complained to the ministry that they (the owners) were trying to steal the locomotive from them and assisting in the decline of the NRC network! Obviously the desired end result was to obtain money from the owners, a trait habitual and traditional in Nigeria. An impasse was quickly reached and this was the situation in April 1995 and was likely to remain so until someone backed down!

During mid-December 1976 the Tyne & Wear Passenger Transport Executive ordered four FS1 0-6-0 diesel electric shunting locomotives for use on its electrified Metro system, which was then still under construction in Newcastle upon Tyne. The locomotives were ordered specifically for

Tyne & Wear Metro 0-6-0 works locomotive WL3 (BEM 803) photographed inside South Gosforth carriage shed on 27th June 1979.

AJ BOOTH

maintenance train haulage, particularly during periods when the overhead supply system was de-energised. Works numbers were 801 to 804 and Tyne & Wear running numbers WL1 to WL4 respectively, the WL prefix indicating Works Locomotive. All the works plates were dated 1977, although deliveries took place early in the following year. A fifth locomotive was ordered in October 1977 as WL5, bearing the works number 805. This also bore the date 1977, but in actual fact the locomotive was not completed until mid-1979. This date discrepancy was caused by the failure to modify the year on the original drawing prior to ordering the extra pair of works plates. The locomotives represented the first shunting locomotive contracts for the home market since the early 1960s, and Brush probably won the orders because of its willingness to tackle the specialised nature of them.

The Metro system itself was part of an integrated transport system in and around Newcastle upon Tyne, itself representing a response to changing conditions in the area. Tyneside was traditionally an area abounding in heavy engineering, shipbuilding and mining, and had been during the early days of the industrial revolution. By the late 1950s and early 1960s changes, many of them social, produced changes common to many British towns as the motor car gained in popularity and commuting to places of work caused traffic problems, often at the expense of public transport. It could not be allowed to continue, but a deteriorating economic situation led even to cutbacks in the local bus services and this compounded the situation further during the mid-1960s. Coincident with this trend a Government White Paper 'Public Transport and Traffic' was published and embodied into the 1968 Transport Act in an attempt to deal with urban transport problems generally.

Under the terms of the Act the Passenger Transport Authority became responsible for transport planning and the Executive was responsible for transport operation and comprised the former municipal transport undertakings of Newcastle, Gateshead, South Shields and Sunderland. Plans materialised into investment in roads and a Metro system linking main centres of Newcastle upon Tyne and Gateshead with new works and adapting existing ones. Eventually the Tyne & Wear Metropolitan Railway Act came in 1973 and construction of the system started during the following year. The rail system was to be 35 miles long and it incorporated 27 miles of former BR track and added eight miles of new railway route.

Almost half of the new route mileage was underground. The overhead supply system was supplied at 1,500 volts DC and the passenger vehicles were lightweight metro cars operating in multiple. Considerable delays were encountered in completing the various parts of the system, but overall it was finished in 1984.

The locomotives ordered from BEM were intended for maintenance purposes long-term, but proved useful during the construction period. Although based upon the established FS1 design supplied previously to WAGR and the NRC the locomotives incorporated extra details and some changes to suit T & W conditions.

The main details and dimensions were as shown in the accompanying table:-

Wheel Arrangement	0-6-0
Track Gauge	4ft 8½ins (1435mm)
Engine Model	Rolls Royce eight-cylinder, DV8N
Engine Rating	300kW at 1,800rpm
Main Generator	TG78-43 Mk4, compound wound, with self-excited shunt, separately excited shunt, run and start series windings
Continuous Ratings	234kW, 355V, 660A, 1,800rpm
	236kW, 750V, 315A, 1,800rpm
Auxiliary Generator	TG28-20 Mk1, 8.8kW, 110V, 80A,1,650/4,243rpm
Traction Motor	TM68-46 Mk4, series wound,(one driving centre axle) axle hung, nose-suspended
Continuous Rating	208kW, 355V, 660A, 522rpm
Length over Buffers	8,520mm
Overall Width	2,820mm
Overall Height	3,556mm
Wheel Diameter	1,086mm
Wheelbase	3,048mm
Minimum Curve Negotiable	50 metres radius
Maximum Speed	50kph (31mph)
Maximum Starting Tractive Effort	80kN
Continuous Tractive Effort	42.7kN at 17.3kph
Fuel Capacity	1250 litres
Weight in Working Order	37.5 tonnes
Water Capacity of Exhaust Gas Conditioning	576 litres

Unusually, the locomotives were equipped with one traction motor, driving the centre axle. They were fitted with several features unique to the Metro system. For example, automatic centre couplers were fitted, in addition to buffers, to enable the locomotives to couple to the multiple unit cars on the system for on line rescue, general movement or shunting operations at the depots. The couplers also featured 52-way electrical connections and could be swung back 90 degrees for stowage on the buffer beam when not required. For multiple-operation with other locomotives or wagons 27-way jumpers were provided, as were conventional side buffers. For tunnel working exhaust gas conditioners were provided, working on the principle of dilution. It is known that the condition of exhaust emission gave considerable trouble during the early service days and personal observation of one locomotive at South Gosforth depot revealed the emission of sparks from the exhaust! Eventually a different arrangement using an air injector was employed, and although it did not clean the exhaust it was found acceptable. Furthermore, following extensive tests, the exhaust was re-routed to come out at rail level. Westinghouse automatic air braking equipment was provided for the locomotive, Westcode E.P. digital brake equipment for the multiple unit stock and for the works wagons was controlled automatic air braking equipment. Radio communication equipment and automatic train stop equipment were fitted. The wheel sets below the cab were provided with additional compensated suspension links.

In outline the locomotives presented a very solid and businesslike appearance, the deck and superstructure overhung the buffer beams quite noticeably and the cab roof was somewhat restricted by the loading gauge. The fuel tank as usual with FS1s constituted the smaller bonnet, but in the case of the Tyne & Wear locomotives it was extended to house the batteries. This added to the top-heavy appearance of the locomotives, but, nonetheless, they were still not unattractive.

The overall livery was Newcastle Cadmium Yellow, one of the colours derived from the former bus livery used by Newcastle Corporation. It conveniently acted as a safety feature in making the locomotives more noticeable to staff. Also yellow were the coupling rods and fly cranks. Inverted black and yellow warning stripes were painted on the buffer beams. The running numbers were applied in transfer form to the bonnet ends and cab sides. The original Tyne & Wear Metro logo was also applied in transfer form to the cab sides on the same level as the running number. It was one of the better-devised logos and indicated the rail network in simplified and mirror image form in black, with a blue horizontal line passing through its centre to represent the River Tyne. The BEM works plates were affixed centrally to the cab sides, at a lower level to the insignia. The cab roof was painted a sensible grey, anticipating the inevitable ultimate weathered colour.

The frame of WL1 was in the Erecting Shop (the former Turbine Shop) by 10th August 1977 and construction advanced over the next few months until on 6th December it was taken out of the shop to the test area, where an extra rail had been added to the test track to provide standard gauge. It moved under its own power on the 20th and suffered a damaged sandbox when it fouled the loading gauge. It was back in the Erecting Shop by 3rd January 1978 and by the 20th was complete and ready for despatch. Despatch was originally scheduled for 16th January, but industrial action in Newcastle upon Tyne caused initial delay and despatch took place on the 23rd. Because the Falcon Works was without a rail link to BR, Leicester Heavy Haulage was employed to take the locomotive by road to Loughborough Midland goods yard, opposite the works. The route was circuitous due to the load limits of the nearby over bridges, but eventually BR lines were gained. The rail journey was not without incident. Coupled to Type 2 No. 25 127 and a BR brake van the short train moved off and almost immediately a sandbox fouled the BR loading gauge! The Tyne & Wear Metro loading gauge was more generous than BR C1. The offending sandbox was removed by the judicious use of oxy-acetylene cutting equipment and the train finally moved off at 19.00 hours. The route for the 'exceptional load' was via Trent Junction, Toton, Clay Cross, Chesterfield, Wath, York, Thirsk, Northallerton, Darlington, Durham, Tyne Yard and finally terminating at the South Gosforth depot. Within a month it had been accepted by the PTE and was being used for driver training purposes.

Number WL2 was despatched on 13th February and while being transferred to the rails in the goods yard at Loughborough, one wheel set was derailed, but it was replaced in time for the scheduled departure.

On 22nd February WL3 was on test, WL4 was still under construction and the frame of WL5 was in the Fabrication Shop. Due to problems with its engine WL3 remained on test for about a month, after which time it returned to the Erecting Shop where the painters had to remove considerable 'traffic film' before it could be finish painted. WL2 had been accepted by 6th April and by that date multiple operations of WL1 and WL2 had been accomplished successfully.

Number WL3 left the Falcon Works on 6th April and was hauled from Loughborough Midland goods yard by Type 4 No. 45 074 at 18.15. WL4 followed on Monday 17th April 1978 at between 18:00 and 19:00 hours.

Meanwhile the later-ordered WL5 reached the Erecting Shop on 8th August 1978, but made several exits and re-entries before settling in for erection. The pace of construction was almost leisurely and it was not until late May of the following year that it was on test, where it spent over three weeks. Despatch finally came on 31st July 1979.

The five locomotives were initially based at South Gosforth and were involved on construction duties during the first years. They were used for works duties, both in the shops and out on the line, but did not come up to expectations generally. By 1982 they could be found not only at the car shed at South Gosforth, but at the Newbridge Street depot also. All were still in use in 1986/7. On 27th August 1987 all five were noted at South Gosforth. Numbers WL1 and WL5 appeared to be working locomotives, while the other three 'looked very woebegone'. By the end of 1988 WL3 and WL5 were out of use.

During early 1990 three Hunslet 26 tonne dual-mode electric locomotives were placed in service on the Metro, to replace the Brush locomotives on engineering trains. They were considered to be more suitable for operations in the tunnels, where exhaust emissions had continued to be a problem.

In September 1991 the five locomotives were purchased from Tyne & Wear Metro by Transmanche-Link (TML) the Channel Tunnel contractor, for use in connection with construction activities in and around the Cheriton site terminal area on the British side of the Channel. Each locomotive cost TML £30,000. WL4 was the first to arrive by road on 7th October and was soon given site number 60. WL1 and WL2 arrived on 12th November and WL3 and WL5 on the 15th. TML renumbered the locomotives 60 to 64 (formerly WL4/2/1/5/3). At least two of them were not in operational condition upon arrival. By 24th November No. 61 had been repainted yellow and renumbered so, and No. 62 was in grey undercoat. Number 60 was being tested with a gantry wagon in connection with side wall fitting operations in the running tunnels. No. 64 was still un-numbered on 8th February 1992 and during the following month was engaged on pilot duties around the Cheriton site, whereas the remainder spent most of their time inside the Tunnel. During the end of April No. 63 was involved with test operations involving BR electric locomotive No. 86 208, Class 47 No. 47 970 and a test car at the British end of the Tunnel. The tests were part of a schedule to determine the effects of AC electric locomotives on the signalling system.

As construction operations proceeded the locomotives were used less, and during March 1994 only Nos 62 and 64 remained, being used by TML to shunt wagons going off hire. TML completed its construction railway work on 30th March and the other three locomotives had already gone to Sevington for disposal.

One of the locomotives was in unserviceable condition due to a damaged power unit, but the remainder were in working order. Their fate was still unresolved by the end of 1994, but there was some interest expressed in them. One possibility considered was for Brush Traction to purchase and overhaul them, then either resell or hire them out. One potential customer for them, following overhaul and modification, was Hong Kong Mass Transit Railway who would use them as interim transport until their newly-ordered dual mode electric locomotives had been supplied from Brush Traction. Whatever the speculation, they remained at Sevington, being noted there in May 1995 and on 5th August 1995. By November 1995 they had been sold.

They had been acquired by Insulated Structures Ltd, Normanby Park, Scunthorpe, the parent company for TP Dibdin Ltd, Neasden, and for Round Oak Rail Ltd of Brierley Hill, Birmingham. Three locomotives were delivered in mid-December 1995, with the remaining two spending the Christmas period in the haulier's yard and being delivered soon after 1st January 1996. Initially they were stored in an open sided workshop at Scunthorpe, pending overhaul and being sent to Neasden and Brierley Hill as required, BEM801 being noted there in 1996/7. During March 1996 Brush Traction was approached regarding details required for overhaul, but no Brush overhaul occurred.

Later BEM801 was transferred to Round Oak Rail Ltd and was noted there in April 1999 in use. It was transferred to Scunthorpe on 15th November 2000, but was sold or scrapped between February 2002 and July 2004. BEM803 was also there in 1999, but undergoing repair in the workshops. It was then noted there in November 2000. The other three locomotives still remained in store at Scunthorpe. Of these three locomotives No. 60 (BEM 804) passed into preservation in July 2000 when it was delivered on the 24th to the Rutland Railway Museum. BEM801, 802 and 805 were scrapped at Insulated Structures, Scunthorpe between 2nd February 2002 and 10th February 2004. BEM803 was acquired by Andrew Briddon for preservation and arrived at Peak Rail, Derbyshire on 21st June 2005. Already in preservation, BEM804 was sold to Ray King and was moved from Rutland Railway Museum to the Mid-Norfolk Railway on 20th April 2007.

During November 1977 a letter of intent to order ten FS1 0-6-0 shunting locomotives was received from the Malayan Railway Administration for the Malayan State Railway (Keretapi Tanah Melayu, abbreviated to KTM). They were given Brush works numbers 806 to 815 and were allocated Malayan Railway numbers 181.01 to 181.10, being designated Class 181 by the Railway. At an early stage running numbers 18.201 to 18.210 were contemplated. The contract was valued at £1.7 million. The order was signed early in 1978 and the works numbers allocated during January of that year.

The locomotives were fitted with six-cylinder, 440kW (600 metric hp) engines manufactured by MTU (Motoren und Turbinen Union) of Germany. They were built to the Malayan track gauge of 1,000mm, but were capable of being converted to 1,067mm should this be required.

The main details and dimensions were as follows:-

Wheel Arrangement	0-6-0
Track Gauge	1,000mm
Engine Model	MTU 6V 396 TC12, six-cylinders
Engine Rating	448kW at 1,800rpm
Main Generator	TG78-43 Mk5 compound wound, with separately excited, self excited and series windings
Continuous Rating	363kW, 413V, 880A, 1,800rpm
	362kW, 274V, 1320A, 1,800rpm
Auxiliary Generator	TG28-20 Mk1, 4.4kW, 110V, 40A,1,770/4,243rpm
Traction Motors (two)	Each TM68-46 Mk6, axle hung, nose-suspended, DC series wound
Continuous Rating	157kW, 274V, 660A, 401rpm
Length over Buffer Beams	7,890mm
Length over Centre Couplers	9,293mm
Overall Width	2,815mm
Overall Height	3,760mm
Wheel Diameter	1,016mm
Wheelbase	3,048mm
Minimum Curve Negotiable	39.62 metres radius
Maximum Speed	24kph
Continuous Tractive Effort	88kN at 12.6kph
Fuel Capacity	1,590 litres
Weight in Working Order	47 tonnes

Braking equipment fitted was straight air and vacuum, the former for the locomotive, the latter the train. In outward appearance the locomotives resembled the Tyne & Wear locomotives, but there were no end overhangs of the superstructure, nor were there battery boxes attached to the fuel tank, but the deck was extended at both ends to allow for pedestrian cross access and in having this feature the they did differ from the Nigerian locomotives.

The first frame entered the Erecting Shop on 18th April 1978 and progressed until the power unit and cab was fitted during June and the completed locomotive went to test on 31st August. It was being painted by 22nd September, not in finish coat, but grey primer/undercoat – the final painting in the yellow livery of the Railway was to be done in Malaysia. The final livery was a rich, yellow, almost orange, with red buffer beams and fly cranks.

The running numbers were applied to the cabsides in large white sans serif numerals between the centrally positioned BEM works plate and the cab side windows. The deck areas and underframes were picked out in black. All the works plates were fitted at Brush and all bore the year 1978.

The first locomotive was noted on a low loader on 13th October 1978 and left the Falcon Works on 1st November, courtesy of Leicester Heavy Haulage, bound for Liverpool Docks. It had taken less than a year to build. It was accompanied by the second locomotive, to Liverpool, the same haulage firm providing the transport.

The ex-works dates were as follows:-

Works No.	Date ex-works	Works No.	Date ex-works
806	01 November 1978	811	c.05 January 1979
807	01 November 1978	812	February 1979
808	c.23 November 1978	813	early March 1979
809	c.23 November 1978	814	early March 1979
810	c.05 January 1979	815	early March 1979

Once in Malaysia they were painted in the livery of the Railway and placed in service. On 11th April 1985 a visitor to the Penang area noted 181.05 on a trip freight at Butterworth Station. Although the locomotives were satisfactory in general terms, one problem experienced was their tendency to hunt at speed. They were much heavier than the other FS1 shunting locomotives, yet the wheelbase was the same, resulting in a higher moment of inertia about a vertical axis yet no greater restoring force. The English Electric shunting locomotives (the Malayan version of BR Class 08) had a longer wheelbase and did not suffer this problem. A visitor to Kuala Lumpur shed on 4th June 1995 found 18 101-3/7/9 present, but it is not certain whether all were in service. By September 1995 it appeared that at least four were still in regular use.

During mid June 1978 some advance news was heard within the works of an impending order for twenty FS1s for the newly constituted Tanzania Railway Corporation (TRC). This translated into fact during the following month, the order being valued at £3.8 million. They were similar to those supplied to the NRC and were fitted with Paxman 8 RPHL engines of 245kW (328bhp) output.

Following the formal break-up of the East African Railways Corporation (East African Railways & Harbours – of Kenya, Uganda and Tanzania) in 1977 TRC had responsibility for its former operations in Tanzania and set about matters arising from the changed circumstances, a need for shunting/transfer locomotives being one of them. The main details and dimensions were as follows:-

Wheel Arrangement	0-6-0
Track Gauge	1,000mm
Engine Model	Paxman 8 RPHL
Engine Rating	245kW (328bhp) at 1,500rpm
Main Generator	TG78-43 Mk6, compound wound with self and separately excited fields, run and start series windings, 6-pole
Continuous Rating	191kW, 255V, 750A, 1,500rpm
	185kW, 140V, 1,320A, 1,500rpm
Auxiliary Generator	TG28-16 Mk3A, 5.63kW, 75V, 75A, 1,578/3,945rpm
Traction Motors (two)	Each TM68-46 Mk6A series wound 69.5kW, 140V, 660A, 4-pole
Length over Bufferbeams	7,254mm
Length over Centre Coupler	8,697mm
Overall Width	3,048mm
Overall Height	3,908mm
Wheel Diameter	1,003mm
Wheelbase	3,048mm
Minimum Curve Negotiable	31.4 metres radius
Maximum Speed	25kph
Maximum Tractive Effort, Starting	11,000kg
One Hour Tractive Effort	8,710kg
Continuous Tractive Effort	7,920kg at 8kph
Fuel Capacity	1591 litres
Weight in Working Order	36.2 tonnes

The twenty locomotives were given works numbers 816 to 835 and TRC numbers 3601 to 3620, the Railway's classification being Class 36. The first underframe was being constructed in the Fabrication Shop early in November 1978 and was moved to the Erecting Shop by 6th December. Progress was swift and by 7th March the following year the resultant locomotive was clear of test. It was fully painted by the end of March and was despatched about a month later.

On completion the locomotive was a splendid sight in the rich blue TRC livery. A broad yellow, horizontal band, edged in red was painted around the locomotive and the undergear was painted black. The fly cranks were picked out in red and the buffer beams were given inverted vee-form yellow and black stripes, the yellow ones being twice the width of the latter. The rectangular works plates were affixed to the cab sides between the pedestrian access and the side grilles. Above the latter and positioned on the yellow band was the running number borne by a cast metal plate (probably stainless steel as no tarnishing occurred) the raised sans serif numerals and border being in polished metal and the remainder being red backed. A matching plate was affixed to the front and rear handrails. The initials of the railway, TR were affixed to the side access doors to the rear of the radiator. The livery style, if not the colours, was derived from that of the old East African Railways. The customary cyclopean lights were fitted in the prominent top and centre position of each bonnet end.

Each locomotive was manufactured in impressive time and the contract of twenty locomotives was completed by the end of November 1979.

The dates for them were as follows:-

TR No.	Works No.	Date to/ex-Erecting Shop	Date ex-works
3601	816	by 06.12.1978/02.04.1979	late 04.1979
3602	817	by 08.01.1979/by 23.04.1979	late 04.1979
3603	818	by 22.01.1979/late 04.1979	late 04.1979
3604	819	by 22.01.1979/by 08.05.1979	late 04 /05.1979
3605	820	by 02.02.1979/08.05.1979	05.1979
3606	821	by 02.02.1979/by 25.05.1979	06.06.1979
3607	822	by 21.02.1979/2by 29.05.1979	06.1979
3608	823	by 01.03.1979/06.1979	by 16.06.1979
3609	824	by 19.03.1979	
3610	825	by 05.04.1979/by 16.08.1979	
3611	826	by 05.04.1979/by 16.08.1979	
3612	827	by 09.05.1979/08.1979	by 24.09.1979
3613	828	by 09.05.1979/09.1979	03.10.1979
3614	829	by 09.05.1979/09.1979	04.10.1979
3615	830	05.1979/by 18.10.1979	c.26.10.1979 *a*
3616	831	by 08.06.1979/late 10.1979	c.26.10.1979 *a*
3617	832	06.06.1979/by 09.11.1979	
3618	833	by 16.06.1979/by 12.11.1979	
3619	834	by 17.08.1979/by 28.11.1979	
3620	835	by 23.07.1979/by 30.11.1979	
a Lost at sea en route for Tanzania			

Number 3620 was the last locomotive to be built in the former Turbine Shop, though not the last to be placed in there. All the locomotives were bound for Dar Es Salaam, the main port of Tanzania. In the days of sailing ships there was always a high risk that some mishap might befall a vessel and cause its loss, but in modern times few cargoes do not reach their destinations. There are exceptions of course, and Nos 3615 and 3616 were chosen by fate to be involved in one of them.

The two locomotives had left the Falcon Works on about the 26th October 1979 by low loader, bound for the King George Docks, Hull. There they were loaded on board the 10,715 tons gross, Greek-registered mv AEOLIAN SKY, built in 1978. She had sailed from London on 21st October to call at Hull to take on more cargo.

When loading was complete, she was carrying a mixed cargo of some 12,500 freight tonnes. As well as the two Brush locomotives she carried a consignment of Land Rovers for Tanzania, a new issue of Seychelles banknotes (face value £1.2 million), nail polish, liquid chlorine, resin, paint, thinners, anhydrous ammonia, Bostik cleaner and other unspecified items.

She sailed from Hull on 2nd November, bound for Dar Es Salaam via Aqaba, Jeddah, Seychelles, Aden and Mombasa.

During the early hours of 3rd November she was in collision with the German flag vessel ANNA KNUPPEL off the Cherbourg Peninsula. The ANNA KNUPPEL was carrying Granite Chips from Cornwall, ex-Newlyn and bound for Hamburg. At 04.56 GMT the AEOLIAN SKY radioed for immediate assistance, reporting that she was holed in No. 1 hold and taking water. The ANNA KNUPPEL, with bow damage, and the bulk carrier RIVERINA stood by. The tug ABEILLE LANGUEDOC sailed from Cherbourg to give assistance and to tow the AEOLIAN SKY to Cherbourg if necessary. Then the master of the AEOLIAN SKY radioed the RIVERINA that the second bulk-head had gone, and two holds were full of water. He feared that he might have to abandon ship. Reliable sources stated at the time that the two Brush locomotives were in the hold near to the point of impact and holing of the hull. In the meantime the AEOLIAN SKY started to settle by the bow and the Dutch destroyer OVERIJSSEL arrived on the scene and assumed duty of on-scene commander. The sea was rough and the weather almost gale-force, with visibility three miles. A rescue helicopter arrived on the scene and lifted some of the crew to the OVERIJSSEL. The ABEILLE LANGUEDEC arrived on the scene and stood by, but then the helicopter was forced to return to Lee-on-Solent with engine trouble, having lifted off sixteen of the crew. A replacement was requested. The remainder of the crew were lifted off after 09.30 GMT. Then the French minesweeper CAPRICORNE also arrived, and stood in attendance. At 10.48 GMT Boulogne Radio cancelled the urgency broadcast. Later the master returned to the AEOLIAN SKY.

A request to tow the stricken vessel to Cherbourg, or indeed any French port, was refused by the French Authorities due to earlier difficulties caused by tanker disasters. She was taken in tow by the ABEILLE LANGUEDEC and it was decided that she should be taken to Southampton instead and two of the crew from the tug joined the master. A small amount of deck cargo was lost overboard and although electric power was still available on the AEOLIAN SKY the pumps refused to work and she shipped even more water.

At 17.15 GMT the position of tug and tow was about twelve miles off St. Catherine's Point and because of her low draught the AEOLIAN SKY was unable to enter the Solent. Portland Bay was the next choice of destination and it was decided to beach her along the coast.

At 03.45 GMT on 4th November, with nobody on board, her bows were well under water and possibly touching the bottom in 30 metres of water, and sinking fast; the end was near. By 04.15 GMT she had sunk and a Trinity House vessel was on the scene near the wreck, some twelve miles off Portland Bill and seven miles off St. Alban's Head. The position of the AEOLIAN SKY was given as Latitude 50 30 31N, Longitude 02 08 23W. With the wind at near Gale Force 7, containers (some measuring 33ft by 15ft), loose deck cargo and spillage of chemicals were threatening the shipping lanes and south coastal areas and as a result, shore patrols went out between Weymouth and Bournemouth. Helicopter surveillance was maintained. Oil slicks, debris and drums headed eastwards. Marking the wreck with buoys was difficult due to bad weather and was not completed until 7th November. On the following day the Corporation of Trinity House took possession of the wreck under the 1894 Merchant Shipping Act, and gave notice that nothing may be taken from it.

On the Isle of Wight a full-scale emergency was declared on 18th December as the Island's biggest-ever pollution problem threatened, with hundreds of containers of highly dangerous chemicals being washed ashore, having drifted at least thirty miles from the wreck. By late January 1979 divers reported that the money bound for the Seychelles was missing; some turned up courtesy of fishermen, at a bank in Weymouth! The pollution problem lasted for over three months and made headline news during that period.

On 25th February 1980, a four-man diving team inspected the AEOLIAN SKY on behalf of the Department of Trade and found that almost all the chemical containers on board the vessel had been washed away and that most of the deck cargo had also gone. This was not surprising, as she was lying on her side. Three more days of surveying the wreck for various purposes revealed that it would need to be cut down by 35 feet to ensure safe navigation and would need to be cut into three or four sections and removed by crane. The whole operation was estimated to be lengthy and expensive, costing about £500,000. As a prelude all the cargo would have to be removed from the holds and all the bunker fuel removed, an estimated 5,000 tons in all.

During June 1980 tenders were invited for clearing oil and cargo from the wreck, and during the following month Trinity House accepted a tender from COSAG of Great Yarmouth for the partial demolition of it to enable the cargo in the forward sections to be removed. Work commenced that month, but the five divers could only safely work half an hour each day due to the strong tides sweeping across the wreck, and consequently by December there were no plans to remove the two Brush locomotives. At the time opinion was that they would be left there, when the wreck was dispersed to ensure safe navigation for shipping.

Some of the items from the wreck were displayed in the shipwreck museum at Charlestown, Cornwall. The owners of the museum, having dived the wreck on occasions, were unaware of the presence of the locos in 1995, although the salvage divers (by this time the wreck's owners) may have been.

Regardless of whether or not the locomotives could be salvaged a decision had to be made regarding their replacement and this occurred within days of the disaster, certainly by 30th November 1979. The matter was placed in the hands of the insurers and by that date replacements were on order, allocated works numbers 840/1 (TRC Nos 3615/6).

The sum insured was barely sufficient to pay the cost of building the two replacements; it costs more per locomotive to build a batch of two than twenty.

They were built in the new purpose-built Erecting Shop, at the rear of the Falcon Works, during 1980 and 1981. By 6th November 1980 No. 3615 had been fitted with its power unit and radiator and No. 3616 had received its power unit. The former left the Falcon Works on Monday 2nd March 1981, sailing from Liverpool aboard the mv JOSEF STEWING two days later. On the day of the sailing No. 3616 was being painted, and left the works about 13th April. It was loaded aboard the LINA FISSER at Birkenhead, leaving three days later. One source reports that the ship left Liverpool on the 22nd, so it is likely that it had to load more cargo there, before finally setting out for Tanzania. Tanzania Railways at last received their Nos 3615 and 3616 and had twenty Brush locomotives at their disposal.

Quite what the Railway did with them is another matter. Within six years of the replacements arriving, all twenty were out of service – observations dated April 1987 noting that they were in sidings becoming overgrown with vegetation due to neglect. It was the old story of lack of finance and proper care and maintenance again.

A visitor to Dar Es Salaam in 1991 found that around the station and beyond were lines of withdrawn, rusting coaches and wagons. The system was generally in run-down condition and staff was hoping for foreign aid to permit refurbishment and the purchase of new equipment. Despite the impression of 1987 some Brush locomotives of 1979 were noted in use.

During the winter of 1992/3 a UK-funded programme included the rehabilitation of nine Class 36 shunting locomotives, and work was directed by John Batley of engineers Haiste International and the Chief Mechanical Engineer of TRC, Mr Michael Kabipe. The Equipment Division ASEA Brown Boveri Transportation won a contract to for the overhaul of eleven of the class, including the supply of spare parts and the expertise to oversee the rebuilding of the locomotives by local labour. There was a possibility that some components would be sent to England for repair. The rehabilitation continued through 1993. In September 1995 Brush Traction sources believed that fourteen locomotives were refurbished and all were currently available for service. In January 2008 some were noted shunting in Malindi yard, Dar es Salaam.

The two replacement locomotives were the last FS1s to be ordered, the last examples of the model to be built and marked the end of an era, by being the last locomotives to be ordered during the 1970s, a somewhat neat datum point.

In conveniently combining the narrative of the two locomotive orders for Tanzania, it is necessary to backtrack slightly to describe the intermediate order received for four locomotives from Chiyoda Chemical Engineering & Construction Company Ltd for its oil refinery in central Nigeria. They were ordered through Crown Agents on 8th October 1979 and received Brush works numbers 836 to 839.

They were very similar those supplied to the Nigerian Railway Corporation and even the livery was similar. They were painted a lighter green and featured the broad, horizontal yellow stripe which omitted only the cabsides. The company insignia and the running numbers occupied the cabside space formed by the break. The company insignia was incorporated within a yellow and red cog-shaped device bearing the title of the parent company, NIGERIAN NATIONAL PETROLEUM CORPORATION. The running numbers were KR01SE to KR04SE, roughly translated as Kaduna Refinery Nos 01 to 04 Shunting Engines.

The main details and dimensions of the locomotives, although very close to those of the NRC locomotives in most cases, were as follows:-

Wheel Arrangement	0-6-0
Track Gauge	1,067mm (3ft 6ins)
Engine Model	Paxman 8RPHXL Mk7
Engine Rating	3,64bhp at 1,250rpm
Main Generator	TG78-43 Mk3, compound wound with self and separately excited fields, and run and start series windings. 6-pole
Continuous Rating	240kW, 250V, 960A, 1,250rpm
	235kW, 178V, 1,320A, 1,250rpm
Auxiliary Generator	TG28-16 Mk3, 3.3kW, 75V, 44A,
	1,580/3,290rpm
Traction Motors (two)	Each TM68-46 Mk7, series wound, 126.4hp, 177V, 660A, 234rpm, 4-pole
Length over Buffer Beams	7,315mm
Length over Centre Coupler	8,560mm
Overall Width	2,946mm
Overall Height	3,962mm
Wheel Diameter	1,086mm
Wheelbase	3,048mm
Minimum Curve Negotiable	39.6 metres radius
Maximum Speed	24kph
Maximum Starting Tractive Effort	13,608kg
Continuous Tractive Effort	8,709kg at 8kph
One Hour Tractive Effort	9,525kg
Fuel Capacity	1,909 litres
Weight in Working Order	40 tonnes

The works plates were rectangular and somewhat complicated affairs situated between the cab pedestrian access and the lower cabside grille s. The bottom line was rendered in smaller characters and the initials HS were in fact the Hawker Siddeley HS logo. The legend on the plates fitted to the first locomotive was as shown in the representation at the foot of the page.

The first locomotive was due by the end of July 1980, but in fact was completed by 6th November and despatched on the 10th of that month. The 6th also saw KR01SE receiving its final coat of paint, KR03SE its undercoat (but not tested) and KR04SE was nearly complete. KR02SE was ex-works on 13th November, the remainder leaving shortly after that date.

Buffer beams were painted in the almost time-honoured yellow and black stripes of inverted vee pattern, and the fly cranks were red. The cab roof was white, at least when new.

Service details are not available, but in September 1995 regular orders for spares continued and it is believed that the locomotives were still in service. At least three (including KR04SE and possibly KR03SE) were noted at NRC workshops in February 1999. They appeared intact (by Nigerian standards) but not in service.

During 1979 the new Locomotive Erecting Shop was built to the rear of the works, adjacent to the Locomotive Superstructure Shops of the 1960s. It was commissioned during the following year and the first locomotives to be constructed in it were the four locomotives for Chiyoda, with the two Tanzanian locomotives following on. Actually at one period locomotives of both contracts were in the shop. Multi-gauge tracks were installed catering for standard, 3ft 6ins and metre gauges and linked the shop with a small test house, situated north of it. Beyond this the test track extended on a curve towards the Great Central railway embankment, terminating abruptly only yards from the end of the formation of the original test track dating from the early 1950s. This was inhabited by rabbits, which lived idyllic lives in the sand, found in great quantities around the surviving buffer stop. After thirty years the colony must have passed through more generations than credited to the Israelites in the Bible! As for the new Locomotive Shop, it was to prove more useful than imagined at the time, as we shall see in Chapters 12 to 17 in the second volume of this work.

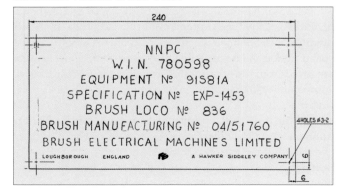

11 – Class 56

It is a far cry from the coalfields of Britain to the battlefields of the Golan Heights and Suez Canal, but in 1973 a link was forged, altering the course of BR locomotive procurement at a time when there seemed little prospect of any heavy freight locomotive requirement.

On 6th October 1973, the Jewish Feast Day of Yom Kippur, Syrian and Egyptian armed forces stormed across the borders of Israel, surprising the Israeli armed forces. Desperate struggles ensued in which the Israelis at first fell back. Gradually, the Israelis counter-attacked and successfully repulsed the invaders at considerable cost to both sides. The USA and USSR intervened, successfully pressurising for a cease-fire, which was to end the war on 24th October.

The consequences of the war were immediate. Firstly, the Suez Canal had been made impassable during the fighting, and secondly, the Organisation of Petroleum Exporting Countries (OPEC), dominated by Middle East countries sympathetic to the Arab cause, set about using the price of oil as a weapon to gain the objectives which the war had failed to achieve, the defeat of Israel and the recapture of territory lost to Israel in previous wars. Their strategy was to pressurise those nations who supported Israel and who were reliant upon oil for their industrial economies. The price of crude oil was increased by 130 percent in December 1973. This huge price increase was not the first; it had been preceded by a massive 70 percent increase in September and October 1973. Whether or not this first move was a coincidence is open to speculation, certainly it was timely. The price of oil per barrel was to quadruple before much time passed, from $3 to more than $12, and by 1980 it reached $30.

The loss of the Suez Canal, the international short cut, diverted traffic around the Cape of Good Hope and forced up the cost of oil further. At regular intervals the oil-producing nations deliberately raised the price. The compounding effect was cumulative and hit industrial nations hard, resulting in monetary inflation worldwide.

The combined price rises of 1973 by OPEC represented an increase of almost threefold. The immediate reactions of affected nations were to conserve stocks and restrict consumption. As further such moves could be expected, the longer-term considered reactions included finding alternative sources for oil and using alternative fuels instead of oil. Britain was among those nations affected, and a decision was made to increase coal production and reduce the dependency upon oil imports. British Government policies on fuel shifted towards a greater use of coal. Likewise, the Central Electricity Generating Board (CEGB) anticipated a large increase in its own coal consumption in its power stations and preparations were made by the National Coal Board (NCB) and BR to cater for the anticipated demand.

The situation facing BR changed very quickly, therefore, and several choices lay open in dealing with the new situation. With the heavy freight locomotives BR had in service it could operate existing ones singly or in multiple, refurbish and uprate existing locomotives, or provide new locomotives. Both the first two choices came with problems, not the least being the age and low power of some of them. In particular the Class 47, which whilst being a good mixed traffic locomotive, would be taxed to the limit under the new and increased haulage requirements. Experience had shown that Class 47s could suffer overload damage on the first long adverse gradient after starting a block train. With already increased train loadings on the mgr circuits, Class 47s were spending too long a time (during initial acceleration and on gradients) at short-term main generator ratings – and for the first time there was an epidemic of generator troubles resulting from high sustained current loadings. As with with most mixed traffic locomotives, extremes of operation with single unit working tended to show up their deficiencies, and multiple-operation of Class 47s would involve modification and divert locomotives away from other duties. This situation held true with other BR diesel classes.

Refurbishing and uprating Class 47s was worth examination and as described in Chapter 6 one member of the class (47 046/47 601) was indeed uprated by drastic rebuilding with higher-powered equipment. It was expensive and would also divert locomotives from other duties, so the only option left was to provide new purpose-built locomotives.

As outlined previously, BR motive power considerations at the end of the 1960s had changed to the point where the mixed traffic concept had given way to designing motive power for specific duties, in other words it was to be a 'horses for courses' policy. One direct result of this policy was the highly successful 125mph High Speed Train, carefully developed and introduced during the 1970s and for many years the mainstay of Intercity services. The development of a heavy freight diesel electric locomotive took a different course and what emerged was the result of necessity and producing what was perceived to be a combination of the best equipment available.

It does appear strange that even in 1970 BR was considering a twin-engined, fast freight locomotive design of 4,500bhp at a time when 'Kestrel' was running on BR and embodying most of the desirable features for a freight locomotive with Co-Co wheel arrangement. The twin-engine principle died hard and 'Kestrel' could not be loaded to the full because no sidings could take the resultant long trains, so 4,500bhp was ambitious unless BR, NCB and the CEGB were to extend facilities for mgr trains. Nevertheless, BR thinking was moving towards introducing heavier block trains requiring higher haulage capacity, but there the matter rested until the events of 1973 changed the situation dramatically.

During the early months of the following year BR considered the new situation and responded quickly by issuing invitations to tender, on a broad-based specification, for thirty heavy freight locomotives. The specification could only be presented in this manner, because the need was so urgent, and furthermore, BREL and BR workshops, committed to other work, could only deliver later rather than sooner. BR had insufficient resources to produce a design in time. Alternatives from North America were considered, but a decision (with Government approval) was quickly made to accept that from Brush. Sixty locomotives were ordered in September 1974, thirty to be built by Brush and thirty by BREL Doncaster. Almost predictably, bearing in mind the situation, the resultant design embodied well-tried and proven components – an amalgam of established practices.

The superstructure was monocoque (derived from Class 47), the engine was of English Electric lineage (in uprated form derived immediately from that fitted to Class 50), and the electrical generating equipment was derived from the latest Brush alternating current (AC) practice as embodied in 'Kestrel'. The DC traction motors were also of Brush design, embodying and updating previous practice of Class 47 and 'Kestrel'. The bogies were of Swiss design, well-proven elsewhere.

The 4,500bhp of the BR twin-engine design of 1970 and the 4,000 metric horsepower of 'Kestrel' were clearly in excess of what could be accommodated in practice, so the 3,250bhp requirement dictated the use of a single engine. The original engine recommendation by GEC Diesels was a twelve-cylinder design based on the 12RKC, but due to the urgency that BR attached to the delivery, there was insufficient time to complete its development programme, which included service trials on 47 601. Instead, BR decided that Class 56 should incorporate a current production engine, the 16RK3CT, and to obtain early operating experience, put it into service on 47 601. In time, the 12RKC completed its test bed development programme and replaced the 16RK3CT. It replaced the engine in 47 601 (which became 47 901) and was proved before being fitted to Class 58 in the 1980s.

The influence of 'Kestrel' was not restricted to the application of AC generating equipment; there were unexpected influences. 'Kestrel', it may be remembered, had been sold to the USSR in 1971 and subsequently made quite an impression upon engineers within Eastern Bloc countries. This interest, mainly concerned with its advanced electrical equipment and electronic control systems, led to an agreement between Brush and Electroputere of Romania to develop jointly a high-power diesel electric freight locomotive for sale in not only Eastern Bloc countries, but also associated countries around the world.

The sudden need for heavy freight locomotives caught Brush without sufficient building facilities consequent of the lack of demand for main line locomotives after 1979 and the resultant utilisation of workshop facilities for other work. Fortunately, the Company still had sufficient design facilities to respond quickly. Although accepting the order for thirty locomotives and an order for the supply of electrical equipment for the remaining thirty locomotives to be built at Doncaster, Brush decided that there was insufficient reason to re-establish main line locomotive construction facilities at the Falcon Works and sub-contracted this work to Electroputere who utilised their facilities at the Craiova Works, in Romania. Most of the components were to be manufactured in Britain and shipped to Romania for installation into the Craiova-built body shells. In retrospect, this arrangement does appear somewhat circumspect and a complication, but in the context of the times it did offer a suitable solution to the requirements of the several parties involved, that of quick delivery without having to set up facilities with a limited and doubtful future. Certainly, the decision to sub-contract in this manner came as a surprise to many outside the Falcon Works and to employees within, but it should be remembered again that production of locomotives had often been intermittent, and that of traction equipment continuous.

The new locomotives were designated Class 56 by BR and Brush was allotted running numbers 56 001 to 56 030 for its contract and BREL Doncaster 56 031 to 56 060. BEM allocated works numbers 750-779 to 56 001-30, though none was ever carried, and the locomotives were produced under BR Lot No. 1507. Doncaster Works produced its thirty locomotives under Lot No. 1508. There may have been an intention to fit works plates to the Brush batch of locomotives because at least one plate existed at the time of delivery, BRUSH 776 of 1976, intended for 56 027. At some stage 170 locomotives of Class 56 were envisaged, but eventual production was curtailed to 135, the balance being produced as the BR designed Standard Class 58. 56 061-90 were produced under Lot No. 1509 and 56 091-135 under Lot No. 1510 (which originally covered 56 091-170). Even in the early years the design appears to have been considered as interim by BR. The Brush order was worth £8.4 million of which £2.6 million was the Romanian portion.

The monocoque body was based upon that applied to Class 47 and 'Kestrel', but where previously there had been a central access door on each side there was now none. Unlike Class 47, which had roof-mounted radiators, side mounted radiators were fitted, so large air intakes (one each side) faced with grilles were provided. They were braced to prevent loss of strength in that area. Behind them were positioned the radiator panels, plus other equipment used for such purposes as providing the cab air-conditioning and forced ventilation for the traction motors, the latter consisting of electrically-driven blowers. The end-loading was distributed to the upper structure members through side trusses, in the established manner and capable of withstanding a buffing load of 200 tons. The roof was made detachable in three sections to facilitate vertical removal of major items of equipment, the sections coinciding with the three main compartments, which in turn were separated by bulkheads. It was liberally provided with air intakes and outlets. Above the radiator compartment Serck Heat Transfer cooling equipment, consisting of two hydrostatically driven cooling fans with thermostatic controls, was housed in the roof section. At the opposite end was the electrical compartment housing the rectifier, another traction motor blower and other various items of electrical equipment. The central section housed the power unit consisting of the diesel engine and brushless alternator set.

Below the body and between the bogies were the fuel oil tank, batteries and sandboxes.

The cabs were fully air-conditioned, well insulated for temperature and noise purposes and aluminium was used extensively for the outer skin. The floors had non-slip surfaces and all windows had toughened safety glass sealed in rubber. The windscreen glass had electrical heating incorporated within it. Two driving positions were provided in each cab, the left for the driver and the right for use by the second man.

The diesel engine was the 16-cylinder 'vee' type GEC Diesels, English Electric Type 16RK3CT capable of 3,520bhp at 900rpm, but rated at 3,250bhp for Class 56 application. Despite its designation it was not of the original RK range. English Electric had two ranges, the 'RK' and the 'V', each a rather different design. Following the amalgamation of English Electric, Ruston & Hornsby and GEC there was a recoding of former English Electric designs into one series, designated 'RK'. One could suggest that a more accurate coding of the 16RK3CT would be 16CSVT Mk3.

The 16RK3CT was applied to Class 56 in turbo-charged and inter-cooled form. It was of monobloc construction, completely enclosed, had integral pumps to circulate cooling water and lubricating oil. Each cylinder had a separate fuel injection pump injecting directly into open-type combustion chambers. A shaft extension drive for the pump motor was taken from the free end of the engine.

The twelve-pole AC generator was directly coupled to the other end of the engine. This was now the standard application, replacing the hitherto standard DC generator for the first time on a BR new production locomotive, other than the HST. With its three-phase output full-wave rectified, controlled and fed into the DC traction motors in an established manner, the AC generator requires little description for this application. The auxiliary AC generator was affixed to the outer end of the main generator and supplied its three-phase AC output to most auxiliary machines without rectification, one of the benefits derived from the new standard resulting in reduced maintenance all round. Six DC series-wound traction motors were permanently connected in series-parallel across the rectified output of the main generator. Each motor was force-ventilated, nose-suspended and axle-mounted.

A 27-way train-wire control system was fitted to enable multiple operation of three locomotives, if required, but the need for more than two was rarely realised in practice. Wheel slip detection was provided by comparing the voltages of two traction motors in each motor circuit. In the event of a wheel slip being detected, power to all six traction motors was cut off and then restored to a level dependent upon the duration of wheelslip when adhesion was restored. Slow-speed control was fitted as standard for mgr duties within colliery and power station yards.

Braking equipment was by Davies & Metcalfe and Westinghouse, providing independent air braking on the locomotive and automatic air braking equipment with proportional control, for train braking. A locomotive parking brake was provided and brake application was by electro-pneumatic means, acting upon the shoes of the inner wheels of each bogie.

The bogies, designated CP2 by BR, were to a Swiss design used extensively on the Romanian State Railways, but adapted for BR use. They were manufactured by Intreprinderia de Constructi de Masini (ICM) at their Resita works in Romania. The manufacturer's plates affixed to the bogies bore the title INTREPRINDERIA DE CONSTRUCTII

DE MASINI and a stylised Resita. The bogies were of welded-frame construction and the cylindrical axle box guides were bolted to the bogie frame. The weight was carried by helical springs supported by equalisers pivoted on the underside of the axle boxes. Friction dampers were fitted within the helical springs. These proved to be erratic in their damping force and one former member of the locomotive design office considers that hydraulic dampers would have been more satisfactory. Secondary suspension was provided by six Flexicoil springs on each bogie, with vertical and lateral hydraulic dampers.

The main details and dimensions were as follows:-

Wheel Arrangement	Co-Co
Track Gauge	4ft 8½ins
Engine Model	GEC Diesels, 16RK3CT, sixteen-cylinder, four-stroke, turbo-charged and charge-air cooled, with 10ins piston diameter and 12ins stroke, and twin-bank arrangement vee form
Engine Rating	3,520bhp at 900rpm full rated output, but set at 3,250bhp for Class 56
Main Generator (alternator)	BA1101A, 12-pole, 3-phase, AC brushless type
Continuous Rating	2,293kW, 840V, 2,730A, 900rpm through rectifier (DC)
	670V, 2,034A line (AC)
	2,310kW, 1,520V, 1,520A, 900rpm
	1,167V, 1,178A line (AC)
One Hour Rating	2,280kW, 760V, 3,000A DC, through rectifier
Auxiliary Generator	BAA602A, 8-pole, 3-phase, AC (alternator) brushless type
Continuous Rating	84kW, 500V, 110A, 900rpm
Machines Spec.	84kW, 500V, 110A, 60Hz
Ratings	41kW, 250V, 108A, 30Hz, 450rpm
Traction Motors (six)	Each TM73-62, series wound, axle-hung, nose-suspended
Continuous Rating	344kW, 910A, 420V, 620rpm
One Hour Rating	336kW, 1,000A, 380V, 538rpm
Length Over Buffers	63ft 6ins
Overall Width	9ft 2ins
Overall Height	12ft 9 3/8ins
Wheel Diameter	3ft 9ins nominal (1,143 and 1,150mm variations)
Total Wheelbase	47ft 10ins
Bogie Wheelbase	13ft 5½ins
Minimum Curve Negotiable	3½ chains radius
Maximum Speed	80mph
Maximum Tractive Effort	61,800lbs
Continuous Tractive Effort	53,950lbs at 16.8mph
Fuel Capacity	1,150 gallons
Weight in Working Order	126 tons
Distance Between Bogie Pivot Centres	37ft 8ins

An early attempt to produce advance publicity views for the Class 56 design saw the artist draw too many zeros for the running number!

BRUSH B405

In outward appearance 56 001 made an impressive sight, and appeared every inch the purposeful and workmanlike machine it really was. Although the outline of the locomotive clearly showed its Class 47 lineage, it appeared different at certain angles, with a 'leaning forward' look when viewed from ahead and from a slightly elevated position. This may have been due to the plain, but domed appearance of the cab roof which lacked the cowl/grille arrangement of Class 47. Within this arrangement were the warning horns, but in Class 56 these were fitted behind a grille on the lower cab front, space being available because roller blind indicators were no longer fitted to new BR locomotives. This position was supposed to reduce draughts in the cab. The black rubber surrounds of the front windows were highlighted against the yellow-painted background afforded by the extended warning panel. A central headlight was fitted to the cab fronts, just below the horizontal handrail that passed below the front windows. An unsightly jumper cable and stowage sockets were fitted to the cab front, as were the customary marker and red tail lights. Circular buffer heads were fitted initially as were the decorative cowlings around the buffer beam areas. Overall Corporate Blue livery was applied in the standard style, with the double arrow emblem placed centrally on the body sides and the running numbers applied to the left of it towards the cab doors. Some of the numerals were non-standard on the Romanian locomotives, the '3' of 56 003 being upside down! Undergear was painted black and plain metal kick plates were fitted below the cab doorways. Red diamonds were painted on cab fronts indicating the multiple-working compatibility.

Class 56 Production and Entry into Service

Class 56 production lasted until 1984 and involved three manufacturing works, the Electroputere Works in Craiova, BREL Doncaster and BREL Crewe. Electroputere was first to lay down the bodywork, in 1975, and in March 1976 No. 56 001 emerged complete, although not finish-painted (official photographs being studio-touched for the initial publicity announcements). The announcements commenced during the following month, The Loughborough Echo of 9th April being among the first. Over the ensuing months 56 001 underwent running tests and trials on the Romanian State Railways (CFR) system around Craiova, hauling freight trains, often consisting of large bogie hopper wagons. During this period 56 001 gained its BR blue livery. Most of the Class 56s were run-in on service trains, both passenger and freight, between Craiova and Bucharest, or Craiova and Tornu Severin. 56 009, in full BR livery, was photographed hauling a coal train of forty bogie hopper wagons for Craiova thermal power station. 56 001 was towed across Europe to Zeebrugge where it arrived on 4th August, in the company of 56 002. The pair made the sea crossing by Sealink ferry and were landed at Harwich (Parkeston Quay) and were drawn off by 0-6-0 diesel shunting locomotive No. 08 767. They remained at Harwich until 7th and then completed the journey under tow by Brush Type 2 No. 31 318, through Colchester, Ipswich, March, Lincoln and Retford to Tinsley depot in Sheffield, where detail commissioning and acceptance was to take place. This delivery procedure was adopted for most of the Romanian batch, although some of the locomotives went to Barrow Hill depot and were placed in store until they could by dealt with. It was expected that once accepted by BR they would be allocated to Tinsley for intensive diagrams on mgr trains between collieries and power stations, and thus meet the expected increased demand for coal. The dates of arrival to Zeebrugge and added to BR stock were as follows:-

Loco.No.	To Zeebrugge	To BR stock
56 001	04 August 1976	28 February 1977
56 002	04 August 1976	28 February 1977
56 003	13 August 1976	28 February 1977
56 004	13 August 1976	28 February 1977
56 005	09 September 1976	14 March 1977
56 006	08 September 1976	25 February 1977
56 007	08 September 1976	13 April 1977
56 008	15 September 1976	13 April 1977
56 009	01 October 1976	27 May 1977
56 010	01 October 1976	28 July 1977
56 011	30 November 1976	29 June 1977
56 012	23 December 1976	18 April 1977
56 013	23 December 1976	01 August 1977
56 014	03 January 1977	28 March 1977
56 015	03 January 1977	21 March 1977
56 016	06 January 1977	27 May 1977
56 017	06 January 1977	13 May 1977
56 018	14 January 1977	23 August 1977
56 019	14 January 1977	13 May 1977
56 020	15 January 1977	20 May 1977
56 021	09 March 1977	17 June 1977
56 022	16 March 1977	24 May 1977
56 023	30 March 1977	11 July 1977
56 024	30 March 1977	15 June 1977
56 025	18 April 1977	05 July 1977
56 026	18 April 1977	15 July 1977
56 027	07 July 1977	19 September 1977
56 028	07 July 1977	14 September 1977
56 029	07 July 1977	12 September 1977
56 030	19 August 1977	21 October 1977

Even when the first locomotive, 56 001, did emerge from the works of Electroputere at Craiova in Romania, it was in primer. Photograph dated 31st March 1976.

BRUSH B600

The conditions which had to be endured with designing and building the locomotives were the worst. Delivering components to Romania and locomotives to Britain were hardly better. Weather, language barriers, different cultures and working practices all conspired to make conditions almost impossible. To add to the confusion, a disastrous earthquake hit the Bucharest and Craiova areas of Romania and it was a miracle that the locomotives remained on the trestles in the Erecting Shop. In many ways the delivery of the locomotives became something of a miracle and the commissioning engineers prayed for something considerably more.

Certainly, the contract was executed in quick time, but it was at some cost in delays experienced in making them suitable for acceptance into BR stock. The table shown left indicates the time spent in achieving acceptance, but the reason for the delay of two and a half months in delivering 56 027 and succeeding locomotives to Zeebrugge is not apparent, but was caused by the serious earthquakes in Romania disrupting production.

Upon receipt at Tinsley, detailed commissioning by Brush service engineers commenced. Immediately it was clear that constructional faults and deficiencies were endemic. Standards and techniques of production and workmanship in Romania were below those found in Britain. For example, gas and water piping was used for cable conduit. Brass collars were not fitted to the ends of the piping, and worse still the ends were rough-finished and resulted in cable insulation being chafed to expose the copper wires and resulted in many earth faults in the wiring systems. Mild steel was used for air pipes, rather than copper, and many of the pipes fitted into

Number 56 001 just after arrival in Britain in 1976. The bodysides show some signs of ripple as the gloss paint catches the sunlight. The Class 47 ancestry is very evident.

BRUSH

Class 56 locomotives were found to be not interchangeable among locomotives because they had not been jig-produced, but hand fitted in situ in each locomotive despite individual drawings for each pipe. Welds were not finished properly, nor sufficiently deep in some cases, and the stressed skin of the bodysides was not finished off to the required standard, evident at certain angles by the ripples which reflected light unevenly. A team of Brush engineers was centred upon Tinsley for over a year sorting out these problems as well as the normal duties expected in commissioning locomotives. Many of the engineers commuted daily from the Loughborough area and came to know the intervening stretch of the M1 motorway well!

Number 56 001 underwent trials between Tinsley and Appleby, on the Settle and Carlisle line, during September 1976, making its inaugural run loaded with 26 HAA type hopper wagons and a brake van on the 24th between Treeton Junction (Sheffield) and Appleby. It returned later in the day, suffering from an overheated axlebox. On the 29th it was noted laid up at Tinsley depot.

On 1st and 2nd November 56 005 was towed to Loughborough in unfinished condition for viewing by members of the Institution of Mechanical Engineers (Railway Division) visiting Brush Electrical Machines Ltd. It was positioned in the former cattle loading bay of Loughborough Midland station and viewed by interested individuals, many of whom were works employees.

On 25th November 56 002 was noted hauling a train through Featherstone, east of Wakefield. By the end of that month eleven of the Class were in Britain. Numbers 56 001/4/7/8 were at Tinsley, 56 002 at Knottingley for crew training purposes, 56 003 at the Railway Technical Centre, Derby. Also at Derby, but in the works, was 56 010, and Doncaster Works held 56 005/6/9/11. By this time out of tolerance faults had been discovered in the machining of the centre axle of each bogie of the eleven locomotives and wheelsets were requiring rectification. Bogie removal took place at Stratford Works and the affected bogies were sent to the Electrical Construction Co. (ECL) at Wolverhampton, ECL being a member company of the Hawker Siddeley Group. There were instances of traction motor pinions coming loose and a whole host of other faults became apparent during the early months.

During mid-December 56 003 remained based at the RTC and was noted there on 17th and 18th. On the 17th 56 001/11 were at Doncaster Works, 56 002 at Knottingley on crew training duties, 56 004/5/7/8/9 were at Tinsley, 56 006 on crew training at Shirebrook, 56 010 at Derby Works and 56 012/3 due to be towed from Harwich on 23rd December. They were indeed noted passing through Stowmarket that day. Meanwhile, commissioning trials had continued when possible, and 56 006 had been noted on 6th December on the Treeton - Blea Moor return working. The load was twenty-six loaded hopper wagons. Two days later the same locomotive continued its test runs with a return trip between Treeton and Marsden. Before the end of the year some Class 56s were working in the Shirebrook area, albeit in pairs and with none fully accepted. Number 56 002 continued to work crew training turns, over the Knottingley line during December, and in January 1977 numbers were swelled by the addition of 56 014 to 56 020 inclusive. Deliveries were to Tinsley, but they were soon sent to Barrow Hill depot for storage until they could be dealt with, due to the continuing problems.

January also saw further trials take place on the Settle - Carlisle line to Appleby where the locomotives ran round their test train, 56 004-7 inclusive being noted on these turns. On 9th February 56 004 ventured north of Doncaster hauling a test train of thirty hopper wagons. Meanwhile, 56 001 was still on trial, being noted on the 16th hauling a train through Chesterfield and the next day hauling a train loaded with steel rails through Holbeck Junction in Leeds. Later in the month 56 001/2/8 were seen on test trains passing through Peterborough. There must have been some relief among engineers when on 25th February 56 006 was accepted into BR stock, followed three days later by 56 001-4. 56 005 joined them on 14th March, all six locomotives being allocated to Tinsley depot. Prior to these dates much effort had been expended in bringing the locomotives up to standard, various visits to Doncaster Works revealing their presence as well as other members of the class. Their first duties included mgr coal trains to High Marnham power station.

About this time rumours were circulating about existing trade union agreements with BR affecting the power rating of Class 56 locomotives. Apparently Type 5 locomotives commanded higher pay if power outputs were set on a par with that of the twenty two Class 55 Deltic locomotives and therefore the setting of Class 56 was made lower at a nominal 3,250bhp, with leeway not to exceed 3,320bhp. The fears were supposedly that of more horsepower leading to longer trains and fewer crews. Perhaps there were fears, but the official output of 3,250bhp had been laid down some time previously and no dispute resulted from the introduction of Class 56. Caution on the part of BR engineers to avoid any repetition of overstressed engines was more of a likely reason. Brush was more confident. Its brochures quoted 3,520bhp, the full output. Nonetheless, with ninety locomotives on order, BR was reported to be seeking tenders for a further eighty locomotives. Its confidence lay elsewhere.

As the summer months passed by more Romanian Class 56s were accepted into stock and more arrived in Britain.

Deliveries ceased with 56 030 in August 1977 and it became the final one to be accepted, in October. All were allocated to Tinsley depot and the commissioning period had been reduced from the seven months of 56 001 to two for 56 030. Almost no time had been saved by early delivery, but in the event the expected massive upsurge of coal traffic had not materialised, offsetting any problems in this respect. What the arrival of Class 56 did achieve was to hasten the fulfilment of the Type 5 heavy freight locomotive role and thus relieve the hard-pressed Class 47s of the heaviest duties.

The first passenger use of a Class 56 came when 56 004 had to take over the failed 10.20 Penzance-Leeds 'Cornishman' at Wincobank, Sheffield, on 22 June 1977. Class 45 number 45 022 had failed, so 56 004 took the train to Sheffield.

During the intervening period 56 008 became the first of the class to be scheduled to haul a passenger train. This occurred on Sunday 24th July when it worked the 'Melton Mowbray Pieman' special train from Barnsley to Melton Mowbray in Leicestershire, via Sheffield and Chesterfield. Melton Mowbray was chosen because it allowed passengers to visit the nearby Stapleford Park of Lord Gretton where there was a miniature railway. A headboard was placed on the locomotive and each passenger was provided with a free Melton Mowbray pork pie.

Number 56 012 standing outside Tinsley motive power depot on 20th March 1977.

A J BOOTH

Locomotives were still making the trip to Stratford Works for bogie removal and following all the commissioning trials a notable final test run for them was from Broughton Lane (Sheffield) - Peterborough and return loaded with a Pullman car and twelve bogie steel wagons carrying old bullhead rails to simulate a commercial load. On 17th June 56 001 was at the RTC at Derby, 56 010 at Doncaster Works for a power unit change, 56 019 was at Stratford DRS for bogie modifications and 56 020 was at Tinsley for repairs to derailment damage. Also at Tinsley were 56 011/3/8/25/6, for commissioning. On 2nd July, of the twenty six locomotives delivered from Romania ten were located at Tinsley, eight at Shirebrook, four at Barrow Hill, one in Doncaster Works and another at Stratford. The latter was still receiving members of the class for attention, 56 012/15-20 during the same month.

The freight duties of Class 56 were not confined to coal traffic. 56 021 was seen hauling a cement train on 17th June, just south of Sheffield Midland station. Early in August fly ash trains began to be worked by Class 56 locomotives, from Ratcliffe and Drakelow power stations to the land reclamation area at Fletton, near Peterborough, a working that continued for many years. At this time block trains of special four-wheel wagons were a familiar sight on these duties and the ash (often sufficiently hot to burn their paintwork) was discharged under pressure into the pits at Fletton. Some of the locomotives involved were ex-Doncaster Works 56 031-4.

By the end of 1977, therefore, Tinsley had its allocation of thirty Class 56s only in theory if one discounts casualties in works. Doncaster Works gained experience of the Romanian locomotives when they came in for attention, and this helped their Class 56 production line, which was building up at this time. 56 031 started to appear in recognisable form during July 1976. The fabricated body of this and sister locomotive 56 032 were noted in the works on the 11th of that month. On 3rd October the Erecting Shop, given over to building new locomotives, contained the bodies of 56 031 to 56 034, by 7th November 56 031 was almost complete and progress with 56 032-6 was being made.

No more bodies had arrived in the New Erecting Shop by 9th January 1977, but 56 031 was expected to leave the works during March. By 6th February 56 031 had progressed to the Paint Shop and 56 032 was nearing completion, with the body of 56 037 already in progress. Exactly a month later 56 031 was noted in the weigh house, still in undercoat, and 56 032 nearly completed in the New Erecting Shop. Numbers 56 033-38 were under construction.

The expected March delivery of 56 031 did not come to pass, indeed the locomotive was next expected to run trials

The first Doncaster-built Class 56, 56 031 'Merehead', in Railfreight livery, ticking over at Leicester on 30th August 1992.

M J STRETTON

from Tinsley on 26th April and was noted on this day passing through Rotherham coupled to 56 011, the pair running light. Obviously, this was a test run and the locomotive was back in Doncaster Works in time for the official handing-over ceremony, which took place there on 29th April. It was noted in the New Erecting Shop, on 1st May. The locomotive represented the first new construction to take place there for over ten years.

Difficulties existed at the works, both in the availability of skilled labour and considerable work in hand, and some components (other than the usual bought out components) were supplied from elsewhere. For example, BREL Swindon supplied radiator housings, air ducting, internal and external doors, and spillage tanks. BREL Ashford Works supplied the roof sections and BREL Eastleigh Works cab desks. Romania supplied the bogies for most of the batch, No. 56 042 being the notable exception, as will be related below. Concurrently, the Works' Value Engineering Committee examined ways of reducing construction and service costs, some of which resulted in modifications (implemented at such times as were convenient).

Some interesting asides occurred. Electroputere supplied a set of drawings for the Doncaster build via Brush and modified drawings were supplied by means of the same route. The drawings were bilingual and the English spelling on some suggests some of the Romanian draughtsmen were copying letter for letter without understanding the language. Perhaps the best of the misunderstandings appeared on the drawing of transit details showing plywood panels covering openings in the body sides and roof (of 56 001-30). The material was stated to be 'fir (tree)', presumably to distinguish from 'fur (cat)'! An inspector at Harwich re-floored his pigeon loft with discarded Romanian plywood.

Regrettably, the Romanian drawings were not up to standard. Doncaster, having made thirty contract sets of components, found that many would not fit together. Over the period of May to September 1977 Brush reinforced its Traction drawing office staff to provide an accurate set of drawings for 56 031-60 while Doncaster worked on 56 061 onwards.

At last, 56 031 was commissioned on 13th May 1977 and was sent southwards to Toton depot soon afterwards for crew training, being noted there on the 29th, the same day it was officially added to revenue-earning stock. Numbers 56 032-4 followed during July and August, 56 032 travelling down to Toton on 20th July. Crew training demands elsewhere soon diverted them away – 56 032 migrated to the West Midlands and was soon replaced by 56 033 which was used during mid-August on the 09.05 Kingsbury-Ironbridge and return while temporarily based at Saltley depot.

Back in Doncaster Works on 21st August 56 035 was in finish-painted condition, 56 036 was in the test house, 56 037 in undercoat and in the New Erecting Shop were 56 038 (complete) and 56 039-44 under construction. On 9th October 56 035 was observed in the yard painted, 56 036 in the test house also painted, while 56 037 and 56 038 (inside the paint shop) were in undercoat.

By 6th November this last pair were fully painted and construction consisted of 56 042-7. By the end of the year 56 035 was the only additional Class 56 from Doncaster to be added to stock, although the following four or five were almost ready for release, the delay presumably due to modifications resulting from running experience with those already in traffic. They entered service in the new year and by the end of February up to and including 56 041 were added to stock and allocated to Toton.

Pioneer 56 001 was a regular test locomotive and had been involved in brake test runs on the Midland Main Line being seen on 20th September 1977 between Derby and Leicester. It was noted on 23rd November at the RTC Derby, presumably between tests.

With thirty Romanian and eleven British locomotives in service some minor external differences were noticeable, partly due to variable availability of materials. The former were almost identical with each other. The latter, however, showed differences not only with the former, but also among themselves. Some of the rubber window surrounds disappeared with the Doncaster locomotives, particularly with regard to the small triangular leading side windows. Where there was a straight horizontal handrail on the cab front below the windows, on the Doncaster examples it was gently curved. With the Doncaster locomotives a diagonal mesh arrangement was fitted to the large body side air intake apertures, replacing the previous vertical/horizontal mesh arrangement. 56 031/2 continued the recessed vertical handrails which flanked the cab doors, but from 56 033 to 56 055 they were not recessed. 56 031 displayed the distinctive cowls around the buffer beam areas, and so did 56 032, but commencing with 56 033 much of this arrangement was dispensed with, leaving a residue consisting of the upper horizontal lip portion. 56 055 was the last to have this feature. Doncaster Works fitted its small rectangular works plate to 56 031, in the unusual position of on the side of the cowls, but did not fit works plates at all on 56 032. 56 033, which now revealed bracing formerly covered by the cowls, continued the lack of works plate trend which ceased when 56 042 appeared with two fitted to the cab sides below the side windows. There was one on each side of the locomotive, on each left hand cab.

From about 56 046 oval buffer heads replaced the former standard circular pattern, presumably because Class 56s were not likely candidates for passing over marshalling yard humps, so the vertical portions were not necessary and probably interfered with good access to the equipment on the buffer beam. The horizontal portions would be necessary due to the severe curvature of track sometimes encountered in colliery and power station environments.

Another difference, affecting 56 031-6 only, was the omission of the kick plate below the cab doors.

Some of these differences may be attributable to the activities of the Doncaster Works Value Engineering Committee, but others are questionable alterations or omissions.

Number 56 022 was involved in a collision during October 1977, being noted at March with a damaged cab on the 26th en route for Stratford Works. Then 56 020 was the first reported Class 56 on Western Region lines when it hauled a train of coal hopper wagons to Didcot power station on 21st November. Testing continued on Class 56 locomotives. On 21st January 1978 56 033 hauled a test train consisting of eleven empty air-braked coaches from Duddeston carriage sidings to Basford Hall, and return. Before the train returned the locomotive had to be turned because the tests required that one cab only should be used for what were described as 'cab instrumentation and riding tests'. 56 036 soon joined 56 001 at the RTC Derby and a trio of test locomotives was made when brand new 56 042 arrived, mounted on bogies of a new design described as CP1. This new design was initiated by BR, before the advent on British metals of the CP2 (fitted to all the other Class 56s). 56 042 had been built by February 1978 and was completed that month.

The CP1 bogie was designed with savings in manufacturing and running costs in mind and as part of a continuing development process, which ideally would result in a standard design of bogie.

It was manufactured as a mild steel fabricated unit using box sections, but with steel castings being used for transoms, which in turn incorporated the traction motor mountings. Secondary suspension between the bogie and underframe of the locomotive was provided by means of flexicoil springs affixed directly to the solebar. Traction links transmitted traction and braking forces between the bogie and body, and also minimized weight transfer effects. The primary suspension between the axles and bogie frame was formed of a rolling rubber ring, which provided lateral stiffness and allowed wheel set yaw. It also replaced the hitherto conventional horn guide arrangement. Coil springs provided vertical suspension stiffness. Floating bearings on the centre axles permitted good negotiation of small radius track curves in collieries and power stations, particularly the former. It appeared somewhat different from the CP2 bogie, mainly because on the latter much of the brake gear, particularly the cylinders and linkages, was mounted on the outer part of the frame and obscured it. The CP1 bogie showed many advantages over the CP2, but they were insufficient to warrant conversion of all the Class 56 locomotives.

Testing lasted some considerable time, long after it had been accepted and the design refined into the CP3 bogie used on Class 58, the heavy freight locomotive design which succeeded Class 56. Number 56 042 was never fitted with any other bogies and ran its whole life with the CP1 type. It was during the same year as 56 042 appeared that the development of the Class 58 concept became more widely known. Meanwhile 56 042 was observed on 10th July during tests conducted between Toton and Brent on a Welbeck-Northfleet train. One of the RTC test cars was included in it, and after uncoupling the car and 56 042 only returned to Derby.

Number 56 034 spent some days at Coalville on trial – the first instance of a long association between the class and the depot. Then, in May 1978 regular appearances were made with Class 56 locomotives, including 56 037/8/40, taking over duties from pairs of Class 20s and single Class 47s. Deliveries from Doncaster continued through the 56 04X series, and on 2nd April 1978 Nos 56 044-53 were in the works, with 56 048-53 under construction. On 14th May present were 56 047-54, 4th June 56 046-56 and 3rd September 56 048-57. The pace was not quick by any standard, but rather gradual. Meanwhile, members of the class continued to stray further

afield, 56 043 being discovered at Reading on 7th May. The 125th Anniversary of Doncaster Works was celebrated by an open day held on 18th June 1978, and among the numerous exhibits on show was sparkling brand new 56 047.

During August 1978 56 036 was repainted at Stratford Works into a striking new livery of Corporate blue with large body side double arrow logos, large running numbers, yellow-painted cabs (extending back to the rear door surround) relieved by black window surrounds, and grey roof. Known affectionately as 'large logo blue' to many railway enthusiasts over the ensuing years, this attractive livery was applied to 56 036 experimentally at the behest of the Railway Design Panel in a conscious effort to improve the appearance of locomotives. Concurrently, similar efforts were being made on other items of rolling stock. The locomotive soon attracted attention and was a familiar sight in the East Midlands for a while before moving to Cardiff.

Class 56 was at the centre of a manning dispute by footplate staff of ASLEF, the issue attracting the attention of the national press during the summer of 1978. The Railway was seeking to introduce single manning of the locomotives, but the union was adhering to agreements and wished to retain two-man crews. 56 040 was sent down to Willesden and on 30th August was inspected by an ASLEF Committee. The single-manning issue was resolved eventually when the two sides reached a new agreement to single man locomotives.

Before 1978 closed some reallocation of Class 56 locomotives occurred as their duties spread, Toton losing 56 031-4 to Tinsley. The former, however, gained new locomotives from Doncaster, deliveries reaching 56 053 by the end of the year. Present at Doncaster Works on 3rd December were 56 052-60. Tinsley had thirty-four Class 56s, covering twenty-eight daily-diagrammed workings and allowing for the remaining six locomotives to be serviced and repaired. The nominal allocation around the district was Tinsley (four), Barrow Hill (five plus one spare), Worksop (two), Shirebrook (ten), Wath (three) and Doncaster (two plus one spare). Life at Tinsley was not without its moments, as demonstrated by 56 003 on 19th December, when it ran away through buffer stops and nearly ventured onto the nearby motorway link road. Master and slave shunting locomotive combination No. 13 003 was used to haul the errant locomotive back onto the track. Runaways also occurred on 21st April 1979 and 5th August 1981. At the end of August 1981 BR announced that a 'safety loop' of track would be built to turn future runaways away from the road.

Various reports of 56 001 being at the RTC Derby continued. On 25th March 1979 Doncaster Works held 56 058-66 and was nearing completion of its first contract and beginning the second order for thirty locomotives placed in August 1976. Numbers 56 054-60 were delivered to Toton during the first six months of the year and by the time the last of the contract had been completed more detail changes were apparent. From 56 056 a new design of 'all-steel' cab was introduced, dispensing with the valance over the buffer beam completely, leaving a clear cut lower edge around the whole cab. Further changes saw the lamp irons move from the buffer casings to the lower portion of the cab front itself. The marker and tail lights were no longer recessed and most noticeable was the revised arrangement for housing the twin warning horns. Gone was the flush pattern, replaced by a slightly prominent rectangular design, which increased the meshed portion to the whole panel area. Also from 56 056 the hand rails adjacent to the cab doors changed pattern from round section to a flat profile and the leading outer ones reached further down than the inner. Some sources report that 56 059/60 had aluminium alloy cabs in the new style, rather than all steel. The new cab also reduced multi-radius curves to a minimum and produced a much 'sharper' appearance. Certainly, the junction between the domed cab roof and the vertical portions of the cab walls was more pronounced. Due to accident damage some of the Romanian locomotives later received replacement cabs of this pattern. From 56 060 the red diamond coupling code was displayed on the nose of Class 56s from new, one diamond being painted on each side of the horn grille.

During this time training of Immingham depot crews commenced and was still underway in May, with 56 013 and 56 022 working oil trains. Other extended duties reached London and included 56 040 being used as a maintenance training locomotive at Cricklewood and 56 049 a driver training locomotive, with the Brent-Stewartby rubbish trains being popular for training purposes. Elsewhere, Class 56s were daily satisfying the needs of Didcot power station, supplying it with coal in six daily mgr turns.

On 10th June 1979 Doncaster Works production was working on 56 060-9 and noted in the weigh shop yard was returned 56 042. In July came the transfer of 56 036/7 to Cardiff Canton depot, with the prospect of a further allocation of ten or twelve examples, some of which were earmarked for working in pairs on the heavy Port Talbot-Llanwern iron ore trains. 56 036 arrived there on the 2nd and was joined by its companion the following day. Fitter and driver training followed and soon they could be seen on steel coil trains. On 25th July BR ran the first Port Talbot-Llanwern Steelworks iron ore train to be hauled by Class 56 locomotives, with 56 036 and 56 035 at its head. This test train consisted of twenty-seven loaded bogie rotary tippler wagons owned by the British Steel Corporation, with a total payload of 2,079 tonnes and a gross trailing weight of 2,740 tonnes. The journey length was forty-six miles and following this successful test run six Class 56s were based in the Cardiff Division providing motive power for regular workings. Transfers of 56 033/7/8/40/1/3 soon followed. Prior to the introduction of Class 56 three English Electric Type 3 locomotives of Class 37 were required to haul these trains, which were the heaviest on BR. In some ways one has cause to reflect that already double heading was being introduced, albeit in one instance, with the latest motive power available. Within a few short years BR would be facing similar changing circumstances on a wider scale.

The final order for Class 56s, placed in August 1977, envisaged that the latest example would be 56 170, but with the advent of the aforementioned Class 58 project the order was curtailed by thirty-five to 135, the balance to form the first examples of the new class. Derby Works was to continue to manufacture bogies for locomotives to 56 090, but thereafter Crewe Works was to supply bogies for the remainder.

On 1st August 56 050, piloting Class 47 327, made the first penetration into North Kent with a coal train to Northfleet.

Another, 56 040, with a Blue Circle coal train, ventured into this area on 18th August. Regular duties between Toton and Northfleet commenced in the October.

On Monday 17th December 56 065 was waiting at Crewe due to travel north into Scotland to undergo trials on Hunterston-Ravenscraig iron ore trains. It was due to travel light, but an unexpected duty befell it when a Class 47 hauling the Euston-Inverness 'Clansman' failed north of Crewe at Winwick. Number 56 065 was sent ahead to act as pilot to Wigan and in the event it hauled the train to Carlisle and was diverted to Newcastle upon Tyne and Edinburgh. There it was detached and made its way to Ravenscraig. The trials took place during the week ending 22nd December and involved trains made up of rotary tippler wagons of 100 tonnes each, formed into rakes of twenty-one, although 56 065 hauled only fourteen.

In the meantime Doncaster Works was proceeding with its gradual production of Class 56s. On 4th November 56 066-78 were in production, with shortages of materials holding up progress on 56 067-72. By the end of the year deliveries had reached 56 071, all of which were allocated to Toton depot. From 56 061 there was a return to the straight version of the horizontal handrail on cab fronts and below there appeared a larger headlight. From either 56 063 or 56 064 the former single skin glass reinforced plastic domed cab roof was replaced by a double skin, single moulded version. Cab doors, previously fabricated, were by now cast in aluminium and the former aluminium cab desk was replaced by one of glass reinforced plastic.

It was intended that twelve Class 56s should be fitted with remote control equipment using the inductive loop system, but initially (and only as it transpired) 56 073/4 were so fitted. This fitting was part of a scheme involving such possible use at Eggborough power station and was installed to facilitate remote control of coal unloading operations. One aerial was mounted under the bogies and another at cantrail level. Orange flashing lights were mounted on the front of the cab roofs immediately above the central window pillar to make the locomotives recognisable. The equipment previously had been fitted to 47 277 and 47 373. Extended trials were conducted, but the equipment was not retained because advances in radio control rendered the remote control equipment obsolete. Nonetheless some progress was made and later members of the class (56 116-35) were built new with all the necessary wiring in place to accept remote control equipment. Transponders were also fitted to all the Healey Mills locomotives (56 020/9, 31-4, 73/4) in connection with the in-motion weighing system at Drax power station that allowed the slow-speed passage of trains to continue through the weighbridge unhindered. This experiment was a forerunner of the Automatic Vehicle Identification system which was fitted to mgr wagons and coal traffic locomotives.

That troubles had been experienced with Class 56 was common knowledge on the railway and within the railway industry in general. The newspapers had long dropped these troubles as no longer newsworthy and never acknowledged the fact that much painstaking and noteworthy work had gone into making matters right.

This was left to railway engineers and subsequently, the objective reporting of the railway magazines. The advantages of Class 56 over Class 47 were correctly acknowledged and the initial problems concerning the Romanian examples were detailed but further problems were brought to a wider attention.

For example, availability for traffic duties had been set at 82% with 77% as an initial starting target, but only 70% had been achieved during the early part of 1977. This had increased to 82%, with a renewed target of 80%, but winter conditions of 1978/9 had reduced actual availability to 70%, thereafter attaining the new target. Another feature, which failed to come up to expected standards was that of cab air conditioning. This had the intention of providing a more comfortable and consistent environment for crews and was recommended by the Chief Inspecting Officer of Railways during the design stage. Indeed, the feature was applied concurrently to the High Speed Trains, but did not translate well when applied to the different cab construction of Class 56, which contained metal rather than the well-insulated glass reinforced plastic conditions of the former. The preset constant temperature was fine in theory, but did not cater for the differing needs of the individual and drivers used to an adjustable system of heat control tended to make amends where possible. Overheating was a problem under certain climatic conditions and the equipment could not be turned off, so an off position was provided retrospectively. The bad winter of 1978/9 brought temporary arrangements in the shape of underseat heaters, ex-Class 24s, and long term remedies of 60 Watt heaters in the driver's safety-device pedal and 500 Watt heaters under each seat. The knee-level air vent was blanked off in favour of a vent placed at an upper level. Experimental work, providing cab heating by engine coolant was conducted on 56 067. These provisions and more thermal insulation were provided on 56 061-90, and from 56 091 onwards pressure ventilation with heating and re-circulation only was fitted, full air conditioning being recognised as impracticable. Electric heaters were provided for pre-heating only.

Engine-exhaust bellows gave trouble and various methods of construction and different materials were tried with varying results, but finally stainless steel bellows provided the solution.

The loss of engine coolant was regarded as the most severe source of trouble at the time, with 'vast amounts' of expensive anti-freeze being lost mainly due to a proprietary coupling used in the pipe between the upper coolant gallery and the cylinder heads.

The CP2 bogies were a variant of the Swiss SLM design, well-proven elsewhere on the European Continent. Unexpected problems arose when irregular noises occurred during running. Investigations showed that bogie components were making irregular contact, and that this was caused by inconsistencies within the hand-wound coil springs making them close prematurely. The remedy was to replace them with more consistent machine-wound springs. Friction dampers, fitted inside the springs, were replaced by viscous dampers, to reduce fierceness of operation. Even with these alterations, not all the problems were cured.

Excessive leakage of gear lubricant occurred through the traction motor gear case sealing joints and these had to be refurbished. The traction motors also suffered from an ingress of water into the suspension tubes which caused corrosion of the bearings during transit from Romania on spare bogies destined for some of the first thirty Doncaster locomotives. New bearings were provided.

Several traction motor blower fans disintegrated, and this was partly due to flimsy construction of the blower stand, so this was later stiffened. Vibration caused a high failure rate of lamp bulbs and fire detector units and partly caused fracturing of the hydrostatic oil system tanks.

Loose tyres and Gibson securing rings were found on several locomotives, but the problem was alleviated by improved fitting standards. In the long term, monobloc disc wheels were fitted as standard. The first examples started to appear on the British-built bogies fitted to locomotives 56 061 onwards. With this change came also an increase in wheel diameter, from 1,143mm maximum to 1,150mm.

During the first instances of Romanian locomotives entering Doncaster Works for classified repairs more constructional deficiencies were discovered. These included hand-filed axle wheel seats and series welding faults. the latter including runs not made continuous where necessary and a lack of full penetration welding, which resulted in effective creation of inbuilt cracks with the potential consequences of reduced fatigue life expectancy. Certainly it was not a good situation. It mainly concerned the Romanian locomotives and components, the latter causing problems within the Doncaster batch. It took a lot of dedication and patience to rectify, but the locomotives were brought up to standard in the long term, although some problems either continued or appeared later. Certainly the issue was controversial.

Progress at Doncaster Works on 17th February 1980 was as follows:- 56 073 complete, 56 074/5 complete but in primer finish, 56 076-8 cabs fitted, 56 079-83 body shells and 56 084 body shell under construction. The schedule was to have up to and including 56 089 completed by the end of the year, with seventeen locomotives each for the successive two years. Training on Class 56s at Healey Mills depot commenced at the end of April and on 11th May fifteen of the class were transferred there for work on the Knottingley mgr trains, where they took over most of the duties. A similar number of Class 47s were displaced. Numbers 56 021-32/4/73/4 were transferred, with 56 020 joining them during July.

From January to June 1980 56 072-7 were delivered from Doncaster, 56 072 going to Toton and the remainder to Tinsley depot. On 8th June 56 079 was complete and almost ready to join them. Number 56 080 was complete, but in primer, 56 081 was in the Paint Shop in primer and 56 082-8 were in the New Erecting Shop under construction. Body shell 56 089 was in the Paint Shop prior to despatch to the Erecting Shop.

Almost new 56 077 participated in the 'ROCKET 150' cavalcade of locomotives which took place on Sunday 25th May at Rainhill in celebration of the 150th anniversary of the Liverpool & Manchester Railway. It pushed the Advanced Passenger Train, a fellow mobile exhibit in the cavalcade, but on 22nd May had towed three steam locomotives from York to Bold Colliery, near Rainhill rather than travel there light.

On 29th September the first thirty-four-wagon train of iron ore from Port Talbot to Llanwern was hauled by 56 037 and 56 041, following on from the exploits of 56 035/6 in July 1979. The leading locomotive, 56 037, was adorned with a large notice proclaiming it to be '3,304 tonnes BRITAIN'S HEAVIEST TRAIN', what was not apparent was that this included the two locomotives, although obviously the diesel engines had to provide power for the whole combination.

On 29/30th July 56 007 and 56 018 were involved in tests between Worksop and Barnetby. They hauled a train of sixty-eight mgr coal wagons during which brake tests were conducted. As in previous tests operations proved constrained because of limited siding facilities at Barnetby, which prevented the locomotives running round the train.

On 11th November 56 081, only a few months in traffic, was derailed at Cottam Power Station, while hauling a train of empty coal hopper wagons. The locomotive remained upright, just, and was rescued two days later by two 75 tonne breakdown cranes sent from as afar as Toton and March, the Tinsley and Doncaster cranes being unavailable at the time.

Doncaster had in progress on 12th October 56 085-94, and also held 56 014 awaiting a decision regarding high repair costs to accident damage. Number 56 084 was a notable example of the recent outshoppings, being conspicuous because of its livery, large logo blue, which adopted that applied experimentally to 56 036. The livery became standard for the class (and also other classes) and although new construction continued the livery, it was some time before repaints of earlier examples appeared in quantity. 56 084 was noted on 16th October entering Newcastle upon Tyne Central Station double-heading a passenger train with a Class 47. On 30th November it was noted back in the works, having accumulated only eighteen hours running.

Towards the end of the year news broke that BREL Crewe was to build 56 091-135 to enable Doncaster Works to commence production of the new Class 58 locomotives unhindered. It transpired that it was to be 56 116-35 instead, with the first one due out for March 1982 and the last one being scheduled for September 1983.

Deliveries did not reach 56 089 by the end of the year as expected but fell short by two, with 56 088/9 following in January 1981. All were allocated to Tinsley depot, with 56 086 first going to the RTC, Derby, on loan. Number 56 090 followed in February, but then there came a lapse in deliveries. It may well be that this was caused by the modifications which were incorporated into 56 091 onwards. As related above, this locomotive saw the application of a pressure ventilation system, which also supplied cab heating derived from the engine coolant. This was applied as a direct result of experiments that were undertaken on 56 067. Electric preheaters were also provided, though they were not fitted to 56 067. A small grille on the cabside revealed which locomotives were so fitted, but for the record 56 091-135 received the equipment.

On 5th April 1981 Doncaster Works was working on 56 091-9 and also in for attention were 56 042, for bogie modifications, and 56 014 which had been out of traffic with accident damage since the previous October and had received a new No. 2 cab. The latter locomotive was due out in the June, but was destined for a much longer stay in the works. By 10th May the new construction present had increased by one bodyshell, 56 100, and 56 101/2 body shells in the Fabrication Shop already being assembled. 56 091 finally left the works in May and was scheduled for test work at Derby RTC, before going into service proper, based at Tinsley depot.

Until this time no Class 56 had been named. Then on 2nd June 1981 Cardiff-based 56 038 was named 'Western Mail' at a ceremony at Cardiff Central Station by Mr Duncan Gardner, editor of the newspaper after which the locomotive was named. More proposed namings were announced, but in some cases there was a delay before it was carried out, depending upon what was being celebrated. The next naming was that of 56 037 on 23rd July when it became 'Richard Trevithick', after the famous engineer, at Merthyr. To complete the ceremony the locomotive hauled a short train consisting of a brake van and a well wagon bearing a replica of Trevithick's locomotive 'Penydarren' of 1804. It retraced the route of the original locomotive from Merthyr to Abercynon. This naming was followed by that of 56 035 which became 'Taff Merthyr' on 9th November, this naming ceremony taking place at Taff Merthyr colliery.

On 14th July 56 092-101 were in Doncaster Works although officially 56 092/3 went into traffic the previous month. They were not present on 26th July, but 56 094 was, together with 56 095-105 which were in progress. Officially, 56 094 went into traffic during July, but was noted at Doncaster on 2nd August. Numbers 56 095/6 officially went into traffic during August and were followed in September by 56 097/8.

On 18th October 56 014 was still under repair at Doncaster, awaiting a cab roof. On the same day 56 099-106 were in progress and 56 098 was also noted on the works. Work had progressed to 56 101-12 by 30th November and by the end of the year deliveries, all to Tinsley, had reached 56 103. Then came a pause in deliveries until February 1982. On 22nd November 1981 56 075/6 were transferred to Gateshead depot and the latter commenced working from Blyth Cambois on the 26th. More Class 56s followed from Tinsley depot.

At Doncaster production of the first Class 58s was already underway, somewhat slowly at first as one might expect. On 10th January 56 104-12 were in progress. On 16th February it was 56 105-12, with the much-delayed 56 014 actually on test. By 23rd March it was still the same batch, but with the members slightly more advanced and 56 014 missing, presumed either out on a test run or in traffic at last. This locomotive, still Tinsley-based, hauled a railway enthusiasts' special from London Bridge to Birmingham on 7th August, with 56 003 (also of Tinsley) hauling it for the return journey. Tinsley depot lent 56 013 and 56 091 to Westbury for crew training purposes, both arriving on 27th February.

Number 56 040 was named 'Oystermouth' at Swansea on 25th March 1982 to mark the 175th Anniversary of the Oystermouth Railway, the world's first passenger-carrying railway, then within three months, on 14th June 1982 56 074 was named 'Kellingley Colliery', the first naming of an ER allocated Class 56. It was so named jointly by the then Chairman of the NCB Sir Derek Ezra and BR Chairman, Sir Peter Parker to mark the importance of the colliery as one of the first serving the mgr system. Another naming in 1982 was that of 56 076 on 8th September, when it became 'Blyth Power' in celebration of the association of mgr workings through Blyth Power Station. It took its first load of coal after naming, from Dawdon Colliery to the power station the same day. 56 104 entered traffic during February 1982 and was followed by the next three in numerical order at the rate of one a month, all going to Tinsley depot. 56 104/5 worked light to South Wales during early May on loan for tests on Port Talbot-Llanwern iron ore trains. In exchange, for the loan period, 56 037/8 were sent to the ER.

Other than several relatively minor accidents Class 56s had escaped really serious mishap. This was brought to an end during the early morning of 30th July when 56 004 was involved in a head on collision near Immingham, South Humberside, while hauling a train of loaded hopper wagons. At just after 08.15 the train was descending the gradient towards Immingham, just past Eastfield Road bridge, when it crashed head-on with the leading locomotive of a double-headed train of tankers loaded with motor spirit from the Conoco oil refinery and bound for Kingsbury. The two crews jumped from their cabs before impact and escaped the collision. The tanker train was hauled by two Brush Type 2s, 31 314 and 31 192. The former locomotive was locked into 56 004, the cab fronts being crushed and flattened by the impact. Thankfully, good locomotive design prevented the localised effects from being more serious than they otherwise would have been. There was further damage, however. The trailing cab of the Class 56 received damage when the leading hopper wagons piled up behind and emptied their load over it. The second Brush Type 2 received body and cab damage. The crash site took days to clear, partly due to the delicate operation of removing the tank wagons and fuel from a damaged wagon and also minimising the fire risk. Limited traffic on the line resumed on 2nd August and the locomotives were parted and re-railed the following day. Removal to Immingham depot for storage took place on the 4th. They were later taken to Doncaster Works. 31 314 was withdrawn and the fate of 56 004 hung in the balance for a while, but eventually it was decided that the somewhat expensive repairs should proceed. It lay at Doncaster, still untouched, on 21st November but had reached the Erecting Shop by mid-February 1983. Progress was painfully slow. It was still inside the works during the early months of 1984 and was observed on test on 20th May of that year and left the works the following month, having spent twenty-two months out of traffic.

The next new locomotive into traffic, 56 108, broke the long-standing trend of either Tinsley or Toton as the first allocation, by being allocated new to Healey Mills depot. This occurred in June 1982, by which time Doncaster Works had under construction 56 115, the last of its allotted build. 56 109 was delivered to Tinsley two months later, after which the pace settled to one a month to the end of the year, not the most impressive of outputs. This left 56 114 and 56 115, which completed the run in January 1983, this latter having been rolled out of the shops early in December. All were provisionally allocated to Healey Mills except for 56 112 which was allocated to Tinsley. In the event the intention was not carried out and all went to Tinsley.

Meanwhile, Crewe Works had commenced work on its

batch of twenty Class 56s. By early February 1982 56 116 was under construction and the next two were recognisable by the end of the month. During the period from March to August 56 116-9 were in progress, but then three more were added by late September to reach 56 124. On 25th November 56 116 was noted on test and was delayed there because of problems. On 9th January it was still in the yard and on 2nd February was noted back in the shops, but still in undercoat finish. By this date 56 117 had made considerable progress and overtaken it, being noted in finish paint condition awaiting trial runs out on the main line. Both were released from Crewe on 13th March, intending to go into traffic from Healey Mills depot.

They were found to be troubled by various faults and returned to the works for rectification, 56 116 being expected to take longer to put right. This pair sported at least two external visual differences to previous Class 56s, with the large air intake grille and surrounds picked out in grey and the longer cab side handrails being fitted with the extension pointing upwards instead of downwards. Presumably the latter was a mistake because the ensuing locomotives conformed to the Doncaster arrangement. The grey embellishment was continued. 56 118 was finish painted during February and 56 119 was on test, with 56 128 the latest construction to be started. Number 56 118 went to Tinsley in April, 56 119/20 in May and 56 121 followed in June.

During the summer months driver training took place at Hither Green and Tonbridge depots. During this period, trains started to enter the south east from other regions in July. In particular, was one from Westbury and one from Mountsorrel. An outward working was a cement train from Malling.

Numbers 56 122/3 were delivered in July and on the last day of that month 56 125 was noted partly painted in the Paint Shop and 56 126 in primer finish. Inside the Erecting Shop were 56 126-30 in varying stages of construction. On 26th August 56 124 was out on the main line on a test run to Shrewsbury and back. It was delivered the next month.

A flurry of naming occurred in the autumn of 1983. First was 56 031, named 'Merehead' on 16th September, second was 56 032 which became bi-lingual 'Sir De Morgannwyg/County of South Glamorgan' on 14th October and thirdly on the 24th, 56 124 which became 'Blue Circle Cement' complete with the blue circle logo on a square plaque mounted above each nameplate. The latter kept its name until September 1989.

At the end of September Class 56 depot allocation ranged from Tinsley and Toton to Bristol, Cardiff, Healey Mills and Gateshead, with the first-listed having the largest allocation.

By 9th October work was already in progress on 56 133 and soon afterwards 56 125 left the works destined for Tinsley depot to join its immediate predecessors.

On 5th November 56 126/7 were complete, the former leaving later in the month and the latter in December, both going to Tinsley. 56 128 was in primer finish, 56 129-32 under construction and 56 133/4 being fabricated. 56 128 left the works during December, being delivered to Tinsley. There were just seven locomotives left to complete at the end of 1983, and in theory the last deliveries should have been quick, but this was not to be. 56 129 was delivered to Tinsley during January

1984 and by the middle of that month 56 130/1 were tested but not painted and 56 132-4 were awaiting power units and 56 135, the final member of the class, was already in progress. After some delay 56 130/1 were delivered to Gateshead depot in April, leaving on works 56 132 in completed condition and 56 133-5 under construction. 56 132/3 were on test on 20th May and on 17th June 56 134 was newly completed and in primer paint and 56 135 under construction. June saw 56 132 go to Gateshead depot.

On 2nd June 56 133 was named 'Crewe Locomotive Works' at a special ceremony held during the mid-afternoon of the works Open Day. This locomotive was the only one in complete condition at the time. The locomotive went into traffic during July, based at Gateshead.

The two remaining locomotives were noted on 27th July as 56 134 completed, but still in undercoat and 56 135 almost complete but expected to be finished in the new Railfreight livery. On 1st September they remained unfinished, 56 134 was still not in blue livery and 56 135 was described as 'almost complete'.

Later that month the penultimate locomotive received its final coats of paint and left Crewe, bound for Gateshead. It was the last new Class 56 locomotive to receive the 'large logo' blue livery. The leisurely pace continued; 56 135 was noted on test on 14th October and was noted on 1st November fully painted in the new livery of grey and red, ready for despatch. It was finally allocated to Tinsley on 4th November. Class 56 was complete.

During October 56 042, the member of the class fitted with the experimental CP1 bogies, was noted on various test runs on the West Coast Main Line north of Crewe, following modifications carried out at Derby. During the latter part of that month and the following month it was running on the North Wales line. It often hauled a test train comprising of Laboratory coaches Nos 1 and 23, and Mk3 coaches 977089/4, all from Derby RTC. It is thought that the bogie testing programme was finally completed during the winter and that the locomotive went into normal traffic without on-board test equipment. The experimental bogies remained with the locomotive, presumably to gain long-term experience with them.

On 13th December 56 035 'Taff Merthyr' caught fire at Hereford while held for attention to faults which had developed while hauling the 19.45 Pengam-Glasgow freightliner train. The local fire service was called to attend to the fire.

By the end of 1984, therefore, Class 56 locomotives were a familiar sight around the country on mgr trains, hauling coal or fly ash, block trains of oil, aggregates, cement, waste, iron ore and steel in various forms. They were no strangers to freightliner trains and often deputised for failed locomotives on other duties. Early in 1982 they had extended their duties to Westbury and in time took over the movement of stone out of the Somerset quarries. Then, later in the year, came the transportation of fly ash from Fiddlers Ferry Power Station to Llandudno Junction in North Wales for use as a road base on the new A55 trunk road, which in places caused the main line to Holyhead to be re-aligned. Certainly for road travellers, the A55 improvements have proved well worth

their somewhat extended efforts over the years. Oil traffic in West Wales saw the introduction of Class 56 locomotives the following year. It is interesting to note that in most cases locomotives were delivered new to either Tinsley or Toton and later if new areas of working were initiated these depots supplied locomotives, second hand as it were.

The initial troubles experienced with the Romanian examples all but disappeared, although some troubles persisted on both these and the British built locomotives. The design was now ten years old and already replaced by Class 58 for new construction of Type 5 heavy freight locomotives.

Afoot were moves by one of BR's aggregate customers to raise reliability stakes not only above those of Class 56, but also that of Class 58. Nevertheless, it has to be stated that Class 56 was demonstrating its worth on BR, though not always at ideal availability. Its equipment generally was proving reliable, particularly the alternator and its associated equipment and the traction motors. The monocoque body shell, as ever, was proving that its immense strength was the vital centre of good design and the engine, despite some continuing problems, very capable. On some workings they worked in tandem, but although triple heading had been part of the original specification of capability it was only used in exceptional cases such as locomotive failure.

Events From 1985

Problems with the turbochargers occurred, limiting their lives to around three to four years. Number 56 051 was fitted with a Brown-Boveri design and for comparison 56 001 received a Napier. The latter was despatched to Westbury in April 1985 and used on the heavy stone trains. After about a year some success appears to have been met with the Napier blower and in August 1986 56 038 came out of Crewe Works following an overhaul similarly equipped, although no trouble appears to have been experienced with the Brown-Boveri blower.

The new livery for Railfreight began to spread among Class 56 locomotives that had been through works for attention. It was smart when new, but tended to dull in service, to its detriment. 56 006 was the first to be repainted, during March 1985. Behind the new livery lay the increasing march of sectorisation, the business-led railway policy which was being moulded in accordance with Conservative Government policy which itself demanded greater efficiency and cost consciousness, and promised less funding from government sources. It also led to sharper management in pursuit of more control of the destiny of the various sectors and sub-sectors of the railway. The whole process was gradual and evolved, gaining momentum during 1986. It may be added that customer demands also shaped the destiny of Railfreight during the mid and late 1980s, and in doing so pointed a finger at the bad availability of Class 56 in certain areas and on certain workings. The WR, and its stone traffic, were particularly poorly-served by the class during the mid 1980s. Failures aroused the local radio stations and provided news items on a regular basis. Elsewhere, workings were disrupted by the notorious miners' dispute and many a Class 56 strayed away from its usual territory. Many more found themselves without work as a consequence. The dispute did no-one any favours – the strike was ill-led and engineered from a distance by discreet Government policy. After almost a year it ended in March 1985. Long term, the railway lost much coal traffic and the mining industry slid into decline.

Early in May the WR received 56 034, after overhaul, in the new Railfreight livery. Then on 5th June it was officially named bi-lingually 'Castell Ogwr/Ogmore Castle' at Bridgend station. On 9th July 56 075 was named 'West Yorkshire Enterprise' and on 29th October 56 135 became 'Port of Tyne Authority'.

Availablility climbed to 70% during the year and further improvement was sought as Ruston engineers sorted out the engine problems. The figure had dropped to around 55%. The various problems co-existed and one persistent problem was that of leakages of engine coolant and of oil from the hydrostatic system, often causing engine failure. A determined 'Stop Leaks' campaign was initiated to target the causes of the leaks and rectify them. It met with success, although with 135 locomotives to be dealt with it did take a long time to implement fully. By 1988 availability was back to 70% and often higher.

The advent of the privately owned Class 59 locomotives was to have a lasting impact upon heavy freight locomotive policy of BR, from 1986, their year of introduction to Foster Yeoman service. Certainly their more specific design features such as heavy freight haulage at lower speed and creep control made a lasting impression. In fairness to Class 56 ten years had seen some proverbial moving of the goalposts as to what was required from a heavy freight locomotive. The American Class 59 was more in the league of 'horses for courses' and was not expected to operate at 80mph on Freightliner services. It also had the benefit of an industry which did not have to cease production for some years due to lack of orders. Continuity helped its cause and dedicated operations and repair facilities more than supported them.

By the end of 1985 over twenty Class 56s were wearing the Railfreight livery and more were on the way. One of the repaints, 56 053, was named in a ceremony at Porth, South Wales, on 17th March 1986. Once again a bi-lingual name was chosen, 'Sir Morgannwg Ganol/County of Mid Glamorgan'. Fortunately Class 56 body sides had large clear areas able to take the large nameplates.

Extra work in the Tyne & Wear area caused Gateshead's Class 56 allocation to be doubled during the middle of the year to eighteen locomotives. Further moves, part of Railfreight's dedicated maintenance plan, occurred in September when at least twenty-nine more moved south from Tinsley to Toton in preparation for the exchange for a similar number of Class 45s, prior to the introduction of the winter timetable. The move left all but three of the Romanian locomotives at Toton, which now had 56 002-28 inclusive on its books. By this time 56 001 had been at Bristol for a while, and Tinsley retained 56 029/30.

On 1st October 56 132 was named 'Fina Energy' at Petrofina's new rail facility at Sunderland. It retained this name until March 1989. Then, on 6th October 56 063 was named 'Bardon Hill' at West Drayton, nowhere near its namesake in Leicestershire, but possibly an abbreviation of Bardon Hill Group plc. The fourth and final naming of 1986

involved 56 134 which became 'Blyth Power' in November, taking its name from 56 076 as a result of the latter's move southwards to Toton from Gateshead. By mid January 1987 the allocation was in excess of eighty.

As part of the new order, Cost Effective Maintenance produced effects familiar elsewhere. One was the suspension of certain activities until accounting niceties were satisfied. This saw 56 012/95 placed in store at Toton until a chronic spare parts situation cleared. Another symptom was the exchange of components among locomotives during overhaul, rather than withdraw them from stores. The new Component Exchange Overhauls (COEs) as part of the new policy of maintenance practice, commenced officially on 1st April 1987.

Railfreight moved steadily along the path of change. By the autumn of 1987 locomotives were now allocated to sub-sectors each with its own dedicated fleet, according to the type of revenue-earning freight hauled. The first application of a dedicated fleet occurred at Leicester, in the previous May, when 56 058-64 arrived. The largest fleet in October became that of Coal in Yorkshire. The North East by this time had increased its Tyne area fleet to twenty-four. For sustained coal traffic Class 56 was in its element, that for which it was designed.

By mid 1987 56 042 had been out of traffic for almost a year. It was in Doncaster Works for attention and examination of its experimental bogies, but as they were the only pair spare parts available were minimal, so as with most unique pieces of equipment delays ensued at times of repair or maintenance. The locomotive was scheduled out of the works in mid-May and was noted at the beginning of July at Old Oak Common depot on crew training duties.

Concurrent with the events culminating in October 1987 was the introduction of the second main Railfreight livery. This has been described in previous chapters with regard to Classes 31 and 47. It reflected the changes taking place and made them more visible, which was not such a bad matter so long as one was involved with or interested in railway events. To many an outsider the new symbols were simply baffling. On the practical side, it did mean that yet another livery came into being with all the others – transition periods overlap in modern times to the extent that few are fully implemented because there is never sufficient time to do so. Privatisation was the first threat to the 1987 Railfreight livery. At the time of its introduction over sixty Class 56s were decked in the original Railfreight livery. The first member of the class to receive the 1987 livery was pioneer locomotive 56 001, wearing it in traffic during the September, one of the very first locomotives to do so and in advance of the official launching of it.

It does appear to be quite deliberate to choose either the first or last of a class for new livery treatment! With Class 58, BR repainted the last of the class, 58 050, in the new livery and of course 58 001 was the first to receive the original one.

56 131 remained in large logo blue, but lost its large running numbers in favour of the standard size! It was in this condition on 20th August when it was named 'Ellington Colliery' at Ellington combined mine in the North East of England. The naming was followed by that of 56 001 on 29th

October when it became 'Whatley' and celebrated the ARC quarries which generated much business for BR. The same day 56 095 was named 'Harworth Colliery'.

The year 1988, therefore, dawned on the new era of business sectors, one from which it appeared might evolve the distant and promised privatisation of the railways. History proved this to be illusory.

Namings continued. On 14th April 1988 56 122, resplendent in the new livery, was named 'Wilton Coalpower' to mark the completion of the changeover of Wilton Power Station, near Middlesborough, to burning coal instead of oil. This Teesside power station, owned by ICI, was the largest privately owned power station in Europe. The locomotive lost its name to 56 117 in March 1992. On 11th May 56 123 was named 'Drax Power Station' at the power station itself, and this naming was followed by 'West Burton Power Station' for 56 028 during September. The latter name remained on the locomotive until October 1992.

A spectacular accident occurred on 15th June when 56 062 of Toton careered down an embankment at speed on the Brighton line at Copyhold Junction, Haywards Heath. It was hauling a train of empty ARC stone wagons, the 09.55 Ardingly-Westbury working, and was severely damaged as it came to rest on its roof. Such was the difficulty in removing the offending locomotive that it was still there in July as details of how to remove it were worked out. The power unit was removed on 24th September to ease the final lifting and it was expected to be re-railed at the end of September. By mid-October operations had been completed and 56 062 was towed to Doncaster for repair on the 29th. Repair and return to traffic was to take several months and many of its components found their way into other Class 56s. Doncaster Works handed the locomotive back for traffic on 28th February 1989, several days ahead of schedule.

Ten years after becoming the pioneer 'large logo blue' locomotive, Cardiff-based 56 036 received the new Railfreight livery.

By the autumn many Class 56s were receiving 'cab to shore' radio telephones as part of a programme to equip both Classes 56 and 58.

On 8th December 56 039 took part in some assessment trials with privately owned 59 004 'Yeoman Challenger'. Foster Yeoman, the owners of the Class 59, lent their locomotive to the Amey Roadstone Corporation Ltd (ARC) to compare the performance of it with the theoretical performance of the newly ordered Brush Class 60 design for BR. ARC wished to assess both designs prior to ordering locomotives for their own use. The Class 56 was used behind 59 004 partly as load and partly as reserve power should it be required. The total train load, including 56 039, was 4,412 tonnes and the test train ran from Whatley Quarry to Westbury, where the Class 59 was removed. ARC required six locomotives and eventually ordered four Class 59s rather than Class 60s.

Accident victim 56 062 finally reappeared into traffic during the early part of 1989. It was a centrepiece of a spectacular show of sound and light on 21st March when it was named 'Mountsorrel' at Barrow upon Soar in Leicestershire by BRB Chairman Sir Robert Reid to mark the signing of a new contract between Railfreight and aggregates firm Redland

Roadstone. Barrow sidings were once rail-connected with the quarries at Mountsorrel but the single line track was removed and a conveyor laid instead in modern times, so this was the nearest point that the ceremony could take place.

A few miles further south, in the premises of Vic Berry of Leicester, 56 065, the first of several Class 56s to be so treated, was repainted under a special contract into the new Railfreight livery. It left on 2nd February and was replaced by 56 031 seven days later. Less than thirty of the original Corporate Blue examples remained in this livery, a total much-reduced before the end of the year.

Commencing with 56 069 and 56 080, derating of certain selected Class 56s to 2,400bhp occurred in 1989. Several reasons were given for this move, but one important one was to gain experience and assess the feasibility of the proposed Class 41 locomotive for short-haul mgr workings. Toton was involved with the necessary work on the former and Doncaster Works the latter. 56 080 was delayed due to the discovery of a major fault necessitating a replacement power unit, suitably modified. Another reason quoted was to attain a reduction in maintenance and fuel costs. It was expected that there would be no adverse effect upon haulage capacity, but there would be reduced acceleration characteristics. Number 56 090 became the third derated example – 56 107 was a further one. The area of operation was a selection of Shirebrook diagrams between Ollerton and Bevercotes Collieries and High Marnham Power Station.

Namings continued in 1989. On 18th June 56 091 was named 'Castle Donington Power Station' at a ceremony held at the Leicestershire power station. Then on 22nd June 56 012 was named 'Maltby Colliery' at that colliery, situated near Rotherham in South Yorkshire. The naming was performed by British Coal's South Yorkshire Area Director, Mr Ted Horton. The rectangular two-line nameplate bore the legend 'British COAL' in the top left-hand corner in black letters on a yellow background, which contrasted well with the remaining polished metal lettering and surround on a black background. The locomotive bore this name until May 1992.

Next in line for naming was 56 099. The name 'Fiddlers Ferry Power Station' was bestowed upon this locomotive on 15th July at the power station situated near Widnes, in Cheshire. The spelling of Fiddlers was often rendered in error as 'Fidlers' due to the abbreviated TOPS spelling!

An Eggborough eagle crest was fitted above each nameplate of 56 030 when it was named 'Eggborough Power Station'. In an official naming ceremony at the power station the nameplates were unveiled on 2nd September. Next came the naming of 56 080 on 30th October, when it became 'Selby Coalfield' at Gascoigne Wood Colliery. The nameplates were of the same pattern as those for 'Maltby Colliery'. Following the ceremony 56 080 left with an mgr train of coal bound for Drax Power Station. Final naming for 1989 was that of 56 093 on 29th November. This locomotive became 'The Institution of Mining Engineers' at Euston Station, named by Lady Haslam, wife of Sir Robert Haslam, President of the Institution.

By October 1989 Railfreight had consolidated its Class 56 operations considerably, making full use of its sub-sector locomotives in operational pools serving specific traffic requirements. These pools were allotted computer codes and it is interesting to note what they were and what they consisted of at this time:-

FAXN was the Leicester 'Construction' Pool, with locomotives based at Toton and serviced at Leicester. Member locomotives were 56 042/54/58-65/70/8/103/5/10.

FAWK was the Western Region 'Construction' Pool, with locomotives based at Cardiff and serviced at Westbury. Member locomotives were 56 001/31-41/43-6/48-53/55-7.

FECN was the Midlands 'Coal' Pool, with locomotives based at Toton and serviced at Toton and Bescot. Member locomotives were 56 002-27.

FEDN was the Yorkshire 'Coal' Pool, with locomotives based at Toton and serviced at Barrow Hill, Shirebrook, Knottingley and Healey Mills. Member locomotives were 56 028-30/47/66-9/71-7/79-99/100-4/6-11/23.

FEEN was the North East 'Coal' Pool, with locomotives based at Toton and serviced at Blyth Cambois. Member locomotives of this pool were 56 112-22/24-35.

Early in 1990 the cost-consciousness within BR, the introduction of Class 60 locomotives and recessionary trends nationally began to cut ever deeper into operations. The diesel locomotive repair programme for the April 1990 to April 1991 financial year envisaged the scheduled withdrawal of numerous locomotives of various classes. Surprising in some aspects was the inclusion of some Class 56s. The normal life-expectancy of such locomotives was thirty-five years. Initial plans earmarked 56 002/5/16/8 for withdrawal and 56 105/10 for storage, this last pair being all the more remarkable choice considering that both dated from 1982. In financial circles reasons for carrying out decisions are extremely elastic and certainly stretch the English language in doing so, euphemisms being part of the tools of the profession. Equally, contradictory moves are similarly explained. As events transpired, the policy was implemented, but did not follow the initial selection of locomotives strictly. The Romanian examples, being the oldest members of the class, were perhaps the most likely choice for withdrawal in some instances, but should any problem beset the non-standard 56 042 this naturally would become a cost-effective repair subject. During February the locomotive was lifted off its bogies at Toton and awaited its fate, stored indefinitely in unserviceable condition. It had been out of service since the previous December awaiting two replacement wheelsets. Repairing the non-standard bogies and modifying the body to accept CP2 bogies clearly were unacceptable choices in economic terms. Taking 56 042 out of service immediately reprieved 56 033 and 56 045 and provided a replacement power unit for 56 103. Either 56 059 or 56 064 were then expected to go into store. By March the list of suggested victims consisted of 56 002/5/16/8/35/41/105/10, with the last pair being reprieved within months.

On a happier note, the namings continued. At midday on 19th March 56 102 was named 'Scunthorpe Steel Centenary' at the British Steel works at Scunthorpe to celebrate a century of steelmaking there. The two-line nameplates bore the British Steel logo in the top right hand corner. Next to be named was 56 101, on 28th April at York station, receiving the name 'Mutual Improvement' to commemorate seventy years of Mutual Improvement Classes on Britain's railways. Mr Ron Fareham, former Area Train Crew Manager at Leeds, performed the unveiling.

Mid-February trials were held in Cornwall to ascertain whether or not Class 56s were suitable for working freight services in the area, in particular replacing Class 37s operating in pairs on some heavy Speedlink trains and on long distance china clay trains. 56 013 travelled south-westwards assisting a failed Class 47 for part of the journey. Tests concluded that running costs were lower and of course one Class 56 released two Class 37s for duties elsewhere, although nothing more has so far resulted from it. In July similar tests were undertaken with a view to displacing Class 20s working in pairs or quadruple on the imported coal traffic from the Gladstone Docks, Liverpool, to Fiddlers Ferry Power Station. Numbers 56 025/6 were involved in clearance tests and haulage runs and 56 014/23 haulage runs only along the route which included a 1 in 60 gradient on a curve. Regular Class 56 haulage commenced the following month, the only snag occurring when the circular buffers of 56 008 did not cope with the sharper curves around Gladstone Dock.

By mid-1990 only seven Class 56s remained in the Corporate Blue livery (56 004/8/10/20-2/6), thirteen in the original Railfreight grey livery (56 002/5/19/24/35/8/40/1/57/8/64/83/7) and ten in the red-stripe modified version of this livery (56 011/44/9/67/8/76/89/100/7/8). Large logo blue examples were 56 103/5/6/9-12/14/16-20/124/6, fifteen in all, with the remainder of the class in the 1987 Railfreight livery.

Numbers 56 083/4/6 became further examples of derated locomotives during 1990 and brought the total to nine (56 025/69/77/80/3/4/6/107/31).

Another naming, on 4th September, saw 56 077 named 'Thorpe Marsh Power Station' on site at the power station, north of Doncaster. On 6th November 56 130 was named 'Wardley Opencast' at the Tyneside site, bringing the total of named Class 56s to thirty, although the total of locomotives having been named was more because of the transfer of names among locomotives.

With more Class 60s emerging from the Falcon Works an increasingly common sight was the pairing of some of them with Class 56s as insurance against failure of the former during their initial acceptance periods. The area close to the Falcon Works and Leicester was popular, with the Mountsorrel-Radlett stone workings providing suitable loads. Later, similar pairings between Toton and Garston Dock were introduced, and when this was not the case they were often headed by pairs of Romanian Class 56s.

56 040 had its 'Oystermouth' nameplates removed during the December and ran nameless until it was reunited with them in January 1992. Only a handful of the class retained the old 'Corporate Blue' livery towards the end of 1990. The locomotives to do so were 56 004/8/10/20-2/6, just seven in total. The 'large logo' blue examples were down to fourteen,

these being 56 103/6/9-12/4/6-20/4/6. By the middle of the following year there were ten, 56 106/9-11 having been repainted. There appeared to be little attempt to repaint the Romanian locomotives into the 1987 Railfreight livery, but then some doubt remained as to what the future held for them at the time.

In February 1991 the Fletton fly ash trains ceased running after twenty-five years. They had been a familiar sight conveying their hot loads from the power stations around the Midlands. Class 20s operating in pairs had been staple motive power during the early years and often hammered their way southwards from Ratcliffe Power Station in noticeable style. Class 56s supplanted them and were there to the end, and it fell to 56 022 to perform the final act leaving Ratcliffe on the 28th with the last load of forty-four wagons. The class also performed another 'last' on 7th February when 56 011, with Class 58 No. 58 042, left Barrow Hill depot, days before it was closed.

During April 56 080 was returned to its original 3,250bhp rating and in May Class 60 locomotives displaced Class 56s which in turn ousted pairs of Class 31s on Ketton cement trains. A drift into Scotland altered a long and rare trend for the class as members became quite common visitors from May.

Some of the earlier members of the class received replacement quartz headlights of the larger version. This involved dividing the horizontal handrail into two parts. Number 56 012 was among the first to be dealt with. Replacement cabs of the newer Doncaster pattern had been fitted over the years to Romanian examples, usually following collision damage to the originals. 56 004/14 were notable examples.

On 17th June 56 002 jumped the rails and came to rest a short distance down an embankment at Caverswall, near Blyth Bridge, between Stoke-on-Trent and Uttoxeter. The locomotive sustained a badly damaged trailing cab as the leading hopper wagon followed and embedded itself. Fortunately, the crew escaped by jumping clear. Crewe and Toton breakdown crews rescued the locomotive several weeks later. It was taken to Toton and declared stored unserviceable on 9th August.

On this day 56 044 was named 'Cardiff Canton' at a ceremony at Cardiff Canton depot, to mark the depot's dedication as a Trainload Metals facility. The pride was obviously there, but one doubts if the casual lineside observer would appreciate the meaning of the name.

Railway enthusiasts obviously appreciated the locomotives. On 18th August 56 025 and 56 022, the latter still in 'Corporate blue' livery, powered the Pathfinder Tours 'Strider' railtour and visited the Morris Cowley branch near Oxford, among other unusual places.

On 27th September the forlorn remains of 56 042 were officially withdrawn from service, making this locomotive the first such example of the class. It was an accounting formality, but as related previously she was non-standard and obviously paid the penalty. Nonetheless, 56 042 was to remain in the Training Compound at Toton depot for some time. The same month saw 56 089 named 'Ferrybridge C Power Station' on the 15th at its namesake location, a few miles north east of Pontefract. The following month 56 094

suffered roof damage to its No. 1 cab as it passed through the loading bunker facility at Selby colliery. It was despatched to Toton for attention.

On 12th November 56 017 was damaged when it collided with Brush Type 2 No. 31 549 near Ashby-de-la-Zouch. This was followed by 56 122 running through the buffer stops at Ryhope Grange Junction, near Sunderland, on the 22nd. The trailing No. 2 cab of 56 122 suffered serious damage. This pair brought the number of class 56s damaged through accidents to four. 56 017 went into store as officially unserviceable on 13th December.

The end of 1991 brought with it the news that the number of British Coal pits was to be drastically reduced from fifty-nine to around fourteen before the end of the century. The cost of deep-mined coal and the freedom of the newly-privatised electricity industry to purchase coal from whom they wished bore heavily upon BR who transported it. Alternative supplies were to come from abroad, and although BR could shift their locomotive operations further traffic reductions were expected. Strange to tell, large-scale reductions were forecast by Arthur Scargill during the prolonged miners' dispute of the mid-1980s. His tactics may have been questionable (as were those of British Coal), but his prophecy eventually came true.

As a result of the various outside influences and internal BR policies further Class 56 locomotives became surplus to requirements during the following year. Some were required to provide much-needed spare parts and others required expensive repairs. Into store, mostly classified as unserviceable, went 56 004/8/12/5/6/22/4/6/8/36/46/66/122. It should be noted that all except one were from the earlier deliveries, accident victim 56 122 being stored at Toton on 13th March and finally withdrawn on 9th October. Of these locomotives a few had temporary periods of storage, some being returned to traffic during the same year. For others the storage was prolonged and, in addition to 56 122, led to official withdrawal for 56 015 and 56 028, both on 26th November 1993. 1992 also saw the withdrawal of accident victims 56 002 and 56 017 on 8th May.

Early in 1992 56 007 was noted in service fitted with rectangular buffer heads, French fashion, adding the third pattern to be fitted to Class 56 locomotives. At this time the number of Class 56s in blue livery were few, with 56 004/8/10/20/6 in 'Corporate Blue' and 56 119/24/6 in the 'large logo blue'. Original Railfreight grey examples were 56 024 and of the red stripe-modified version only 56 011/9/48/9/108 remained.

Resplendent in Coal Sub-Sector grey, 56 014 worked the first Class 56-hauled passenger train on a private line on 10th May when it powered the 13.40 Kidderminster-Bewdley on the Severn Valley Railway. This was on the occasion of the preserved line's gala weekend.

An example of the way Class 56 workings were being reduced was the cessation of bringing in of coal to Willington Power Station by rail. On 17th July 56 021 brought in the final train, ending ten years of mgr operation. The power station had considerable stocks of coal and intended to run these down and then have coal brought in by road haulage.

The naming of Class 56 locomotives continued, despite

(and sometimes because of) the demise of some of them. Upon its transfer to the Nottinghamshire coal pool 56 128 inherited the name 'Maltby Colliery' from stored 56 012 in July at Toton Traction Maintenance Depot. Then, on 6th September, 56 110 was named 'Croft' at Leicester TMD after the South Leicestershire village or its traffic-generating quarry. The same month saw 56 117 named 'Wilton-Coalpower' at Thornaby TMD, an inheritance from sister locomotive 56 122. In December, at Cardiff Canton depot, 56 060 received the name 'Cardiff Rod Mill' formerly carried by English Electric Class 37 No. 37 712. Originally, it was thought that 56 048 would receive the name. Although the renaming of locomotives only minimally affected Class 56, the localised nature of some of the names and the transfer away of some of their holders led to a practice somewhat akin to the game of 'pass the parcel'!

Previous mention was made above of 56 066 being placed in store. On 13th November at 22.15 while hauling a Millerhill-York loaded coal train, she ran into the rear of the empty Leith-Hartlepool pipe train at Morpeth. The latter was standing at Clifton Lane crossing, south of Morpeth station. Tragically, her 33 year old driver was killed. The main line was blocked for over twenty-four hours and, remarkably for the economic climate of the day, 56 066 despite its badly damaged No. 2 cab, was eventually repaired and returned to traffic.

During December 56 031, 56 036 and 56 049 were transferred to the Network SouthEast Civil Engineer's Department for heavy ballast workings. They went into Doncaster BRML for Cost Effective Maintenance overhaul and received the appropriate 'Dutch' grey and yellow livery in the process, adding another colour variation to the Class. Their entry into service working on Meldon Quarry duties was early in 1993. Apparently, non-Romanian examples were specifically requested. A fleet of twelve was envisaged to replace double-heading ballast trains with Class 33s, but before other events overtook the arrangement the fleet numbered six, Nos 56 031/36/46-9.

By the end of the year there were four Class 56s withdrawn from stock, these being 56 002/17/42/122. 'Corporate Blue' examples remained at six (56 004/8/10/20/2/6) and the two remaining 'large logo' were 56 124/6. Of the original Railfreight grey, only 56 024 remained and the red stripe version had four survivors, 56 011/9/48/108. 'Dutch' members apart the rest of the class were painted in the variations of the 1987 Railfreight grey livery. December 1992 saw 56 044 'Cardiff Canton' receive the addition of 'Quality Assured' to its name at Cardiff Canton depot. Also at Cardiff was stored 56 046, soon to be returned to traffic as one of the 'Dutch' six.

The contracts between British Coal and the power generating companies ran out in March 1993 and following the last-minute rush to fulfil deliveries there came a change to importing cheaper coal. There was no guarantee that levels of rail haulage would be maintained, but at least BR changed its operating patterns to meet the new circumstances. Later in the year Immingham depot received an allocation of Class 56s for

Doncaster-built 56 034 'Castell Ogwr – Ogmore Castle' passing Challow on 26th September 1990, at the head of a bin-liner waste train.

M J STRETTON

the first time and commenced haulage of trains of imported coal in October. The first allocations were 56 084/5/8/9/90 and were employed on workings to and from Scunthorpe. 56 003 also went to Immingham to allow fitter training to take place as it was envisaged that some maintenance work would be transferred from Toton.

Active naming and renaming of Class 56s continued. In February 56 128 became 'West Burton Power Station', gaining the name from 56 028. This was followed in March by the naming of 56 073 'Tremorfa Steelworks' at BRML Doncaster. In April 56 094 became 'Eggborough Power Station' at Toton TMD after the plates were removed from stored 56 030. Also stored, in unserviceable condition, was pioneer member 56 001 'Whatley'. It resided at Stewarts Lane depot, but was later restored to active use, a common happening with quite a few Class 56s at this time. By July only eight Romanian locomotives were active, these being 56 005/6/7/9/10/1/8/21. The state of some of the withdrawn locomotives was one of dereliction, with most re-usable parts removed. Number 56 002, at Doncaster depot, was a grounded and empty hulk with severe cab damage. The state of 56 017 at Toton was similar, but because one end drooped because of collision damage it was mounted on blocks to maintain a level plane. In addition to the previously-mentioned 56 007, 56 083 was noted in service during 1993 with rectangular buffers, but only at one end!

May was a good month for naming. Number 56 054 gained the name 'British Steel Llanwern' previously carried by Class 37 No. 37 902, and 56 076 became 'British Steel Trostre'. Both sets of plates were fitted at Cardiff Canton depot. The following month at Stewarts Lane depot 56 051 received the name 'Isle of Grain', a name previously attached to Class 33 No. 33 050. In July at Thornaby depot 56 069 appropriately

became 'Thornaby TMD', inheriting it from Class 37 No. 37 714. By this time only one Class 56 remained in the 'large logo' blue livery, 56 126, though not for long because it was in Doncaster Works during September for CEM Repair and of course a repaint into the 1987 Railfreight livery.

At 15.00 on Thursday 29th July 1993 the situation regarding the thirty Romanian locomotives was as follows:-

56 001	stored at Stewarts Lane
56 002	withdrawn at Doncaster
56 003/4	out of service at Toton
56 005	under repair at Shirebrook
56 006	in service (Leicester)
56 007-9	out of service at Toton
56 010	stabled at Worksop
56 011-3	out of service at Toton
56 014/5	out of service at Doncaster
56 016	out of service at Toton
56 017	withdrawn at Doncaster
56 018	in traffic, (Brookgate-Toton)
56 019/20	out of service at Toton
56 021	in traffic, Drakelow Power Station
56 022-30	out of service at Toton

Most of those described as out of service were stored and some were later returned to traffic, in particular 56 004. Others were not so fortunate and were withdrawn. First were 56 015/28/30 on 26th November and then 56 013/23 on 17th December, making a total of nine locomotives withdrawn from stock.

The pioneer Class 56, 56 001 stored at Cardiff Canton depot on 24th October 1994.

M J STRETTON

Of the remaining 126 locomotives on the books, 120 were allocated to Trainload Freight and six to Network SouthEast.

A sign of the times perhaps, was the formation of 'The Class 56 Group' with two main aims of promoting interest in the class and to maintain a preserved example in full working order. This was a good, healthy and welcome move, prompted by the early withdrawal of Class 56s. Stored 56 001 'Whatley' was an obvious candidate, being the pioneer member of the class, but it had an uncertain future. Sister locomotive 56 004, one of the 'Corporate Blue' survivors, was treated to a repaint in the same livery early in 1994, but with additional, cast, double arrow symbols on the cab sides, thus attracting attention from railway enthusiasts.

April 1st 1994 saw the long-expected start of the privatisation of British Rail. Trainload Freight was divided into three separate companies, Trainload Freight West, Trainload Freight North and Trainload Freight South East. The first was allocated sixty Class 56s (13 based at Motherwell and 47 at Cardiff) and the second was allocated 66 (57 based at Immingham and 9 at Thornaby). The third did not receive any. The official day required preparation and to this end the weekend of 19/20th March was the culmination of it all, although in practice locomotives were trickling to new locations for several months after. By far the greatest loser of Class 56s was Toton, which found itself with no allocation at all, for the first time since the early days of the Class. Another loser was Network SouthEast, which lost its six 'Dutch'-liveried Class 56s. One seriously has to consider whether or not the new order was necessary overall, at least from the operating and maintenance points of view. Surely, all those years of patiently building up the business sectors into workable organisations should have progressed further into companies not geographically-based, assuming of course that privatisation was necessary in the first instance. Unlike the previous politically inspired upheavals of 1923 and 1948, the new order appeared unclear and ill-conceived to many within and without the Railway Industry. Certainly, the politicians appeared confident, but then they often do.

During the run-up to these events some 'tidying up' of dead locomotives was deemed necessary. One notable operation was the clearing of long-withdrawn locomotives dumped at March. Another was the cutting up of withdrawn Class 56s. During mid-February 1994 a list was issued by the BRB requesting tenders for the scrap of many locomotives, including five Class 56s. First to go was 56 002 at Doncaster TMD. Scrapping of this locomotive was undertaken by Ronald Hull Junior Ltd of Parkgate, and the work was well advanced by 25th March. During mid-April 56 042 was noted cut into two sections at Toton, and disappeared soon afterwards, probably by the 15th. The work was undertaken by Coopers who turned their attention to 56 017 and completed it by 6th May.

Scrapping Class 56s ensured that the class would never be completely in one uniform livery, and privatisation ensured that the remainder would not either. In May 1994 the livery situation was as follows. Remaining in 'Corporate' blue were 56 004/8/10/20/2/6, in the original Railfreight grey was 56 024 and the red stripe version 56 019. The six 'Dutch' grey and yellow locomotives were 56 031/6/46-9 and the remainder

bore the variations of the 1987 Railfreight triple grey livery representing the Construction, Coal and Metals sub-sectors. Some bore no sub-sector symbols, but in all cases the basic livery was to all intents and purposes the same.

Little time passed before someone produced new liveries for the new companies. Number 56 039 was part of the initial unveiling events of the Load-Haul company's (formerly Trainload Freight North East) new image at the Doncaster Works Open Days of 9/10th July. Gone was the triple grey and in its place was a mainly semi-gloss black scheme relieved by stylised yellow ends with lower cab sides picked out in orange. Cab window surround areas were black as were undergear. The Load-Haul logo was affixed in transfer form to the body side, 'load' being rendered in dark grey lower case italics on a white background, with 'haul' similarly below in white on a grey background. An orange highlight was to the left and below the combination. 'Corporate' numerals in black were provided for the cab side running numbers. In the manner of then contemporary British Telecom vans, the logos were made luminous to glow in the dark, surely a novelty introduction on the British scene! The livery was devised by Venture Design Consultants.

For triple grey locomotives with good paintwork the main application was to be the logo and minimal orange inboard of the cab side doors. At least when new the work done on 56 039 was practical and superb in both finish and appearance.

It shortly received the name 'ABP Port of Hull' at the King George Dock, Hull, on 19th July. Numbers 56 034 and 56 074 soon followed in receiving the new livery whilst 56 022, one of the last Class 56s to still wear the 'Corporate Blue' livery, was placed back in traffic in the Railfreight triple grey, but without sub-Sector markings, at the end of May, perhaps one of the last to do so. The last Class 56 to retain 'red stripe' Railfreight grey livery, 56 019, continued to do so in the autumn of 1994, albeit in work-worn condition, whilst 56 072 received TRANSRAIL markings on its triple grey livery.

By the end of the summer withdrawn Class 56s could be found at a couple of locations. 56 015 was at BRML Doncaster and the remainder, 56 013/023/028/030/122, were at Toton. Number 56 042 by this time had been cut up and only the cab of 56 017 had survived, mainly due to kindly scrap men leaving it until resident fledglings had left the nest. Meanwhile, 56 029 had been resurrected from storage by this time, but 56 066, the unfortunate Morpeth accident victim of 13th November 1992, was still confined to BRML Doncaster under repair. Stored locomotives were 56 001/3/8/12/16/20/4/6/7, all at Immingham except for 56 001/16/20, which were at Cardiff. Happily, before the year was out, 56 003 and 56 027 were taken to Doncaster for overhaul. Officially, 126 of the original 135 locomotives were still on the books.

On Wednesday 18th January 1995 56 107 arrived at the Falcon Works for a Class 'G' general overhaul. This was a pilot effort by Brush Traction for evaluation purposes to enable the Company to effectively undertake further such work on a regular basis, in lieu of orders for new locomotives. It had been reported several months previously that the Company was seeking approval for undertaking Level 5 overhaul work. The locomotive was soon stripped until only a shell remained, and was noted inside 25 Shop off its bogies on

2nd February. Various components removed could be seen in several locations, all of them in absolutely filthy condition. Initial comments, by personnel engaged on such work, was unprintable! Some of the wiring registered only 0.5 Megohms insulation resistance due to oil and other contamination.

Work undertaken in overhauling this locomotive proved to be of the highest order; in some instances certain items requested as replacements proved how thorough the work was. Load-Haul were impressed from an early stage of the overhaul.

Number 56 107 regained the rails at the Falcon Works during late April and was moved to the new test house, and then to the load bank. It spent most of May in this vicinity before being transferred to the paint shop where the new Load-Haul livery of black and orange was applied. A new version of the Brush Traction works plate was fitted to each side of the locomotive. Sadly, these plates survived for only a few months of service, being removed illegally.

Number 56 107 left the works at 12.40 on Wednesday 7th June, and on 24th July was part of a changeover from pairs of Class 47 to Class 56 haulage of the Felixstowe Freightliners. On this day it, 56 003 and 56 106 were all noted on these trains. Early June had seen trials with various members of the class to evaluate their suitability on such services. News filtered back to Loughborough that 56 107 was performing well and the operators were very satisfied.

Among the withdrawn locomotives, 56 015 was languishing at Doncaster RML, 56 028/30 were at Margam and 56 013/023/122 were at Toton. Number 56 089 lost its name 'Ferrybridge 'C' Power Station' to 56 006 and 56 128 had its 'West Burton Power Station' plates removed. One of the class, 56 010, became the first member to run on the preserved Torbay & Dartmouth Railway in Devon, when it hauled the 'Cream T' railtour from Manchester. By the summer, repairs to the accident victim 56 066 were nearly complete at the ABB Doncaster Works. The locomotive returned to traffic during the second half of July, having been out of service since November 1992.

Following the success of 56 107, Brush Traction received 56 102 'Scunthorpe Steel Centenary' on Thursday 24th August and 56 075 'West Yorkshire Enterprise' on Thursday 28th September. The former was slightly delayed entering the shops, but the latter, which had failed at Holgate Bridge Junction near York on 26th July, received immediate attention. The standard of work on 56 102 was again high, and on 29th September the locomotive was on the stands in the erecting shop being refitted. The large nameplates had been removed and all associated bolt holes sealed by welding.

Another member of the class was reported to have lost its name by December. This was 56 076 'British Steel Trostre'. Despite this, another naming occurred on 4th October 1995 when 56 086 was named 'The Magistrates' Association' at Euston station in London. It was an unusual place to find a Class 56 and also an unusual name for a heavy freight locomotive.

Number 56 033 was officially named 'Shotton Paper Mill' at a ceremony held on 18th December 1995 at Chester Wagon Repair Depot to commemorate the signing of a five-year contract by Transrail securing the transport of 100,000 tonnes of timber annually from Scotland. A little earlier 56 068 had arrived at the Falcon Works for an intermediate examination on 17th November, joining 56 041 in the Erecting Shop for stripping. By this time the remains of long withdrawn 56 122 had just been cut up at Toton.

On 18th January 1996 56 102 left the works, resplendent in Load-Haul black and orange livery. It soon returned, suffering from a wheelslip detection problem at 5mph, a speed not sustainable within the works confines. That day the works still held 56 098, a shell mounted on Class 20 bogies, awaiting its turn to go into the Erecting Shop where 56 041 and 56 068 were being reassembled.

Meanwhile, events elsewhere resulted in a period of uncertainty. The entry of Wisconsin Central, upon purchase of the three freight companies, naturally led to this as existing managements awaited possible changes in policy direction. Most visible signs of this came when the repainting of locomotives was stopped at the undercoat stage, 56 041 emerging from the Falcon Works in this condition during March 1996. The resultant 'albino' appearance was not unattractive, although some of the paint staff at the works considered that the absorbent nature of the paint might prove troublesome when it came to removing oil and dirt prior to applying the final coat.

Wisconsin Central's newly formed English Welsh & Scottish Railway Ltd, soon adopted maroon and gold as its new livery and declared that plans were drawn up for re-engining some of the Class 56s and the upgrading of other equipment. On the other hand, should substantial failures or serious collision damage occur, the locomotives concerned would be withdrawn.

At least the future of Class 56 appeared assured for some years to come, despite nine of the class already scrapped or withdrawn from service and 56 005 recently placed in store. Indeed, plans to modify and improve Class 56s were already in hand as a result of the experience gained during the overhauls at the Falcon Works and a contract for such work was gained for the works during the early part of 1996.

Concurrently, the Class 56 Group began to set aside funds to purchase a Class 56 locomotive when the opportunity arose.

Ten Class 56s were scheduled to undergo intermediate overhaul at the Falcon Works and by the end of 1996 most had either been dealt with or were being dealt with. They were easily distinguishable by the red and gold livery of EW&S, whereas light repairs and modification warranted no repaint.

Following the cutting up of 56 015 earlier in the year, two more derelict Romanian examples were brought into the Falcon Works for stripping prior to scrapping. These were 56 005 and 56 024, both leaving the works with interiors that would be the pride of anyone's scrap skip! Number 56 009 came in for a different reason, that of conversion to a mobile engine test bed. This was to facilitate engine testing when a locomotive was not available and also gain time and therefore return locomotives to traffic quicker. The well worn grey hulk was described as sold to BEM in September 1996 and thereafter could be seen either serving its purpose alongside the load bank or being towed by SPRITE. Pioneer locomotive

56 001 was withdrawn in October and despite reports that it might be preserved, was cut up at Cardiff Canton depot the following May. In pitiful condition on withdrawal much useful equipment had been removed, so there was little left to preserve. One day railway enthusiasts will bemoan its loss, in principle at least.

The lives of the Romanian-built examples were clearly limited, more limited than the remainder of the class, accidents excepted, but with an upturn in EWS traffic their future appeared more secure as time passed. Scrapping of the derelict examples continued however during 1997. At the beginning of the year eleven Romanian Class 56s remained in active service (56 003/4/6/7/ 10/18/21/22/25/27/29). Despite fire damage and languishing at the depot for several months, 56 011 was undergoing repair at Toton during early 1997. Of the British-built examples 56 060 languished at Cardiff Canton awaiting its fate, its name 'The Cardiff Rod Mill' passing to 56 052. A surprise move for the locomotive was its transfer to Brush during the first week of August.

Due to the upturn in traffic and particularly to the success of the modifications and overhauls at the Falcon Works the future of Class 56 appeared to be brighter. Better availability led to an appraisal which tended to support a longer-term fleet of 113 locomotives rather than the fifty envisaged in 1996. Sadly, 56 020 met its fate under the torches of Booth Roe Metals of Rotherham.

Members of the class which had undergone a general overhaul by the autumn of 1997 were 56 032/37/51/59/65/67/87/88/103/ 105/114/117/120. Their transformations were remarkable; those examples wearing the maroon EWS livery bore it better than any previous livery.

In the meantime, 56 103 had been named STORA on 18th July 1997. The maroon and gold locomotive received this name in celebration of one million tonnes of reeled newsprint paper carried in six years from Stora's warehouse in Immingham Docks to Ripple Lane, in London. The one millionth tonne of Swedish paper was carried on 6th August. In the ever-shifting renaming of locomotives the name 'ABP Port of Hull' found its way onto 56 087. Its previous carrier Load-Haul black and orange liveried 56 039, soon found its way into the Falcon Works for a 'G' Exam, following fire damage. Numbers 56 032 and 56 037 also lost their names during the summer.

During the course of the year 56 019, still in somewhat worn red stripe Railfreight grey livery, was gradually returned to working condition, mainly due to the efforts of staff at Knottingley depot. It had been in store at Springs Branch for a long time and on 30th September it was sufficiently advanced to be started for running light tests. Within weeks the locomotive was based at Immingham, working local runs on iron ore trains to and from Scunthorpe. Another Romanian-built example returned to traffic after collision repairs had been effected. Damaged during the previous summer months, 56 027 worked again for the first time on 10th December working a Toton-Milford coal train. Toton depot staff had made good body damage and had transferred a cab from withdrawn 56 013.

Following such returns to traffic there remained Romanians 56 008/012/014 stored at Immingham, 56 091 at Thornaby,

56 028/030 at Margam Wagon Works and 56 011/013/023 at Toton. Long withdrawn 56 122 was also at Toton, being little more than a shell. By the close of 1997 56 062 and 56 007 in turn had been based at Aberdeen and used for crew training purposes, the latter being the first use of a Class 56 between Aberdeen and Inverness. Replacement 56 088 was in use on 6th January 1998.

Reliability modifications (mini-mods) and 'G' Exams continued to be undertaken at the Falcon Works. On 8th January 1998 56 108 was present undergoing the former with 56 018/039/060/069 in for 'G' Exam. 56 108 had left the previous day, following its modifications and 56 018 proved to be the last Romanian example to receive such an overhaul, being outshopped in EWS maroon livery. In contrast, Romanian 56 020 was cut up at the Booth Roe Metals scrap yard in Rotherham by mid-January. The remains of 56 122 were moved by road to the scrap yard in April and quickly broken up. 56 028/030 had moved from Margam to Crewe for stripping by this time. They were scrapped on site during late September 1998.

Number 56 049 was damaged in a shunting accident at Warrington Arpley in mid-January and sustained a crushed No. 2 cab, whereas the recently resurrected 56 019 found a variety of work, including Virgin passenger duties.

During the first week in April 1998 56 009 was taken into the paint shop at the Falcon Works for a repaint. The mobile engine test bed was in scruffy condition and although the repaint was cosmetic it certainly smartened its external appearance considerably. It received British Steel blue, using paint left over from the two repainted Class 60s 60 006/033, with black roof and yellow warning panels on each end. Repainting was completed by 16th April. No markings were applied at this time and it remained anonymous for some months. Unofficially it was planned to give the former 56 009 a new number to confuse railway enthusiasts but by the time numerals were located the surprise element had vaporised. The new number 56 201 was applied to each cab on the driver's side on 3rd December 1998 and two spare Hong Kong MTR logos from 1996 followed on 15th August 1999, being placed immediately below the numbers. Its last Class 56 engine test occurred at the end of June 1999.

Other Class 56s receiving attention at the Falcon Works in mid-April 1998 were 56 039/046/ 049/ 059/ 069/091. The works continued to deal with Class 56s throughout the year. Two namings occurred during the summer months when 56 069 was named 'Wolverhampton Steel Terminal' on 22nd July and 56 091 was named 'Stanton' on 29th August, the latter at the Toton Open Weekend.

The class continued almost unscathed for the remainder of the year, but with the introduction of Class 66 in large numbers and EWS financial stringencies the situation was to change during 1999. Hints of what were to come were leaked from EWS that should major out of course repairs be needed, withdrawal might result, otherwise budgeted overhauls would continue. By this time many people were used to seeing the 'thin end of the wedge' approach to locomotive matters and (correctly as it transpired) read into it more serious implications. Very quickly it became known that 56 123 and 56 135, the latter the last to be built and only fourteen years

56 029 is seen stored unserviceable at Toton on 20th June 1993.

M J STRETTON

56 037 at Cardiff Canton (Transrail) in October 1994. Note the surviving evidence for the intended cowling above the buffers.

M J STRETTON

56 039 at the launch of the Load Haul livery at Doncaster Works open day 10th July 1994.

M J STRETTON

56 042 parked at Leicester, 2nd June 1989. This locomotive was the only example fitted with CP1 bogies.

M J STRETTON

old, had been stored. 56 121/125 soon followed, although 56 110 partly offset this when it came out of store.

During early March 1999 it was decided to move 56 121 from Crewe to the recently established Component Recovery Centre at Wigan Springs Branch. Unfortunately, the driver of the low loader took a wrong turning in the Wigan area and the trailer portion with its locomotive load had to be left parked with a weight restricted bridge ahead of it until the situation could be sorted. Aptly, the parking location was 'Cemetary Road'. In the event after five days the ensemble returned to the haulier's yard at Studley.

During March 1999 news emerged that EWS planned to store up to seventy Class 56s by the end of March 2000, to leave around fifty in service. Such planned moves suggested economies and accountancy decisions within the company, presumably with finances being directed towards the lower maintenance costs of the new Class 66s entering service.

At this time 56 019 ended its reprieve and was placed into store and the Brush involvement with Class 56 dwindled as existing work was completed. 56 011 left the works on 22nd February and 56 038 finally left on 31st March. Recent arrival 56 031 still remained, but departed on 24th April. This completed the involvement and with no more such work in the offing, confirmed EWS policy further.

Fire damaged 56 035 was placed in store and moved to Wigan as were 56 066/092/121/126. May 4th saw even more storages when blue-liveried 56 004 and 56 046/052/097/131 went, followed next day by 56 003 and 56 099, leaving ninety-eight in service. Then, the fourth EWS locomotive sales advertisement of May/June 1999 offered 56 013 and 56 023 for sale. By early August the operational fleet totalled eighty-seven examples. Stored 56 006 was repainted BR blue at Old Oak Common for the East Lancashire Railway's Classic Traction event of 10-12th September. Although the locomotive was in action during the event it was not expected to be used afterwards, but was to be retained for the August 2000 London EWS/RAIL open weekend at the Old Oak Common depot.

Further withdrawals from traffic reduced the operational total to eighty-one and further advertisements offered 56 008/014/035/ 092/097/102/126 for sale before the end of 1999. Number 56 126 was scrapped during November 1999. With the new century only days old the operational fleet was down to seventy examples.

More were then taken out of traffic and placed in storage, until around fifty operational examples remained by mid-March. Scrapping of some of the derelict Class 56s was authorised, but other members of the class stored at Barry were reported as tentatively earmarked for further service in Bulgaria. Clearly, the introduction of the General Motors Class 66 locomotives not only drastically reduced the operational total in the class, but almost resulted in repatriation to Eastern Europe. Almost was the word, for nothing came of such rumours, but indeed during mid-2000 six of those stored were earmarked for a return to traffic.

In the meantime Raxstar had scrapped 56 008/12/14 on site at Immingham by early April and EWS had scrapped 56 035 at the component recovery centre, Springs Branch, Wigan in June.

Erstwhile stored 56 006 was revived, repainted into its first BR blue livery and placed into the unofficial EWS heritage fleet, notably for the Old Oak Common Open Weekend (London 2000) of 5/6th August. Following this event it made its way to the Severn Valley Railway at Kidderminster for storage. By mid-November 2000 there were sixty Class 56s officially in service, slightly up on previously-stated EWS requirements. By mid-February 2001 there were 58 in service, 56 were in store and 21 had been scrapped.

Following its visit to the Severn Valley Railway, unofficial heritage locomotive 56 006 went to Old Oak Common depot in London on 28th February 2001. It was noted there shunting on 18th March. During May the heritage traction pool became official, WMOC. Included among its ranks were BR blue 56 004 and 56 006, the former for spare parts and the latter being operational. By that summer EWS was considering reinstating twenty Class 56s, among them was 56 006. July saw 56 092 scrapped at Springs Branch, Wigan.

EWS then made it known that at least twelve (later fifteen) would be reinstated to allow twelve Class 66s to be released for work connected with the construction of the Channel Tunnel Rail Link in the autumn. Numbers 56 004/6 were sent to Toton on 27th September for the latter to receive the bogies from donor 56 004 to allow it to return to revenue earning traffic. Already 56 072/100/109/129 had returned to traffic a few days previously. Others found their way out of EWS ownership, 56 023/080 to unspecified buyers (and ultimately scrap) and 56 097 to preservation, with the Type 3 Traction Group, which moved it to South Wales where it became resident at Cathays Carriage & Wagon Works, Cardiff on 6th March 2002. Then 56 006/033/049/070/077/083/099/104/107/123/ 133 were returned to traffic during the autumn and winter of 2001. In January 2002 there were 67 in traffic, in the WGAT and WGAI pools, based at Thornaby and Immingham depots respectively. They mainly operated in the North East and Eastern areas, but could stray into the Midlands and Scotland on occasions.

On 21st January 2002 56 115 was named 'Barry Needham' in memory of EWS logistics manager killed in the Great Heck accident on 28th February 2001 whilst travelling as a passenger in the GNER train. The private ceremony was held at Doncaster Royal Mail terminal.

In April 2002 four Class 56s were stored, 56 025/059/100/110 being despatched to the WNXX pool. More storages followed to WNTR and WNTS pools during the following months, with 56 006 returning briefly to heritage status proper, and its donor 56 004 coming out and allocated to WNYX in September and being despatched to the component recovery centre at Springs Branch on 6th December. 56 006, in the meantime, was used on the seasonal upturn of coal traffic.

As 2003 opened, withdrawals increased among those in the ranks with wear and tear to contend with. 10,000 engine hours and worn tyres would mean heavier than usual expenditure and such afflicted locomotives might be replaced by those stored in better condition. On the other hand bogie swaps might effect an economic solution where applicable. By April 2003 there were just over forty of the class in service, this total slipping to below forty by September.

With a deadline of 15th July 2003 EWS offered 56 019/022/

047/123/125/135 for sale. All were stored at Immingham and in poor condition. Four went for scrap, but Fragonset Railways bought two, 56 022 and 56 125. While not committing itself to any definite plan for their future the locomotives continued in storage in new ownership and still had not returned to traffic in 2005. 56 135 was the final member of the class to be built, at Crewe Works in 1984.

Often a portent of things to come are heritage or specially revived liveries. During September 2003 56 078 was sent to the Toton paint shop for repainting, this time it was BR large logo blue. It had never received this livery before and it was applied specially for the event it would be a guest at, the three-day gala held on the Severn Valley Railway 3-5th October. At the event it was named 'Doncaster Enterprise' on 4th October and hauled the Riviera Trains Mk2 coaching stock, in BR style blue and grey livery, on the preserved railway.

In November EWS let it be known that considerable fleet reductions were planned before the new financial year started in April 2004, particularly with Classes 37, 47 and 56. Class 58, by this time, was completely non-operational in Britain and Class 56s numbered 43 at this time. EWS then continued to shuffle the Class 56 pack in and out of store, but with losses outweighing gains. By 9th December the total was 33 and almost a month later it was 25, with most working in North East England between Doncaster, Immingham and Thornaby.

Before the end of 2003 Fragonset Railways purchased 56 066 as a source of spare parts for its other Class 56s and followed this by adding 56 061 to its non-operational fleet in June 2004.

The official notification that EWS would stand down its operational Class 56 fleet by 31st March came early in February 2004. The intention was that the company would concentrate its fleet on Classes 60, 66 and 67. The last-named was soon to show signs of attrition, despite its apparent immunity. Class 56, meanwhile, came down to 21 in early February and 13 by the middle of the month. Stored Class 56s were scattered around the depots, Immingham having an accumulation of nearly fifty.

During February 2004 celebrity locomotive 56 078 spent two days at Eastleigh for inspection by representatives of various foreign railways interested in hiring locomotives on infrastructure contracts abroad in the manner of EWS locomotives already working in Spain. Presumably, as a result of this occasion, events later in the year were a direct consequence.

By late March there were only ten Class 56s left in traffic – 56 059/060/071/078/081//087/091/094/095/115.

The last Romanian built example to be in traffic was 56 018. It suffered a failed turbocharger and became *hors de combat*. All except 56 078 and 56 115 went into store (WNTR) on 29th March.

Pathfinder Tours, in the business since 1983, arranged a Class 56 farewell tour at short notice for 31st March, a Bristol-York return. Locomotives used were EWS red 56 115 'Barry Needham' on the 'Twilight Grids' tour from Bristol to York, then BR large logo blue 56 078 'Doncaster Enterprise' on a round tour back to York. The return to Bristol was double-headed 56 115 and 56 078. The very last working was the

following morning when 56 078 headed the 06.08 Hams Hall - Daventry and returned light locomotive.

On 4th April 56 090/117/118 from Crewe to Bristol Barton Hill depot, one of three depots used for preparing EWS locomotives for foreign hire arrangements (Eastleigh and Old Oak Common, London, being the other two). Negotiations were now afoot to send some locomotives to the Continent.

By May a number of such moves were under way.

More cheerful news at this time was the securing of 56 003 for preservation, from the scrapyard of Booths of Rotherham. Due to lack of space, that it was not a designated locomotive and apparently not an historically significant locomotive design, the National Railway Museum turned down the offer of EWS to donate 56 006 to its collection. This may appear strange to many railway enthusiasts in the light of the NRM accepting 47 798 to its collection, presumably because of its 'royal' connection. Class 56 was significant because it was the first production locomotive design to utilise an AC alternator for generating electrical power instead of a DC generator. 56 006 was moved to Old Oak Common for bodywork repairs prior to being sent to Doncaster and then Barrow Hill preservation site in time for the '1979' gala of 10/11 July.

A few Class 56s had passed into scrap dealers' hands by this time and EWS sold more to Booth's of Rotherham, in May 2004. These were 56 029/050/075/130. With a deadline of 22nd June EWS advertised 56 004/034/036/121/132 for sale.

In June it became known that EWS was close to signing a contract with Keolis, for the hire of 14 Class 58s and 26 Class 56s for despatch to France to undertake infrastructure train haulage in connection with the construction of the TGV Est high speed line. This line was being built between Paris and Baudrecourt in eastern France, and three sites were earmarked as locomotive bases, one at St. Hilaire, near Reims and at Ocquerre and Pagny, both near Metz.

Toton soon had 56 078 back in its paint shop in June to give the locomotive a new livery of grey with French operator Fertis markings. A new pool was created for those Class 56s destined for France, WZGF, and locomotives were constantly on the move from storage to restoration sites.

A private buyer acquired 56 045 from HNRC in July for preservation. It had lain at Immingham since withdrawal by EWS in 1999, but its new owner soon transferred it to Barrow Hill. Next came 56 057 for preservation. This locomotive arrived on the Nene Valley Railway on 8th July in faded original style EWS livery. It also had been stored in 1999.

The first Fertis Class 56 to go to France under a two-year hire deal was the former celebrity 56 078, on 9th September with 58 046, being hauled through the Channel Tunnel by 92 028 and 92 043. Numbers 56 087 and 56 118 went through on 1st October , with 56 059/60 on the 9th and 56 090 on the 19th. Also in France by 22nd October were 56 038, 56 069 and 56 117. By Christmas 2004, more had been allocated to the WZGF pool, although the October total of nine had not increased.

Those in France worked weekdays from Vadenay St. Hilare au Temple near Reims. Most worked ballast trains with two Class 56s at the head and a Class 58 at the rear. Three ballast trains daily left at 06.00, returning at 13.00. Two Class 56s were working close to the Franco German border at Creutzwald yard.

By March 2005 further allocations to WZGF had been made and one, 56 099 had been removed to WNXX, due to being unsuitable for return to traffic. Movements occurred frequently as locomotives were prepared and painted, prior to despatch to France. In the first few months of 2005 there were around 33 Class 56s stored at Immingham, six at Ferrybridge and fourteen at Healey Mills. Not only did demands for France see members leave, but also 56 124 for preservation by Edward Stevenson was poised to go. Eight left Immingham for storage at Healey Mills during April. By the end of May it became apparent that more were due as Immingham was to be cleared of Class 56s, to allow concentrated storage of Class 60s. By the end of May Healey Mills held nineteen.

Four more Class 56s were sent to France during April and May, increasing the total to sixteen, over half of the planned allocation. The final total of thirty Class 56 locomotives sent to France was as follows:

No.	WZGF	Date to France
56 007	01.05	01.09.05
56 018	03.05	04.05.05
56 031	01.05	28.06.05
56 032	03.05	14.05.05
56 038	06.04	07.10.04
56 049	06.04	26.05.05
56 051	06.04	22.06.05
56 058	?	15.06.05
56 059	06.04	12.10.04
56 060	06.04	12.10.04
56 065	06.04	26.05.05
56 069	06.04	30.09.04
56 071	03.05	24.08.05
56 074	01.05	06.09.05
56 078	06.04	09.09.04
56 081	06.04	01.07.05
56 087	06.04	05.10.04
56 090	08.04	19.10.04
56 091	03.05	23.06.05 *(a)*
56 094	03.05	21.07.05
56 095	03.05	12.07.05
56 096	12.04	27.04.05
56 103	07.05	03.11.05
56 104	07.05	21.10.05
56 105	12.04	27.04.05
56 106	12.04	04.05.05
56 113	11.05	03.11.05
56 115	07.05	04.11.05
56 117	06.04	05.10.04
56 118	06.04	30.09.04

(a) 56 091 was returned to UK (Old Oak Common) for repairs 02.04.06 and returned to France 03.05.06

Preserved 56 097, which had previously made its way from South Wales to Brush, was repaired on behalf of the preservation group 'Type 3 Traction Group' and despatched from the works to the Great Central (North) railway during late August 2005.

In the EWS sale of 38 locomotives, part of the EWS Component Recovery and Distribution Centre at Springs Branch, Wigan, six were Class 56s. Numbers 56 004/036/121/132 were purchased by CF Booth for scrap and 56 029/34 were purchased by Harry Needle Railroad Co. While the Booth purchases were all scrapped, the latter pair were destined to be resold and moved to Brush on 17th August and 2nd September 2005 respectively, as sources of spare parts for rebuilding other Class 56s for Jarvis Fastline.

A further sale of locomotives in August offered eight more, listed below with recipients:-

56 011	FM Rail
56 021	FM Rail
56 040	Edward Stevenson for Class 56 Group (Mid-Norfolk Rly)
56 044	CF Booth 09.05, Jarvis Rail, to Brush 28.04.06
56 063	CF Booth 09.05, Jarvis Rail, to Brush 04.11.05
56 098	Edward Stevenson 09.05, Pres 11.05 Northampton & Lamport Rly
56 128	HNRC Long Marston
56 131	CF Booth 09.05, Jarvis Rail, to Brush 03.11.05

Those sent to the Brush Falcon Works were a source of spare parts for rebuilding other Class 56s and were still on site in February 2007.

Rebuilding Class 56s occurred after infrastructure company Jarvis Rail decided to operate freight services and infrastructure trains using Type 5 traction. The company had been considering various options for a while, and it decided initially to operate three Class 56s. Two were to be rebuilt by Brush Traction and were purchased by Jarvis Rail for this purpose and the third was to be leased from FM Rail following overhaul by that company at Derby.

The former were to be rebuilt from 56 045 and 56 124, which had passed from HNRC ownership in June 2004, then into preservation in July 2004 and April 2005, to Edward Stevenson. Although accorded preservation status at this time, the pair was resold in August 2005 to Jarvis Rail. Number 56 045 arrived at the Falcon Works on 9th August 2005 and 56 124 on 9th September. Edward Stevenson replaced his locomotives with the above 56 040 and 56 098, from the August sale. FM Rail selected its 56 125 as the third candidate for Jarvis Rail.

Number 56 045 was shunted into 25 Shop during the first week of September, was parted from its bogies and moved into the adjacent 34 Shop and placed on stands. It was joined by 56 124 within a fortnight. Other than visiting the pressure wash and paint shop for internal and underside painting, 34 Shop was to be their home whilst stripping and rebuilding took place over the ensuing months.

FM Rail 56 125 had previously had some work undertaken, but this was accelerated and in October 2005 it was reported to have received its OTMR (On Train Monitoring and Recording) and TPWS (Train Protection Warning System).

On 3rd November 2005 56 103 and 56 113 arrived in France. They were followed by 56 115 the next day, and in doing so it become the thirtieth and final member of the class to arrive in France for infrastructure duties with Fertis. The thirty locomotives worked hard in France, together with their companion Class 58s, although the following month 56 118 caught fire while working in multiple near Ocquerre and 56 091 returned to Britain for attention during April 2006, after suffering engine problems. It returned to France on 3rd May.

Number 56 040 became news again in December, when Edward Stevenson sold the locomotive to The Class 56 Group. Still at Immingham, the locomotive was prepared for removal to the Mid-Norfolk Railway.

During the course of 2005 a total of two Class 56 locomotives had been scrapped.

Meanwhile, at the Falcon Works much work had been done to strip, clean, renovate and rebuild the two Class 56s for Jarvis Rail. Indeed, although selected as in better condition than many Class 56s available for sale in 2005, storage had not been kind to either locomotive. Both were repainted very early in their stay, receiving the basic grey livery before the end of the year. Number 56 045 was moved from 34 Shop to 25 Shop on 1st February 2006 and re-bogied within a fortnight, reaching the New Test House by 15th February. By 1st March it had progressed to load banking and 56 124 had been placed on its bogies in 25 Shop. A week later it was still on the load bank, and the latter in the New Test House.

Both locomotives were renumbered during the latter part of 14th March 2006, 56 045 becoming 56 301 and 56 124 becoming 56 302. Initially, black numerals were used but proved almost invisible. White numerals replaced them, before despatch. When the livery was completed Jarvis subsidiary Fastline branding was applied to the body sides in large lower case letters 'fast' being rendered in black and 'line' in yellow. Black upper parts on a line with the cabside windows were painted black, this portion being carried around the cab side and front windows. Prominent on the body sides were two raked yellow lines and three white grouped together. The former crossed from the grey area on to the black, whereas the latter remained in the grey portion. An additional lone pair of white raked lines featured further along the grey portion. The overall effect was neat and attractive. It was reported at the time that each locomotive cost around £1.5 million to rebuild.

Number 56 302 reached the load bank by the third week in March and FM Rail 31 128 collected 56 301 during the afternoon of 27th March. The pair, with 56 301 powered and leading, and the Class 31 present for insurance, made the journey northwards from Loughborough to Doncaster. All three 56/3s were to be based at the Jarvis depot at Roberts Road, Doncaster, initially for testing in Yorkshire. Following the initial period Fastline planned to work intermodal trains between Doncaster and Thamesport using newly-built 60ft container flat wagons. Additionally, the locomotives would be used on engineering trains.

Number 56 301 returned to the Falcon Works on 6th April, for attention to its wheelsets, and was replaced by 56 302, which left the works at 15.15 on 10th April. Tests continued during April and it finally left the Falcon Works on 5th May.

Meanwhile at FM Rail in Derby, still bearing its old number, 56 125 was started up for the first time on 20th April, after a lapse of seven years. By mid-May it had been repainted in Fastline colours and renumbered 56 303 at Barrow Hill. On 18th May the locomotive ran from Barrow Hill to Doncaster coupled to 56 301 for insurance. Once accepted it made its first revenue earning run for Fastline on 23rd May heading 56 301 and the 10.45 Barrow Hill-Rugby infrastructure train.

On 20th May 56 302 rescued a 'Steamy Affairs' Birmingham-Keighley charter rail tour at Newark and hauled it and its pair of Class 33s to Doncaster. This was the first, albeit impromptu, instance of a Class 56/3 working a passenger train. Number 56 302 became the first of the trio to reach Scotland on 29th August, when it hauled a track slinger from Doncaster to Glasgow, returning the next day.

During May 2006, therefore, thirty EWS Class 56s were busy at work in France, three were working for Fastline and several were active in preservation. Due to fire damage 56 118 was returned to England for assessment, and in the event did not return to France. At this time FM Rail started to concentrate its scattered inactive locomotives to its new premises at Coalville and on 26th June 56 021, in EWS red livery and 56 011, still wearing Load-Haul black and orange livery, were towed there together with various coaches by 33 103.

The former 'Heritage Fleet' retained by EWS for several years, was offered for sale during the summer of 2006. The only Type 5 within it was 56 006, but it remained with the company for the time being.

With ballast and track work nearing completion in France, the Type 5 locomotives started to trickle back to England. August saw the first Class 58s return and in September 56 081 became the first intentional returnee. More followed (56 051/058/060/065//090/095/113/117 towards the end of October alone) making the return journey over the ensuing months. Once through the Channel Tunnel they usually paused at Dollands Moor, before moving north to Wembley and most, though not all, then on to Old Oak Common depot for storage.

With preserved 56 003 visiting various preserved railways over the months and 56 057 operating regularly on the Nene Valley Railway, a third active Class 56 burst onto the scene on 5th October. This was 56 098 resplendent in Railfreight grey with red stripe livery working on the Northampton and Lamport Railway – another credit to the volunteers of the preservation movement.

The class was further reduced by four due to scrapping during 2006, and with former Fertis examples returning home for storage, the new year started with only a few Class 56s in operation, in Britain notably the three Fastline and three preserved locomotives, with another seven in France. Five more returned in January, leaving just 56 078 and 56 106 working in France.

Following the voluntary administration of FM Rail in December 2006, the administrator offered for sale its stock

Above: Brush Traction's future 56 201 in its original identity as 56 009 photographed in the Falcon Works Test Yard on 28th February 1998.

G TOMS

Right: 56 301 takes shape having just been gutted in 34 Shop, photographed on 11th September 2005.

G TOMS

Donor locomotive 56 034 sheeted over to protect its equipment in the Test Yard on 21st January 2006.

G TOMS

56 301 takes shape in 34 Shop at a time when this number had not been decided upon, and the shops were still using the old identity as can be seen.

G TOMS

Above: Completed 56 301 in mint condition outside the new Test House in the Test Yard on 15th March 2006.

G TOMS

The black numerals on 56 302 were too small and should have been white – they were short-lived. Photograph taken alongside the load bank platform on 18th March 2006.

G TOMS

One of the works plates fitted to 56 302. It bears the standard Brush Traction logo of the time, with the 'long-legged' letter R in the word Traction.

G TOMS

Pioneer Class 56 locomotive brand new at its birthplace in Romania, 1976.

ELECTROPUTERE

of locomotives. Although it was not clear of what its fate was regarding ownership, 56 303 returned to traffic with Fastline, after repairs at Derby, on 5th February 2007.

By early March 2007, 56 301 was at Derby undergoing maintenance to its engine and bogies. Stored 56 011/021/022 meanwhile passed from FM Rail to the mysterious Nemesis Rail on 26th February and then to the then equally mysterious Mainline Rail stored fleet.

During the weekend of 3/4th March 2007 the Nene Valley Railway was showing off three Class 56s, 56 003/057/098 all being in traffic for visitors and the last making its debut in preservation.

The Fastline donor locomotives at Brush Traction were sold for scrap. Number 56 029 was collected from the Falcon Works on 14th March 2007 and scrapped the following month at EMR at Kingsbury. Number 56 044 left on 18th May and was followed by 56 034 on 21st May, both bound for Booth's at Rotherham. Last out was 56 131 on 23rd May for the same destination.

Preserved 56 057 was sold in May 2007 to an unspecified buyer with a reported intention to return it to main line service. The locomotive was transferred to Rail Vehicle Engineering at Derby and eventually it emerged that Hanson Traction was the new owner.

Around 24th June 2007 the French saga of Class 56 came to an end when 56 106 came home and was stored at Dollands Moor.

Fastline 56 302 was named 'Wilson Walshe' at the National Railway Museum, York, on 1st October 2007. This commemorated the late Mr Walshe, the Jarvis' Engineering Standards Manager involved with the firm's Class 56 project, who had died earlier in the year. Fastline also saw the return to traffic of 56 301 that month following a prolonged stay at Derby under repair with engine and bogie problems.

Meanwhile, Mainline Rail moved at least three of its Class 56s which were in storage. Number 56 022 was moved from Immingham to the Weardale Railway on 18th September for further storage, and on 19th November the final clearance of former FM Rail stock from Coalville saw 56 011 and 56 021 moved from there to Long Marston depot.

Number 56 063 was scrapped at Booth's in Rotherham in November 2007, followed by 56 131 the following month. Hanson Traction purchased 56 003 out of preservation in December, followed by 56 128 from HNRC and both were moved to the Nene Valley Railway in January 2008. Both locomotives, together with previously purchased 56 057, were intended to be returned to main line use. Number 56 057 itself was re-registered for main line use in February 2008 and was reported to be undergoing repainting and that it would be renumbered 56 311 before re-entering traffic.

In March the news emerged that Mainline Rail had ceased running. Owned by Ealing Community Transport, the Company had operated for about a year and among its assorted locomotives were 56 011 and 56 021, both former FM rail locomotives and stored for some years. By May they had passed into HNRC ownership.

Hanson Traction's 56 057 had progressed well at RVEL in Derby, and in due course re-entered traffic for Fastline as 56 311 on 3rd June 2008 in plain grey livery. It was seen behind Fastline 56 301 on Grain-Doncaster Fastline empty container traffic two days later, and on 10th June running singly on another empty Grain-Trafford Park, Manchester roster. It continued these workings on a spot hire basis, in the absence of a long-term contract.

Hanson's former 56 003 progressed its overhaul on the Nene Valley Railway at Wansford, and by early July had emerged into the yard as 56 312, wearing a pleasing purple livery, albeit without branding. With work almost complete on this locomotive, Wansford's attention started to turn to Hanson Traction's third Class 56, No. 56 128, to transform it into a main line serviceable unit as 56 313, ready for Spring 2009, with the expectation of another different livery. Number 56 312 was used on the Nene Valley Railway for testing purposes by September, and gained what must surely be the largest rending of a name ever to grace a locomotive – it bore the name ARTEMIS in vinyl form and in almost luminous green letters. It was expected to go to RVEL at Derby and to gain the main line in November 2008. In due course there was the prospect of six Class 56s back in revenue earning traffic on the main line in Britain.

The four locomotives that were in revenue earning service by the Autumn of 2008 experienced various troubles. Indeed 56 301 and 56 302 were briefly at Brush Traction, and 56 311 at Wansford for attention, but it was hoped that as the owners gained experience some of the foibles of the Class could be mastered to gain better reliability.

In October 2008 EWS offered 44 locomotives for sale, including a number of Class 56s which had been out of service for a long time. These were 56 025/27/43/52/64/76/84/89/101/ 114, none of which had seen service in France. One that had seen service in France, 56 007, by now languishing at Old Oak Common, had been chosen in the meantime to be fitted with GSM-R radio communication equipment on a trial basis.

Elsewhere, in preservation, 56 040 'Oystermouth' had been started up on the Mid-Norfolk Railway on 4th May, by the Class 56 Group. On 12th October the Great Central Railway (North) saw preserved 56 097 enter passenger service on this line. At the head of a train of ex-Gatwick Express and Anglia coaches, the locomotive shone in its 1987 Railfreight Coal grey livery. The work of the preservationists was ensuring a future for Class 56 units off the main line.

In November 2008, therefore, it appeared that Class 56 had a future, albeit for just a few examples, unless the ones that had seen service in France were found new work by EWS abroad. We shall be able to review the situation in the second volume of the Brush story.

12 – Overseas Miscellany

Brush number 800 of 1977 was supplied to the Ashaka Cement Company in Nigeria. Indeed such was the supposed urgency that it was diverted from the second **NRC** contract at a late stage of building. Had this not occured it would have become **NRC** number 955 (Brush number 784). Instead it became Ashaka 001, but only after some indecision on the part of the customer.

BRUSH

In 1980 four FS1s were built for the Chiyoda Chemical Engineering & Construction
Company of Nigeria. They were destined for the Kaduna plant and were numbered
KR01 SE - KR04 SE (BT 836-9). The livery closely followed that of the NRC locomotives.
They were the first locomotives to be built in the new erecting shop, adjacent to the old
superstructure shop. The first one is seen here outside the shop.

BRUSH

Tanzanian Railway Corporation number 3604 at work shunting in its home country.

BRUSH

Malayan locomotive 181.04 on shunting operations.

BRUSH

One of the traditional Brush Traction group photographs, taken in 1981 inside the then brand-new erecting shop. The locomotive in the background is number 3615 of Tanzanian Railway Corporation (BT 840), one of the two replacements for those lost at sea.

BRUSH

This Volume takes the building of Brush locomotives at Loughborough to circa 1980, with Class 56s still being built elsewhere until 1984. The service histories, of course, are brought to modern times, where known. It is a convenient break point between volumes, and Volume 2 will continue to chronicle events from this time, with a change in demand from overseas customers and the entry of Brush into electric locomotive building, following on with Classes 60, 92 and the Euroshuttle. With leaner times in the 1990s, Brush Traction diversified, and with considerable success, sufficient to keep a momentum well into the 21st Century. The considerable run of re-engineering HST power cars receives mention, not being Brush locomotives in the strictest sense, but the re-engineering of Euroshuttle locomotives and Class 57s receive more, of course. Volume 2 is scheduled to be published during 2010 and will be advertised by the Publisher and also MDS Book Sales, both at 128 Pikes Lane Glossop, SK13 8EH.

The new and the old in Sri Lanka (Ceylon). An interesting comparison of 30 years of Brush locomotive design progress between number 799 (BT 842) and number 562 (BB 3048).

BRUSH

Index

A

Accidents.... 75, 79, 81, 148, 150, 151, 159, 160, 162, 178, 275, 277
Ace 14, 17, 34, 64
'Aeolian Sky', mv 256, 257
Ashaka Cement Co. of Nigeria 251

B

Bagnall, WG Ltd 26, 28, 31, 52
Battelle Research Institute.......................... 200 et seq
Beasant, F 217
Beevor, Miles 19, 37, 54
Beyer Peacock & Co. 52, 58-64, 222-226, 238
Bond, R C 54
BREL, Crewe 271-273
BREL, Doncaster........................260, 266-272
British Railways 49
    Modernisation Plan 49
    Loco. Classification (1968)..............................149
British Steel Corporation.............................. 223
British Transport Commission............................. 200
Brush Bagnall 28
Brush Bagnall Traction Ltd 28
Brush Electrical Engineering Co. Ltd, The............. 13
Brush Electrical Machines Ltd .... 248 et seq
Brush Group, The.................................. 59, 98
Brushless alternators for ETH (D1960/61) 143
Brush logo (sans serif)................................. 209, 244
Brush Research & Development Division..... 201, 202, 206
Brush traction policy (1964)................................ 241
Brush Type 2 locomotive .... 49 et seq
    Fortieth anniversary 86
Brush Type 4 original names (1965).............. 136, 137
BRC&W 'Lion' prototype. 102, 105, 106, 110, 111, 119

C

Ceylon Government Railways .... 31 et seq
Chiyoda Chemical Engineering & Construction Co. Ltd 257
CIE... 21
CIE 0-6-0 locomotives 21, 22
Class 31 names circa 1988-1992 81-83
Class 56.. 259 et seq
Class 56 engine test bed locomotive (56 201) 282
Class 56 engine test bed locomotive (47 601)152-154
Class 56 locomotives to France 286, 287
Class 57..182-184
Class 58 engine test bed locomotive (47 901)155-157
Clayton Equipment Co............................... 233 et seq
Colas Rail 196
Cotswold Rail.........88, 93, 95, 188, 190-192, 194-197

Cox, ES 54
CP1 bogie.. 268
CP2 bogie.. 268, 270
CP3 bogie.. 268
Crewe Locomotive Works............. 115, 122, 123, 125, 127-130, 132, 134-141, 143
Cuban National Railways 233-237
Cuban sugar railways (MINAZ) 244, 246, 247
Cwm Colliery 0-6-0s 42, 43

D

Dainton Bank 105, 117
Dilley, Bob.. 19, 20
Direct Rail Services 188, 194-197
Draycott, John 105
Durber, JM 249
'Dutch' grey and yellow livery 81, 83

E

Ealing Community Transport 97
Electric Heating Units/locomotives 58, 90
Electric Train Heat conversions. 74, 77, 150, 151, 163
Electroputere 260-263, 267
Eley, Geoffrey 54
Ell, SO 104
English Electric DP2 prototype....... 102, 110, 111, 119
English Welsh & Scottish Railway 85, 181, 281
    Locomotive disposals..........................87, 182, 192
Experimental Brush/Beyer Peacock 0-6-0..... 64, 215, 216

F

Falcon name plates and motifs.............. 105, 106, 108
'Falcon' prototype .... 98 et seq
Falcon Engine & Car Works Ltd, The.................... 12
FM Rail 90, 91, 95, 191, 193, 194, 197, 287, 288, 294
Fragonset Railways...87-91, 182, 184, 186, 188, 191, 196, 286
Freightliner container trains 148, 149

G

Gimbert GC, Benjamin 160, 161
Good, Alan P 14, 17, 21, 23, 26
Goodlet, BL... 55, 67, 98, 110
GW Railway... 23
GWR 0-6-0 locomotive (15107)........................ 23, 4

H

Hall, Sir Arnold.. 211
Harrison, JF 109
'Hawk' Project... 198 et seq

I

Ivatt, HG 34, 54

J

Jarvis Rail (Fastline) 287, 288

K

'Kestrel' project .... 207 et seq, 259
'Kestrel' weights (actual) 211
'Kestrel' on Shap incline 212

L

Lever Bros. 28-30
Lickey Incline 104, 105, 117
Liner Trains 144, 145
LMS Railway 14, 98
Locomotives, steam 12
LNE Railway 14, 17

M

Mainline Rail 95, 96, 294
Malayan State Railway (KTM) 254, 255
Matthews, Sir Ronald 14, 36
Maybach Motorenbau GmbH 98
Mays, Neville 86
Mirrlees, Bickerton & Day 14
Mirrlees JVS12T engine problems 71, 72
Mobile fuel carriers 231
Monocoque design (D1500) 111, 112

N

National Coal Board 42, 43, 64, 65
National Railways of Zimbabwe 231
Nemesis Rail 95, 96
Network Rail 95, 96
New Brush Workshops (1959/60) 69
New Locomotive Erecting Shop (1980) 257, 258
Nigerian Railway Corporation 248-251
Nightall GC, James 160, 161

P

Painting Brush Type 4s at Derby Works 127
Panay Island Railway 244-246
Park Gate Iron & Steel Co. Ltd 222-224
Petters Ltd 14
Pioneer Brush Type 4 preserved (D1500) 174
'Premonition locomotive' 47 299 .... 161, 162
Privatisation of BR 280
Proposed locomotives, 1949 .... 24, 25
Proposed locomotives (mid 1960s) 240, 241
Proposed 'Peregrine' locomotive 206
Prototype 0-6-0 (15004) 18-21

Push-pull 47/7 locomotives 158, 159

R

Rail Blue livery.. 73, 74, 142, 143, 148, 149, 275, 276, 278
Railfreight grey livery (1982) 78, 79, 273, 276, 278
Railfreight grey livery (1987) 77, 79-81, 273, 275, 276
Raine & Co. 225
Rampala, BD 31
Renishaw Iron Co. 224
Rhodesia Railways DE4 locomotives .... 226 et seq
Richards, HWH 18
Riviera Trains 194
Rugby Testing Station 204, 205

S

Senior, Herbert V 14
Shcherbinka 219-221
Skopje Steelworks 238-240
Smyth, WA 31
Soviet visit to Falcon Works 217
Sprite (first) 13-17
Sprite (second) 32, 33, 64
Sprite (third) 62, 63
Squirrel Cage traction motors 204
Staged crashes 93, 95
Steel Company of Wales, The 27
    Locomotives, Bo-Bo 37-41, 46-48, 58
0-6-0 .... 28, 30, 40, 41
0-4-0 .... 37, 38, 40, 41, 44-48, 58, 59
Stewarts & Lloyds 43, 44
Stock locomotives.. 26, 27, 60-64, 125, 126, 222, 225, 238-240
Sulzer Bros. 109, 207
Sulzer engine problems 146, 147

T

Tanzania Railway Corporation 255-257
Thunderbird locomotives 176
TOPS locomotive classification 72
    Class 31 .... 57, 72, 74
    Class 47 numbering 152
Traction Department (Brush) 18
Transmanche-Link (TML) 253
Tulloch Ltd 241-244
Turbine Shop 69, 115, 253, 256
Tyne & Wear Metro 252, 253
Type 5 locomotive requirement 206

U

USSR Ministry of Transport & Energy
    Machine building 218

W

Waterman, Pete.................................... 175, 178, 181
West Coast Railway Co................. 192, 194, 195, 197
Western Australia Government Railways ... 242 et seq
Wilkes & Ashmore 102, 110, 111
Wood, FH 28, 49, 54, 71, 211, 216, 218, 237, 240

X

XP64 livery (D1733) 131

Y

Yom Kippur War, 1973... 259

Z

Zebrugge 263